Praise for *Business Ethics*

"Boylan appropriately encourages the reader first to 'know thyself,' since construction of effective decision-making models begins with introspection. His guidance certainly is well-placed, given lessons of the past decade—and before. *Business Ethics* proceeds to equip its readers with the tools necessary to continue to construct those models while allowing for diverse results. Throughout the text, we are offered varying perspectives on classic ethical questions, allowing each of us to hone both our view of ourselves and our worldview, while also developing a more concise vocabulary for that articulation through the case response method.

Boylan's text is both a challenge and a delight to read, as one is reminded that great minds do not always think alike; sometimes, what makes them great is that they offer exceptionally exquisite arguments on differing sides of ethical debates."

—Laura P. Hartman, *DePaul University*

"Carefully crafted, this book contains a pedagogical gold mine of cases and essays on the key issues in business ethics today. It serves as a perfect introduction to the complex equation of balancing business and ethics."

—Al Gini, Quinlan School of Business, *Loyola University Chicago*

"In the information age, corporate stakeholders are increasingly 'connected' to a global marketplace yet may find themselves strangely isolated, even alienated, within it. Taking as their starting point Michael Boylan's 'personal worldview imperative,' which mandates that we cultivate comprehensive and coherent worldviews that inspire action toward the good, the dialogical essays collected in Boylan's *Business Ethics* offer more than an introduction to ethics applied to business concerns. They provide a compass with which we may chart distinctive courses toward market relationships of integrity and satisfaction."

—Sybol Anderson, *St. Mary's College of Maryland*

Business Ethics

Second Edition

Edited by Michael Boylan

WILEY Blackwell

This edition first published 2014
© 2014 John Wiley & Sons, Inc

Edition history: Prentice Hall (1e, 2001)

Wiley-Blackwell is an imprint of John Wiley & Sons, formed by the merger of Wiley's global
Scientific, Technical and Medical business with Blackwell Publishing.

Registered Office
John Wiley & Sons, Ltd, The Atrium, Southern Gate, Chichester, West Sussex, PO19 8SQ, UK

Editorial Offices
350 Main Street, Malden, MA 02148-5020, USA
9600 Garsington Road, Oxford, OX4 2DQ, UK
The Atrium, Southern Gate, Chichester, West Sussex, PO19 8SQ, UK

For details of our global editorial offices, for customer services, and for information about how
to apply for permission to reuse the copyright material in this book please see our website at
www.wiley.com/wiley-blackwell.

The right of Michael Boylan to be identified as the author of the editorial material in this work has
been asserted in accordance with the UK Copyright, Designs and Patents Act 1988.

Library of Congress Cataloging-in-Publication Data

Business ethics / edited by Michael Boylan. – 2nd edition.
    pages   cm
  Revised edition of: Business ethics / Michael Boylan. c2001.
  Includes bibliographical references.
  ISBN 978-1-118-49474-5 (pbk. : alk. paper)   1.   Business ethics–Case studies.
I. Boylan, Michael, 1952–
  HF5387.B86673 2015
  174′.4–dc23

                           2013017492

A catalogue record for this book is available from the British Library.

Cover image: Maidenhead Bridge, Berkshire © Martin Stavars, martinstavars.com
Cover design by www.simonlevy.co.uk

Set in 10.5/12.5pt Dante by SPi Publisher Services, Pondicherry, India
Printed in Singapore by Ho Printing Singapore Pte Ltd

1   2014

For Éamon

Contents

Notes on Contributors

Jane Aronson is professor and director of the faculty of social sciences, McMaster University, Hamilton, Canada.

Michael Boylan is professor and chair of philosophy at Marymount University.

Marvin T. Brown teaches business and organizational ethics in the philosophy department, University of San Francisco and in the organizational systems program at Saybrook University in San Francisco.

Thomas L. Carson is professor of philosophy at Loyola University of Chicago.

Stephen Cohen is professor of philosophy at the University of New South Wales.

Thomas Donaldson is the Mark O. Winkelman Professor of Legal Studies and Business Ethics at the Wharton School, The University of Pennsylvania.

Ronald Duska is Charles Lamont Post Chair of Ethics and the Professions at The American College.

Mary Jane Eichorn is an investor reporting specialist at the Navy Federal Credit Union.

Amitai Etzioni is university professor at the George Washington University.

Peter A. French is the Lincoln Chair in Ethics, professor of philosophy, and the director of the Lincoln Center for Applied Ethics at Arizona State University.

Kenneth E. Goodpaster is the David and Barbara Koch Endowed Chair in Business Ethics at the University of St. Thomas.

Erika Henik is an affiliate professor at the Wesley J. Howe School of Technology Management at Stevens Institute of Technology.

Tony L. Henthorne is associate professor of marketing at the University of Southern Mississippi.

Nien-hê Hsieh is associate professor of legal studies and business ethics and co-director of the Wharton's Ethics Program at the Wharton School, The University of Pennsylvania.

Rekha Karambayya is associate professor of organization studies and chair of organizational behaviour/industrial relations at York University, Canada.

Michael S. LaTour is associate professor of marketing at Auburn University.

William W. Lowrance is a consultant in health research ethics and policy, based in La Grande Motte in the south of France.

Alexei M. Marcoux is an honorary lecturer in philosophy at the department of philosophy, University of East Anglia.

John B. Matthews, Jr. is a professor at the Graduate School of Business Administration, Harvard University.

David E. McClean is a lecturer at Rutgers University and also the principal at David E. McClean Associates, a financial services consulting group.

Terrance McConnell is professor of philosophy at the University of North Carolina at Greensboro.

Sheila M. Neysmith is professor, associate dean of research, and RBC Chair in Applied Social Work Research, McGill University, Montreal, Canada.

Michael Philips is professor emeritus of philosophy at Portland State University.

Behnaz Z. Quigley is professor of accounting at Marymount University.

Farhad Rassekh is associate dean for academic management and professor of economics at the University of Hartford.

Jeffrey Reiman is William Fraser McDowell Professor of Philosophy at the American University in Washington, DC.

David M. Schilling is a United Methodist minister and director of Global Corporate Accountability at the Interfaith Center on Corporate Responsibility in New York.

Robert Simon is Marjorie and Robert W. McEwen Professor of Philosophy at Hamilton College in New York.

Edward H. Spence is a senior lecturer in moral philosophy and professional ethics in the School of Communication, Charles Sturt University, Australia. He is also a senior research fellow at the Centre for Applied Philosophy and Public Ethics (CAPPE) in Canberra.

Mariarosaria Taddeo is research fellow in Cyber Security and Ethics, PAIS, University of Warwick, England, and research associate, Uehiro Centre for Practical Ethics, University of Oxford.

Judith Jarvis Thomson is professor of philosophy at Massachusetts Institute of Technology.

Scott Turow is an author and practicing attorney.

Jane Uebelhoer is associate professor of business ethics at Marymount University.

John Weckert is professor of computer ethics in the School of Humanities and Social Sciences and professorial fellow at the Centre for Applied Philosophy and Public Ethics (CAPPE) in Canberra, Australia.

Preface to the Second Edition

Business Ethics is one of my three texts on applied ethics that is now being published by Wiley-Blackwell. The idea behind each of the books, in general, is to present some of the most pressing questions in applied ethics through a mixture of classic essays and some new essays commissioned precisely for these volumes. The result is a dialogue that I think readers will find enriching.

In addition to the essays, there is an ongoing pedagogical device on how to write an essay in applied ethics—using case response as the model. To this end, the major chapters of the book are followed by two sorts of cases: macro cases and micro cases. In macro cases the student takes the role of a supervisor and must solve a problem from that perspective. In the micro cases the student becomes a line worker and confronts dilemmas from that vantage point. Some felicity at both perspectives can enable the student better to understand the complication of using ethical theories (set out in Chapter 1) to real-life problems.

Others using the book may choose instead to evaluate selected essays through a "pro" or "con" evaluation. This approach emphasizes close reading of an article and the application of ethical theory (set out in Chapter 1) to show why you believe the author is correct or incorrect in her/his assessment of the problem. In order to make this approach appealing to readers, some effort has been made to offer different approaches to contemporary questions in healthcare ethics.

What is new in this second edition:

- Over half of the selections have been replaced (most with new original essays solicited especially for this volume).
- The book is introduced with a new discussion on ethical decision-making by the editor.
- Two original essays ground two different but compelling visions of global economic justice. These two essays provide a theoretical context for the succeeding essays.
- The section on the corporation as an individual is given a new context with the US Supreme Court case: *Citizens United v. FEC*.
- An extended examination of business as a community: stakeholder theory.
- The information technology chapter has been completely redone with new cutting-edge essays.

- A new section on the financial services industry has been created, with new original essays.
- A new section on globalization has been created, with new original essays.
- Many cases have been updated to reflect current problems.

It is my hope that this second edition will meet the needs of classroom instruction in a unique way while recognizing that responsible business practice occurs within a diverse context that must be understood in order to be effective. The world moves on and now, more than ever, we need vehicles to stimulate our students to be aware of how they can integrate social responsibility into the way they make decisions—either at the micro or macro level. To this end, students must learn when and how to adapt the principles of its theoretical core in order to meet these practical demands.

As is always the case in projects like this there are many to thank. I would first like to thank all the scholars who have written original essays expressly for this edition. Their fine work has added a unique character to the book. To the anonymous reviewers of this book, a thank-you for your thoughtful comments. I would also like to thank Jeff Dean, my editor, for his support of the project and the whole Wiley-Blackwell team.

I would also like to thank my research team at Marymount: Tanya Lanuzo and Lynn McLaughlin. Their expertise helped with my original essays that are in this volume. Finally, I would like to thank my family: Rebecca, Arianne, Seán, and Éamon. They continually help me grow as a person.

Source Credits

Chapter 5

William W. Lowrance, "Of Acceptable Risk." From *Of Acceptable Risk* (Los Altos, CA: William Kauffmann, 1976).

Sheila M. Neysmith and Jane Aronson, "Working Conditions in Home Care: Negotiating Race and Class Boundaries in Gendered Work." Reprinted by permission of the publisher from *International Journal of Health Services* 27, 3 (1997): 479–499. Copyright ©1997 Baywood Publishers.

David M. Schilling, "Sneakers and Sweatshops: Holding Corporations Accountable." Reprinted by permission from *The Christian Century*, October 9, 1996: 240–244. Copyright © 1996 Christian Century Foundation.

Judith Jarvis Thomson, "Preferential Hiring." Reprinted with permission of Princeton University Press from *Philosophy and Public Affairs* 2.4 (1973): 364–384. Copyright © 1973 by Princeton University Press.

Robert Simon, "Preferential Hiring: A Reply to Judith Jarvis Thomson." Reprinted with permission of Princeton University Press from *Philosophy and Public Affairs* 3.3 (1974): 312–320. Copyright © 1974 by Princeton University Press.

Michael Boylan "Affirmative Action: Strategies for the Future." Reprinted with permission from *Journal of Social Philosophy* 33.1 (2002): 117–130.

Rekha Karambayya, "In Shouts and Whispers: Paradoxes Facing Women of Colour in Organizations." Reprinted with kind permission of Springer from *Journal of Business Ethics* 16 (1997): 891–897. Copyright © 1997.

Terrance McConnell, "Whistle-Blowing." Reprinted with permission of John Wiley & Sons Ltd from R.G. Frey ed., *A Companion to Applied Ethics: Blackwell Companions to Philosophy* (2003); 570–582.

Erika Henik, "Mad as Hell or Scared Stiff? The Effects of Value Conflict and Emotions on Potential Whistle-Blowers." Reprinted with permission of Springer from *Journal of Business Ethics* 80.1 (June 2008): 111–119.

Chapter 6

Michael Philips, "Bribery," *Ethics* 94 (July 1984): 621–636. © 1984 by The University of Chicago. All rights reserved.

Thomas L. Carson, "Bribery and Implicit Agreements: A Reply to Philips." Reprinted with kind permission of Springer from *Journal of Business Ethics* 6 (1987): 123–125. Copyright © 1987.

Scott Turow, "What's Wrong with Bribery?" Reprinted with kind permission of Springer from *Journal of Business Ethics* 4 (1985): 249–251. Copyright © 1985.

Ethical Reasoning

Michael Boylan

What is the point of studying ethics? This is the critical question that will drive this chapter. Many people don't think about ethics as they make decisions in their day-to-day lives. They see problems and make decisions based upon practical criteria. Many see ethics as rather an affectation of personal taste. It is useful only when it can get you somewhere. Is this correct? Do we only act ethically when there is a *win–win* situation in which we can get what we want and also seem like an honorable, feeling, and caring person?

A Prudential Model of Decision-Making

In order to begin answering this question we must start by examining the way most of us make decisions. Everyone on earth initiates the decision-making process with an established worldview. A worldview is a current personal consciousness that consists of one's understanding about the facts and values in the world. It is the most primitive term to describe our factual and normative conceptions. This worldview may be one that we have chosen or it may be one that we have passively accepted as we grow up in a particular culture. Sometimes the worldview is wildly inconsistent. Sometimes the worldview has gaping holes so that no answer can be generated. Sometimes it is only geared to perceived self-interest. And sometimes it is fanciful and can never be put into practice. Failures in one's personal worldview model will lead to failures in decision-making.

One common worldview model in the Western world is that of celebrity fantasy. Under this worldview, being a celebrity is everything. Andy Warhol famously claimed that what Americans sought after most was *15 minutes of fame*.[1] Under this worldview model we should strive to become a celebrity if only for a fleeting moment. What does it mean to be a celebrity? It is one who is seen and recognized by a large number

Business Ethics, Second Edition. Edited by Michael Boylan.
© 2014 John Wiley & Sons, Inc. Published 2014 by John Wiley & Sons, Inc.

of people. Notice that this definition does not stipulate that once recognized the object is given positive assent. That would be to take an additional step. To be seen and recognized is enough. One can be a sinner or a saint—all the same. To be recognized is to be recognized. If this is the end, then it is probably easier to take the sinner route. In this way, the passion for celebrity is at heart contrary to ethics.

Another popular worldview model is one of practical competence. Under this model the practitioner strives to consider what is in his or her best interest and applies a practical cost–benefit analysis to various situations in order to ascertain whether action x or action y will maximize the greatest amount of pleasure for the agent (often described in terms of money). Thus, if you are Bernie Madoff (a well-known financial swindler) you might think about the risks and rewards of creating an illegal Ponzi scheme as opposed to creating a legitimate investment house that operates as other investment houses do. The risk of setting off in your own direction is that you might get caught and go to prison. The rewards are that you might make much more money than you would have under the conventional investment house model. Since you think you are smarter than everyone else and won't get caught, the prudential model would say—*go for it!* Madoff did get caught, but who knows how many others don't? We couldn't know because they *haven't been caught*. But, even if you aren't caught, is that the best worldview approach? The prudential model says yes.

Possible Ethical Additions to the Prudential Model

Some people, including this author, think that the prudential model is lacking. Something else is necessary in order have a well-functioning worldview by which we can commit purposive action (here understood to be the primary requirement of fulfilled human nature). First, we have to accept that the construction of our worldview is within our control. What I suggest is a set of practical guidelines for the construction of our worldview: *"All people must develop a single comprehensive and internally coherent worldview that is good and that we strive to act out in our daily lives."* I call this the personal worldview imperative. Now one's personal worldview is a very basic concept. One's personal worldview contains all that we hold good, true, and beautiful about existence in the world. There are four parts to the personal worldview imperative: completeness, coherence, connection to a theory of ethics, and practicality. Let's briefly say something about each.

First is *completeness*. Completeness is a formal term that refers to a theory being able to handle all cases put before it and to determine an answer based upon the system's recommendations. In this case, I think that the notion of the good will provides completeness to everyone who develops one. There are two senses of the good will. The first is the rational good will. The rational good will means that each agent will develop an understanding about what reason requires of one as we go about our business in the world. In the various domains in which we engage this may require developing different sorts of skills. In the case of ethics it would require engaging in a rationally based philosophical ethics and abiding by what reason demands.

Another sort of good will is the affective good will. We are more than just rational machines. We have an affective nature, too. Our feelings are important, but just as was the case with reason, some guidelines are in order. For ethics we begin with sympathy.

Sympathy will be taken to be the emotional connection that one forms with other humans. This emotional connection must be one in which the parties are considered to be on a level basis. The sort of emotional connection I am talking about is open and between equals. It is not that of a superior "feeling sorry" for an inferior. It is my conjecture that those who engage in interactive human sympathy that is open and level will respond to another with care. Care is an action-guiding response that gives moral motivation to acting properly. Together sympathy, openness, and care constitute love.

When confronted with any novel situation one should utilize the two dimensions of the good will to generate a response. Because these two orientations act differently it is possible that they may contradict each other. When this is the case, I would allot the tiebreaker to reason. Others demur.[2] Each reader should take a moment to think about her own response to such an occurrence.

Second is *coherence*. People should have coherent worldviews. This also has two varieties: deductive and inductive. Deductive coherence speaks to our not having overt contradictions in our worldview. An example of an overt contradiction in one's worldview would be for Sasha to tell her friend Sharad that she has no prejudice against Muslims and yet, in another context, tell anti-Muslim jokes. The coherence provision of the personal worldview imperative says that you shouldn't change who you are and what you stand for depending upon the context in which you happen to be.

Inductive coherence is different. It is about adopting life strategies that work together. When they work against each other it is inductive incoherence. In inductive logic this is called a sure loss contract. For example, if a person wanted to be a devoted husband and family man and yet also engage in extramarital affairs he would involve himself in inductive incoherence. The very traits that make him a good family man: loyalty, keeping your word, sincere interest in the well-being of others are damaging to a philanderer, who requires selfish manipulation of others for his own pleasure. The good family man will be a bad philanderer and vice versa. To try to do both well involves a sure loss contract. Such an individual will fail at both. This is what inductive incoherence means.

Third is *connection to a theory of being good, that is, ethics*. The personal worldview imperative enjoins that we consider and adopt an ethical theory. It does not give us direction, as such, as to which theory to choose except that the chosen theory must not violate any of the other three conditions (completeness, coherence, and practicability). What is demanded is that one connects to a theory of ethics and uses its action guiding force to control action.

The final criterion is *practicability*. In this case there are two senses to the command. The first sense refers to the fact that we actually carry out what we say we will do. If we did otherwise, we'd be hypocrites and also deductively incoherent. But second, it is important that the demands of ethics and social and political philosophy be doable. One cannot command another to do the impossible! The way that I have chosen to describe this is the distinction between the utopian and the aspirational. The utopian is a command that may have logically valid arguments behind it but is existentially unsound (meaning that some of the premises in the action-guiding argument are untrue by virtue of their being impractical). In a theory of global ethics if we required that everyone in a rich country gave up threequarters of their income so that they might support the legitimate plight of the poor, this would be a utopian vision. Philosophers are very attracted to utopian visions. However, unless philosophers want to be marginalized, we must situate our prescriptions in terms that can actually be used by policy makers. Beautiful visions that can never be should be transferred to artists and poets.

How to Construct Your Own Model

The first step in creating your own model for which you are responsible is to go through personal introspection concerning the four steps in the personal worldview imperative. The first two are global analyses in which an individual thinks about who he or she is right now in terms of consistency and completeness. These criteria are amenable to the prudential model. They are instrumental to making whatever worldview one chooses to be the most *effective* possible. This is a prudential standard of excellence. What constitutes the moral turn is the connection to a theory of the good: ethics.

Thus the third step is to consider the principal moral theories and make a choice as to which theory best represents your own considered position. To assist readers in this task, I provide a brief gloss here of the major theories of ethics.

Theories of ethics

There are various ways to parse theories of ethics. I will parse theories of ethics according to what they see as the ontological status of their objects. There are two principal categories: (a) the realist theories that assert that theories of ethics speak to actual realities that exist;[3] and (b) the anti-realist, that assert that theories of ethics are merely conventional and do not speak about ontological objects.

Realist theories
Utilitarianism is a theory that suggests that an action is morally right when that action produces more total utility for the group as a consequence than any other alternative. Sometimes this has been shortened to the slogan, "The greatest good for the greatest number." This emphasis upon calculating quantitatively the general population's projected consequential utility among competing alternatives, appeals to many of the same principles that underlie democracy and capitalism (which is why this theory has always been very popular in the USA and other Western capitalistic democracies). Because the measurement device is natural (people's expected pleasures as outcomes of some decision or policy), it is a realist theory. The normative connection with aggregate happiness and the good is a factual claim. Utilitarianism's advocates point to the definite outcomes it can produce by an external and transparent mechanism. Critics cite the fact that the interests of minorities may be overridden.

Deontology is a moral theory that emphasizes one's duty to do a particular action just because the action, itself, is inherently right and not through any other sorts of calculations—such as the consequences of the action. Because of this nonconsequentialist bent, deontology is often contrasted with utilitarianism, which defines the right action in term of its ability to bring about the greatest aggregate utility. In contradistinction to utilitarianism, deontology will recommend an action based upon principle. "Principle" is justified through an understanding of the structure of action, the nature of reason, and the operation of the will. Because its measures deal with the nature of human reason or the externalist measures of the possibility of human agency, the theory is realist. The result is a moral command to act that does not justify itself by calculating consequences. Advocates of deontology like the emphasis upon acting on principle or duty alone. One's duty is usually discovered via careful rational analysis of the nature of reason or human action. Critics cite the fact that there is too much emphasis upon reason and not enough on emotion and our social selves situated in the world.

Swing theories (may be realist or anti-realist)

Ethical intuitionism can be described as a theory of justification about the immediate grasping of self-evident ethical truths. Ethical intuitionism can operate on the level of general principles or on the level of daily decision-making. In this latter mode many of us have experienced a form of ethical intuitionism through the teaching of timeless adages such as "Look before you leap," and "Faint heart never won fair maiden." The truth of these sayings is justified through intuition. Many adages or maxims contradict each other (such as the two above), so that the ability properly to apply these maxims is also understood through intuition. When the source of the intuitions is either God or Truth itself as independently existing, then the theory is realist, the idea being that everyone who has a proper understanding of God or Truth will have the same revelation. When the source of the intuitions is the person herself living as a biological being in a social environment, then the theory is anti-realist because many different people will have various intuitions and none can take precedent over another.

Virtue ethics is also sometimes called agent-based or character ethics. It takes the viewpoint that in living your life you should try to cultivate excellence in all that you do and all that others do. These excellences or virtues are both moral and nonmoral. Through conscious training, for example, an athlete can achieve excellence in a sport (nonmoral example). In the same way a person can achieve moral excellence, as well. The way these habits are developed and the sort of community that nurtures them are all under the umbrella of virtue ethics. When the source of these community values is Truth or God, then the theory is realist. When the source is the random creation of a culture based upon geography or other accidental features, then the theory is anti-realist. Proponents of the theory cite the real effect that cultures have in influencing our behavior. We are social animals and this theory often ties itself with communitarianism, which affirms the positive interactive role that society plays in our lives. Detractors often point to the fact that virtue ethics does not give specific directives on particular actions. For example, a good action is said to be one that a person of character would make. To detractors this sounds like begging the question.

Anti-realist theories

Ethical noncognitivism is a theory that suggests that the descriptive analysis of language and culture tells us all we need to know about developing an appropriate attitude in ethical situations. Ethical propositions are neither true nor false but can be analyzed via linguistic devices to tell us what action-guiding meanings are hidden there. We all live in particular and diverse societies. Discerning what each society commends and admonishes is the task for any person living in a society. We should all fit in and follow the social program as described via our language and society. Because these imperatives are relative to the values of the society or social group being queried, the maxims generated hold no natural truth value and as such are anti-realist. Advocates of this theory point to its methodological similarity to deeply felt worldview inclinations of linguistics, sociology, and anthropology. If one is an admirer of these disciplines as seminal directions of thought, then ethical noncognitivism looks pretty good. Detractors point to corrupt societies and that ethical noncognitivism cannot criticize these from within (because the social milieu is accepted at face value).

Ethical contractarians assert that freely made personal assent gives credence to ethical and social philosophical principles. These advocates point to the advantage of the participants being happy or contented with a given outcome. The assumption is that within a context of competing personal interests in a free and fair interchange of values that those principles that are intersubjectively agreed upon are sufficient for creating a moral "ought." The "ought" comes from the contract and extends from two people to a social group. Others universalize this, by thought experiments, to anyone entering such contracts. Because the theory does not assert that the basis of the contract is a proposition that has natural existence as such the theory is anti-realist. Proponents of the theory tout its connection to notions of personal autonomy that most people support. Detractors cite the fact that the theory rests upon the supposition that the keeping of contracts is a good thing, but why is this so? Doesn't the theory presuppose a meta-moral theory validating the primacy of contracts? If not, then the question remains, "What about making a contract with another creates normative value"?

For the purposes of this text, we will assume these six theories to be exhaustive of philosophically based theories of ethics or morality.[4] In subsequent chapters you should be prepared to apply these terms to situations and compare the sorts of outcomes that different theories would promote.

The fourth step in modifying one's personal worldview (now including ethics) is to go through an examination of what is possible (aspirational) as opposed to what is impossible (utopian). This is another exercise in pragmatic reasoning that should be based on the agent's own abilities and situation in society given her or his place in the scheme of things. Once this is determined, the agent is enjoined to discipline herself to actually bring about the desired change. If the challenge is great, then she should enlist the help of others: family, friends, community, and other support groups.

How Do Ethics Make a Difference in Decision-Making?

In order to get a handle on how the purely prudential worldview differs from the ethically enhanced worldview, let us consider two cases and evaluate the input of ethics. First, we will consider a general case in social and political ethics and then one from business ethics. The reader should note how the decision-making process differs when we add the ethical mode. In most cases in life the decisions we make have no ethical content. It doesn't ethically matter whether we have the chocolate or vanilla ice cream cone. It doesn't ethically matter if we buy orchestra seats for the ballet or the nosebleed seats. It doesn't ethically matter if I wear a red or a blue tie today. The instances in which ethics are important form a small subset of all the decisions that we make. That is why many forego thought about ethical decision-making: it is only important in a minority of our total daily decisions. In fact, if we are insensitive to what *counts* as an ethical decision context, then we might believe that we are *never* confronted with a decision with ethical consequences.

To get at these relations let's consider a couple of cases in which the ethical features are highly enhanced. Readers are encouraged to participate in creating reactions to these from the worldviews they now possess.

Case 1: Social/Political Ethics
The Trolley Problem

You are the engineer of the Bell Street Trolley. You are approaching Lexington Avenue Station (one of the major hub switching stations). The switchman on duty there says there is a problem. A school bus filled with 39 children has broken down on the right track (the main track). Normally, this would mean that he would switch you to the siding track, but on that track is a car filled with 4 adults that has broken down. The switchman asks you to apply your brakes immediately. You try to do so, but you find that your brakes have failed, too. There is no way that you can stop your trolley train. You will ram either the school bus or the car killing either 39 children or 4 adults. You outrank the switchman. It's your call: what should you do?

Secondary nuance: What if the switchman were to tell you that from his vantage point on the overpass to the Lexington Avenue Station there is a rather obese homeless man who is staggering about. What if (says the switchman) he were to get out of his booth and push the homeless person over the bridge and onto the electric lines that are right below it? The result would be to stop all trains coming into and out of the Lexington Avenue Station. This would result in saving the lives of the occupants of the two vehicles. Of course it would mean the death of the obese homeless person. The switchman wants your OK to push the homeless man over the bridge—what do you say?

Analysis

This case has two sorts of interpretations: before and after the nuance addition. In the first instance, you are faced with a simple question: should you kill 4 people or 39? The major moral theories give different answers to this question. First, there is the point of view of utilitarianism. It would suggest that killing 4 causes less pain than killing 39. Thus you should tell the switchman to move you to the siding.

There is the fact that when the car was stuck on the siding, the driver probably viewed his risk as different from being stuck on the main line. Thus, by making that choice you are altering that expectation—versus the bus driver who has to know that he is in imminent danger of death. Rule utilitarians might think that moving away from normal procedures requires a positive alternative. Killing four people may not qualify as a positive alternative (because it involves breaking a rule about willful killing of innocents). Thus, the utilitarian option may be more complicated than first envisioned.

Rule utilitarianism would also find it problematic to throw the homeless person over the bridge for the same reason, though the act utilitarian (the variety outlined above) might view the situation as killing 1 versus 4 or 39. However, there is the reality that one is committing an act of murder to save others. This would be disallowed by the rule utilitarian. If the act utilitarian were to consider the long-term social consequences in sometimes allowing murder, he would agree with the rule utilitarian. However, without the long-term time frame, the act utilitarian would be committed to throwing the homeless person over the rail.

The deontologist would be constrained by a negative duty not to kill. It would be equally wrong from a moral situation to kill *anyone*. There is no *moral* reason to choose between the car and the bus. Both are impermissible. However, there is no avoidance alternative. You will kill some group of people unless the homeless person is thrown over the wall. But throwing the homeless person over the wall is murder. Murder is impermissible. Thus, the deontologist cannot allow the homeless person to be killed—even if it saved 4 or 39 lives. Because of this, the deontologist would use other normative factors—such as aesthetics—to choose whether to kill 4 or 39 (probably choosing to kill 4 on aesthetic grounds).

The virtue ethics person or the ethical intuitionist would equally reply that the engineer should act from the appropriate virtue—say justice—and do what a person with a just character would do. But this does not really answer the question. One could construct various scenarios about it being more just to run into the school bus rather than the car when the occupants of the car might be very important to society: generals, key political leaders, great physicists, etc. In the same way, the intuitionists will choose what moral maxim they wish to apply at that particular time and place. The end result will be a rather subjectivist decision-making process.

Finally, noncognitivism and contractarianism are constrained to issues like, "What does the legal manual for engineers tell them to do in situations like this?" If the manual is silent on this sort of situation, then the response is what is the recommended action for situations *similar* to this in some relevant way? This is much like the decision-making process in the law, *stare decisis et non quieta movere* 'support the decisions and do not disturb what is not changed'. In other words, one must act based upon a cultural or legal framework that provides the only relevant context for critical decisions.

In any event, the reader can see that the way one reasons about the best outcome of a very difficult situation changes when one adds ethics to the decision-making machinery. I invite readers to go through several calculations on their own for class discussion. Pick one or more moral theory and set it out along with prudential calculations such that morality is the senior partner in the transaction. One may have to return to one's personal worldview (critically understood—as per above) and balance it with the practical considerations and their embeddedness to make this call.

Case 2: Business Ethics
Accountant at Alpha-Male Sport Shoes

You are a midlevel accountant at Alpha-Male Sport Shoes. Your company competes with the big brands like Nike and Adidas but you offer cheaper prices and more garish fashionable colors. The brand has been doing reasonably well. Your factories are in Vietnam. Your sales are in the USA. The company also has a venture capital arm that seeks to find new avenues to diversify the company in new global markets.

Your boss, Cora, calls in sick and asks you to handle any emergencies. She gives you her computer access code. After you finish your work for the day, you make one last check on Cora's account and in the process of following up upon a routine inquiry you discover that one of the venture capital accounts, Elysium Fields, is a totally bogus operation. This bothers you. You decide to stay late at work and subsequently discover that it is some sort of phony operation. Lots of company monies go into the venture capital arm and especially into Elysium Fields through various foreign bank accounts that offer secrecy and do not report to the Internal Revenue Service (IRS). You are convinced that something terribly wrong is happening. Your company is breaking the law. Just before you leave for the day you discover a suspicious e-mail that ties Elysium Fields into the illegal drug trade from Vietnam. You print out the suspicious files and accounts transactions. Then you go home with the copies.

You are a Vietnamese citizen of the USA, Thuy Nguyen. You are a single mother with a seven-year-old daughter. You have heard over and over again about the pain that illegal drug traffic has caused in the USA. Your own brother died of a drug overdose. You feel that Alpha-Male Sport Shoes is a front company for illegal drug traffic. You have enough evidence in your briefcase to go to the Federal Bureau of Investigation (FBI) and open an investigation that will probably lead to a conviction. However, this will disrupt your life. You will be put into the witness protection program, which will greatly disrupt your and your daughter's lives. If you do nothing, more people will die via this particular drug outlet. If you shut them down, then your own family life is permanently disrupted. What should you do? Do you go to the FBI?

Analysis

The prudential viewpoint begins with the individual involved, Thuy Nguyen. You want to keep your job so that you can pay your bills and look after your daughter. People in the witness protection program are often more prone to psychological stress—this would not be good for your daughter as she develops. Such possible practical consequences would suggest that you keep quiet and pretend nothing has happened.

If we extend the prudential viewpoint, then certain assumptions must be made about the case. Will the prosecution be successful? Will your life be in danger? Even though there may be good to others prudentially, it would be overridden by the possible negative effects to you. Again, the prudential viewpoint seems clearly against taking any action: mum's the word.

If we begin the ethical analysis with noncognitivism, then we must specify which culture we are talking about when we analyze the language of morals. Is the language that of the Vietnamese organized crime families? If so, then there is probably a code of looking the other way so that the profits might be made. Is the language that of recent naturalized Vietnamese citizens? How about naturalized citizens, in general? US citizens? It might make a difference which community is chosen as being operative in this particular situation. Once a choice is made, the analysis of the normative discourse within that sociological group will be rather straightforward. Thus, it is possible to get a range of recommendations under this approach (including some that are contradictory).

The same sort of dynamic might apply to contractarianism, intuitionism, or virtue ethics if one were to understand the contract, ethical adages, or community values to be relative to the sociological group chosen. In each case these anti-realist approaches will invoke a moral relativism such that one would have to decide which community is primary and hang her hat there.

The realist theories would operate differently. Utilitarianism would suggest an analysis of how much harm illegal drugs cause people in that and other communities. We are probably talking about tens of thousands of people who become addicts and have their lives torn apart. Thus we have a very large amount of pain multiplied by tens of thousands (including your own brother). That is a pretty strong argument against continuing where you are. You and your daughter count as two against many thousands. You are deciding about taking on risk to save lives. It would seem that utilitarianism would vote for your contacting the FBI.

Deontology would examine the relevant duties involved under some proper description of the action. Some of the duties might include: Thuy has a duty to her daughter to raise her with the basic goods of agency (such as she can), love, and moral training.[5] The first two are compatible with either choice, but the latter suggests contacting the FBI. Thuy also has a duty to her profession: accounting. She must report accurately and not distort reality for internal, selfish purposes. The goal is a transparent rendering of operations. Her professional duty is to go to the FBI. Then there is her general duty as a citizen of the USA. This is a duty to report violations of the law so that the purpose of the law might be upheld: the conviction of the guilty and the acquittal of the innocent. This duty also suggests reporting the company's activity to the FBI.

Both realist theories require Thuy to report what she has discovered as an accountant to the FBI. (We are assuming that the option of Thuy going to her bosses to tell them what she has discovered in order to get them to change would be rejected on prudential grounds.)

Readers are encouraged to try to take one of the moral theories and set out a decision-making scenario that involves both ethical and prudential criteria.

Conclusion

This chapter began by asking the rhetorical question, "What is the point in studying ethics?" The examination of the question took us various places. First it took us to prudential decision-making and possible problems many decision models face because of unreflective worldviews. Next, some suggestions were made to remedy this problem including the personal worldview imperative. Finally, the chapter worked through two case studies in which difficult decisions were presented. In this context, the prudential models were supplemented with an overlay of some ethical theories that might offer more coherent direction in decision-making. The slant of this author was toward the realist ethical theories and the swing theories interpreted realistically. However, each side was presented in order that the reader might make up her own mind on how she intends to adopt the overlay of ethics into her worldview and into her decision-making model. This is an important, ongoing task. I exhort each reader to take this quest seriously. It may be just the best investment of time you've ever made!

Notes

1 Cited in *The Philosophy of Andy Warhol* (New York: Harcourt, Brace, Jovanovich, 1975). At an art exhibition in Stockholm, Sweden he is reported to have said, "In the future everyone will be world-famous for fifteen minutes." Since that time, the quotation has morphed into several different formulations.

2 This is particularly true of some feminist ethicists. See Rosemarie Tong, "A Feminist Personal Worldview Imperative" in *Morality and Justice: Reading Boylan's* A Just Society, ed. John-Stewart Gordon (Lanham, MD and Oxford: Lexington/Rowman and Littlefield, 2009); 29–38.

3 Another popular distinction is *natural* versus *non-natural*. This is a subcategory of realism. For example, the philosopher G.E. Moore was a realist about the existence of "good" but he felt that "good" was an non-natural property. Thus realists can be naturalists and non-naturalists. Anti-realists are neither natural nor unnatural—they don't think that the good (for example) actually exists at all: in or out of nature.

4 For the purposes of this book the words "ethics" and "morality" will be taken to be exact synonyms.

5 I have argued for this in more detail in "Duties to Children," in *The Ethics and Global Justice Reader*, ed. Michael Boylan (Boulder, CO: Westview, 2011); 385–403.

Theories of Economic Justice

Overview: Business does not exist in a vacuum. Rather, it must be situated within a context. The context has many layers: form of government, social institutions, historically based folkways, etc. However, one of the most fundamental of these environmental givens is the received theory of economic justice that is adopted by the society. Economic justice covers the distribution of goods and services within a society. There are many possible models for basing these distributions ranging from raw "might makes right" to theories of justice that are based upon ethical principles.[1]

One way to parse the landscape is to focus upon individual oriented theories (liberal theories)[2] and those that are more community oriented (such as virtue ethics or utilitarianism). Each approach has advantages and drawbacks. This dichotomy of approaches continues into the next chapter in more concrete terms.

The student of business ethics should try to decide which of these ways of thinking about how to ground a theory of economic justice makes the most sense to him or her.

In Jeffrey Reiman's essay he puts together an intriguing alternative to the usual libertarian approach. Most liberal or libertarian thinkers believe in negative duties only. The difference between a negative and a positive duty is that: (a) negative duties are those incurred when one injures another and *must* (in virtue of the negative duty incurred) bring the person injured back to a pre-loss condition; and (b) positive duties are those incurred through a duty to rescue another who is in distress (even though the agent had nothing to do with the conditions causing the distress). Since negative duties only apply to harms caused by the agent, and since there is often a very high barrier to determining these, the end result is often a very small number of redistribution cases.

What makes Reiman's approach novel is his broadening of what constitutes a harm—thus generating negative duties. Using principles from Karl Marx and John Rawls, Reiman creates a context by which a libertarian approach can be an engine for progressive social policy, hence the paradoxical title of his essay.

Business Ethics, Second Edition. Edited by Michael Boylan.
© 2014 John Wiley & Sons, Inc. Published 2014 by John Wiley & Sons, Inc.

Marvin T. Brown takes a different approach. He approaches justice from the point of view of the community. This is the "commonwealth" in the title of his essay. Because of this foundational choice, Brown is committed to positive duties as well as negative duties. Brown begins with an examination of the privatization of the commons. This is an important concept because, by keeping alive the notion of the commons, there is a commitment towards a community sensibility: the common wealth that emphasizes shared provision, land as a provider, and membership (rather than ownership). From this worldview perspective Brown wants to fashion a standpoint for public policy—a civic commonwealth. In this civic commonwealth all sectors of the community are key stakeholders. This means that all of their interests must be addressed in the three core concerns: to provide for one another, to protect one another, and to find reasons for doing so. Governments should use persuasion, incentives, and regulations to address these primal functions.

Notes

1   I set out this landscape in greater detail in Chapter 7 of Michael Boylan, *A Just Society* (Lanham, MD and Oxford: Rowman and Littlefield, 2004).
2   This meaning of "liberal" is obviously different from the *liberal* versus *conservative* use of the term that is often applied in the evening newspapers. Rather, this sense goes back to the era of Thomas Jefferson in which individual liberty was most at issue.

Marxian Liberalism

Jeffrey Reiman

Marxian Liberalism[1] is a theory of justice that results from combining the liberal belief that people have a natural right to liberty understood as a right to be free of unwanted coercion, with some Marxian beliefs, most importantly, that private property is coercive. A crucial result of this combination is that *on liberal grounds*, to be justified, a right to private property must be consented to by all affected by it, which means by all present and future humans. Consequently, that consent must be *theoretical*, not a matter of asking actual people to sign on the dotted line, and I shall explain why theoretical consent is satisfactory in this context. To determine what sort of right to private property would receive this theoretical consent, I deploy an imaginary contracting situation modeled on John Rawls's original position and veil of ignorance,[2] but with a special difference: The knowledge that the parties in this original position possess includes certain liberal and certain Marxian beliefs. I contend that the parties in this Marxian-Liberal original position will agree to a right to property limited by an egalitarian requirement, namely, Rawls's *difference principle*.[3] In fact, I will argue that this provides the deduction of the difference principle that Rawls aimed for but did not think he accomplished in *A Theory of Justice*.[4] Apart from its role in Marxian Liberalism, this deduction will tell us something interesting about the difference principle.

Marxian Liberalism should not be confused with Left-libertarianism. Left-libertarians start from two independent moral principles, first, that individual human beings own themselves and, second, that all humans own the world.[5] Marxian Liberalism makes neither claim, though possession of the right to liberty effectively amounts to individual self-ownership.[6] For reasons that will emerge in what follows, I believe that ownership and its rights should be derivative in a theory of justice rather than foundational. The authors of a recent defense of Left-libertarianism hold that: "Left-libertarianism seems promising because it recognizes both strong individual rights of liberty … and also grounds a strong demand for some kind of material equality."[7] Marxian Liberalism seems promising for the same reasons, plus it better satisfies Occam's razor by starting with one moral principle—the right to liberty— rather than two.

I will give a Lockean defense of the natural right to liberty based on a secular interpretation of his theory. Then, I will present the Marxian idea that private ownership of means of production is coercive and note its antecedents in Locke, Rousseau, and Kant. These latter thinkers recognized that property limits nonowners' liberty, but it was Marx who saw that it was coercive. Moreover, he discovered the mechanism by which this coercion functions. I call this mechanism *structural coercion*: the way patterns of social behavior work to constrain people's choices beyond the limits of nature or morality. Beyond the normal use of force to protect persons and property, structural coercion works without overt violence. Accordingly, it tends to be invisible. The invisibility of structural coercion is the core of ideology in capitalism. Its result is that transactions in capitalism appear free because they are free of overt violence. Libertarian defenses of capitalism characteristically fall prey to this ideology. Seeing no special power in great property holdings, they think that all that is necessary for justice is that transactions be free of overt force. Likewise, though modern-day liberalism has distinguished itself from liberalism by effectively recognizing that racism and sexism are forms of structural coercion from which people must be protected,[8] liberalism generally shares libertarianism's ideological blindness to the coerciveness of private property itself. Marxian Liberalism corrects this blindness.

To overcome resistance to the unlikely marriage of Marxism and liberalism, I shall point out that Locke saw implicitly, and Rousseau and Kant saw explicitly, that property was a restriction on liberty, and that Marx viewed liberalism as progressive and endorsed the value of individual freedom. However, I am more interested in the theory that results from combining liberal and Marxian elements, than in fidelity to the sources. I exercise a fair amount of selectivity in choosing, and philosophical license in interpreting, the elements of Marxian Liberalism as I join them together. Moreover, in trying to present a whole theory of justice in this brief space, I cannot give the elements of that theory the extended defenses they need. I hope that the theory that results is interesting enough to justify the shortcuts that I will take.

My argument unfolds in the following order. In section I, "The Natural Right to Liberty," I present my interpretation of Locke's argument for the natural right to liberty. In section II, "Property: Expression of Liberty and Constraint on Liberty," I follow Locke as he moves from that right to a right to large and unequal property. In section III, "Property and Structural Coercion," I argue that Marx went beyond Locke, Rousseau, and Kant, in seeing that property not only constrained liberty but that it was a form of coercion. I contend that Marx's *dereified* view of social phenomena enabled him to see this, and led him to discover a new social mechanism of coercion which I call "structural coercion." That it is coercive makes it necessary *on liberal grounds* that private property be consented to, to be justified. In section IV, "The Marxian-Liberal Original Position," I formulate a Marxian-Liberal version of Rawls's original position, and argue that the parties therein will consent to a right to property subject to Rawls's difference principle. In section V, "The Just State," based on the natural right to liberty and the difference principle, I sketch Marxian Liberalism's conception of the just state.

I. The Natural Right to Liberty

The right to liberty is a right not to be subject to unwanted coercion.[9] I call it a *natural* right, because it does not require any act of consent or authorization by others to exist, nor is it derived from some more basic right. It's a *negative* right because it is a right to noninterference, rather than to some particular performance on the part of others. The right to liberty might be established in numerous ways, so Marxian Liberalism is not limited to the way in which I defend the right here. Nonetheless, since liberals often appeal to Locke's views on rights to liberty and property, I will present a Lockean argument for the natural right to liberty in this section, and trace his defense of the right to property in the next.

I contend that we can make the best sense out of Locke's argument for the natural right to liberty by taking that argument to presuppose that rational human beings have the competence to make correctly some simple inferences from facts to normative conclusions. I shall argue that that same presupposed rational competence can account, in Locke's theory, for how we know that we have the natural right to liberty, for why people are morally responsible, for when people gain the right to liberty, and for why people are morally obligated to respect it. These are not claims about what Locke actually thought he was doing. They are claims about how to make the best sense for us—for whom appeals to God carry little weight in philosophical argument—out of Locke's theory of the right to liberty.[10]

I understand Locke to be reporting an exercise of this rational competence when he writes in the *Second Treatise of Government*: "The state of Nature has a law of Nature to govern it, which obliges every one, and *reason*, which is that law, *teaches all mankind who will but consult it*, that being all equal and independent, no one ought to harm another in his life, health, liberty or possessions" (*ST*, ii:6; emphasis added). What Locke calls the "state of Nature" is the human world with social and political authority imagined away. The "equality" of which he speaks is the absence of any natural authority of one sane adult over another. The "independence" is their physical separateness. Understood as a report of an exercise of the competence to make correct normative inferences, Locke's statement means that rational human beings, imagining the natural condition they share with their fellows, will infer from the equality and independence of humans that each human has a right not to be interfered with in his or her life, health, or liberty.

I omitted the term "possessions" from Locke's famous phrase here, because it is ambiguous between "what we physically possess" and "what we rightfully possess." Since, as Locke recognized, justifying property is a separate matter, the inference that all have an equal right to liberty is made about us simply as corporeal rational beings. This is essentially an equal right not to have one's body interfered with, a *natural negative right to bodily liberty*. I call it simply the *natural right to liberty*.

Our rational competence to make correct moral inferences is not infallible. Its exercises need corroboration. However, since the inferences that result from its exercise are substantive moral judgments, they cannot be proven true by comparing them to facts. Neither can they be proven true by showing that their denial is self-contradictory. Their only corroboration lies in the fact that normal rational human beings tend to make those inferences. Like agreement among scientific experimenters, widespread agreement on such inferences is evidence that they are sound exercises of the competence so to infer, and thus true. This idea is not as strange as it may seem. It is, for example, assumed by the common moral-philosophical strategy of appealing to widely held intuitions to support moral principles. Such intuitions would be of no probative value if they didn't represent inferences (from situational facts to normative judgments) that humans are thought normally competent to make correctly.

Moreover, some normative inferences are so nearly universally made that they become part of the rationality that we require for people to be held morally responsible for their actions. Such rationality is *substantive*; it is not limited to logical consistency. Seriously deranged people can be (maddeningly!) logically consistent in their beliefs. They are held to be insane, and thus not morally responsible, because they fail to make certain substantive inferences, including normative ones. The traditional M'Naghten test for legal insanity includes inability to distinguish right from wrong, that is, lack of the competence to make certain substantive moral inferences correctly. The inference that, in the absence of social and political authority, people have a natural right to liberty is such an inference. When social and political authority are not in play, virtually everyone recognizes that it is wrong to harm innocent nonthreatening human beings in their life, health, or liberty. Those who do not recognize this are not sufficiently rational to be morally responsible.

Locke presupposes something like this when he affirms that a person gains the right to liberty when he reaches a "[s]tate of maturity, wherein he might be supposed capable to know that law [of nature] ... When he has acquired that state he is presumed to know how far the law is to be his guide, and how far he may make use of his freedom, and so he comes to have it" (*ST*, vi:59). The substantive rational competence that enables one to know the right to liberty provides the necessary condition for moral responsibility, and entitles one to exercise the right to liberty. This means that the right is possessed by actual humans who are judged rational enough to be morally responsible by commonsense standards. It is not based on an ideal of perfect rationality or perfect freedom. Thus it does not justify forcing adults to become more rational, nor, in Rousseau's famous and ominous words, *forcing people to be free*.

Finally, the rational competence that accounts for our knowledge of the natural right to liberty, for moral responsibility, and for when people gain the right, also helps us to make sense of Locke's account of the moral obligation to respect that right. That all rational people can be expected to make the inference that people have a natural right to liberty means that all people know that all other people recognize that right, and thus that all can expect all others to respect it. Then, anyone who does not respect it is consciously flouting the reasonable expectations of his fellows. Such a person is reasonably judged a threat by the others, and reasonably dealt with defensively. Thus, writes Locke,

> In transgressing the law of Nature, the offender declares himself to live by another rule than that of reason and common equity … and so he becomes dangerous to mankind; … which being a trespass against the whole species, and the peace and safety of it, provided by the law of Nature, every man upon this score, by the right he hath to preserve mankind in general, may restrain, or where it is necessary, destroy things noxious to them, and so may bring such evil on any one who hath transgressed that law, as may make him repent the doing of it, and thereby deter him, and by his example, others from doing the like mischief. (*ST*, ii:8)

In short, the natural right of liberty obligates us both because it is a reasonable judgment in response to our shared human condition—acting contrary to it is unreasonable—and because defensive action against those who are not willing to respect the right to liberty is the reasonable response to them. As might be expected, a Lockean theory of obligation is grounded both in reason and in the threat of sanction.[11]

II. Property: Expression of Liberty and Constraint on Liberty

From the right to liberty, Locke argues for a right to property. He starts by claiming, based presumably upon the natural right to liberty, that people own themselves and their labor. He takes this to mean that they own what unowned stuff they mix their labor with. This is a very limited property right, since it applies only to what people can consume before it spoils—and it is constrained by what comes to be called the *Lockean proviso*,[12] namely, that there be "enough and as good left in common for others" (*ST*, v:27). Though Locke constrains this limited right to property for consumption so that it doesn't harm others, significantly he does not appeal to consent to justify it. He treats the right as an extension of the natural right to liberty.

Locke goes on to argue for a larger right to property, the right to own as much as one can justly accumulate including what can be stored in the form of money. This *right to large and unequal property* is essentially the right to property one finds in modern Western nations, such as the USA. That Locke argues for this larger right in the state of nature—prior to the formation of the state—makes him the odd man out among social contractarians. Hobbes, Rousseau, and Kant all held that the larger right to property emerges only *after people have left the state of nature* by consenting to form a state. Thus Hobbes, Rousseau, and Kant took the right to property to be, not a natural right, but one that is created by the agreement of those affected by it. However, Locke's difference from these other social contractarians is less than it seems to be. Though it appears in the state of nature, Locke argues that the larger right to property is based on people's consent. He contends that since the value of money is conventional, it has been consented to. And since money makes possible large and unequal property holdings, they too have been consented to (*ST*, v:50). Locke effectively gives us, in the state of nature, a pre-contract contractarian argument for the right to large and unequal property. By my definition, even for Locke this right is not a natural right.

Locke's argument for consent to this right is not very persuasive.[13] More important than the quality of the argument however, is that Locke thought he had to make it. I think he did because the right to large and unequal property is a substantial restriction of the natural right to liberty. Go back in the state of nature to the point at which the natural right to liberty exists, and other rights do not yet exist. At that point, all of us have the right to go wherever we wish, as long as we do not trespass upon others' bodies. When we add the natural right to property for consumption before spoilage, it brings only minor additional limits. Now we also may not trespass on whatever little pile of things others have accumulated and are about to consume. These limits are naturally small and, since our bodies and our capacities for consumption are similar, the limits are virtually the same for all. Thus, the rights to liberty and to property for consumption keep relations between humans symmetric: we all have roughly the same amount of freedom and authority vis-à-vis one another.

When we add a right to large and unequal property, things change dramatically. When this large piece of land is now my rightful property, you may no longer walk on it without my permission. Since there is little limit on how much land I may own, this can be a very substantial restriction on where you were previously free to walk. And, since there is no assurance that you own an equally large tract of land or any land at all, this is a restriction on you that is not necessarily balanced by an equal restriction on me. You and I may now stand in an asymmetrical relation in which I have significantly more freedom to go where I wish than you do.

I surmise that Locke saw (or, at least, sensed) that the right to large and unequal property introduced a new order of unequal liberty and authority into social life. For Locke, the state must be consented to because people have a natural right to liberty that a state's authority may significantly restrict. That right to liberty entails that such a restriction on liberty may not legitimately be imposed on anyone without her *exercising her right to liberty by* authorizing that restriction. Since the larger right to property may also significantly restrict liberty, the larger right must be consented to for the same reason that the authority of the state must be consented to. Indeed, the right to large and unequal property is a kind of authority over others. You cannot walk on or use my property unless I give you permission to do so. Then, the larger right to property is exactly on a par with the authority of the state, albeit parceled out to some individuals. If the state is imposed without consent, it violates the natural right to liberty—and the same is true if the right to large and unequal property is imposed without consent.

Though Locke saw or sensed that large property rights constrained liberty, he did not contemplate how great this constraint would be once virtually everything is owned by someone. Rousseau recognized the implications of this fateful moment:

> When inheritances so increased in number and extent as to occupy the whole of the land, and to border on one another ...; the supernumeraries, who had been too weak or too

indolent to make such acquisitions ... were obliged to receive their subsistence, or steal it, from the rich; and this soon bred, according to their different characters, dominion and slavery, or violence and rapine.[14]

Kant rejected Locke's notion that the right to property was a result of mixing one's labor with unowned stuff, and replaced it with the claim that property was an essential condition of liberty. No matter what one freely does, one must use some part of nature to do it, at very least the ground upon which one stands.[15] Accordingly, Kant saw the right to property as an expression of the natural right to liberty, even more directly than did Locke. However, Kant also recognized that the right to property was a constraint on the liberty of nonowners. In the *Metaphysics of Morals*, he wrote: "When I declare ... that something external is to be mine, I thereby declare that everyone else is under obligation to refrain from using that object of my choice, an obligation no one would have were it not for this act of mine to establish a right."[16] Kant saw as well that this could lead to significant inequality such that "the welfare of one very much depends on the will of another (that of the poor on the rich), [and thus] one must obey ... while the other commands, one must serve (as laborer) while the other pays."[17]

Note, before proceeding, that Marxian Liberalism is not tied to any particular derivation of the right to property from the right to liberty, just as it is not tied to the Lockean argument for the right to liberty that I presented in the previous section. There are numerous routes by which liberals may go from the right to liberty to the right to property. Robert Nozick draws on the Lockean notion that property arises from mixing one's labor with unowned stuff (*ASU*, 174–178). By contrast, Jan Narveson makes an argument closer to Kant's, namely, that the right to liberty directly entails the right to property.[18] In section IV, I shall suggest historical and even Marxian reasons for linking the right to property to the right to liberty. All that Marxian Liberalism needs is the link.

III. Property and Structural Coercion

Locke, Rousseau, and Kant all saw that property limited liberty, but they did not yet see it as coercive. That fell to Marx. In the half century that separated him from Kant, Marx saw the emergence of a class of workers possessing no property beyond the muscles in their backs confronting a capitalist class owning all the means for earning a living—which is to say, all the means for living. To live at all, the workers had to work for capitalists. Thus Marx characterized the worker in capitalism as "a man who is compelled to sell himself of his own free will."[19] Private ownership of means of production by capitalists coerces workers in the same way that some group's private ownership of all sources of available oxygen would coerce the rest of society. Beyond what was necessary to defend this group against challenges to its ownership of the oxygen, no overt violence would be necessary for the coercion to operate. It would operate quite effectively by means of bargains freely struck in which the nonoxygen owners had to offer something to the owners to get the chance to breathe. They, too, would be compelled to sell themselves of their own free will.

But Marx went further. "The dull compulsion of economic relations," he wrote, "completes the subjection of the labourer to the capitalist. Direct force, outside economic conditions, is of course still used, but only exceptionally" (*C*,I, 737). With these words, Marx announced the discovery of the mechanism by which private property coerces, namely, economic relations themselves. The existence of a social structure defined by private ownership of means of production by some, and nonownership for the rest, is what coerces the worker to work for the capitalist. Marx was able to see that this was indeed coercion, rather than mere constraint, because of his *dereified* view of social reality. He saw social structures as patterns of human behavior. Of capitalism, Marx wrote, "capital is not a thing, but a social relation between persons, established by the instrumentality of things" (*C*, I, 766).[20] Marx saw the institution of property in capitalism as a complex system of human behavior in which humans effectively forced one another to act in certain ways. I call this mechanism of compulsion *structural coercion*.

The term "structural" is appropriate for such coercion because it works the way that a physical structure such as a *traffic bottleneck* works to imposes fates on groups, forcing a majority of cars to slow down while leaving it to chance and other factors who makes up that majority and who the minority that slips easily through. The institution of private property is like a bottleneck. A large number of people play roles—as judges, lawyers, police officers, laborers, employers, buyers, sellers, real estate agents, and so on—in that institution. It is the overall pattern of behavior determined by those roles that forces a certain pattern of options on the people subject to it.[21] Though the force works to make the class of nonowners serve the class of owners, it is not the owning class that forces the nonowning class. It is the social structure determined by ownership that forces this service. *The social structure is virtually everyone acting to force virtually everyone to constrain their behavior in certain ways*. Precisely because the social structure is a pattern of human behavior (not externally necessitated like a traffic bottleneck), it is human beings acting on human beings, and thus it is coercion.

Interestingly, this view of social structure is shared by Rawls. For example, Rawls contends that "unjust social arrangements are themselves a kind of extortion, even violence" (*TJ*, 302). Since extortion and violence are coercive acts of human beings, this requires seeing the social structure in a dereified way, that is, as human beings acting on human beings. And Rawls sees it that way. "The social system," he writes, "is not an unchangeable order beyond human control but a pattern of human action" (*TJ*, 88).

Since any right to property (beyond a right to what one needs for consumption) will determine the shape of a social structure and thus enable some form of structural coercion, the liberal natural right to liberty dictates that a right to property must be consented to, to be justified. But the issue is not simply will a right to property be consented to or not. The issue is what sort of right, if any, will be consented to. Liberals characteristically think that the right to property has one shape, namely, absolute ownership, the right to do with one's property whatever one wishes—limited only by others' rights to liberty and their equally absolute ownership rights. This is mistaken in principle and in history. Once we recognize that a right to property must be consented to to be justified, the only limit in principle on the strings that might be attached to the right—as conditions of consent—is that the right remain a recognizable right to property. But rights to property almost always come with limits built into them, with no one thereby doubting that they are rights to property. Ownership comes in many forms. It is "a bundle of rights, privileges, and obligations ... Ownership does not always mean absolute ownership."[22] Ownership in *fee simple* is the most complete form of individual ownership of property in common law countries, but it is not without limits. It is subject to taxation, *easements*, and the government's power of eminent domain.[23] Limits are also built into property rights in the legal traditions of other cultures and other eras.[24] In short, property rights normally have limits built into them without stopping being property rights. Thus, the issue is not merely whether a right to property is justified, but what *sort* of right to property, if any, is justified.

IV. The Marxian-Liberal Original Position

Since any human being living now or in the future may have her liberty limited by a right to property, the consent that can justify such a right must be theoretical rather than actual. It may well be asked how theoretical consent—consent that it would be rational for people to give, but that they do not actually give—can justify anything. In response, consider first that, for critical decisions that must be made when actual consent is impossible and actual preferences unknown (say, the decision whether to treat an unconscious person who will die without treatment), it is common to accept *consent that it would be rational for people to give* as equivalent to actual consent. Further, the difference between theoretical and actual consent is less than it seems. For its audience, even "actual" consent is theoretical. The uttering of "yes" is not consent, since it might be uttered by someone not competent to consent, a child or a crazy person. We infer consent from the uttering of "yes" coupled with evidence that the individual is competent. Part of that evidence is that it would be rational to consent in this case.[25] Combining these ideas, we can treat theoretical consent to some right to property as equivalent to actual consent because it concerns a critical decision that must be made when actual consent is impossible, actual preferences unknown, and the only evidence we possess that people do consent is that it would be rational for them to consent. Note further, that there is no other way that a right to property can be consented to but theoretically, since a right to property that must wait on the actual consent of every newly appearing human being is no right at all. Once it is accepted that property is coercive, the only way in which it can be justified is by theoretical consent.

Defenders of the right to large and unequal property tend to offer capitalism's great productivity as a reason people would consent to that relatively unlimited right to property. Locke does it (see, e.g., *ST*, v:43); and Nozick does too (*ASU*, e.g., 117). But this move is a bit too quick. It would not be rational for people to consent to what leads to greater productivity as an *end in itself*, that is, without assurance that they will benefit from it—especially knowing that they are agreeing to potentially large limits on their natural right to liberty. Thus, the right to property that can be justified by consent of those affected by it will be a right with, at a minimum, limits built into it that guarantee that everyone will end up with a decent share. But this is just a minimum, and a vague minimum at that.

When, however, we pose the question of what sort of right to property would be consented to by parties in an original position informed by liberal and Marxian beliefs, we get a much more specific notion of the necessary limits on the right of private property. In the imaginary choice situation that Rawls calls the "original position," parties, representing everyone in a society, must consent unanimously to rules of justice. A veil of ignorance denies them knowledge of facts about their personal characteristics, including what generation they are in, and especially what position they will be in, in the economic system they agree to.[26] Moreover they are prohibited from gambling on what position they will be in.[27] However, the parties in Rawls's original position are stipulated to have general factual knowledge.[28] In the Marxian-Liberal original position, this factual knowledge includes key beliefs from liberalism and from Marxism.

On Marxian and liberal grounds, I take parties in the Marxian-Liberal original position to have an interest in maximizing their ability to act freely, that is, to be as little subject to coercion as possible. The specific liberal beliefs they hold are that people already have natural rights to liberty, that private property is a necessary condition of individual liberty, and that a state is needed to protect the rights to both liberty and property. The specific Marxian beliefs are that coercion can function structurally (as already discussed), that *a moral version of the labor theory of value* is needed to evaluate property systems, and what I shall call *the equivalence of material and social subjugation*. I will elaborate on these beliefs in what follows. It's important to note that, apart from the natural right to liberty already established, none of these beliefs is a moral principle. They are factual beliefs that could in principle become part of generally accepted knowledge and thus part of the knowledge possessed by parties in Rawls's own version of the original position. The beliefs get what moral force they have by being coupled with the natural right to liberty.

That people enter the original position already possessing natural rights to liberty shows that Marxian Liberalism is more a Lockean than a Rawlsian form of contractarianism. Unlike Rawls's contract, here the parties are not trying to determine all their rights including that to liberty. Like Locke's contract, the parties are contracting precisely because they already have a right to liberty that requires their consent to other moral or political arrangements that might threaten that liberty.

Though the natural right to liberty is a liberal principle, it is not in conflict with Marxian theory. A right to individual freedom from coercion is not ideological, since freedom must be guaranteed to individuals to be real at all. Nor does such a right deny the social nature of human beings. It is recognition of people's actual physical separateness, which makes it possible for an individual to suffer or be oppressed even if others are not. Individuals must be protected from coercion precisely because the individual is the smallest unit of oppressibility. Moreover, Marx recognized the importance of liberal individual rights. In "On the Jewish Question," he wrote: "Political emancipation [exemplified by the liberal rights granted in the French *Declaration of the Rights of Man and the Citizen*, and in the revolutionary era American state constitutions of Pennsylvania and New Hampshire] is indeed a great step forward."[29]

In addition to knowing that they have natural rights to liberty, the parties believe, from liberalism and Locke and Kant, but also from history and (surprisingly) as an implication of their Marxian beliefs, that private property is essential for liberty. That ownership of means of production is coercive is a Marxian reason for doubting that individual freedom can exist if such ownership is taken out of individuals' hands and placed under state (or other collective) control. The oppressive nature of 20th-century communist states is powerful evidence for such doubt.[30] The parties also understand from history that a state is needed to protect both the natural right of liberty and whatever right of private property would be consented to.

In addition to an understanding of structural coercion, parties in the Marxian-Liberal original position hold what I call a *moral version of the labor theory of value*.[31] This version of the theory does not claim to account for prices. It is a theory of what is exchanged in economic systems that is suited to the moral evaluation of such systems. We need such a theory because, in order to take up the question of what sort of property right would be consented to, we need a measure of what participants give and receive under different property regimes that does not presuppose the validity of any particular property right. When nothing that presupposes the validity of the property system can be used, all that remains that workers give in production (and receive in the form of goods purchased with their wages) is their time and energy, in a word, their labor, or as Marx put it, their "labor-time" (which he understood to include a standard measure of energy expended).[32] Materials do not count since they are only given if owned, which presupposes a right to property. Talent is not given because it is not depleted in being exercised. Labor-time is really given in the sense that it is *used up*— workers have only finite time and energy, and thus less left over when they have labored.[33] It might be objected that counting labor as given by workers presupposes that workers have a property right to it. But it only presupposes that labor is *physically their own*, as their pains and their deaths are their own. This is a natural fact. People literally use themselves up in laboring. *Labor done, however willingly or even joyously, is life itself spent.*

Because of the moral version of the labor theory of value, parties in the Marxian-Liberal original position understand that the money or goods that a person gets in an economic system are not simply "his" money or goods, but "other people's labor." Thus, inequalities in people's economic shares are not merely distributive differences. Indeed, since a property regime is a system of structural coercion, inequalities represent the fact that some people are being forced to work more for others than those others work for them. Because of the complexity of a modern economy, this is spread through the system, not limited only to relations between capitalists and workers. That is, if the average worker's salary is $20,000 a year, then someone who earns $100,000 a year has the labor-time of five workers at his disposal in return for his own labor-time (and not even for that much, if his earnings are from stocks or other investments). And given that the property system coerces this arrangement, the result is a relationship of forced servitude mediated by the economic system. I call this forced servitude *social subjugation* because it is a matter of people being subjugated by other people. We need distributive measures for this because the invisibility of structural coercion hides the fact of social subjugation.[34]

Since they understand distributive inequalities as measures of social subjugation, the parties—desiring to maximize their ability to act freely—will not consent to distributive inequalities unless there is a counterbalancing gain in freedom. However, the parties in the Marxian-Liberal original position also believe in *the equivalence of material subjugation and social subjugation*. And this belief points the way to a counter-balancing gain in freedom that make it reasonable to consent to distributive inequalities that represent social subjugation.

Material subjugation refers to the constraints on freedom that come from the fact that human beings' freedom is subject to the constraints of the material world, such that (a) they need material objects to have genuine freedom in the sense of the real possibility of acting on their choices (this includes obvious things that enhance people's ability to act on their choices, such as food and phones and cars, but also cures to diseases and other protections against life's perils),[35] and (b) they must work on nature to wring from it the objects covered under (a). The belief that an ample supply of material goods is a necessary condition of genuine freedom is behind the Marxian critique of liberal rights as merely formal: rights without material means to act on them give no real freedom.[36] And Marx is clear that ultimately freedom requires the end, or the dramatic reduction, of necessary labor: "the realm of freedom," he writes, "actually begins only where labour which is determined by necessity and mundane considerations ceases" (*C*, III, 820).

The equivalence of material subjugation and social subjugation holds that for equal deprivations of freedom, being constrained by material deprivation is equivalent to being constrained by human coercion. The belief that material and social subjugation are equivalent is implicit in Marx's view that history is progressive. "In broad outline," writes Marx, "the Asiatic, ancient, feudal and modern bourgeois modes of production may be designated as epochs marking progress in the economic development of society."[37] About capitalism in particular, Marx writes: "It is one of the civilizing aspects of capital that it enforces this [extraction of] surplus-labour in a manner and under conditions which are more advantageous to the development of the productive forces, social relations, and the creation of the elements for a new and higher form than under the preceding forms of slavery and serfdom, etc." (*C*, III, 819). Since, for Marx, history—up to and including capitalism—is a story of human subjugation accompanied by increasing power over nature, the progressivity of history implies that such social subjugation is a price worth paying for the reduction in material subjugation that increasing power over nature brings, and thus that social and material subjugation are comparable, one can rationally be traded for the other.[38] And I take this to mean that, for equal deprivations of freedom, social and material subjugation are equivalent.

Accordingly, social subjugation could be accepted if it were compensated for by a reduction in material subjugation, either in the form of more material goods or less required labor. Since workers even in the most advanced nations are far from having all the material goods they need to be able generally to subject their lives to their choices, I shall assume that for the near term, the gain in freedom from overcoming material subjugation must take the form of increases in workers' material standard of living (later I shall relax this assumption). Then, parties in the Marxian-Liberal original position can accept inequalities (measured in labor-time) that amount to social subjugation, if they are counterbalanced by the freedom from material subjugation that comes from increases in the workers' standard of living (measured in goods).

Since the parties in the Marxian-Liberal original position do not know and cannot gamble on what position they will occupy in society, they will measure a whole society's material standard of living by the size of the poorest people's distributive shares (measured in goods) since that is the smallest share they will possess. They will know, as part of their general knowledge, that increases in the material standard of living tend to be cumulative, and thus that any rise in the standard of living will normally raise the floor for all subsequent generations. And, where the floor rises, the shares of all those above the floor normally rise as well. It follows that everyone stands to gain more in freedom from reductions in material subjugation than from reductions in social subjugation. This is all the more so in the near term since, even if social subjugation were eliminated, workers would still be required to work to produce their material goods. Thus they would simply exchange social for material subjugation, with little appreciable gain. This point gains even more force from the presence of the natural right to liberty, since it eliminates the worst forms of social subjugation, serfdom and slavery.

Accordingly, parties in the Marxian-Liberal original position will seek the greatest possible reduction in material subjugation. For ease of expression, let us call reduction in material subjugation *material dominion*. Then, the parties will accept social subjugation when it is necessary to maximize material dominion. That means that they will accept the minimum amount of social subjugation needed to produce maximum material dominion. Translating social subjugation back into distributive inequalities (understood in terms of labor-time), and maximization of material dominion into the poorest workers' material standard of living (understood in terms goods), we can say that parties in the Marxian-Liberal original position will find it rational to consent to inequalities in distributive shares if they are the minimum necessary to maximize the poorest people's share of goods.

This standard is equivalent to Rawls's *difference principle*, which calls for reducing inequalities to the minimum necessary to maximize the absolute size of the worst-off social group's lifetime share[39] of socially produced goods.[40] The absolute size of the worst-off group's lifetime share (measured in goods) reflects the degree in which people achieve material dominion. The inequalities that the difference principle allows (measured in labor-time) represent the least amount of social subjugation necessary to maximize material dominion for the worst-off group—and thereby for every group more fortunate than it in the social system. Accordingly, people in the imaginary Marxian-Liberal original position will consent to a right to property governed by Rawls's difference principle.

This provides a deduction of the difference principle. Since structural coercion amounts to virtually everyone forcing virtually everyone else, economic subjugation will be spread through society, to the detriment and benefit of numerous people. Nonetheless, subjugation is a greater constraint on freedom the relatively poorer one is, since the relatively poorer one is, the more one is forced to work for others compared to how much those others work for one. Accordingly, parties in the Marxian-Liberal original position, not knowing (and unable to gamble on) which position they will occupy in whatever distributive scheme they agree to, and wanting to maximize their ability to act freely, will want to reduce material subjugation from the bottom of society working up. Imagining themselves in the poorest position, they will insist that their lifetime share be the largest it can be. Then, imagining themselves in each better position one after another, they will insist that the shares at each position be the largest they can be without reducing the shares below them.

Think of the positions in the distributive scheme as arrayed on a ladder, with the smallest share at the bottom, and shares getting larger as they ascend the ladder. Then, the lifetime share at the lowest rung must be the largest it can be, the share on the second rung must be the largest it can be without making the one below it yet smaller, the share on the third rung must be the largest it can be without making the two lower than it still smaller, and so on all the way to the top. This is precisely how Rawls understands the difference principle to work. Though Rawls focuses on the fate of the worst-off group, he assumes that the logic of the difference principle will apply to all groups working upwards from the worst off. If it doesn't, then Rawls contends that an expanded version of the difference principle, which he calls the *lexical difference principle*, should be applied. It holds:

> in a basic structure with n relevant representatives, first maximize the welfare of the worst-off representative man; second, for equal welfare of the worst-off representative, maximize the welfare of the second worst-off representative man, and so on until the last case which is, for equal welfare of all the preceding n − 1 representatives, maximize the welfare of the best-off representative man. (*TJ*, 72)

Note that, for Marxian Liberalism, this is more than a principle of distributive justice. It is a principle for making the structural coercion built into the property system such that people would consent to it. Thus it makes for a property system that, albeit coercive, is compatible with the natural right to liberty.

Before ending this section, it's worth noting that Marxian Liberalism entails some theoretical limits on the difference principle. Marxian Liberalism understands the goods that workers receive back for their labor under the difference principle as means to freedom. It is, however, implausible to think that freedom will increase endlessly with endlessly increasing shares of material goods. If so, then there must be a point after which additional material goods will no longer increase freedom. When this point is reached, rational Marxian Liberals will opt for cutting back on work rather than for getting more stuff, or they will work for the pleasure of it. The difference principle will still hold, but it will be applied in reverse, that is, toward reducing the amount of labor required to provide people with sufficient goods for real freedom. The amount of goods that suffice for freedom will change historically, and will surely be difficult, controversial, and maybe impossible to identify, so in practice the difference principle will still call for maximizing shares of goods for the worst off on up, and we will have to leave it to workers to choose between more goods or less work. (Something analogous will apply to the difference principle considered simply as a principle of distributive justice: when additional goods are no longer attractive—that third dishwasher, that eighth TV—inequalities will not be justified by piling more goods onto workers, and rational workers will take their additional benefits in leisure, or work because it pleases them to do so.) In any event, as long as workers can stop laboring at the point at which they have goods sufficient for genuine freedom, work they choose to do beyond this is not coerced.[41]

A further limit on the difference principle entailed by Marxian Liberalism is this: like Marx himself, Marxian Liberalism looks forward to a time when technology will produce all the goods that people need and want (when "the springs of cooperative wealth flow more abundantly"), and people will labor for the pleasure of it (when "labour has become . . . life's prime want"). At that point, the difference principle would be replaced by the principle: "From each according to his ability, to each according to his needs."[42] This principle announces the end of economically mediated coercion because it no longer makes what workers receive depend on the labor they give. Until then, the difference principle would make for the least possible coercion in the economy, and thus make private property such that people could consent to it.

V. The Just State

A state would be chosen in the Marxian-Liberal original position because it is necessary to specify and enforce the rights to liberty and property. The just state must protect every sane adult's natural negative right to be free from unwanted coercion, and it must assure that the economy works in conformity with the difference principle. Though I speak here of the state and the economy, Marxian Liberalism does not accept the distinction between the political and economic realms that Marx attacked in his essay "On the Jewish Question."[43] That distinction is ideological because it suggests that while the state is coercive, the economy is not. It is of a piece with the ideological invisibility of the structural coercion built into private property. For Marxian Liberalism, the economy must be governed by the difference principle precisely because it is a realm of coercion. For this reason, unlike Rawls's theory of justice, the protection of natural liberty and the implementation of the difference principle are not characterized by lexical priority of the first over the second (cf., e.g., *TJ*, 53–54). Both principles hold fully and simultaneously, because both are meant to protect individuals from coercion. Therefore, also unlike Rawls's theory of justice, both principles are constitutional principles to be enforced by the equivalent of a Supreme Court.[44]

The just state is limited in its activity to enforcing these two principles, and providing the conditions necessary to their functioning. Under the first principle, the just state will outlaw physical assaults, and fraud as well, since it functions like coercion to undermine choice. That principle also dictates that preference be given to private—that is, voluntary—solutions to public problems. Under the second principle, the government will assure that distributive outcomes conform to the difference principle, and that the conditions for the effective functioning of the economy are in place. Because racism and sexism are forms of structural coercion, the government will combat them and other (perhaps as yet unidentified) "isms" that are structurally coercive as well. For this reason (plus the provision for education of children mentioned below), the difference principle need not be associated with a principle of fair opportunity, as it is in Rawls's version (*TJ*, 226, see also 77–78).

Decisions about how the just state will satisfy these requirements will be made democratically—based on the principle of one person, one vote. That assures that all people have equal ability to determine their society's conduct, and thus their own conduct as members of that society. In that sense, democracy is the collective expression of each person's natural right to liberty. For that reason, the just state will also make sure that private property is not used in ways that undermine people's equal rights to shape their society's conduct.[45]

Note that by protecting liberty for all and implementing the difference principle, the just state is an egalitarian state. The right to liberty is possessed equally by all, and the difference principle is egalitarian because it calls for the greatest degree of equality that can be had without making the poorest people even poorer.[46] Compared to simply leaving the economy to exchanges undertaken without threat of force or fraud, the difference principle is a principle of redistribution. That redistribution is necessary to make the coercion built into property ownership such that all can freely consent to it. It is not redistribution in the sense of taking from anyone what they were justly entitled to; it is redistribution to get people the shares to which they are justly entitled. Nonetheless, the government of the just state will be more active than the minimum *nightwatchman* state preferred by some liberals. For the following reasons, it is, nonetheless, still truly a liberal state:

There will be no morals legislation, no victimless crime laws and the like. These are constitutionally prohibited by the natural right to liberty. That the state will engage in public projects necessary for protection of liberty and conformity to the difference principle only when these cannot be assured privately[47] is guaranteed by that same constitutional right to liberty.

The only paternalism in which the just state will engage is where paternalism is appropriate, namely, the treatment of children. Since children are unable to provide for themselves, and unable to decide how to use freedom, the state will have to assure that they receive the care and education needed to develop into adults who can provide for themselves and decide how to use their freedom. Here too, if such care and education can be provided privately, then it will be.

More deeply, however, the just state is a liberal state because in it, all laws, as well as the state itself, exist only to protect people against unwanted coercion. The just state appears to be doing more than this because of the general invisibility of structural coercion. Since the just state both protects the right to liberty and limits social subjugation in the economic system to the minimum needed to maximize people's shares in the material means of freedom, it arguably provides overall for the greatest amount of freedom possible.

Notes

1   This essay is a very brief version of the argument that I set out at length in Jeffrey Reiman, *As Free and as Just as Possible: The Theory of Marxian Liberalism* (Oxford: Wiley-Blackwell, 2012).

2   "In justice as fairness the original position of equality corresponds to the state of nature in the traditional theory of the social contract ... It is understood as a purely hypothetical situation characterized so as to lead to a certain conception of justice. Among the essential features of this situation is that no one knows his place in society, his class position or social status, nor does anyone know his fortune in the distribution of natural assets and abilities, his intelligence, strength, and the like ... The principles of

justice are chosen behind a veil of ignorance. This ensures that no one is advantaged or disadvantaged in the choice of principles by the outcome of natural chance or the contingency of social circumstances." John Rawls, *A Theory of Justice*, rev. ed. (Cambridge, MA: Harvard University Press, 1999); 11 (hereafter cited as *TJ*).

3 "Social and economic inequalities are to be arranged so that they are ... to the greatest benefit of the least advantaged" (*TJ*, 266). Rawls writes also that "the difference principle is a strongly egalitarian conception in the sense that unless there is a distribution that makes both [the more advantaged and the less advantaged] persons better off ..., an equal distribution is to be preferred" (*TJ*, 65–66).

4 "One should note that acceptance of [the principles of justice in the original position] is not conjectured as a psychological law or probability. Ideally anyway, I should like to show that their acknowledgment is the only choice consistent with the full description of the original position. The argument aims eventually to be strictly deductive ... Unhappily the reasoning I shall give will fall far short of this, since it is highly intuitive throughout" (*TJ*, 104–105).

5 Peter Vallentyne, Hillel Steiner, and Michael Otsuka, "Why Left-Libertarianism Is Not Incoherent, Indeterminate, or Irrelevant: A Reply to Fried," *Philosophy & Public Affairs*, *33*(2) (2005): 201; on the independence of the two basic principles, see 208–210.

6 Locke appears to infer self-ownership from the right to liberty, and uses it as part of his argument for the right to own property for consumption. Kant rejects self-ownership, holding that only things, and not persons, can be owned. He argues directly from the right to liberty to the right to property. John Locke, *The Second Treatise of Government*, in John Locke, *Political Writings*, David Wooton, ed. (Indianapolis, IN: Hackett Publishing, 2003; the *Second Treatise* orig. pub. 1689), chapter v, section 27 (hereafter cited as *ST*, followed by chapter and section numbers). Immanuel Kant, *The Metaphysics of Morals* (Cambridge: Cambridge University Press, 1996; the two parts of *The Metaphysics of Morals*, "The Doctrine of Right" and "The Doctrine of Virtue," orig. pub. separately in 1797); 41, 56.

7 Vallentyne et al., "Why Left-Libertarianism Is Not Incoherent," 201.

8 By employers systematically choosing not to hire women or blacks for certain jobs, for example, women and blacks are deprived of a large range of options that white men have.

9 I say "unwanted" here because, with this right, people may voluntarily subject themselves to coercion, say, by signing a contract. Moreover, people are also rightly subject to coercion necessary to enforce this right for all. I will henceforth assume that this is understood, and not continue to use the term "unwanted."

10 Jeremy Waldron has argued that Locke's theory of rights cannot be understood apart from Locke's theistic views. See Waldron, *God, Locke, and Equality: Christian Foundations of Locke's Political Thought* (Cambridge: Cambridge University Press, 2002). For a defense of a secular reading of Locke's theory against Waldron's claim, see Jeffrey Reiman, "Towards a Secular Lockean Liberalism," *Review of Politics*, *67*(3) (Summer 2005): 473–493. Another philosopher who reads Locke's theory in secular terms is A. John Simmons. See Simmons, *The Lockean Theory of Rights* (Princeton, NJ: Princeton University Press, 1992); 10.

11 On Locke's views about the ground of moral obligation, see the discussion in Simmons, *Lockean Theory of Rights*, 26–28.

12 Robert Nozick, *Anarchy, State, and Utopia* (New York: Basic Books, 1974); 174–182 (hereafter cited as *ASU*).

13 That the value of money is conventional does not imply that it is consented to, and, even if it did, it would not imply consent to everything that money makes possible. The meanings of words are conventional, but that hardly means they are consented to, and, even if it did, it would not imply consent to everything that words make possible, such as lying.

14 Jean-Jacques Rousseau, *A Discourse on the Origin of Inequality*, in *The Social Contract and Discourses* (London: Dent & Sons, 1973; orig. pub. 1755); 87.

15 Kant, *Metaphysics of Morals*, 41.

16 Kant, *Metaphysics of Morals*, 55.

17 Immanuel Kant, "On the Proverb: That May Be True in Theory, But Is of No Practical Use," in *Perpetual Peace and Other Essays* (Indianapolis, IN: Hackett, 1983; orig. pub. 1793); 73.

18 Jan Narveson, "Property and Rights," *Social Philosophy and Policy*, *27*(1) (2010): 112–115.

19 Karl Marx, *Capital* (New York: International Publishers, 1967; orig. pub.: vol. I, 1867, vol. II, 1893, vol. III, 1894; hereafter cited as *C*, plus vol. number), I; 766.

20 Marx may have been influenced by Kant here, since Kant recognized that property ownership was not a

relation of a person to a thing, but "a relation of a person to persons." See Kant, *Metaphysics of Morals*, 55.

21 Because, like the traffic bottleneck, the institution of private property affects people as groups rather than determining the outcome for each individual, it is compatible with G.A. Cohen's claim that individual members of the proletarian are free to leave the working class (they can borrow money and establish small shops, for example), but collectively the members of the working class are not free to do so (only a few could set up businesses before the opportunities would be closed off). See G.A. Cohen, "The Structure of Proletarian Unfreedom," *Philosophy & Public Affairs*, 12(1) (Winter 1983): 14; "Are Workers Forced to Sell Their Labor Power?" *Philosophy & Public Affairs*, 14(1) (Winter 1985): 102. It is, of course, a standard ideological gambit to claim in defense of capitalism that, because some can leave the working class, all can.

22 *Corpus Jurus Secundum: Property* 73, sec. 43 (Eagan, MN: Thomson West, 2004); 48.

23 W.L. Burdick, *Handbook of the Law of Real Property* (St Paul, MN: West Publishing, 1914); 61–67.

24 See V.G. Kiernan, "Private Property in History," in Jack Goody, Joan Thirsk, and E.P. Thomson, eds., *Family and Inheritance: Rural Society in Western Europe, 1200–1800* (Cambridge: Cambridge University Press, 1976); 376, 376–377, 387–391; Peter Garnsey, *Thinking about Property: From Antiquity to the Age of Revolution* (Cambridge: Cambridge University Press, 2007); 186–188; and Alan Watson, *Roman Law and Comparative Law* (Athens, GA: University of Georgia Press, 1991); 49.

25 "[T]he very fact that a choice clearly is extremely detrimental to [individuals] may itself be grounds for concluding that it was made in a moment of incompetence; at that point it becomes reasonable to respect the choices they *would* have made had they been competent rather than the choices they actually made." Steven Luper, *The Philosophy of Death* (Cambridge: Cambridge University Press, 2009); 161.

26 See note 2, above.

27 Though Rawls offers arguments to prove that gambling on the position one will end up in is not rational in the original position (e.g., *TJ*, 134–135; see also 149–150), I think he should have ruled gambling out in the very design of the original position. Rawls expressly designed his original position "to lead to a certain conception of justice," in particular one that honors the inviolability of humans (*TJ*, 3). This is one reason that decisions in the original position must be unanimous. But gambling takes back what unanimity gives. If the rewards of some arrangement are great enough and the risk of a negative outcome small enough, a group of rational individuals who are permitted to gamble will find it rational to agree to that arrangement no matter how badly it treats a few. Accordingly, gambling is prohibited in the design of the Marxian-Liberal original position.

28 "It is taken for granted that [the parties in the original position] know the general facts about human society. They understand political affairs and the principles of economic theory; they know the basis of social organization and the laws of human psychology. Indeed, the parties are presumed to know whatever general facts affect the choice of the principles of justice" (*TJ*, 119).

29 Karl Marx, "On the Jewish Question," in *Karl Marx, Writings of the Young Marx on Philosophy and Society*, eds. L. Easton and K. Guddat (Indianapolis, IN: 1997; "On the Jewish Question" orig. pub. 1843); 227, 234–237. That liberalism is the ideology of capitalism does not imply that it is wholly false or regressive. It is no accident that democracy only stops being a bad word after the advent of capitalism, that feminism arises after the arrival of capitalism, that even the communist movement depends on the existence of capitalism. Ideology must itself be in some measure progressive to work as ideology.

30 In my view, private, and thus relatively decentralized, ownership of property is the material basis for the freedoms that generally characterize capitalist societies and that have been generally absent from communist ones.

31 Here and for the following several paragraphs, I generally follow the analysis in Jeffrey Reiman, "The Labor Theory of the Difference Principle," *Philosophy & Public Affairs*, 12(2) (Spring 1983): 133–159.

32 "The labour-time socially necessary is that required to produce an article under the normal conditions of production, and with the average degree of skill and intensity prevalent at the time" (*C*, I, 39). Note that Marx insisted that the amount of labor-time embodied in the value of commodities was equal to *socially necessary* labor-time to avoid the implication that the less efficiently goods were produced the higher their value would be. G.A. Cohen has argued that this leads to a problem for Marxian theory: the value of actual commodities does not necessarily correspond to the actual labor that went into them,

and thus surplus value cannot be taken as equivalent to unpaid labor extracted from workers. See G.A. Cohen, "The Labor Theory of Value and the Concept of Exploitation," *Philosophy & Public Affairs*, 8(4) (Summer 1979): 338–360. Since the moral version of the labor theory of value is not concerned with determining prices, it can take commodities as representing the actual labor that went into producing them, and thus it does not fall prey to Cohen's criticism.

33 Marx writes that "however varied the useful kinds of labour ... may be, it is a physiological fact, that they are functions of the human organism, and that each such function, whatever may be its nature or form, is essentially the expenditure of human brain, nerves, muscles, &c.... . In all states of society, the labour-time that it costs to produce the means of subsistence, must necessarily be an object of interest to mankind" (*C*, I, 71).

34 In *Capital*, Marx took distributive measures as indications of exploitation: "The rate of surplus-value [the ratio between the surplus value received by the capitalist and the variable capital that the capitalist gives to the worker in the form of his wage] is ... an exact expression of the degree of exploitation ... of the labourer by the capitalist" (*C*, I, 218).

35 This general idea is accepted by Philippe van Parijs in *Real Freedom for All: What (if Anything) Can Justify Capitalism?* (Oxford: Oxford University Press, 1995), and by Amartya Sen in *The Idea of Justice* (Cambridge, MA: Harvard University Press, 2009).

36 Rawls addresses this Marxian critique with respect to political rights. See John Rawls, *Justice as Fairness: A Restatement*, ed. Erin Kelly (Cambridge, MA: Harvard University Press, 2001); 177.

37 Karl Marx, "A Preface to *A Contribution to the Critique of Political Economy*," in Karl Marx, *Early Writings* (New York: Vintage Books, 1975; *A Contribution* was originally written in 1859); 426.

38 This is most evident if Marx is taken as subscribing the view sometimes voiced by Engels, that the earliest societies were characterized by a so-called primitive communism. Since those societies were more egalitarian than the ones that followed, history could only count as progressive if those subsequent societies were seen as trade-offs necessary for increasing human power over nature. See Frederick Engels, *The Origin of the Family, Private Property and the State* (New York: International Publishers, 1970; orig. pub. 1884); 103, 112–114.

39 Rawls is clear that the difference principle is about people's shares over the course of their lifetimes. When he talks about how the principle operates, he speaks of "life prospects" or "expectations" (*TJ*, 67–68), and he makes clear that individuals' "expectation indicates their life prospects as viewed from their social station" (*TJ*, 56).

40 Rawls's version of the idea that inequalities are necessary to maximize distributive share of the poorest people is that—at least for some stretch of history—inequalities are necessary as incentives for higher productivity, especially since we want to avoid using coercion for that end. This is tied to the emphasis on lifetime shares in the difference principle, just mentioned. Without the emphasis on lifetime shares, one might think the difference principle requires equality right now because by making everyone equal right now, we maximize the share of the worst off (without making anyone else still worse off than them). However, if inequalities are necessary as incentives for higher productivity, making everyone equal right now will eventually undermine productivity and cause the worst-off group to be even worse off over the course of their lifetimes.

41 I take it as obvious that, even in the advanced nations of the world, the point has not been reached at which everyone has goods sufficient for genuine freedom.

42 Karl Marx, "Critique of the Gotha Program," in R. Tucker, ed., *The Marx-Engels Reader*, 2nd edition (New York: Norton, 1978); 531.

43 Marx, "On the Jewish Question," 216–248.

44 John Rawls, *Political Liberalism* (New York: Columbia University Press, 1993); 230.

45 Rawls refers to this as guaranteeing the fair value of political liberties. See Rawls, *Justice as Fairness*, 148–150.

46 "According to the difference principle, [inequality in life prospects between entrepreneurs and unskilled workers] is only justifiable if the difference in expectation is to the advantage of the ... unskilled worker. The inequality in expectation is permissible only if lowering it would make the working class even more worse off" (*TJ*, 68).

47 For example, some part of people's shares in the distributive scheme might take the form of health services that would be provided by the state if that were the only way to provide them efficiently and reliably.

Reframing the Commonwealth
Commercial or Civic

MARVIN T. BROWN

What do we really want from the businesses in our communities? Jobs? Affordable products? Safe workplaces? Good wages? Donations? Happiness? Perhaps we first need to ask: what kind of community do we want? Can we say we want our community to be wealthy—to enjoy a common wealth? And what would that entail? We can use Amartya Sen (1999) and Martha Nussbaum's (2011) definition of human development to answer that question. They propose that human development can be measured by the capacity of a community's members to acquire what they have reason to value. People may disagree about what that would include, but, in general, it would at least include security, significant relationships, possibilities for self-development, and some control over one's existence. If we did understand common wealth in this way, then what would be the role of business, and of business ethics, in such a community?

The idea of a commonwealth has been around since the 18th-century Enlightenment. One thinks of the British Commonwealth, the Commonwealth of Nations, or even the Commonwealth of Virginia. Four states in the USA are named commonwealths. For the most part, the notion of the common wealth has had a double meaning: a referential meaning of government and a more symbolic meaning of wealth-in-common. Perhaps one could combine these two meanings with the notion of a government for the common good (wealth). Uniting these two meanings of common wealth, however, is not as easy as it might seem. In fact, since the beginning of capitalism, we have lived in an economy where much of what was a common wealth has been privatized (Bollier 2003). Before we can understand the role that businesses, and business ethics, should play in our communities, we need to first understand what has happened to our common wealth and how we could build a new commonwealth for all of us. We begin with the 18th-century privatization of the commons.

The Privatization of the Commons

The economist Karl Polanyi called the privatization of the commons part of the "great transformation" of early capitalism (1957). Land that had been open for common use was "enclosed" by legislative acts beginning in the 15th century and continuing until the 18th. The land became the private property of the landowner.

Before the enclosures, commoners or peasants had various common rights. They included the right to access the fields and forests around villages for grazing livestock, gleaning leftover grain, gathering fodder for animals, as well as the right to wood and other materials for fuel. With these rights, many commoners were able to provide for their families by sharing land with others and taking on extra work when they needed to (Neeson 1993, p. 42). The enclosures resulted in the loss of these rights and most of the commoners either moved to the cities and became dependent on wages for their survival or immigrated to the colonies.

A similar enclosure or privatizing of the commons occurred in the American colonies. Stuart Banner describes the parallels between the English enclosure movements and the privatization of land in the Americas this way:

> Enclosure meant the conversion of an ancient system of property rights, in which individuals and groups often possessed rights to use particular resources scattered in various places, into the familiar modern property system, in which individuals possess all the resources within a given area of land ... Indian property arrangements were similar in some respects to the English common fields. The combination of individual planting rights in particular plots of land and group resource-gathering right in the remainder would have reminded many English colonists of property systems back home. (Banner 2005, p. 58)

Instead of sharing land with others, which was the practice of many native tribes, the Europeans believed that ownership gave them exclusive use of the land, and others were guilty of trespassing if they walked across it. Although these different enclosures happened centuries ago, their legacy continues to influence our views of what we share in common and what we own by ourselves. A key source of this ideology has been Adam Smith's *The Wealth of Nations* (1776), where we find the promotion of what he called a "commercial society" (Smith 1944, p. 24).

Adam Smith's "Commercial Society"

The book's title is already revealing. Why the wealth of "nations," and not the wealth of the "commons," or the wealth of the "commonwealth"? Smith does use the term "commonwealth" in Book V of *The Wealth of Nations*: "Of the Revenue of the Sovereign or Commonwealth" (1944, p. 747). Book V has little to do with either the commons or with wealth, but rather with the costs involved in the government protection of the commercial society. Smith's use of the term "nation" appears to refer much more to a social grouping than to the political state. At the beginning of Book V, he writes of four different nations: the nation of hunters, the nation of shepherds, the nation of husbandmen, and then the nation of Smith's time: "a civilized nation."

These four "nations" require different levels of government (the sovereign or commonwealth) because they have different amounts of property. The evolution of these four types of nations is a story of the evolution of property—from a hunter nation that does not accumulate property to a "civilized nation" that is characterized by property and property relations. This nation is the last stage of human evolution, wherein, as Smith writes: "Every man thus lives by exchanging or becomes in some measure a merchant, and the society itself grows to be what is property called a commercial society" (1944, p. 24). In Smith's "commercial society," all properties—labor, land, or money—are owned by individuals. The commons is effectively eliminated in Smith's "economics of property." The only "commons" one can find here would be the market itself, or to use Smith's phrase, the invisible hand. The common, in other words, has become the commercial.

The Legacy of Smith's "Commercial Society"

The connection of a civilized nation with a commercial society has erased, for the most part, the commons of our communities. It created an economic framework that focuses on "me, myself, and I," rather than on "we." Wealth, for the most part, is measured by the exchange of commodities and only those who have commodities to exchange can have a "piece of the action," so to speak. The commercial market includes anything that can be transformed into something that can sell and excludes everything else. In this framework, instead of seeing families and communities, one sees a labor market; instead of seeing the natural living planet, one sees real estate; instead of seeing money as credit for economic growth, one sees money as a commodity in financial markets. Even our participation in higher education, in this commercial society, becomes a means to increase the property value of our knowledge, skills, and gregariousness.

In this commercial commonwealth, businesses have found an accepting framework for focusing on cheap products and high profits. Yes, they may engage in various programs to meet their responsibilities to stakeholders, but, at their core, they see themselves "in business" to increase the value of what they own. In this world, individuals may be rich or poor, depending on their effort and luck, but the commons is either ignored or taken for granted.

The overlooking of what we share in common, and the assumed independence of the commercial from the political, has created a commercial framework not only for businesses, but also for much of business ethics. In contrast to the Western origin of ethics in the civic realm, this can be seen as a privatization of business ethics.

The Privatization of Business Ethics

In the history of ethics as a discipline, it began as a civic or public ethic. In the first textbook on ethics, Aristotle's *Nicomachean Ethics*, we learn that since ethics is an inquiry into the good for man, not only as an individual but also for the community, it is a sort of political science (1999, p. 2). Most people in the field of business ethics have not followed Aristotle's view of ethics as belonging to politics. The ethicist Robert Solomon wrote the following in his popular book, *Ethics and Excellence* (1993, pp. 123–124):

> The very structure of our society, its ample leisure and personality, are created by business, by the way business spurs and makes productivity possible and the way it distributes the goods throughout society and the world. Indeed, the values of our society— for better or worse—are essentially business values, the values of "free enterprise," the values of necessity and novelty and innovation and personal initiative. But that does not mean that is it "everyone for himself or herself," a "dog-eat-dog world, or a world in

which "everything goes." To the contrary, it is a world defined by tacit understandings and implicit rules, a practice defined, like all practices, by mutual understandings and underlying trust, and justified not by its profits but by the general prosperity it brings about.

Solomon's reference above to "mutual understandings and underlying trust" shows his awareness of the role of what we will see later as the reality of the commons, but what is most significant about his statement is its assertion that "the very structure of society" is "created by business." In fact, both the implicit commons and the explicit social structures have been privatized. Solomon is not alone, of course. Many in business ethics believe that we should not think beyond what is called the "business case for ethics," which is that businesses should not have any obligations that harm their "bottom line." Maybe we should not expect anything else as long as the default framework for business ethics is a commercial society.

Business ethics, in other words, has tended to work within the framework of a commercial society rather than a civic society. Operating in this commercial framework has not prevented ethicists from recognizing the existence of the commons, as we noticed in the quote from Robert Solomon, but we must say that it has not facilitated perceptions of what we actually do hold in common or share with each other. It has operated, in other words, mostly within the framework created by the enclosure of the commons, which has led us to focus on what we own and relationships among owners, not relationships among commoners or citizens.

The truth of the matter, however, is that we need many things we cannot own, and much that we do claim to own actually comes from a common resource. The ideas in this essay, for example, draw on common knowledge about business and society that many have contributed to and are now available to anyone who visits a library, goes online, or talks with colleagues. Music, stories, rituals, and many other things that enrich (en-rich) our lives are part of our common wealth. In fact, much that our commercial markets now threaten—air quality, fresh water, ecosystems, and even the planet—are commons that belong to all of us. For the sake of a viable future, it is time to renew our connections to the commons.

The Idea of the Commons

In its broadest sense, the "commons" refers to things that cannot or should not be exclusively owned. The commons is the polar opposite of commodities. A widespread image of the commons is a pasture used by several, but owned by no one. This was the image used by Garrett Hardin in his famous piece on "the tragedy of the commons" (1968). He argued that if there were several shepherds using a common pasture each one's self-interest would lead him to increase his flock of sheep and, if each one did the same thing, the pasture would be overgrazed and destroyed. The "tragedy," according to Hardin, was that what looked like an abundant resource from an individual point of view was actually a limited resource from a bird's-eye view. The lesson from Hardin's narrative seemed to be that the best way to manage the commons was by ownership.

In the 1990s, the economist Elinor Ostrom demonstrated that Hardin was mistaken. She investigated communities that had used and protected what she called common polled resources for hundreds of years (Ostrom 1990). In her research on governing the commons, she found numerous cases where communities did share a commons to everyone's benefit. Her first case, in fact, described how the citizens of a village in Switzerland had set up rules for sharing a common pasture. One of the rules was that no one could put more cattle on the pasture than they could care for in the winter (1990, p. 61). This community, and others as well, did not experience the commons as a "tragedy," but as a source of wealth.

Ostrom's research serves as one of the foundations for current conversations about the commons. David Bollier's work is another. He makes a clear distinction between a market economy and gift economy (Bollier 2003, p. 48). Bollier makes the following distinctions between the two economies: in a market economy, relations are impersonal and based on property relations. In a gift economy, relationships are personal and based on caring and meeting people's needs. A gift economy is based on trust in personal relations in contrast to the market economy that is based on trust in the market (the invisible hand). As Mark Brown has pointed out, not all gift economies are based on personal relations:

> Science is a gift economy based on impersonal relations and motivated not by "caring and meeting people's needs," but by (at least in part) egoistic efforts to establish and enhance one's reputations among colleagues. The greatest honors go to those who give the most, and people "give" not to specific personal others but to the abstract community as a whole. (Brown, personal communication)

Some of the most thought-provoking ideas about the commons have come from thinkers who see the creative sharing and innovation on the Internet as a commons. Michel Bauwens, the founder of the P2P (peer to peer) Foundation has given a new perspective of the commons that focuses on the processes of sharing. He writes that P2P processes:

- produce use-value through the free cooperation of producers who have access to distributed capital: this is the P2P production mode, a "third mode of production" different from for-profit or public production by state-owned enterprises. Its product is not exchange value for a market, but use-value for a community of users.
- are governed by the community of producers themselves, and not by market allocation or corporate hierarchy: this is the P2P governance mode, or "third mode of governance."
- make use-value freely accessible on a universal basis, through new common property regimes. This is its distribution or "peer property mode": a "third mode of ownership," different from private property or public (state) property. (Bauwens 2005)

These three premises ensure that the mode of production is open to all those who have something to contribute to the process, the community is self-governed, and that the product itself is not something that becomes a commodity, but remains useful for others who can benefit from it. Bauwens is searching not for the rules that will protect the commons, but for the common processes that will make such rules unnecessary.

I am not sure if common processes will be enough to secure "all that we share," to use the title of a recent book edited by Jay Walljasper. All that we share turns out to be a long list. It includes the following (Walljasper 2010, pp. 7–8):

> Air & water, the land, the Internet, parks, libraries, streets, and sidewalks, dance steps, the airwaves, holiday traditions, music, games, biodiversity, Famous stories, open-source software, the oceans, jokes, and outer space.

As you review this list, and perhaps add to it, you will find that some are abundant, and some are scarce. Some are things that belong to culture and society, such as music or games, and some belong to the biosphere. If we understand wealth as the capacity to acquire what we have reason to value, then many things on this list are sources of wealth. They are also quite different from our commercial wealth.

Commercial and Common Wealth

In a commercial society, what counts as wealth is what can be treated as a commodity in the market. In a common society, wealth will not be limited to what we can purchase, but will include all that we need for a good life. People will acquire much that they need through sharing and giving. Instead of focusing on the accumulation of property, the focus will be on the making of provisions. A common society will provide for one another though processes that are based on shared endeavors, as well as on individual efforts.

A common society will also allow us to recognize the planet as a living provider instead of only seeing its property value. Most importantly, instead of treating the planet as an object we control, we can see it as something to which we belong. This means that inhabitants of the planet can relate to one another not primarily as owners, but rather as members of a commons. Table 2.1 highlights these differences.

These differences are not absolute. It would be a mistake to see the distinction between commercial and common wealth as an either/or choice. We need commercial activities and property ownership. I am not trying to do away with either one, but

Table 2.1 Two kinds of wealth

Commercial wealth	Common wealth
Private property	Shared provision
Land as commodity	Land as provider
Ownership	Membership

rather trying to put them in their place in a commonwealth that actually provides wealth for everyone. This requires a rejection of Adam Smith's belief that a commercial society was the final stage of human evolution. We need to begin with what we have in common, and then to see how commerce fits with it. What kind of relationship, in other words, should we build between the commons and the commercial?

This may seem like *the* question for business ethics today. How can businesses function in such a manner that our common resources remain available to all? Can businesses help to make water, clean air, and knowledge available to all and owned by none? Well, it depends on your view of business.

Does business also belong to the commons? Not as we know it. In fact, business today is usually about the commodity market, about property relations. It belongs to commerce. It is commerce. If people share cars, for example, that would be bad for business, because people would buy fewer cars. Perhaps business and the commons are really mutual enemies, and they actually pose threats to each other's existence. If we remain in a commercial framework for thinking about the role of business in society, we easily come to these conclusions. Another option is to create another platform, so to speak, on which we could stand and from this vantage point reconfigure the relationship between the commons and commercial. I want to suggest that we should construct a civic platform for developing a new framework for a contemporary commonwealth.

A Civic Platform

In terms of individual identity, we are all commoners, consumers, and citizens. As commoners, we share with others what is available to all. As consumers, we select commodities in the market based on our preferences. Most of us are probably quite familiar with the identity of consumers. Who does not like to go shopping? The identity of commoners is more challenging. In fact, there is a strong fashion in modern cultures not to be common, but to be special. This fashion, however, echoes the pervasiveness of the commercial culture that values what we "have," instead of what we share in common. In any case, the most thought provoking is the third form of identity—our identity as citizens.

To be a citizen is to be a member of a city (that is actually its original meaning). In other words, you cannot be a citizen alone. Our identity as a citizen, to quote the political theorist Sheldon Wolin, "provides what other roles cannot, namely an integrative experience which brings together the multiple role activities of the contemporary person and demands that the separate roles be surveyed from a more general point of view" (2004, p. 389). This more general point of view is not to be found in the mind of the individual, but in conversations among citizens. It is the mutual learning from engagement in conversations with others that allows an expansion of each person's knowledge as well as the creation of collective knowledge. We can assume that such conversations have been occurring, in some fashion, in many different communities. The patterns and expectations that civic conversations create and maintain can serve as a platform for seeing the economy itself as a mixture of the common and the commercial, or a civic commonwealth.

A Civic Commonwealth

A civic commonwealth can be created and maintained by the decisions, actions, and policies that emerge from civic conversations among citizens about how we should provide for all. These conversations must both recognize the differences between the commercial and the common, and yet still integrate the two. This process of integration depends on answers to three questions: (1) How should we design an economy that makes provisions for everyone? (2) How should we deal with disagreements among citizens? and (3) How should we govern a civic commonwealth?

An economy that provides for everyone

As we have seen, common wealth is inclusive, while commercial wealth is exclusive. How do we integrate these two types of wealth into our economy? We can begin by examining how we actually gain access to the things we have reason to value. Some of the things we value, such as practical wisdom or community celebrations, can be acquired through sharing—a gift economy. Others can be shared through mutual coordination. Groups agree to take turns to use parks, have street fairs, and so on. People will acquire what they have reason to value, in other words, in a variety of ways.

Many provisions originate in the commons, and are transformed into consumer products by the commercial. From a civic perspective, the commercial functions as a transformative process of changing common resources into provisions for our families and communities. Food, for example, comes from the earth, lives in a common biosphere, and is processed and distributed in common spaces (cities and infrastructures). The commercial belongs to this process of making food available for all, from farming to processing, shipping, and selling in markets. From a civic perspective, however, food should not be treated only as private property.

Imagine a farmer who decides to burn a cornfield instead of harvesting it and sending it to market. Has not he destroyed our common wealth? Of course, from the perspective of commercial wealth, the corn is his private property. But from a civic commonwealth framework, the corn belongs to the commons, and should be brought to market. There, the farmer can ask for a good price for the corn and receive his due for his work, and even honor for taking care of the land for this and future generations. Actually, the movement from the cornfield to the table involves many agencies that together comprise what can be called a system of provision.

For those of us who live in urban cities, most common resources become available to us only through elaborate systems. To get a drink of water in San Francisco, for example, we rely on a complicated water system that brings the melted snow from the Sierra mountain range on the other side of the state. In the greater San Francisco Bay Area, from Santa Rosa to Santa Cruz, we are around 8 million people. Every morning, there is food for almost all of us. It comes from local, regional, national, and international sources. In the best of times, our milk and apples could come from within California. Our bananas will not, neither will some other products. In fact, the "food system" is a vast and multidimensional system that includes many different organizations from the land to the grocery store and restaurant. In a nutshell, the food system

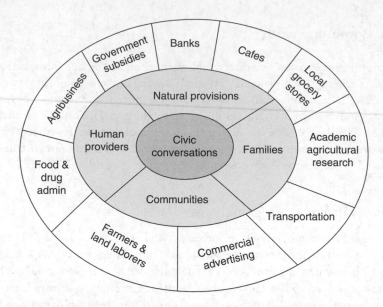

Figure 2.1   Key stakeholders of the food system
Source: M. Brown, *Civilizing the Economy: A New Economics of Provision*, Cambridge: Cambridge University Press, 2010, p. 195.

transforms things from the land (a commons) into products (through commerce) that provide daily nutrition for all of us.

At the core of any system of provision—whether it is food, housing, or healthcare—there should be citizens deliberating about the design of the system. Such civic conversations can occur in any of the organizations that have a stake in the system, from farmworkers to research scientists. All the key stakeholders of this system can be seen as engaged in the civic process of directing the whole system toward its goal of making provisions for all. We actually can imagine three concentric circles here. The inner circle is composed by civic conversations. This circle is surrounded by the basic activity of a civic commonwealth: human providers transforming natural provisions into accessible provisions for our families and communities, and then an outer circle of the key stakeholders of the system. Figure 2.1 shows these concentric circles for the food system.

Other systems of provision, of course, have other stakeholders, and yet most have some of the same. Banks, for example, have an important role in most systems of provisions, from housing to healthcare, because most systems need credit and money as a means of exchange. A good bank is one that fulfills its systemic function. The system of provision, in other words, determines the bank's purpose. It would be a mistake if the bank were to take the debt that it received from extending credit and turn it into a commodity that it could sell for a profit in a financial market. Banks, like other stakeholders in the system of provision, find their purpose in their contribution to the success of the whole system to which they belong.

And what is a good system? A good system, I would suggest, fulfills its purpose, fits in with other systems, and protects the significant characteristics of its parts. So a good food system provides good food for people, does it in such a way that it fits in with larger social and natural systems (promotes justice and sustainability), and protects the labor, land, and investments that energize the system. Moving any system of provision toward these general ideas of the good is possible through the strategies of persuasion, incentives, and regulation. Before we review these three forms of governing, we need to address our second question: how to deal with disagreements (see Brown, 2003).

Dealing with disagreements

Would it not be nice if some "invisible hand" or "divine providence" took care of our conflicts and dilemmas, and somehow, behind our back, so to speak, would wring some good out of whatever we did? While the civic provides a platform for connecting the commons and the commercial, and allows the commons to be the foundation for the commercial, it does not resolve disagreements and conflicts about how we should design the different systems of provision that make up a civic commonwealth. There are differences of opinion about how all this should fit together, and no group has all the right answers or even the right questions. In fact, it is only by tolerating disagreement that the participants in civic conversations can both individually know more than they knew before and as a group see their way toward a course of action that is supported by the best contributions of all sides. To engage in this process, participants must take on the identity of citizens and members of a civil society that transcends their social differences, but does not erase them. Diversity is essential for making the best decisions possible.

The process of dealing with disagreement involves more than listening to and learning from different points of view. It also requires a common acceptance of the general principles that we outlined previously about a good system of provision—fulfills its purpose, fits in the larger whole, and protects the value and dignity of its parts. These general norms provide a common basis for dealing with disagreement (people will only effectively disagree with each other when they share some broader agreements) and also provide some normative standards for evaluating the different positions. Successful civic conversations, in other words, must be guided by civic norms.

Where do such conversations take place? They can occur in any of the organizations that are contributing to the goal of any system of provision. In fact, if we are to actually change from a commercial to a civic commonwealth, they need to occur in businesses and corporations as well as in nonprofits, government agencies, and voluntary associations. Civic conversations, in other words, are not limited to some special civic location, such as city hall, but rather are limited by the openness of different types of organizations to facilitate a civic identity and conversation in their offices and workplaces.

Facilitating such conversations would appear to be one significant contribution that business ethics could make not only to business but also to the work of designing effective systems of provision. This does not mean that we should make corporations "citizens." Just as we do not name religious organizations or nonprofits "citizens," nor should we give the name to corporations. They are not citizens, but we can institute civic conversations among their members. In fact, that may be one of the most important civic obligations of corporations. Businesses and corporations, in other words, should participate in the governing of a civic commonwealth, but they should also recognize the limits of their reach.

Governing the civic commonwealth

Governing is about steering systems of provision toward making provisions for all, and, at the same time, moving toward a just and sustainable economy. The old economics of property assumed that all we really had to do was to protect individual rights to property and most other things would take care of themselves. This has turned into one of the biggest mistakes in human history. It has placed our whole planet in danger. Through the privatization of land, labor, and money, we have stretched the bonds of human communities about as far as they can go. Considering this situation, one can sympathize with those who have given up on government, on democracy, and on our capacity for collective action. The fact is, however, the ship of state is heading toward disaster and we need to take hold of the steering tools we have and to change course.

Borrowing from Kenneth Boulding's work on managing systems, we can posit three different types of steering mechanisms: (1) persuasion—getting people to share similar values and visions; (2) incentives—rewarding people for doing what needs to be done, and (3) regulations—forcing people to obey laws and regulations (Boulding 1989). Although all three are always present in any successful system, each one has its own possibilities. Unfortunately, corporations control many of these possibilities. If we are to move from a commercial to a civic commonwealth, we will need to make some changes.

Governing by persuasion

Contrary to what many may believe, persuasion is perhaps the most powerful of the three. Persuasion is what maintains the current emphasis on economic growth, even in the light of solid evidence that such growth is totally unsustainable. Corporations spend around $200 billion a year in advertising. Shopping has become not only an American pastime, but even an important part of the American Dream. In light of the corporate control of the mainstream media, some people have given up on traditional educational institutions. Others see another option. For them, the Internet and social media offers a new means of educating citizens about what is actually happening in the world as well as new opportunities for engagement in making significant changes.

Still, the education we need is civic education. We need people to understand themselves as citizens, as members of the same generation whose decisions will affect future generations. It would certainly help if employees gained the rights of citizens in the workplace. That would require that they have a voice in the design of their workplaces and even a voice in the distribution of company profits. It would mean, in other words, a shift from property relations to civic relations at work. Some people in business ethics have argued for this, but it has not been a major theme (see Brenkert 1994; Brown 2005; McMahon 1994). Perhaps it should become one.

If people spend most of their lives in organizations that do not recognize their civic identity, then these institutional denials of their civic rights may be more persuasive than all the books on business ethics. Crucial are the expectations of the groups in which we live and work. Most of us live up (or down) to group expectations, and if we are to use persuasion to change the systems in which we live, we will need to learn how to change expectations. Few would deny that corporations are governing (steering) our social lives today, but mostly from a commercial rather than a civic perspective, especially when it comes to using the second way of changing systems: incentives.

Governing by incentives

If some have difficulty understanding the power of persuasion, few will doubt the power of incentives. Isn't it true that whoever has the money has the power? Here we need a bit of reflection. Power, in the modern world, does not really reside in money, but rather in organizations and systems. If you are the CEO of a large corporation, for example, you have power in your position, but if you leave the position, you leave the power. Also if one redesigns an organization's structure, one also changes the power of different positions, and therefore also the structures of incentives.

Since electoral politics in the USA are currently structured so an individual's money can buy capacity to reach voters, money does make a difference. Changing the process of elections could change this. Social media, for example, may provide an alternative means of communicating about the election that is not dependent on corporate incentives. In any case, perhaps there is no more important issue to address than the use of corporate incentives to influence government. In many ways, the power of regulation has become dominated by the power of incentives, which means that we still live in a world where the commercial dominates the civic. This must change if we are to have a viable future for everyone. The question is who should control regulation.

Governing by regulation

For regulation to be an effective means of governing, it must not be dominated by financial incentives, but rather grounded in civic norms. Perhaps we need to apply the principle of the separation of church and state to the relationships between corporations and governments. Just as the state should not become the servant of any religion, nor should it become the servant of corporations, or, more generally, the world of commerce. At the same time, corporations are also governing bodies, and their regulations (policies and procedures) that pertain to their function in a particular system of provision should not be taken over by government.

Government needs to protect not only the civic sphere, but also the civic character of market competition. When necessary, government should develop standards of corporate conduct to ensure that workers and others are treated as citizens. Government can also create an even playing field for business competitors by developing environmental and social standards that all competitors must follow. Corporations can also participate in the development of regulation in the system of provision in which they operate. In fact, knowledge from corporate experience can be very helpful in developing smart regulation for any system of provision. At the same time, corporations should not participate in systems of provision in which they do not belong, such as the system that provides us with our political leaders—our system of democratic elections. Regulations should maintain the boundaries between different systems of provision, and prevent agencies that have legitimate influence in one system from using that influence in another where they do not belong.

If we locate the role of regulation in the various systems of provision, then its primary role will be to protect the providers of wealth—planet and people—and to provide guidelines for all participants in these systems to fulfill their systemic function. The political community has resources for legitimizing and for enforcing its regulations: constitutions, legislation, and law enforcement. As long as these instruments of regulation remain available, the state has the "power" to regulate corporations, if it has the will.

Conclusion

If we step back for a minute, we can say that human communities have three basic tasks: to provide for one another, to protect one another, and to find reasons for doing so. Persuasion, incentives, and regulation connect to these tasks. Persuasion maintains a meaningful world, whether by myths and rituals or corporate commercials; incentives motivate us to provide for one another, whether by norms of reciprocity or by selfishness; and regulations protect us, whether by protecting privileges or protecting equal opportunity. As a community, we must decide what types of persuasion, incentives, and regulations will enable to move us toward a mature and stable human community. This will require us to move from the current commercial commonwealth to a civic commonwealth.

Current research and reflection of the commons has given us a chance to actually develop a new understanding of "common wealth." We live in a world of abundance. The sun shines on all the planet. It is the ultimate commons that gives our planet life. This living planet is the source of our common wealth, for this and future generations. Today, we cannot transform our common sources into human resources, however, without commercial enterprises. At the same time, we cannot survive if the commercial defines our life together. The work ahead, I believe, is the work of citizens, who through civic conversations give shape to a viable relationship between the commons and the commercial. Business leaders can participate in this work by exploring the role of their business in a particular system of provision. Ethicists and other can help to facilitate such conversations, so that the civic defines our commonwealth rather than the commercial.

This essay expands on some of the arguments made in Marvin T. Brown, *Civilizing the Economy: A New Economics of Provision*, Cambridge: Cambridge University Press, 2010.

References

Aristotle (1999) *Nicomachean Ethics*, 2nd edn, trans. Terence Irwin, Indianapolis, IN: Hackett.

Banner, S. (2005) *How the Indians Lost Their Land: Law and Power on the Frontier*, Cambridge, MA: Belknap Press.

Bauwens, M. (2005) "The Political Economy of Peer Production." Retrieved March 7, from http://www.informatik.uni-leipzig.de/~graebe/Texte/Bauwens-06.pdf

Billier, D. (2003) *Silent Theft: The Private Plunder of Our Common Wealth*, New York: Routledge.

Boulding, K. (1989) *Three Faces of Power*, Newbury Park, CA: Sage.

Brenkert, G. (1992) "Freedom, Participation and Corporations: The Issue of Corporate (Economic) Democracy," *Business Ethics Quarterly*, 2(3): 251–269.

Brown, M. (2003) *The Ethical Process: An Approach to Disagreements and Controversial Issues*, 3rd edn, Upper Saddle River, NJ: Prentice-Hall.

Brown, M. (2005) *Corporate Integrity: Rethinking Organizational Ethics and Leadership*, New York: Cambridge University Press.

Brown, M. (2010) *Civilizing the Economy: A New Economics of Provision*, Cambridge: Cambridge University Press, 2010.

Hardin, G. (1968) "The Tragedy of the Commons," *Science*, 162: 1243–1248.

McMahon, C. (1994) *Authority and Democracy: A General Theory of Government and Management*, Princeton, NJ: Princeton University Press.

Neeson, J.M. (1993) *Commoners: Common Right, Enclosure and Social Change in England, 1700–1820*, Cambridge: Cambridge University Press.

Nussbaum, M.C. (2011) *Creating Capabilities: The Human Development Approach*, Cambridge, MA: Belknap Press.

Ostrom, E. (1990) *Governing the Commons: The Evolution of Institutions for Collective Action*, New York: Cambridge University Press.

Polanyi, K. (1957) *The Great Transformation: The Political and Economic Origins of Our Time*, Boston, MA: Beacon Press.

Sen, A. (1999) *Development as Freedom*. New York: Alfred A. Knopf.

Smith, A. (1944) *The Wealth of Nations*, ed. Edwin Cannan, New York: Random House.

Solomon, R. (1993) *Ethics and Excellence: Cooperation and Integrity in Business*, Oxford: Oxford University Press.

Walljasper, J. (2010) *All That We Share: A Field Guide to the Commons*, New York: The New Press.

Wolin, S. (2004) *Politics and Vision: Continuity and Innovation in Western Political Thought*, expanded edn, Princeton, NJ: Princeton University Press.

Evaluating a Case Study
Developing a Practical Ethical Viewpoint

Your goal in this book is to respond critically to case studies on various aspects of Business Ethics. To do this, you must be able to assess the ethical impact of some critical factor(s) in situations that pose ethical problems. One factor in accessing the case is the ethical impact of the project/policy/action. At the end of the Reacting to a Case Study essays, you should be better prepared to do just that. This chapter and Chapters 3 through 6 end with an "Evaluating a Case Study" section that focuses on a particular exercise. These sections include case studies to which you can apply the insight you gained from the readings and discussions in the chapter. Because the information presented in the "Evaluating a Case Study" is cumulative, you should be able to write a complete critical response to a case study by the end of Chapter 6.

These essays seek to bridge the gap between Normative Ethics and Applied Ethics. Skill in Applied Ethics is very important, for this is where the practical decision making occurs. My approach in these essays is to allow you to employ techniques that you have been taught elsewhere along with those found in this text. Depending on your background in business, you can write a critical response to a case study that demonstrates your professional acumen along with your sensitivity to the ethical dimensions found in the situation you are examining. Classes that have few students with business backgrounds will deemphasize the business fundamentals and concentrate instead on a less technical response.

Business people often become so enmeshed in the practice of business that they lose the ability to discern and react to possible ethical dilemmas, a difficulty experienced in all professions.[1] But this is wrong. The "Evaluating a Case Study" sections will help you analyze both ethical and practical situations. The approach will invoke a technique that rates a proposal as having three levels of complexity: surface, medium, and deep. The level of interaction allows you to see at a glance how the competing areas of interest and ethical value conflict.

The five essays in this series are intended to sequentially lead you to develop the abilities to write a critical response to a case study: (a) Developing a Practical Ethical Viewpoint, (b) Finding the Conflicts, (c) Assessing Embedded Levels, (d) Applying Ethical Issues, and (e) Structuring the Essay.

At the end of Chapters 3 through 6, you will be presented case studies to which you can apply your newfound skills. By the end of the term, you should be able to create an ethical impact statement of some sophistication.

Let us begin first by choosing an ethical theory and then proceed to developing a practical viewpoint. Few people bother to choose an ethical theory, most pick up a few moral maxims that they apply when the occasion seems appropriate. The manner of this acquisition is often environment dependent, that is, having to do with their upbringing, friends, and the community(ies) in which they live. As such, their maxims reflect those other viewpoints.

The Personal Worldview Imperative enjoins us to develop a single comprehensive and internally coherent worldview that is good and that we strive to act out in our lives (see Chapter 1). One component of this worldview is an ethical theory. Thus, each of us must *develop* an ethical theory. This does not mean we must all start from scratch. Those before us have done too much good work. But we must personally choose an ethical theory and assume ownership for it as being the most correct theory in existence. It is not enough merely to accept someone else's theory without any active work on our part. We must go through the process of personal introspection and evaluation to determine what we think is best and to be open to ways we can improve the theory (in concept or in practice).

This process of making an ethical theory our own can take years. This course lasts only a few months. Does this pose a problem? Not really when you consider that part of the process of making an ethical theory our own involves provisional acceptance and testing of various moral maxims. Obviously, this testing has a limit. We should not test whether it is morally permissible to murder by going out and murdering various people. The testing I am advocating is a way to examine various moral commands and evaluate whether their application is consonant with other worldview values we hold. The process will perhaps go back and forth in a progressive dialectic until we have accepted or rejected the commands.

To begin this process of testing, we must read about some of the most prominent ethical theories. We must identify the major ethical theories and their tenets. Many books survey and evaluate the major ethical theories. In the series of textbooks, *Basic Ethics in Action*, I have written one such survey entitled *Basic Ethics*. I would suggest that you either refer to that book or another like it to obtain enough information to enable you to begin the process of choosing an ethical theory.

For the purposes of this book, I will highlight four major theories: Utilitarianism, Deontology, Intuitionism, and Virtue Ethics. To begin the process, I recommend that you choose a single theory from these four (or from others your instructor may suggest) as your critical tool as you prepare for class. You might ask, How do I know which viewpoint to choose? This is a difficult question. It concerns the justification of the various ethical theories.

Many criteria can be used to justify an ethical theory. One criterion is Naturalism. Each theory presupposes a naturalistic or nonnaturalistic epistemological standpoint. Naturalism is complicated; for our purposes, let us describe it as a view that holds that no entities or events are in principle beyond the domain of scientific explanation. Cognitive claims are valid only if they are based on accepted scientific modes.

Ethical Naturalism states that moral judgments are also merely a subclass of facts about the natural world that can be studied scientifically. From this study, we can determine moral correctness as a corollary of certain facts that can be scientifically investigated (e.g., how much pleasure various alternatives will produce for the group). Thus, utilitarians believe that moral judgments *are* judgments about which alternative will be most beneficial to some group's survival.

A utilitarian might point to the scientific study of nature and say that the instinct to seek pleasure is evidenced in all species. Furthermore, an evolutionary advantage seems to exist for those species that act for the benefit of the group that does not exist for those who do not act in this way.

Many sociobiologists make this sort of claim. The main imperative is that a person's own genes be passed on to another generation. If passing a person's genes is impossible, the next best thing is to pass on the genes of the individual's relatives. Thus, seemingly altruistic behavior (such as a bird that stays behind in dangerous situations so that the group might survive) is really selfish because helping the group *is* helping the bird to pass on its genes (or those of its relatives).

Sociobiology, of course, is not universally accepted, nor is it necessary for a utilitarian to be a sociobiologist. However, this example does illustrate a type of justification that the utilitarian might make. He could move from the concept of group happiness in animals and extrapolate to humans. The supporting data are scientific; therefore, the theory is naturalistic.

Deontologists may or may not be naturalists. Since Deontology involves a duty-based ethics, the key question to be asked concerns how we know whether a binding duty exists to do such and such. Are all moral "oughts" derivable from factual, scientifically ascertainable "is" statements? If they are, then the deontologist is a naturalist. If they are not, then the deontologist is not a naturalist.

In his book *Reason and Morality*, Alan Gewirth claims to derive ought from is. There is no reference to knowledge claims that are not compatible with the scientific inquiry of natural objects. This would make Gewirth a naturalist. Kant and Donagan are somewhat different. Each refers to supernatural entities that are not scientifically supported. Kant spends considerable effort trying to define those boundaries in the "Transcendental Dialectic" section of his book *The Critique of Pure Reason*. This aside, neither Kant nor Donagan considered that a problem about integrating the factual and the normative existed.

If you are inclined to view reality as an extension of evolutionary biology or to believe that group advantage immediately entails a moral ought, then you are leaning toward Utilitarianism. If you think that people should act from pure duty alone without reference to anything except the rightness of the action, however, then Deontology is probably your preference.

The is-ought problem was sharpened by intuitionist G.E. Moore,[2] who rejected Ethical Naturalism because he believed it contained a fallacy (which he dubbed *the naturalistic fallacy*). This fallacy claims that it is false to define goodness in terms of any natural property. This is so because good is not definable and because good is not subject to scientific examination. This is true because the factual is realm is separate from the normative ought realm. The chasm between the two cannot be crossed.

Good for Moore is a unique, unanalyzable, non-natural property (as opposed, for example, to yellow, which is a natural property). Clearly, scientific methods are of no use. Science can tell us things about yellow but can tell us nothing about the meaning of good. Other intuitionists also hold that we understand important moral terms and/or moral maxims by cognitive means that are not scientific. Generally, these are immediate and cannot be justified in factual "is" language.

Intuitionism is therefore a non-naturalistic theory. Still, it has some remote connections to Naturalism. For example, one can point to the *plausibility* of accepting certain common moral maxims—such as a prohibition against murder—by reference to other societies. (In other words, since all societies prohibit murder, the prohibition against murder must be immediately apparent to all.) However, plausibility is not the same as exhaustive scientific demonstration. Justification in Intuitionism lies in its alleged unarguable truth that can be grasped in principle immediately by all.

If you are having trouble adopting any of the theories and believe that acceptance or rejection of an ethical theory comes to some sort of brute immediate acceptance, then you will probably want to accept Intuitionism as your ethical theory.

Finally, we turn to Virtue Ethics. This theory seems at first to be naturalistic. Aristotle lends credence to this when he talks about relying on the common opinions of people about what is considered to be a virtue. The common opinions could be gathered and reviewed much as a sociologist or anthropologist might do, and this "scientific" method would yield definitive results. Aristotle believed that some common agreement about a core set of virtues existed.

Justification, therefore, was not an issue for Aristotle. If we accept a worldview such as Aristotle presents, then we would all agree that everyone considers courage (for example) to be a virtue. The confirming data can be gathered and scientifically studied; ergo, it is naturalistic. The proof depends on the community that values these traits. This emphasis on community makes Virtue Ethics a favorite theory among those who call themselves *communitarians*. The communitarian begins with the group and its intuitions and depends on individual members to submit to the authority of the group (or to change the group in ways acceptable to the group).

How does Communitarianism affect today's pluralistic society? Some might argue that consensus about the virtues no longer exists, nor does a single community to which we all belong. If there is no consensus as Aristotle envisioned, then what constitutes a virtue may collapse into a form of Intuitionism. For example, I think that X is a virtue. You think Y is a virtue. X and Y are mutually exclusive traits. You and I come from different communities/societies; therefore, we cannot come to an agreement.

All each of us can say is that I am right and you are wrong. Personal insight (Intuitionism) is all we have to justify our practices (to ourselves and to others).

If you believe that courage, wisdom, self-control, piety, and so forth are virtues in every society, then perhaps you will choose Virtue Ethics as your model.

To help you choose an ethical theory, try the following exercise. Examine one or more of the following moral situations and (a) interpret what is right and wrong according to each of the four theories, (b) then give an argument that each theory might provide, and (c) state your own assessment of the strengths of each theory.

Situation One

You are the constable in a small, remote, rural town in Northern Ireland that is divided into the Catholics (20 percent minority) and the Protestants (80 percent majority). All Catholics live in one section of town on a peninsula jutting into the river just east of the main part of town.

One morning a young Protestant girl is found raped and murdered next to the town green. According to general consensus, a Catholic must have committed the crime. The Protestants form a citizens' committee that demands the following of the constable: "We believe you to be a Catholic sympathizer, and we don't think you will press fast enough to bring this killer to justice. We know a Catholic committed the crime. We've sealed off the Catholic section of town; no one can go in or out. If you don't hand over the criminal by sundown, we will torch the entire Catholic section of town, killing all 1,000 people. Don't try to call for help. We've already disabled all communications."

You made every effort to find out who did it, but you made no progress. You could not find out. At one hour before sundown, you do not know what to do. Your deputy says, "Why don't we just pick a random Catholic and tell them he did it? At least we'd be saving 999 lives."

"But then I'd be responsible for killing an innocent man!" you reply. "Better one innocent die and 999 be saved. After all, there's no way the two of us can stop the mob. You have to give them a scapegoat," the deputy responds.

Describe how each ethical theory might approach this situation. Which one is most consonant to your own worldview, and why?

Situation Two

You are on the executive committee of the XYZ organization of health care professionals. Each year the committee gives an award to one of its members who display high moral character in his or her work. This year you are among the four judges for the award. There is some disagreement among the judges, however, about what constitutes a good person. The judges, besides yourself, are Ms. Smith, Mrs. Taylor, and Mr. Jones. The candidates for the award are Mr. Little and Mrs. Big.

Ms. Smith said that the award should go to Mrs. Big because she saved a man from drowning. However, Mr. Jones demurred, saying that Mrs. Big's motives are suspect because the man she saved was in the midst of a very big financial deal with Mrs. Big. If the man had been allowed to drown, Mrs. Big would have lost a lost of money. Ms. Smith said motives are not important but that the goodness of the act counts and the man who was saved runs a big business in town. Many people besides Mrs. Big would have been hurt if Mrs. Big had not saved the man.

Mr. Jones said the award should go to Mr. Little because he performed a kind act of charity in chairing the town's United Way Campaign last year. Surely such an act could not be said to benefit Mr. Little in any way (unlike Mrs. Big).

Mrs. Taylor said that she is somewhat unsure about either Mrs. Big or Mr. Little because both of them have been recommended on the basis of a single good act. Mrs. Taylor believed that it would be better to choose a candidate who has shown over time to have performed many good actions and to be of good character. "After all," she said "a single swallow does not make a spring." Mr. Jones and Ms. Smith scratched their heads at this remark and turned to you. Who is right?

Describe how each ethical theory might approach this situation. Which one is most consonant to your own worldview, and why?

Choosing an ethical theory is only the first step in developing a practical ethical viewpoint. A link between the Normative Theory and application of the theory is needed. In Chapter 1, I outlined my basic position concerning personal worldview and how it might be utilized when applying an ethical theory. In the last section Chapter 1, I outlined a principle of fair competition that I believe can be used to apply the general theory chosen and to the moral decision at hand.

The point is that one important aspect of developing a practical ethical viewpoint is to challenge ourselves to think about and provisionally accept certain necessary tenets to effectively apply ethical principles to practice. These concepts should allow professionals to connect normative theories to the real-life problems that confront them.

Before addressing ethical cases, try first to provisionally accept one moral theory. Then try to determine what connecting principles or concepts are necessary to translate theory to practice. Concentrate your efforts on these connections. They will be useful to you as you address what you see as the important issues resident in each case.

Notes

1 For a fuller discussion of this, see *Basic Ethics*, chap. 7.
2 I cannot stress too much the impossibility of completely pigeonholing philosophers. In some important ways, Moore was an intuitionist. "Good" had to be accepted as an unanalyzable, unnatural fact. Toward the end of *Principia Ethica*, he sounds much like an agathistic utilitarian, however, one who wishes to maximize the group's good. This mixture of labels among philosophers shows only that labels are limited in what they can do.

Ross and Rawls have deontological and intuitionistic aspects to their theories. Therefore, one label alone cannot adequately capture the spirit of their philosophy. In an introductory text, such as this one, labels are used to simplify—but hopefully not obfuscate—the dynamics present in these thinkers.

What Is a Corporation?

General Overview: One important element that is fundamental to our study of business ethics is to determine the nature of the corporation. Is a corporation merely a piece of property owned by its shareholders? Is it a combination of the shareholders, directors, and top executives? Perhaps a corporation is an abstract entity that belongs to all of those who are affected by its activities? These questions force us to view the corporation as either an individual entity or as a community. The duties and responsibilities of what we can expect from a corporation vary according to the model we choose.

The individual model would see the corporation as having the same sort of rights and responsibilities that characterize other individuals in the society. In philosophical logic the status of an individual is different from that of a group. The individual approach imposes a set of essentialist characteristics. The group approach embraces diversity and uses statistical modeling to create empirical generalizations, but these are seen to make a different ontological assertion than the individual approach.[1]

A. The Corporation as an Individual

Overview: Our goal in defining a corporation as an individual is to be able to create a model that requires it to be morally responsible for what it does. The "corporate veil," originally created to absolve directors, officers, and stockholders from personal liability resulting from the company's actions, has often created a situation in which *no person or entity* is ever responsible for anything.

In the first article, by Kenneth E. Goodpaster and John B. Matthews, Jr., the authors contrast two different imperatives that might guide corporate decision-making: the invisible hand and the government hand. In the former imperative, the sole obligations of the

Business Ethics, Second Edition. Edited by Michael Boylan.
© 2014 John Wiley & Sons, Inc. Published 2014 by John Wiley & Sons, Inc.

corporation are to make money and to obey the law. The forces of the market will control the corporation's activity. If the public is upset with the company with the company's behavior, then the public will vote with its pocketbooks and force the company to go under.

The imperative of the government is to marshal the activity of the corporation toward the common good. In this model, government policy is toward ethical concerns so that the corporation (as individual) can be held responsible for its actions.

In the second article Peter A. French more explicitly advances the concept of the corporation as an individual. French wants to assert that thinking of the corporation as an individual is more than an analogy. He thinks that the corporation really *is* a moral person. He bases his argument on a theory of personhood that is rooted in the action theory of Donald Davidson and the functionalism of Daniel Dennett. If we can identify the structural features of an action description, then we can ascribe agency to the alleged actor. This does not depend upon biology (such as a living, breathing organism).

French believes that, if the corporation is a moral actor, metaphysical personhood follows as well. He cites two theories to prove his point: the fiction theory and the reality theory. The former has a thorough legal grounding of the person; the latter is pre-legal. He contrasts these views with the standard theories (as characterized by the legal aggregate theory) that identify a corporation with its human stakeholders. French's argument is important because the rights and responsibilities that a corporation enjoys are a function of its metaphysical and moral status.

Thomas Donaldson replies to French by emphasizing that a corporation does not have the same rights as a person (such as the right to vote) and that the origin of the corporation's rights (unlike human persons') cannot be natural. Natural rights are important because some oppressed people (such as African Americans in the USA) were legally denied rights but surely possessed them despite the fact that legal institutions did not recognize them. If they had these rights, then how did they possess them? Presumably, they possessed them by natural right. If natural rights are more basic than legal rights, then how can we explain that corporations have natural rights?

In the United States Supreme Court *Citizens United v. Federal Election Commission* case, we have the status of corporations as individuals set in a different sense. In this case the issue is whether corporations, like individuals, have the First Amendment rights to free speech—and, if free speech entails the ability to give unlimited amounts of campaign contributions, then corporations can give unlimited amounts of campaign contributions (just as individuals can). Previously, corporations and labor unions were heavily restricted in this regard.

The way we conceptualize corporations and their ability to act within society is an important question for business ethics.

B. The Corporation as a Community: Stakeholder Theory

Overview of Stakeholders: Though there are different ways to explore the corporation as a community (e.g., via organizational culture) the most common and popular approach of understanding of the corporation as a community comes from stakeholder theory. A stakeholder is a part of the collage of relationships that includes virtually any agent or group that works for, or is affected by, the company or its policies. The *stake* is the interest, share, or claim that an agent or group has against a company. Those who possess these stakes, whether they be legal, economic, political, moral, or so on, are called *stakeholders*.[2] R. Edward Freeman depicts stakeholders as "any individual or group who can affect or is affected by the actions, decisions, policies, practices, or goals of the organization."[3] Under this model, we can distinguish between the company's primary stakeholders (owners, customers, employees, and suppliers) and secondary stakeholders (all other interested groups such as the general public, government, competitors). Primary stakeholders weigh more heavily in the decision-making process than do secondary stakeholders, but even primary stakeholders possess stakeholders of their own, so that the societal web becomes very complex.

Proponents of stakeholder theory point to the way that it *situates* a company into a community. It forces the company to view itself as being contained within a series of social environments that often intersect. In this way, a company must accommodate its actions with the needs and interests of all its stakeholders. If morality is about ameliorating an individual's interests given those of the broader group (a crucial tenet of utilitarianism), then stakeholder theory provides a way to integrate ethics into daily business decisions. Virtue ethics (either by itself or integrated with communitarianism)[4] is also a possible theory that distributes interests among stakeholders in an ethical fashion.

Stakeholder theory is meant to contrast with a traditional view of whose interests ought to be considered (viz., those of the owners of the company: the stockholders). Under traditional theory a contract exists between the stockholders and the company's board of directors that the latter will do everything in their power to continue in the company's historical mission and maximize wealth for the stockholders. Such an agreement incurs a fiduciary responsibility on the part of the officers and directors of the corporation to the stockholders.

It is clear, however, that this fiduciary responsibility is *not* carte blanche. If the company were *merely* concerned with making money, it could engage in illegal gun sales, money laundering, and drug smuggling, for example. The stockholders do not have the right to expect the officers and directors to make *the most money possible* because this could involve the company in illegal activity and is wrong on three counts: (a) the company would be breaking the law and faces fines and sanctions if caught (a prudential reason), (b) the company is veering away from its historical mission (the basis on which the stockholders invested in the company—a moral reason via promise keeping, and (c) the company should not engage in an illegal or immoral activity (an ethical reason—but the basis is rather unclear without further justification).

Under the traditional analysis, it is not entirely clear why a company should not "ride the line" of legality and illegality in an attempt to weigh the risk versus rewards of extra profits against the possibility of getting caught. If the company's sole mission were to make money for the stockholders, then it should do all that it can to fulfill that mission. It should operate near the edge of the law, occasionally challenging the barrier when the risks/rewards calculus dictates that it is prudent to do so. The late Nobel laureate Milton Friedman has been a proponent of this strategy.[5]

Thus the stakeholder theory is one alternative to the traditional stockholder model. (The corporation as a morally responsible individual, as we have seen above, is another.) One of the key issues that stakeholder theory must address is how it claims to be a normative theory. It is one thing to say that a company's actions affect many individuals and groups. One can describe the sociology of decision-making and the dynamics of the political process. All of this is a *descriptive* process. It is another thing to be able to show how some claims *should* trump others and how sometimes a moral argument will carry the day. This latter mission of how ethics can trump other considerations is a normative exercise. In business ethics, we are ultimately interested in the normative exercise.

In the first essay Amatai Etzioni begins by reviewing the shift from shareholder notions to those of stakeholders. The beginning point of his argument is that "private property" and "incorporation" are social constructs. This is because the real power-brokers in a practical sense are the managers of the company, and because the rules of private property are set by the country in which the business is domiciled (and subject to political and cultural constraints). This said, Etzioni believes that there are many ways to *invest* in a corporation. Stakeholder theory captures this and the ensuing rights and duties that flow from this investment. The act of investing creates a relationship between the parties. This relationship creates a positive duty of fairness toward those in the relationship (the stakeholders).

Some examples of investment are very tangible. Some communities build roads to service a corporation or provide special tax rates or rezone property. These are financial investments by the community for a private company. Fairness would dictate some reciprocity. But often this is not the case. It is often a one-sided transaction. Creditors also help the corporation by providing start-up capital that often exceeds that of the stockholders. Where this leads us is the concept of the common good (a critical concept in utilitarianism and virtue ethics—especially when it teams up with communitarianism). By considering the stakeholders' interest and not just stockholders' interests the common good is enhanced in a far greater way than just considering the latter. Thus, stakeholder theory is upheld as a model to view business that leads to ethical outcomes by enhancing the common good.

In the second essay of this section, Kenneth Goodpaster takes the position that stakeholder theory, as generally presented, leads to a so-called stakeholder paradox. This paradox may be put into a dilemma situation (that one is both enjoined and not enjoined to perform some action). This paradox results from the phenomena of multifiduciary responsibilities that is the natural consequence of multiple (often contradictory) stakeholder interests. If Goodpaster is correct, then stakeholder theory must be corrected. The essence of this correction will revolve around the notions of different types of responsibilities. In other words, a fiduciary relationship is not the only type that directors should recognize, but there must be a way to adjudicate between these different types of obligations.

In his excerpted essay, Stephen Cohen offers a way to deal with various conflicting stakeholder interests (such as those mentioned by Goodpaster) through the concept of *consent*, which emphasized here is deliberate, future-oriented consent. What consent does to the decision-making equation is to create a political framework through which problems might be solved among stakeholders. Cohen cites various criteria that are utilized in the process of group consent. The reader must determine for herself whether the normative question raised by Goodpaster has been satisfied.

In the final essay of this section Alexi M. Marcoux raises another issue about stakeholder theory: that it does not privilege the moral status of shareholders. Stakeholder theorists reply that there is nothing morally significant about shareholders that can underwrite those fiduciary duties. Marcoux advances a counterargument that seeks to demonstrate both the special moral status of shareholders in a firm and the concomitant moral inadequacy of stakeholder theory. Marcoux argues that: (a) if some relations morally require fiduciary duties, and (b) the shareholder–manager relation possesses the features that make fiduciary duties morally necessary to those relations, then (c) stakeholder theory (which denies this) is morally lacking.

Because of the importance of stakeholder theory in the literature, these searching examinations and counterarguments are important for going forward in this depiction of the corporation as community.

Notes

1 This same conundrum between individual and group exists in evolutionary biology as it seeks to understand what is "the unit of selection." The traditional neo-Darwinists, such as E.O. Wilson and Elliott Sober, seek the group approach whereas David Hull and his group seek a model that characterizes the species as an individual.

2 For further discussion on the origins of this definition see Archie Carroll, *Business and Society: Ethics and Stakeholder Management* (Cincinnati, OH: South-Western Publishing, 1989) and Joseph Weiss, *The*

Management of Change: Administrative Logics and Actions (New York: Praeger, 1986).

3 R. Edward Freeman, *Strategic Management: A Stakeholder Approach* (Boston: Pitman, 1984); 25.

4 A sketch of virtue ethics in the context of communitarianism can be found in Michael J. Sandel, *Liberalism and the Limits of Justice*, 2nd edn (Cambridge: Cambridge University Press, 1998); 76–77, 88–89, 98–99.

5 Milton Friedman, "The Social Responsibility of Business is to Increase its Profits," *New York Times Sunday Magazine*, September 13, 1970: 32–33, 122–126.

A. The Corporation as an Individual

Can a Corporation Have a Conscience?

Kenneth E. Goodpaster and John B. Matthews Jr.

During the severe racial tensions of the 1960s, Southern Steel Company (actual case, disguised name) faced considerable pressure from government and the press to explain and modify its policies regarding discrimination both within its plants and in the major city where it was located. SSC was the largest employer in the area (it had nearly 15,000

Kenneth E. Goodpaster and John B. Mathews Jr., "Can a Corporation Have a Conscience?" Reprinted by permission of *Harvard Business Review* from *Harvard Business Review*, 60 (Jan./Feb. 1982): 132–141.

workers, one-third of whom were black) and had made great strides toward removing barriers to equal job opportunity in its several plants. In addition, its top executives (especially its chief executive officer, James Weston) had distinguished themselves as private citizens for years in community programs for black housing, education, and small business as well as in attempts at desegregating all-white police and local government organizations.

SSC drew the line, however, at using its substantial economic influence in the local area to advance the cause of the civil rights movement by pressuring banks, suppliers, and the local government.

"As individuals we can exercise what influence we may have as citizens," James Weston said, "but for a corporation to attempt to exert any kind of economic compulsion to achieve a particular end in a social area seems to me to be quite beyond what a corporation should do and quite beyond what a corporation can do. I believe that while government may seek to compel social reforms, any attempt by a private organization like SSC to impose its views, its beliefs, and its will upon the community would be repugnant to our American constitutional concepts and that appropriate steps to correct this abuse of corporate power would be universally demanded by public opinion."

Weston could have been speaking in the early 1980s on any issue that corporations around the United States now face. Instead of social justice, his theme might be environmental protection, product safety, marketing practice, or international bribery. His statement for SSC raises the important issue of corporate responsibility. Can a corporation have a conscience?

Weston apparently felt comfortable saying it need not. The responsibilities of ordinary persons and of "artificial persons" like corporations are, in his view, separate. Persons' responsibilities go beyond those of corporations. Persons, he seems to have believed, ought to care not only about themselves but also about the dignity and well-being of those around them—ought not only to care but also to act. Organizations, he evidently thought, are creatures of, and to a degree prisoners of, the systems of economic incentive and political sanction that give them reality and therefore should not be expected to display the same moral attributes that we expect of persons.

Others inside business as well as outside share Weston's perception. One influential philosopher—John Ladd—carries Weston's view a step further:

> It is improper to expect organizational conduct to conform to the ordinary principles of morality. We cannot and must not expect formal organizations, or their representatives acting in their official capacities, to be honest, courageous, considerate, sympathetic, or to have any kind of moral integrity. Such concepts are not in the vocabulary, so to speak, of the organizational language game.[1]

In our opinion, this line of thought represents a tremendous barrier to the development of business ethics both as a field of inquiry and as a practical force in managerial decision making. This is a matter about which executives must be philosophical and philosophers must be practical. A corporation can and should have a conscience. The language of ethics does have a place in the vocabulary of an organization. There need not be and there should not be a disjunction of the sort attributed to SSC's James Weston. Organizational agents such as corporations should be no more and no less morally responsible (rational, self-interested, altruistic) than ordinary persons.

We take this position because we think an analogy holds between the individual and the corporation. If we analyze the concept of moral responsibility as it applies to persons, we find that projecting it to corporations as agents in society is possible.

Defining the Responsibility of Persons

When we speak of the responsibility of individuals, philosophers say that we mean three things: someone is to blame, something has to be done, or some kind of trust-worthiness can be expected. (See the *Exhibit*.)

Holding accountable

We apply the first meaning, what we shall call the *causal* sense, primarily to legal and moral contexts where what is at issue is praise or blame for a past action. We say of a person that he or she was responsible for what happened, is to blame for it, should be held accountable. In this sense of the word, *responsibility* has to do with tracing the causes of actions and events, of finding out who is answerable in a given situation. Our aim is to determine someone's intention, free will, degree of participation, and appropriate reward or punishment.

Rule following

We apply the second meaning of *responsibility* to rule following, to contexts where individuals are subject to externally imposed norms often associated with some social role that people play. We speak of the responsibilities of parents to children, of doctors to patients, of lawyers to clients, of citizens to the law. What is socially expected and what the party involved is to answer for are at issue here.

Decision making

We use the third meaning of *responsibility* for decision making. With this meaning of the term, we say that individuals are responsible if they are trustworthy and reliable, if they allow appropriate factors to affect their judgment; we refer primarily to a person's independent thought processes and decision making, processes that justify an attitude of trust from those who interact with him or her as a responsible individual.

The distinguishing characteristic of moral responsibility, it seems to us, lies in this third sense of the term. Here the focus is on the intellectual and emotional processes in the individual's moral reasoning. Philosophers call this "taking a moral point of view" and contrast it with such other processes as being financially prudent and attending to legal obligations.

To be sure, characterizing a person as "morally responsible" may seem rather vague. But vagueness is a contextual notion. Everything depends on how we fill in the blank in "vague for_____purposes."

In some contexts the term "six o'clockish" is vague, while in others it is useful and informative. As a response to a space-shuttle pilot who wants to know when to fire the reentry rockets, it will not do, but it might do in response to a spouse who wants to know when one will arrive home at the end of the workday.

We maintain that the processes underlying moral responsibility can be defined and are not themselves vague, even though gaining consensus on specific moral norms and decisions is not always easy.

What, then, characterizes the processes underlying the judgment of a person we call morally responsible? Philosopher William K. Frankena offers the following answer:

> A morality is a normative system in which judgments are made, more or less consciously, [out of a] consideration of the effects of actions ... on the lives of persons ... including the lives of others besides the person acting. ... David Hume took a similar position when the argued that what speaks in a moral judgment is a kind of sympathy. ... A little later, ... Kant put the matter somewhat better by characterizing morality as the business of respecting persons as ends and not as means or as things. ...[2]

Frankena is pointing to two traits, both rooted in a long and diverse philosophical tradition:

1. Rationality. Taking a moral point of view includes the features we usually attribute to rational decision making, that is, lack of impulsiveness, care in mapping out alternatives and consequences, clarity about goals and purposes, attention to details of implementation.
2. Respect. The moral point of view also includes a special awareness of and concern for the effects of one's decisions and policies on others, special in the sense that it goes beyond the kind of awareness and concern that would ordinarily be part of rationality, that is, beyond seeing others merely as instrumental to accomplishing one's own purposes. This is respect for the lives of others and involves taking their needs and interests seriously, not simply as resources in one's own decision making but as limiting conditions which change the very definition of one's habitat from a self-centered to a shared environment. It is what philosopher Immanuel Kant meant by the "categorical imperative" to treat others as valuable in and for themselves.

It is this feature that permits us to trust the morally responsible person. We know that such a person takes our point of view into account not merely as a useful precaution (as in "honesty is the best policy") but as important in its own right.

These components of moral responsibility are not too vague to be useful. Rationality and respect affect the manner in which a person approaches practical decision making: they affect the way in which the individual processes information and makes choices. A rational but not respectful Bill Jones will not lie to his friends *unless* he is reasonably sure he will not be found out. A rational but not respectful Mary Smith will defend an unjustly treated party *unless* she thinks it may be too costly to herself. A rational *and* respectful decision maker, however, notices—and cares—whether the consequences of his or her conduct lead to injuries or indignities to others.

Two individuals who take "the moral point of view" will not of course always agree on ethical matters, but they do at least have a basis for dialogue.

Projecting Responsibility to Corporations

Now that we have removed some of the vagueness from the notion of moral responsibility as it applies to persons, we can search for a frame of reference in which, by analogy with Bill Jones and Mary Smith, we can meaningfully and appropriately say that corporations are morally responsible. This is the issue reflected in the SSC case.

To deal with it, we must ask two questions: Is it meaningful to apply moral concepts to actors who are not persons but who are instead made up of persons? And even if meaningful, is it advisable to do so?

If a group can act like a person in some ways, then we can expect it to behave like a person in other ways. For one thing, we know that people organized into a group can act as a unit. As businesspeople well know, legally a corporation is considered a unit. To approach unity, a group usually has some sort of internal decision structure, a system of rules that spell out authority relationships and specify the conditions under which certain individuals' actions become official actions of the group.[3]

If we can say that persons act responsibly only if they gather information about the impact of their actions on others and use it in making decisions, we can reasonably do the same for organizations. Our proposed frame of reference for thinking about and implementing corporate responsibility aims at spelling out the processes associated with the moral responsibility of individuals and projecting them to the level of organizations. This is similar to, though an inversion of, Plato's famous method in the *Republic*, in which justice in the community is used as a model for justice in the individual.

Hence, corporations that monitor their employment practices and the effects of their production processes and products on the environment and human health show the same kind of rationality and respect that morally responsible individuals do. Thus, attributing actions, strategies, decisions, and moral responsibilities to corporations as entities distinguishable from those who hold offices in them poses no problem.

And when we look about us, we can readily see differences in moral responsibility among corporations in much the same way that we see differences among persons. Some corporations have built features into their management incentive systems, board structures, internal control systems, and research agendas that in a person we would call self-control, integrity, and conscientiousness. Some have institutionalized awareness and concern for consumers, employees, and the rest of the public in ways that others clearly have not.

As a matter of course, some corporations attend to the human impact of their operations and policies and reject operations and policies that are questionable. Whether the issue be the health effects of sugared cereal or cigarettes, the safety of tires or tampons, civil liberties in the corporation or the community, an organization reveals its character as surely as a person does.

Indeed, the parallel may be even more dramatic. For just as the moral responsibility displayed by an individual develops over time from infancy to adulthood,[4] so too we may expect to find stages of development in organizational character that show significant patterns.

Evaluating the Idea of Moral Projection

Concepts like moral responsibility not only make sense when applied to organizations but also provide touchstones for designing more effective models than we now have for guiding corporate policy.

Now we can understand what it means to invite SSC as a corporation to be morally responsible both in-house and in its community, but *should* we issue the invitation? Here we turn to the question of advisability. Should we require the organizational agents in our society to have the same moral attributes we require of ourselves?

Our proposal to spell out the processes associated with moral responsibility for individuals and then to project them to their organizational counterparts takes on added meaning when we examine alternative frames of reference for corporate responsibility.

Two frames of reference that compete for the allegiance of people who ponder the question of corporate responsibility are emphatically opposed to this principle of moral projection—what we might refer to as the "invisible hand" view and the "hand of government" view.

The invisible hand

The most eloquent spokesman of the first view is Milton Friedman (echoing many philosophers and economists since Adam Smith). According to this pattern of thought, the true and only social responsibilities of business organizations are to make profits and obey the laws. The workings of the free and competitive marketplace will "moralize" corporate behavior quite independently of any attempts to expand or transform decision making via moral projection.

A deliberate amorality in the executive suite is encouraged in the name of systemic morality: the common good is best served when each of us and our economic institutions pursue not the common good or moral purpose, advocates say, but competitive advantage. Morality, responsibility, and conscience reside in the invisible hand of the free market system, not in the hands of the organizations within the system, much less the managers within the organizations.

To be sure, people of this opinion admit, there is a sense in which social or ethical issues can and should enter the corporate mind, but the filtering of such issues is thorough: they go through the screens of custom, public opinion, public relations, and the law. And, in any case, self-interest maintains primacy as an objective and a guiding star.

The reaction from this frame of reference to the suggestion that moral judgment be integrated with corporate strategy is clearly negative. Such an integration is seen as inefficient and arrogant, and in the end both an illegitimate use of corporate power and an abuse of the manager's fiduciary role. With respect to our SSC case, advocates of the invisible hand model would vigorously resist efforts, beyond legal requirements, to make SSC right the wrongs of racial injustice. SSC's responsibility would be to make steel of high quality at least cost, to deliver it on time, and to satisfy its customers and stockholders. Justice would not be part of SSC's corporate mandate.

The hand of government

Advocates of the second dissenting frame of reference abound, but John Kenneth Galbraith's work has counterpointed Milton Friedman's with insight and style. Under this view of corporate responsibility, corporations are to pursue objectives that are rational and purely economic. The regulatory hands of the law and the political process rather than the invisible hand of the marketplace turns these objectives to the common good.

Again, in this view, it is a system that provides the moral direction for corporate decision making—a system, though, that is guided by political managers, the custodians of the public purpose. In the case of SSC, proponents of this view would look to the state for moral direction and responsible management, both within SSC and in the community. The corporation would have no moral responsibility beyond political and legal obedience.

What is striking is not so much the radical difference between the economic and social philosophies that underlie these two views of the source of corporate responsibility but the conceptual similarities. Both views locate morality, ethics, responsibility, and conscience in the systems of rules and incentives in which the modern corporation finds itself embedded. Both views reject the exercise of independent moral judgment by corporations as actors in society.

Neither view trusts corporate leaders with stewardship over what are often called noneconomic values. Both require corporate responsibility to march to the beat of drums outside. In the jargon of moral philosophy, both views press for a rule-centered or a system-centered ethics instead of an agent-centered ethics. In terms of the *Exhibit*, these frames of reference countenance corporate rule-following responsibility for corporations but not corporate decision-making responsibility.

The hand of management

To be sure, the two views under discussion differ in that one looks to an invisible moral force in the market while the other looks to a visible moral force in government. But both would advise against a principle of moral projection that permits or encourages corporations to exercise independent, noneconomic judgment over matters that face them in their short- and long-term plans and operations.

Accordingly, both would reject a third view of corporate responsibility that seeks to affect the thought processes of the organization itself—a sort of "hand of management" view—since neither seems willing or able to see the engines of profit regulate themselves to the degree that would be implied by taking the principle of moral projection seriously. Cries of inefficiency and moral imperialism from the right would be matched by cries of insensitivity and illegitimacy from the left, all in the name of preserving us from corporations and managers run morally amok.

Better, critics would say, that moral philosophy be left to philosophers, philanthropists, and politicians than to business leaders. Better that corporate morality be kept to glossy annual reports, where it is safely insulated from policy and performance.

The two conventional frames of reference locate moral restraint in forces external to the person and the corporation. They deny moral reasoning and intent to the corporation in the name of either market competition or society's system of explicit legal constraints and presume that these have a better moral effect than that of rationality and respect.

Although the principle of moral projection, which underwrites the idea of a corporate conscience and patterns it on the thought and feeling processes of the person, is in our view compelling, we must acknowledge that it is neither part of the received wisdom, nor is its advisability beyond question or objection. Indeed, attributing the role of conscience to the corporation seems to carry with it new and disturbing implications for our usual ways of thinking about ethics and business.

Perhaps the best way to clarify and defend this frame of reference is to address the objections to the principle found in the ruled insert here. There we see a summary of the criticisms and counterarguments we have heard during hours of discussion with business executives and business school students. We believe that the replies to the objections about a corporation having a conscience are convincing.

Leaving the Double Standard Behind

We have come some distance from our opening reflection on Southern Steel Company and its role in its community. Our proposal—clarified, we hope, through these objections and replies—suggests that it is not sufficient to draw a sharp line between individuals' private ideas and efforts and a corporation's institutional efforts but that the latter can and should be built upon the former.

Does this frame of reference give us an unequivocal prescription for the behavior of SSC in its circumstances? No, it does not. Persuasive arguments might be made now and might have been made then that SSC should not have used its considerable economic clout to threaten the community into desegregation. A careful analysis of the realities of the environment might have disclosed that such a course would have been counterproductive, leading to more injustice than it would have alleviated.

The point is that some of the arguments and some of the analyses are or would have been moral arguments, and thereby the ultimate decision that of an ethically responsible organization. The significance of this point can hardly be overstated, for it represents the adoption of a new perspective on corporate policy and a new way of thinking about business ethics. We agree with one authority, who writes that "the business firm, as an organic entity intricately affected by and affecting its environment, is as appropriately adaptive ... to demands for responsible behavior as for economic service."[5]

The frame of reference here developed does not offer a decision procedure for corporate managers. That has not been our purpose. It does, however, shed light on the conceptual foundations of business ethics by training attention on the corporation as a moral agent in society. Legal systems of rules and incentives are insufficient, even though they may be necessary, as frameworks for corporate responsibility. Taking conceptual cues from the features of moral responsibility normally expected of the person in our opinion deserves practicing managers' serious consideration.

The lack of congruence that James Weston saw between individual and corporate moral responsibility can be, and we think should be, overcome. In the process, what a number of writers have characterized as a double standard—a discrepancy between our personal lives and our lives in organizational settings—might be dampened. The principle of moral projection not only helps us to conceptualize the kinds of demands that we might make of corporations and other organizations but also offers the prospect of harmonizing those demands with the demands that we make of ourselves.

Notes

1 See John Ladd, "Mortality and the Ideal of Rationality in Formal Organizations," *The Monist*, October 1970: p. 499.

2 See William K. Frankena, *Thinking About Morality* (Ann Arbor: University of Michigan Press, 1980); p. 26.

3 See Peter French, "The Corporation as a Moral Person," *American Philosophical Quarterly*, July 1979: p. 207.

4 A process that psychological researchers from Jean Piaget to Lawrence Kohlberg have examined carefully; see Jean Piaget, *The Moral Judgment of the Child* (New York: Free Press, 1965) and Lawrence Kohlberg, *The Philosophy of Moral Development* (New York: Harper & Row, 1981).

5 See Kenneth R. Andrews, *The Concept of Corporate Strategy*, rev. ed. (Homewood, Ill.: Dow Jones-Irwin, 1980); p. 99.

The Corporation as a Moral Person

PETER A. FRENCH

In his *New York Times* column, Tom Wicker expressed his aroused ire at a Gulf Oil Corporation advertisement that "pointed the finger of blame" for energy shortages and high prices at virtually every element of our society except the oil companies. Wicker, as might be expected, attacked Gulf Oil and the petroleum industry as the major, if not the sole, perpetrators of that crisis and most every other social ill, with the possible exception of venereal disease.

In a courtroom in Winamac, Indiana, in 1979–80, the Ford Motor Company was tried for reckless homicide in the deaths of Judy, Lyn, and Donna Ulrich. The three teenagers were incinerated when the Ford Pinto in which they were driving was hit in the rear at a speed differential of around thirty miles per hour. One of the law professors who worked as a consultant for the prosecution recently wrote: "What we were saying is that a corporation like all other persons must be forced at times to look at the very personal tragedies it causes."[1] The prosecution's case was directed at demonstrating the moral and criminal capacity for responsibility of the Ford Motor Company. No attempt was made to prosecute individual Ford executives or engineers. We need not concern ourselves with whether Wicker was serious or merely sarcastic when he made his charges against Gulf. Most certainly the prosecution in the Pinto case was serious and, although Ford Motor Company was acquitted of the charges, the concept of corporate moral and legal responsibility was not discredited. Indeed, it was provided with a landmark of courtroom precedent and popular acceptance. In this essay I will examine the sense ascriptions of moral responsibility make when their subjects are corporations. I hope to provide the foundation of a theory that allows treatment of corporations as full-fledged members of the moral community, of equal standing with the traditionally acknowledged residents: human beings. With such a theory in hand we should treat moral-responsibility ascriptions to corporations as unexceptionable instances of a perfectly proper sort and not have to paraphrase or reduce them. Corporations as moral persons will have whatever privileges, rights and duties as are, in the normal course of affairs, accorded to all members of the moral community.

It is important to distinguish three quite different notions of what is it to be a person that are frequently entangled throughout the various aspects of our tradition: the metaphysical, moral, and legal concepts of personhood. The entanglement is clearly evident in John Locke's account of personal identity. He writes that the term "person" is "a *forensic* term, appropriating actions and their merit; and so belongs only to *intelligent agents*, capable of law, and happiness, and misery." He goes on to say that by consciousness and memory persons are capable of extending themselves into the past and thereby become "concerned and *accountable*."[2] Locke is historically correct in citing the law as a primary origin of the term "person." But he is incorrect in maintaining that its legal usage entails its metaphysical sense, agency; and whether or not either sense, but especially the metaphysical, is interdependent on the moral sense, accountability, is surely controversial.

There are two distinct schools of thought regarding the relationship between metaphysical and moral persons. According to one, to be a metaphysical person is only to be a moral one; to understand what it is to be accountable, one must understand what it is to be an intentional or a rational agent and vice versa. According to the other, being an intentional agent is a necessary but not a sufficient condition of being a moral person. Locke appears to hold the interdependence view, with which I agree, but he roots both moral and metaphysical persons in the juristic person, which is, I think, wrongheaded. The preponderance of current thinking in moral and social theory, however, endorses some version of the necessary precondition view. Most of those holding such a position do exhibit the virtue of treating legal personhood as something apart from moral and metaphysical matters.

It is of note that many contemporary moral philosophers and economists both defend a precondition view of the relationship between the metaphysical and moral person and also adopt a view of the legal personhood of corporations that excludes corporations per se from the class of moral persons. Such philosophers and economists tend to champion the least defensible of a number of possible interpretations of the juristic personhood of corporations, but their doing so allows them to systematically sidestep the question of whether corporations can meet the conditions of metaphysical personhood.[3]

John Rawls is, to some extent, guilty of fortifying what I hope to show is an indefensible interpretation of the legal concept and of thereby encouraging an anthropocentric bias that has led to the general belief that corporations just cannot be moral persons. As is well known, Rawls defends his two principles of justice by the use of a thought experiment that incorporates the essential characteristics of what he takes to be a premoral, though metaphysical population and then derives the moral guidelines for social institutions that they would accept. The persons (or parties) in the "original position" are described by Rawls as being mutually self-interested, rational, as having similar wants, needs, interests, and capacities and as being, for all intents and purposes, equal in power (so that no one of them can dominate the others). Their choice of the principles of justice is, as Daniel Dennett has pointed out,[4] a rather dramatic rendering of one version of the compelling (though I think unnecessarily complex) philosophical thesis that only out of metaphysical persons can moral ones evolve.

But Rawls is remarkably ambiguous (and admittedly so) regarding who or what may qualify as a metaphysical person. He admits into the category, in one sentence, not only biological human beings but "nations, provinces, business firms, churches, teams, and so on," then, perhaps because he does not want to tackle the demonstration of the rationality of those institutions and organizations, or because he is a captive of the traditional prejudice in favor of biological persons, in the next sentence he withdraws entry. "There is, perhaps, a certain logical priority to the case of human individuals: it may be possible to analyze the actions of so-called artificial persons as logical constructions of the actions of human persons...."[5] "Perhaps" is, of course, a rather large hedge behind which to hide; but it is, I suppose, of some significance that in *A Theory of Justice* when he is listing the nature of the parties in the "original position" he adds as item c "associations (states, churches, or other corporate bodies."[6] He does not, unfortunately, discuss this entry on his list anywhere else in the book. Rawls had hold, I think, of an important intuition: that some associations of human beings should be treated as metaphysical persons capable, on his account, of becoming moral persons, in and of themselves. He shrunk, however, from the task of exploring the implications of that intuition and instead retreated to the comfortable bulwarks of the anthropocentric bias.

Many philosophers, including (I think) Rawls, have rather uncritically relied upon what they incorrectly perceive to be the most defensible juristic treatment of corporations as a paradigm for the treatment of corporations in their moral theories. The concept of corporate legal personhood under any of its popular interpretations is, I want to argue, virtually useless for moral purposes.

Following a number of writers on jurisprudence, a juristic person may be defined as any entity that is a subject of a right. There are good etymological grounds for such an inclusive neutral definition. The Latin *persona* originally referred to *dramatis personae*, but in Roman law the term was adopted to refer to anything that could act on either side of a legal dispute. (It was not until Boethius' definition of a person: *"Persona est naturae rationabilis individua substantia"* [a person is the individual subsistence of a rational nature] that metaphysical traits were ascribed to persons.) In effect, in Roman legal tradition persons are creations or artifacts of the law itself, i.e., of the legislature that enacts the law, and are not considered to have, or only have incidentally, existence of any kind outside of the legal sphere. The law, on the Roman interpretation, is systematically ignorant of the biological status of its subjects.

The Roman notion applied to corporations is popularly known as the Fiction Theory. Frederick Hallis characterizes that theory as maintaining that "the personality of a corporate body is a pure fiction and owes its existence to a creative act of the state."[7] Rawls' view of corporate persons, however, is not a version of the Fiction Theory. The theory draws no dichotomy between real and artificial persons. All juristic persons, on the theory, are creations of the law. The Fiction Theory does not view the law as recognizing or verifying prelegally existing persons; it maintains that the law creates all of its own subjects. Second, the theory, in its pure form at least, does not regard any juristic persons as composites. All things which are legislatively created as subjects of rights are nonreducible or, if you will, primitive individual legal persons. It is of some note that the Fiction Theory is enshrined in English law in regard to corporate bodies by no less an authority than Sir Edward Coke, who wrote that corporations "rest only in intendment and consideration of the law."[8]

The Fiction Theory's major rival in American jurisprudence and the view that does seem to inform Rawls' account is what I shall call the Legal Aggregate Theory of the Corporation. It holds that the names of corporate organizations are only umbrellas that cover (but do not shield) a specific aggregate of biological persons. The Aggregate Theory allows that biological status has legal priority and that a corporation is but a contrivance, the name of which is best used for summary reference. (Aggregate Theorists tend to ignore employees and identify corporations with directors, executives, and stockholders. The model on which they stake their claim is no doubt that of the primitive partnership)...

The third major rival interpretation of corporate juristic personhood resides in Germanic legal tradition. Primarily because of the advocacy of Otto von Gierke, the so-called Reality Theory recognizes corporations to be prelegal existing sociological persons. Underlying the theory is the view that law cannot create its subjects; it can only determine which societal facts are in conformity with its requirements. Law endorses the prelegal existence of persons for its own purposes. Gierke regards the corporation as an offspring of certain social actions and as having a de facto personality, which the law declares to be a juridical fact.[9] The Reality Theory's primary virtue is that it does not ignore the nonlegal roots of the corporation while it, as may the Fiction Theory, acknowledges the nonidentity of the corporation and the aggregate of its directors, stockholders, executives, and employees. The primary difference between the Fiction and Reality Theories, that one treats the corporate person as de jure and the other as de facto, turns out to be of no real importance, however, in regard to the issue of the moral personhood of a corporation. Admittedly the Reality Theory encapsulates a view at least superficially more amenable to arguing for discrete corporate moral personhood than does the Fiction Theory just because it does acknowledge de facto personhood, but theorists on both sides will admit that they are providing interpretations of only the formula "juristic person = the subject of rights," and as long as we stick to legal history, no interpretation of that formula need concern itself with metaphysical personhood or intentional agency. The de facto personhood of the Reality Theory is that of a sociological entity only, of which no claim is or need be made regarding agency, or rationality, or any of the traits of a metaphysical person. One could, without contradiction, hold the Reality Theory and deny the metaphysical or moral personhood of corporations. What is needed is a Reality Theory that identifies a de facto metaphysical person not just a sociological entity.

Underlying all of these interpretations of corporate legal personhood is a distinction, embedded in the law itself, that renders them unhelpful for our purposes. Being a subject of rights is often contrasted in the law with being an administrator of rights. Any number of entities and associations can and have been the subjects of legal rights. In earlier times, animals have been given legal rights; legislatures have given rights to unborn human beings; they have reserved rights for human beings long after their death; and in some recent cases they have invested rights in generations of the future. Of course such recipients of rights, though, strictly speaking, legal persons, cannot dispose of their rights. They also cannot administer them, because to administer a right one must be an intentional agent, i.e., able to *act* in certain ways. It may be only an historical accident that most legal cases are cases in which "the subject of right X" and "the administrator of right X" are coreferential. It is nowhere required by law, not under any of the three theories just discussed or elsewhere, that it be so. Yet, it is possession of the attributes of an administrator of rights and not those of a subject of rights that constitutes the generally accepted conditions of moral personhood. It is a fundamental mistake to regard the fact of juristic corporate personhood as having settled the question of the moral personhood of a corporation one way or the other.

Two helpful lessons are learned from the investigation of the legal personhood of corporations: (1) biological existence is not essentially associated with the concept of personhood (only the fallacious Aggregate Theory depends upon reduction to biological beings), and (2) a paradigm for the form of an inclusive neutral definition of a moral person is provided: a subject of a right. I shall define a moral person as a referent of any proper name or of any noneliminatable subject in an ascription of moral responsibility. The non-eliminatable nature of the subject should be stressed because responsibility and other predicates of morality are neutral as regards person and person-sum predication.[10] I argued [elsewhere] that ascriptions of moral responsibility involve the notions of accountability and being held liable for an answer. These notions presuppose the existence of responsibility relationships, and one of their primary foci is on the subject's intentions. To be the subject of an ascription of moral responsibility, to be a party in responsibility relationships, hence to be a moral person, the subject must be at minimum an intentional actor.[11] If corporations are moral persons they will evidence a noneliminatable intentionality with regard to the things they do.

For a corporation to be treated as a moral person, it must be the case that some events are describable in a way that makes certain sentences true: sentences that say that some of the things a corporation does were intended by the corporation itself. That is not accomplished if attributing intentions to a corporation is only a shorthand way of attributing intentions to the biological persons who comprise, e.g., its board of directors. If that were to turn out to be the case, then on metaphysical if not logical grounds, there would be no real way to distinguish between corporations and crowds. I shall argue, however, that a Corporation's Internal Decision Structure (its CID Structure) provides the requisite redescription device that licenses the predication of corporate intentionality....

The important point is that metaphysical personhood depends on the possibility of describing an event as an intentional action. Often a single event can be correctly described in a number of different and nonequivent ways. With respect to some events, there are layers of nonintersubstitutable true descriptions. Some layers merely describe the event as a movement or a piece of behavior. Other layers describe the same event as the effect of prior causes that are reasons or desires and beliefs. Significantly, a single event may be described as the effect of different sets of reasons, even of different kinds of reasons, so there may be more than one layer of true descriptions of an event at which it is appropriate to identify it as an intentional action. At every layer at which it is proper to describe an event as an intentional action, there is a metaphysical person, an actor.

Certainly a corporation's doing something involves or includes human beings doing things, and the human beings who occupy various positions in a corporation usually can be described as having reasons for *their* behavior. In fact, in virtue of those descriptions, they may be properly held responsible for their behavior, ceteris paribus. What needs to be shown if there is to be corporate responsibility is that there is sense in saying that corporations and not just the people who work in them have reasons for doing what they do. Typically, we will be told that corporate reasons are to be identified with the reasons and desires of the directors or of certain high-level managers and that, although corporate action may not be reducible without remainder, corporate intentions are always reducible to such executive intentions. Such a view is, in fact, captured in English legal precedent, specifically in the 1971 case of *Tesco Supermarkets Ltd. v. Nattcass*. The supermarket company was charged under a section of the Trade Descriptions Act of 1968. The case involved false price advertising. An assistant had replaced reduced-priced soap boxes with those marked at regular prices. The assistant did not notify the store manager who is responsible for seeing that sales items were properly priced. The manager failed to check the pricing on his own. The company argued that it had exercised due diligence and that the negligence was that of a person too far down in the corporate hierarchy to be identified with the intentions of the corporation itself. The House of Lords found in the company's favor, thereby endorsing the idea that corporate reasons are the reasons of senior executive staff members. Such a view, I shall argue, is not adequate to the understanding of corporate intentionality. It should, however, be strikingly plain that finding directional negligence, for example, is not necessarily finding corporate negligence. If an underling can act for personal, self-serving reasons, so can a director, and his doing so may have nothing to do with the corporation's business practices. In fact those practices may make his self-serving possible by creating a climate of trust and honesty in which he can operate.

Every corporation has an internal decision structure. CID Structures have two elements of interest to us here: (1) an organizational or responsibility flowchart that delineates stations and levels within the corporate power structure and (2) corporate-decision recognition rule(s) (usually embedded in something called corporation policy). The CID Structure is the personnel organization for the exercise of the corporation's power with respect to its ventures, and as such its primary function is to draw experience from various levels of the corporation into a decision-making and ratification process. When operative and properly activated, the CID Structure accomplishes a subordination and synthesis of the intentions and acts of various biological persons into a corporate decision. When viewed in another way, as already suggested, the CID Structure licenses the descriptive transformation of events, seen under another aspect as the acts of biological persons (those who occupy various stations on the organizational chart), to corporate acts by exposing the corporate character of those events. A CID Structure *incorporates* acts of biological persons. For illustrative purposes, suppose we imagine that an event E has at least two aspects, that is, can be described in two nonidentical ways. One of those aspects is "Executive X's doing y" and one is "Corporation C's doing z." The corporate act and the individual act may have different properties; indeed they have different causal ancestors, though they are causally inseparable. (I hope to show that the causal inseparability of these acts is a product of the CID Structure; X's doing y is not the cause of C's doing z; nor is C's doing z the cause of X's doing y; although if X's doing y causes event F, then C's doing z causes F and vice versa.)

J.K. Galbraith rather neatly captures what I have in mind, although I doubt he is aware of the metaphysical reading that can be given to this process, when he writes in his recent popular book on the history of economics: "From [the] interpersonal exercise of power, the interaction ... of the participants, comes the *personality* of the corporation."[12] I take Galbraith here to be quite literally correct, but it is important to spell out how a CID Structure works this miracle.

In philosophy in recent years we have grown accustomed to the use of games as models for understanding institutional behavior. We all have some understanding of how rules in games make certain descriptions of events possible, which would not be so if those rules were nonexistent. The CID Structure of a corporation is a kind of constitutive rule (or rules) analogous to the game rules with which we are familiar. The organization chart of a corporation distinguishes players and clarifies their rank and the interwoven lines of responsibility within the corporation. An organizational chart tells us, for example, that anyone holding the title "Executive vice-president for finance administration" stands in a certain relationship to anyone holding the title "director of internal audit" and to anyone holding the title "treasurer," etc. In effect it expresses, or maps, the interdependent and dependent relationships, line and staff, that are involved in determinations of corporate decisions and actions. The organizational chart provides what might be called the grammar of corporate decision-making. What I shall call internal recognition rules provide its logic.

By "recognition rule(s)" I mean what Hart, in another context, calls "conclusive affirmative indication," that a decision on an act has been made or performed for corporate reasons.[13] Recognition rules are of two sorts. Partially embedded in the organizational chart are procedural recognitors: We see that decisions are to be reached collectively at certain levels and that they are to be ratified at higher levels (or at inner circles, if one prefers that Galbraithean model). A corporate decision is recognized internally, however, not only by the procedure is its making, but by the policy it instantiates. Hence every corporation creates an image (not to be confused with its public image) or a general policy, what G. C. Buzby of the Chilton Company has called the "basic belief of the corporation," that must inform its decisions for them to be properly described as being those of that corporation. "The moment policy is side-stepped or violated, it is no longer the policy of that company."[14]

Peter Drucker has seen the importance of the basic policy recognitors in the CID Structure (though he treats matters rather differently from the way I am recommending). Drucker writes:

> Because the corporation is an institution it must have a basic policy. For it must subordinate individual ambitions and decisions to the *needs* of the corporation's welfare and survival. That means that it must have a set of principles and a rule of conduct which limit and direct individual actions and behavior.[15]

Suppose, for illustrative purposes, we activate a CID Structure in a corporation, Tom Wicker's whipping boy, the Gulf Oil Corporation. Imagine that three executives, Jones, Smith, and Jackson have the task of deciding whether or not Gulf Oil will join a world uranium cartel. They have before them an Everest of papers that have been prepared by lower-echelon executives. Some of the papers will be purely factual reports, some will be contingency plans, some will be formulations of positions developed by various departments, some will outline financial considerations, and some will be legal opinions. Insofar as these will all have been processed through Gulf's CID Structure system, the personal reasons, if any, individual executives may have had for writing their reports and recommendations in a specific way will likely have been diluted by the subordination of individual inputs to peer group input and higher level review and recommendation before Jones, Smith, and Jackson deal with the matter. A vote is taken, as is authorized procedure in the Gulf CID Structure, which is to say that under these circumstances the vote of Jones, Smith, and Jackson can be redescribed as the corporation's making a decision: that is, the event "Jones, Smith, and Jackson voting" may be redescribed to expose an aspect otherwise unrevealed, quite different from its other aspects, e.g., from Jones's (or Smith's or Jackson's) voting in the affirmative. Redescriptive exposure of a procedurally corporate aspect of an event is not to be confused with a description of an event that makes true a sentence that says that the corporation did something intentionally. But the CID Structure, as already suggested, also provides the grounds in its other type of recognitor for such an attribution of corporate intentionality. Simply, when the corporate act is consistent with an instantiation or an implementation of established corporate policy, then it is proper to describe it as having been done for corporate reasons, as having been caused by a corporate desire coupled with a corporate belief and so, in other words, as corporate intentional.

An event may, under one of its aspects, be described as the conjunctive act "Jones intentionally voted yes, and Smith intentionally voted yes, and Jackson did so as well" (where a "yes" vote was to vote in the affirmative on the question of Gulf oil joining the cartel). Within the Gulf CID Structure we find the conjunction of rules that tell us that when the occupants of positions *A*, *B*, and *C* on the organizational chart unanimously vote to do something that is consistent with an instantiation or an implementation of general corporate policy and ceteris paribus, Gulf Oil Corporation has decided to do it for corporate reasons. The event of those executives voting is then redescribable as "the

Gulf Oil Corporation decided to join the cartel for reasons consistent with basic policy of Gulf Oil, e.g., increasing profits," or simply as "Gulf Oil Corporation intentionally decided to join the cartel." This is a rather technical way of saying that in these circumstances the executives voting is, given its CID Structure, also the corporation deciding to do something. Regardless of the personal reasons the executives have for voting as they do, and even if their reasons are inconsistent with established corporate policy or even if one of them has no reason at all for voting as he does, the corporation still has reasons for joining the cartel, that is, joining is consistent with the inviolate corporate general policies, as encrusted in the precedent of previous corporation actions, and its statements of purpose as recorded in its certificate of incorporation, annual reports, etc. The corporation's only method of achieving its desires or goals is the activation of the personnel who occupy its various positions. However, if Jones voted affirmatively purely for reasons of personal monetary gain (suppose she had been bribed to do so) that does not alter the fact that the corporate reason for joining the cartel was to minimize competition and hence pay higher dividends to its shareholders. Corporations have reasons because they have interests in doing those things that are likely to result in realization of their established corporate goals, regardless of the transient self-interest of directors or managers. If there is a difference between corporate goals and desires and those of human beings, it is probably that the corporate ones are relatively stable and not very wide ranging, but that is only because corporations can do relatively fewer things than human beings, being confined in action predominantly to a limited socio-economic sphere. It is, of course, in a corporation's interest that its component membership views the corporate purposes as instrumental in the achievement of their own goals. (Financial reward is the most common way this is achieved.)...

The CID Structure licenses both redescriptions of events as corporate and attributions of corporate intentionality, while it does not obscure the private acts of executives, directors, etc. Although Jones voted to support the joining of the cartel because she was bribed to do so, Jones did not join the cartel, Gulf Oil Corporation joined the cartel. Consequently, we may say that Jones did something for which she should be held morally responsible, yet whether or not Gulf Oil Corporation should be held morally responsible for joining the cartel is a question that turns on issues that may be unrelated to Jones' having accepted a bribe.

Of course Gulf Oil Corporation cannot join the cartel unless Jones or somebody who occupies position *A* on the organizational chart votes in the affirmative. What that shows, however, is that corporations are organizations or associations including human beings. That should not, however, rule out the possibility of their having metaphysical status, as being intentional actors in their own right, and being thereby full-fledged moral persons.

This much I hope is clear: we can describe many events in terms of certain physical movements of human beings, and we also can sometimes describe those very events as done for reasons by those human beings, but further we can sometimes describe the same events as corporate and still further as done for corporate reasons that are qualitatively different from whatever personal reasons component members may have for doing what they do.

Corporate agency resides in the possibility of CID Structure licensed redescription of events as corporate intentional. That may still appear to be downright mysterious, although I do not think it is, for human agency as I have suggested, resides in the possibility of description as well.

Notes

1 Bruce Berner, "Letter to William Maakestad," published in "The Ford Pinto Case and Beyond." A paper presented by F. Cullen, W. Maakestad, and G. Cavender at the 1983 Meeting of the Academy of Criminal Justice Sciences, 1983.

2 John Locke, *An Essay Concerning Human Understanding*, P. H. Nidditch, ed. (Oxford: Oxford University Press, 1975); Book II, ch. 27, p. 346.

3 For a particularly flagrant example see Michael Jensen and William Meckling, "Theory of the Firm: Managerial Behavior, Agency Costs and Ownership Structure," *Journal of Financial Economics* (1976), 3:305–60. On page 311 they write, "The private corporation or firm is simply one form of legal fiction which serves as a nexus for contracting relationships."

4 Daniel Dennett, "Conditions of Personhood," in A. O. Rorty, ed., *The Identities of Persons* (Berkeley: University of California Press, 1976); pp. 175–96.

5 John Rawls, "Justice as Reciprocity," in Samuel Gorovitz, ed., *John Stuart Mill*, *Utilitarianism* (Indianapolis: Bobbs-Merrill, 1971); pp. 244–45.

6 John Rawls, A *Theory of Justice* (Cambridge: Harvard University Press, 1970); p. 146.

7 Frederick Hallis, *Corporate Personality* (Oxford: Oxford University Press, 1930); p. xlii.

8 *Coke's Reports* 253, see Hallis, *Corporate Personality*, p. xlii.

9 See in particular Otto von Gierke, *Die Genossenschaftstheorie* (Berlin, 1887).

10 See Gerald Massey, "Tom, Dick, and Harry and All the King's Men," *American Philosophical Quarterly* (April 1976), 13(2):89–108.

11 I am especially indebted to Donald Davidson, "Agency," in Robert Binkley, Richard Bronaugh, and Ausonio Marras, eds., *Agent, Action, and Reason* (Toronto: University of Toronto Press, 1971).

12 John Kenneth Galbraith, *The Age of Uncertainty* (Boston: Houghton Mifflin, 1977); p. 261.

13 H. L. A. Hart, *The Concept of Law* (Oxford, Oxford University Press, 1961); ch. 6.

14 G. C. Buzby, "Policies—A Guide to What A Company Stands For," *Management Record* (March 1962), 24:5–12.

15 Peter Drucker, *The Concept of Corporation* (New York: Crowell, 1972); pp. 36–37.

Personalizing Corporate Ontology
The French Way

Thomas Donaldson

The trickiest philosophical problems are those for which we choose alternative and self-contradictory solutions. The problem of corporate agency appears to be of this kind, at least insofar as leading theorists investigating it have divided their opinions dramatically, one side declaring the corporation to be an impersonal machine incapable of even modest moral attributes, and the other proclaiming it to be a person

Thomas Donaldson, "Personalizing Corporate Ontology: The French Way." Reprinted with kind permission of the editor and the author from *Shame, Responsibility and the Corporation*, ed. Hugh Curtler (New York: Haven Publishing, 1986); 101–112.

with similarities to human beings, similarities sufficient, indeed, to warrant sponsoring the development of moral faculties such as "consciousness" in the corporation analogous to those on the level of flesh and blood people.[1] Logic tells us that the corporation cannot be both machine and person, but which side of the dilemma are we to choose?

When a penetrating mind encounters a dilemma, it often refuses to be pigeonholed by either side. This seems to characterize Peter French who, despite subtle suggestions now and then that his view remains the same, began his writing on the subject strongly emphasizing the similarities between corporations and human beings—he began, one might say, as an unabashed moral person theorist—and has ever since been modifying his view in the opposite direction. In this article I investigate French's shift of view in detail, for I believe it provides a clue to a problem underlying his entire analysis. I argue that in the end he is driven to propose a modified set of conditions for moral personhood that are insufficient for his task, and that, although he manages to clarify key problematic issues, he nonetheless fails in his primary mission of bridging the conceptual gap between corporations and human beings. His mission fails, I believe, because it is a mission impossible.

Through a series of separate writings,[2] we find French moving from a view which presumes that the set of rights and duties held by traditional persons can be held by corporate "persons," to one that denies the legitimacy of presuming without independent evidence that rights and duties attaching to human beings have straightforward counterparts in the corporation. In an early writing, "The Corporation as Moral Person," for example, we find in the opening paragraph a statement of vigorous personalism: he writes "I hope to provide the foundation of a theory that allows treatment of corporations as members of the moral community, of equal standing with the traditionally acknowledged residents: biological human beings, and hence treats ... responsibility ascriptions as unexceptionable instances of a perfectly proper sort without having to paraphrase them. In short, corporations can be full-fledged moral persons and can have whatever privileges, rights, and duties as are, in the normal course of affairs, accorded to moral persons."[3]

Now to assert that whatever privileges, rights, and duties are normally accorded to ordinary moral persons, can also be possessed by corporations is a vigorous assertion of moral similarity between corporations and people. It would appear that once we are happy with the list of rights and duties that we think characterize normal, adult human beings, we can then apply that list *en toto* to corporations—at least corporations that meet certain structural and procedural conditions.[4] Think of the list the average person would draw up for flesh and blood persons, and then think of it applied to Exxon or Union Carbide. Such a list would include, I suppose, all ten items in the U.S. Constitution's Bill of Rights, including rights to privacy, property, and freedom from cruel and unusual punishment, and also those rights highlighted in the preamble to the Declaration of Independence, e.g., to life, liberty, and the pursuit of happiness.

One almost begins to suspect that Professor French did not intend such a strong statement; in any case, he clearly wishes in later writings to establish limits on the ascription of rights to corporations. In his recent book, for example, he responds to a criticism I had made in this regard.

(Donaldson) tells us "If, morally speaking, corporations are analogous to persons, then they should have the rights which ordinary persons have." The idea is that we will be aghast at this notion and give up the theory as having an absurd corollary. But does it? . . . (Donaldson) claims that it would be implausible for corporations to have the right to vote and to draw Social Security benefits. Yes it would definitely be implausible, indeed it would be stupid.[5]

So one thing is clear. Professor French wants to deny attribution of at least some rights to corporations. Does he then wish to persist in maintaining that corporations are directly analogous to human persons? Apparently so. Notice that his question in the above paragraph, i.e., "But does it (have an absurd corollary)?" suggests that he is less than aghast at maintaining strong moral interchangeability. And in the next line he writes:

But that proves absolutely nothing. Twelve-year-old human children do not have either the right to vote or the right to draw Social Security benefits. And why not? Because legislated rights are not always, in fact rarely are they, nonrestrictive. The fact that a perfectly competent sixteen-year old woman does not have the right to vote says nothing at all about her moral status.[6]

So now he appears able to defend the claim that corporations are directly analogous to human persons, since even in the instance of ordinary persons, not *all* rights are possessed by *all* persons. The key to his defense is the notion of the general restrictiveness of rights in application to persons. Sixteen-year old women do not have the right to vote, and corporations do not have the right to draw social security presumably because legislated rights typically have classificatory restrictions built into their application; and yet their not having such rights makes them no less "moral persons." Of course, he concludes, "Donaldson might have argued that corporations cannot be said to have natural rights. That, of course, is unexceptionable. To have natural rights something must be natural. Corporations are clearly not . . . (Hence) Donaldson's argument from rights is utterly beside the point, misguided, and irrelevant.[7]

Something is wrong here. The above remark implies both that corporations *do* have those rights that are granted to them by duly authorized legislative bodies, and do *not* have those rights that traditionally are classified as "natural." But *prima facie* this is niggardly from the perspective of corporate rights. Among the rights counted as "natural" are those such as the right to property and to free speech, ones which Professor French—and excepting Marxists everyone else—wants to grant. Surely corporations have rights to property and free speech, and surely we must, in turn, adjust our interpretation of Professor French's account to square with this obvious fact.

Now this problem can be remedied only by adding the caveat that corporations possess rights to, e.g., property and speech, but that in the case of the corporation these are not "natural" rights, but instead have their epistemological source elsewhere, perhaps in legislation. But the remedy in this instance is worse than the disease. For either it is the case that corporations have rights to all the things that normally are counted as the objects of natural rights, or it is not. If it is, then an obvious objection arises, namely, that it is silly to imagine corporations having rights to life or unhindered worship, since they have neither lives nor religious sentiments.

If it is not, then a plethora of interconnected difficulties arises. First this contradicts the earlier assertion that corporations "can have whatever privileges, rights, and duties as are, in the normal course of affairs, accorded to moral persons." The caveat that legislated rights are restrictively applied is of little help here; in other words, it will not do to claim that a corporation's lack of the right to freedom of religious worship is like a non-citizen's lack of a right to vote, or like an ineligible person's lack of a right to draw medicare benefits. Unlike legislated rights (which are usually called "legal" rights in the literature) those rights contained in the package known as "natural rights" are understood by scholars to apply without exception to all adult, rational human beings. The only exceptions Locke makes in the application of rights are for children and those lacking human rationality. Hence all adult persons have *all* natural rights, e.g., to life, liberty, property, and so on, with the result that, unless we wish to exclude corporations on grounds of being "children" or "insane," then a commitment to the idea that corporations are directly analogous to human persons will involve attributing to them the entire list of rights included in the package of natural rights (although we may refuse to call them "natural" rights on the ground that corporations are not natural entities). But, again, this fails because some members of that list are simply inappropriate for corporate entities.

Second, claiming that corporations possess some but not all the rights usually called "natural" prompts the obvious question of how we know *which* rights are included in the "some." The first answer that comes to mind, and the one French seems to be hinting at in the remarks above, is that they have precisely those rights granted to them by duly authorized legislatures, or duly convened court sessions. Hence, the answer comes by looking at statutory and common law in the legal jurisdiction the corporation happens to inhabit. But this answer must be rejected as French himself notes in other writings. To claim that corporations have only those rights granted through law would be to consider them simply as juristic persons, as persons with exclusively legal personalities from the standpoint of morality. And while this constitutes much of the rationale behind the traditional concept in law of the corporation as a "persona ficta,"[8] it fails utterly as a canon of moral analysis. Juristic rights and duties can be poor or misleading guides to the determination of moral rights and duties. For example, the deceased in a probate case is a juristic person with certain legal rights (to have his will executed properly, for instance), but this fact is inadequate for establishing that the deceased is a moral agent, because, except for his or her past deeds, a deceased person cannot be held *morally* responsible for anything. Legal rights are typically distinguished from moral rights and for good reason. Consider the best accepted current definition of a right, which is offered by Joel Feinberg. A right, says Feinberg, is a "valid claim *to* something and *against* someone which is recognized by the principles of an enlightened conscience."[9] In other words, any right makes a claim *to* something, as a right to free speech is a right to speak freely, or a right to equal treatment is a right to be treated as all others would be in relevantly similar situations. At the same time, any right makes a claim *against* someone, in the sense that my right to free speech must also be a claim against those who are obliged to allow me to speak, or my right to equal treatment is a claim against those who are obliged to treat me equally.

Now most important in this definition is the idea that rights are entities or attributes recognized by the principles of an enlightened conscience and not by courts or legislatures. The U.S. Congress did not recognize the right of American blacks to not be slaves in 1850, but blacks then had a right to be free nonetheless. And today, the Soviet Union may not recognize the legal right of its citizens to free speech, but they have a right to speak freely nonetheless. Indeed, it is this notion of a right as a claim or entitlement that is justified not by law but by the nature of reason and reality that lies behind the notion of some rights as being "natural," and not so much, as Professor French seems to suggest, the idea that humans have rights because they are biological, i.e., "natural," creatures. In any event, this is another reason why it is crucial to distinguish legal rights and duties from moral ones and not to suppose that we can determine the rights or duties of any moral agent, corporation or human person, by merely consulting the law books. If the corporation is to be a moral person, and not merely a juristic person, it must possess some of its moral characteristics *qua* moral person, and not *qua* legal person. Finally, and most important, this constitutes a second reason why the other side of French's dilemma, in which he is forced to grant that only some of those rights called "natural" apply to corporations, is unacceptable. It is unacceptable because, once cut free from the appeal to courts and legislatures, we are entirely at sea when it comes to saying which "natural" rights do, and which do not, characterize the corporation.[10] This is a shaky platform, indeed, from which to proclaim the profound similarity between corporations and ordinary moral agents.

Having seen the problem, it remains to identify its theoretical source. Where did French go wrong, and why is he driven in the end to moderate so completely his earlier assertions about corporate personalism? My own suspicion is that die is cast early, about the time he attempts to ground the moral agency of the corporation on its status as an intentional or Davidsonian agent. Now were it true that plain, unmodified Davidsonian agency were sufficient to ground moral agency, then given French's supplementary argument that corporations are Davidsonian agents, it is a short step to the conclusion that whatever basic moral attributes are possessed by people are also possessed by corporations. After all, it appears reasonable that the same set of conditions that ground the moral agency and fundamental moral properties of humans, will also, when shown to be operative in the instance of the corporation, ground a similar agency and set of moral properties. And so long as one simply uses the term, "moral person," as a convenient placeholder for the concept of a full-fledged moral agent—which French does throughout his writings—then the term "moral person" will be no less appropriate when applied to a corporation than to one's spouse.

And yet the search for a set of characteristics which both grounds moral agency and is possessed by corporations and humans has proven elusive. Here too French has altered his views, beginning with a straightforward inference from Davidsonian agency to moral personhood and ending with a reasonably complex constellation of conditions, complete with subsidiary caveats, meant to serve as a criterion and explanation of moral personhood. In this alteration of his original opinions, Professor French has been wise, for he has recognized problems that demanded solutions and provided them. Moreover, this increasing sophistication has tended, as we have seen, to soften the connection he sees between human and corporate agency, and to make his view more alert to the genuine differences between them. But the price of increasing sophistication has been a sacrifice of his original goal; for, as I shall show, he no longer is left with a theory that can explain moral personhood.

Let us review quickly a key transformation of French's views that occurred prior to the writing of the present article. It was prompted in part, interestingly, by a criticism of my own.

Willing to grant that his own view as articulated in his earlier writings entailed that anything that can behave intentionally, i.e., a Davidsonian agent, is a moral person, French confronted in Chapter Twelve of his *Collective and Corporate Responsibility* a counterexample I offered. I had written that "some entities appear to behave intentionally which do not qualify as moral agents. A cat may behave intentionally when it crouches for a mouse. We know that it intends to catch the mouse, but we do not credit it with moral agency ... One seemingly needs more than the presence of intentions to deduce moral agency.[11] Now French first appears to reject this criticism, for he remarks: "With the dash of a philosophical swashbuckler, Donaldson cavalierly leaps from a somewhat noncommital 'may behave' to a very staunch epistemological claim about the way cats think."[12] But later, having acknowledged that respected philosophical psychologists such as Aristotle[13] and Daniel Dennett[14] do regard lower animals as intentional agents, he is persuaded to conclude:

> Rather than wasting time poking fun at Donaldson's example, we are in a position to offer our modification of the account of moral personhood to satisfy the concern that seems to have motivated Donaldson's comments, while yet preserving the basic theory of the corporation as a moral person.... Donaldson's cats and other lower animals are to be excluded from the class of moral persons because, although they may behave intentionally in some rather restricted way that I should not like to try to specify, they can neither appreciate that an event for which their intentional or unintentional behavior has been causally responsible is untoward or worthy nor intentionally modify their way of behaving to correct the offensive actions or to adopt the behavior that was productive of worthy results. In short, they are just not full-blooded intentional actors. Simply, they are not intentional actors.[15]

Clearly, French is wise to alter his account of personal moral agency so as to exclude lower animals, and he is, I think, correct to say that a critical difference is that merely intentional agents such as dogs and chimps cannot "appreciate" the moral "untowardness" (irresponsibility) of their acts or intentionally modify their ways of behaving to correct the offensive actions. French later suggests, I think also correctly, that this latter condition is linked to his principle of responsive adjustment. And finally, there is nothing objectionable about redefining the notion of "intentional" so that the only agents qualifying as intentional are those above the level of the lower animals.[16]

French's overall argument could be arranged in the form of a syllogism, namely:

If A has x, then A is a moral person.
Most corporations have x.

Therefore, most corporations are moral persons.

Here x stands for the conditions of moral personhood, and it is crucial that these conditions be sufficient, and not merely necessary ones, for if not the syllogism cannot be constructed. French seems to forget this at one point when he speaks of his conditions as only "minimal" ones and writes, "if … something is to be counted as a moral person, it must, minimally, be a Davidsonian agent with the capacity or ability to intentionally modify its behavior patterns, habits, or modus operandi after learning that untoward events were brought about by its past pieces of behavior."[17] But later he is more careful to make the stronger claim: "How then does the concept of a moral person fare? What entities ought to be included in the moral census? A moral person, we should say, is a Davidsonian agent with the capacity to respond and responsively adjust to moral evaluation."[18] Business corporations, he adds, "cannot be locked into purely programmed decision structures."[19] Here, then, we seem to have the characterization we are looking for. Stripped of its Davidsonian jargon it means:

> A moral person is something that can act intentionally and respond to moral evaluation.[20]

In this way French has finally provided substance to the value of "x" in his premise, "If A has x, then A is a moral person." And, happily, so long as the concept of x has been discovered without included as a precondition that x must be a property held by corporations, then French's overall argument is not circular. But is x a sufficient, and not merely necessary, condition? Again, it must qualify as a sufficient condition to make his argument go through, and yet I am afraid it fails on this score.

Can we imagine an entity able both to behave intentionally and respond to moral evaluation that is not a moral person? Let us grant that when considering the class of all existing biological agents known, so long as any known biological agent can behave intentionally and respond to moral evaluation (i.e., so long as it possesses x), then we may infer that the entity is a moral person. Quite simply, the only agents in this class that qualify are human beings. But this does not show that logically speaking there is a necessary inference to be drawn from the possession of x to moral personhood.

Imagine a hypothetical extraterrestrial being. Let us call him the Creature-without-a-heart, or for short, Heartless. Now Heartless, let us suppose, belongs to a species of creatures that is rational and intentional in every way. Heartless plans, schemes, worries, adjusts opinions to meet facts, and in every other way displays rational control over his behavior. Heartless plays chess like a demon, has an I.Q. of 160, and has read and thoroughly absorbed Kant's *Groundwork for the Metaphysics of Morals*. But Heartless hasn't a heart. He never concerns himself with others except insofar as their lives impact on him. He never worries about others but only about himself, and, indeed, it is natural for him to do so since all other members of the species to which he belongs are similarly disposed. And although Heartless knows that the essence of morality lies in acting in accordance with such maxims as "Act so that the principle of your act can be universalized," and "Do unto others as you would have them do unto you," and certainly *could* act in accordance with such maxims if he wished, he does not so wish. That is, he can see no reason why he *should* act in accordance with them because he places no value on the pains, desires, feelings, and existence of anyone other than himself.

Is Heartless a moral person? It strikes me that only the most extreme rationalists in ethics (of a kind that even Immanuel Kant was not) would answer "yes." Heartless is not a moral person because, as a matter of his innate nature, he lacks the ability to sympathize with others.[21]

And here is the rub for French. Do corporations have hearts? Do the rules and procedures of corporate decision-making, their "CID structures" as French calls them, entail that they recognize and respect the fact that other moral agents, in particular human beings, have value in themselves, value over and above the corporate ends they may aid or hinder? I am not at all sure how to answer such questions, but I am certain that I cannot claim to know that most corporations are moral persons in this sense. My inclination would be to say that the rules and procedures of some corporations push them close to the status of "having a heart" and others do not. But in any case, supporting such an inclination would be the subject of a lengthy investigation into the structure of corporations, and is a topic for another occasion. What the preceding analysis has shown is that French's attempt to posit the sufficient conditions of moral personhood misses the mark insofar as it fails to compass all requisite conditions. To put it in Kantian language, showing that an agent is able to act in *accordance* with true moral principles (principles Kant refers to as the "Moral Law") is not sufficient to conclude that an agent is able to act *out of respect* for true moral principles. Perhaps Professor French will respond that it is possible to infer from the fact that a corporation is made up of individual moral persons that the corporation, and not merely its individual members, can act *out of respect* for morality. I hope, indeed, that such a demonstration is possible; and yet, I think even French would grant that his work to date has offered no such demonstration.

Hence we are brought full circle in our investigation. Having started by questioning the stark parity French appears to grant in his early writings between corporations and human beings, we are once again asking about such parity. We asked at the beginning about the correctness of claiming that whatever rights and duties are possessed by ordinary moral agents are also possessed by corporations, a claim that French himself seemed later to moderate. And now at the end of our inquiry, we are asking about the correctness of claiming that the underlying conditions sufficient for moral personhood are actually present in corporations. It appears that, even if the set of conditions identified by French for moral personhood is present both in humans and corporations, the set he identifies is insufficient to guarantee moral personhood.

The two problems are not unconnected. French's motivation behind asserting a parity of basic rights and duties in corporate and human agents was no doubt tied to an underlying conviction that the essence of moral personhood was present in both instances, that, in other words, whatever makes something a moral person is equally present in corporate as well as individual human agents. Hence the difficulty of discovering a consistent, satisfactory account of the rights and duties of corporations and humans examined in the first part of the paper, is inextricably linked to the difficulty of articulating the essence of moral personhood examined in the second part.

Thus French has made a heroic attempt to bridge the conceptual moral gap between corporations and human beings, and yet the gap looms large as ever. One's recognition that this attempt, undertaken by a gifted scholar in a thoroughgoing way, has failed, may prompt one to look in another theoretical direction entirely. Instead of assuming that a single concept of moral agency underlies both human and corporation, why not consider the prospect of a double concept? Why not consider the possibility that both human and corporation qualify as moral agents, and yet refuse to reduce each agency to a common denominator? Such an approach would preserve the moral quality of corporate decision-making without sacrificing rational and moral consistency. The final acceptability of such a view would depend on its capacity to be worked out in detail; but *prima facie* it seems plausible. On such a view, Exxon, Incorporated, and Mr. John Jones would look like very different creatures indeed.

Notes

1 John Ladd is a popular representative of the former view, see, e.g., "Morality and the Ideal of Rationality in Formal Organizations," in *The Monist*, 54 (1970), pp. 488–516; while Kenneth Goodpaster is frequently associated with the latter, see, e.g., "Morality and Organizations," in *Ethical Issues in Business: A Philosophical Approach*, ed. Thomas Donaldson and Patricia Werhane (Englewood Cliffs, N.J.: Prentice-Hall, Inc., 1983).

2 Three of these writings are: "The Corporation as a Moral Person," *American Philosophical Quarterly*, 16 (July 1979): 207–15. *Collective and Corporate Responsibility* (New York: Columbia University Press, 1984), and "Principles of Responsibility, Shame and the Corporation," (this volume).

3 *Moral Person*, p. 207.

4 See Thomas Donaldson, *Corporations and Morality* (Englewood Cliffs, N.J.: Prentice-Hall, Inc., 1982); Chapter 2.

5 French, *Collective and Corporate Responsibility*, pp. 169–70.

6 French, *Collective and Corporate Responsibility*, p. 170.

7 French, *Collective and Corporate Responsibility*, p. 170.

8 The view of juristic personhood has evolved from Roman law and seems well entrenched in legal practice.

9 See Joel Feinberg, "Duties, Rights and Claims," *American Philosophical Quarterly*, 3 (1966): 137–44. Also Feinberg, "The Nature and Value of Rights," *Journal of Value Inquiry*, 4 (1970): 243–57.

10 The only mode left for determining the class of rights and duties characterizing corporate entities is dead reckoning, a mode which Professor French finally relies upon. But appeals to our intuitions about corporations and their moral attributes are inappropriate if the purpose of one's argument is to show why corporations are on all fours with other moral agents and to provide a theory of corporate moral agency.

11 Donaldson, *Corporations and Morality*, p. 22.

12 French, *Collective and Corporate Responsibility*, p. 166.

13 French, *Collective and Corporate Responsibility*, p. 166.

14 See French, "Principles of Responsibility, Shame, and the Corporation," p. 16, in this volume; and Daniel Dennett, "Conditions of Personhood," in *The Identities of Persons*, ed by Amelie Rorty (Berkeley: University of California Press, 1976); p. 179.

15 French, *Collective and Corporate Responsibility*, p. 166.

16 This is the force of the transition from "full-blooded intentional actors" to "intentional actors" in the passage quoted from French, i.e., his remark that "In short, (lower animals) are just not full-blooded intentional actors. Simply, they are not intentional actors."

17 French, "Principles of Responsibilities, Shame, and the Corporation" in this volume, p. 27.

18 French, *Ibid.*, p. 29.

19 French, *Ibid.*, p. 29.

20 It is interesting to notice the striking similarity between this revised analysis of moral agency and the one I offered in *Corporations and Morality* that French has so frequently criticized. There I wrote that in order to qualify as a moral agent a corporation must have the capacity to use moral reasons in decision-making as well as the ability to employ such a moral decision-making process to control not only its overt acts, but the structure of its policies and rules. See Donaldson, *Corporations and Morality*, p. 30.

21 He may be able to empathize, but he cannot sympathize.

October Term, 2009 Supreme Court of the United States

Syllabus

CITIZENS UNITED *v.* FEDERAL ELECTION COMMISSION
APPEAL FROM THE UNITED STATES DISTRICT COURT FOR THE
DISTRICT OF COLUMBIA

No. 08–205. Argued March 24, 2009—Reargued September 9, 2009—Decided January 21, 2010

As amended by §203 of the Bipartisan Campaign Reform Act of 2002(BCRA), federal law prohibits corporations and unions from using their general treasury funds to make independent expenditures for speech that is an "electioneering communication" or for speech that expressly advocates the election or defeat of a candidate. 2 U. S. C. §441b. An electioneering communication is "any broadcast, cable, or satellite communication" that "refers to a clearly identified candidate for Federal office" and is made within 30 days of a primary election,§434(f)(3)(A), and that is "publicly distributed," 11 CFR §100.29(a)(2),which in "the case of a candidate for nomination for President ... means" that the communication "[c]an be received by 50,000 or more persons in a State where a primary election ... is being held within 30 days," §100.29(b)(3)(ii). Corporations and unions may establish apolitical action committee (PAC) for express advocacy or electioneering communications purposes. 2 U. S. C. §441b (b) (2). In *McConnell* v. *Federal Election Comm'n*, 540 U. S. 93, 203–209, this Court upheld limits on electioneering communications in a facial challenge, relying on the holding in *Austin* v. *Michigan Chamber of Commerce*, 494 U. S. 652, that political speech may be banned based on the speaker's corporate identity.

In January 2008, appellant Citizens United, a nonprofit corporation, released a documentary (hereinafter *Hillary*) critical of then-Senator Hillary Clinton, a candidate for her party's Presidential nomination. Anticipating that it would make *Hillary* available on cable television through video-on-demand within 30 days of primary elections, Citizens United produced television ads to run on broadcast and cable television. Concerned about possible civil and criminal penalties for violating §441b, it sought declaratory and injunctive relief, arguing that (1) §441b is unconstitutional as applied to *Hillary;* and (2) BCRA's disclaimer, disclosure, and reporting requirements, BCRA §§201 and 311, were unconstitutional as applied to *Hillary* and the ads. The District Court denied Citizens United a preliminary injunction and granted appellee Federal Election Commission (FEC) summary judgment.

Held:

1. Because the question whether §441b applies to *Hillary* cannot be resolved on other, narrower grounds without chilling political speech, this Court must consider the continuing effect of the speech suppression upheld in *Austin*. Pp. 5–20.

   (a) Citizen United's narrower arguments—that *Hillary* is not an "electioneering communication" covered by §441b because it is not "publicly distributed" under 11 CFR §100.29(a)(2); that §441b may not be applied to *Hillary* under *Federal Election Comm'n* v. *Wisconsin Right to Life, Inc.*, 551 U. S. 449 *(WRTL)*, which found §441b unconstitutional as applied to speech that was not "express advocacy or its functional equivalent," *id.*, at 481 (opinion of ROBERTS, C. J.), determining that a communication "is the functional equivalent of express advocacy only if [it] is susceptible of no reasonable interpretation other than as an appeal to vote for or against a specific candidate," *id.*, at 469–470; that §441b should be invalidated as applied to movies shown through video-on-demand because this delivery system has a lower risk of distorting the political process than do television ads; and that there should be an exception to §441b's ban for nonprofit corporate political speech funded overwhelming by individuals—are not sustainable under a fair reading of the statute. Pp. 5–12.

   (b) Thus, this case cannot be resolved on a narrower ground without chilling political speech, speech that is central to the First Amendment's meaning and purpose. Citizens United did not waive this challenge to *Austin* when it stipulated to dismissing the facial challenge below, since (1) even if such a challenge could be waived, this Court may reconsider *Austin* and §441b's facial validity here because the District Court "passed upon" the issue, *Lebron* v. *National Railroad Passenger Corporation*, 513 U. S. 374, 379; (2) throughout the litigation, Citizens United has asserted a claim that the FEC has violated its right to free speech; and (3) the parties cannot enter into a stipulation that prevents the Court from considering remedies necessary to resolve a claim that has been preserved. Because Citizen United's narrower arguments are not sustainable, this Court must, in an exercise of its judicial responsibility, consider §441b's facial validity. Any other course would prolong the substantial, nationwide chilling effect caused by §441b's corporate expenditure ban. This conclusion is further supported by the following: (1) the uncertainty caused by the Government's litigating position; (2) substantial time would be required to clarify §441b's application on the points raised by the Government's position in order to avoid any chilling effect caused by an improper interpretation; and (3) because speech itself is of primary importance to the integrity of the election process, any speech arguably within the reach of rules created for regulating political speech is chilled. The regulatory scheme at issue may not be a prior restraint in the strict sense. However, given its complexity and the deference courts show to administrative determinations, a speaker wishing to avoid criminal liability threats and the heavy costs of defending against FEC enforcement must ask a governmental agency for prior permission to speak. The restrictions thus function as the equivalent of a prior restraint, giving the FEC power analogous to the type of government practices that the First Amendment was drawn to prohibit. The ongoing chill on speech makes it necessary to invoke the earlier precedents that a statute that chills speech can and must be invalidated where its facial invalidity has been demonstrated. Pp. 12–20.

2. *Austin* is overruled, and thus provides no basis for allowing the Government to limit corporate independent expenditures. Hence, §441b's restrictions on such expenditures are invalid and cannot be applied to *Hillary*. Given this conclusion, the part of *McConnell* that upheld BCRA §203's extension of §441b's restrictions on independent corporate expenditures is also overruled. Pp. 20–51.

   (a) Although the First Amendment provides that "Congress shall make no law . . . abridging the freedom of speech," §441b's prohibition on corporate independent expenditures is an outright ban on speech, backed by criminal sanctions. It is a ban notwithstanding the fact that a PAC created by a corporation can still speak, for a PAC is a separate association from the corporation. Because speech is an essential mechanism of democracy—it is the means to hold officials accountable to the people—political speech must prevail against laws that would suppress it by design or inadvertence. Laws burdening such speech are subject to strict scrutiny, which requires the Government to prove that the restriction "furthers a compelling interest and is narrowly tailored to achieve that interest." *WRTL*, 551 U. S., at 464. This language provides a sufficient framework for protecting the interests in this case. Premised on mistrust of governmental power, the First Amendment stands against attempts to disfavor certain subjects or viewpoints or to distinguish among different speakers, which may be a means to control content. The Government may also commit a constitutional wrong when by law it identifies certain preferred speakers. There is no basis for the proposition that, in the political speech context, the Government may impose restrictions on certain disfavored speakers. Both history and logic lead to this conclusion. Pp. 20–25.

   (b) The Court has recognized that the First Amendment applies to corporations, *e.g., First Nat. Bank of Boston* v. *Bellotti*, 435 U. S. 765, 778, n. 14, and extended this protection to the context of political speech, see, *e.g., NAACP* v. *Button*, 371 U. S. 415, 428–429. Addressing challenges to the Federal Election Campaign Act of 1971, the *Buckley* Court upheld limits on direct contributions to candidates, 18 U. S. C. §608(b), recognizing a governmental interest in preventing *quid pro quo* corruption. 424 U. S., at 25–26. However, the Court invalidated §608(e)'s expenditure ban, which applied to individuals, corporations, and unions, because it "fail[ed] to serve any substantial governmental interest in stemming the reality or appearance of corruption in the electoral process," *id.*, at 47–48. While *Buckley* did not consider a separate ban on corporate and union independent expenditures found in §610, had that provision been challenged in *Buckley*'s wake, it could not have been squared with the precedent's reasoning and analysis. The *Buckley* Court did not invoke the over breadth doctrine to suggest that §608(e)'s expenditure ban would have been constitutional had it applied to corporations and unions but not individuals.

Notwithstanding this precedent, Congress soon recodified §610's corporate and union expenditure ban at 2 U. S. C. §441b, the provision at issue. Less than two years after *Buckley, Bellotti* reaffirmed the First Amendment principle that the Government lacks the power to restrict political speech based on the speaker's corporate identity. 435 U.S., at 784–785. Thus the law stood until *Austin* upheld a corporate independent expenditure restriction, bypassing *Buckley* and *Bellotti* by recognizing a new governmental interest in preventing "the corrosive and distorting effects of immense aggregations of [corporate] wealth . . . that have little or no correlation to the public's support for the corporation's political ideas." 494 U. S., at 660. Pp. 25–32.

(c)   This Court is confronted with conflicting lines of precedent: a pre-*Austin* line forbidding speech restrictions based on the speaker's corporate identity and a post-*Austin* line permitting them. Neither *Austin*'s antidistortion rationale nor the Government's other justifications support §441b's restrictions. Pp. 32–47.

(1)   The First Amendment prohibits Congress from fining or jailing citizens, or associations of citizens, for engaging in political speech, but *Austin*'s antidistortion rationale would permit the Government to ban political speech because the speaker is an association with a corporate form. Political speech is "indispensable to decision making in a democracy, and this is no less true because the speech comes from a corporation." *Bellotti, supra*, at 777 (footnote omitted). This protection is inconsistent with *Austin*'s rationale, which is meant to prevent corporations from obtaining "'an unfair advantage in the political marketplace'" by using "'resources amassed in the economic marketplace.'" 494 U. S., at 659. First Amendment protections do not depend on the speaker's "financial ability to engage in public discussion." *Buckley, supra*, at 49. These conclusions were reaffirmed when the Court invalidated a BCRA provision that increased the cap on contributions to one candidate if the opponent made certain expenditures from personal funds. *Davis* v. *Federal Election Comm'n*, 554 U. S. ___, ___. Distinguishing wealthy individuals from corporations based on the latter's special advantages of, *e.g.*, limited liability, does not suffice to allow laws prohibiting speech. It is irrelevant for First Amendment purposes that corporate funds may "have little or no correlation to the public's support for the corporation's political ideas." *Austin, supra*, at 660. All speakers, including individuals and the media, use money amassed from the economic marketplace to fund their speech, and the First Amendment protects the resulting speech. Under the antidistortion rationale, Congress could also ban political speech of media corporations. Although currently exempt from §441b, they accumulate wealth with the help of their corporate form, may have aggregations of wealth, and may express views "hav[ing] little or no correlation to the public's support" for those views. Differential treatment of media corporations and other

corporations cannot be squared with the First Amendment, and there is no support for the view that the Amendment's original meaning would permit suppressing media corporations' political speech. *Austin* interferes with the "open marketplace" of ideas protected by the First Amendment. *New York State Bd. of Elections* v. *Lopez Torres*, 552 U. S. 196, 208. Its censorship is vast in its reach, suppressing the speech of both for-profit and nonprofit, both small and large, corporations. Pp. 32–40.

(2) This reasoning also shows the invalidity of the Government's other arguments. It reasons that corporate political speech can be banned to prevent corruption or its appearance. The *Buckley* Court found this rationale "sufficiently important" to allow contribution limits but refused to extend that reasoning to expenditure limits, 424 U.S., at 25, and the Court does not do so here. While a single *Bellotti* footnote purported to leave the question open, 435 U. S., at 788, n. 26, this Court now concludes that independent expenditures, including those made by corporations, do not give rise to corruption or the appearance of corruption. That speakers may have influence over or access to elected officials does not mean that those officials are corrupt. And the appearance of influence or access will not cause the electorate to lose faith in this democracy. *Caperton* v. *A. T. Massey Coal Co.*, 556 U. S. ___, distinguished. Pp. 40–45.

(3) The Government's asserted interest in protecting shareholders from being compelled to fund corporate speech, like the antidistortion rationale, would allow the Government to ban political speech even of media corporations. The statute is under inclusive; it only protects a dissenting shareholder's interests in certain media for 30 or 60 days before an election when such interests would be implicated in any media at any time. It is also over inclusive because it covers all corporations, including those with one shareholder. p. 46.

(4) Because §441b is not limited to corporations or associations created in foreign countries or funded predominately by foreign shareholders, it would be overbroad even if the Court were to recognize a compelling governmental interest in limiting foreign influence over the Nation's political process. Pp. 46–47.

(d) The relevant factors in deciding whether to adhere to *stare decisis*, beyond workability—the precedent's antiquity, the reliance interests at stake, and whether the decision was well reasoned— counsel in favor of abandoning *Austin*, which itself contravened the precedents of *Buckley* and *Bellotti*. As already explained, *Austin* was not well reasoned. It is also undermined by experience since its announcement. Political speech is so ingrained in this country's culture that speakers find ways around campaign finance laws. Rapid changes in technology—and the creative dynamic inherent in the concept of free expression—counsel against upholding a law that restricts political speech in certain media or by certain speakers. In addition, no serious reliance issues are at stake. Thus, due consideration leads to the conclusion that *Austin* should be overruled. The Court returns to the principle established in *Buckley* and *Bellotti* that the Government may not suppress political speech based on the speaker's corporate identity. No sufficient governmental interest justifies limits on the political speech of nonprofit or for-profit corporations. Pp. 47–50.

3. BCRA §§201 and 311 are valid as applied to the ads for *Hillary* and to the movie itself. Pp. 50–57.

  (a) Disclaimer and disclosure requirements may burden the ability to speak, but they "impose no ceiling on campaign-related activities," *Buckley*, 424 U. S., at 64, or " 'prevent anyone from speaking,' " *McConnell, supra*, at 201. The *Buckley* Court explained that disclosure can be justified by a governmental interest in providing "the electorate with information" about election-related spending sources. The *McConnell* Court applied this interest in rejecting facial challenges to §§201 and 311. 540 U. S., at 196. However, the Court acknowledged that as-applied challenges would be available if a group could show a " 'reasonable probability' " that disclosing its contributors' names would " 'subject them to threats, harassment, or reprisals from either Government officials or private parties.' " *Id.*, at 198. Pp. 50–52.

  (b) The disclaimer and disclosure requirements are valid as applied to Citizens United's ads. They fall within BCRA's "electioneering communication" definition: They referred to then-Senator Clinton by name shortly before a primary and contained pejorative references to her candidacy. Section 311 disclaimers provide information to the electorate, *McConnell, supra*, at 196, and "insure that the voters are fully informed" about who is speaking, *Buckley, supra*, at 76. At the very least, they avoid confusion by making clear that the ads are not funded by a candidate or political party. Citizens United's arguments that §311 is under inclusive because it requires disclaimers for broadcast advertisements but not for print or Internet advertising and that §311 decreases the quantity and effectiveness of the group's speech were rejected in *McConnell*. This Court also rejects their contention that §201's disclosure requirements must be confined to speech that is the functional equivalent of express advocacy under *WRTL*'s test for restrictions on independent expenditures, 551 U. S., at 469–476(opinion of ROBERTS, C.J.). Disclosure is the less-restrictive alternative to more comprehensive speech regulations. Such requirements have been upheld in *Buckley* and *McConnell*. Citizens United's argument that no informational interest justifies applying §201 to its ads is similar to the argument this Court rejected with regard to disclaimers. Citizens United finally claims that disclosure requirements can chill donations by exposing donors to retaliation, but offers no evidence that its members face the type of threats, harassment, or reprisals that might make §201 unconstitutional as applied. Pp. 52–55.

  (c) For these same reasons, this Court affirms the application of the §§201 and 311 disclaimer and disclosure requirements to *Hillary*. Pp. 55–56.

Reversed in part, affirmed in part, and remanded.

KENNEDY, J., delivered the opinion of the Court, in which ROBERTS, C. J., and SCALIA and ALITO, JJ. joined, in which THOMAS, J., joined as to all but Part IV, and in which STEVENS, GINSBURG, BREYER, and SO-TOMAYOR, JJ., joined as to Part IV. ROBERTS, C. J., filed a concurring opinion, in which ALITO, J., joined. SCALIA, J., filed a concurring opinion, in which ALITO, J., joined, and in which THOMAS, J., joined in part. STEVENS, J., filed an opinion concurring in part and dissenting in part, in which GINSBURG, BREYER, and SOTOMAYOR, JJ. joined. THOMAS, J., filed an opinion concurring in part and dissenting in part.

B. The Corporation as a Community: Stakeholder Theory

Corporations as Communities

Amitai Etzioni

Corporations—the term brings to mind the profit-making ones—are not constituted in ways that make communities. However, to the extent that they adopt the concept of stakeholders, they can move in a communitarian direction.

Several powerful arguments have been advanced for a shift from a shareholder approach to a stakeholder approach towards corporate governance.[1] These include works by R. Edward Freeman,[2] articles by Thomas Donaldson and Thomas Dunfee,[3] as well as by L.E. Preston,[4] Max Clarkson,[5] Margaret Blair,[6] and Robert A. Phillips.[7] Reference here is limited to the literature that focuses on the normative issues raised by the stakeholder approach.[8] There is a much larger body of writing that deals with the pragmatic merits of taking into account the needs and values of various nonshareholder constituencies out of utilitarian consequentialist considerations.[9] Nell Minow makes the distinction clear in legal terms when she points to the difference between allowing corporate executives to take into account the needs of constituents other than the shareholders (e.g., giving money to charity) and legally entitling groups other than the shareholders to have a say in the management of the corporation.[10] This pragmatic literature is not discussed here, as my interest is limited to adding a normative note to the existing literature that justifies the chartering of stakeholders.

My note is based on the communitarian thinking I have elaborated elsewhere.[11] It points to the idea that all those involved in the corporation are potentially members of one community; while they clearly have significantly divergent interests, needs, and values, they also have some significant shared goals and bonds.

I. "Private Property" and "Incorporation" as Social Constructs

My starting point is the elementary observation that the concepts of "private property" and "incorporation" (the legal and social basis of corporations) are social constructs, that is, concepts that reflect the particular values, interests, and needs of the society in which these concepts are recognized in a given historical period. They are not an expression of some kind of "natural," self-evident, absolute, uncontestable right. Specifically, there is no a priori reason to argue that the current model of property relations and of governance by shareholders is more natural than any other. In this context, it is worth remembering, as Berle and Means pointed out long ago, that the notion that shareholders govern the corporation is largely a fiction; typically, executives have the main power, although shareholders have a measure of influence.[12] Thus, the question is if the executives should (and can) be made responsive, to some extent, to groups other than the shareholders.

Most important, as the legitimacy of both private property and the way corporations are owned and managed is conditioned by society to begin with, society is free and able to change these social arrangements; society gives these licenses and it can take them away or modify them. As Edward S. Mason has pointed out, "[T]he corporation is an evolving entity, and the end of its evolution is by no means in sight. There is every reason to believe that the business corporation a century hence will be a rather different institution from the one we now behold."[13]

To begin, the claim that private property rights are "natural" and hence uncontestable, or that those who do contest them are challenging a sanctified law, flies in the face of a wealth of historical and sociological evidence and experience. The evidence shows unmistakably that property, as has often been observed, is not an object nor an innate attribute, but a relationship of one or more persons to specified objects.[14] And the nature of this relationship is determined by the legal system and moral beliefs of the society that defines property. Thus, in some countries individuals cannot own land, oil, or beaches because these are construed to be exclusively public properties. Before the 1980s, many Mexican industries were not allowed to be privately owned. And I know from personal observation that in the early kibbutzim, not only the means of production but also the items of consumption, including the shirt on one's back, were considered communal property.

Moreover, *all* societies set some limits on the extent to which owners can control and benefit from "their" property, and on the specific ways they must go about using it—even for those items a society characterizes as the private property of a given individual. Some societies greatly restrict the extent to which ownership can be transferred from generation to generation (for instance by imposing hefty estate taxes); others have few such restrictions. Jewish law calls for letting the land lie fallow every seven years. American law imposes numerous restrictions on what one may do with what people consider "their" private property. For instance, if it is declared as an historical trust, owners cannot modify its appearance without prior permission.[15] They cannot use their property in ways that may produce many kinds of pollution, noise above a given amplitude, or erect what the community considers eyesores, cause erosion of the soil or flooding or the seeping of chemicals into the water, or threaten endangered species, and so on. Moreover, property laws have been greatly changed over the years as societal values, interests, and needs have evolved.[16] In short, voluminous historical and sociological experience suggests that changing property rights is far from unprecedented, indeed rather common. R. Edward Freeman and his associates write, "Moral rules that apply to private property apply to corporate property. No one, or their agent, may use his or her property to harm others (at least without their permission)."[17]

All these statements apply with even greater force to the corporation. While the beginnings of the notions of private property are shrouded in the mysteries of early history and, most likely, prehistory, the corporation is a relatively recent legal and social invention. The permission to incorporate was, to begin with, granted by the state as a charter or license as a matter of privilege, not of right, to some members of society under conditions the state determined. Typically, in their petition for incorporation, the organizers of the first manufacturing company in Massachusetts in 1789 asked "to be incorporated 'with such immunities and favors' as the legislators should think necessary ..."[18] And, as limited liability was introduced as a corporate feature, it granted shareholders an extra privilege of great value. It stands out when shareholders are compared to partners in a business, the main form of amassing capital prior to the existence of corporations. Partners must keep close tabs over their business because if it fails, they may have to sacrifice their personal assets to satisfy those who have claims against the business. This, in turn, limits the extent to which a partnership can grow. In contrast, shareholders' "liability" is limited to the share price, enabling them to invest while they are preoccupied elsewhere, without extensive scrutiny of the enterprise they are "involved" in, and enabling the corporation to amass large amounts of capital. Joshua Margolis and James P. Walsh write, "Even as business organizations may be imperfect instruments for advancing a narrowly construed wealth-maximizing objective, ironically, they may also be the entities of last resort for achieving social objectives of all stripes."[19]

In short, corporations are a societal creation and society grants shareholders a valuable privilege in exchange for which the society can seek some specific consideration.

II. Corporations Are the Property of ALL Who Invest in Them

While society has legitimate and legal authority to determine who will own, control, and benefit from the corporations it created, it needs to justify the reason it grants this authority to some groups and not to others. The discussion here focuses on one idea, namely that the right to participate in the governance of a corporation should be shared by all stakeholder groups rather than only by shareholders. The discussion deliberately focuses on the question of whether a compelling case can be made for a *right* to participate rather than a privilege voluntarily granted by the shareholders should they be so inclined or find it beneficial. That is, the arguments advanced are held to a much higher level of scrutiny because the claim of a right is much stronger than an expression of a desire to be indulged.

The affirmative response to this question is based on the same basic notion that has compelled many to recognize that the corporation should be treated as the property of those who invest capital in it, the shareholders. Or, as it is sometimes put, the corporation "belongs" to the shareholders because they invested their money in it; it is an extension of their private property.[20]

The stakeholder argument, as I see it, accepts the moral legitimacy of the claim that shareholders have the said rights and entitlements, but argues that *the same basic claim should be extended to all those who invest in the corporation*. This often includes employees (especially those who worked for a corporation for many years and loyally); the community (to the extent it provides special investments to a corporation, for instance, if it builds an access road at its own cost, as distinct from providing an environment that is generally favorable to business); creditors (especially large, long-term ones); and, under some conditions, clients. I proceed by briefly discussing what the concept of investment entails, as a moral (and legal) claim rather then merely as an economic concept, before I discuss how one establishes such a claim as a legitimate one.

Investment is defined as the outlay of money for profit. Investment thus differs from a donation or act of charity, in which one gives up the resources one commands without expectations of a specific return. At the same time, investment differs from a sale of one's assets in that investment *forms a relationship* between investors and that in which they invest—a relationship that has a futuristic element because the consummation of the investment relationship presumes continuity, while a sale is typically a discrete transaction, complete in and of itself. The underlying difference is that while, in the case of a sale, the full compensation is typically collected at the time of the transaction or close to it (or a full commitment is made to provide a specific return at specific dates) and above all, the compensation is considered to complete the transaction, in the case of investment, the return constitutes a future stream of yield which is typically far from secure or specified and which may rise or fall, or even be wholly lost, depending on the ways the investment is used. While sellers typically give up their rights to benefit in the future of the sold property and to have a say in the ways it is used, the opposite is true of investors. They give up some immediate benefits and voice in order to seek a better return in the future. Investors, so to speak, not only have yet to be compensated for their investment, but grant their investment on the condition that they will be able to participate to some extent, even if indirectly via directors of pension funds and mutual funds, in the decisions that affect what their return may be in the future. Margaret Blair has emphasized the legitimate interest shareholders have in limiting the risk to which their investment is put.[21] Their interest in enhancing the upside is akin to their interest in minimizing the downside, so to speak. In effect, the fact that they invest in shares rather than in bonds reflects their interest in accepting a less secure return for a possibly higher one. Hence, they are keenly interested not merely in minimizing the risks (avoiding bankruptcies or declines in the size of dividends paid and the price of the shares) but also in increasing the upside potential of higher dividends and share prices. Most important for the discussion that follows, the fact that investors draw some benefits in the short run from their investments (typically in the form of dividends) is not and should not be considered a full compensation for the use of their assets and an abdication of their right to participate in the governance of the corporation.

The preceding statements are widely accepted, indeed considered uncontestable to the point they are rarely even mentioned when the rights of shareholders are discussed.

The fact that shareholders receive a flow of dividends (when this is the case) does not preempt their right to participate in the governance of the corporation. This is traditionally explained by saying that shareholders should monitor the corporation because it is their money that is being managed. However, as we have already indicated, ownership of corporations, like other laws, is defined by people and societal influences, and both have the power to change the definition. Edward S. Mason puts it this way: "most of the elements that are emphasized as essential attributes of the modern business corporation are the product of social invention and have not been characteristic of business corporations from their beginning."[22] As I see it, shareholders' rights are ultimately based on a conception of fairness: society recognizes that shareholders are provided with no compensation for the use of their assets at the point of investment; that their compensation lies in a future flow of dividends and appreciation of share prices which are expected but explicitly not guaranteed. Hence, the investors have a right to ensure that the tree they helped plant will be properly cultivated so it will bear fruit, hopefully increasing its value.

My main argument is that *from a moral viewpoint this concept of fairness applies to all stakeholders and not merely to shareholders*. While this view may seem visionary, I will show that it is already reflected, albeit in a rather limited extent, in various laws and corporate practices. I proceed to support these two claims, focusing first on employees.

The employees' investment in the corporation, often referred to as human or social capital, is very different in appearance from that of the shareholders but similar in principle. They invest years, sometimes a lifetime, of their labor in the corporation. While an economist may argue that the employees "sell" their labor and are compensated for their work and hence no longer have any rights to the products of their labor, there can be little doubt that a significant part of the employees' compensation lies in the future, in the expectation of being employed and paid in the future. Moreover, workers anticipate, and are often encouraged to believe, that if they work harder and with more dedication and loyalty, the corporation will fare better than it would otherwise. And they are also encouraged to expect to share in future gains, both in continued flow of wages and in higher wages. Thus, employees have a keen interest in ensuring the future flow of benefits (an issue that often arises in the discussion of job security), the level of benefits the corporation will be able to afford and allot to them in the future (comparable to shareholders' concerns with the size of dividends), and the viability of the corporation (an issue that arises most sharply when corporations are teetering, and most especially when workers are expected to accept cuts in wages and other benefits to help ensure the corporation's future). Like shareholders, the employees' investment in the corporation is endangered when the corporation is managed recklessly or in violation of the law. And, employees, like shareholders, have a social interest in participating in the decisions concerning the asocial and antisocial use of assets they help create by their investment.

The notion that employees have some rights akin to shareholders is far from fanciful. Several theorists have suggested that workers be assigned a fundamental property right to their jobs.[23] John Locke wrote, "[E]very man has a property in his own person; this nobody has any right to but himself. The labor of his body and the work of his hands, we may say, are properly his. Whatsoever then he removes out of the State that Nature has provided and left it in, he has mixed his labor with, and joined to it something that is his own, and thereby makes it his property."[24] A fair number of court decisions recognize an employee's right to employment by the corporation for which he has been working, based on good faith implied by longevity of satisfactory service.[25] This right may be seen as a precursor or a rather primitive treatment of employees as stakeholders.

Also, in some instances, employees have been granted representation in the governance of the corporations. For example, German companies use codetermination—the requirement to include voting employee representatives on corporate policy-making boards. German workers also have the right to influence decisions at the shop floor level. The popularity of Quality of Life circles in the USA shows that giving the workers a role in corporate decision making, albeit on a low level, far from damages its traditional goals.

Communities also invest in corporations through such means as building special access roads at public cost, providing free land, offering loans at below the interest rates, and suspending or granting exemptions from various rules and regulations that apply to others, from pollution controls to noise abatement, from zoning regulations to traffic requirements, among others. Reference is to specific investments on the behest of specific corporations rather than to general investments in an area, to make it attractive for all corporations (for instance, improving the local schools and public safety).

Communities are rarely, if ever, compensated for their investments at the point of investment. Thus clearly the economic acts at issue do not constitute a sale. Nor do they constitute charity for the corporations. Communities invest in corporations with the implicit understanding that they will benefit from the business in the future—by job creation, tax collection, or other benefits. Hence, communities have a similar interest to others who invest in the corporations to ensure both the future viability of the corporations they have invested in and that the corporations be managed in ways that will increase rather than diminish their contributions to the community. The notion that a corporation has some obligation to the community is recognized already, albeit to a very limited extent and indirectly, in laws that require corporations to notify communities before they close a local plant or move out of the community in order to allow the communities time to react. Even though some community members may not interact with certain companies directly (e.g., as customers or investors), they are still involved with different forms of a company's infrastructure and are "impacted directly by tax revenues and physical environmental protection (or degradation)."[26]

Creditors invest in corporations by providing start-up, working, and expansion capital, not infrequently in amounts that match or exceed that capital provided by shareholders. Creditors especially extend themselves when they provide capital to the corporation when it is at high risk or provide the capital below market rates. The right of large credit investors to participate in the management of corporations they invest in is widely recognized by law in Western Europe. In the USA, the 1933 Glass-Steagall Act mandated the separation of the banking and securities industries. However, recently several pieces of legislation have been advanced in Congress to reduce the strictures imposed by the Glass-Steagall Act, reflecting the fact that allowing creditors a voice in corporate governance is not considered particularly visionary or far-fetched.

Finally, clients invest in corporations when they continue to purchase a business's products out of loyalty to their source of supply even when they could either obtain more advantageous terms or products of better quality elsewhere. (Reference is not to brand loyalty by retail consumers but by wholesale clients.) True, in each case an argument can be made that the continued commitment relies on some narrow self-serving grounds. The fact is, though, that such calculations are often difficult to make with any degree of precision. (For instance, if a defect is found in a product, the question whether to seek the product elsewhere or stick with the source will be affected by how long it will take to fix the problem, which is often rather difficult to establish before the repair takes place. Here, loyalty of the client, often a large-scale one, to the supplier will influence the decision of whether or not the client will choose to invest in the corporation by sticking it out rather than withdrawing orders.) More generally, by staying with one source especially, but not only, during down times, instead of constantly searching for other sources, large scale clients invest in the corporation.

For all these stakeholders, the *longer* the relationship, the larger the investment is. A worker's investment over a lifetime is much larger than for one who works for a given corporation for a few months. A client who remains loyal for decades invests more than one who stayed loyal for a year. Even capital investors who do not pull their share out with every down quarter, but keep their investments for years, invest "more" in this sense.

III. Stakeholders and the Common Good

An argument can be made that, while all stakeholders and not only shareholders have fair claims to a voice in corporate governance, recognizing such claims may be damaging to the well-being of the economy, and hence injurious to the common good. Such considerations should outweigh the fairness claim. For instance, it might be argued that workers would seek to maximize their wages and thus damage the ability of the corporation to invest for the long run; that creditors would be more inclined to favor a conservative course, and so on. To examine the effects of granting some measure of representation on the corporate governance to all stakeholder groups, which make the corporation much more of a community and democratize its government, would take us into a highly speculative direction, as no such corporations exist. However, several preliminary observations can be made. First of all, there is no systematic evidence that in those corporations in which nonshareholders have been given some rights of representation (for instance, creditors gained membership on the board or codetermination), have been less successful than others.[27] Moreover, many corporations have increasingly learned to take the needs and demands of nonshareholders into account in their decision-making for various pragmatic considerations (e.g., labor peace, good credit rating). Also, corporations are not the only groups with a perceived self-serving nature. Some public agencies have issues serving the community due to a tendency to serve their own interests and achieve their political objectives at the risk of harming or ignoring the needs of the greater public.[28] The only change suggested here is to make such participation a right rather than a privilege granted by the sufferance of the executives or the shareholders, or both. Last, but not least, the myopic tendency of shareholders and executives has often been criticized as damaging to corporations. Workers, whose future is often much more closely tied to a specific corporation than that of shareholders is (who can exit with one phone call and very readily find a new investment), may serve as a force to ensure longer-run perspectives.[29] In fact, William D. Leach and Paul A. Sabatier ran a study on stakeholders and found that "stakeholders' perceptions of procedural fairness and legitimacy [are] better predictors of interpersonal trust than is the partnership's track record of producing policy agreements."[30] Fairness, in this case, would be achieved by providing a fair representation of the perspective of workers. Creditors may balance adventurous executives; communities may curb antisocial interests of shareholders. In short, while groups other than shareholders may tilt the corporation into a different course than it would follow if it was responding only to shareholders, it is by no means a foregone conclusion that this course would be less compatible with the common good, even if this good is defined only in narrow economic terms, and it is even less likely to be injurious if other social considerations are taken into account (for instance, concern for the environment and social peace).

Notes

1 For different concepts of stakeholder theory see Robert Phillips, R. Edward Freeman, and Andrew C. Wicks, "What Stakeholder Theory Is Not," *Business Ethics Quarterly*, 13(4) (2003): 479–502; Rogene A. Buchholz and Sandra B. Rosenthal, "Stakeholder Theory and Public Policy: How Governments Matter," *Journal of Business Ethics*, 51(2) (2004): 143–153.

2 R. Edward Freeman, *Strategic Management: A Stakeholder Approach* (Boston: Pitman, 1984); "The Politics of Stakeholder Theory: Some Future Directions," *Business Ethics Quarterly*, 4(4) (1994): 409–421.

3 Thomas Donaldson and T.W. Dunfee, "Towards a Unified Conception of Business Ethics: Integrative Social Contracts Theory," *Academy of Management Review*, 19 (1994): 252–284.

4 Thomas Donaldson and L.E. Preston, "The Stakeholder Theory of the Corporation: Concepts, Evidence, and Implications," *Academy of Management Review*, 20 (1995): 65–91.

5 Max B.E. Clarkson, "A Stakeholder Framework for Analysing and Evaluating Corporate Social Performance," *Academy of Management Review*, 20 (1995): 92–117.

6 Margaret M. Blair, *Ownership and Control: Rethinking Corporate Governance for the Twenty-First Century* (Washington, DC: Brookings, 1995).

7 Robert A. Phillips, "Stakeholder Theory and a Principle of Fairness," *Business Ethics Quarterly*, 7(1) (1997): 51–66.

8 Steven M.H. Wallman, "The Proper Interpretation of Corporate Constituency Statutes and Formulation of Director Duties," *Stetson Law Review*, 21(1) (1991): 163–196.

9 Irwin M. Stelzer, "The Stakeholder Cometh," *Weekly Standard* (February 5, 1996): 16–17.

10 Nell Minow, "Shareholders, Stakeholders, and Boards of Directors," *Stetson Law Review*, 21(1) (1991), 197–243.

11 Amitai Etzioni, The New Golden Rule: *Community and Morality in a Democratic Society* (New York: Basic Books, 1996).

12 Adolfe A. Berle and Gardiner C. Means, *The Modern Corporation and Private Property* (New York: Macmillan, 1932).

13 Edward S. Mason, "Corporation," in David L. Sills, ed., *International Encyclopedia of Social Sciences* (New York: Macmillan, 1968); 397.

14 William Chambliss and Robert Seidman, *Law, Order, and Power* (Reading, MA: Addison-Wesley, 1982); 88–92.

15 Ronald E. Voogt, "'Taking': Real Estate Owners, Rights and Responsibilities," *The Responsive Community*, 2(2): 7–10.

16 For example, American property law changed during the 19th century from a "natural use" conception

of property which favored agrarian uses to a "reasonable use" conception which favored industrial uses. William Chambliss and Robert Seidman, *Law, Order, and Power* (Reading, MA: Addison-Wesley, 1982); 89–90.

17 R. Edward Freeman, Andrew C. Wicks, and Bidhan Parmar, "Stakeholder Theory and 'The Corporate Objective Revisited'," *Organization Science*, 15(3) (2004): 368.

18 E. Merrick Dodd, "The Evolution of Limited Liability in American Industry: Massachusetts," *Harvard Law Review*, LXI(8) (1948): 1361.

19 Joshua D. Margolis and James P. Walsh, "Misery Loves Companies: Rethinking Social Initiatives by Business," *Administrative Science Quarterly*, 48(2) (2003): 296.

20 Marleen A. O'Connor, "Restructuring the Corporation's Nexus of Contracts: Recognizing a Fiduciary Duty," *North Carolina Law Review*, 60 (1991): 1189–1199.

21 Margaret M. Blair, *Ownership and Control: Rethinking Corporate Governance for the Twenty-First Century* (Washington, DC: Brookings, 1995).

22 Edward S. Mason, "Corporation," *International Encyclopedia of the Social Sciences* (New York: Macmillan, 1968); 396.

23 See Rick Molz, "Employee Job Rights: Foundation Considerations," *Journal of Business Ethics*, 6 (1987): 449–458.

24 John Locke, *The Second Treatise of Government*, Thomas P. Peardon, ed. (New York: Bobbs-Merrill, 1952); 17.

25 For example, see Clear v. American Airlines, Inc. (1980), Pugh v. See's Candies (1981), and Monge v. Beebe Rubber Co. (1974).

26 A.J. Hillman and G.D. Keim, "Shareholders, Stakeholders and Social Issue," *Strategic Management Journal*, 22 (2001): 127.

27 I write typically because nonvoting shares are an exception.

28 Steven M.H. Wallman, "The Proper Interpretation of Corporate Constituency Statutes and Formulation of Director Duties," *Stetson Law Review* 21(1) (1991): 163.

29 Mark Lubell, Adam Douglas Henry, and Mike McCoy, "Collaborative Institutions in an Ecology of Games," *American Journal of Political Science*, 54(2) (2010): 288.

30 William D. Leach and Paul A. Sabatier, "To Trust an Adversary: Integrating Rational and Psychological Models of Collaborative Policymaking," *American Political Science Review*, 99(4) (2005): 500.

Business Ethics and Stakeholder Analysis

Kenneth E. Goodpaster

So we must think through what management should be accountable for: and how and through whom its accountability can be discharged. The stockholders' interest, both short- and long-term, is one of the areas. But it is only one.

Peter Drucker, *Harvard Business Review*, 1988

Kenneth Goodpaster, "Business Ethics and Stakeholder Analysis." Reprinted with permission of the Philosophy Documentation Center from *Business Ethics Quarterly* 1 (1991): 52–71.

What is ethically responsible management? How can a corporation, given its economic mission, be managed with appropriate attention to ethical concerns? These are central questions in the field of business ethics. One approach to answering such questions that has become popular during the last two decades is loosely referred to as "stakeholder analysis." Ethically responsible management, it is often suggested, is management that includes careful attention not only to stockholders *but to stakeholders generally* in the decision-making process.

This suggestion about the ethical importance of stakeholder analysis contains an important kernel of truth, but it can also be misleading. Comparing the ethical relationship between managers and stockholders with their relationship to other stakeholders is, I will argue, almost as problematic as ignoring stakeholders (ethically) altogether—presenting us with something of a "stakeholder paradox."

Definition

The term "stakeholder" appears to have been invented in the early 1960s as a deliberate play on the word "stockholder" to signify that there are other parties having a "stake" in the decision-making of the modern, publicly held corporation in addition to those holding equity positions. Professor R. Edward Freeman, in his book *Strategic Management: A Stakeholder Approach*, defines the term as follows: "A stakeholder in an organization is (by definition) any group or individual who can affect or is affected by the achievement of the organization's objectives."[1] Examples of stakeholder groups (beyond stockholders) are employees, suppliers, customers, creditors, competitors, governments, and communities....

Another metaphor with which the term "stakeholder" is associated is that of a "player" in a game like poker. One with a "stake" in the game is one who plays and puts some economic value at risk.[2]

Much of what makes responsible decision-making difficult is understanding how there can be an ethical relationship between management and stakeholders that avoids being too weak (making stakeholders mere means to stockholders' ends) or too strong (making stakeholders quasi-stockholders in their own right). To give these issues life, a case example will help. So let us consider the case of General Motors and Poletown.[3]

The Poletown Case

In 1980, GM was facing a net loss in income, the first since 1921, due to intense foreign competition. Management realized that major capital expenditures would be required for the company to regain its competitive position and profitability. A $40 billion five-year capital spending program was announced that included new, state-of-the-art assembly techniques aimed at smaller, fuel-efficient automobiles demanded by the market. Two aging assembly plants in Detroit were among the ones to be replaced. Their closure would eliminate 500 jobs. Detroit in 1980 was a city with a black majority,

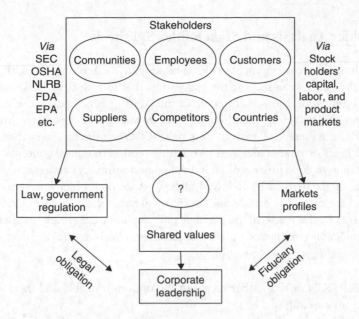

Figure 3.1 Business decision-making and ethical values

an unemployment rate of 18 percent overall and 30 percent for blacks, a rising public debt, and a chronic budget deficit, despite high tax rates.

The site requirements for a new assembly plant included 500 acres, access to long-haul railroad and freeways, and proximity to suppliers for "just-in-time" inventory management. It needed to be ready to produce 1983 model year cars beginning in September 1982. The only site in Detroit meeting GM's requirements was heavily settled, covering a section of the Detroit neighborhood of Poletown. Of the 3,500 residents, half were black. The whites were mostly of Polish descent, retired or nearing retirement. An alternative "green field" site was available in another midwestern state.

Using the power of eminent domain, the Poletown area could be acquired and cleared for a new plant within the company's timetable, and the city government was eager to cooperate. Because of job retention in Detroit, the leadership of the United Auto Workers was also in favor of the idea. The Poletown Neighborhood Council strongly opposed the plan, but was willing to work with the city and GM.

The new plant would employ 6,150 workers and would cost GM $500 million wherever it was built. Obtaining and preparing the Poletown site would cost an additional $200 million, whereas alternative sites in the midwest were available for $65-80 million.

The interested parties were many—stockholders, customers, employees, suppliers, the Detroit community, the midwestern alternative, the Poletown neighborhood. The decision was difficult. GM management needed to consider its competitive situation, the extra costs of remaining in Detroit, the consequences to the city of leaving for another part of the midwest, and the implications for the residents of choosing the Poletown site if the decision were made to stay. The decision about whom to talk to and *how* was as puzzling as the decision about *what* to do and *why*.

Stakeholder Analysis and Stakeholder Synthesis

Ethical values enter management decision-making, it is often suggested, through the gate of stakeholder analysis. But the suggestion that introducing "stakeholder analysis" into business decisions is the same as introducing ethics into those decisions is questionable. To make this plain, let me first distinguish between two importantly different ideas: stakeholder analysis and stakeholder synthesis. I will then examine alternative kinds of stakeholder synthesis with attention to ethical content.

The decision-making process of an individual or a company can be seen in terms of a sequence of six steps to be followed after an issue or problem presents itself for resolution.[4] For ease of reference and recall, I will name the sequence PASCAL, after the six letters in the name of the French philosopher–mathematician Blaise Pascal (1623–62), who once remarked in reference to ethical decision-making that "the heart has reasons that reason knows not of."

1. PERCEPTION or fact-gathering about the options available and their short- and long-term implications;
2. ANALYSIS of these implications with specific attention to affected parties and to the decision-maker's goals, objectives, values, responsibilities, etc.;
3. SYNTHESIS of this structured information according to whatever fundamental priorities obtain in the mindset of the decision-maker;
4. CHOICE among the available options based on the synthesis;
5. ACTION or implementation of the chosen option through a series of specific requests to specific individuals or groups, resource allocation, incentives, controls, and feedback;
6. LEARNING from the outcome of the decision, resulting in either reinforcement or modification (for future decisions) of the way in which the above steps have been taken.

We might simplify this analysis, of course, to something like "input," "decision," and "output," but distinguishing interim steps can often be helpful. The main point is that the path from the presentation of a problem to its resolution must somehow involve gathering, processing, and acting on relevant information.

Now, by *stakeholder analysis* I simply mean a process that does not go beyond the first two steps mentioned above. That is, the affected parties caught up in each available option are identified and the positive and negative impacts on each stakeholder are determined. But questions having to do with processing this information into a decision and implementing it are *left unanswered*. These steps are not part of the *analysis* but of the *synthesis, choice* and *action*.

Stakeholder analysis may give the initial appearance of a decision-making process, but in fact is only a *segment* of a decision-making process. It represents the preparatory or opening phase that awaits the crucial application of the moral (or nonmoral) values of the decision-maker. So, to be informed that an individual or an institution regularly makes stakeholder analysis part of decision-making or takes a "stakeholder approach" to management is to learn little or nothing about the ethical character of that individual or institution. It is to learn only that stakeholders are regularly identified—*not why and for what purpose*. To be told that stakeholders are or must be "taken into account" is, so far, to be told very little. Stakeholder analysis is, as a practical matter, morally *neutral*. It is therefore a mistake to see it as a substitute for normative ethical thinking.[5]

What I shall call "stakeholder synthesis" goes further into the sequence of decision-making steps mentioned above to include actual decision-making and implementation (S, C, A). The critical point is that stakeholder synthesis offers *a pattern or channel by which to move from stakeholder identification to a practical response or resolution*. Here we begin to join stakeholder analysis to questions of substance. But we must now ask: What kind of substance? And how does it relate to *ethics*? The stakeholder idea, remember, is typically offered as a way of integrating *ethical* values into management decision-making. When and how does substance become *ethical* substance?

Strategic Stakeholder Synthesis

We can imagine decision-makers doing "stakeholder analysis" for different underlying reasons, not always having to do with ethics. A management team, for example, might be careful to take positive and (especially) negative stakeholder effects into account for no other reason than that offended stakeholders might resist or retaliate (e.g. through political action or opposition to necessary regulatory clearances). It might not be *ethical* concern for the stakeholders that motivates and guides such analysis, so much as concern about potential impediments to the achievement of strategic objectives. Thus positive and negative effects on relatively powerless stakeholders may be ignored or discounted in the synthesis, choice, and action phases of the decision process.[6]

In the Poletown case, General Motors might have done a stakeholder analysis using the following reasoning: our stockholders are the central stakeholders here, but other key stakeholders include our suppliers, old and new plant employees, the City of Detroit, and the residents of Poletown. These other stakeholders are not our direct concern as a corporation with an economic mission, but since they can influence our short- or long-term strategic interests, they must be taken into account. Public relations costs and benefits, for example, or concerns about union contracts or litigation, might well have influenced the choice between staying in Detroit and going elsewhere.

I refer to this kind of stakeholder synthesis as "strategic" since stakeholders outside the stockholder group are viewed instrumentally, as factors potentially affecting the overarching goal of optimizing stockholder interests. They are taken into account in the decision-making process, but as external environmental forces, as potential sources of either goodwill or retaliation. "We" are the economic principals and management; "they" are significant players whose attitudes and future actions might affect our short-term or long-term success. We must respect them in the way one "respects" the weather—as a set of forces to be reckoned with.[7]

It should be emphasized that managers who adopt the strategic stakeholder approach are not necessarily *personally* indifferent to the plight of stakeholders who are "strategically unimportant." The point is that *in their role as managers*, with a fiduciary relationship that binds them as agents to principals, their basic outlook subordinates other stakeholder concerns to those of stockholders. Market and legal forces are relied upon to secure the interests of those whom strategic considerations might discount. This reliance can and does take different forms, depending on the emphasis given to market forces on the one hand and legal forces on the other. A more conservative, market-oriented view acknowledges the role of legal compliance as an environmental factor affecting strategic choice, but thinks stakeholder interests are best served by minimal interference from the public sector. Adam Smith's "invisible hand" is thought to be the most important guarantor of the common good in a competitive economy. A more liberal view sees the hand of government, through legislation and regulation, as essential for representing stakeholders that might otherwise not achieve "standing" in the strategic decision process.

What both conservatives and liberals have in common is the conviction that the fundamental orientation of management must be toward the interests of stockholders. Other stakeholders (customers, employees, suppliers, neighbors) enter the decision-making equation either directly as instrumental economic factors or indirectly as potential legal claimants. . . . Both see law and regulation as providing a voice for stakeholders that goes beyond market dynamics. They differ about how much government regulation is socially and economically desirable.

During the Poletown controversy, GM managers as individuals may have cared deeply about the potential lost jobs in Detroit, or about the potential dislocation of Poletown residents. But in their role as agents for the owners (stockholders) they could allow such considerations to "count" only if they served GM's strategic interests (or perhaps as legal constraints on the decision).

Professor Freeman appears to adopt some form of strategic stakeholder synthesis. After presenting his definition of stakeholders, he remarks on its application to any group or individual "who can *affect* or is *affected by*" a company's achievement of its purposes. The "affect" part of the definition is not hard to understand; but Freeman clarifies the "affected by" part:

> The point of strategic management is in some sense to chart a direction for the firm. Groups which can affect the direction and its implementation must be considered in the strategic management process. However, it is less obvious why "those groups who are affected by the corporation" are stakeholders as well . . . I make the definition symmetric because of the changes which the firm has undergone in the past few years. Groups which 20 years ago had no effect on the actions of the firm, can affect it today, largely because of the actions of the firm which ignored the effects on these groups. Thus, by calling those affected groups "stakeholders," the ensuing strategic management model will be sensitive to future change.[8]

Freeman might have said "who can actually or potentially affect" the company, for the mindset appears to be one in which attention to stakeholders is justified in terms of actual or potential impact on the company's achievement of its strategic purposes. Stakeholders (other than stockholders) are actual or potential means/obstacles to corporate objectives. A few pages later, Freeman writes:

> From the standpoint of strategic management, or the achievement of organizational purpose, we need an inclusive definition. We must not leave out any group or individual who can affect or is affected by organizational purpose, *because that group may prevent our accomplishments.*[9]

The essence of a strategic view of stakeholders is not that stakeholders are ignored, but that all but a special group (stockholders) are considered on the basis of their actual or potential influence on management's central mission. The basic normative principle is fiduciary responsibility (organizational prudence), supplemented by legal compliance.

The question we must ask in thinking about a strategic approach to stakeholder synthesis is this: Is it really an adequate rendering of the *ethical* component in managerial judgment? Unlike mere stakeholder analysis, this kind of synthesis does go beyond simply *identifying* stakeholders. It integrates the stakeholder information by using a single interest group (stockholders) as its basic normative touchstone....

Many, most notably Nobel Laureate Milton Friedman, believe that market and legal forces are adequate to translate or transmute ethical concerns into straightforward strategic concerns for management. He believes that in our economic and political system (democratic capitalism), direct concern for stakeholders (what Kant might have called "categorical" concern) is unnecessary, redundant, and inefficient, not to mention dishonest:

> In many cases, there is a strong temptation to rationalize actions as an exercise of "social responsibility." In the present climate of opinion, with its widespread aversion to "capitalism," "profits," the "soulless corporation" and so on, this is one way for a corporation to generate good will as a by-product of expenditures that are entirely justified in its own self-interest. If our institutions, and the attitudes of the public make it in their self-interest to cloak their actions in this way, I cannot summon much indignation to denounce them. At the same time, I can express admiration for those individual proprietors or owners of closely held corporations or stockholders of more broadly held corporations who disdain such tactics as approaching fraud.[10]

Multi-Fiduciary Stakeholder Synthesis

In contrast to a strategic view of stakeholders, one can imagine a management team processing stakeholder information by giving the same care to the interests of, say, employees, customers, and local communities as to the economic interests of stakeholders. This kind of substantive commitment to stakeholders might involve trading off the economic advantages of one group against those of another, e.g. in a decision to close a plant. I shall refer to this way of integrating stakeholder analysis with decision-making as "multi-fiduciary" since all stakeholders are treated by management as having equally important interests, deserving joint "maximization" (or what Herbert Simon might call "satisficing").

Professor Freeman contemplates what I am calling the multi-fiduciary view at the end of his 1984 book under the heading "The Manager As Fiduciary To Stakeholders":

> Perhaps the most important area of future research is the issue of whether or not a theory of management can be constructed that uses the stakeholder concept to enrich "managerial capitalism," that is, can the notion that managers bear a fiduciary relationship to stockholders or the owners of the firm, be replaced by a concept of management whereby the manager *must* act in the interests of the stakeholders in the organization?[11]

… We must now ask, as we did of the strategic approach: How satisfactory is multi-fiduciary stakeholder synthesis as a way of giving ethical substance to management decision-making? On the face of it, and in stark contrast to the strategic approach, it may seem that we have at last arrived at a truly moral view. But we should be cautious. For no sooner do we think we have found the proper interpretation of ethics in management than a major objection presents itself. And, yes, it appears to be a *moral* objection!

It can be argued that multi-fiduciary stakeholder analysis is simply incompatible with widely held moral convictions about the special fiduciary obligations owed by management to stockholders. At the center of the objection is the belief that the obligations of agents to principals are stronger than or different in kind from those of agents to third parties.

The Stakeholder Paradox

Managers who would pursue a multi-fiduciary stakeholder orientation for their companies must face resistance from those who believe that a strategic orientation is the only *legitimate* one for business to adopt, given the economic mission and legal constitution of the modern corporation. This may be disorienting since the word "illegitimate" has clear negative ethical connotations, and yet the multi-fiduciary approach is often defended on ethical grounds. I will refer to this anomalous situation as the *Stakeholder Paradox*: It seems essential, yet in some ways illegitimate, to orient corporate decisions by ethical values that go beyond strategic stakeholder considerations to multi-fiduciary ones. I call this a paradox because it says there is an ethical problem whichever approach management takes. Ethics seems both to forbid and to demand a strategic, profit-maximizing mindset. The argument behind the paradox focuses on management's *fiduciary* duty to the stockholder, essentially the duty to keep a profit-maximizing promise, and a concern that the "impatiality" of the multi-fiduciary approach simply cuts management loose from certain well-defined bonds of stockholder accountability. On this view, impartiality is thought to be a *betrayal of trust*.

Professor David S. Ruder, a former chairman of the US Securities and Exchange Commission, once summarized the matter this way:

> Traditional fiduciary obligation theory insists that a corporate manager owes an obligation of care and loyalty to shareholders. If a public obligation theory unrelated to profit maximization becomes the law, the corporate manager who is not able to act in his own self interest without violating his fiduciary obligation, may nevertheless act in the public interest without violating that obligation.

He continued:

> Whether induced by government legislation, government pressure, or merely by enlightened attitudes of the corporation regarding its long range potential as a unit in society, corporate activities carried on in satisfaction of public obligations can be consistent with profit maximization objectives. In contrast, justification of public obligations upon bold concepts of public need without corporate benefit will merely serve to reduce further

the owner's influence on his corporation and to create additional demands for public participation in corporate management.[12]

Ruder's view appears to be that (a) multi-fiduciary stakeholder synthesis *need not* be used by management because the strategic approach is more accommodating than meets the eye; and (b) multi-fiduciary stakeholder synthesis should not be invoked by management because such a "bold" concept could threaten the private (vs public) status of the corporation.

In response to (a), we saw earlier that there were reasonable questions about the tidy convergence of ethics and economic success. Respecting the interests and rights of the Poletown residents might really have meant incurring higher costs for GM (short-term as well as long-term).

Appeals to corporate self-interest, even long-term, might not always support ethical decisions. But even on those occasions where they will, we must wonder about the disposition to favor economic and legal reasoning "for the record." If Ruder means to suggest that business leaders can often *reformulate* or *re-present* their reasons for certain morally grounded decisions in strategic terms having to do with profit maximization and obedience to law, he is perhaps correct. In the spirit of our earlier quotation from Milton Friedman, we might not summon much indignation to denounce them. But why the fiction? Why not call a moral reason a moral reason?

This issue is not simply of academic interest. Managers must confront it in practice....

The Problem of Boldness

What appears to lie at the foundation of Ruder's cautious view is a concern about the "boldness" of the multi-fiduciary concept ((b) above).[13] It is not that he thinks the strategic approach is always satisfactory; it is that the multi-fiduciary approach is, in his eyes, much worse. For it questions the special relationship between the manager as agent and the stockholder as principal.

Ruder suggests that what he calls a "public obligation" theory threatens the private status of the corporation. He believes that what we are calling multi-fiduciary stakeholder synthesis *dilutes* the fiduciary obligation to stockholders (by extending it to customers, employees, suppliers, etc.) and he sees this as a threat to the "privacy" of the private sector organization. If public organizations are understood on the model of public sector institutions with their multiple constituencies, Ruder thinks, the stockholder loses status.

There is something profoundly *right* about Ruder's line of argument here, I believe, and something profoundly *wrong*. What is right is his intuition that if we treat other stakeholders on the model of the fiduciary relationship between management and the stockholder, we will, in effect, make them into quasi-stockholders. We can do this, of course, if we choose to as a society. But we should be aware that it is a radical step indeed. For it blurs traditional goals in terms of entrepreneurial risk-taking, pushes decision-making toward paralysis because of the dilemmas posed by divided loyalties, and, in the final analysis, represents nothing less than the conversion of the modern private corporation into a public institution and probably calls for a corresponding restructuring of corporate governance (e.g. representatives of each stakeholder group on the board of directors). Unless we believe that the social utility of a private sector has disappeared, not to mention its value for individual liberty and enterprise, we will be cautious about an interpretation of stakeholder synthesis that transforms the private sector into the public sector.

On the other hand, I believe Ruder is mistaken if he thinks that business ethics requires this kind of either/or: either a private sector with a strategic stakeholder synthesis (business without ethics) or the effective loss of the private sector with a multi-fiduciary stakeholder synthesis (ethics without business).

Recent debates over state laws protecting companies against hostile takeovers may illustrate Ruder's concern as well as the new challenge. According to journalist Christopher Elias, a recent Pennsylvania antitakeover law

> does no less than redefine the fiduciary duty of corporate directors, enabling them to base decisions not merely on the interests of shareholders, but on the interests of customers, suppliers, employees and the community at large. Pennsylvania is saying that it is the corporation that directors are responsible to. Shareholders say they always thought they themselves were the corporation.[14]

Echoing Ruder, one legal observer quoted by Elias commented with reference to this law that it "undermines and erodes free markets and property rights. From this perspective, this is an anticapitalist law. The management can take away property from the real owners."

In our terms, the state of Pennsylvania is charged with adopting a multi-fiduciary stakeholder approach in an effort to rectify deficiencies of the strategic approach which (presumably) corporate raiders hold.

The challenge with which we are thus presented is to develop an account of the moral responsibilities of management that (1) avoid surrendering the moral relationship between management and stakeholders as the strategic view does, while (2) not transforming stakeholder obligations into fiduciary obligations (thus protecting the uniqueness of the principal–agent relationship between management and stockholder).

Toward a New Stakeholder Synthesis

We all remember the story of the well-intentioned Doctor Frankenstein. He sought to improve the human condition by designing a powerful, intelligent force for good in the community. Alas, when he flipped the switch, his creation turned out to be a monster rather than a marvel! Is the concept of the ethical corporation like a Frankenstein monster?

Taking business ethics seriously need not mean that management bears *additional* fiduciary relationships to third parties (nonstockholder constituencies) as multi-fiduciary stakeholder synthesis suggests. It may mean that there are morally significant *nonfiduciary* obligations to third parties surrounding any fiduciary relationship (see

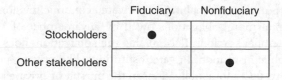

Figure 3.2 Direct managerial obligations

Figure 3.2). Such moral obligations may be owed by private individuals as well as private sector organizations to those whose freedom and well-being is affected by their economic behavior. It is these very obligations, in fact (the duty not to harm or coerce and duties not to lie, cheat, or steal), that are cited in regulatory, legislative, and judicial arguments for constraining profit-driven business activities. These obligations are not "hypothetical" or contingent or indirect, as they would be on the strategic model. They are not rooted in the *fiduciary* relationship, but in other relationships at least as deep.

It must be admitted in fairness to Ruder's argument that the jargon of "stakeholders" in discussions of business ethics can seem to threaten the notion of what corporate law refers to as the "undivided and unselfish loyalty" owed by managers and directors to stockholders. For this way of speaking can suggest a multiplication of management duties *of the same kind* as the duty to stockholders. What we must understand is that the responsibilities of management toward stockholders are of a piece with the obligations that *stockholders themselves* would be expected to honor in their own right. As an old Latin proverb has it, *nemo dat quod non habet*, which literally means "nobody gives what he doesn't have." Freely translating in this context we can say: I cannot (ethically) *hire* done on my behalf what I would not (ethically) *do* myself. We might refer to this as the "Nemo Dat Principle" (NDP) and consider it a formal requirement of consistency in business ethics (and professional ethics generally):

(NDP)   Investors cannot expect of managers (more generally, principals cannot expect of their agents) behavior that would be inconsistent with the reasonable ethical expectations of the community.[15]

The NDP does not, of course, resolve in advance the many ethical challenges that managers must face. It only indicates that these challenges are of a piece with those that face us all. It offers a different kind of test (and so a different kind of stakeholder synthesis) that management (and institutional investors) might apply to policies and decisions.

The foundation of ethics in management—and the way out of the stakeholder paradox—lies in understanding that the conscience of the corporation is a logical and moral extension of the consciences of its principals. It is *not* an expansion of the *list* of principals, but a gloss on the principal–agent relationship itself. Whatever the structure of the principal–agent relationship, neither principal nor agent can ever claim that an agent has "moral immunity" from the basic obligations that would apply to any human being toward other members of the community.

Indeed, consistent with Ruder's belief, the introduction of moral reasoning (distinguished from multi-fiduciary stakeholder reasoning) into the framework of management thinking may *protect* rather than threaten private sector legitimacy. The conscientious corporation can maintain its private economic mission, but in the context of fundamental moral obligations owed by any member of society to others affected by that member's actions. Recognizing such obligations does *not* mean that an institution is a public institution. Private institutions, like private individuals, can be and are bound to respect moral obligations in the pursuit of private purposes.

Conceptually, then, we can make room for a moral posture toward stakeholders that is both *partial* (respecting the fiduciary relationship between managers and stockholders) and *impartial* (respecting the equally important nonfiduciary relationships between management and other stakeholders). As philosopher Thomas Nagel has said, "In the conduct of life, of all places, the rivalry between the view from within and the view from without must be taken seriously."[16]

Whether this conceptual room can be used *effectively* in the face of enormous pressures on contemporary managers and directors is another story, of course. For it is one thing to say that "giving standing to stakeholders" in managerial reasoning is conceptually coherent. It is something else to say that it is practically coherent.

Yet most of us, I submit, believe it. Most of us believe that management at General Motors *owed* it to the people of Detroit and to the people of Poletown to take their (nonfiduciary) interests very seriously, to seek creative solutions to the conflict, to do more than use or manipulate them in accordance with GM's needs only. We understand that managers and directors have a special obligation to provide a financial return to the stockholders, but we also understand that the word "special" in this context needs to be tempered by an appreciation of certain fundamental community norms that go beyond the demands of both laws and markets. There are certain class-action suits that stockholders ought not to win. For there is sometimes a moral defense.

Conclusion

The relationship between management and stockholders is ethically different in kind from the relationship between management and other parties (employees, suppliers, customers, etc.), a fact that seems to go unnoticed by the multi-fiduciary approach. If it were not, the corporation would cease to be a private sector institution—and what is now called business ethics would become a more radical critique of our economic system than is typically thought. On this point, Milton Friedman must be given a fair and serious hearing.

This does not mean, however, that "stakeholders" lack a morally significant relationship to management, as the strategic approach implies. It means only that the relationship in question is different from a fiduciary one. Management may never have promised customers, employees, suppliers, etc. a "return on investment," but management is nevertheless obliged to take seriously its extra-legal obligations not to injure, lie to, or cheat these stakeholders *quite apart from* whether it is in the stockholders' interests.

As we think through the *proper* relationship of management to stakeholders, fundamental features of business life must undoubtedly be reorganized: that corporations have a principally economic mission and competence; that fiduciary obligations to investors and general obligations to comply with the law cannot be set aside; and that abuses of economic power and disregard of corporate stewardship in the name of business ethics are possible.

But these things must be recognized as well: that corporations are not solely financial institutions; that fiduciary obligations go beyond short-term profit and are in any case subject to moral criteria in their execution; and that mere compliance with the law can be unduly limited and even unjust.

The Stakeholder Paradox can be avoided by a more thoughtful understanding of the nature of moral obligation and the limits it imposes on the principal–agent relationship. Once we understand that there is a practical "space" for identifying the ethical values shared by a corporation and its stockholders—a space that goes beyond strategic self-interest but stops short of impartiality—the hard work of filling that space can proceed.

Notes

1 R. Edward Freeman, *Strategic Management: A Stakeholder Approach* (Pitman, 1984); p. 46.

2 Strictly speaking the historical meaning of "stakeholder" in this context is someone who literally *holds* the stakes during play.

3 See K. Goodpaster and T. Piper, *Managerial Decision Making and Ethical Values*, Harvard Business School Publishing Division, 1989.

4 See K. Goodpaster, "PASCAL: A Framework For Conscientious Decision-Making," (1989). Unpublished paper, University of St. Thomas.

5 Actually, there are subtle ways in which even the stakeholder identification or inventory process might have *some* ethical content. The very process of *identifying* affected parties involves the use of the imagination in a way that can lead to a natural emphathetic or caring response to those parties in the synthesis, choice, and action phases of decision-making. This is a contingent connection, however, not a necessary one.

6 Note that including powerless stakeholders in the analysis phase may indicate whether the decision-maker cares about "affecting" them or "being affected by" them. Also, the inclusion of what might be called secondary stakeholders as advocates for primary stakeholders (e.g. local governments on behalf of certain citizen groups) may signal the values that will come into play in any synthesis.

7 It should be mentioned that some authors, most notably Kenneth R. Andrews in *The Concept of Corporate Strategy*, 3rd edn (Irwin, 1987) employ a broader and more social definition of "strategic" decision-making than the one implied here.

8 Freeman, *Strategic Management*, p. 46.

9 Ibid., p. 52 (emphasis added).

10 Milton Friedman, "The Social Responsibility of Business is to Increase its Profits," New York Times Magazine, Sept. 13, 1970.

11 Freeman, *Strategic Management*, p. 249.

12 Ibid., pp. 226, 228–9. Ruder recently (in 1989) reaffirmed the views expressed in his 1965 article.

13 "The Business Judgement Rule" gives broad latitude to officers and directors of corporations, but calls for reasoning on the basis of the long-term economic interest of the company. And corporate case law ordinarily allows exceptions to profit-maximization criteria only when there are actual or potential *legal* barriers, and limits charitable and humanitarian gifts by the logic of long-term self-interest. The underlying rationale is accountability to investors. Recent work by the American Law Institute, however, suggests a rethinking of these matters. See appendix.

14 Christopher Elias, "Turning Up the Heat on the Top," *Insight*, July 23, 1990.

15 We might consider the NDP in broader terms that would include the relationship between "client" and "professional" in other contexts, such as law, medicine, education, government, and religion, where normally the community's expectations are embodied in ethical standards.

16 T. Nagel, *The View from Nowhere* (Oxford University Press, 1986); p. 163.

Stakeholders and Consent[1]

Stephen Cohen

In this essay, I suggest that it might be fruitful to consider the notion of stakeholders from the perspective of consent-theory. Neither talk about stakeholders *per se* nor, particularly, talk about consent-theory is itself novel. However, I believe that the suggestion that consent-theory can shed some light on the position of stakeholders does provide something new, as does the suggestion that what I shall call "putative consent" and "future-oriented consent" both have important roles to play in discussions of stakeholders.

★ ★ ★

Stakeholders' Interests

What is it, then, to take account of the interests of stakeholders? The simple answer is that it is to calculate the impact of an action or a practice on the stakeholders, and to figure into the overall calculation about what to do an element of the effect of the practice or action on the stakeholders. Standardly, this is conceived of as a matter of calculating the utility or disutility of a proposed practice for the stakeholders, recognizing that various stakeholders (or groups of stakeholders) have different stakes in the possible outcomes of some activity.[2]

Reaching a decision about whether a possible practice would be advantageous or disadvantageous to a particular group need not involve actual consultation with that group itself. Sometimes, the options available and the choices to be made are such that it is not presumptuous for someone other than the stakeholders to decide what is in the stakeholders' interest. If a certain practice would endanger the health of a group of stakeholders, and offer no prospects of advantage to them or to anyone else, it would not be presumptuous to calculate accordingly, without consulting with the stakeholders themselves. In such a case, we probably would not consider the decision not to endanger their health as being a paternal one or as preempting the decision of the interested parties. It would, rather, simply be deciding not to engage in some activity because of its possible harmful effects on some group—effects which are not offset by anything else.

More typically, however, decisions about whether to engage in an activity are based on trying to take account of the group's welfare in the context of some competing

Stephen Cohen, "Stakeholders and Consent." Reprinted with permission of the Philosophy Documentation Center from *Business and Professional Ethics Journal* 14, 1 (1995): 3–16.

claims about that welfare, or at least in the context of there being both minuses and pluses associated with the activity (e.g., fluoridation of a community's water supply or stringing powerlines over the homes of numbers of the members of a community, at some risk to those residents). Here, to decide to act one way or another because of the benefit to the group can well be to engage in a paternalistic decision: "We'll do this, because it'll be for their good"; or, "we'll allow this risk, because the likely benefits are such as to make it a risk worth taking"; or "we'll do this, because the disadvantages or losses are outweighed by the benefits which will accrue." In such cases, someone decides the matter for those who will be affected by the activity. This differs from the earlier case (where there was nothing but disadvantage), inasmuch as in that case, there was, in effect, nothing to decide—because the proposed activity had no benefits to offset its likely disadvantages, and so nothing to raise the question of whether to engage in that activity. And it also differs from a case in which one decides that the possible disadvantage to one group is outweighed by the possible advantage to another, where, of course, the first group would dislike the activity, and where there would be no point in further taking their interests into account—precisely because one's calculation in the first place was to sacrifice that group's welfare for something else.[3]

As an alternative to paternalistic decision-making and the possibility of disinterested arm's-length calculation of utility by whoever has the power or the authority (governmental body, professional organization, business entity, or individual), it is important to keep in mind the possibility of taking account of the wishes or decision of the potentially affected group itself. It is important to recognize that stakeholders are not only to be taken account of, but, when appropriate, to be given a voice. Sometimes this is so (should be so) because the stakeholders can give a worthwhile opinion about the costs and benefits of the proposed activity—they have an opinion worth consulting about whether the benefits of the proposed activity do, in fact, outweigh the disadvantages. Further, there might be a real question of what that group would consent to. Given that there are some disadvantages or some risks associated with a possible gain for the group concerned, there might be a real question of whether incurring those disadvantages or those risks is worth the possibility of that gain—whether it is worth it *to them*. And there it should be recognized that it is not always the case (perhaps it is hardly ever the case) that only one decision is *the* rational (or even *the reasonable*) one. That being so, there is something to be decided, some choice to be made, on grounds other than simply, say, "the dictates of rationality." Here, very importantly, is an occasion for taking account of the interests of stakeholders. And here is an occasion where being informed of the actual view or the opinion of the stakeholders themselves is important for being able to properly take account of their interests.

Consent

Classical consent-theory in political philosophy argues that legitimate authority is exercised over people only with their consent. A central feature of human beings is their capacity to make decisions for themselves. Respect for agent autonomy is the hallmark of consent-theory. If this is so, then it is vitally important that the integrity of an environment in which human beings as agents engage in individual (and group) decision-making be maintained. This requires not only that a serious role be allowed for consenting, but also that the agents be in a position where their consent is meaningful and significant. In a word, it requires that the consent be "informed."

Informed Consent

The notion of "informed consent" has occupied an important position in discussions of the relation between individuals and medical procedures and to the medical profession generally, and also in discussions of people's relation to lawyers. The idea is that the only adequate justification for doing some things to people is that those people have been sufficiently informed about their situation, and have consented to the medical or legal activity concerning them. Without their consent, those activities are unjustified impositions on people. The context in which "informed consent" has been important has been where it is seen as unjustified, unacceptable behavior for a practitioner to judge that some proposed course of action would be for the subject's own good, or that it amounts to a risk worth taking (or avoiding), and hence, to unilaterally decide on that course. This paternalistic stance is seen to provide an insufficient justification; it does not allow the subjects themselves to make decisions for themselves, or even to be significantly involved in the making of those decisions which affect them. . . .

Consent and Stakeholders

Sometimes actual, express consent is not obtained (and need not be obtained), but is still the case that the subject could be said to have consented to something. The consent might be implied by something which the subject does. Sometimes implied consent can be explicit—it can be very clear that the subject consents, even though the subject never says "I consent," or words to that effect.

I suggest that the applicability of the notion of consent to a responsibility to take account of the interests of stakeholders is important, obvious, and largely neglected in discussions about stakeholders. Whether some risk or disadvantage should be imposed on some group for the purpose of some possible gain is a matter about which that group itself has an important opinion—possibly a decisive opinion. Imposition without the group's consent can be unjustified.

Discussions of stakeholders largely either neglect the possible role of stakeholders' consent or present stakeholder analysis as paternal, in contrast to consent theory. Mike Martin and Roland Schinzinger are exceptional in this respect. In suggesting that engineering should be viewed as social experimentation, they say,

> We believe that the problem of informed consent, which is so vital to the concept of a
> properly conducted experiment involving human subjects, should be the keystone in the
> interaction between engineers and the public.[4]

Putative Consent and Future-Oriented Consent

As I have indicated, sometimes consent can be literal and explicit, and sometimes it can be something else. There is also a place for what might be called "putative consent" and for what might be called "future-oriented consent," notions which are related but not identical, and which, I believe, should be particularly important with respect to taking account of stakeholders' interests. Putative consent amounts to imputing consent to someone. This might be because rationality requires consent to some particular thing, and so, of course this person consents to it. They needn't be asked whether or not they consent. Some such claims have played a role in arguments concerning the necessity of acquiring actual consent in matters relating to certain medical procedures: "only someone who was irrational or did not understand would refuse this procedure; therefore, the question need not actually be put." Putative consent also applies to imputation of consent to someone in situations where you know that they would consent if they were asked, not because consent is required by rationality, but rather because of the particular person that they are: "I went ahead and did such-and-such, because I knew that that's what you would want me to do"; or, "I went ahead and did such-and-such, because I knew that you would have agreed to it, if I had asked you." In such cases, application of putative consent requires that one know something about the particular person or group, because it is precisely in virtue of what one knows about them (perhaps their preferences, perhaps their desires, perhaps their character, perhaps their relation to the one who is wondering, . . .) that consent can be assumed or imputed.

I think that "future-oriented consent" is an important and useful notion here, as well:[5] I do something to you now, recognizing that you have not consented to it (either express or implied), and I claim as my justification not that I know what is best for you and am requiring that you do (or submit to) something which I know to be for your own good, but rather that if you had been in a position to know, etc., then you would have consented; or that when, in the future, you come to be in such a position, you will then consent to my having done this thing to (or for) you now—it is something that you will want that I have done. Future-oriented consent can differ from putative consent, in that an ascription of future-oriented consent does not necessarily carry with it a belief that if the consenter were asked now that he/she would consent. As an example of future-oriented consent, we might think of various things a parent might require that a certain child do. Some of those things are required simply because the parent knows best and requires that the child act according to the parent's will: "you simply have to take the swim lessons; I knew they will be good for you." These are cases of pure justified paternalism. Other things, however, might be required of the child because the parent knows that particular child well enough to know that when the child reaches the "age of reason," the child will want that such-and-such had happened to him/her at that earlier age. The point here is that the parent knows the particular child well enough so that the parent might require something of the child or inflict something on the child or do something for the child—sometimes even contrary to the child's express wishes at the time—in the name of the child's consenting to it: "Given the kind of person you are, with your athletic and competitive nature, you will thank me for signing you up as a member of the tennis squad; you will want me to have done this—despite what you are saying now."

It is important to recognize a couple of features of—and some dangers associated with—future-oriented consent. It is something different from paternalism—different, at least, from any straightforward type of paternalism. Nevertheless, in invoking the notion of future-oriented consent, there is a particular danger of it functioning only as a "justification" for someone (e.g., a parent, a public utility, or a corporation) inflicting their preferences on someone else. There is a danger of someone's inappropriately taking licence, inflicting something on someone, while incorrectly claiming as a justification the presence of consent. We must be clear, however, that this would be a *misapplication* of the notion. It would be an *incorrect* claim about the consent of the subject. It is not a feature of future-oriented consent itself. Given the nature of future-oriented consent—in particular, that the subject's current preferences, etc. might legitimately be dismissed, while maintaining a legitimate reference to the subject's future preferences—there is the further danger of simply dismissing as irrelevant even explicit protestations by a subject that they do not consent. Perhaps the trickiest and most treacherous danger of all associated with the notion is the danger that in inflicting something on someone in the name of future-oriented consent, that which is inflicted is itself such as to produce the future consent of the subject. The extreme, of course, is brainwashing, where the activity itself might be designed specifically to achieve that result. This serious danger aside, however, I believe that there is an important place for considerations of consent—including putative and future-oriented consent—in discussion of the interests of stakeholders.

Conclusion

Reference to future-oriented consent, putative consent, and even, surprisingly, express consent have been largely absent from discussions of the relevant considerations which should be taken into account in having proper regard for the interests of stakeholders. The process of making a decision about what is to the advantage of a group or what advances *that group's* welfare should often (usually) involve considering *that group's* opinion. There are at least two reasons for this, the first (and maybe also the second) of which was advocated by John Stuart Mill.[6] (1) That group is usually particularly well-placed to evaluate what is and what is not in its own interest. By itself, this concern has nothing to do with respect for agent-autonomy. (2) In many matters involving some decision procedure, there is no single exclusively rational decision. There can be a number of possibilities. For example, the degree of risk which one or a group might be willing to take for some possible gain is, within limits, not a matter which can be specified as a directive of rationality. It can be a matter of preference, public policy, or any other of a number of other legitimate, appropriate concerns. And, I suggest, more often than not, it is the affected group itself which should have a major say in what course of action should be taken. What that group consents to should be an important element involved in arriving at a decision about matters concerning or affecting that group.

The process of making a decision about what is to the advantage of a group of what advances some group's welfare should often involve considering the opinion of the stakeholders in the activity which would bring about that effect. This is a broader claim, which involves eliciting the opinion of stakeholders in general, while realizing that from at least some perspectives (and perhaps from an overall perspective), it might be seen as desirable (or at least as satisfactory) that the interests of some be sacrificed for the benefit of some others. Even here, however, it seems to me appropriate that all the stakeholders have a say; even here, there is room for eliciting stakeholders' opinions and considering what they do actually or would consent to.[7] As with the situation in which the stakeholders are the ones for whose benefit an activity is proposed to be undertaken, here, too, the operable consent might be expressed, implied, putative, or future-oriented. Perhaps the groups can be consulted directly; but perhaps for any of a great number of reasons, some group cannot be so consulted. Either way, there is room for taking account of the important consideration of the groups' consent to the activity.

Notes

1 I have benefitted from the comments and suggestions I have received at a number of points in the development of this essay from Damian Grace, Neil Harpley, and Michael Jackson, and for the ongoing dialogue about stakeholders which I have with Damian Grace. The general and specific critical comments from this journal's editor have been particularly helpful.

2 Kenneth Goodpaster in "Business Ethics and Stakeholder Analysis" (*Business Ethics Quarterly* 1 (1991): 53–71) and Damian Grace in "Stakeholders" (unpublished) make the important point that merely identifying some group as stakeholders in some activity does not, by itself, point in any direction at all toward a correct or appropriate ethical analysis of the activity. It might be a significant prerequisite to moral reasoning, but it is not more than this. Further, Grace and I suggest that a danger with 'stakeholder analysis' is that as a phrase it might simply become synonymous with 'social responsibility,' while at the same time presenting a misleading impression (a) that there is some methodological substance to it as a *type* of analysis, and (b) that there should be a special status accorded to stakeholders, who as stakeholders have entitlements different from or additional to those present for society at large (*Business Ethics: Australian Problems and Cases* (Sydney: Oxford U.P., 1995); ch. 3). To talk about "stakeholder analysis" and "rights of stakeholders" without articulating what gives someone a stake can be misleading and dangerous. While I have nothing to add here to this general point, I do believe that the injection of a consent requirement into a stakeholder analysis amounts to

recognition of a terribly important element in moral reasoning.

3 Perhaps this is not a good thing to do. Perhaps it could never be justified. Nevertheless, if it *were* the case, there would be no point in taking further account of the group whose interests were to be sacrificed. Nothing more could be learned about that group.

4 Mike W. Martin and Roland Schinzinger, *Ethics in Engineering*, second edition (New York: McGraw Hill, 1989); p. 68. It is not clear how far Martin and Schinzinger would be prepared to generalize this point to include other professions and, more importantly, to include other practices which do not so easily fit the model of social experimentation.

5 What I am suggesting here is a relative of Gerald Dworkin's "hypothetical consent." ("Paternalism, *The Monist* 56 (1972): 64–84; and "Paternalism: Some Second Thoughts," in *Paternalism*, ed. Rolf Sartorius (Minneapolis: U. of Minnesota P., 1983); 105–112.)

6 Mill, however, regarded these reasons as decisive. I am suggesting only that they are important considerations, and that they might, at the end of the day, be outweighed by other considerations on any particular occasion.

7 This would be a more easily supportable claim if made from a position analogous to John Rawls' claims about permissible inequalities within a society in general. We might argue that any satisfactory justification for advancing the welfare of one group above that of another must be such to help the lesser-advantaged groups, as well. And if this is so, then the consent of even the lesser-advantaged stakeholders might be gained from an appeal to their own self-interest alone.

A Fiduciary Argument against Stakeholder Theory

Alexei M. Marcoux

Critics attack normative ethical stakeholder theory (hereinafter, "stakeholder theory") for failing to recognize the special moral status of shareholders that issues in and justifies the fiduciary duties owed to them at law by managers.[1] Proponents of stakeholder theory and fellow-travelling others reply that there is nothing morally significant about shareholders that can underwrite the fiduciary duties owed to them at law by managers.[2] In the present paper, I advance an argument that seeks to demonstrate both the special moral status of shareholders in a firm and the concomitant moral inadequacy of stakeholder theory. By examination of representative non-business fiduciary relations (doctor-patient, attorney-client, guardian-ward) I intend to show that at least some fiduciary duties are morally important to the relations to which they attach, not as a matter of "public policy," but as a matter of what is morally owing to the objects of those relations.[3] Thereafter, I argue that the manager-shareholder relation exhibits the same, essential features in virtue of which fiduciary duties are morally necessary to the above-referenced relations. In other words, I argue that (i) if some relations morally require fiduciary duties, and (ii) the shareholder-manager relation possesses the features that make fiduciary duties morally necessary to those relations, then (iii) stakeholder theory—which is constrained to deny that shareholders are owed fiduciary duties—is morally lacking.

In part 1, I argue that the manager-stakeholder relation contemplated by stakeholder theorists is necessarily non-fiduciary. In part 2, I argue that at least some fiduciary relations are morally deep. Rather than being justified as matters of mere public policy, they are instead a morally necessary aspect of the relations to which they attach, independent of the social good that they may bring. In part 3, I argue that the manager-shareholder relation possesses features analogous to those that make the fiduciary relations discussed in part 2 morally necessary. In part 4, I argue that the manager-(non-shareholding) stakeholder relation lacks the features that make fiduciary relations morally necessary. In part 5, I conclude (A) that shareholders, as a result of the arguments of parts 2 and 3, are owed fiduciary duties morally; (B) that non-shareholding stakeholders, as a result of the arguments of parts 2 and 4, are not owed fiduciary duties morally; and (C) that the stakeholder theory is morally lacking because (i) it fails to account for shareholders being owed fiduciary duties, and (ii) it treats all stakeholders' interests equally

Alexei Marcoux, "A Fiduciary Argument against Stakeholder Theory." Reprinted with permission of the Philosophy Documentation Center from *Business Ethics Quarterly* 13.1 (Jan., 2003): 1–24.

despite the shareholders' legitimate claim to managerial partiality as required by the fiduciary duties owed to them.

I. Non-Fiduciary Stakeholder Theory

Offered in contrast and opposition to *shareholder* theory, which holds that managers are fiduciaries for and ought to manage firms in the interests of shareholders, stakeholder theory holds that firms ought to be managed so as to coordinate the interests of their various stakeholders, usually shareholders, employees, customers, suppliers, and communities.[4] Each stakeholder's interest is to be treated equally in the formulation of business policy. Interests are to be "coordinated" or "balanced" by "trading-off" competing interests (although in terms of what interests are to be coordinated, balanced, and/or traded-off is not clear).[5]

A. Multi-fiduciary stakeholder theory

Some stakeholder theorists (e.g., Freeman) contend that theirs is a *multi-fiduciary* stakeholder theory. Multi-fiduciary stakeholder theory holds that managers are fiduciaries for, and ought to manage in, the interests of all of a firm's stakeholders.[6] In their landmark article, "A Stakeholder Theory of the Modern Corporation: Kantian Capitalism," Evan and Freeman argue for a "stakeholder fiduciary principle," the substance of which is that the interests of all of a firm's stakeholders are to be the object of the fiduciary duties of management.[7] In other words, their theory is multi-fiduciary because it ostensibly extends the fiduciary duties owed solely to shareholders at law to non-shareholding stakeholders, as well. In sum, multi-fiduciary stakeholder theory apparently holds that (i) fiduciary duties are morally important, and (ii) non-shareholding stakeholders are among those to whom it is morally important to extend fiduciary duties.

I will argue, however, that in fact the stakeholder theory demands that manager-stakeholder relations be *non*-fiduciary in character. Rather than *extending* the fiduciary duties historically owed to shareholders alone to non-shareholding stakeholders as well, the stakeholder theory instead *eliminates* fiduciary duties from all manager-stakeholder relations. Whatever moral duties managers have to stakeholders according to the stakeholder theory, they are not—and indeed, *cannot* be—fiduciary duties.

B. Fiduciary relations

In order to recognize this point, one must be clear about the nature of the fiduciary relation. The fiduciary relation is a triadic relation existing among and between two parties and some asset or project.

> The term [fiduciary] is derived from the Roman law, and means (as a noun) a person holding the character of a trustee, in respect to the trust and confidence involved in it and the scrupulous good faith and candor which it requires. A person having duty, created by his undertaking, to act primarily for another's benefit in matters connected with such undertaking.[8]

The fiduciary relation may be schematically represented as follows:

> where a fiduciary duty exists
> (i)   a party *p* (the fiduciary) is obligated to advance primarily
> (ii) the interests of another party *q* (the beneficiary) in
> (iii) acting upon and administering *r* (some asset[s] or project[s]).[9]

To act as a fiduciary means to place the interests of the beneficiary ahead of one's own interests and, obviously, those of third parties, with respect to the administration of some asset(s) or project(s).[10]

An example of a fiduciary relation is that of a doctor to her patient. In satisfying the duties that she takes on upon entering the relationship, the doctor must place the interests of the patient ahead of her own (i.e., serve the patient's interests even to the detriment of her own) with respect to the project of maintaining the patient's health. Note two important aspects of the relationship: (1) the *loyalty* of the fiduciary to the beneficiary's interests, as against her own and those of others; and (2) the *limitation* of that loyalty *to a particular project or asset*. The first aspect demands the advancement of a single party's interests (the beneficiary's) and partiality toward those interests in the formulation of an action plan. The second aspect limits the fiduciary's loyalty to the project for which the relationship exists. The doctor need not consider, let alone advance, the interests of her patient when, e.g., buying an automobile, even if the patient has interests in *that* project that could be advanced in some way (e.g., if the patient were an automobile dealer).

C. Stakeholder theory and fiduciary relations

If the multi-fiduciary stakeholder theory prescribes manager-stakeholder relations that are fiduciary in character, it must insist that managers are fiduciaries for the shareholders, employees, customers, suppliers, and communities of the firm—in short, for *all* the firm's stakeholders. But of course, managers cannot be fiduciaries for all of these groups. This is so for two reasons.

(1) It is conceptually impossible to simultaneously place the interests of the shareholders ahead of all the others, the interests of employees ahead of all the others (including shareholders), the interests of customers ahead of all the others (including shareholders and employees), the interests of suppliers ahead of all the others (including shareholders, employees, and customers), etc.

(2) It is practically impossible to serve the interests of each of these groups simultaneously. As most everyone recognizes, the interests of shareholders, customers, suppliers, employees, and communities in the management of a firm's assets are conflicting.[11]

As such, it is manifest that managers cannot be fiduciaries for all of these groups in the management of the firm, for to advance some stakeholder interests would be to frustrate at least some other stakeholder interests and hence to fail to act in a fiduciary capacity with respect to those others. In other words, the nature of the fiduciary relation is such that it is impossible for one to act as a fiduciary for multiple parties where the interests of those parties are (or are likely to be) in conflict. John Hasnas puts the point well:

> This feature of the normative stakeholder theory immediately gives rise to the objection that it is based on an oxymoron. Given the meaning of the word 'fiduciary,' it is impossible to have a fiduciary relationship to several parties who, like the stakeholders of a corporation, have potentially conflicting interests. Further, even if this did make sense, placing oneself in such a position would appear to be unethical. For example, an attorney who represented two parties with conflicting interests would clearly be guilty of a violation of the canon of ethics.[12]

As stakeholder theory demands that the interests of all stakeholders be counted, and presumably served equally (i.e., non-partially) in the governance of the firm, and as fiduciary duties require partiality toward the interests of some (the beneficiaries) over others, it follows that stakeholder theory is non-fiduciary in character.

D. The stakeholder theorist's reply

The stakeholder theorist might reply that the multi-fiduciary stakeholder theory demands that managers be partial to (and hence fiduciaries for) *stakeholders*, as opposed to non-stakeholders. Indeed, Freeman makes exactly this claim when criticizing Goodpaster:

> Plainly, unless [Goodpaster's] "argument" [that multi-fiduciary stakeholder theory is contrary to widely-held moral intuitions about the fiduciary nature of the manager-shareholder relation] has some merit, there is no paradox, for the Multi [sic] Fiduciary Interpretation *need only hold that managers bear fiduciary, or "special fiduciary" obligations to stakeholders*.[13]

This move may address the problem of partiality, insofar as it makes managers partial to *some* interests over others, but it fails to contend with the problem of conflict. A fiduciary has a conflict of interest if those for whom he is to act in a fiduciary capacity have conflicting interests in the asset or project to which the fiduciary duties attach. In other words, as Hasnas notes, it is *unethical* to take on fiduciary obligations to parties with conflicting interests in the same asset or project because there will come a time when it will be impossible to act as a fiduciary for all of them. As such, managers cannot be fiduciaries for stakeholders (as opposed to non-stakeholders) because, as is observed above (and is readily conceded by most stakeholder theorists), stakeholder interests are in fundamental conflict. In other words, contrary to Freeman's claim, the multi-fiduciary stakeholder theory *cannot possibly* hold "that managers bear fiduciary, or 'special fiduciary' obligations to stakeholders" on any plausible understanding of the fiduciary relation.

It is instructive, as well as exceedingly helpful to the present argument, that proponents of the multi-fiduciary stakeholder theory do not pretend to hold that managers ought to place the interests of any stakeholder constituency above that of any other (i.e., ought to be fiduciaries to any of them), as a matter of policy. Instead, they contend that managers ought to "coordinate" or "balance" these interests, "trading-off" one against another in the formulation of strategy and policy for the firm. The managerial practice that emerges from the multi-fiduciary stakeholder theory, therefore, is not one of loyal and partial advancement of some party's interests with respect to some asset(s) or project(s), but one of weighing and balancing (and hence often frustrating) the competing interests of many parties in a(n apparent) consequentialist calculus.[14]

E. Summary

The multi-fiduciary stakeholder theory, rather than extending the fiduciary duties of managers to non-shareholding stakeholders (because it is conceptually and practically impossible), *eliminates* fiduciary duty altogether in favor of a consequentialist-like weighing and balancing of admittedly competing stakeholder interests. The managerial practice prescribed by the stakeholder theory is thus, on any plausible understanding of the fiduciary relation, incompatible with the existence of morally substantial fiduciary relations. In short, stakeholder theory is necessarily non-fiduciary in character.

II. Morally Substantial Fiduciary Relations

The argument of part 1 is of no consequence to stakeholder theory, except that variant that styles itself "multi-fiduciary," if the fiduciary relation is morally insubstantial. Stakeholder theorists, recognizing the incoherence of multi-fiduciary stakeholder theory, may be happy to jettison fiduciary duties altogether if they have no moral basis or if their moral status is based upon the contingency that they make society in general better off, i.e., as a matter of public policy.[15] Here I will argue that at least some of the fiduciary relations recognized at law are not grounded in the morally thin contingencies of public policy but are instead morally substantial, constitutive of justice or fairness in the relations to which they attach. That is, it would be morally wrong for the relations *not* to be fiduciary in character—whatever the effect (or lack of same) on society in general.

A. Fiduciary relations at law

Doctors have fiduciary duties to their patients. Attorneys have fiduciary duties to their clients. Guardians have fiduciary duties to their wards. Why? One answer is because these duties are provided for by law. The more interesting question is *why* they are provided for by law and *whether* there are any deep moral reasons that might ground these legal duties. That is, is there something about these relations that make fiduciary duties morally appropriate, or even necessary, to them?

The legal definition and treatment of the fiduciary relation gives some clue as to why it might be morally significant. The fiduciary relation arises "whenever confidence is reposed on one side, and domination and influence result on the other."[16] It exists "when there is a reposing of faith, confidence and trust, and the placing of reliance by one upon the judgement and advice of the other."[17] Indeed, the

> [f]iduciary relation is not limited to cases of trustee and cestui que trust, guardian and ward, attorney and client, or other recognized legal relations, but exists in all cases where confidence is reposed on one side and resulting superiority and influence on the other side arises.[18]

Moreover:

> [The f]iduciary relation not only includes all legal relations such as attorney and client, broker and principal, executor or administrator and heir, legatee, or devisee, factor and principal, guardian and ward, husband and wife, partners, principal and agent, trustee and cestui que trust, but it extends to every possible case in which a fiduciary relation exists in fact and in which there is confidence reposed on one side and resulting domination and influence on the other. It is not necessary that the relation and duties involved be legal; they may be either moral, social, domestic, or merely personal. The origin of the confidence and the source of the influence are immaterial.[19]

B. Vulnerability

The common thread running through the myriad relations listed in the above-quoted passages is that each relation entails trust and confidence on one side of the relation and a corresponding influence and potential for domination on the other. The influencing and potentially dominating party bears fiduciary duties to the trusting and confiding party. In other words, the focus of the legal justification for fiduciary relations appears to be the *vulnerability* of one party (the beneficiary) to the other party (the fiduciary) in the relation.

Robert Goodin adverts to the explanatory power of vulnerability for widely held intuitions about many morally considerable relations in his book, *Protecting the Vulnerable*.[20] Goodin's principal objective is to show how vulnerability explains our moral intuitions about the obligations we have in a variety of contexts, as well as to justify still other obligations that may or may not accord with our intuitions because of the vulnerabilities that some people have. In his discussion of the special duties of doctors and lawyers to their patients and clients, Goodin writes:

> Why a professional person should have these obligations to his clients, and only his clients, is ordinarily explained in quasi-contractual terms of voluntary undertakings. Here again, the model of self-assumed obligations is thought to apply. Yet closer investigation once again shows the model to be inadequate. The peculiar vulnerability of clients to their doctors, lawyers, and so forth, offers a more satisfactory explanation for both the existence and the peculiar strength of the special professional responsibilities.[21]

Of course, this is not to say that vulnerability *alone* gives rise to fiduciary duties. Fiduciary duties constitute a special class of vulnerability-based moral obligations as they typically do not arise as a result of vulnerability alone, but instead are parasitic upon the voluntary undertaking of the superior and/or inferior parties, usually (though not exclusively) via contract. That is, there are voluntary relations (usually contractual) that give rise to certain kinds of non-fiduciary duties (e.g., duties attendant to contracts), but the presence of what Goodin calls a "peculiar vulnerability" on the part of one of the parties to the voluntary relation demands that the other act in a fiduciary capacity. A lawyer is not a fiduciary to me before I retain his services. However, upon retaining his services, my vulnerability to him gives rise to fiduciary duties on his part.

This concept of a peculiar vulnerability attending certain types of relations affords one a powerful tool with which to understand and explain some key relations to which fiduciary duties are typically thought to attach.

1. *Doctor-Patient*. Patients find themselves at a special disadvantage both before and upon entering the doctor-patient relationship. The doctor is possessed of all the relevant knowledge about the patient's health and about the treatment strategies that would serve the patient best. The patient lacks an effective means of protecting himself in a world of disease and injury generally, let alone against a doctor who chooses to serve her own interests or those of others in formulating a treatment strategy. As such, the law demands of the doctor that she act as a fiduciary for her patient. In formulating a treatment strategy, the doctor has a duty to subordinate her (and all other) interests to those of the patient, because otherwise the patient's interests are wholly at the mercy of the doctor.

2. *Attorney-Client*. Similarly, clients find themselves at a special disadvantage both before and upon entering the attorney-client relationship. The attorney is expert in assessing the client's legal status and the client lacks an effective means of availing himself of legal remedies and defenses, let alone to check an attorney serving her own interests or those of others at the expense of the client. Here, too, the law demands of the attorney that she act as a fiduciary for her client. In advising the client, the attorney has a duty to subordinate her (and all other) interests to those of her client because otherwise the client's interests are wholly at the mercy of the attorney. Moreover, because of the special vulnerability of the client, the attorney is morally obligated not to withdraw from representing the client until a suitable replacement can be found.[22]

3. *Guardian-Ward*. Similarly, wards find themselves at a special disadvantage in the guardian-ward relationship. The guardian is in near-complete control of the affairs of the ward. The guardian may determine, e.g., when and whether the ward is fed, clothed, attended to by medical or dental professionals, and educated. Here, the law demands that the guardian act as a fiduciary for the ward. In managing the affairs of the ward, the guardian has a duty to subordinate his (and all other) interests to those of his ward because otherwise the ward's interests are wholly at the mercy of the guardian.

4. *Summary*. Although the fiduciary duties of doctor to patient, attorney to client, and guardian to ward are provided for in the law, they are undoubtedly moral duties, as well. If the doctor orders unnecessary tests to be done in a lab in which she owns an interest, or shortens the regimen of treatment to contain costs and satisfy the insurance company and the patient dies as a result, it should be clear that she has committed a serious moral, as well as legal, wrong. If the criminal defense attorney fails to bring motions and raise objections at trial upon which an appeal can be mounted, and the client is convicted and incarcerated as a result, it should be clear that she has committed a serious moral, as well as a legal, wrong. If the guardian forbids the ward food or medical attention, and the ward suffers hunger, pain, or disease as a result, it should be clear that he has committed a serious moral, and not merely legal, wrong.[23] Indeed, the law here stands as a usually reliable (if not always infallible) guide to our moral intuitions.[24]

C. Vulnerability reconsidered

But note that this account of the moral basis of fiduciary duties is not completely satisfactory. Many people are beneficiaries of fiduciary duties who are not in positions of vulnerability, at least as it is normally understood. If you are my lawyer defending me against criminal charges, you have fiduciary duties to me whether I am rich or poor, brilliant or dull, legally trained or not. Similarly, if you are a doctor treating my heart condition, you have fiduciary duties to me whether I am a cardiac surgeon of equal or superior training and experience, or medically and scientifically ignorant. Moreover, if you administer a trust set up for my benefit, you have fiduciary duties to me whether I am a computer whiz of genius IQ or mentally defective.[25]

Clearly, if the fiduciary duties owed to those who are, as in the above examples, legally trained, medically trained, or of significant mental agility have a moral basis, it cannot be in virtue of garden-variety concerns about their vulnerability. For these examples suggest that if anyone is lacking in vulnerability to their fiduciaries, it is those who possess the capacities that permit them to evaluate the conduct of their fiduciaries. Indeed, perhaps only the computer whiz is unable to evaluate the conduct of the administrator of his trust. Nonetheless, I will argue that these beneficiaries *are* vulnerable to their fiduciaries in significant, though perhaps not readily apparent, ways.

1. *Control Vulnerability*. First, note that fiduciaries exercise a considerable degree of *control* over the affairs of their beneficiaries. Upon hiring a doctor or lawyer, I relinquish to her a considerable control over my medical or legal affairs. This should not surprise, for fiduciaries are always *agents* of their beneficiaries, and hence are empowered to act on behalf of those beneficiaries. Clothed with the authority to act on my behalf, fiduciaries can do many potentially damaging things that I may undo only with considerable difficulty—even if I am rich, intelligent, and knowledgeable about the subject of their agency. Call this type of vulnerability *control vulnerability*. Even if I am not vulnerable to my fiduciary in the way Goodin stresses, I almost invariably find myself control vulnerable in a relationship to which fiduciary duties attach.

2. *Information Vulnerability*. Second, fiduciaries typically have privileged access to *information* about the affairs of the beneficiary. Though I may myself be a doctor or lawyer, my doctor or lawyer typically has access to information about my medical or legal affairs that I may obtain, if at all, only through her. Although I may be *initially* more knowledgeable about my circumstances, the fiduciary occupies a position of informational superiority, at least with respect to information about the transactions or projects over which the fiduciary relationship exists. As new information is acquired, the fiduciary has it and the beneficiary does not. Call this type of vulnerability *information vulnerability*. Upon entering into a fiduciary relationship with my doctor or lawyer, I become information vulnerable to her.

   There exists a further aspect of information vulnerability. The fiduciary's control over my affairs and informational superiority make it possible for her to *control the flow of information to me*. Thus, though I may be quite knowledgeable at the outset of the relationship, the fiduciary can control what I know and discover thereafter. Like the ministers of propaganda in totalitarian regimes behind the former Iron Curtain, the fiduciary is uniquely positioned to control the information that becomes available to me—even if I am quite knowledgeable about my affairs and about the fiduciary's area of expertise. Thus, whether I am a doctor who hires a doctor, a lawyer who hires a lawyer, etc., I am vulnerable to my hire because she can control the flow of information that I receive about my legal affairs, my medical affairs, or whatever else is the subject of our fiduciary relationship.

3. *Implications.* Note that the very viability of the relationships to which fiduciary duties attach depends critically upon the existence of control vulnerability and information vulnerability. The doctor-patient relation is a prime example.

> The difference in information between the patient and the physician implies that the former has relatively little check on the latter. He may never be in a position to know whether the physician did as well as he could; if the patient knew that much, he would be a physician.... It is for this reason that ethical indoctrination of physicians is of crucial importance.[26]

If I could protect myself from both classes of vulnerability with respect to my doctor, I would have no use of her services. It is only the existence of both classes of vulnerability, coupled with fiduciary obligations on the part of the stronger party, that make it worthwhile and sensible to enter into relationships of this kind.

4. *Summary.* Fiduciary relations constitute a special class of moral relations where the duties of one party to a relationship are enhanced or extended by the vulnerability of the other party. Vulnerability consists not merely in physical, mental, or financial weakness, but also in deficits of control and information that arise from the relationship, even in the absence of physical, mental, or financial weakness. Vulnerability alone, i.e., in the absence of a special undertaking on the part of one or both of the parties, does not give rise to a fiduciary obligation or relation.[27] But the taking on of a relationship to those exhibiting a peculiar vulnerability carries with it an enhanced or extended set of obligations that exceeds those of ordinary contracts.

D. The moral core of fiduciary relations

The beneficiaries of fiduciary duties at law exhibit morally salient features that appear to make fiduciary duties morally obligatory. If I transact with another in a situation in which she has all of the relevant knowledge and virtually all control over my assets, both the law and the moral intuitions supporting it suggest that she exercise a special duty of care for my interests. The fact that we have contracted gives rise to ordinary, contractual obligations on both our parts. The fact that I am vulnerable to her gives rise to special, fiduciary obligations on her part. I am vulnerable to her as she carries out the project for which we have transacted. Lacking both knowledge and control, I am without ready recourse if my interests are subordinated. Indeed, it is because of the harm that I may all-too-readily suffer at the hands of a doctor, attorney, or guardian— harm that I am ill-equipped to anticipate and counteract, and that is entirely within the control of the doctor, attorney, or guardian—that fiduciary duties are owed to me.

In a fiduciary relationship, ... because one party is in a more advantageous position, he or she has special obligations to the other. The weaker party depends upon the stronger in ways in which the other does not and so must *trust* the stronger party.[28]

The point of the foregoing observation is that it is something about *me*, and something about *my* situation, that would make the failure to exercise fiduciary duties morally wrong. *I* may suffer harm if fiduciary duties are not carried out, and the nature of the relationship is such that *I* cannot protect my interests. Though collaterally this may affect society as a whole, the effect is only collateral. The moral wrongness of subordinating the interests of the beneficiary exists quite apart from the aggregate effects on society.

1. *Governing Fiduciary Relations in Non-Fiduciary Ways.* In order to see the moral necessity of at least some fiduciary relationships, one need only imagine one of the exemplar fiduciary relationships ungoverned by fiduciary duties. Suppose that the doctor owed no fiduciary duties to her patient. Instead, suppose that she is obligated only to coordinate the interests of the many parties that have an interest in the patient's medical condition. These would include, presumably, the patient, his family, his employer, his insurer, the doctor, the hospital, and the community.

   Rather than subordinate all interests to those of the patient (as fiduciary obligation would require), suppose that the doctor, in treating her patient's illness, were to "trade-off" the different and competing interests of the various interested parties. In formulating a treatment strategy, the doctor would have to weigh, for instance, (a) the patient's interest in effective treatment against the insurer's interest in cost-containment; (b) the hospital's interest in sufficient observation and monitoring of the patient's progress (in order to avoid malpractice or wrongful death liability) against the family's interest in minimizing the portion of the medical bill not covered by insurance (lest it threaten their interest in the patient's estate); and (c) the patient's interest in a period of prescribed, recuperative rest against the employer's and the community's interest in getting the patient back on the shop floor and the tax rolls.

   What should be clear is that the doctor who pursues the treatment of her patient in this manner is treating the patient in a morally deplorable manner—a manner that undermines the trust that the patient places in the doctor to serve his interests, and a manner of treatment whose defects he may not be able discover and from which he may not be able to escape. Indeed, who in his right mind would place himself under the care of a doctor who lacked fiduciary duties toward him and would treat him in this manner?

   Interestingly, this thinly-veiled stakeholder model of the doctor-patient relationship both exhibits and exacerbates all of the features of current American health care practice that most everyone finds so deplorable. In fact, the important social policy debate over health care is motivated, in part, by the implicit recognition that stakeholder-oriented management (as it has come to be practiced in the health care industry), and its concomitant anti-fiduciary implications, are *problems* to be *overcome* through public policy rather than an aim or object of public policy. Indeed, President Clinton's call in the 1998 State of the Union Address for important medical decisions to be made by doctors and not by insurance company bureaucrats stands as a concrete example of the view that decisions based on medical criteria are consistent with fiduciary obligations owed to the patient, whereas decisions based upon financial criteria are not. In fiduciary terms, the beneficiary's interests ought not to be traded-off against the interests of other stakeholders in the formulation of treatment strategies. In short, it would be morally wrong to deny patients the protections of fiduciary duties.

2. *Summary*. The point of this thought experiment is that fiduciary obligation captures something morally important about the way those who are vulnerable (in one or another sense) ought to be treated by those who are possessed of all of the relevant knowledge and control pertaining to the relationship into which they have contracted themselves. To eliminate the fiduciary aspect from the doctor-patient, attorney-client, or guardian-ward relations—that is, to permit doctors, attorneys, or guardians to treat the interests of their patients, clients, or wards as but some among many to be considered in determining what ought to be done— undermines the moral character of the relation and invites an *abuse* of those already at a marked disadvantage in the relation. Moreover, this abuse is "local"— i.e., in the relation itself—and is not a matter of what harms the interests of society in general. In other words, the fiduciary relation, in at least these cases, is morally substantial, not as a matter of what benefits society in general (i.e., public policy), but as a matter of what is due morally to one party in the relation—quite independent of the benefits to society in general.[29]

III. The Manager-Shareholder Relation

One may agree that the argument of part 2 is substantially correct and that the fiduciary aspect of the doctor-patient, attorney-client, and guardian-ward relations is morally substantial, and yet still deny that managers are morally required to have fiduciary duties to shareholders. That is, one may deny that the manager-shareholder relation possesses the features of the doctor-patient, attorney-client, and guardian-ward relations that make the fiduciary duties that attend them morally substantial.[30] In part 3, I will argue that the manager-shareholder relation *does* possess those features.

A. Control and information vulnerabilities revisited

The discussion in part 2 reveals that fiduciary duties are most morally pressing where one party is at a special disadvantage with respect to the other. Fiduciary relations arise where there is a special disadvantage, and a corresponding repose of trust and confidence, of one party with respect to the other. It is because of the special disadvantages of patients, clients, and wards that the fiduciary duties owed to them by doctors, attorneys, and guardians are morally substantial. If one can demonstrate that shareholders stand in the same disadvantageous position with respect to managers that patients, clients, and wards stand with respect to doctors, attorneys, and guardians, then one will have demonstrated that shareholders are proper moral objects of fiduciary duties.

Recall from part 2 the discussion of control vulnerability and information vulnerability. Shareholders suffer the special disadvantage of having their assets in the hands of a management team in possession of all of the relevant knowledge, in control of all aspects of their investment, and in control of the flow of information to the shareholders.

Shareholders exhibit control vulnerability because managers are entirely in control of shareholders' investments in the firm. Shareholders may regain control of their investments only if they can find another willing to assume their relationship with the firm (i.e., buy their shares) at or above the price at which shareholders initially acquired them.

Shareholders exhibit information vulnerability because managers have access to information about the day-to-day operations, the successes and failures, and the financial inflows and outflows of the firm. Shareholders generally lack and cannot easily acquire this sort of information. Shareholders are further information vulnerable because managers both have access to the information that shareholders generally lack and control the flow of information to shareholders. That is, managers may control who comes to acquire that important information and when or whether they acquire it.

Shareholder interests are protected only to the extent that managers take it upon themselves to advance the interests of shareholders and to apprise shareholders of their success or failure in that project. As such, shareholders generally lack the ability to monitor effectively their investment and the orientation of the firm's business policies toward their interests. This is not surprising, for it is difficult to evaluate distributions of profit and fluctuations in share price to determine whether management is doing well or poorly by equity investors. Dividends of $1.25 / share and a four-point increase in share price since the last quarter may be exemplary or poor, depending upon what the best efforts of management would bring, what opportunities were available, etc. In their book, *The Economic Structure of Corporate Law*, Easterbrook and Fischel[31] make this quite plain:

> The corporate contract locates the uncertainties in the holders of the residual claims—conventionally the equity investors. They receive few explicit promises. Instead they get the right to vote and the protection of fiduciary principles: the duty of loyalty and the duty of care... .[T]hese attach to the residual claim because the holders of these claims bear the marginal risks of the firm and so have the best incentives to make the optimal investment and management decisions—not perfect incentives, just best.[32]

That is, shareholders are the object of the fiduciary duties of managers because their contracts with the firm are fundamentally *incomplete*. "If contracts can be written in enough detail, there is no need for 'fiduciary' duties as well."[33] It is both exceedingly difficult and prohibitively costly, however, to foresee and provide for the myriad contingencies in which shareholder interests could potentially be subordinated. Therefore,

> [t]he only promise that makes sense in such an open-ended relation is to work hard and honestly. In other words, the corporate contract makes managers the agents of the equity investors but does not specify the agents' duties. To make such an arrangement palatable to investors, managers must pledge their careful and honest services.[34]

Moreover, shareholders generally lack the ability to insulate themselves against adverse policy once they have invested.

> Detailed contracting, costly enough at the outset of the venture, is almost impossible once a firm has been established. After the firm has raised the necessary capital, investors have no practical way of revising the articles on their own to overcome intervening legal surprises.[35]

Shareholders have no contractual guarantees that they will receive a return and, having once invested, may recoup their investment only if they can find another who will take their place (by purchasing their shares)—and do so at or above the price of their original investment. Indeed, the law recognizes this special vulnerability of the shareholder:

> A director of a corporation, though not a trustee in the strict sense for reason that he has not title to the estate, is a fiduciary *because he and his fellow directors have control of the corporate property*, and, upon violating his fiduciary obligation, whether by sheer embezzlement, the director comes under same obligation to his company that any agent is under who is faithless to his trust, and if corporation becomes insolvent its claim against director for an accounting, restitution, or equitable damages passes to its liquidator along with its other assets.[36]

Just as patients lack the ability to monitor their own health and the orientation of the doctor's treatment strategy towards their interests (and to easily insulate themselves against a doctor bent on using their health to advance other interests), as clients lack the ability to monitor their legal status and the orientation of the attorney's legal strategy toward their interests (and to easily insulate themselves against an attorney bent on using their legal status to advance other interests), and as wards lack the ability to monitor the care they receive (and to insulate themselves against a guardian willing to subordinate it to other interests), so too does the shareholder lack the ability, having once invested, to protect his interests against corporate managers in control of his investment and possessed of all the relevant knowledge. As such, the shareholder is a prime candidate for fiduciary duties from managers.

B. Reply: The ready-market-for-shares argument

Stakeholder theorists typically counter that shareholders are protected against these eventualities by the existence of a ready market for their shares.[37] The argument is that, because they may easily dispose of their shares and recoup the current market value of their investment, shareholders are protected against managerial practices adverse to their interests in a way that, e.g., employees are not. Call this the *ready-market-for-shares* argument. There are two important observations to make about this line of argument that cast doubt upon its ultimate usefulness to stakeholder theorists and its merit.

1. *Publicly-Traded Corporate Form*. To the extent that it is relied upon exclusively to demonstrate the lack of any special shareholder vulnerability, this argument cedes enormous ground to the shareholder theorist. That is, if it is only the availability

of a ready market for shares that vitiates shareholders' vulnerabilities to managers, then the argument is limited in its application almost solely to firms in the publicly-traded corporate form—and then, only so long as there are, in fact, buyers ready to purchase the shares of the firm. Sole proprietorships, partnerships, many (though not all) limited partnerships, and closely-held corporations all typically lack a developed and ready market for their equity.[38] If it is only the existence of a ready market for equity holdings that defeats shareholders' special vulnerability and their concomitant claims to fiduciary duties from managers, then it is only in firms of the large, publicly-traded variety that shareholders lack the special vulnerability that justifies fiduciary duties owed to them. In all other legal forms, stakeholder theorists seem constrained to acknowledge the special vulnerability of equity holders, because equity holders in those legal forms have no ready market for shares that could defeat their vulnerability to managers.[39]

2. *What Protection?* It is unclear why the existence of a market for shares, *even* in the case of large, publicly-traded firms, is to be regarded as a protection. Typically, the decreasing orientation of a firm's management to profitability and other shareholder interests is reflected in share prices, and is so reflected before most shareholders can discover the underlying reasons themselves.

Some have argued that portfolio diversification can protect against this eventuality. But note two things about portfolio diversification. First, although portfolio diversification can ensure that management practices adverse to my interests will not swallow the whole of my net worth, it does nothing to protect whatever stake I *do* have in the firm that engages in those practices. Simply put, portfolio diversification does not protect my stake. Second, portfolio diversification cannot protect shareholders if stakeholder-oriented management becomes widespread (as stakeholder theorists surely hope). That is, if *all* firms exhibit a decreasing orientation to shareholder interests, then a diversified investment strategy can hardly insulate shareholders from the share-price-diminishing effects of a management that considers the interests of a shareholders merely some among many to be considered in determining what to do. Indeed, if stakeholder-oriented management were adopted universally, one would expect a universal collapse of equity markets and the inability of firms to obtain equity capital (because, as Easterbrook and Fischel note, arrangements of this sort would hardly be palatable to investors). Equity markets offer no protection once the damage of stakeholder-oriented management is done.

Indeed, the existence of a market for shares is no more a protection of shareholders' investments in their firms than is the existence of wrecking yards a "protection" of car owners' investments in their cars. It would be absurd to suggest that car owners have no need, e.g., of automobile insurance because there is a ready scrap market willing to buy damaged cars at a substantial discount. By the same token, it is absurd to suggest that shareholders have no need of fiduciary duties from managers because there is a ready market whose participants are willing to buy—again, at a substantial discount—the shares of firms whose managements accord shareholder interests no privileged place.

In short, the shareholder is either (i) unaware of, and hence unable to protect himself from, managerial practices that are detrimental to his interests, or he is

(ii) aware of them, but so is everyone else, and hence share prices will already reflect the decreased orientation of the firm toward shareholder interests. How the existence of a ready market for shares constitutes a protection to shareholders—one that vitiates their vulnerability to management and hence their legitimate claim to fiduciary duties—is unclear at best.

C. Summary

In sum, shareholders exhibit a special vulnerability to managers that arises out of their contract to provide equity capital to the firm secured only by a residual interest in the firm. Shareholders exhibit control vulnerability and information vulnerability to the managers of firms in which they hold equity positions. Their vulnerabilities are acute because even if they possess much of the information to which managers have access, they generally lack the ability to evaluate the wisdom of managerial decisions unless they know what the alternatives were, what the outcomes would be, and the like. That is, it is only if one knows, or can discover, what the counterfactual case would hold that one can evaluate managerial performance and determine whether it is exemplary or poor. Indeed, this inability is one generally shared by courts and, as such, underwrites the standard of review inherent in the business judgment rule. That is, just as shareholders are ill-equipped to evaluate the wisdom of managerial decisions (and so are information vulnerable and hence the proper objects of fiduciary duties), so too are courts ill-equipped to evaluate the wisdom of corporate decisions (and so will not second-guess managerial judgment absent a showing of gross negligence or breach of loyalty).

IV. The Manager- (Non-Shareholding) Stakeholder Relation

If the argument of part 3 is correct, then shareholders seem to be morally necessary beneficiaries of fiduciary duties—and not merely as a matter of public policy. But perhaps it is the case that some or all *non-shareholding* stakeholders stand in the same relationship with respect to managers. One of the central arguments of Freeman and Evan is that stakeholders with *asset-specific* investments stand at as much (or more) of a disadvantage as shareholders and, consequently, should be afforded representation on corporate boards.[40] In part 4, I will argue that the manager- (non-shareholding) stakeholder relation lacks the characteristics that would make non-shareholding stakeholders proper moral objects of fiduciary duties. In other words, the relationship of non-shareholding stakeholders to the firm is of a morally different kind.[41]

Non-shareholding stakeholders lack the special disadvantages that justify fiduciary obligations. Although they may possess certain disadvantages with respect to managers, these are comparatively small, and non-shareholding stakeholders are not without effective and beneficial recourse if their interests in the firm are harmed.

A. Employees and suppliers

Unlike shareholders, non-shareholding stakeholders like employees and suppliers do not invest the entirety their labor and goods in the firm up front. Instead, they contract with the firm to provide labor and goods incrementally over time and, if they receive less than they bargained for, may terminate their relationship with the firm and sue for damages. Whatever labor or goods they have invested in the firm give rise to a legal right of compensation at the agreed-upon rate. Whether the firm fares well or ill, employees and suppliers are legal claimants on the firm and the firm is obligated to compensate them for what they have put into it.

Stated in terms of control and information vulnerability, employees and suppliers exhibit only limited control vulnerability. They turn control of their labor and goods over to the firm, but that control is limited by the relative ease with which employees can withdraw their labor from the firm and suppliers may interrupt the flow of their goods to the firm.

Employees and suppliers generally lack information vulnerability because their contracts with the firm require periodic specific performances by management. If the employee's bi-weekly paycheck is short or missing entirely, that conveys an enormous amount of information about whether the firm is keeping its end of the bargain. Similarly, if the employee's contract provides for medical coverage but the employee is turned away by her HMO, this too conveys an enormous amount of information about whether the firm is discharging its duties to the employee. The same analysis applies to suppliers. If the firm fails to pay the supplier in a timely manner or terminates a supply contract without the agreed-upon notice, then the supplier is apprised of the firm's performance on the contract and may then take steps to secure its interests.

By the same token, employees and suppliers generally lack that variant of information vulnerability that concerns the flow of information. This is because both action *and* inaction on the part of management conveys information about the course of performance on the contract. It is extremely difficult for managers to obscure the fact that they are not performing on their contracts with employees and suppliers. Checks that never come, meetings that go unattended—these are the telltale signs that one's stake in the contract is in jeopardy. Moreover, these can be pointed to in court as conclusive evidence of the failure to perform.[42] Compare the shareholder, who may not conclude from the fact that the firm declares no dividend or that share prices fall that managers are not acting in his interests.

It would be truly strange, therefore, to extend the benefits of fiduciary duties to employees and suppliers.

B. Customers

Although, like shareholders, customers may invest money in the products of the firm up front, but they are otherwise unlike shareholders. Like employees and suppliers, customers may, with relative ease, discover failures of the firm to live up to its contract (by failing to deliver what was bargained for). Moreover, they can easily terminate their relationship with the firm (by refusing to purchase more) and sue for damages if the firm has failed to live up to the bargain.

Like employees and suppliers, customers exhibit only limited control vulnerability, but generally lack information vulnerability. Therefore, it would be strange to extend fiduciary duties to customers.

C. Communities

Although, like shareholders, communities cannot readily sever their relationship with the firm, they are otherwise unlike shareholders. Communities may, by way of the law, seek to insulate themselves against losses due to their dealings with the firm through taxation, regulation, and, in extreme cases, exercise of eminent domain or outright proscription of entire industries and industrial activities within their borders. That is, communities possess significant powers via political and legal mechanisms to determine the nature and extent of their relationship with the firm. Moreover, they often have contractual agreements with firms not to relocate for a period of years in return, e.g., for tax rebates, charges for schools, sewage, and road costs. In these circumstances, communities are like other non-shareholding stakeholders: they are creditors of the firm who may easily discover breaches of their contracts and seek legal recourse for failure to perform.

In short, like employees, suppliers, and customers, communities generally exhibit at most limited control vulnerability. They do not, however, generally exhibit information vulnerability. Therefore, it would be strange to extend fiduciary duties to communities.

D. Summary

Unlike shareholders, non-shareholding stakeholders may readily compare what they receive from the firm with what they were contractually promised by the firm. Even where communities lack contracts with the firm, they may readily compare the conduct of the firm with the requirements of the law. Whatever their informational disadvantages with respect to managers, non-shareholding stakeholders may relatively easily identify discrepancies that, in turn, give rise to legally cognizable claims against the firm. In short, unlike shareholders, non-shareholding stakeholders have complete or near-complete contracts with the firm and it is the completeness of their contracts that obviates the need for fiduciary obligations. Indeed, Easterbrook and Fischel say as much: "If contracts can be written in enough detail, there is no need for 'fiduciary' duties as well."[43]

Non-shareholding stakeholders are more accurately characterized as arm's-length contractors with the firm. Arm's-length contractors typically do not have fiduciary duties owed to them.[44] They offer no investment in trust and confidence to management that places them at a special disadvantage.[45] Their relationships are easily monitorable and severable and give rise to specific, legally protected claims on the assets of the firm. As such, non-shareholding stakeholders are not proper objects of fiduciary duties.

V. The Moral Inadequacy of the Stakeholder Theory

From part 1 we recognize that stakeholder theory denies all fiduciary duties of managers. To be a fiduciary for someone is to be partial to that someone's interests and to promote them within a certain domain, but the stakeholder theory demands impartiality among and between the admittedly competing interests of stakeholders. Therefore, the stakeholder theory demands that managers be fiduciaries to no one.

From part 2 we recognize that some fiduciary relations—doctor-patient, attorney-client, guardian-ward—are morally deep. That is, fiduciary duties are morally appropriate to those relations not because of the social benefit they bring, but because of the nature of the relations themselves, the vulnerability of the weaker parties to those relations, the intentions and expectations of the parties, and the concomitantmoral badness of governing those relations in a non-fiduciary way (witness, e.g., the non-fiduciary doctor-patient relationship).

From part 3 we recognize that shareholders occupy a vulnerable position with respect to managers that is analogous to the vulnerable position of patients with respect to doctors, clients with respect to attorneys, and wards with respect to guardians. That is, the manager-shareholder relation shares the features of the doctor-patient, attorney-client, and guardian-ward relations that make the fiduciary duties that attend them morally substantial. As such, the fiduciary duties of managers to shareholders are morally substantial, as well.

From part 4 we recognize that although there are some risks and some corresponding moral obligations that attend becoming a non-shareholding stakeholder in a firm, non-shareholding stakeholders do not stand in a position of vulnerability analogous to that of a shareholder or any other proper moral object of fiduciary duties. As such, non-shareholding stakeholders lack a just claim to fiduciary duties from managers.

If the arguments of parts 1–4 are correct, they underwrite three conclusions, none of which is welcome news for the stakeholder theorist.

A. Shareholders

The first conclusion is that shareholders have a legitimate moral claim to fiduciary duties from managers. This follows from the moral substance of the fiduciary duties owed by doctors, attorneys, and guardians to patients, clients, and wards argued for in part 2 and the relevantly analogous features of the manager-shareholder relationship to the doctor-patient, attorney-client, and guardian-ward relationships argued for in part 3.

B. Non-shareholding stakeholders

The second conclusion is that non-shareholding stakeholders do not have a legitimate moral claim to fiduciary duties from managers. This follows from the features of morally obligatory fiduciary relationships identified in part 2 and non-shareholding stakeholders' lack of them argued for in part 4.

C. Stakeholder theory

The third, and most important, conclusion is that stakeholder theory cannot account for the moral duties of managers toward their shareholders. This follows from the non-fiduciary character of the manager-stakeholder relations contemplated by stakeholder theorists argued for in part I and the legitimacy of shareholders' claims to fiduciary duties that falls out of the arguments of parts 2 and 3.

If shareholders have a legitimate moral claim on managers to act as fiduciaries for them, and stakeholder theory demands that managers not act as fiduciaries for anyone (including shareholders), then stakeholder theory fails to account for the legitimate moral claims of shareholders. Moreover, as stakeholder theory demands that managers be impartial among and between competing stakeholder interests, and as the very nature of a fiduciary duty requires that the one owing it practice partiality, the legitimacy of shareholders' claims to fiduciary duties from managers (and the lack of legitimacy of similar claims on the part of non-shareholding stakeholders) demonstrates that managers *cannot* be obligated to be impartial. Hence, stakeholder theory stands as a profoundly mistaken account of the moral obligations of managers generally.[46]

Notes

1 See, generally, Kenneth E. Goodpaster, "Business Ethics and Stakeholder Analysis," *Business Ethics Quarterly* 1 (1991): 53–73; Kenneth E. Goodpaster and Thomas Holloran, "In Defense of a Paradox," *Business Ethics Quarterly* 4 (1994): 423–429. I shall employ the term "managers" throughout as a shorthand for the officers and directors of firms. I trust no argument will turn on this generic use of the term "managers" and that its use will make my exposition less cumbersome than would frequent recourse to the less felicitous "officers and directors."

2 See John R. Boatright, "Fiduciary Duties and the Shareholder-Management Relation: Or, What's So Special About Shareholders?" *Business Ethics Quarterly* 4 (1994): 393–407, and the favorable reception of same in R. Edward Freeman, "The Politics of Stakeholder Theory: Some Future Directions," *Business Ethics Quarterly* 4 (1994): 409–421, 413.

3 The intended target of this argument is Boatright, who argues that the fiduciary duties historically owed to shareholders from managers are not morally deep, but instead find their way into the law as a matter of what will make society in general better off. See, generally, his "Fiduciary Duties and the Shareholder-Management Relation," op. cit.

4 Some accounts of narrowly interpreted stakeholder theory include managers in this list, as well. Whether they may be subsumed by the "employees" heading or must be regarded as a separate constituency of the firm is a matter that need not detain us here. I trust that no argument offered here will turn on whether or not managers constitute a separate stakeholder group.

5 The "coordinating" characterization is found in William M. Evan and R. Edward Freeman, "A Stakeholder Theory of the Modern Corporation: Kantian Capitalism," in *Ethical Theory and Business*, Tom L. Beauchamp and Norman Bowie, eds., 3rd ed., (Englewood Cliffs, N.J., 1988); 103; and Freeman, "The Politics of Stakeholder Theory," op. cit., 413. The "balancing" characterization is found in Thomas Donaldson and Lee E. Preston, "The Stakeholder Theory of the Corporation: Concepts, Evidence, and Implications," *Academy of Management Review* 20 (1995): 65–91, 79. The "trading-off" characterization is found in Goodpaster, "Business Ethics and Stakeholder Analysis," op. cit., 61.

6 Some refer to the stakeholder theory as "multi-fiduciary" in scare quotes, as I have done here (see, e.g., Goodpaster, "Business Ethics and Stakeholder Analysis," op. cit.), suggesting the view that the stakeholder theory is not fiduciary in character. Others employ the term without scare quotes (see, e.g., Freeman, "The Politics of Stakeholder Theory," op. cit.), suggesting that the stakeholder theory extends truly fiduciary duties to non-shareholding stakeholders.

7 They write:

> Management bears a fiduciary relationship to stakeholders and to the corporation as an abstract entity. It must act in the interests of the stakeholders as their agent, and it must act in the interests of the corporation to ensure the survival of the firm, safeguarding the longterm stakes of each group.... [This] we might call The Stakeholder

Fiduciary Principle ... (Evan and Freeman, "A Stakeholder Theory of the Modern Corporation," op. cit., 103–104).

8 "Fiduciary," in *Black's Law Dictionary*, 5th ed. (St. Paul, Minn.: West, 1979); 563.

9 Thus, fiduciary relations can be represented in first-order predicate calculus by sentences of the form 'Fpqr', where p holds or administers r for q's benefit in an F way.

10 That the fiduciary must also place the beneficiary's interests ahead of those of third parties is obvious because were the fiduciary to subordinate only his own interests to those of the beneficiary, but not those of third parties, then there would be no sense in which the beneficiary (or class of beneficiaries) is treated any differently than third parties. The fiduciary would not have entered into any special relationship with the supposed beneficiary, but rather would merely have made an altruistic commitment to the world at large not to pursue his own interests over the project or asset he manages.

11 Evan and Freeman are perfectly aware of this point. They write:

> [M]anagement, especially top management, must look after the health of the corporation, and this involves balancing the multiple claims of *conflicting* stakeholders. Owners want more financial returns, while customers want more money spent on research and development. Employees want higher wages and better benefits, while the local community wants better parks and daycare facilities. ("A Stakeholder Theory of the Modern Corporation," op. cit., 103, emphasis added.)

I say *most* everyone recognizes this because there exist at least some adherents of the stakeholder theory who regard conflicts among the interests of the various stakeholders in a firm as rare. See, e.g., Lee E. Preston and Harry J. Sapienza, "Stakeholder Management and Corporate Performance," *Journal of Behavioral Economics* 19 (1990): 361–375, cited approvingly in Thomas W. Dunfee and Thomas Donaldson, "Contractarian Business Ethics: Current Status and Next Steps," *Business Ethics Quarterly* 5 (1995): 173–186, 183.

12 John Hasnas, "The Normative Theories of Business Ethics: A Guide for the Perplexed," *Business Ethics Quarterly* 8 (1998): 19–43, 39 n. 32.

13 Freeman, "The Politics of Stakeholder Theory," op. cit., 410, emphasis added.

14 I say "apparent" because although the language of consequentialist weighing and balancing is most often employed by those advancing the stakeholder theory, none explicitly regards the theory as consequentialist in character. Evan and Freeman ("A Stakeholder Theory of the Modern Corporation," op. cit.) conceive of the stakeholder theory as essentially Kantian—an implication and application of the practical imperative. The more recent Freeman ("The Politics of Stakeholder Theory," op. cit.) and (sometimes) Donaldson (Donaldson and Preston, "The Stakeholder Theory of the Corporation," op. cit.) see their stakeholder-theoretic projects within the tradition of rights theory. In a more recent paper, Donaldson and Dunfee, "Integrative Social Contracts Theory: A Communitarian Conception of Economic Ethics," *Economics and Philosophy* 11 (1995): 85–112, see their project as contractarian, but, as the title indicates, yielding a "communitarian conception of economic ethics." In other words, by all accounts the stakeholder theory functions in a consequentialist manner, but its partisans advance theoretical bases for it that range all over the map of non-consequentialist ethical theories.

15 This, apparently, is Boatright's view. See, generally, "Fiduciary Duties and the Shareholder-Management Relation," op. cit. Of course, this would require Evan and Freeman to jettison, or at least rename, their Stakeholder Fiduciary Principle.

16 *Matter of Heilman's Estate*, 37 Ill. App. 3d 390, 345 N.E.2d 536, 540.

17 *Williams v. Griffin*, 35 Mich.App. 179, 192 N.W.2d 283, 285.

18 *Schweikhardt v. Chessen*, 161 N.E. 118, 123, 329 Ill. 637.

19 *Patton v. Shelton*, 40 S.W.2d 706, 712, 328 Mo. 631.

20 Robert Goodin, *Protecting the Vulnerable* (Chicago: University of Chicago Press, 1985).

21 Goodin, *Protecting the Vulnerable*, op. cit., 62.

22 Charles Fried, "The Lawyer as Friend: the Moral Foundations of the Lawyer-Client Relation," *Yale Law Journal* 85 (1976): 1060–1089, 1077.

23 The discussion here is borrowed from James W. Child and Alexei M. Marcoux, "Stakeholder Theory's Ephemeral Normative Core," presented at the Society for Business Ethics session, Central Division Meetings of the American Philosophical Association, Pittsburgh, April 24, 1997.

24 Indeed, Goodin treats it as such, writing that in his consideration of professional obligations he "shall continue to look to the law as the principal guide to our settled moral intuitions ..." (*Protecting the Vulnerable*, op. cit., 62).

25 I am indebted to Elaine Sternberg for these observations.

26 Kenneth Arrow, "Government Decision Making and the Preciousness of Life," in *Ethics of Health Care*, L. R. Tancredi, ed. (Washington, D.C.: National Academy of Sciences, 1974); 33–47, 37, quoted in Goodin, *Protecting the Vulnerable*, op. cit., 66 n. 35.

27 Although, as Goodin notes, it may give rise to an obligation on the part of a professional providing fiduciary services to avoid driving hard bargains in contracting out their services and to avoid declining to serve those who might be left helpless without the professional's services (*Protecting the Vulnerable*, op. cit., 67).

28 M. D. Bayles, *Professional Ethics* (Belmont, Calif.: Wadsworth, 1981), 69, quoted in Goodin, *Protecting the Vulnerable*, op. cit., 66–67.

29 This discussion intentionally leaves unanswered a number of interesting conceptual and practical puzzles that attend the fiduciary relation. These puzzles form the basis of another project by the present author.

The Anglo-American law generally conceives of fiduciary duties as requiring that the fiduciary maximize for the beneficiary. That is, within the scope of the project over which the fiduciary owes fiduciary duties to the beneficiary, the fiduciary is obligated to make her best efforts to maximize for the beneficiary, subject to the legitimate legal claims of others (e.g., a fiduciary cannot steal from another for the benefit of the beneficiary). This requirement of constrained maximization in the interests of the beneficiary poses no apparent difficulty if the fiduciary has only a single beneficiary and a single project. Many professionals, however, are in the business of providing fiduciary services for multiple beneficiary-clients. The typical personal injury attorney, for example, carries a caseload of 200–300 cases, making her a fiduciary for some 200–300 people over some 200–300 separate projects. Medical doctors typically have many regular patients. Surely, the fiduciary duties of lawyers and doctors to one client do not bar them from serving the interests of other clients. As such, the constrained maximization interpretation of fiduciary relations is not as straightforward as it might first appear. Among the side-constraints on maximizing for a beneficiary are not only the legitimate claims of non-beneficiaries (e.g., not to be thieved from), but also the positive claims of other beneficiaries on the time and resources of the fiduciary. How do we reconcile the legitimate claims of other beneficiaries with the idea that the fiduciary is a constrained maximizer of the interests of the beneficiary?

Similarly, fiduciaries, like normal people, presumably may rest, take vacations, attend to their families, and the like, using for these purposes time that *could* be spent in the service of one or another of their beneficiaries. How are we to reconcile these legitimate pursuits with the constrained maximization model of fiduciary relations?

In other words, the fiduciary relation is ripe for a detailed conceptual treatment, one that takes important steps towards an account of the bounds within which the fiduciary must maximize for the beneficiary—an account that is consistent with the prevalent practice of professional fiduciaries serving many beneficiaries over many projects, as well as being consistent with the concept of exerting reasonable (as opposed to super-human) efforts on behalf of one's beneficiaries.

30 This is one way to read Boatright's argument in "Fiduciary Duties and the Shareholder-Management Relation," op. cit.

31 Frank H. Easterbrook and Daniel R. Fischel, *The Economic Structure of Corporate Law* (Cambridge, Mass.: Harvard University Press, 1991).

32 Easterbrook and Fischel, *The Economic Structure of Corporate Law*, op. cit., 90–91.

33 Easterbrook and Fischel, *The Economic Structure of Corporate Law*, op. cit., 90.

34 Easterbrook and Fischel, *The Economic Structure of Corporate Law*, op. cit., 90–91.

35 Easterbrook and Fischel, *The Economic Structure of Corporate Law*, op. cit., 93.

36 *Gochenour v. George & Francis Ball Foundation*, D.C.Ind., 35 F.Supp. 508, 515 (emphasis added).

37 See, e.g., Freeman and Evan, "Corporate Governance: a Stakeholder Interpretation," *Journal of Behavioral Economics* 19 (1990): 337–359, 340–342; Boatright, "Fiduciary Duties and the Shareholder-Management Relation," op. cit., 396.

38 I owe this observation to Jim Child.

39 This is one of the strangest aspects of stakeholder theory: it is apparently a theory of the moral

obligations of managers that is limited to firms doing business in the publicly-traded corporate form. As such, stakeholder theorists might object to ABC Corporation's decision to close its plant in Fort Wayne, Indiana, on the grounds that it failed to consider properly the interests of employees and the community in reaching that decision. However, were the managers of to take ABC private (e.g., as a closely-held corporation or limited partnership) before reaching that decision, stakeholder theorists—according to their own theory—have no grounds upon which to object. Why the legal form assumed by ABC should determine the propriety of closing its Fort Wayne plant is a mystery.

Apparently, I am not alone in this concern. An earlier iteration of the Wharton Ethics Program website reveals that stakeholder theory's exclusive focus on the corporate form is an area of interest and concern for Thomas W. Dunfee, who is generally sympathetic to the stakeholder theory.

40 "Corporate Governance: A Stakeholder Interpretation," op. cit., 342–344. Boatright advances similar arguments ("Fiduciary Duty and the Shareholder-Management Relation," op. cit., 396), although not for the purpose of advocating stakeholder representation on boards.

41 Note that the argument is not that the relationship of non-shareholding stakeholders to the firm is morally empty. The argument I advance is perfectly consistent with the view that firms have obligations—perhaps negative, perhaps positive, perhaps both—to non-shareholding stakeholders. I deny only that those obligations are or should be fiduciary, i.e., that they include advancing the interests of non-shareholding stakeholders as the object of managerial action. As such, managers may have extensive obligations to non-shareholding stakeholders, but they must stand as *side constraints* on the pursuit of the interests of shareholders—a pursuit that is morally obligatory via fiduciary obligations owed to shareholders. (For the seminal discussion of side constraints, see Robert Nozick, *Anarchy, State and Utopia* [New York: Basic Books, 1974]; 28–35.)

It is this constrained maximization view of the moral obligations of managers to stakeholders that I take to be anathema to, and the principal competitor of, stakeholder theory, for it is the one which Freeman most strongly criticizes in a recent article:

The mythology of laissez-faire capitalism is unfortunately easily propped up by arguments that claim, of course managers have the same moral obligations that you and I have, even if they disregard them in favor of invisible hand explanations. Economists, business theorists and evidently some business ethicists think that it is enough to see morality as a side-constraint on the maximization of stockholder wealth, justifiable only if a greater good or other moral end is served. ("The Politics of Stakeholder Theory," op. cit., 411–412.)

It is also the view advanced by Child and Marcoux, "Stakeholder Theory's Ephemeral Normative Core," op. cit.

42 The same analysis applies to debt-holders, who are for all intents and purposes ordinary suppliers, albeit of debt capital. Unlike employees and ordinary suppliers, debt-holders typically do invest everything up front. However, like employees and other suppliers, they may readily discover whether the firm is holding up its end of the bargain and they have legal recourse if it does not.

43 Easterbrook and Fischel, *The Economic Structure of Corporate Law*, op. cit., 90.

44 Easterbrook and Fischel write that, "Fiduciary principles are uncommon in contractual relations" (*The Economic Structure of Corporate Law*, op. cit., 90).

45 Margaret Blair, *Ownership and Control* (Washington, D.C.: Brookings 1995), and others argue that employees and suppliers make asset-specific investments in the firm and that this constitutes a vulnerability that justifies a claim to management in behalf of their interests. Assuming, for the sake of argument, that this is true, why does this legitimate vulnerability give rise to claims that firms be managed in employees' and suppliers' behalf? Why does it not merely give rise to certain threshold claims on the firm, e.g., to notice and/or severance before closing a plant or terminating a supply arrangement? How does such reliance justify a blank check on (or equal participation in) managerial care and concern?

46 This paper was presented at the Society for Business Ethics Annual Meeting in San Diego, 1998. It has benefitted considerably from discussion with, and suggestions from, John Boatright, Jim Child, John Hasnas, Elaine Sternberg, and Sean Whyte.

Evaluating a Case Study
Finding the Conflicts

After establishing an ethical point of view (including a segue to application), we are ready to approach cases. The first stage in handling cases effectively is to analyze the situation according to normal practice and potential ethical issues. Obviously, sometimes ethical issues are involved in what one will do, and at other times they are not. It is your job to determine when ethical issues are involved. Let us consider specific cases.

Case 1

You are a sales manager at a Fortune 1000 company. You have several large deals that are just about to close, but for some reason they have been hung up over some details. The sales in your division have been down for five consecutive quarters. If you show one more decline, you are history and many others in your division will be history, too. You could "fudge" your report and show two of the three pending deals as sold and thereby avoid being sacked. After all, you are very sure they will go through. Anyway, it buys you a little time even if they do not.

Does this case involve any ethical issues? If so, what are they? How do they affect normal practice?

Case 2

You work in the accounting department of a small company. You notice that Mr. Jones has been "hitting on" Ms. Smith. This takes up a lot of time for both of them, and the other accountants must work even harder to make up for the time Mr. Jones and Ms. Smith lose. Your department is small, so this situation is especially difficult and irritating.

Does this case involve any ethical issues? If so, what are they? How do they affect prudential (self-interested) concerns? What about issues of professional practice?

Checklist for Detecting Issues Concerning Professional Practice

Directions: Read your case carefully and determine what (if any) relevant points of professional practice are at stake. Identify the individual in the case from whose perspective you will develop your comments. Determine whether there are any clear violations of professional practice. Identify these violations and the various risks that such behavior entails. Next go through the checklist for detecting ethical issues.

Checklist for Detecting Ethical Issues

Directions: Read your case carefully. Determine your ethical viewpoint (as per "Developing a Practical Ethical Viewpoint," p. 32. Create one or more detection questions that identify ethical issues. These detection questions will follow your own ethical perspective. For example, from my own practical ethical perspective I have chosen the following two detection questions to bring ethical issues to my attention. These questions follow from a deontological viewpoint.

1. *Is any party being exploited solely for the advantage of another?* (Exploitation can include instances of lying, injuring, deliberately falsifying, creating an unequal competitive environment, and so forth.)
2. *Is every effort being made to assist and affirm the human dignity of all parties involved?* (Affirming human dignity can include instances of encouraging the fulfillment of legal and human rights as well as taking personal responsibility for results that are consonant with these principles. Thus, you cannot hide behind nonfunctioning rules.)

By asking these questions within the context of the case, I am able better to understand the moral dimensions that exist with other professional concerns.

A few other comments may be useful concerning my detection questions. Question 1 concerns "prohibitions" (i.e., actions that you must refrain from doing). Question 2 concerns "obligations" (i.e., actions that you are required to do). Anything that is not an ethical obligation or a prohibition is a "permission" (i.e., actions that you may do if you choose). Thus, if the case you present does not invoke a prohibition or an obligation, then you may act solely according to the dictates of your professional practice. It is often useful to group your detection questions as prohibitions and obligations, which emphasizes different types of moral duty.

Try creating detection questions and apply them to the two earlier cases. What do they reveal about the ethical issues involved in the cases? How do different detection questions emphasize different ethical issues? How different are these perspectives? How similar are they?

Once you have completed this preliminary ethical assessment, you can return to the ethical theory you have chosen and to determine *how* and *why* the prohibitions and obligations are applicable to this theory.

Read the following macro and micro cases and complete the steps outlined:

1. List the professional practice issues at stake.
2. Identify your practical ethical viewpoint including any linking principles.
3. Determine which character's perspective you will adopt.
4. Identify two or more detection questions that define obligation and prohibition within the ethical theory you have chosen.

5. Apply the detection questions to the cases to bring attention to the ethical issues.
6. Discuss the interrelationships between the dictates of the ethical issues and those of the professional practice. How might they work together? How might they be opposed?

Macro and Micro Cases

The cases section of this book is divided into two categories, macro and micro. Each type of case employs a different point of view.

Macro Case. The macro case takes the perspective of someone in an executive position of authority who supervises or directs an organizational unit. His or her decisions will affect many people and resonate in a larger sociological sphere.

Micro Case. The micro case examines the perspective of someone at the proximate level of professional practice, such as a salesperson, accountant, or lower level manager. Obviously, this case applies to more people than does the macro case.

Case Development. This book suggests one way to develop critical evaluations of ethical cases. In the "Evaluating a Case Study" sections, you will be asked to apply a specific skill to the cases presented. At the end of Chapter 6, you will be able to write an essay concerning the application of an ethical perspective to a specific problem.

Please note that although the cases presented here have fictional venues, they are based on composites of actual business practice.

Macro Case 1 You are the operations director for *XYZ Sports Apparel*. XYZ has recently opened a factory in Guadalajara, Mexico to make various casual sports apparel. Your product twist is that XYZ's tops are treated with a chemical that blocks harmful ultraviolet sunlight, thus protecting customers from the major cause of melanoma in their torso region. The problem is that this chemical has been anecdotally linked to miscarriages. Your company has met all of Mexico's published safety standards (though the chemical has not yet been approved in the USA and is banned in Europe). You believe the case is still out on the chemical. However, melanoma is the number one cause of skin cancer deaths in the USA. The potential "health" appeal could be tremendous. You are not breaking any laws in the USA or Mexico by manufacturing this product. However, your management team is still restless. How would a solution to this problem go forward using the "corporation as an individual model" versus the "corporation as a community model"? Write a memo to your vice president of marketing in your US home office making your recommendation using one of these two models and employing practical and ethical considerations.

Macro Case 2 You are the new chairperson of the board at Drummond Defense Contractors, which has experienced some ethical problems in the past. The company made its reputation through very cagey and aggressive business dealings. This means operating as far below the law as possible without being caught. These dealings have brought stockholders large profits. You want to change the company's dealings from being on the edge of legality to being fully compliant with the professional standards of good business practice. You realize that this suggestion is controversial since it could mean that the company's bottom line might suffer (most certainly will suffer is more accurate).

You know that you will need more than a whim to make your case to the other directors. You know that there are various ways to look at a corporation (i.e., as a moral agent, as the representative of stakeholders' interests, and as some other property-oriented aggregate, as you learned in college when you studied philosophy). You also know that the other directors think that philosophy is basically worthless (fit only for the feeble minded and the insane). You cannot present your case in philosophical terms or you will be out of a job. Instead, you must find a way to convince Drummond to revise its practices of doing anything to obtain specs on competitive bidding and to find out *beforehand* what other companies are bidding. Your job is to make the argument so that your board will accept it.

Macro Case 3 You are the head of the federal Food and Drug Administration (FDA). You have learned that numerous vitamin companies are making claims about the efficacy of their over-the-counter products that are not entirely correct and in some cases are patently wrong. It has been agency policy to treat over-the-counter vitamins largely as unregulated so long as the products actually contain what the label says (e.g., vitamin E in a vitamin E pill).

The current situation worries you. More and more vitamins and herbal medications are available in increasingly potent amounts and pose health problems to people who use them improperly. Some affect heart rate, and others are mood altering. This poses a difficulty to your understanding of the professional responsibility incumbent in your position. You believe that your job is to protect the public; however, when you bring this up in a staff meeting, it becomes apparent that at least three clear positions emerge. First is the position that the marketplace will police itself and the media will inform the public of excesses and problems, which will result in putting financial pressures on those companies to reform themselves.

The second position is that only the government can treat corporations as moral entities with the moral (and legal) responsibility to act responsibly (with a high level of care and professionalism). Those who say that companies ought to be made accountable use language suggesting that these companies are persons in their own right.

A third position is to view the situation as the interface of stakeholders' intersts.

Obviously, these three positions predict radically different solutions to what everyone agrees is a disaster waiting to happen. You have an appointment with the secretary of Health and Human Services to discuss this problem. Write a position paper noting the practical and professional issues and the way you characterize a corporation.

Micro Case 1 You work for *Tough Dude Cycles* (a major competitor to Harley Davidson). Your union has made a special assessment withholding from your paycheck of $48 to fund the campaign of Lila Lefty, a political candidate you detest. You don't want to pay. You go to your shop steward and voice your complaint. Your shop steward says, "When you join a union you work together as a unit. We rise and fall together. Get lost!" But you don't want to get lost. What do you do?

Micro Case 2 You are the manager of a discount computer software and hardware store that is part of a chain. The final decision-making authority lies with the home office. Each store is rated against other stores in the chain, and those that score poorly experience lower pay and higher layoffs. It is a very competitive system.

One practice mentioned at a recent meeting of store managers is customer service exhaustion (CSE). Under CSE, the store classifies customer service requests as trivial and nontrivial. The classification depends on the cost to solve the problem. Problems costing the company $10 or less are trivial; all others are nontrivial. CSE has trivial requests processed promptly. Nontrivial requests are addressed under a calculated system of delay based on the "principle of five," which means that the client must be turned down at least five times. The rationale behind the principle of five is that few customers will have the endurance to continue the process of having a customer service associate meet with superiors and return time and again without approval to address the problem. The customer service associate assumes the role of the "good guy," and the superiors making the decisions are the "bad guys."

Employing CSE works; fully 70 percent of the customers walk away, saving the company the expense of seeking recompense from the supplier (a difficult operation at best). Stores that utilize CSE consistently outperform those that do not.

CSE does not fit the values of your personal worldview, however. You believe that CSE is simply a strategy to cheat the customer and make money for the company. You are a steward of the company's resources; the stockholders' money is in your hands. If you press forward your ideas of ethics and morality, you are concerned that you are adding a new element to your job description (preserving the company as a moral entity) and it is rather presumptuous of you to do so. Shouldn't you just do whatever is necessary to increase the profit of the company to the benefit of the real owners, the stockholders? What about the stakeholders?

You are very conflicted by this. Write a report for your own benefit to justify the action you will take. Be sure to take into account practical issues, professional issues, and your personal conception of what a corporation should be.

Micro Case 3 You are a life insurance salesperson whose company has a new marketing campaign: "Rising to the Top of the Pyramid: Retirement Security." The essence of the campaign is to approach businesses and sell them on the fact that $50,000 of life insurance can be purchased by an employer and remain tax free. By "overpaying" a universal or variable life policy to the maximum under regulations, a person can create a pool of money that enjoys tax-deferred status. This is touted as an ideal plan for employers who wish to leverage their benefits as much as possible (in some cases, the corporation itself can be the beneficiary of the death benefit until the employee retires).

The problem is that although the life insurance policy is currently paying 5.5 percent and is guaranteed to pay 3.0 percent, this is deceptive in comparison to other investment vehicles. These figures are based on the net cost (i.e., before deducting the death benefit costs and administrative fees). Once these costs are deducted, the real return is approximately 0.75 percent.

You firmly believe that although life insurance is a legitimate financial planning tool and that every working person with a family should have 3 to 5 times the annual salary protected by life insurance, this campaign deceptively sells insurance as a retirement vehicle or an investment tool.

The problem is that you do not believe in the company's marketing plan. It violates the values supported by your personal worldview. Should you go along with the campaign? What do you owe the company? What do you owe the company's stockholders? Should you just continue to sell in your traditional way? What if everyone did that? If the company is wrong in its moral direction and if you think of the company as a moral entity, then perhaps you are doing the company a favor by not going along with its new campaign. If the company is a moral entity and is consciously moving in this direction, what does this say about the relationship between your own moral views and those of your employer? Does stakeholder analysis alter your evaluation?

This is a complicated set of questions. Choose the ones that seem most appropriate to you and write a report supporting your position. Be sure to make a copy and keep it in your safe deposit box in the bank in case there is an investigation.

What Are Proper Business Practices?

General Overview: When we talk about *practices* we are exploring how we go about doing something. For example, some sports teams try to win by creating an explosive offence while others concentrate upon a formidable defense. This level of analysis constitutes strategic planning. The way you go about creating a top offense or robust defense means adopting specific methods of bringing about one's goals. These methods are the practices.

In business within a modified capitalistic structure there is no getting around it being about competition. Only in command economies (such as China) can one get away from competition (and even then not entirely). Since the focus of this volume concerns modified capitalistic countries (most of the wealthiest countries in the world), we will only examine competition from that perspective.

Practices are often related in a nested fashion. For example, one's attitude towards competition may affect the way one chooses to advertise or use IT. The relationship between these master practices and their subordinates is often opaque to participants so they don't really see that the reason that they may be involved in unethical advertising or information technology is as a result of a skewed understanding of competition. Therefore, it is towards competition that we will turn first.

A. Competition and the Practice of Business

Overview: In the first essay in this section, I take a rather broad perspective to competition. This begins with the worldview perspectives that lie at the heart of competition. One of these is that competition turned bad. Some people use the name "competition" to hide a kraterist sensibility. (Kraterism is the name I give to those who think that the bald exercise of power is self-justifying.)[1]

Business Ethics, Second Edition. Edited by Michael Boylan.
© 2014 John Wiley & Sons, Inc. Published 2014 by John Wiley & Sons, Inc.

The second worldview stance is competition as a force for good. This can be exhibited in social interest competition. The act of competition is imbedded in a clear social context by which others gain while I gain.

These two versions of competition can be fit into models that become good or bad in the way they implement competition. This fits the question of competition as implemented into a framework of justice. Several philosophers on justice are brought forward in order to fashion a view of competition that highlights the good aspects and minimizes the bad (thus the Janus faces turned somewhat to the right side).

In the second essay, my vantage point is rather more focused. I try to set out the practice of business competition into the model of professionalism. Professionalism, broadly conceived, refers to a specialized notion of a practice. A community of professionals defines best practices and professional malpractice. It is this community working together that seeks to set the standards and often to monitor them as well (as in the paradigm cases of doctors and lawyers).

Competition that is viewed from this perspective must accept as a given that a businessman has accepted an understanding of practice that is not just some legal set of statutes that could land him in jail. The principle of *fair* competition envisions a community originated set of professional practices that are consistent with one of the theories of morality. Virtue ethics, for example, seems to do exceptionally well under this standard.

B. Advertising

Overview: Edward Spence's essay brings to the fore the association of consumer products with human values as a fundamental description of the moral landscape. Advertising seeks to create a positive impression in the hearts and minds of the consumers who have become predisposed to the products advertised in this way. This association of products to values may, however, have the undesirable effect of diminishing the importance of those values. Worse still, it may encourage the view, especially among children exposed to these advertisements, that values and people (just like consumer products) are tradable, replaceable, and expendable. Key values such as freedom, friendship, and happiness that are fundamental to our ethical and axiological understanding of society may become subverted and corrupted through the constant association of these values with brands of commodities.

In the second essay, Tony L. Henthorne and Michael S. LaTour examine another specific issue in advertising: the use of sexually suggestive models to sell products (which consumers know is not a new phenomenon). The authors use a psychologically multidimensional scale to evaluate responses to such ads. For example, if it is taken as a given that a small erotic stimulus catches the audience's attention and (if the ad is sufficiently benign, according to the personal worldviews of those viewing the ad), attention is gained and may generate a positive feeling for the product. But if the advertiser goes too far, she risks a backlash on the part of the audience. Readers also may question the validity of even so-called successful uses of this strategy in the communication flow between media and the intended audience.

C. Information Technology

Overview: Since the 1990s the use of information and communication technologies has defined the Information Revolution that has (in much of the world) redefined the workplace. This revolution, claims Mariarosaria Taddeo, has both a technological character as well as a philosophical one. To properly understand these dimensions in this context a greater understanding is required of how the technology affects semantic information, transparency in the marketplace, online trust, and privacy. A definition of (semantic) information as true semantic data raises the three problems of transparency, online trust, and privacy. This essay highlights how the ethical misuse of information can create problems and impede the promise of the fourth revolution of information.

John Weckert's essay narrows the scope of analysis to workplace monitoring and surveillance (which impinges on "trust"). To begin, Weckert allows that some monitoring of workers' activity has always occurred. Supervisors often walked the floor to make sure that employees were doing their job. The floorwalker has been replaced by closed circuit television, monitoring of phone calls, GPS devices in company cars to insure that there are no detours, and radio-frequency identification (RFID) devices to monitor employee productivity. Though there are justifications for these measures by employers who want to increase profits, there are some concerns as well. Primary among these is the loss of privacy that can lead to employee health problems. At the heart of this problem, conceptually, is the issue of trust. Weckert depicts it this way: "If A trusts B to achieve some goal X, then A chooses to rely on B making certain choices." Of course this model assumes that A believes B to be capable of achieving X. If this is the case, then B may make certain choices to achieve X that may differ from A. This is due to B's individuality as an agent and his autonomy to choose. This attitude will bring about a "seeing as" disposition: "If A trusts B then A *sees* B's behavior *as* being trustworthy." This "seeing as" disposition moves us into some questions in the recent history of the philosophy of science. These distinctions are very important because the concept of *trust* is a rich and multidimensional one. However, Weckert argues that coming to terms with the concept of trust is essential as business goes forward within the context of the problem of electronic monitoring and surveillance of employees.

Note

1   I discuss this at greater depth in Chapter 8 of *A Just Society* (Lanham, MD: Rowman and Littlefield, 2004).

A. Competition and the Practice of Business

The Janus Faces of Competition

Michael Boylan

Janus was the Roman god of doorways. In every doorway there is an entry and an exit. Janus was thus depicted as two-faced and looking in opposite directions. He heralded both happiness and despair, beginnings and endings.[1] With this sun–moon emblem of opposites in our minds, I suggest we consider the role of competition in our lives.

Competition brings us the thrill of victory and the agony of defeat (or so says the intro for ABC's "Wide World of Sports" since the 1960s). In this way competition can be a powerful motivational tool that will convince athletes to undergo great physical pain in order to beat the other guy. Salespeople may attain new levels of productivity when spurred by competition. In this way competition brings out the best in us.

Competition can also motivate people to break the law. Some athletes, for example, are so keen at winning that they will do more than become disciplined and motivated—they go to the next step and take illegal performance-enhancing drugs (some of which may bring about their deaths).[2] Some businesspeople will fake sales figures or engage in other lies and deceptions in order to make a big sale. These individuals will do anything to win. In this way competition brings out the worst in us.

So what is it? Is competition bad or good? This essay will contend that it's both. If we want to promote the good and demote the bad, then we have to get to the center of what makes competition such a powerful force.

What Is Competition?

Etymology

Competition comes from a Latin compound: *com* 'together' + *petere* 'to strive or seek'. In the active form it refers to striving or seeking together. In the passive form it indicates meeting together in a common purpose.[3] In Latin literature the active form often refers to contending against one's peers. It is a part of the ancient world's understanding of contending against one another to seek a personal prize.[4]

When one observes the word in its etymological origins it seems that there is a Janus-faced depiction of the word according to whether it is in the active or passive voice. In the active voice there is an aggressive contending after the prize. In the passive voice there is a cooperative striving for some common goal. If we believe that language reflects popular sentiments (what this author depicts as the shared community worldview), then this exposition of origins describes deeply felt cultural sensibilities.

From its etymological beginnings competition is two faced.

Psychology

Have you ever tried to take a bone from a dog that is chewing on it? If you haven't, then *don't*. You will get a dog bite. Why is this? It is because deep within us is a natural instinct for the preservation of what we perceive to be ours. What applies to dogs is also resident in all *Homo sapiens*. It is sometimes referred to as the *fight or flight* response. It is a very strong biological drive that is connected to competition. We want to protect what we have. This also extends to protecting what we reasonably seek to achieve and, by extension, what we think that we might be able to garner. In the lingua of sales this means that one must meet one's sales goals and *that it would be a good thing* to approach the "stretch" goals.

Behind competition is this biological imperative born in an era in which many starved to death. One needs to eat. It would be nice to eat and be filled. However, this life-or-death imperative can also include imperviousness to those we push aside in our own quest for the good. Again, Janus' double face presents itself in personal versus community values.

Competition as Bad

In Lisa Newton's recent book, *Permission to Steal*, she discusses competitive approaches that emphasize achieving a certain bottom line: whatever it takes.[5] Certainly in the corporate scandals after the new millennium this often seemed to be the case. The reason is simple: when there are two competitors of equal ability and one of them cheats, then the cheater wins (unless he is caught). I experienced this when I was an American Athletic Union (AAU) cross-country runner in the 1970s. The 10,000-meter course was too long to have judges everywhere so they had an honor system to follow the course. There was one competitor I remember who was about the same ability as myself. But he often cut the corners so that he was running a shorter course than I was. It was no surprise that he generally beat me.

This is the reason that people cheat in competition: cheaters win more often than the rest of us—unless they are caught. The possession of the "prize" at the end of the day is so important to the cheater that he will do anything (or almost anything) to attain it. It is as if the "rules" of the competition are morphed to resemble some sort of "state of nature" scenario. It is not a coincidence that many in the corporate world employ metaphors of hunting for food in a wild jungle to describe the role of competition in their work life. Such a worldview can readily justify *doing whatever it takes* to close the deal. Recent history has shown this to be true. Janus must shut his eyes on the just to focus his other face upon the expedient.

Competition as Good

The failure of corporate greed is not the only story that competition can tell. Competition can also be seen as a positive force for good. This section will discuss two large categories of competition that aspires to be good: social interest competition and personal interest competition.

Social interest competition

When I was a boy scout in the 1960s I was told that the troop was in financial trouble. We didn't have enough money to continue. Therefore, the scoutmaster gave us a task of selling boxes of popcorn (pre-microwave). The troop got 50% of the gross revenue per sale. We were trying to imitate the girl scouts who had a lock on the cookie market (though they only got a 4% return on gross receipts). But the time horizon was short. For this reason, the scoutmaster told us that there would be a competition in the troop. The top three sellers would be given the huge fathers' tent at the next campout as well as unlimited "smores."[6] We were provided no directions on how to sell these boxes of nutritional fluff. I just went along with the party line: "Our Boy Scout troop is in trouble; would you please buy this popcorn so that we might continue?"

What was left out of this pitch was: (a) Is this popcorn you are selling any good? (b) If you are in trouble, then why don't your parents bail you out?

I came in second in the sales contest. However, the prize was not very enjoyable. I had to sleep next to a boy who thrashed around in his sleeping bag and kept me from my rest. I also didn't like smores. What made me persevere to get second place in a troop of 75 boys? For me it wasn't the short-term personal prize. I wanted our troop to continue another year so that I might reach Eagle Scout (that I did reach). I was connected to my personal goals within the context of the group. If the group failed, then I assumed that I, also, would fail. This gave a twist to competition.

In the business world there are countless examples of competition also bringing out the best in this way. For example, the Chrysler Corporation and United Airlines fought off bankruptcy by inspiring their employees to rise to new production heights and to engage in salary and benefit give-backs in order to meet the guidelines set out by the bankruptcy court. This, in turn, motivated others to arrive at novel solutions—such as the government bail out of Chrysler and the employee stock program at United. Like the scout popcorn case above, this sort of competition is set in a social framework. People are moved to extraordinary actions to avoid negative consequences that are proximately directed at the group but also involve individual interests as well (such as keeping your job!). Let's call this sort of competition *social interest competition* (*competere* in the passive form).

There are other examples of social interest competition as well, some good and some bad. For example, in the late 1980s the USA was beset by competition from Japan. First, it was from Toyota and Honda, that were able to produce a significantly higher quality fuel-efficient automobile at a much lower price than the big three US companies. Second, the Japanese also threatened to dominate in computer technology and its commercial applications. These two events led to some anti-Japanese feeling in the USA. In one case in Louisiana, an exchange student was murdered in an action that some attribute to this corrupt side of social interest competition.[7]

On the positive side, many companies in the USA responded via social interest competition as an incentive to their workers. The vision presented to workers was that if they didn't respond to this economic threat, their jobs and the country's entire standard of living might be significantly diminished.

The US commercial sector responded. The USA pulled ahead in computer technology. They were *not* successful in auto manufacturing. There the USA rode a wave of cheap gas prices and an allure of large, luxury-styled cars/trucks (sport utility vehicles, SUVs) that sold at huge profit margins. At the writing of this essay, the price of oil has again become a public issue of concern. SUV sales have tanked and Toyota has taken over first place in world auto sales.

Though it is never entirely successful, it is still the case that social interest competition can be a powerful motivator for generally positive results.

Personal interest competition

A second competitive motivator for performance is individual competition (*competere*, in the active voice). Most stories on competition lead with this. For example, Zaholan Chang was a bubble in the enormous sea of people that is the Peoples' Republic of China. She worked hard at her sales job so that she might travel to the USA and get a second degree that might launch her to a higher level of management when she returned. Zaholan was a student of mine. What motivated her to work so hard and to accomplish so much for herself (and by extension for her company—which paid for her way to the USA)? It was *personal interest competition*.

Personal interest competition is the sort of motivating force that pushes many forward to help both themselves (proximately) and others (remotely). It is this sort of vision of competition that spurred the vision of Mandeville's beehive.[8] If each of us works toward his own interest, then the society is benefited. By extension, if each of us is spurred by personal interest competition, then the society wins. Hey, what's to hate? If I work for myself, then I'm helping everyone! Maybe they should nominate me for sainthood!

Plato's *Republic* presents a similar image: if all the classes work together on what they are able to do, then the society (as a whole) will prosper. The underlying idea is that the model of society—presented in this way—is right. It's natural.

So what is there about this model of personal interest competition that makes it feel so right to most Americans and those of other G-8 countries? Well, the answer is: meritocracy.

Competition and Merit

Meritocracy is the underlying justification for most competitive situations. Who could be against it? Adam Smith, Milton Friedman, Friedrich Hayek, et al. have purported unfettered competition based upon the assumption of meritocracy as the driving engine of growth and productivity for society. In the microperspective the person who deserves something by his or her hard work within the competitive environment is rewarded regardless of race, gender, or religious orientation. Isn't this Thomas Jefferson's America?[9] The term "meritocracy" refers to the practice of rewarding or allocating according to those who are excellent or deserving. The word comes from the Latin *merere*, which means to receive one's share as pay for work done. Thus, in its simplest form, meritocracy can be seen as a way to reward producers. For example, it is often the cases that some of the higher-compensated employees in a company are the top salespeople who are paid on commission. Most companies are happy to provide a competitive rate of commission to salespeople who produce for them. Given this incentive, there are many salespeople who are quite talented and work very hard to earn handsome incomes—especially in such industries as financial services, real estate, and big-ticket manufacturing and services contracts.

On the next level things become a little more difficult. How is it that we judge "merit" or "deserts"? This is the more difficult question and links the question of meritocracy with that of distributive justice. Three views will be examined: (a) the traditional position (represented by Daniel Bell), (b) a social welfare-based position (represented principally by John Rawls), and (c) a deserts-based position (represented principally by this author).

The Traditional Position

Daniel Bell says that meritocracy is made up of those who have earned their authority through individual achievement.[10] This is a functionally based understanding. In a sales contest a company might offer a vacation to Hawaii to anyone selling 50 000 widgets in the latest financial quarter. Under the traditional position, if Andy sells 50 000 widgets, then Andy merits or deserves the vacation. The traditional interpretation of meritocracy is behind much of US and global business assumptions. This is because of the strong link to classical models of capitalism. These models suggest a reward formula "to each according to his valued work." Thus, within the rules of fair competition, a person is rewarded more if he produces tangible output that the society values. It is not the case that any means of production is allowable (since, at the extreme, one could kill another and snatch *his* output). Therefore, within the framework of rewarding according to work is a caveat that all the applicable rules of competition have been obeyed.

Implicit in classical models of capitalism is also a vision of useful synergy between various production engines within the society. Behind Andy's vacation reward, for example, is the notion that the company's functional standards should be seen in the context of larger interdependent markets. No single business can be accurately separated out. In macroeconomic terms the traditional model supports distributing according to social usefulness (which fits the relatively unfettered operation of capitalism à la Friedrich Hayek or Milton Friedman). In theory, those who will acquire the most resources will be those who offer a social benefit to those who are able to compensate them for said benefit. In practice, the traditional understanding of meritocracy operates through a dynamic interaction between business and society.

The state steps in to establish fair rules and then acts as a referee only when someone breaks the rules. Aside from that, each person gets what she can with whatever resources she has at her disposal (such as her IQ or her hard work) within the competitive environment.

The Social Welfare-Based Position

For John Rawls, the question of distributive justice is rather different.[11] He is not content to say that any person begins at some point in the process of acquisition and then is merely constrained by a set of rules and procedures to insure fairness. Rather, the socioeconomic position of the agent is also considered.

Let's return to Andy and the sales contest. In the traditional position, the only thing we had to consider was whether there were clear rules and that everyone in the sales force was following these rules. This is because what is important is whether someone sells 50,000 widgets or not. If you do, you get the trip. If you don't, you stay at home.

What Rawls wants to ask is *why* Andy is such a good salesman and whether there is some level on which justice might redistribute outcomes for others not as gifted as Andy. Rawls bases his query upon *how* the agent is presented with his distribution of talents and social position. His conclusion is that these distributions are accidental and arbitrary. It is an accident that someone is born with whatever natural traits he may possess. For example, let us consider two traits only: being a fast runner and being a fast talker (meaning a persuasive salesman). Now if Sam is a fast runner he is so because he was born with certain physical traits that made him that way, such as an efficient Krebs cycle in respiration, lung capacity, and so forth. If Jamal is a fast talker, this may also be due to certain natural attributes such as neural wiring that permits quick thinking and an ability to be singleminded and not subject to hormonal interference (such as might cause anger or upset). Neither Sam nor Jamal can claim credit for their natural abilities that were given to them by their parents in a natural genetic lottery. Thus, if these natural abilities are the basis of societal reward, then in a strong sense neither Sam nor Jamal *deserve* what they have achieved. In this case, the question is raised whether a meritocracy based upon natural abilities is thus unfair. Some might contend, for example, that even if we do not deserve our natural abilities it is not unfair if we reap the rewards of those abilities because the system of reward is independent of the system of deserts.

However, Rawls makes the case that social position is also random and arbitrary. For example, if you put Sam the fast runner into a hunting society, he may garner the most goods because his speed makes him a better hunter. However, if you put him into the information-based service society, then speed is irrelevant. He will not be rewarded. The same may be said of Jamal in reverse (he would do poorly in the hunting society, but would prosper in the information-based service society). Neither Sam nor Jamal could help growing up in the society in which they were born. It was an accident. Thus, the fact that their natural abilities may or may not be rewarded in that society is also an accident. To be rewarded based merely upon an accident is not deserved. Thus, a meritocracy that is based upon reward from undeserved social position is similarly unfair.

Therefore, both natural abilities and social position may not be the basis of distributive justice because they are unfair. The naturally advantaged are not to gain merely because they are more gifted. The rectification of these disparities in Rawls is his difference principle that makes all inequalities subject to the stipulation that the least advantaged will benefit from them.

Since competition is the motivational engine within which striving occurs, for competition to be just, Rawls would contend, there must be various mechanisms in place to ensure that the competition is a fair one. These might include affirmative action or extra educational opportunities to those who have been shortchanged in the lottery of natural abilities and social position. Thus, according to this model, only competition that takes steps aimed at lessening these disparities can be called fair.

The Debate Reconsidered

How do these two positions, the traditional approach and the social welfare-based approach, view each other? The traditional approach responds to Rawls that distributive justice does not require that each agent *deserve* everything she has obtained, merely that she has played by the rules (enforced by the government). As Robert Nozick once famously said, it need not be that the foundations underlying desert are themselves deserved, *all the way down*.[12] Under this account, it is irrelevant to justice whether one deserves one's natural or social advantages. They are what one is given. So long as one goes forth from the starting point and obeys all the rules, then justice is upheld. However, Rawls would demur by claiming that natural talents are collectively held. If this is so, then the least advantaged has some claim upon the goods possessed by those who are society's winners in the key competitions of life because of natural talent or social position.

Those evaluating the arguments supporting the above positions should note that much depends upon the understanding of the agent and her role in society. If the agent is primarily seen as a largely separate autonomous entity acting for herself as much as possible, then the traditional position will seem most appealing. The individual cannot help how she begins life. Why make her "pay" for her positive talents and advantages as she competes for life's more exotic prizes? If one begins at a fundamental position of a Lockean state of nature, then it is after all one's use of natural resources that would determine ownership. For Locke, the process of making a valid property claim depends upon one actually using what is claimed. If one fails to use the land or ceases to use the land, then there is no valid claim. (This "use" principle is also behind the concept of adverse possession that entitles one to engage in a valid taking of another's property if the owner is not using it and does not defend it.) The "use" principle is based upon a presupposition that it is individual effort that counts the most in competing for goods.

Hobbes complicates the picture even further by suggesting that all agents are different but equal. If one person has natural advantage A to the nth degree then another will have a different but equally as effective natural advantage B to a degree such that both can compete upon an equal footing. If one finds these depictions of the state of nature fundamentally correct, then the individualistic position again seems most plausible.

However, if one sees the individual as contextually linked in a kingdom of ends, then the story plays out differently. For the social welfare advocate to make her case, it is necessary to conceptualize society as radically interdependent. The ideas of John Donne ("No man is an island entire of itself, every man is a piece of the Continent, a part of the main" *Meditation* XVII, l.5) or Martin Luther King, Jr. ("Injustice anywhere is a threat to justice everywhere" *Letter from a Birmingham Jail*) describe a society in which there are no largely separate individuals. Each person in society is connected to every other person such that the proposition that natural assets are collective is entirely plausible. Competition under this model is quite different from the individualistic account. Second, Rawls's difference principle can be seen as a response to the question of moral luck. How much should one's personal happiness depend upon factors outside one's control? How much should our judgment of others depend upon luck (natural talents or social position)? If it seems *wrong* for luck to be determinant without recompense from the community, then you are probably on the side of social welfare.

The Deserts-Based Position

Joel Feinberg has said that desert without a basis is simply not a desert.[13] Feinberg then calls for some sort of basis so that if a person is deserving of some sort of treatment, he must, necessarily, be so in virtue of some possessed characteristic or prior activity.

The traditional position asserts that reward is based upon merit and merit is based upon achievement (as per Andy and the sales contest). The deserts position agrees with this in part. Janus affords one of his gazes in this direction. The traditional and the deserts-based positions concur that merit is based upon achievement, but the traditional position measures achievement as an outcome only. The deserts position turns Janus' face the other way, as he measures achievement on the basis of work done by the individual without the advantage of any preferment. Thus, if you were a manager for the ABC Widget Corporation and your northeast sales staff was dominated by a producer named Andy who has family connections that allow him uniquely to always lead the company in sales, if you wanted to have a sales contest that would motivate producers and increase production, you should make the sales contest based upon bettering your last year's rolling average by some percentage. Such a sales contest would reward those who improve from where they are and mute the undeserved advantages Andy has due to family. Thus, in hiring and compensation practices, advocates of the deserts position strive to look at how far each individual has gone and strive to encourage and reward personal growth (and not just absolute outcomes).

In contrast to Rawls's social welfare conception, the deserts position judges merit upon past actions and not upon some sort of social, utopian goal.

The traditional meritocracy model of competition might ask, for example, "Who do you want doing your newly mandated Sarbanes-Oxley corporate audits each year— a person who has graduated from a top business school or someone who went to a mid-tier or lower-tier school and was probably admitted under Affirmative Action?" The assumption under the traditional model is that the former person has reached some higher level of technical competency and therefore merits the contract. Those advocating the deserts model would ask further questions about both candidates.

It might be the case that the latter candidate has had to work very hard for everything he's gotten while the former candidate got into school because his family has always given a lot of money to the school. The former candidate's status of achievement may not be indicative of how well he might perform over the long haul. Since so much has been given to him, and since the latter candidate has already demonstrated an ability to overcome adversity, the deserts model would suggest hiring the mid or lower-tier graduate (because of his previous degree in the school of hard knocks).

Obviously, this is a case at the extremes. However, it is put forth to make an abstract point about merit and competition. Like the social welfare-based approach, the deserts model recognizes that some people have natural and environmental advantages that can include some or all of the following when it comes to the ability to compete for society's goods:

- adequate food, clothing, shelter, and protection from unwarranted bodily harm;
- basic educational opportunity;
- being treated with dignity and love for who you are;
- a nurturing home environment;
- parental models for patterning behavior (that the society views positively);
- freedom from disabling disease, whether it be mental or physical;
- inside connections affecting admission to universities and to the professions;
- affluence.[14]

Obviously, this list could go on and on. But when Mr. B speaks with hubris about how he has become a partner in the accounting firm, it may be important to know that Mr. B's father is the senior partner in the firm and got B his job in the first place (and has been holding B's hand all his life). This is the life of preferment that allows parents to present to their children an easy road. All the child has to do is not to screw up too badly and he's set for life.

This preferment list need not merely include socioeconomic factors. Race and gender may also be factors. According to the deserts-based model, this is *not* competitive success by merit; it is success by unmerited preferment. Thus, the deserts-based approach contends that it combines the definition of competitive merit (from the traditional model) with the concern for the distribution of natural and social advantage (the social welfare-based approach). Competition under this blended approach seeks the advantages of both standpoints.

Conclusion

This essay has presented several faces of competition. Social interest competition can be a powerful force for good. It appeals to our social human nature. However, it can be corrupted when the system within which one is striving is also corrupt—such as fascist and communist regimes that preach social virtues that really hide a totalitarian allocation policy of enriching those in charge because of their power.

More common in our world today is self-interested competition. Its traditional form can push people beyond the pale so that they break the rules and invalidate the meritocracy that is meant to be behind the competitive machinery. How do we run competitions so that they are fair? This essay has set forth three answers: the traditional position based upon unfettered individualism, the social welfare position based upon making allocations to certain competitors who seem to be disadvantaged at the outset (through no fault of their own), and the deserts position that seeks to reward what people have actually achieved on their own. The writer of this essay is most keen on the third interpretation of competition and merit.

Each of these three models of competition presents some partial truths about competition (no matter which is one's personal favorite). Further, it is necessary to view competition primarily within one of these contexts in order for there to be a rich enough concept that might drive social policy. Just as it is important to know where you are going in order to decide if you are to enter or exit the doorway, so also it is essential to be able to contextualize competition within a theory of merit in order to chart our social and political direction. Janus was the god of doorways, but it is up to us to discover which direction is the right one.

Notes

1   Janus had various temples in ancient Rome, but all of these temples ran east–west so that they could depict the sun rising and setting. Often Janus also had two doors between which stood his statue. These doors would only be closed when there was peace in Rome. In the first 700 years of these temples the doors were only closed three times: Edith Hamilton, *Mythology* (Boston: Little Brown, 1942); p. 51.

2   Two introductions to this subject include: Michael A. Bahrke and Charles E. Yesalis, *Performance-Enhancing Substances in Sport and Exercise* (Champaign, IL: Human Kinetics Publishers, 2002) and William Morgan (ed.) *Ethics in Sport* (Champaign, IL: Human Kinetics Publishers, 2007).

3   Charlton T. Lewis, Charles Short, and William Freund, *A Latin Dictionary* (Oxford: Oxford University Press, 1956).

4   For an overview of this sense of competition see the enormously influential A.W.H. Adkins, *Merit and Responsibility* (Oxford: Blackwell, 1959).

5   Lisa Newton, *Permission to Steal* (Oxford: Blackwell, 2006).

6   Smores are a wonderful concoction of graham crackers, marshmallows, and chocolate. This is the equivalent of "heaven" to boy scouts of this era.

7   On October 17, 1992, Yoshihiro Hattori, a Japanese exchange student in Baton Rouge, Louisiana, mistakenly knocked on the wrong door and was shot by the homeowner who reported rage at Japan for taking away American Jobs.

8   Bernard Mandeville, *The Fable of the Bees* (Indianapolis, IN: Hackett, 1997 [1714]).

9   Readers of this essay may want to look at my encyclopedia entry on Thomas Jefferson in *The Encyclopedia of Philosophy*, 2nd edn, ed. Donald M. Borchert (Farmington Hills, MI: Macmillan, 2006).

10 Daniel Bell, *The Coming of Post-Industrial Society* (New York: Basic Books, 1976).

11 John Rawls, *A Theory of Justice* (Cambridge, MA: Harvard University Press, 1971).

12 Robert Nozick, *Anarchy, State, and Utopia* (New York: Basic Books, 1974).

13 Joel Feinberg, *Doing and Deserving* (Princeton, NJ: Princeton University Press, 1970).

14 I discuss this in further detail in *A Just Society* (Lanham, MD: Rowman and Littlefield, 2004), Chapters 3 and 7.

The Principle of Fair Competition

MICHAEL BOYLAN

I believe that a businessperson faces the following factors when making a decision:

1. *Professional considerations (broadly conceived)*. Here I follow Alasdair MacIntyre, who uses a sense of practice to develop the internal perspective of the shared community worldview.[1] MacIntyre says, "A practice involves standards of excellence and obedience to rules as well as the achievement of goods. To enter into a practice is to accept the authority of those standards and the inadequacy of my own performances as judged by them."[2] For our purposes, this definition provides the following.

First, to attain the products of the profession, a person must accept the internal rules to the practice. This means that she must accept the profession as being worthy, as being governed by rules, as having an authority, and that to enter into the profession, she must submit to its authority and its rules.

Second, accepting authority entails the following: (a) realizing that an individual is incapable as an agent to judge or alter the rules until that person has mastered them, (b) accepting the fact that to become a master of the rules, the individual must give herself over to the rules, and (c) that she must consequently give herself over to the rules.

Third, giving herself over to the rules entails (a) accepting the authority of the shared community's worldview over her personal worldview and (b) accepting the authority of the shared community's worldview when specific tenets of the shared community worldview conflict with her personal worldview.[3]

MacIntyre's design is to tie excellence in attaining the goods internal to the profession to turning oneself over to it. This excellence is virtue (in the traditional sense of Aristotle and Aquinas), and the internal structure of the profession ties together the practitioners (present, past, and future); therefore, the foundation of excellence is social. This constitutes an argument for Virtue Ethics.

I suggest that the internal practice constitutes the internal standpoint of the shared community worldview. In the context of Professional Ethics, this can be understood as the profession itself.

2. *Cost considerations*. These are self-evident (whatever will increase *benefit* on a cost-benefit analysis).[4]

3. *Worldview interactions*. Whatever personal worldview values an individual possesses interact with the shared community's worldview. The personal worldview dictates what each of us thinks are "fair" parameters for competition. The shared worldview dictates what is professionally acceptable for competition. These acceptable practices may vary from profession to profession.

An original essay from the 1st edition of this volume.

For example, in one case an individual's personal worldview may dictate less restrictive guidelines than the professional shared worldview. In another case, the personal worldview may be more restrictive than the professional worldview. (In some cases—quite the minority, I believe—an individual's worldview may exactly mirror the professional worldview.) In the less restrictive and the more restrictive situations, the individual is at a disadvantage (in the former because he will possess a flawed worldview and in the latter because he will be at a competitive disadvantage).

In the first case, a salesperson, manager, or executive may exceed what is considered to be professionally acceptable to make the sale. Let us assume, for example, that a life insurance salesperson has created a computer printout as a marketing tool for a prospective universal life policy showing that particular interest rates will be credited to excess monies in the account. In our example, the salesperson has used interest rate assumptions that are higher than the company pays its current policies. Thus, the salesperson is acting contrary to the industry practice of quoting only what the company is currently paying for such policies.

By projecting higher interest rates than the company actually pays, the salesperson will probably make more sales, but what justifies the person's taking a less restrictive worldview in this situation? Clearly, the justification is a primary emphasis on cost considerations and personal gain. As a primary emphasis, this worldview trumps most other considerations and may express itself through selfish egoism.[5] I have detailed my problems with selfish egoism elsewhere.[6] In short, it seems to me that selfish egoism fails the consistency test of the Personal Worldview Imperative (PWI): All people must develop a single comprehensive and internally coherent worldview that is good and that we strive to act out in our daily lives.[7]

Therefore, unless we alter our worldview to become ethical egoists or adopt a complicated supernatural superstructure to support it,[8] we are involved in an inconsistent position when we assert an egoistic position. Individuals whose personal worldview violates the PWI will be forced (on the pain of being irrational)[9] to alter their position. They must conform (at least) to the minimal professional standard.

In the second case, individual values are more restrictive than the professional standard. In this situation, the individuals involved are at a competitive disadvantage, but this does not necessarily mean failure. In many environments, competition is not overly fierce and there is enough business for anyone willing to work hard and provide superior service. This strategy implies failure only when intense competition exists; in this event, entering an arena with one hand tied behind your back will put you at a disadvantage. I believe this to be a fact but this is not always bad, in my opinion. This is so because I do not believe that totally maximizing prudential benefits is an imperative (by itself alone) that is fruitful to follow. If a person found herself in a business so competitive (meaning many people working in a very limited market) that only those who violate standard professional practice (not to mention the law, in many cases) were able to succeed, then she should either discover a novel marketing slant (honestly outthinking her adversaries) or leave that field. There are always other ways for her to use her skills. Most business skills such as sales and customer relations are clearly transferable to other business venues and to more specialized endeavors, such as law and accounting.

The old adage that behind every challenge there is an opportunity may be pertinent here. By acting contrary to an individual's personal worldview, he will either hate himself or become so numb that much of what makes life worthwhile may disappear.[10] A person cannot authentically act contrary to her worldview because such action fragments who she is by forcing her to adopt multiple, conflicting personal and shared community worldviews. Thus, unless a person can find a legitimate approach by which to succeed (through honest innovation), she should move to something else, even if this entails temporary financial insecurity. Such an action promotes wholeness, that is to say, *integrity*.[11]

I view these relationships on a continuum of functional excellence. At one level is the *krateristic* group of people who live in a worldview of unbridled selfish egoism; in other words, they believe that might makes right. They would be very at home with Plato's depiction of Thrasymachus and Callicles.[12] These men believed that in life the powerful take what they can get; the more powerful restrained them. If someone could put them in jail, then they would pay attention to that person who had the power to do so. Otherwise, these men acted on the sole imperative of pleasing themselves and gratifying their personal whims.

The next level represents the law. All countries have legal principles to stop the most egregious selfish egoists. Of course, these laws must be enforced, but enforcement in many countries of the world (now and throughout history) has been the exception rather than the rule. The rich and powerful selfish egoists are allowed to have their own way even though they have broken the law.

The third level is based on the standards of professional practice. Our broad sense of profession outlined earlier stated that the hallmarks for professionalism are that one must accept that (a) the practice is worthy, (b) the practice is governed by rules, (c) whatever governs the practice has authority within the province of the practice, and (d) to enter into the practice, a person must submit to the authority of the practice and its rules.

Set in this way, the level of the standard of professional practice is more exacting that the legal standard (although in some cases the law may punish those who stray from the professional standard). Thus, in some instances, the legal and professional standards are the same. However, even in those instances there is really another, informal sense of the professional standard that separates itself from the *de jure* enforced standard and outlines what a good practice is.

Beyond the professional standard is another picture of an excellent member of the profession. This individual exceeds professional standards and is considered excellent to a high degree. This is the individual who has been able to compete in the world of business and still maintain wholeness. This is the person of integrity.

The person of integrity stands as the most admired of all who value the standards of the profession. This person accepts the constraints and limitations of the profession—and more. Even with these constraints (and in some cases *because* of these constraints), the person still excels in the practice of the occupation.

This continuum can be depicted in Figure 4.1. Thus, those who choose to compete at the levels of X and Y are lawbreakers driven by selfish egoism. I am sorry to say that in many professions, this group of individuals represents (by far) the largest group of people. These people thrive because it is generally impossible to bring every lawbreaker to justice (barring a significant hundredfold increase in law enforcement personnel). Thus, this group plays the odds that they will not be caught. Because they have such a

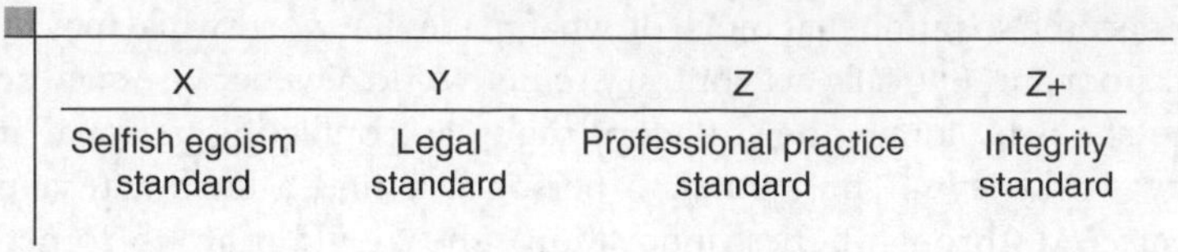

X	Y	Z	Z+
Selfish egoism standard	Legal standard	Professional practice standard	Integrity standard

Figure 4.1   Standards for Competition

competitive advantage over those playing by the rules, this is the group that includes most tycoons of the world.

The next largest group of individuals operate between Y and Z. These individuals do not break the law, but they are not exemplary members of their profession. They look for a smaller competitive edge by acting within the law but sometimes unprofessionally.

The penultimate group consists of those who always strive to meet the professional standards. These people cannot be faulted for their behavior because they always seek to do exactly what a member of the profession should do. However, as good as this group is, it is not as high as those who rise to the level of integrity.

People of integrity seek to affirm all of their worldview values by their professional lives, which creates wholeness and requires them to fulfill additional standards in executing their professional roles (community worldviews).

It is not uncommon for a person who has a coherent, consistent personal worldview to seek to become a member of a community that shares the individual's worldview. Such a person exhibits a desire for wholeness; to be one person at work and another at home creates an unacceptable incoherence within the person's worldview. Therefore, a person should actively seek a business situation in which his personal and ethical values are not violated by working in the particular profession.

Such a depiction of the competitive arena underlies my Principle of Fair Competition, which can be stated formally: All businesspeople should strive always to compete at or above the level of accepted professional practice with a view toward advancing toward the level of integrity. This principle assumes several things. First, it assumes that the creation of the standard of professional practice occurs in a free and open way from the bottom up. That is, it is created by people who actually do the work involved. The personal worldview of these people interacts with the shared community worldview of the emerging profession. It is assumed that if the practices are open and responsive to the members of the profession, sound ethical rules that reflect the practical needs of the profession will develop.

Of course, one can imagine that in totalitarian top-down regimes, standards are *imposed* on the members of a profession and are shams. They are not authentic professional standards and thus do not fall under the purview of the principle of fair competition.

The principle of fair competition seeks to offer concrete direction as to how a person should behave as a businessperson. If a person is operating within a free and open society, then the person should first discover what the law is, second what the professional standard is, and third who the most admired practitioners are. A person should begin with the professional standard and seek to emulate the behavior of the most admired practitioners.

Some might say that this approach is rather idealistic. They might suggest that people who have jobs are lucky and jeopardize those jobs if they demand that their employers adhere to professional standards. This is a real problem. The power situation between employer and employee is vastly unequal, and good jobs are not easy to obtain.

This vast power inequality between employer and employee is the source of many problems in the workplace, including sexual harassment. For example, Mr. Big approaches a subordinate and interacts with her. His position of power eliminates any true sense of "consensual" behavior because what seems consensual to him is *not* necessarily consensual to her. The reason for this is that he holds a power advantage over her. Therefore, if she consents, she may do so because she is thinking of how much she needs her job to support herself and her family. She may be thinking that if she refuses, she might be fired (not for refusing sex, for no employer would fire an employee for that reason) but for some other reason. (When a boss wants to fire a person, she will find a way within the limits of the law.)[13]

In the rare (lucky) circumstance in which an employee is so valuable to his employer that he can dictate his own terms, this power dynamic is not a problem in the workplace. Even when it is the case, most employers try to pretend that many other people can perform the employee's job. The employer emphasizes how lucky the person is to have the job. This is a fact; we are all lucky to have the jobs we have. Does this mean, however, that we must abnegate our personal dignity to keep our jobs? Absolutely not. The basic rights we are entitled to morally are not a function of our bargaining position. If any person X deserves Y, then what X deserves does not depend upon Y's coming-to-be (based on some irrelevant set of circumstances or other fictions).

I believe that the essential point to be made in business ethics is that most cases in real life involve conflicts among professional values, cost issues, and our personal worldview (which determines all that we personally value, including ethics). Seldom are there easy, totally fair adjudications. People who obey the rules often lose to those who do not—this is a fact. However, this fact does not provide a license to do whatever selfish egoism dictates; instead, it is an admission that the final goals in life must be more than obtaining the most money and power. This is a state of balanced consciousness in which a person is content knowing that she is living within chosen guidelines that compose her individual worldview. Such a state of balanced consciousness supersedes the imperatives of winning.

I offer an analogy to sports to illustrate this point. I have been an athlete of sorts and a coach of youth sports for more than thirty-five years. The way athletes compete has always been a point of fascination to me. Some athletes openly violate the sport's standards. I once was in an AAU crosscountry regional meet in which the runner just in front of me cut the corners on the turns and did not obey the flags posted to define the course. This runner's ability was probably equal to mine, but I lost because he cut the turns and I did not.

Other athletes adhere to a standard but push the envelope to enhance the professional practice standard. This is especially true in basketball. Basketball players are often trained to develop "tricks" (such as thrusting his hand into the abdomen of the shooter he is guarding to throw off the shooter's concentration or to "undercut" the shooter early in the game so that later he will fear injury on some crucial jump). Basketball players learn these and many other tricks to give them the competitive edge. Sports in general support the adages that nice guys finish last and that winning is not the most important thing—it is the only thing. Do we agree with this?

Most of us do not agree. We believe that fair competition begins at the standard of professional practice—this is the benchmark. Those who operate at any lower level are behaving badly and thus diminish themselves. When we exceed the standard of acceptable professional practice, we move toward the goal of professional or personal integrity, a level of excellence in which the practitioner exceeds the standard of professional practice by integrating her worldview into the shared community worldview. When one achieves the level of professional or personal integrity, she rises to a level of personal excellence that defines *telos* of all human endeavor.

In order to engage the reader further to the model I am presenting, let me pose some questions that have been put to me as I have lectured on this topic over the past few years.

Q: You describe the principle of fair competition as a linking principle to moral action. Describe in more detail just how it operates between the theoretical and the practical.

A: All moral linking principles (as I conceive of them) must have some logical origin in theory. However, they must also contain a high amount of empirical content so that everyone can readily apply them to action. This property must be very clear or the linking principle will be of very limited value.

First, in the case of the Principle of Fair Competition ("All business-people should strive always to compete at or above the level of accepted professional practice with a view toward advancing toward the level of integrity"), we must start with its link in moral theory. This link is established because the level of accepted professional practice is grounded in the fair and open interplay between individual worldviews (all of which will reflect various moral theories) and the shared community worldview (that will be the synthesis of the functional demands of the profession in light of the values of its members).

Second is the level of practice. Because the principle is also grounded in the functional demands of the profession, it will always be action guiding in its prescriptions.

Q: Isn't this theory of personal excellence (fair competition) rather remote for the average person?

A: Not really. It is a myth that people are most concerned with selfish egoism before all else. In my own experience on this earth (which includes a dozen years at or below the poverty level), I have found that people in lower economic circumstances are most often concerned with being true to their core worldview values. It is all that they have of any worth. Oddly enough, I believe that it is often the affluent who are overly concerned with maximizing their prudential gains.

This is not an overly idealistic prescription because it is something that is in our personal control. All of us can practice our jobs at the level of professional practice and above. Not all of us can become wealthy. Why not fulfill what is within our power when the rewards of personal harmony are there for the taking? This is a linking principle for everyone.

Q: What about the "owners" of the corporation—the stockholders—don't we owe them the highest possible return on their investment?

A: No. This is another myth. Investors deserve the highest possible return, all things considered. This caveat means the following:

1. Investors do not own the employees of the corporation. This means that the people who make up the company should be *expected* to express their highest values as they perform their jobs. Why sort of company would want less? Only one that wants to exploit its workers; only one that seeks to control people as if they were cogs in some giant machine. Such a company has an immoral purpose.
2. Investors cannot reasonably expect the company to break the law. They should not expect the company to operate only at the standard of the law. Such an attitude fosters a "wink-and-nod" mentality that is really nothing more than the standard of selfish egoism.
3. Companies that embrace the highest values within their employees' personal worldviews will foster a loyal and committed workforce that will honorably and fairly compete in the marketplace.

Thus, I believe that investors deserve to have everyone work hard, work honestly, work professionally, and, within those parameters, bring in the highest possible profit.

Q: When you say that people ought to leave overly competitive situations that are fraught with immoral business practices, aren't you really becoming part of the problem by not advocating a solution?

A: Perhaps. This is meant to be a practical prescription rather than a "perfect world" direction. Certainly, if one could *change* a widespread, immoral business practice, then she or he should do it. But most of us don't have such power; we are bits of sand in a landscape dominated by mountains. My point is that we should not just accept that the marketplace in which we are making our money is corrupt, and therefore, we should be corrupt, too (because that's the only way to make a living there).

It may be a fact that the marketplace is corrupt and that the only way to make a living there is to be corrupt also, but this fact does not compel *us* to be corrupt. We can get out of that marketplace. Even those with highly specialized skills can adapt their skills to a new venue. Unless they do so, they will fragment themselves and thus lead a life that is less satisfactory (assuming that the integrated personal worldview is more satisfactory than the disjointed, fragmented worldview).

Q: Since the Principle of Fair Competition depends on the accepted level of professional practice, isn't it really just another form of ethical relativism?

A: Not really. This is because, as a linking principle to moral action, the Principle of Fair Competition has ties to moral theory. I have described the societal circumstances that might foster proper standards for professional practice (free and open societies). In other situations, it is possible that professional standards that are ethically abhorrent might emerge. This is not the fault of the Principle of Fair Competition but of the oppressive totalitarian society. Any clear thinking, rational person will be able to see through such a sham.

The professional standard is functionally tied to the demands of the profession. From this, an *ethos* develops that considers the functional needs of the profession with the moral expression so that any and all practitioners can feel secure because clear guidelines have been established on how this job (all things considered) *ought* to be performed. Clear and fair rules mean that all businesspeople should strive always to compete at or above the level of accepted professional practice with a view to advancing toward the level of integrity.

The arena for this agreement will proximately occur in the national marketplace. It can also occur in our global economy. I believe that such agreement can spread across nations to create international standards of acceptable practice. It is when we achieve such agreement that the term *business ethics* will cease to be an oxymoron to many people and will instead express our highest aspirations about how people can and should act.

Notes

1 I develop the concepts of worldview, shared worldview, and the Personal Worldview Imperative in my book *Basic Ethics* (Upper Saddle River, NJ: Prentice Hall, 2000).

2 Alasdair MacIntyre, *After Virtue: A Study in Moral Theory*, 2d ed. (London: Duckworth, 1985); p. 190.

3 My comments here should clearly indicate that these consequences of accepting a practice, as defined by MacIntyre, come from my critical understanding of this process and are not meant to be an exact paraphrase of MacIntyre.

4 This is obviously a complicated issue. Many factors must be considered, such as the time frame of expected results, relation to strategic plan, crucial environmental effects, and so forth. For this analysis, let the benefit stand for (all things considered) the highest prudential consequential advantage to the company.

5 I intend *selfish egoism* to refer to a decision-making mechanism that looks to personal, prudential benefit above all else when making an action decision.

6 For a discussion of some of the most important issues involving egoism see the introduction to my text *Basic Ethics* (Upper Saddle River, NJ: Prentice Hall, 2000).

7 I outline an argument for the Personal Worldview Imperative in *Basic Ethics*.

8 I am thinking here of Plato's theory of reincarnation (very similar to Hinduism). One *could* by fiat create a situation in which the ethical action would always be to one's ultimate advantage. The issue is how much one must give up, logically speaking, to accept these added tenets?

9 My position here is that to be irrational is to violate one's human nature. We are, by nature, rational animals. This is not to exclude other aspects of our nature, such as human love and sympathy, but these are always to be understood in relation to rationality.

10 I also believe that many personally self-destructive behaviors, such as alcoholism and drug abuse, may begin this way.

11 This assumes, of course, that a person is not in a position to revise the system and expel those who are violating the professional standards. This would be an ideal answer but is rarely a practical alternative.

12 These characters are famous advocates of might makes right and selfish egoism is all that counts. See Plato, *Republic* I and *Gorgias*.

13 This scenario obviously works in the other direction, too. When one factors in homo-sexual situations, the possibilities increase, but the same principle still holds.

B. Advertising

The Advertising of Happiness and the Branding of Values

EDWARD H. SPENCE

1. Introduction

The object of this essay is to offer an ethical analysis and evaluation of the strategy and practice in advertising of associating brands with values so as to render those brands more marketable and ultimately more saleable. To that end, the methodology employed, as befits the discipline of moral philosophy and applied ethics, is conceptual analysis supported by sound rational arguments. This analysis will attempt to demonstrate that the association of brands with values is ethically problematic. The primary purpose of the essay is to explore if there is a prima facie ethical problem concerning the systematic and pervasive association of commodity brands with values. A second, related but independent, purpose, one not pursued in this essay, is to establish the initial motivation and basis for a further empirical investigation, through interdisciplinary research, of the ethical impact that the association of brands with values has on consumers, and especially on young people and children.

2. The Manufacturing of Happiness

"Happiness is . . . Hyundai" boldly declares an advertisement for Hyundai, the South Korean car manufacturer. Nice use of alliteration, but is it true? As an identity statement of the type X = Y it can't of course be true, as "happiness" is not strictly speaking the same thing as a "car with the brand name "Hyundai." Perhaps the statement merely suggests, implicitly if not explicitly, that the possession of a Hyundai car can make a person that owns one, happy. Even if not intended as a true statement in this secondary sense, the statement seems at least designed, through its association of "happiness" with the brand "Hyundai," to create a favorable impression and a pro-attitude towards the brand in the mind of the consumer. It is designed to do so by the creation of a conceptual link of something highly valued and desired, such as happiness, to a specific brand name of a car. By doing so, it is hoped that the high value and desirability that people usually attribute to happiness will be transferred in the mind of the consumer to the brand of the car itself.[1]

The Japanese car manufacturer Toyota seems to attempt something not dissimilar with their well-known and now instantly recognizable ad jingle "Oh what a feeling, Toyota!" which is usually accompanied by a picture of a seemingly jubilant Toyota owner jumping in the air with joy. At least that seems to be a reasonable interpretation of the ad, based on how those words and human movements are normally understood in popular culture. Not missing out on the happiness bandwagon, the cosmetics company Clinique uses an ad caption for one of its perfumes to proclaim, "Happy"— "Clinique happy" next to a picture of a young woman's seemingly contorted face of happiness. In its advertising campaign for Kraft Singles sliced cheese, Kraft joins the chorus with "Have a happy sandwich."[2]

3. The Association of Brands with Values

Another way in which consumer brands are associated with the concept of happiness is indirectly through the association of those brands with values and attributes that are generally highly regarded and valued in their own right but also valued as being conducive to happiness. Values and attributes such as "friendship," "truth," "romance," "grace," "elegance," "carefree," "freedom," "independence," "beauty," and "love," to name but a few, have been regularly associated with various consumer brands. For example: *friendship* with bourbon in the Jim Beam ad, "Real friends. Real bourbon"; *truth* with the Calvin Klein perfume "Truth"; *amazing grace* with a woman's watch in an ad by Pulsar; *romance* with the perfume "Romance" by Ralph Lauren; *elegance* with a watch in an ad by Longines; *carefree* with a brand name for tampons; *a declaration of independence* with the perfume "Tommy Girl"; and, not least, *lovable* with "Lovable," a brand of women's lingerie. Philosophy, the pursuit of wisdom, is not spared either. *Philosophy* is also a brand name for ladies handbags.

Insofar as those attributes and values are generally seen as contributing factors to people's happiness and wellbeing, their ubiquitous association with consumer products is ethically problematic in the way that will be explained under four separate arguments below. Additionally, insofar as those attributes and values are in themselves considered highly valuable and important by most people, and not merely by virtue of being viewed as contributing factors to happiness, then their pervasive and cumulative association with consumer products in advertisements can also be seen as ethically problematic. For the arguments are intended to show that such an association diminishes and degrades those attributes and values—it *devalues* them.

In summary, the association of brands with values deceives people by the implied suggestion that they too can have independence, beauty, friendship, elegance, romance, truth, and love in their lives simply by wearing a certain watch, perfume, or lingerie (the argument from deception). It exploits the gullibility of the young and vulnerable by that implied suggestion (the argument from exploitation). Insofar as it subverts the importance of those attributes and values, it sets up a bad example for children, thus undermining the importance of those attributes and values for future generations of citizens (the argument from setting a good example and protecting the vulnerable). And finally, it is paradoxical as it generates an internal inconsistency within the advertising messages themselves (the argument form paradox). In doing so, it undermines a fundamental and necessary epistemological condition for all communication of information, that of rational consistency. For communication that violates the basic principle of noncontradiction, namely, "Not 'A and not A'," at the same time and in the same respect, is epistemologically problematic in that it can cause confusion and ambiguity in meaning that undermines all meaningful communication. As a persuasion strategy this might seem acceptable and instrumentally useful but ethically it might prove to be objectionable if it misleads or exploits its intended audience.

Aspirational values,[3] attributes, and feelings, such as happiness, freedom, friendship, independence, beauty, elegance, grace, love, and truth, amongst others, comprise our common cultural, aesthetic, and ethical heritage which creates the moral environment in which we socially interact as citizens. It is indeed paradoxical how as *consumers* we, through ignorance, or indifference, or negligence, allow those aspirational values, attributes, and feelings, that give social, aesthetic, and ethical meaning and direction to our lives as *citizens*, to be subverted and corrupted by pervasive advertising. This is done through their constant and cumulative association with commodities and brands for the sake of satisfying our collective craving for more consumer products.

4. The Feel Good Argument

As an advertising strategy, the association of consumer products or services (for simplicity, the term "products" will henceforth refer to both products and services) makes rational instrumental sense. Consider the following argument—let us refer to this argument as the "Feel Good Argument":

1. The ultimate object of advertising is to persuade consumers to feel predisposed towards a particular product in the hope that consumers may actually become disposed to purchasing that product.
2. People are generally pro-disposed to their own happiness and the things that contribute directly or indirectly to their happiness.
3. The association of consumer products with the concept and images of happiness are designed to create in consumers the same pro-attitude or predisposition towards the products advertised as people have towards their own happiness and its contributing associated values.
4. If the association of consumer products with the concept and images of happiness in the relevant ads is successful, it is very likely that consumers will be persuaded through that association to feel pro-disposed to the advertised consumer products and become inclined to purchase those products.
5. Therefore, insofar as the strategy of associating consumer products with the concept of happiness is likely to succeed and prove effective that strategy seems eminently instrumentally rational. For, if successful, it utilizes effective means in achieving the ultimate goal of advertising: the promotion of the sale of consumer products. Moreover, it does so without offering much information about the products other than the implied suggestion that possession of those products is likely to make one feel happy.
6. Thus the strategy of associating consumer products with the concept and images of happiness if successful proves to be information efficient as it persuades through minimal content of product information. Moreover, in a market saturated with consumer products that prima facie at least have product parity, differentiating a specific product like a car or a perfume from other similar competitors through

the association of that product with aspirational values, such as happiness for example, seems to make good professional and business sense.

The "Feel Good Argument" seems to indicate that the advertising strategy of associating consumer products with the concept of happiness is instrumentally rational. This may help to partly explain the pervasive use of this strategy in contemporary advertising. For the strategy, if successful, promises, at least in its design, to achieve the ultimate goal of advertising, namely, the maximization of persuasion power over consumers to purchase consumer products at minimal information cost.

However, even if it is instrumentally rational, is the strategy of seeking to persuade people to purchase consumer products through their association with the highly valued and desirable state of happiness, and its associated values, ethical? Does the association of products with the concept of happiness and other values amount to a suggested promise of elusive happiness acquisition through a never-ending spiral of possession and consumption of material goods? Goods that the targeted consumers may not in fact need or the possession of which is unlikely to make those consumers happy? Is this a case of a false promise or perhaps a case of a promise that cannot be fulfilled and, if so, does the mere implied suggestion of such promises constitute a type of deception? If it does, is this type of deception a form of exploitation—a strategy of seeking to persuade people to acquire products by misleadingly appealing to their highest aspiration for happiness attainment?

5. The Ethical Dimension of Happiness

Before attempting to answer these questions, let us first look briefly at the concept of "happiness." According to the Greek philosopher Aristotle the ultimate goal in life for every person is to be happy (Aristotle 1953). For who wouldn't want to be happy? People may pursue its attainment in many different ways, some through wealth, fame, job satisfaction, social status, having a family, good health, and good friends, but all these things are intermediate means towards the ultimate goal of being happy. Perceived by Greek and Roman philosophers including Aristotle, Plato, the Epicureans, and the Stoics to be of fundamental importance to our lives, happiness or *eudaimonia* was placed at the center of their respective philosophical systems.[4] These philosophers understood happiness or *eudaimonia* not merely as short-term gratification but, far more importantly, as long-term self-fulfillment or self-actualization. Aristotle referred to a happy life as a *flourishing* life. Thus a key practical goal of these philosophies was to at once explore the nature of happiness and determine the best possible means for its attainment. Conceived as *the art of living* (*techne biou*), Greek and, later, Roman philosophy sought to systematically explore and discover the best way to live one's life so as to attain maximum and long-lasting happiness or *eudaimonia*.

Although these philosophers argued about the nature of happiness and the means of its attainment in different and sometimes opposing ways, they all thought that an essential condition for being truly happy was the adoption of an ethical lifestyle that emanated from a virtuous character, the idea being that unethical conduct undermined one's integrity and corrupted one's character, which, in turn, could, at least potentially, undermine one's chances for real and lasting happiness. Unethical conduct was thus perceived as self-defeating. It was seen as using unsuitable means that were, at least potentially, more conducive to the defeat than to the fulfillment of one's ultimate goal of attaining happiness. An example of this would be a corrupt police officer. His acceptance of bribes for financial gain, for example, undermines his personal and professional integrity and risks a shameful dismissal and judicial punishment. This is self-defeating as it could, potentially at least, have the opposite effect to his desired goal of being happy. Martha Stewart's conviction and imprisonment for insider trading in America and that of Rene Rivkin in Australia for a similar offence are examples of how greed proves self-defeating because it potentially results in unhappiness, not happiness.[5]

The connection between ethics and happiness, even if not as close as the Greek and Roman philosophers thought it was, is nevertheless an important one. For it is reasonable to claim that, even if ethical conduct is not always essential for living a happy life, it is at least conducive to a happy life. At the very least it is conducive to the happiness of others who might otherwise suffer harm as a result of our own unethical conduct. For even if unethical conduct does not undermine our own happiness, doubtful as this may be, especially in the long run, it can nevertheless undermine the happiness of others. Thus, insofar as there seems to be a connection between ethics and happiness, the concept of happiness in professional and corporate practice generally, and advertising practice in particular, is an ethically important concept. It must therefore inform all professional and corporate practices and policies, including those of advertising. In the case of advertising, the conceptual connection between happiness and ethics is close and challenging since advertising is by and large in the business of creating and manufacturing images of "happiness." Hyundai's "Happiness is . . . Hyundai" and McDonald's "Happy Meal," are just two examples amongst many others.

6. Plato's Quarrel with the Poets: What Plato Can Teach Us about Advertising Ethics

Plato addresses his complaint against the poets in Books 2 and 3 of the *Republic*. In those passages Socrates, the protagonist of Plato's dialogues, is having a dialectical conversation with Adeimantus about the appropriate education for the guardians of the state.

To Adeimantus' astonishment, Socrates finds fault with two of the greatest poets of the time, Homer and Hesiod. The thrust of his complaint is that these and other poets "who have ever been the great story-tellers of mankind" (Plato, 1952) lie. In short, they lie about the true nature of the gods and that of heroes. They misrepresent the gods by depicting them as cunning, dissembling, profligate, quarrelsome, lascivious, hot-tempered, self-seeking, and self-serving, vain individuals who are morally no better, and sometimes worse, than ordinary men and women.

Socrates gives several examples of depictions by Homer of gods behaving badly. One in particular which he alludes to is the various transformations of Zeus, father of the gods, who changes into bulls, swans, and other disguises so that he may seduce and have his carnal way with earthly women. According to Socrates, "it is impossible that

God should ever be willing to change; being, as is supposed, the fairest and the best that is conceivable, every God remains absolutely and for ever in his own form." He goes onto say that "God is perfectly simple and true both in word and deed; he changes not; he deceives not, either by sign or word, by dream or waking vision," and concludes that "the gods are not magicians who transform themselves, neither do they deceive mankind in any way." Socrates' argument about the true nature of God is based on a conceptual analysis that ascribes to God, as the best of all that there is in the whole of existence, the quality of perfection. Being perfect, God would not want to change to something less perfect, especially as a self-seeking means for deceiving humans for his or her own selfish ends.

According to Socrates, the poets not only misrepresent the gods but they also misrepresent the true nature of heroes by depicting them as grabbing, selfish, arrogant, greedy, and callous egotists who, like Achilles, would only fight for ransom and gifts from the Greeks after his slave girl is taken from him by Agamemnon. He acts like a thug when after killing Hector he desecrates his body by tying it to his chariot and dragging it around the walls of Troy, refusing to surrender it for burial in contravention of divine and human laws. Is such a depiction of Achilles, the greatest of all the heroes, a true representation of what a hero is or at least ought to be? And what of the harmful effect that such a depiction might have on the impressionable minds of children? As Socrates claims "the young man should not be told that in committing the worst of crimes he is far from doing anything outrageous." He goes on to say that "a young person cannot judge what is allegorical and what is literal; anything that he receives into his mind at that age is likely to become indelible and unalterable; and therefore it is most important that the tales which the young first hear should be models of virtuous thoughts."

We can see now that Socrates' complaint against the poets is a fundamental and deep concern for moral education and how false depictions of gods and heroes in the poetry of his time can have a detrimental effect on the character of children and impressionable young persons who are not yet capable of critical and reflective thinking that allow them, through knowledge or experience, to discern truth from falsehood.

Socrates' arguments against the false depictions of gods and heroes in Homer's poetry are of two kinds. First, a *deontological argument* seeks to demonstrate that the depictions of gods and heroes by poets are inherently inconsistent since those depictions are in direct negation of the essential attributes that characterize gods and heroes alike. A deontological argument is a rational argument that purports to show that an action is morally wrong, or at least ethically problematic, if it is informed and motivated by thinking that involves an inherent logical contradiction. Immanuel Kant's *Categorical Imperative*,[6] for example, is based on this type of argument. So gods and heroes cannot behave badly and immorally in a way that denies their inherent excellence of character and divine perfection respectively. For vices are inconsistent with excellence of character and divine perfection. Given that heroes by definition possess or should possess excellence of character instantiated by virtues and the absence of vices, and gods possess perfect natures which cannot of necessity admit the imperfection of vices, depictions of gods and heroes that are inconsistent with the heroes' and gods' essential characteristics amount thus to lies.

So, for example, Achilles as a hero par excellence cannot, by definition, be ill tempered, arrogant, petulant, greedy, malicious, cruel, and unjust in the way described by Homer in the Iliad, just because those are vices that are in direct negation of the cardinal virtues such as courage, moderation, prudence, and justice that a hero must of necessity possess. Note also that, according to Plato and later the Stoics, virtues come in a package, so that if one is virtuous one must be in possession of all the cardinal virtues such as courage, prudence, moderation, and justice and not just some of them—it's either all or nothing. For even if we grant that Achilles was brave, the absence of moderation, prudence, and justice in his character would render him vicious, not virtuous.

To be courageous, one must sometimes moderate one's anger, which can take more courage than merely giving vent to it and seeking revenge at all costs. To be prudent, one must also be reverential to the gods as Achilles wasn't when he desecrated Hector's body and refused to give it back to the Trojans for burial. To be just, one must sometimes constrain one's self-interest with regard to the legitimate interests of others. Achilles, by contrast, allowed his self-interest and sulking pride to jeopardize the interests of his fellow Greeks by withdrawing from battle in a way that almost cost the Greeks the war.

So either Achilles, as depicted by Homer, was not a hero or he was a hero and was falsely depicted by Homer as being vicious rather than virtuous. Either way Homer lied about the true nature of heroes or about the true character of Achilles. So Homer's depiction of heroes generally, and his depiction of Achilles' character specifically, was a misrepresentation and thus a lie.

The second argument that Socrates uses against false poetical depictions of gods and heroes is a *consequentialist argument* which demonstrates that children and young people can be adversely influenced by these false depictions of gods and heroes and, furthermore, that encouraged by those depictions they may learn to act viciously and immorally as their false models of gods and heroes do. Consequentially, this could prove detrimental to the good of the state. A consequentialist argument is a rational argument that purports to show that an action is morally wrong if it results in bad consequences overall.

By combining the two arguments Socrates can rationally conclude that the false representations of gods and heroes in poetry is ethically problematic. The poets engaging in such false representations should be asked to carefully consider for themselves the inherent inconsistency and potential harmful consequences of their false representations and desist from doing so on the basis of their own self-censorship. Moreover, he goes on to argue that the young must be educated to be sceptical and critical of such poetry, thus being equipped and able to recognize the many ways in which poets such as Homer distort the truth of many things, including the truth about gods and heroes.

7. The Devaluation of Happiness and Values by Advertising

There are several reasons that can be offered to show that the association of the concept of happiness and other associated values with consumer products by advertising can be viewed as ethically problematic. In this section, I will use the two types of arguments used by Plato in his complaint against the poets, to support those reasons, three deontological and two consequentialist arguments.

7.1 Three deontological arguments

The argument from the diminution of values
As an important and highly valued personal and social goal for most people, the constant association of the concept of happiness and its associated values, either directly or indirectly, with consumer products diminishes and degrades the importance and value of that concept. For most people the acquisition of a new car or a new perfume might be desirable and contribute in some way to their short-term pleasure or happiness but it seems implausible to suggest that the serial and cumulative acquisition of commodities alone can constitute the whole of one's happiness. Happiness is a rich and complex tapestry comprising many different things, such as love, friendship, work satisfaction, family, education, social acceptance, travel, holidays, a stroll on the beach, creativity, the arts, and sport. It cannot, therefore, be reduced merely to the acquisition and consumption of products and their brands without degrading the richness and complexity of that concept. It cannot, without severely diminishing its value, be associated exclusively with a particular car, perfume, or any other specific consumer product. To be sure, the piecemeal association of the concept of happiness with a particular consumer product by a specific commercial may not necessarily undermine the value of that concept. Nevertheless, it is reasonable to postulate that the *cumulative* effect of many such commercials for many different products over a protracted period of time may have a degrading and diminishing effect on that concept.

The suggestion that a single type of consumer product can exclusively be identified with the concept of happiness, if taken seriously, would amount to a perversion or a subversion of the concept of happiness. On the other hand, that suggestion may not be taken seriously, for most people would probably recognize the identification of the concept of happiness with a particular product, be it a car or perfume, as merely an advertising gimmick, puffery, and exaggeration. But even the latter suggestion seems to amount to a diminution of the value and importance of the concept of happiness. For under the second suggestion, the concept of happiness is presented as something that can be treated lightly and trifled with. If people's happiness is not a trifling matter, as assuredly it is not, then it should not be treated as such. For to treat happiness as a trifling matter, in associating it with particular consumer products, is to treat the concept of happiness with disrespect. And by extension and parity of argument to also treat the majority of people who attach great value and importance to that concept with disrespect, even if unintentionally so. Ignorance, however, in treating others with disrespect by unintentionally diminishing the things they consider highly valuable, is not a valid excuse and doesn't let those who do it off the ethical hook. Thus ignorance of appropriate ethical conduct, like ignorance of the law, is not a valid defense against ethical transgressions. At best it is a form of moral negligence and that is equally ethically problematic.

The argument from deception
The association of a particular consumer product with the concept of happiness in the form of a straight identity claim of the sort Y = X ("Happiness . . . is Hyundai") is clearly

false. Happiness is neither identical with a car nor a perfume nor any other consumer product. However, the association in all probability is merely intended as an implied suggestion that the exclusive acquisition of a particular consumer product that is directly associated with the concept of happiness will somehow render the person who acquires and consumes it happy. This suggestion also seems, if not false, at least greatly exaggerated. It is highly unlikely that the exclusive acquisition and use of a specific consumer product could render one happy. For, as we all know, happiness is a multifaceted and multisplendored thing that comprises many different things, not all of which are consumer products, let alone one single individual consumer product or brand.

Gross exaggeration can be viewed as a form of deception, for it misrepresents a particular state of affairs. For if you boast to others that the proverbial fish you have caught far exceeds its actual size your exaggeration is a form of deception. Similarly, the implied suggestion that the acquisition of a specific product associated with the concept of happiness in an ad can make one happy seems like a gross exaggeration. If it is a gross exaggeration then it qualifies as a form of deception. Since all forms of deception, insofar as they seek to take an unjustified advantage over others, are generally considered to be unethical, deception through gross exaggeration must also be viewed as unethical.

Moreover, insofar as the association of happiness with consumer products cumulatively distorts the nature and significance of happiness through that association, that distortion could also be viewed as a form of deception and thus unethical.

The argument from paradox
The association of consumer products with the concept of happiness in advertising is paradoxical and involves a rational inconsistency. On the one hand, the concept of happiness is associated with consumer products in ads precisely because the creators and producers of those ads want to impart the same high value that people place on happiness to the associated advertised products. In other words, it is precisely because advertisers[7] take the generally recognized importance of happiness seriously that they choose to associate it with consumer products in the hope this will promote the sales of those products. On the other hand, however, the association of consumer products with the concept of happiness diminishes and thus degrades the value and the importance of that concept. This seems to suggest that, contrary to the generally recognized and acknowledged importance of happiness, the advertisers are not taking that importance seriously, at least ethically seriously. Thus those advertisers paradoxically at once acknowledge and undermine the importance of happiness. But this is ethically problematic. For something that is generally recognized and acknowledged as something highly valuable, and for that reason associated with consumer products, is nevertheless devalued though that association.

7.2 Two consequentialist arguments

The argument from setting a good example and protecting the vulnerable
The Crosby, Stills, Nash, and Young song "Teach Your Children Well" has a few valuable lessons for advertisers too. Do we collectively as a society treat our children well when we might be encouraging them through a plethora of ads to associate happiness with the sole acquisition of consumer products? Even if those ads are not

targeted at children, the pervasiveness and ubiquity of advertising can reach children through many different mediums and at different times. Insofar as the direct association of happiness with consumer products diminishes its value and perverts its significance (and that of its associated values) the effect of that diminution on children over a long period of time could have a negative effect on children's appreciation of the importance of values, such as happiness.

Related to this is the problem that children and other vulnerable groups of reduced critically informed judgment may come to believe the unbelievable, namely, that the sole acquisition of consumer products will render them happy. This perception could potentially result in serious repercussions of severe disappointment or unhappiness when the acquisition of those goods is not forthcoming or, if forthcoming, fails to live up to expectation. Society at large, including the advertising industry, has an ethical responsibility to safeguard the interests of the vulnerable members in our society. Encouraging them to identify the highly valued and important concept of happiness exclusively with the acquisition of specific consumer products is thus ethically undesirable.

The problem of child obesity is presently becoming so acute that the advertising industry in the UK, USA, and, currently, in Australia, has come under increasing community and government pressure to introduce regulatory guidelines that reduce if not eliminate junk food advertising to children. Under such proposed guidelines, McDonalds' "Happy Meal," for example, could be perceived as a case of manipulative advertising that targets children through an association of junk food with the concept of happiness. Consequently, such ads could become subject to regulation that discourages manipulative advertising strategies that target children with junk food commercials.

The argument from exploitation

Happiness is undoubtedly, as Aristotle pointed out 2,500 years ago, the ultimate goal in life for most, if not all, people, and its attainment highly prized. Those who design ads that directly associate consumer products like cars and perfume with the concept of happiness could be seen as exploiting the deep-felt desire and high aspiration that people have for being happy. Insofar as the implied suggestion that the acquisition of a specific consumer product can make a person happy is a gross exaggeration and thus a form of deception, that implied suggestion is also exploitative. For the deceptive implied suggestion plays on the deep desire that people have for happiness. It plays, in a sense, with people's deep-felt feelings associated with the paramount desire to be happy. Hence, insofar as that is the intention of those ads, then those ads are exploitative and, since exploitation is generally considered unethical, then those ads that exaggerate the association between consumer products and the concept of happiness are unethical. At the very least, they are ethically problematic and should be avoided.

Objection: One objection to the above arguments might be as follows: "Lighten up, you are taking this too seriously. The ads that directly associate consumer products with the concept of happiness are meant to be taken humorously and with a generous pinch of salt. Your own serious reaction to a light-hearted association of products to happiness *is* the exaggeration!"

Response: In response, I reiterate that happiness, as something that is highly valued by most people, should be taken seriously, just as friendship and other highly prized values are. To associate happiness exclusively with specific consumer products is to diminish the value and importance of happiness and by extension and parity of argument it amounts to treating all the people who value happiness highly with disrespect. Insofar as the association of consumer products with happiness and its other related aspirational values, such as self-fulfillment, self-actualization, and wellbeing, degrades the concept of happiness and its related aspirational values, that association indirectly degrades the people who consider those values both significant and important. And to the extent that most people highly value happiness, then its degradation through advertising is no laughing matter.

It is, moreover, precisely because the advertisers themselves recognize the importance and significance that people attach to happiness and its related aspirational values, that they design to associate consumer products with the concept of happiness and its related aspirational values. That goes to show the advertisers themselves take the association of happiness with consumer products seriously! At least they take it commercially seriously.

8. Plato's Relevance and Lessons for Advertising of Brands

Since values are generally seen as contributing factors to people's happiness, their association with consumer products is ethically problematic in the way indicated above under Plato's deontological and consequentialist arguments. Note that Plato's deontological and consequentialist arguments run parallel and inform my own arguments concerning the devaluation of happiness and values generally, in section 7. Just as the descriptions of gods and heroes by the poets in Plato's time ascribe characteristics and attributes to the gods and heroes which are inherently inconsistent with their true nature, so too the commodification of happiness and other aspirational values by advertisers, which ascribes to those values characteristics such as manufacturability, consumption, expendability, replacement, exchangeability, tradability, exhaustion, depreciation, and price, are directly and inherently inconsistent with the true nature of those values. Unlike consumable products that one trades for a price in the marketplace, our aspirational values as a society are nonmanufacturable, nonconsumable, nonexpendable, nonreplaceable, nonexchangeable, nontradable, nonexhaustible, nondepreciable, and, ultimately, priceless.[8] Values are generally considered more ideal and spiritual than commodities and other material objects, no matter how valuable (in terms of price value) those commodities and objects are. Thus values should not be compared and associated to commodities since they are essentially and inherently different types of things. Moreover, insofar as the association of values to consumer products degrades those values as argued above, there is a case to be made for some form of self-regulation within the advertising industry along similar lines suggested by Plato's arguments for the self-censorship of poets. For, just as those poets degraded both gods and heroes through exaggerations and misstatements regarding their nature and character, so too the exaggerated and misstated claims made about human values through their constant association with consumer products degrades those values. And, to the extent that we as a society value those values highly, we should be ethically concerned about their degradation. We should require collectively as citizens that the advertising industry act responsibly by agreeing to some form of self-regulation to combat this problem, or, if that proves impractical, a form of co-regulation between the advertising industry, appropriate government bodies, and citizen groups.

In keeping with the dialectical approach of this essay, the regulation envisaged and suggested here is one that emanates from informed and rational balanced dialogue among all the relevant stakeholders, including the media, academics, the government, and the community at large. As such, it is a bottom-up (dialectical) not a top-down (didactic) approach to regulation.

9. Conclusion

It has often been said advertising does not construct social reality, it merely reflects it. If that is true then the association of consumer products with values by advertising does not accurately or adequately reflect social reality. For people generally do not think of values solely in terms of the acquisition of individual and specific consumer products. Moreover, most people do not think that the exclusive acquisition of consumer products will provide them with happiness, grace, elegance, beauty, freedom, truth, friendship, or romance. Insofar as some people might believe the exclusive acquisition of specific advertised consumer products will provide them with all or some of those things, this possibility may be viewed as a case where advertising no longer merely reflects social reality but actually constructs it. If this is the case, it raises the question of whether this is ethically desirable. Namely, whether it is ethically desirable to create in some people the belief that the mere acquisition of consumer products will somehow provide them with happiness or with the attributes and values that are generally thought to contribute to a happy life.

The answer seems to be that such a construction of social reality by advertising through the association of consumer products with values is not ethically desirable for all the reasons adduced above. Moreover, such a construction of social reality is a perversion of our highest aspirational values and attributes, which diminishes and thus degrades our collective humanity. For just as the triumph of Olympic athletes elevates our collective humanity by allowing us to share vicariously and symbolically in their inspiring achievements, so too the mugging of an old lady on her way home by a thug diminishes and denigrates our collective humanity. Analogously, but of course not to the same degree, insofar as the association of consumer products with our collective aspirational values degrades those values, our collective humanity is by extension and by parity of argument also degraded.

As a diminution and degradation of our collective humanity I believe that such a construction of social reality by advertising is thus unethical and should be avoided. The advertising industry has a moral responsibility to ensure that our aspirational values are not diminished and degraded through the uncritical and arbitrary association of consumer products with those values. This conclusion is in keeping with Immanuel Kant's central idea, articulated in his *Categorical Imperative*, namely, that people should not be used merely as means to other people's ends as this degrades their inherent human value and moral worth. By extension of that argument, we can say the use of aspirational values merely as a means for the end of promoting consumer products degrades our collective humanity, as those values constitute an important component of our collective human identity and dignity, one that should not be traded away for the sake of advertising brands.

The purpose of this essay has been to provide a preliminary conceptual and normative analysis of various ethical issues concerning the *pervasive* and *cumulative* association of consumer products and brands with values. Further collaborative and interdisciplinary research involving social scientists, including sociologists, psychologist and advertisers is required to establish empirically the extent, if any, to which the consumers' notions of values are influenced by advertising. This essay has hopefully established that there is at least a prima facie case for ethical concern regarding the *systematic* degradation of values by advertising through the pervasive and cumulative association of those values with commodities.

An earlier version of this chapter appeared as a paper "The Commodification of Values: What Plato and Epicurus Can Teach us about Advertising Ethics—Ancient Wisdom for a New World" in Ioanna Papasolomou (ed.) (2005) *Proceedings of the 10th International Conference on Corporate and Marketing Communications*. Nicosia, Cyprus: Intercollege; pp. 14–29.

Notes

1 A similar conclusion is reached by Debasish Roy (2011).

2 Elliott (2007).

3 Understand *aspirational* as referring to ideal values, attributes, and feelings that people generally aspire to possess because they are normally regarded very highly, socially, aesthetically, and ethically, at least in Western democracies, even if they are not always actualized in practice. Typically, such values, attributes, or affective states are not limited but transcend the material and other physical or psychological conditions that pertain to those who aspire to them. It is in that sense that they can be considered "ideal" but capable of being actualized.

4 For an excellent and informative exposition and analysis of Hellenistic and related Roman philosophy, see Long (1986).

5 Rene Rivkin got depressed and committed suicide whereas Martha Stewart apparently bounced back and was back to business as usual.

6 A formulation of Kant's celebrated argument is as follows: "Always act in accordance with a rule or maxim that you can at the same time consistently will that it should become a universal law." Thus, deception, for example, can be considered unethical or at least ethically problematic under Kant's Categorical Imperative, since one cannot consistently will that deception as a favored rule or maxim should become a universal law. For all trustworthy communication will break down to the detriment of everyone including the person who stands to occasionally benefit from deception exercised selectively in his favour.

7 The term "advertisers" as used here is intended to denote both advertisers and advertising agencies.

8 Ironically, MasterCard ads uses the term "priceless" in its successful ad campaign to show that values such as friendship and love cannot be bought even with a credit card simply because they are "priceless."

References

Aristotle (1953) *Nichomachean Ethics*, trans. J.A.K. Thomson. Harmondsworth: Penguin Classics.

Elliott, S. (2007) "The Pursuit of Happiness in a Grilled Cheese Sandwich," *The New York Times*, October 1.

Retrieved February 25, 2013 from http://www.nytimes.com/2007/10/01/business/media/01adcol.html

Long, A.A. (1986) *Hellenistic Philosophy: Stoics, Epicureans, Sceptics*. Berkeley and Los Angeles: University of California Press.

Plato (1952) *The Dialogues of Plato*, trans. Benjamin Jowett. Chicago: Encyclopaedia Britannica.

Roy, D. (2011) "Brand Implies the Happiness that a Customer Associates with," *The Economic Times*, Apr 24. Retrieved February 25, 2013 from http://articles.economictimes.indiatimes.com/2011-04-24/news/29469200_1_brand-trade-mark-indian-business

Spence, E. (2005) The Commodification of Values: What Plato and Epicurus Can Teach Us about Advertising Ethics—Ancient Wisdom for a New World. In Ioanna Papasolomou (ed.), *Proceedings of the 10th International Conference on Corporate and Marketing Communications*. Nicosia, Cyprus: Intercollege; pp. 14–29.

Spence, E., and Van Heekeren, B. (2005) *Advertising Ethics*. Upper Saddle River, NJ: Pearson/Prentice Hall.

A Model to Explore the Ethics of Erotic Stimuli in Print Advertising

Tony L. Henthorne and Michael S. LaTour

The use of female nudity/erotic stimuli in print advertising has become quite commonplace. Ads characteristic of the genre, such as the continued run of controversial print advertisements for "Obsession" perfume and cologne by Calvin Klein, typically feature a nude couple or solitary female in a suggestively compromising position. Just as memorable are many of the print advertisements for jeans by Calvin Klein. Ads of this type are designed to elicit what the originators hope is a vicarious experience of sensuality without the result being extreme levels of anxiety or discomfort (LaTour and Henthorne, 1993).

The employment of sexual (or erotic) communication appeals in print advertising continues to be a controversial topic, as evidenced by the strength and variability of reactions to its usage. This study evaluates the impact of a sexual appeal by testing a hypothetical model incorporating linkages between the ethical dimensions of the Reidenbach-Robin (1988, 1990) multidimensional ethics scale and resulting attitude toward the ad, attitude toward the brand, and purchase intention.

Background

The use of erotic stimuli in print advertising has become almost commonplace in current advertising practices (LaTour and Henthorne, 1994). It is not unusual to find provocatively posed and attired (or unattired) models promoting any number of items in general-interest consumer magazines. This routine use of erotic stimuli in print advertising has resulted in mixed consumer responses. Prior empirical studies have shown both positive reactions and negative reactions from viewers of such ads (see, for example, the works of Alexander and Judd, 1986; Henthorne and LaTour, 1994; LaTour, 1990; LaTour and Henthorne, 1993; Sciglimpaglia et al., 1978). One of the central issues of the erotic stimuli controversy currently facing advertisers is believed to be the perception of continued traditional sex-role stereotyping of women (Boddewyn and Kunz, 1991). This traditional sex-role stereotyping is thought to focus on the most efficacious treatments, regardless of cost. We believe that there are two major obstacles to the attainment of this objective:

- First, the current absence of accountability in the field denies insurance companies access to actuarial data on which they could measure their exposure.
- Second, the high incidence of multiple pregnancies associated with IVF often transforms a medical triumph into a costly human catastrophe.

It is poetic justice that by addressing the obstacle of accountability through a verifiable and independent audit, we at Pacific Fertility Medical Centers now can address the issue of multiple births with IVF. Traditionally, IVF outcome has been expressed in terms of the pregnancy or birthrate per transfer of multiple embryos at one time. The Arthur Andersen accounting firm recently sanctioned our reporting pregnancy or birthrates as a function of the number of cycles of ovarian stimulation and egg retrieval as a separate category. This means that we now can transfer one embryo at a time until conception or until the supply of embryos has been exhausted. Once implemented, the single embryo transfer procedure will allow us to refocus on the overall chance of a baby being born following one egg retrieval, regardless of the number of embryo transfers performed.

We maintain that a national audit of all IVF programs will go a long way toward resurrecting the credibility of our discipline and will take us one giant step closer to universal insurance coverage. In the process, it likely would remove the need for advertising and outcome-based pricing altogether.

It is our sincere hope that this presentation will provoke a healthy debate that will focus on the imperative of linking advertising to disclosure and accountability in the field of IVF. To approach ethics from a narrow perspective and sidestep the larger issues of honesty, integrity, and accountability is to create a smoke screen that perpetuates an unacceptable status quo.

Pacific Fertility Medical Centers of California claims the right to continue honest marketing of its services supported by full disclosure and outcome-based fee structures that are linked to fully verifiable performance criteria. We deem such practices to meet the highest standards of morality and ethics and, most importantly, to serve the best interests of our patients. by many social critics to contribute to the perceived continuing injustice and inequality for many women. Additionally, there appears to be no reduction in perceived "sex objectification" in recent years even though female roles have substantially changed to more professional depictions (Ford and LaTour, 1993). Meanwhile, the advertising industry has come under increasing and consistently strong pressure from various outside sources (including well known feminists and feminist groups) who argue that the dignity of women has been lowered by their continued portrayal as sex objects (Kilbourne, 1987; Soley and Kurzbard, 1986). Because the whole issue of sex, sexual innuendo, and what is considered decent, moral, and/or acceptable in a culture or society is in constant evolution (Boddewyn, 1991), advertisers are finding it increasingly difficult to determine whether their viewers will perceive ads containing a relatively high level of female nudity as "sexy" or "sexist" (Lipman, 1991; Miller, 1992). Women's perceptions, in particular, of such female role portrayals have been shown to have a substantial impact upon purchase intention and perceived overall image of the sponsoring corporation (Ford and LaTour, 1993; Lundstrom and Sciglimpaglia, 1977). To assist in coping with this precarious situation, advertising agencies are bringing in increasing numbers of female consultants to provide input on ads which may be viewed as potentially offensive to women (Lipman, 1991). Clearly, with such important and pragmatic concerns at stake, the impact of the use of such advertising on society should be examined.

The influence of ethics

One step toward understanding the impact of the use of erotic stimuli in print advertising is to examine the ethical dilemmas emanating from such use. Gould (1994) states that insight into these positive and negative consumer reactions may arise from an investigation of the basic concepts contained in normative ethical theories of moral philosophy. Normative ethical theories of moral philosophy may generally be classified as either deontological or teleological, with the principal difference being in the basic focus of the framework (Murphy and Laczniak, 1981).

Deontological philosophies focus on the specific actions of the individual without regard to the consequences of those actions. The deontological viewpoint is concerned with the inherent rightness of the individual act. Actions should be judged by the actions themselves, without regard to the eventual outcome.

Conversely, teleological philosophies focus primarily on the outcomes and consequences of actions and behaviors in the determination of "worth" (Ferrell and Gresham, 1985). An individual behavior is considered ethical if it produces the greatest balance of good over bad, when compared with all other alternative actions (Hunt and Vitell, 1986). From a teleological perspective, many times the use of erotic stimuli in print advertising is not appealing to viewers and may actually exist in the generation of unintended (i.e., negative) side effects (for example, gratuitous sex). Therefore, these side effects of the use of erotic stimuli in print advertising, as well as the fundamental moral rightness of its use are of interest (Gould, 1994).

Reidenbach and Robin (1988) contend that individuals do not use the clearly defined concepts of deontology or teleology in making specific ethical judgements. They contend that a mixing or combining of the philosophies is more the norm in ethical

Table 4.1 The multidimensional ethics scale

The moral equity dimension
Fair—Unfair
Just—Unjust
Morally right—Not morally right
Acceptable to my family—Unacceptable to my family
The relativistic dimension
Culturally acceptable—Culturally unacceptable
Traditionally acceptable—Traditionally unacceptable
The contractualism dimension
Violates an unspoken promise—Does not violate an unspoken promise
Violates an unwritten contract—Does not violate an unwritten contract

decision making. This belief is based in the work of Frankena (1963). Frankena (1963) advocated a view blending the seemingly mutually exclusive requirements of teleology and deontology.

The Reidenbach-Robin ethics scale

Normative ethical philosophy, containing a number of overlapping theoretical ideals, was used as the basis for the development of the Reidenbach and Robin (1988, 1990) multidimensional ethics scale. (For a detailed discussion of the moral philosophy base of the scale the reader is referred to the work of Reidenbach and Robin [1990].) The scale has typically distilled the three dimensions of "moral equity," "relativism," and "contractualism" (see Table 4.1).

The "moral equity" dimension is composed of four items:

1. Fair–Unfair
2. Just–Unjust
3. Morally right–Not morally right
4. Acceptable to my family–Not acceptable to my family.

According to Reidenbach and Robin (1990), this dimension is believed to be based on lessons from early in life gained through basic institutions (such as family and religion) regarding such elemental constructs as fairness, equity, and right and wrong. The insights achieved from such institutions are considered decisive in establishing what individuals consider to be decent (positive) or objectionable (negative) in advertising (Gilly, 1988; Reid *et al.*, 1984).

The "relativistic" dimension is composed of two items:

1. Culturally acceptable–Culturally unacceptable
2. Traditionally acceptable–Traditionally unacceptable.

Dimension two is concerned with the social/cultural influences, guidelines, and parameters as they impact the individual. How we work to interpret individual events

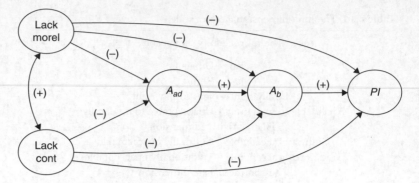

Figure 4.2 Hypothetical model

may be impacted by the items forming this dimension (Reidenbach and Robin, 1990). The possibility of a linkage between the ethical evaluative process and the social/ cultural influences on the individual has been examined by Hunt and Vitell (1986). The current level of sex and eroticism in advertising may simply be a mirror of what is now acceptable social behavior (Courtney and Whipple, 1983).

Given the overlapping theoretical dimensions fundamental to the various ethical philosophies utilized in the initial distillation of the scales, it is not surprising to find a high degree of correlation between some of the various constructs. Specifically, dimensions one and two frequently have been shown, to combine into a single comprehensive dimension (Reidenbach and Robin, 1990; Reidenbach *et al.*, 1991).

The final dimension, "contractualism," is composed of two items:

1. Violates an unspoken promise–Does not violate an unspoken promise
2. Violates an unwritten contract–Does not violate an unwritten contract.

This dimension is centered around the concept of a "social contract" between the individual and society (Reidenbach and Robin, 1990). Implied obligation or contract is the fundamental issue addressed.

The Hypothetical Model

Figure 4.2 reveals the structural relationships posited as linkages between the ethical dimensions of the Reidenbach-Robin conceptualization and the resulting attitude toward the ad (A_{ad}), attitude toward the brand (A_b) and, ultimately, purchase intention (*PI*). Figure 4.2 displays the two-dimensional structural outcome of the Reidenbach-Robin model. (Preliminary factor analysis of the present study's data supports this structural interpretation.)

It is hypothesized that a perceived lack of "Moral Equity/Relativism" (Lack Morel) associated with the use of the treatment ad will result in a negative relationship with attitude toward the ad (A_{ad}), attitude toward the brand (A_b), and purchase intention (*PI*). In addition to these "direct effects," it is hypothesized some of the negative impact of "Lack Morel" will be indirect. For example, "Lack Morel" may be found to impact purchase intention through the variables of attitude toward the ad (A_{ad}) and attitude toward the brand (A_b). It is further hypothesized the same type of relationships will exist between the endogenous variables and a perceived lack of contractualism. Based on prior research (e.g., Burke and Edell, 1989; LaTour *et al.*, 1990), the present model indicates attitude toward the ad (A_{ad}) should be positively associated with attitude toward the brand (A_b) which, in turn, should be positively linked with purchase intention (*PI*). This hypothetical model significantly extends previous research by providing a statistical test of linkages between moral philosophical dimensions and advertising response outcomes in one complete model.

The Study

Data collection and ad stimuli

Data were collected by trained interviewers through the use of a mall intercept in a large regional mall located in a culturally dynamic and growing SMSA in the mid-gulf coast region. Following procedures suggested by Nowell and Stanley (1991), data collectors were rotated in random patterns throughout the mall during all hours of the mall's operation over a period of one week. Over 80% of individuals approached agreed to participate in the study. Each respondent completed the questionnaire in private, yet was monitored from a distance by research assistants. The use of the mall intercept as a data collection technique is commonly used in research such as this and has been shown to produce a significant cross-section of respondents (Bush and Hair, 1985). Such a cross-section will include older individuals which may be outside of the target market for youth-oriented products. However, the inclusion of such "non-targeted" individuals in the study is of importance due to their possible exposure to the ad and the resulting unintended social consequences for the advertiser (e.g., the perceived degradation of women) (Gould, 1994).

A high quality copy of a black and white print ad was used in the treatment. The selected ad stimulus was part of a collection of black and white photographs promoting a well known brand of jeans and used in a metropolitan area different from where the current study was being conducted. As part of the treatment selection process, a focus group of adults ranging in age from 21 to 50 was used to select an ad from this promotional outset perceived to contain substantial erotic content and nudity. The focus group selected ad featured a nude female model, with her body up against a chain link fence while at the same time being sexually embraced and kissed by a male model wearing only jeans with the fly unzipped. The ad contained the brand name of the jeans at the bottom. Each respondent was given the ad followed by the questionnaire.

Operationalization

Respondents completed two series of three seven-point items which were summed to measure attitude toward the ad (A_{ad}) and attitude toward the brand (A_b) (See Table 4.2).

Table 4.2 Variables used in the study

Attitude toward the ad (A_{ad})*	*Attitude toward the brand* (A_b)*
1. High quality	1. High quality
2. Interesting	2. Distinctive
3. Appropriate	3. Appealing

*Purchase intention**
The next time I purchase jeans I will purchase [brand name] jeans.

*Lack morel composite dimension***	*Lack contractualism dimension***
1. Unjust	1. Violates an unspoken promise
2. Unacceptable to my family	2. Violates an unwritten contract
3. Unfair	
4. Not morally right	
5. Not culturally acceptable	
6. Not traditionally acceptable	

*Measured on 7-point scales anchored by "Yes definitely" = 7 and "No definitely not" = 1.
**Measured on 7-point bi-polar adjective item scales.

The items were selected on the basis of focus group research and their use in related advertising research (e.g., Henthorne *et al.*, 1993; LaTour *et al.*, 1990).

In order to evaluate ethical dimensions associated with the ad stimulus, respondents were asked to respond to a series of eight items in terms of their beliefs about the promotional use of the ad they had just seen. As discussed earlier, these eight items were identical to those which were distilled from an earlier instrument based on moral philosophy and validated by Reidenbach and Robin (1988, 1990) (refer again to Table 4.2).

In previous validation research, both a three factor structure solution (Reidenbach and Robin, 1990) and a two factor structure solution (Reidenbach *et al.*, 1991) have been extracted. In the two factor solution, items representing the moral equity and relativism dimensions join to form a single composite dimension. According to Reidenbach *et al.* (1991), a possible explanation to the two dimensional structure may include the effects of a "natural relation expected between what people perceive to be culturally acceptable and what is just (p. 86)." The authors go on to say that the meaning of "fairness" comes to us in part through our culture and that, therefore, such a composite makes intuitive sense.

Next, selected demographic information was collected. Finally, purchase intention was measured by a seven-point item which read "The next time I purchase jeans I will purchase [brand name] Jeans." This scale was anchored by "yes definitely" and "no definitely not."

Preliminary analysis and profile of the sample

Factor analysis indicated the two factor structure (as previously discussed). As in previous research (Reidenbach *et al.*, 1991), a composite dimension (six items) was distilled (entitled "Lack Morel" in the present study) along with the "contractualism" dimension (entitled "Lack Contractualism"). All tests of internal consistency of

Table 4.3 Variable averages

Variable	Mean	S.D.
Lack morel	29.50	10.68
Lack contract	7.69	3.40
A_{ad}	9.75	5.93
A_b	13.26	5.75
PI	2.67	1.69

summed scales indicated adequate levels for basic research (e.g., Cronbach alpha tests greater than or equal to 0.70) (see Bagozzi, 1978; Nunally, 1967).

Table 4.3 indicates the per-item average on "Lack Morel" was above the midpoint on a 7-point scale ($29.50/6 = 4.91$). In contrast, the per-item average on the "Lack Contractualism" dimension was not found to be above the midpoint ($7.69/2 = 3.84$). Attitude toward the ad per-item average and Purchase Intention per-item average were below the midpoint ($9.75/3 = 3.25$ and 2.67, respectively). Finally, attitude toward the brand per-item average was found to be above the midpoint ($13.26/3 = 4.42$). However, all the scales had either sizable standard deviations (refer to Table 4.3) indicating substantial variability in responses. It stands to reason that individuals differ in the degree to which they react to such ad stimuli.

Of the 103 total useable responses, 44 were male and 59 were female. The average age of the sample was approximately 34 years, with a standard deviation of 14.7 years. 19.6% of the sample were African-American, 75.5% were white, 2.9% were Asian, with the remainder indicating "other." Income levels were widely dispersed across several categories and generally reflected the income levels of the population surrounding a ten-mile radius of the mall (as supplied by mall management). The average number of years of education (high school = 12 years) was 13.6 years, with a standard deviation of 2.9 years. As mentioned previously, due to the importance of nontargeted individuals, based on their possible exposure to the ad and the subsequent possible negative social consequences of their viewing of the ad (e.g., perceived debasement of women) (Gould, 1994), no attempt was made to exclude nontargeted individuals from the study.

Results of the test of the hypothetical model

Maximum likelihood estimation was used to model the posited relationship of the variables. Figure 4.3 reveals strong goodness of fit indices of the data to the parameters specified in the hypothetical model. The chi-square index was nonsignificant, which in the case of causal modeling is an indicator of good fit. The percentage of variance explained by the structural equations representing the effects of other variables upon A_{ad}, A_b, and PI were 64%, 18%, and 30%, respectively. While this indicates appreciable amounts of variance remaining unexplained, it does establish that the structural relations featured in this model play a major role in these complex variable relationships and that the theoretical linkages were supported.

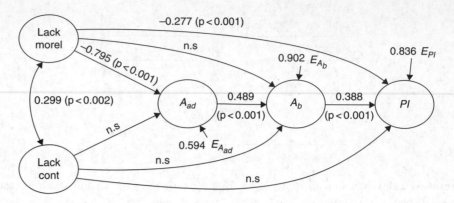

Figure 4.3 Chi-square=0.828, p=0.36 1 d.f., Bentler-Bonett Normed Fit Index=0.99, Bentler-Bonett Nonnormed Fit Index=1.01, Comparative Fit Index=1.00.

Analysis of the specific paths reveals a perceived "Lack of Moral Equity/Relativism" ethical dimension ("Lack Morel") associated with the use of the featured ad. This dimension was strongly negatively associated with A_{ad} (standardized coefficient = −0.795, $p < 0.001$). The relationship between "Lack Morel" and Purchase Intention (PI) was also found to be significant (standardized coefficient = −0.277, $p < 0.001$), but not as strong as the link from "Lack Morel" to A_{ad}. The link between "Lack Morel" and A_b was non-significant. Apparently, the main direct impact of "Lack Morel" is upon the perceptions of the stimulus and, to a lesser extent, perhaps a desire to "boycott" the offending ad sponsor. "Lack Morel" also had a significant (standardized coefficient = −0.388, $p < 0.001$) negative indirect effect on A_b, through A_{ad} (via the paths from "Lack Morel" to A_{ad} and from A_{ad} to A_b).

While the correlation between "Lack Contractualism" and Lack Morel" was positive and significant, none of the paths from "Lack Contractualism" to the endogenous variables were significant. It seems intuitively reasonable that the "Lack Morel" composite dimension would be more clearly associated with an advertising issue due to its focus on "moral acceptability" to society. Conversely, violation of an unwritten social promise or contract may not seem as relevant in this particular context as it is when, for example, a retailer promises some product performance characteristics that are not readily forthcoming.

As expected, the paths from A_{ad} to A_b, and from A_b to PI were all positive and significant. This supports the well developed arguments found in the advertising literature (e.g., Burke and Edell, 1989) that such linkage are a significant part of the "causal chain" of advertising events.

Discussion

The use of female nudity and erotic content in print advertising evokes dynamic reactions from viewers. However, the feelings which result from exposure to such strong stimuli may not be exactly what the advertiser intended (LaTour and Henthorne, 1994). As product marketers strive to differentiate and draw attention to their product offering, the use of erotic content has become increasingly common. It is suggested that such content be used with discretion and caution.

The results of this study indicate that the use of high levels of female nudity/erotic content in print ads may not be perceived as morally right or culturally acceptable to viewers of such ads. While the use of such stimuli may draw additional attention to the ad, the outcome of the use of such high degrees of erotic stimuli may, in fact, be negative. In other words (as indicated by the results of the test of the hypothetical model), the perceived lack of moral equity/relativism associated with the use of high levels of female nudity in print advertising appears to result in negative feelings toward the advertisement and indirectly toward the brand. Additionally, a direct "product boycott" effect from perceived "Lack of Moral Equity/Relativism" is supported. The lack of contractualism impact, at least in the test of this data, does not appear to be relevant to the advertising ethics environment.

Findings such as these should give advertisers pause as they prepare to use prominent levels of erotic content in print advertising. Care and consideration should be directed to predetermining the reaction of their particular target market to print ads containing high levels of nudity and/or erotic content. Additionally, advertisers must consider the likely exposure of individuals outside of the selected target market and the subsequent possible negative social consequences (e.g., perceived sex objectification; Ford and Latour, 1993), perceived degradation of women (Gould, 1994), increased promiscuity (Boddewyn and Kunz, 1991), negative word of mouth (Miller, 1992) to the exposure.

Finally, future endeavors should examine this issue from a cross-cultural perspective. In fact, the controversy surrounding perceptually negative female portrayals in advertising has been shown to be a growing international phenomenon (Ford *et al.*, 1994). As world-wide societal change accelerates due in part to rapidly communicated social norms (such as the roles and portrayals of women in the media) of and among people of widely diverse cultures (Ford *et al.*, 1994), this controversy will become an even more visible and central issue to be deliberated.

References

Alexander, M.W. and B. Judd, Jr.: 1986, 'Differences in Attitudes Toward Nudity in Advertising', Psychology: *A Quarterly Journal of Human Behavior* 23(1): 27–29.

Bagozzi, R.D.: 1978, 'Salesforce Performance and Satisfaction as a Function of Individual Difference, Interpersonal, and Situational Factors', *Journal of Marketing Research* 15: 517–531.

Boddewyn, J.J.: 1991, 'Controlling Sex and Decency in Advertising Around the World', *Journal of Advertising* 20(4): 25–35.

Boddewyn, J.J. and H. Kunz: 1991, 'Sex and Decency Issues in Advertising: General and International Dimension', *Business Horizons*: 13–19.

Burke, M.C. and J.A. Edell: 1989, 'The Impact of Feelings on Ad-Based Affect and Cognition', *Journal of Marketing Research* 26: 69–83.

Bush, A.J. and J.F. Hair, Jr.: 1985, 'An Assessment of the Mall Intercept as a Data Collection Method', *Journal of Marketing Research* 22: 158–167.

Courtney, A.E. and T.W. Whipple: 1983, *Sex Stereotyping in Advertising* (Lexington Books, Lexington, MA).

Ferrell, O.C. and L. Gresham: 1985, 'A Contingency Framework for Understanding Ethical Decision Making in Marketing', *Journal of Marketing* 49 (Summer): 87–96.

Ford, J.B. and M.S. LaTour: 1993, 'Differing Reactions to Female Role Portrayals in Advertising', *Journal of Advertising Research* 33(5): 43–52.

Ford, J.B., and M.S. LaTour, E.D. Honeycutt, Jr., and M. Joseph: 1994, 'Female Role Portrayals in International Advertising: Should Advertisers Standardize in the Pacific Rim?', *American Business Review* 12(2): 1–10.

Frankena, W.: 1963, *Ethics* (Prentice-Hall, Inc., Englewood Cliffs, NJ).

Gilly, M.C.: 1988, 'Sex Roles in Advertising: A Comparison of Television Advertisements in Australia, Mexico, and the United States', *Journal of Marketing* 52: 75–85.

Gould, S.J.: 1994, 'Sexuality and Ethics in Advertising: A Framework and Research Agenda', *Journal of Advertising* 23(3): 13–80.

Henthorne, T.L., M.S. LaTour, and R. Nataraajan: 1993, 'Fear Appeals in Print Advertising: An Analysis of Arousal and Ad Response', *Journal of Advertising* 22(2): 59–69.

Kilbourne, J.: 1987, 'Still Killing Us Softly', (Cambridge Documentary Films, Cambridge, MA).

LaTour, M.S.: 1990, 'Female Nudity in Print Advertising: An Analysis of Gender Differences in Arousal and Ad Response', *Psychology and Marketing* 7(1): 65–81.

LaTour, M.S. and T.L. Henthorne: 1993, 'Female Nudity: Attitudes Toward the Ad and the Brand, and Implications for Advertising Strategy', *Journal of Consumer Marketing* 10(3): 25–32.

LaTour, M.S. and T.L. Henthorne: 1994, 'Ethical Judgements of Sexual Appeals in Print Advertising', *Journal of Advertising* 23(3): 81.

LaTour, M.S., R.E. Pitts, and D.C. Snook-Luther: 1990, 'Female Nudity, Arousal, and Ad Response: An Experimental Investigation', *Journal of Advertising* 19(4): 51–62.

Lipman, J.: 1991, 'Sexy or Sexist? Recent Ads Spark Debate', *The Wall Street Journal* (Sept. 30): B1.

Lundstrom, W.J. and D. Sciglimpaglia: 1977, 'Sex Role Portrayals in Advertising', *Journal of Marketing* 41: 72–79.

Miller, C.: 1992, 'Publisher Says Sexy Ads Are OK, But Sexist Ones Will Sink Sales', *Marketing News* 26(24): 8–9.

Murphy, P. and G.R. Laczniak: 1981, 'Marketing Ethics: A Review with Implications for Managers, Educators and Researchers', *Review of Marketing 1981* (American Marketing Association, Chicago, IL); pp. 251–266.

Nowell, C. and L.R. Stanley: 1991, 'Length-Biased Sampling in Mall Intercept Surveys', *Journal of Marketing Research* 28: 475–479.

Nunally, J.C.: 1967, *Psychometric Theory* (McGraw-Hill, New York).

Reid, L.N., C.T. Salmon, and L.C. Soley: 1984, 'The Nature of Sexual Content in Television Advertising: A Cross-Cultural Comparison of Award-Winning Commercials', in R.W. Belk (ed.), *AMA Educators' Proceedings* (American Marketing Association, Chicago, IL); pp. 214–216.

Reidenbach, R.E. and D.P. Robin: 1988, 'Some Initial Steps Toward Improving the Measurement of Ethical Evaluations of Marketing Activities', *Journal of Business Ethics* 7: 871–879.

Reidenbach, R.E., D.P. Robin, and L. Dawson: 1991, 'An Application and Extension of a Multidimensional Ethics Scale to Selected Marketing Practices and Marketing Groups', *Journal of the Academy of Marketing Science* 19(2): 83–92.

Sciglimpaglia, D., M.A. Belch, and R.F. Cain: 1978, 'Demographic and Cognitive Factors Influencing Viewers' Evaluations of 'Sexy' Advertisements', in William L. Wilkie (ed.), *Advances in Consumer Research*, Vol. 6 (Association for Consumer Research); pp. 62–65.

Soley, L. and G. Kurzbard: 1986, 'Sex in Advertising: A Comparison of 1964 and 1984 Magazine Advertisements', *Journal of Advertising* 15(3): 45–54, 65.

C. Information Technology

The Importance of Information in Business Ethics

Mariarosaria Taddeo

1. Introduction

In the last two decades the use of ICTs (information and communication techno-logies) determined the so-called information revolution, which changed the way individuals manage their communications and daily practices, from working and reading books and listening to music, to shopping and driving. At a social level, ICTs reshaped social interactions with the dissemination of social networks, like Facebook, Twitter, or Flickr for example. The same applies at the institutional level, where ICTs provide new tools for the management of information and bureaucracy (Ciborra 2005; Saxena 2005), and at military level, where ICTs determine the latest revolution in military affairs (Taddeo forthcoming-a). The information revolution also affects the way companies manage their activities and, in general, conduct business, the diffusion of chatrooms and e-mail as well as the increasing expansion of e-commerce provide just two examples of the effects of ICTs on companies' business management.

The information revolution is a twofold phenomenon; it has both a technological and a philosophical nature. The technological breakthrough initiated a series of trans-formations affecting individual and social activities, which have philosophical conse-quences as they radically change the way human beings interact with their environment. Floridi stresses this aspect of the information revolution when he calls it the *fourth revolution* (Floridi 2009), to highlight that—like the previous three revolutions, Darwinian, Copernican, and Freudian—the information revolution changes deeply the way human beings perceive themselves in the universe and interact with their environment.

Among the peculiarities of the fourth revolution, one is of particular relevance. This is that it changes fundamentally the way reality is perceived and understood. In Floridi's words: "[The information revolution] is updating our everyday perspective on ourselves and on the ultimate nature of reality, that is, our metaphysics, from a mate-rialist one, in which physical objects and processes play a key role, to an informational one. Objects and processes are increasingly seen as *de-physicalised*, in the sense that they tend to be treated as support-independent" (Floridi 2010, p. 2; emphasis added).

The process described by Floridi leads to the erosion of the boundaries between the online and off-line domains, from which a new heterogenic environment emerges, where the analogue and digital domain are both included, and artificial agents interact with human agents on a regular basis, and have rights concerning their status and well-being (Floridi 2008b).

In such a new environment information plays a central role, and it becomes increasingly important to treat—that is, to elaborate, communicate, and destroy—information *fairly*, as the mismanagement of information may lead to the breach of individuals' rights. The need to define a set of ethical guidelines suitable for addressing problems related to the fair treatment of information becomes a crucial and pressing issue.

In the rest of the essay, attention will be focused on three problems, *transparency*, *online trust*, and *privacy*, which are all concerned with the ethical treatment of information. The goal of the essay is to describe an information-oriented approach to these three problems and to their solutions. In order to achieve this goal, the concept of *semantic information* will first be introduced and will be then deployed in the remaining sections to address the ethical problems posed by transparency, online trust, and privacy.

2. Semantic Information

Information is a term whose meaning may change depending on the context in which it is used; here, information indicates some meaningful, true data (Floridi 2005). Information defined in this way is called *semantic* information. Semantic information is used in everyday communication and it is part of several epistemic processes (Floridi forthcoming; Taddeo forthcoming-b). It is noteworthy that semantic information is compounded by data but it is not only data.

A datum is "lack of uniformity" (Floridi 2008a). It is something that "'makes a difference' and, as such, can be perceived, measured and captured via an interaction. Data can be thought of as a precondition for the experience, pre-epistemic entities the existence of which is empirically inferred" (Turilli & Floridi 2009, p. 108). Data may originate from the interaction of an agent with the environment; the data stored on your digital camera after last summer's holiday provides a good example. Data can also be elaborated; this is the case, for example, of you tagging your pictures on Facebook.

Semantic information derives from the elaboration of data. More explicitly, semantic information exists only as the result of a process of data elaboration. An example may clarify the relation between data and semantic information. Consider the raw data of an experiment collected by a scientist working on evolution. The data by themselves do not convey any information until the scientist does elaborate them and derives the information that, for example, when environmental resources decrease the agents in the environment become more aggressive. In the same way, in economics the information about the financial status of a country is derived by elaborating a set of data concerning, for example, the average debt and the level of industrial production and the level of international exports and imports. The process of data elaboration is called *semanticization*.

Semanticization produces information only if the elaborated data are truthful. Elaborated false data do not convey any information. Recalling our scientist, the result of the elaboration of false experimental data may be meaningful, as it conveys a message that can be understood by other agents, but it is not informative about the evolution process occurring in a given section of the environment, as the data do not reflect the facts.

Now that the reader is more acquainted with the concept of semantic information, we can turn our attention to the problem of information transparency.

3. Transparency

In considering transparency two aspects are usually stressed: the disclosing of some information (DiPiazza and Eccles 2002; Vaccaro and Madsen 2006), and the use that one could make of the disclosed information for his or her decision-making processes (Winkler 2000). This distinction reflects the two perspectives from which transparency is usually considered: the perspective of those to whom the information is disclosed, and the perspective of the information providers, who decide what information will be disclosed, and the way in which it will be disclosed.

When considered from an ethical perspective, the problem posed by transparency concerns what kind of information should be made available. The issue arises because, if on the one hand information plays a crucial role in the decision-making process of an agent and hence the more an agent is informed the better he can make his decision, on the other hand the disclosure of some information may breach ethical principles, like privacy or anonymity. For example, a lawyer may be in a better position to defend her client if she can gain access to the information about the crime rate in the client's neighbourhood, but at the same time it is possible that in doing so the lawyer could access personal information concerning the client's neighbors and hence violate their right to privacy.

An interesting analysis of the ethical implication of transparency has been provided by Turilli and Floridi (2009, p. 107). They argue that transparency is not per se an ethical principle as

> the disclosed information may be ethically neutral, it may not affect ethical principles and have only ethically unrelated effects, if any effect at all. For example, the user interface of operating systems (e.g. Windows, OSX or Linux) often discloses information about the underlying computational processes without any ethical consequence. Users may be informed whether their interaction with a program is correct, whether they have received new e-mails or whether there are new upgrades to install.

On the basis of this analysis the authors conclude that transparency should be considered an *ethically enabling* factor rather than an ethical principle per se. Transparency can enhance the morality of a given scenario, if the information made available facilitates the application of some ethical principles.

In more detail, Turilli and Floridi identify two types of relationships between the disclosed information and ethical principles: dependence and regulation. A principle depends on some information when some amount of information is necessary to apply that principle. Ethical principles regulate the flow of information by providing criteria for its access, usage, dissemination and storage. Given these two types of relationships,

> transparency is ethically enabling when it provides the information necessary for the endorsement of ethical principles (dependence) or (and this might be an inclusive or) when it provides details on how information is constrained (regulation). Conversely, ethical principles can be impaired if false details (misinformation) or inadequate or excessive amounts of information are disclosed. (p. 107)

For example, transparency enables accountability, as this principle depends on the disclosure of some information about the author of a given action or decision in order to be applied. In the same way, transparency enables privacy and anonymity by providing the constraints for the disclosure of information to the public.

As transparency can both enable and impair ethical principles, the authors consider it ethically neutral. Such neutrality uncovers the importance of transparency and the delicacy required in the processes of disclosing information, as it can be both ethically enabling and ethically impairing. This makes it even more urgent to define the best possible way to decide what information should be made available. As the authors put it, "radical approaches to information transparency—such as full disclosure or completely withholding information relative to the activity of an organisation—merely fail to guarantee positive ethical implications while risking the promotion of negative ones" (p. 108). The solution suggested by Turilli and Floridi focuses on the elaboration process of information (semanticization as defined in section 2). They argue that semanticization is not ethically neutral and is relevant when considering the ethical implication of disclosing or withholding some information.

The case of the evolutionary scientist will help to clarify this aspect. It is necessary to know how the data of the experiment were collected and elaborated in order to assess whether the resulting information has been elaborated ethically. This means that it is necessary to know that the process of information elaboration described in the previous section occurred "respecting ethical principles of, for example, accuracy and fairness, and whether the semantic content produced is veridical about its subject matter (i.e. agent's actions)" (Turilli and Floridi 2009, p. 109). Suppose that some information about company governance is disclosed to enable the principle of accountability, so that information about the outcomes of one's actions is made available to the public. The point stressed by the authors is that the disclosing of information itself is not enough to enable the principle, as it is also necessary to disclose the process of information elaboration in order to provide evidence that the disclosed information is true and has been produced fairly.

On the basis of this analysis, it follows that, as transparency can be a pro-ethical condition, it becomes a valuable tool for making evident the ethical principles endorsed by companies and organizations. A consequence of the approach proposed by Turilli and Floridi is that the ethical commitments of organizations, companies, or public institutions will not be limited to public declarations of intent, as they will have to provide evidence showing how the ethical principles, to which they commit, are prioritized and applied to their activities.

We can now focus on the case for online trust.

4. Online Trust

Trust is generally considered a fundamental aspect of social interactions; following the fourth revolution and the development of the Internet as a new domain where social and commercial activities are developed, it became a fundamental aspect of online interactions as well, giving rise to a new phenomenon. This is "online trust," understood as the occurrence of trust in the digital environment. The development of online trust gives rise to a set of conceptual and ethical problems. In particular, two topics are at the centre of the debate concerning online trust; one concerns the analysis of the minimal requirements for the emergence of online trust, and the other focuses on the definition of the criteria for the development and maintenance of *fair* online trust. In the rest of this section I will focus on the latter, I shall brush away the former by summarizing briefly the discussion on online trust.

The debate revolves around the analysis of two conditions disputed to be necessary for the occurrence of online trust: (a) the presence of a shared cultural and institutional background; and (b) the ascertainment of the trustee's identity. The debate leads to two opposing positions. Some scholars (Nissenbaum 2001; Pettit 1995; Seigman 2000) defend the thesis that (a) and (b) cannot be satisfied in an online environment and hence deny the possibility of the presence of trust in such an environment. Others (Papadopoulou 2007; Vries 2006; Weckert 2005) argue in favour of the presence of online trust, stating that either (a) and (b) are not necessary conditions for the emergence of trust or that it is actually possible to satisfy (a) and (b) in online interactions.

We can now focus on the analysis of the conditions that need to be satisfied for developing a fair online trust. This issue concerns the debate both in computer and business ethics, as it mainly relates to companies' practices to acquire customers' trust in online interactions (Ess 2010; Taddeo & Floridi 2011). In the digital environment, where customers do not have the possibility of trying or seeing the objects that they would like to buy, and where there are no physical interactions between buyers and sellers, trust plays a fundamental role in the decision-making process. The problem arises of defining a fair way for establishing and maintaining trust in online interactions.

An analysis of this problem has been provided in Turilli, Vaccaro, & Taddeo (2010). The proposed analysis rests on two pillars, Taddeo's (2010) definition of trust as a second order property qualifying first order relations and the consideration of the informational nature of the online interactions. Let us consider first Taddeo's definition of trust.

Trust is generally understood as a decision taken by an agent A (the trustor) to rely on another agent B (the trustee) to perform a given action. A's decision to trust B rests on the assessment of B's trustworthiness. The act of trusting implies some risks: the trustee can betray the trustor by behaving differently from what was expected or agreed. Usually the trustor mitigates the risk of being betrayed by seeking some guarantees on the trustee's behavior, assessing, in this way, whether the trustee is trustworthy (Gambetta 1998; Luhmann 1979) and establishing the risk threshold he is willing to run depending on the availability of assurances of the damages he may suffer.

According to Taddeo's analysis, the trustor decides to *delegate* to the trustee a given task functional to the achievement of the trustor's goal.[1] The trustor *does not supervise* the trustee's performances and decisions as the trustee is considered trustworthy. Delegation and absence of supervision are then the defining characteristics of the occurrence of trust. On the basis of this analysis Taddeo concludes that trust is a *property of relations*, not a relation itself. Trust qualifies the relations occurring among the agents of a system, changing the way in which they occur. This analysis of trust particularly emphasizes that a relation qualified by trust has the property of being *advantageous* for the trustor, because it minimizes the trustor's effort and commitment in achieving his or her own goal. So, for example, in the case of e-commerce, the buyer (B) is said to trust the seller (S) when:

- B and S communicate, indirectly through the content and functionalities of S's website;
- B delegates to S the task of finding out and locating the item B desires to buy, to assess its cost and quality, and to determine the costs and time of delivery; and
- B does not supervise S's performances of any of these actions nor does she verify the information communicated by B.

Taddeo's analysis points out that trust implies the prospect of a significant advantage for the trustor in achieving his goal. Such advantage is the reason for which an individual considers the possibility of trusting other individuals, and to take related risks. Hence the presence of trust *facilitates* the emergence of social behaviors and the growth of social capital, as it facilitates the interactions among the agents operating in the environment.

This analysis becomes particularly relevant for addressing the case of online trust, when considering the nature of the online environment. Such an environment affords so-called computer-mediated communications, and is the *locus* for the communication of information. Online interactions are about the communication of some information, not only in the obvious cases of chats and e-mails but also, for example, when online sellers communicate to online buyers information concerning the offered products, their honesty, efficiency, loyalty, and so on (Corritore, Kracher, & Wiedenbeck 2003). In the case of online interactions, trust affects the relations of computer-mediated communication occurring among individuals. By means of his website, the seller in an online shop communicates to the buyer the cost of the desired good, the quality, the delivery time, and so on.

It follows that online trust is a particular instance of the second order property of trust, characterized by occurring in an online environment and qualifying only first order relations of communication. Like off-line trust, online trust is grounded on the trustee's trustworthiness. Since online trust is successful when the communication between two individuals is honest and transparent, then *honesty* and *transparency* are the criteria that should be endorsed in the assessment of the potential trustee's trustworthiness. On the basis of this analysis, online trust is defined as "a specific instance of the second-order property of trust. Such instance has the peculiarity of exclusively qualifying first-order relations of communication . . . occurring in online environment and has the effect of producing some advantages[2] for the trustor" (Turilli et al. 2010, p. 342).

In summary, online trust makes interactions advantageous for the trustor, hence provides an incentive for the trustor to interact with other individuals. As a consequence, online trust initiates a virtuous circle that leads to a selection process, according to which trustworthy individuals are involved in a growing number of interactions, whereas, in the long run, untrustworthy individuals are progressively marginalized and eventually excluded from the social system. These dynamics are quite evident when considering online communities, such as e-Bay or Amazon.

It follows that online trust is successful when communication is *honest* and *transparent*, that is, when the trustee does not lie and does not hide anything from the trustor. Lack of transparency and dishonesty are the ways of betraying online trust. Consequently, transparency and honesty are two main parameters in assessing the potential trustee's trustworthiness. The virtuous circle initiated by online trust enhances the dissemination of honest and transparent interactions. This becomes clear if one considers, for example, the strategies implemented by e-sellers to obtain the trust of Internet users. Transparency on company policies, stock availability, time-line dispatch procedure, even on prices, is one of the most common policies put in place, together with the commitment to act honestly by delivering what the customer has seen on the website (Corritore et al. 2003).

With the analysis of online trust in place, we can now turn our attention to the problem of privacy.

5. Privacy

When considering privacy, one should remember that one thing that has been made easier by the dissemination of ICTs is access to information. Nowadays it is as simple as inserting a query into a search engine to get information about virtually everything one could think of. Scholars know this quite well; with the Internet the search for an article, which a few years ago could have taken hours in a library, is now done in a matter of minutes, if not seconds. It is not only the time spent in searching but also the scope of the information one can access that has increased in the last decades. With the same effort one can now access information from how to build a piece of furniture to (allegedly) classified information about the US government or personal information. This last case gives rise to the problem of privacy, which leads to calls for regulation of access to personal information.

Two aspects need to be taken in consideration to understand the importance of privacy. The first one is the so-called *greased information*, "greased information is information that moves like lightning and is hard to hold onto" (Moor 1997, p. 27). Information greasiness refers to the fact that ICTs facilitate the processes of information creation and communication, but also provide the tools for facilitating information storage and access, making easier to retrieve (personal) information and allowing one to use that information in unexpected ways. This brings us to the second aspect to be taken into account, namely, the ethical value of privacy.

Different positions have been held in the extant literature with respect to the value of privacy and its nature; some scholars consider privacy a "core value," which needs to be safeguarded, others defend the thesis that privacy is an individual preference, culture-relative. For example, Rachaels argues that "privacy is valuable because it enables us to form varied relationships with other people" (Rachaels 1975, p. 323), while Johnson's account of privacy considers "privacy as an essential aspect of autonomy" (Johnson 1994, p. 89). Others, like Fried for example, suggest that "privacy is not simply an absence of information about us in the minds of others, rather it is the *control* we have over information about ourselves" (Fried 1984, p. 209). With this respect is of particular value the analysis of privacy provided by Moor (1997).

Moor's analysis ascribes an instrumental value to privacy. He suggests that there are some values that are at the core of every culture: life, happiness, freedom, knowledge, ability, resources, and security are examples of such values. According to Moor, even the most primitive society rests on an at least implicit acknowledgment of the values, as they are closely related to the survival of the members of society. In this context, privacy has a (instrumental) value because it enables respect of the core values, in particular of the value of security. In Moor's words: "without protection species and cultures don't survive and flourish. All cultures need security of some kind, but not all need privacy. As societies become larger, highly interactive, but less intimate, privacy becomes a natural expression of the need for security" (1997, p. 29). A need that becomes more urgent in contemporary society, given the greasiness of information, where individuals' right to be safe and protected includes the protection of their privacy.

On the basis of this analysis, Moor develops what he defines as a control/restricted access analysis of privacy. According to which, "an individual or group has normative privacy in a situation with regard to others if and only if in that situation the individual or group is normatively protected form intrusion, interference, and information access by others" (p. 30). This definition of privacy rests on the consideration of the way the concept of privacy has changed over time, passing form the conceptualization of privacy as nonintrusion, especially with respect to government activities, to noninterference in one's private decisions, to the identification of privacy with the restriction of the access to personal information. This last conceptualization follows from the consideration of information greasiness and the subsequent need for making sure that relevant information is accessed only by the "right people . . . at the right time."

The importance of safeguarding personal information and the relation between personal information and personal identity is stressed even more by the analysis of privacy proposed by Floridi (2006). He grounds his analysis on an *informational ontology*, according to which all entities existing in the environment, including human beings and their actions as social agents, share an informational nature. This means that "each person [is] constituted by his or her information" (2006, p. 194); in other words an individual's identity is constituted by her information and therefore any access or use of that information which violates the right to privacy is a violation of personal identity. In Floridi's words "the right to informational privacy . . . shields one's personal identity. This is why informational privacy is extremely valuable and ought to be respected" (p. 195).

When considered in relation to personal identity, the definition of ethical guidance for policies for the management of privacy becomes an even more compelling task. In this respect, three noteworthy principles are provided in Moor's analysis: the publicity principle, the justification of exceptions principle, and the adjustment principle. The publicity principle states "rules and conditions governing private situations should be clear and known to the persons affected by them" (1997, p. 32). Moor suggests that privacy is better protected once the scope of the information that can be accessed, under what conditions, and to whom information will be disclosed is clarified. For example, if a user knows in advance that by searching the web with a given search engine access to personal information is given to a third party, then he or she may decide not to use that search engine at all, or to limit its usage only to certain types of queries. This principle encourages informed consent and rational decision-making. The justification of exceptions principle states that breach of privacy is justified if there is a great likelihood that the harm caused by the disclosure of the accessed information will be inferior to the harm prevented by not disclosing the same information. This may be the case, for example, for unveiling someone's search on the Web for child pornography material. Finally, the adjustment principle prescribes that if special circumstances justify a change in the parameters regulating information access, then the change should be made explicit and included in the rules governing privacy.

The analyses of privacy described in this section stress the importance of regulating access to personal information and the need to make some effort, which should be a concern for both policy making and for the development and design of privacy enhancing technologies (PET), "which may allow users to design, shape and maintain their identities as informational agents" (Floridi 2006, p. 195).

6. Conclusion

In this essay the reader's attention has been drawn to information-related problems; that is, those problems that arise in the age of the fourth revolution from the mistreatment of information. A definition of (semantic) information as true semantic data has been provided. Then the analysis focused on three problems: transparency, online trust and privacy, and on the solutions developed in the extant literature for these problems, with the purpose of providing the reader with an overview of the most important positions held with respect to these issues.

The goal of this essay was to highlight the ethical implications of the misuse of information and the need to establish some ethical guidelines for the management of information. Such a need should not be mistaken for a theoretical necessity; on the contrary, it concerns quite concrete aspects of our lives. It concerns us as individuals, as citizens, and eventually as users and consumers. Being able to safeguard personal information, that is, the right to privacy, or to access information about the environment in which we live, or about the agents with whom we interact, that is, the right of being informed, prove to be fundamental rights. Should they be breached, then our daily activities will be affected, and we would witness the impairment of our freedom, autonomy, and decision-making power.

In the age of the fourth revolution information is the ultimate good, and as such, we need to recognize its value and to treat it fairly. Such a need concerns individuals, governments, and social institutions, but also companies and firms. In order to be considered ethically oriented, treating information ethically should be a necessary condition.

Notes

1 Please note that the task that an agent is trusted to perform may entail both performing or not performing a given action. Consider for example the cases in which A may trust B not to sell her a faulty product. In this case A expects B to perform the task of providing a perfectly working product. In the same way, if A trusts B not to be violent, A is actually expecting B to be patient or quiet.

2 Please note that no assumption is made on the type of advantage enjoyed by the trustor nor on whether it can be quantified.

References

Ciborra, C. (2005). Interpreting e-government and development: Efficiency, transparency or governance at a distance? *Information Technology & People*, 18(3): 260–279.

Corritore, C.L., Kracher, B., & Wiedenbeck, S. (2003). On-line trust: Concepts, evolving themes, a model. *International Journal of Human-Computer Studies*, 58(6): 737–758.

DiPiazza, S.A., & Eccles, R.G. (2002). *Building public trust: The future of corporate reporting*. New York: Wiley.

Ess, C.M. (2010). Trust and new communication technologies: Vicious circles, virtuous circles, possible futures. *Knowledge, Technology and Policy*, 23(3–4): 287–305.

Floridi, L. (2005). Is information meaningful data? *Philosophy and Phenomenological Research*, 70(2): 351–370.

Floridi, L. (2006). The ontological interpretation of informational privacy. *Ethics and Information Technology*, 7(4): 185–200.

Floridi, L. (2008a). Data. In W.A. Darity (Ed.), *International encyclopedia of the social sciences*. Detroit: Macmillan.

Floridi, L. (2008b). Information ethics, its nature and scope. In J. v. d. Hoven, & J. Weckert (Eds.), *Information Technology and Moral Philosophy* (Vol. 40–65). Cambridge: Cambridge University Press.

Floridi, L. (2009). The information society and its philosophy. *The Information Society*, 25(3): 153–158.

Floridi, L. (forthcoming). Semantic information and the network theory of account. *Synthese*.

Fried, C. (1984). Privacy. In E.D. Schoeman (Ed.), *Philosophical dimensionsof privacy* (pp. 203–222). New York: Cambridge University Press.

Gambetta, D. (1998). Can we trust trust? Trust: Making and breaking cooperative relations. In D. Gambetta (Ed.), *Trust: Making and breaking cooperative relations* (pp. 213–238). Oxford: Blackwell.

Johnson, D. (1994). *Computer ethics* (2nd ed.). Englewood Cliffs, NJ: Prentice Hall.

Luhmann, N. (1979). *Trust and power*. Chichester: John Wiley & Sons.

Moor, J.H. (1997). Towards a theory of privacy in the information age. *SIGCAS Computer and Society*, 27(3): 27–32.

Nissenbaum, H. (2001). Securing trust online: Wisdom or oxymoron. *Boston University Law Review*, 81(3): 635–664.

Papadopoulou, P. (2007). Applying virtual reality for trust-building e-commerce environments. *Virtual Reality*, 11(2–3): 107–127.

Pettit, P. (1995). The cunning of trust. *Philosophy & Public Affairs*, 24(3): 202–225.

Rachaels, J. (1975). Why is privacy important? *Philosophy and Public Affairs* (Summer), 323–333.

Saxena, K.B.C. (2005). Towards excellence in e-governance. *Journal of Public Sector Management*, 18(6): 498–513.

Seigman, A. B. (2000). *The problem of trust*. Princeton, NJ: Princeton University Press.

Taddeo, M. (2010). Modelling trust in artificial agents, a first step toward the analysis of e-trust. *Minds and Machines*, 20(2): 243–257.

Taddeo, M. (forthcoming-a). Information warfare: A philosophical perspective. *Philosophy and Technology*.

Taddeo, M. (forthcoming-b). An information-based analysis for the puzzle of testimony and trust. *Social Epistemology*.

Taddeo, M., & Floridi, L. (2011). The case for e-trust. *Ethics and Information Technology*, 13(1): 1–3.

Turilli, M., & Floridi, L. (2009). The ethics of information transparency. *Ethics and Information Technology*, 11(2): 105–112.

Turilli, M., Vaccaro, A., & Taddeo, M. (2010). The case of on-line trust. *Knowledge, Technology and Policy*.

Vaccaro, A., & Madsen, P. (2006). Firm information transparency: Ethical questions in the information age. In *Social informatics: An information society for all? In remembrance of Rob Kling* (pp. 145–156). New York: Springer.

Vries, P. d. (2006). Social presence as a conduit to the social dimensions of online trust. In W. IJsselsteijn,

Y. d. Kort, C. Midden, B. Eggen, & E. v. d. Hoven (Eds.), *Persuasive technology* (pp. 55–59). Berlin: Springer.

Weckert, J. (2005). Trust in cyberspace. In R.J. Cavalier (Ed.), *The impact of the Internet on our moral lives* (pp. 95–120). Albany: State University of New York Press.

Winkler, B. (2000). Which kind of transparency? On the need for clarity in monetary policy-making. Frankfurt: European Central Bank.

Workplace Monitoring and Surveillance
The Problem of Trust

JOHN WECKERT

Introduction

> Out west, near Hawtch-Hawtch,
> there's a Hawtch-Hawtcher Bee-Watcher,
> His job is to watch . . .
> Is to keep both his eyes on the lazy town bee.
> A bee that is watched will work harder, you see.
>
> (Dr. Seuss 1973)

The residents of Hawtch-Hawtch are not the only people interested in monitoring the activities of their workers and we will return to them later. According to a recent survey, "From e-mail monitoring and Website blocking to phone tapping and GPS tracking, employers increasingly combine technology with policy to manage productivity and minimize litigation, security, and other risks" (AMA 2007). According to this report, more employers electronically monitor their employees than do not. Given developments in the workplace in the last couple of decades this is hardly surprising. Employers have always had legitimate reasons to keep track of what their employees are doing while at work but current computer and communication technologies (ICT) together with cameras, sound recording devices, global positioning systems (GPS), and other technologies, this tracking has been made much easier. Additionally, the boundaries of the workplace have become indistinct. We can work from home and from just about anywhere with Internet access, depending of course on what our work is. Most workplaces are now heavily computerized, networked, and connected to the Internet. This undoubtedly has many benefits for efficiency, productivity, and flexibility for employees but has also enabled much more efficient monitoring and surveillance of their activities. This too has benefits but is not an unmitigated good.

Although monitoring and surveillance do not mean quite the same thing in all contexts, here for the most part the two will be used interchangeably. Monitoring is generally more focused than surveillance but for most of our purposes the difference is unimportant. We will however return to this briefly at the end of the essay.

Types of Workplace Surveillance

Some monitoring of workers' activity has always occurred. Bosses or supervisors could periodically walk around the factory floor or the office to ensure that all was proceeding as it should be. New technologies, however, particularly ICT technologies, have dramatically increased the possibilities for keeping track of what employees are doing. Closed circuit television (CCTV) is used extensively and in some contexts telephone calls are monitored. This latter monitoring is particularly true of call centers and helplines generally where we commonly hear "Your call is being monitored . . .". Keystroke monitoring is another well-known method of surveillance. One advertisement says:

> With Activity Monitor, SoftActivity™ TS Monitor and SoftActivity™ Keylogger solutions you have your hand on the pulse of what is going on in your LAN [local area network]. This unique spy software allows remote computer monitoring and keylogger recording in real time. The outstanding built-in keystroke recorder allows you to know everything user types in his emails, chats and other programs, including passwords. View and record Internet activity, trace all programs started and run by your network members. (Softactivity n.d.)

One suggested use for this software is "Employee activity monitoring. Find out what they are doing when they are assumed to be working." This advertisement points to another much discussed kind of workplace monitoring, that is, e-mail monitoring and Web activity more generally. The following advertisement is more explicit:

> Employers seeking to regain discipline in their employees' Internet activity commonly use Net Spy Pro. Many companies are faced with employees who waste time online while a supervisor has their back turned. Finding out the TRUTH about what they are doing and correcting an employee's bad behavior couldn't be easier! (Net Spy Pro n.d.)

Many occupations involve travelling between different work sites, delivering products, visiting clients, and so on. Until fairly recently the employee was relatively independent and free from observation on such trips but that has changed, largely as a result of mobile phone and GPS technology. In a recent report in Australia a union official called for tighter legislation on worker surveillance "because plumbers, electricians and others in the service industry were being monitored by GPS in their cars or phones" (Bali 2011).

One product designed for this purpose is SmartTrack:

> When used in a commercial environment the *SmartTrack* solution provides a powerful tool to improve the efficiency of your organisation. The *SmartTrack* fleet management system provides the ability to reduce fuel costs, streamline the dispatch of mobile workforces, meet legislative requirements (e.g. hours worked) or just track where vehicles are located at any chosen minute of the day or night. (SmartTrack n.d.)

Finally, radio-frequency identification (RFID) chips are beginning to be used for employee monitoring. The common use of RFIDs is to embed them in supermarket products, pallets of goods in warehouses, books in libraries, clothes for sale and the like. This allows for much more efficient tracking of products, but

> Companies are also using RFID to track how quickly employees work and have them compete with each other in order for everyone to work faster. If a task normally takes two minutes and an employee finds a more efficient way to get it done in one minute, then the standards are changed . . . (Barker 2009)

This is just a selection of types of electronic monitoring currently being used or under consideration but it is indicative of the current situation and of developments. For a more detailed account see Ciocchetti (2011). We now turn to some justifications of employee monitoring before considering concerns.

Workplace Surveillance Justifications

There are many reasons why employers electronically monitor their employees and they fall into three overlapping kinds. The justification can be in terms of employers, of customers, or of employees. The most obvious is that with better monitored employees, efficiency and profitability will be greater because it will help ensure that they are doing their jobs properly. After all, employers need to make profits or they will not need any employees. Efficiency and productivity are probably the most common reasons given for monitoring. Another advantage to employers is the security of products and especially of intellectual property. Vast amounts of data are collected and stored and this has high value for the running of the business and often in its own right, as well, if it can be sold or if it gives a business an advantage over its rivals. It is clearly in the employer's interests that this data is kept secure and most of the ways of doing this will involve technologies that can be used for monitoring that only legitimate users access the various parts of the system.

An important motivation, and in fact one of the most compelling, is vicarious liability, the liability that employers have for the actions of their employees while at work. *Black's Law Dictionary* gives this definition:

> Vicarious liability: Liability that a supervisory part (such as an employer) bears for the actionable conduct of a subordinate or associate (such as an employee) based on the relationship between the two parties. (Garner 2004, p. 934)

Given this, it seems irresponsible of an employer not to monitor the activities of employees and in particular their use of the Internet or the business's local network. The widespread employment of ICTs has created many new opportunities for criminal and corrupt activities, both online and off, so the employer can be liable for breaches of the law with respect to, for example, defamation, copyright infringement, and obscene material (Cutler 1998; see also Miller et al. 2001).

Another reason for monitoring is safety, something that can be a benefit to both employers and employees alike. Employers are responsible for the safety of their workers and monitoring behavior is an aid to its maintenance and improvement. This is obviously to the employee's advantage but also to the employer's to minimize the risk of being legally responsible for worker injuries. Additionally, surveillance can help reduce bullying and harassment of employees by their co-workers or supervisors.

Other benefits of monitoring for employees concern education and training. This is a commonly stated objective of the monitoring of telephone calls to helplines. It is also sometimes suggested that it helps employers make better decisions regarding promotions by making available more objective measures of the person's abilities.

The third kind of reason relates to customer benefits. The better that employees work, the better the service and the products that customers receive.

These are all, to a greater or lesser extent, persuasive justifications for workplace monitoring and surveillance but not everyone is convinced that it does not require regulation. Along with the undoubted benefits, various concerns have been raised and to these we now turn.

Workplace Surveillance Concerns

Back in 1999, Scott McNealy, the chief executive officer of Sun Microsystems, made the frequently quoted statement "You have zero privacy anyway, get over it" (Sprenger 1999). This was directed at consumer privacy concerns but could easily be applied more generally. The problem with that exhortation is that we do not seem to want to "get over it." Our privacy, at least in some contexts, does concern us to varying degrees and is the most discussed worry for employee monitoring. Monitoring and surveillance can be seen as a violation of the rights of employees to privacy or it can be seen as giving employers too much power over their employees. The more that others know about us the greater can be their control over us. The privacy issue has been discussed extensively so little more will be said about it here except to mention briefly three arguments against a violation of privacy rights.

One of these arguments is that the employees, because they are being paid, have no, or few, privacy rights at work so no rights are violated by monitoring Web use, for example. Another is that, because they are using their employer's computing equipment, no rights are violated if their activity on that equipment is monitored. Neither of these replies is entirely convincing. People are still people when at work and arguably should still have their rights to privacy protected. Another reply is that, providing that the employees are informed of the monitoring, then if they are still willing to work there, they have consented to be monitored. In some contexts this may be reasonable but in situations in which employment is scarce there may be no real alternative to that job. Then consent has little force (Miller and Weckert 2000).

Another worry concerns the health of workers. There is some evidence that monitoring and surveillance can lead to health problems, especially stress-related ones, and be detrimental to employees' wellbeing more generally. It has been argued that electronically monitored employees suffer health, stress, and morale problems to a higher degree than other employees (Bewayo 1996; Kolb and Aiello 1996).

These issues, while important, have received considerable attention, particularly privacy, but here the focus will be on trust. Trust is not often discussed as a concern in the context of workplace surveillance, possibly because of different ways of looking at what trust is. On one type of account, monitoring and surveillance would in fact enhance trust but it will be argued here that this is mistaken. On the account of trust to be outlined in this essay, trust cannot flourish in a context of monitoring and surveillance and, given the importance of trust, this is an issue worthy of further examination. First though, it is worth briefly looking at how trust is commonly discussed in ICT.

Trust in ICT

In the computing industry, trust is often seen purely as a technical security issue. What matters is to make the whole networked system secure. According to Schneiderman, "the trustworthiness of an NIS [Networked Information System] encompasses correctness, reliability, security (conventionally including secrecy, confidentiality, integrity, and availability), privacy, safety, and survivability" (1999, p. 14). More recently there has been discussion of trusted computing and of trust management. The Trusted Computing Group is "a not-for-profit organization formed to develop, define and promote open, vendor-neutral, industry standards for trusted computing building blocks and software interfaces across multiple platforms." By incorporating the trusted computing standards, users will be able to

- Protect Business Critical Data and Systems
- Secure Authentication and Strong Protection of User IDs
- Establish Strong Machine Identity and Integrity
- Ensure Regulatory Compliance with Hardware-Based Security
- Reduce Total Cost of Ownership Through "Built In" Protection. (TCG n.d.)

Another approach is trust management, which, according to a recent discussion, "forms the basis for communicating policy among system elements and demands credential checking for access to all virtual private service resources— along with careful evaluation of credentials against specified policies—before a party can be trusted" (Blaze et al. 2009, p. 44). Furthermore "[t]rust negotiation policies direct the participants' behavior—they describe which credentials are required to access some resource, and which can be disclosed during the negotiation" (Skogsrud et al. 2009, p. 54).

These, together with the closely related identity management, are valuable approaches to improving the reliability and security of computer systems and the argument in this essay is in no way disparaging of these activities. For the effectiveness of large and networked computer systems, this work is absolutely necessary and of very high importance. The argument here is simply that the way that these approaches talk about trust leaves out much of what is important about trust between people. Maybe that does not matter and perhaps having reliable systems is enough, but we will argue later that it is not. The reason that these ways of talking about trust in the computing industry are relevant to the current discussion is that, on this view, trust is under no threat from workplace monitoring and surveillance. In fact, the monitoring and surveillance, or the technologies that enable it, may be part of the overall trustworthy system. In the next section an account of trust will be outlined that is threatened by monitoring and surveillance.

Accounts of Trust

In this section an account of trust will be described in some detail in order to show that an important sense of trust, in fact the most important, is not captured well by the typical approaches in ICT as outlined above. It is this sense of trust that is threatened by monitoring and surveillance. It might be thought at the outset that if there is a sense of trust that is not threatened, why worry about another sense in which it is? This is a legitimate query and the detailed answer will be left until later but the short answer is that trust between humans is a rich concept and something important is lost by monitoring and surveillance.

Accounts of trust have been categorized as cognitive, that is, based primarily on belief and evidence, and noncognitive, with attitudes being most important. At the simplest level, if person A trusts person B to do something X, then on a cognitivist view this means that A believes that he has good evidence that B will do X. On a noncognitivist account it is rather that A has a particular attitude towards B. Such a view will be spelt out shortly, but first some comments on the difference between trust and reliance to highlight some important features of the former.

We regularly rely on other people or on things in order to achieve our goals. Sometimes I rely on my friend to take me to work and other times I rely on my bicycle to get me to work. In both cases if something goes wrong, if my friend forgets to pick me up or of if my bicycle tyres get punctured, I am disadvantaged. These two cases are significantly different. In both cases we can talk of trust; I trust my friend and I trust my bicycle, but in no interesting sense do I trust the latter even though I certainly do rely on it. On the other hand, when I rely on my friend to take me to work, I do trust him to do it. The main difference between these cases is that my friend can choose to take me or not; he can choose to help or harm me. While it makes sense in English to say that I trust the bicycle, that is a very different sense of trust, and a much thinner one, than the sense in which I trust my friend. Trust involves the trustee, the person trusted, having the ability and opportunity to make a choice. But the trustor, the person trusting, must also be in a position to choose to trust or not to trust. A beggar may rely on passers-by for sustenance, but have no trust that his needs will be met—he simply has no choice. Trust involves choices. The trustor chooses to rely on the trustee making a particular choice. Reliance, on the other hand, might or might not involve choice. In general then, if A trusts B to achieve some goal X, then A chooses to rely on B making certain choices.

More must be said here because choosing to rely on choices in itself is not enough. It must be reliance on a choice made for certain reasons. Relying on the choice of an enemy does not sound like a good idea. Annette Baier (1986) argues that trust is reliance on a person's goodwill towards one. If A trusts B then A relies on B's goodwill toward A, that is, A relies on B's choice because of B's goodwill towards A. Something like this seems right but to allow for cases where there is little goodwill, we will say that if A trusts B then A relies on B's disposition to behave favorably toward A, whether it be because B has the required goodwill, or is a moral person who wants to do the right thing even to those he does not like.

As noted at the beginning of this section, cognitive accounts of trust are based on rational choice. On this view, if A trusts B to do X then A believes or expects that B will do X. Coleman emphasizes this in the following:

> the elements confronting the potential trustor are nothing more or less than the considerations a rational actor applies in deciding whether to place a bet . . . The potential trustor must decide between not placing trust, in which case there is no change in his utility, and placing trust, in which case the expected utility relative to his current status is the potential gain times the chance of gain minus the potential loss times the chance of loss. A rational actor will place trust if the first product is greater than the second . . . (Coleman, 1990, p. 99)

One problem with this type of account is that it does not reflect well how trust actually works. Typically we do not consciously make decisions after weighing up the evidence before each occasion on which we trust. Another worry has been alluded to earlier. Certain conditions that strengthen beliefs about whether or not the trustee will do as expected actually reduce the space for trust rather than strengthening it. That is, some conditions that strengthen beliefs that someone will do as expected should strengthen trust but in fact they make it less likely or impossible because they reduce space for it. This is true for example if I constantly monitor my employees. My belief that they are doing their jobs properly is strengthened, I have more confidence that they are doing so, but my space for trusting them is reduced (this will be examined in more detail later).

This however is not the case with all belief-strengthening conditions. Conditions which lead me to believe that I am loved by someone strengthen my beliefs about that person's behavior toward me, but that does not reduce the space for trust, it broadens it. It is the kind of *conditions* that are important. This argument, however, that *some* of the conditions that strengthen expectations regarding behavior reduce space for trust, remains a significant difficulty for purely cognitive views.

An alternative to the cognitive type of account is to consider trust in terms of attitudes. Uslander, for example, says that trust (specifically, generalized trust) does not depend on evidence (2002, p. 32). He sees trust as primarily an optimistic way of viewing the world, in other words, an attitude. His argument is that trust as we know it just cannot be explained adequately in terms of beliefs. If I trust more or less anyone with whom I come into contact, it is not because I have beliefs and expectations about each of them, it is rather that I have an optimistic attitude to people in general. These ideas have something in common too, with Olli Lagerspertz, who says that to trust "is to present behavior in a certain light" (1998, p. 5). Explaining trust in terms of attitudes seems plausible and is also an important aspect of Annette Baier's account, but the cognitive aspect is also present, something supported by Baier, who includes cognitive, affective, and conative aspects (Baier 1994, p. 132).

Trust as "Seeing As"

Here trust will be explained in terms of *seeing as* and this will help highlight at least the attitudinal and cognitive aspects. If A trusts B then A *sees* B's behavior *as* being trustworthy or, simply, A *sees* B *as* trustworthy. Another way of putting it is that A sees B as someone who will, typically, do as he or she says, who is reliable, who will act with the interests of A in mind, and so on. For the sake of brevity however, we will talk of A's seeing B as someone trustworthy. The idea is similar to that of seeing the ambiguous Jastrow duck-rabbit drawing as a duck or as a rabbit. It is not merely that I know that it can be taken as either the picture of a duck or of a rabbit. The important point is that I can *see* it as a duck or as a rabbit. When shown the picture I can truthfully say "I see a duck" or "I see a picture of a duck." That is stronger than merely knowing that it can be seen as a duck picture or a rabbit picture (see Wittgenstein 1968, pp. 193–195). "A sees B as trustworthy" can be explained similarly. If I see my employee as trustworthy, I could say "He is trustworthy" or "He is reliable, will do as he says, will work conscientiously, has my interests in mind and so on." This does not mean that beliefs and expectations are not in some way involved, but more on that shortly.

Looking at trust in this way makes it resemble a Kuhnian paradigm (Kuhn 1970). Thomas Kuhn argued that scientists normally undertake their research within a fixed and assumed framework. This "normal science" operates within a generally accepted paradigm and it is this that enables the puzzle-solving activity of this science. Unless there are good reasons to, scientists normally do not question their underlying basic theories or the framework within which they are working. These are held constant in order to solve the problems that arise within those paradigms.

The argument is that trust is of the ilk of normal science. In most cases when A trusts B to do X, A does not go through some rational decision procedure, weighing up the options and examining the evidence before deciding to trust or not to trust. A just trusts B to do X (or just does not trust, as the case may be). Trust can be seen as a paradigm for puzzle-solving; the puzzle to be solved being whether or not to rely on B to do X. Where there is trust, that is, where the potential trustor is operating within a trusting paradigm, there will not be, in most cases, any conscious thought. A will just trust as a matter of course.

This seems to be what commonly happens. If asked why I trust even some stranger, I may not be able to articulate my reasons, at least not easily and quickly, and may resort to saying that I have no reason not to. Trust here is the default position. I trust unless I have good reason not to. This, however, does not show that I have no beliefs about the stranger (or about people in general), just that I have no *explicit* beliefs that I can easily verbalize. Michael Polanyi argued that we know more than we can say, and that this *more* could be explained in terms of tacit knowledge (Polanyi 1967). Whether any knowledge is inherently tacit does not matter here; that at any point in time some knowledge, but not necessarily the same knowledge, is always tacit, is enough. Substituting "belief" for "knowledge," we can say that we always hold some tacit beliefs. While it may be true that I have no explicit beliefs about people in general being trustworthy, it does not follow that I have no such tacit beliefs. A tacit belief, in the way that it is meant here, is nothing mysterious. We hold a vast number of beliefs that we seldom bother to even try to articulate, and we must do this if meaningful communication is to be possible. These can be called background beliefs, or common-sense beliefs. Most of these, unless we have reason to think of them, are held tacitly. Not all background beliefs are commonsense or held by all. My background beliefs in the general trustworthiness of others, even strangers, may not be widely held.

This approach does highlight some of the important features of trust. One is that we can see people as trustworthy, and in fact trust them, without having any explicit beliefs about the matter. We do not normally think about trust too much, or some-one's trustworthiness, except when something goes wrong. If I trusted someone and was let down, then I think about it. It is similar to normal science being conducted within an unquestioned paradigm as described by Kuhn. A second feature of this approach is that it shows, or provides a way of explaining, the intertwining of the attitudinal and the cognitive. Beliefs play a role in our attitudes but much of the time they are tacit.

A third feature of trust that it highlights the robustness of trust. Trust contains an element of commitment that is often overlooked, in much the same way that scientists are committed to paradigm in normal science, as Kuhn describes. This model chal-lenges the common view that while trust is difficult to build it is rather fragile and easy to demolish. (Govier raises this issue in the first sentence of her book, 1997, p. 3, where she writes "The human capacity for trust is amazing.") It is not clear that trust is so difficult to build, but of more importance here is the claim that it is fragile. It is not as fragile as is often claimed. This view of the fragility of trust seems to be based on something like a Popperian falsificationist view of science. According to Karl Popper (1963), while a scientific theory cannot be verified, an incompatible observation falsifies it. We know that in science the situation is more complicated than that. A well-known historical example comes from astronomy. The Ptolemaic view of earth at the center of the solar system did not fit well with observations of the movements of the planets but, instead of taking these as falsifying the theory that the earth was at the center, modifications were made to the theory to try to make it fit. None of these proved to be very satisfactory but were considered to be better than rejecting the theory. This was largely because there was nothing better with which to replace it. It is similar with respect to trust. It is probably true that if I know that A has *deceived* me in a situation in which I trusted him, my trust will be weakened or, perhaps, extinguished. According to Descartes "a wise man never entirely trusts those who have once cheated him" (1964, p. 62). But most cases are not like this. When expectations are not met, deceit is not always, and probably not usually, involved. Suppose that I trust A to do X but he does not do X. It is unlikely that I will stop trusting him on the basis of one, or even a few, lapses of this kind, unless, of course, I do suspect deceit. There could be many reasons why A did not do X. There may have been some misunderstanding between us and he did not realize that I expected him to do it. He might have had good reasons for not doing it which are unknown to me, but such that if I did know of them I would approve of his not doing it. I do *not* immediately see A's behavior as being untrustworthy, just as in science where, if there is incompatibility between an observation and a theory, there is more than one way to explain the incoherence. One need not reject the theory, or the trust, outright. Willard van Orman Quine's *maxim of minimum mutilation* is relevant here (Quine 1970, p. 7). Quine says that if our observations do not fit our theories, we modify our views in a way that minimally upsets, or mutilates, our total set of beliefs. Similarly Imre Lakatos talks of a hard core at the center of scientific research programmes, which is surrounded by a protective belt of auxiliary hypotheses (Lakatos 1974, p. 133). If that hard core is challenged by observations, the auxiliary hypotheses are changed first in order to save the central theories. The hardcore belief that the sun was at the center was protected by auxiliary hypotheses of epicycles. Our most cherished beliefs and attitudes, or this hard core, are affected least, or mutilated least; they are protected by the auxiliary hypotheses. And trust in someone is frequently cherished. I will, if I can, find some explanation that does not involve rejecting my trust. Just like Kuhn in his explanation of defending scientific paradigms, I will most likely treat the actions as anomalies to be explained by "auxiliary hypotheses." Suppose that I have a highly trusted employee who on one occasion unexpectedly does something quite out of character and appears to have let me down badly. Rather than immediately losing trust in this person, as would be the case if trust were fragile, I will most like try to find explanations for the behavior. He might have misunderstood my instructions, he may have become sick or had an accident or received upsetting news. A host of "auxiliary hypotheses" could save my "hardcore" trust in him.

This view of trust is supported by some empirical research as well. According to Rempel, Ross, and Holmes (2001, p.58) talking of trust in close relationships, "trust can act as a filter through which people interpret their partner's motives." People in high trust relationships interpret their partner's actions "in ways that are consistent with their positive expectations," while those in low trust relationships "are less likely to attribute their partner's behavior to benevolent motives."

Something must now be said about when, or under what circumstances, it is reasonable or rational to trust. Not all trust is reasonable; some can be just silly. On a cognitive account of trust, such as Coleman's, A's trust in B to do X is reasonable when there is good evidence that it B will do X. A's trust in B is reasonable if A knows or justifiably believes that B is trustworthy, or if A justifiably believes that most people are trustworthy most of the time and justifiably believes that he has no reason to distrust B on this occasion. The next step is to spell out the conditions under which it justifiable to believe in B's trustworthiness in this case.

A different type of justification for trusting behavior must be given for the "seeing as" account of trust. Consider the duck-rabbit drawing again. While it can be seen as a duck or as a rabbit, it would require extreme imagination in normal circumstances to see it as a cucumber or as a dictionary of quotations. Only some *seeings*, or interpretations, are plausible. It should be noted too that the duck-rabbit drawing itself is most ambiguous when context free. If seen in the context of rabbit stories and unambiguous rabbit pictures it is most plausible to see it as a rabbit. While it is still certainly possible to see it as a duck, it is more reasonable to see it as a rabbit unless there is good reason not to, for example if the caption is "Spot the duck in the colony of rabbits." The situation is similar in the case of an instance of trust. The reasonableness must be in terms of the reasonableness of the *seeing as*. A's seeing B as trustworthy is reasonable to the extent that A's seeing B in this way gives a coherent account of B's behavior. In a particular instance of A trusting B, A will of course have an expectation of B's trustworthiness *in this instance* and this expectation will be based on past experience of, not only B's behavior, but also of that of many of the other people with whom A interacts. This makes it look as if the justification of trust is similar in this account to that of a more purely cognitive account. The difference is that, if A is operating within a trusting paradigm, no weighing up of evidence or options typically occurs when A trusts B. He just trusts. Beliefs will still be involved in the sense that A has tacit beliefs regarding B's trustworthiness and that of others. If questioned he could most probably articulate his reasons for trusting B and for trusting most other people most of the time. But normally, unless something untoward happens, he trusts without much thought; he is working within his accepted paradigm.

On this view, a few cases of possibly untrustworthy behavior will not count against the reasonableness of the overall trust. To recap what was said previously, those cases can be counted as just anomalies to be explained away. A will try to "minimally mutilate" his view of B just as I try to in the case of the trusted employee who behaves anomalously. If there are too many anomalies, of course, such a stance becomes no longer viable and maintaining trust will be unreasonable. This is similar to Kuhn's view of paradigm change. Where the threshold is will vary, depending on the strength of the trust. Where the trust is very strong, say the trust in a parent, the trust "paradigm" will be very resistant to challenge. The "protective belt" will surround the beliefs in trustworthiness. Too much is at stake to reject those beliefs. Where the trust is less, there will be a correspondingly weaker resistance to change. The important point is that trust can reasonably be maintained when isolated cases of apparent untrustworthiness occur. When there are too many of these "anomalies" and trust is lost, there will be something like a "gestalt switch." After the switch, A will see B as untrustworthy, and possibly trustworthy actions will be interpreted as anomalies and explained away. Again close parallels exist with Kuhn's description of paradigm change in science.

Finally, something needs to be said about the application of this model. So far it has been applied to trust relationships between individuals only, but this requires qualification. Often we trust a person in some respect rather than in all respects. A might trust B to care for his children, but not to be punctual for a meeting. An employee might be trusted to work conscientiously but not to remember appointments. Trust is frequently relative to contexts but that is compatible with the seeing as model. A sees B as trustworthy in context C, but not necessarily in context D. This model of trust can also accommodate trust of institutions. For example, A sees the government as trustworthy, or A sees business X as trustworthy. Again, these could be relativized to particular contexts.

Earlier in this section it was claimed that monitoring and surveillance in the workplace reduce the space for trust. The next section develops and explains this.

Trust and Surveillance

To show that surveillance is detrimental for trust, it will first be argued that surveillance reduces scope for autonomy and then that autonomy is essential for trust. From this it will follow that surveillance reduces scope for trust.

Surveillance reduces scope for autonomy

For our purposes here an employee is autonomous in the workplace to the extent that he or she can make decisions and act on them. There are obvious limits, of course. An employee making truck tyres cannot reasonably decide to tie pink ribbons around Easter eggs and act on that decision, in that workplace. The decisions will normally be limited to how hard to work, how best to do what has to be done, and so on, but, in the workplace context, this amount of autonomy is significant. It allows the employee to demonstrate that he or she is a conscientious worker, has initiative and the like. Without this level of autonomy these attributes cannot be demonstrated. In a heavily monitored workplace I cannot show that I am a good worker. There is no freedom to do the right thing without the possible, and plausible, retort "He is only doing it because he knows the he is being monitored." This is a general point and not limited to the workplace. I have little freedom to show that I have no inclination to take a handgun onto an aeroplane. Airport surveillance almost ensures that no handguns are taken on board planes but this is not a restriction on my autonomy that bothers me. The benefits of a safe flight clearly outweigh the costs. It may also be true that the benefits of workplace surveillance outweigh the costs of loss of autonomy but we will say more about this shortly.

Autonomy is essential for trust

It was argued earlier that trust is only possible in situations where both the trustor and the trustee have autonomy. The former must be in a position to choose to trust and the latter free to do or not do what the trustor wants. Trust is only possible where the trustor can be let down by the trustee. When we trust we become vulnerable and in situations where either the trustor or the trustee lacks autonomy this is not possible. We can justifiably rely on someone but that is similar to relying on a chair to take my weight. While we do use "trust" in this way, it is a much thinner sense than that outlined earlier. Trust between people is much richer than that and this is the important sense here. Autonomy is necessary for this thick trust between people.

Surveillance reduces scope for trust

That surveillance reduces the space for trust follows directly from the previous two claims. Consider a maximum security prison where the prisoners are locked up and under constant surveillance. The prison officers have no need to trust the prisoners simply because the prisoners have little choice but to do as they are told. But not only do the officers not need to trust them, there is no room left for trust.

The difficulty of developing trust in this environment is outlined well by Bertram Raven:

> Having used coercive power, along with surveillance, the power holder attributes any successful influence to the power holder, rather than to the target, tending thereby to further devalue and distrust the target. Further influence attempts will be even more coercive, more distrusting, and will tend to further devalue the target . . . (Raven 1993, p. 242)

If this is right, there is no scope for me to impress either my superiors or my fellow workers. I do what I ought to but the perception is that I only do it because I have no choice. Carl Botan and Mihaela Vorvoreanu argue too, on the basis of their research, that surveillance communicates "the overwhelming meta-message" to employees that they are distrusted. They continue "Many subjects also see surveillance as communicating the fact that management feels that they deserve to be treated as children" (Botan & Vorvoreanu 2005, p. 135). To be treated as a child is to be treated as one who as yet does not possess the maturity to be trusted. Here there is no room to enhance my reputation or gain esteem.

This might all be true but someone could argue that it does not matter. Just as some have suggested that privacy is an outdated notion, workplace trust might be too, at least the sort of trust outlined in the previous section. With all of the possibilities for monitoring and surveillance, why worry about trust? This question will be answered now.

Does It Matter?

Various concerns have been expressed about workplace monitoring and surveillance, some of which were mentioned earlier and will not be rehearsed again. Here we will consider why the kind of trust just outlined matters, from a moral point of view. If it does matter and if it is threatened by monitoring and surveillance, then we have another argument for carefully considering how that activity should be undertaken.

The issues will be considered from three ethical perspectives: consequentialism, deontology, and virtue theory. Some of the concerns, however, arise from more than one of the perspectives.

First, from a consequentialist point of view, is reducing the space of trust a good idea, particularly with regard to productivity and efficiency? Trust, it is generally claimed, increases efficiency. According to Francis Fukuyama, "People who do not trust one another will end up cooperating only under a system of formal rules and regulations . . . This legal apparatus, serving as a substitute for trust, entails what economists call "transaction costs" (Fukuyama 1995, pp. 11, 27–28).

Trust is spoken of as social capital (Putnam 1994) and in high trust situations people work and the community in general runs with a minimum of supervision and rules and therefore with low transaction costs. Returning now to Hawtch-Hawtch, Dr. Seuss puts these transaction costs clearly on display. Unfortunately, employing someone to watch the town bee did not seem to produce the desired increase in production, so it was assumed that the bee-watcher was not doing his job, so a bee-watcher-watcher was employed. But while

> The Bee-Watcher Watcher watched the Bee-Watcher.
> He didn't watch well. So another Hawtch-Hawtcher
> had to come in as a Watch-Watcher-Watcher.

That did not solve the lazy bee problem either so eventually the whole town was either a bee-watcher, a bee-watcher-watcher, or a watcher-watcher of a higher order. But we are given no evidence that the bee's output increased much even then. Even if it did, however, the town had to bear considerable transaction costs for a small increase in honey or flower fertilization. The moral of the tale is that high and often unrecognized costs are associated with lack of trust. In some circumstances the benefits most likely do outweigh the costs but even here it would be better to try to find a way of creating and maintaining trust than to simply resort to monitoring and surveillance.

Another consideration for a consequentialist, at least for a utilitarian, is that one should always act to maximize happiness and a strong case can be made that trusting people is good for them. According to David Hume

> Our reputation, our character, our name are considerations of vast weight and importance; and even the other causes of pride; virtue, beauty and riches; have little influence, when not seconded by the opinions and sentiments of others. (Hume 1975, p. 316)

This might not be true for everyone but it surely is for the vast majority and showing someone that he is trusted is evidence that he is held in high regard, at least in certain respects. If it is obvious to me that someone trusts me, I feel better about myself than if I know that I am not trusted. Being trusted is good for one's self-esteem. While this is certainly not an overriding consideration, on consequentialist grounds it must be taken into account.

Second, not trusting does not fare well from a deontological point of view either. Immanuel Kant argued that people should always be treated as ends and not purely as means to achieve some purpose. People are owed respect as autonomous human beings and not merely for what they can do. Given this, there is a duty to trust others in order to allow them to act as autonomous humans. Not trusting someone is not respecting that person. In the workplace, not trusting employees to do what they are supposed to do is a sign of disrespect and is a case of treating them as means to an end and not as ends in themselves. Clearly some qualifications are required. First, Kant's point was not that people cannot ever be treated as means. What is important is that they are not treated *merely* as means. We regularly treat people as means in order to achieve a goal. My taxi driver is a means for me to get to the airport but I should not treat him just as a means like I might treat the taxi. He is a person who deserves my respect. The same is obviously true of employers and their employees. The employees are of course a means for the achievement of a goal but they are more than that. They are not simply commodities necessary for production. As autonomous humans they deserve respect and in general deserve to be trusted. The "in general" is important here. People deserve respect so the default should be that I trust someone unless there is good reason to think otherwise. This is the reverse of what is commonly stated, that people should not be trusted until they have demonstrated that they are trustworthy.

Finally, from a virtue ethics perspective, one ought to develop virtues as much as one can. Trust, as developed here, is important for this to be achievable. Trust enables people to act autonomously and develop certain virtues that are difficult to develop in its absence. In a highly monitored workplace, for example, it is difficult for an employee to use his autonomy to develop the virtue of conscientiousness, simply because his autonomy is restricted. As noted earlier, when we trust we become vulnerable to the trustee. He or she is in a position to harm us in a way that is not possible when not trusted. The trusted person therefore is in a much better position to develop virtues associated with doing the right thing and caring for others than someone not trusted. From a virtue ethics point of view trust is valuable too.

Workplace Monitoring and Surveillance Revisited

Throughout this essay monitoring and surveillance have been used as if they were the same thing and for the purposes so far the differences are insignificant. Now however it is necessary to look a little more closely at them in order to distinguish instances of monitoring and surveillance that are more trust threatening from those that are less so. In general, the activities of a person or a group are monitored for a particular reason, whereas surveillance is less focused and is more concerned with seeing what is happening. This distinction is certainly not sharp. Monitoring someone continuously could be described as keeping him under surveillance and typical airport security could be called either monitoring passengers for weapons or keeping all passengers under surveillance. While nothing very much hinges on whether something is called monitoring or surveillance, there are two important underlying issues for our discussion of trust in the workplace. The first is related to authentication. A core issue for a computer system, and especially for networked systems, is how best to ensure that users can only access those parts of the system for which they have authorization. This is obviously necessary but it involves monitoring. Each time that a user tries to gain access to some part of the system, usernames and passwords must be checked against a list of authorized users. Firewalls established to keep unwanted people out of the system are similar. These can loosely be called blocking technologies. Their aim is to block unauthorized people from entering the system as a whole or from certain areas of it. This kind of monitoring (but it is not normally called monitoring), is not significantly trust threatening. It might be better if it were not necessary but it limits our autonomy only minimally. This is similar to locking houses and offices and only giving keys to certain people.

This kind of monitoring is very focused and in general focused monitoring does not reduce the space for trust very much. If an employer justified suspicion that an employee is engaged in criminal activities, harassing a colleague, is not working properly or suchlike, monitoring this employee for those particular misdemeanours is also of minimal concern. Quite different is surveillance that is essentially a "fishing expedition," that is, keeping workers under surveillance in case they do something wrong or that the employer does not like. The technologies outlined earlier, if not explicitly designed for this purpose, can all easily be employed for that kind of surveillance. That is the surveillance that seriously endangers trust.

Conclusion

The electronic monitoring and surveillance of employees in their workplaces has been raising concerns for the last few decades. Most concerns have been about employee privacy and some about health. In this essay it has been argued that dangers to trust are also significant and need to be examined. Dangers to trust have not been widely recognized and this is unfortunate. In the computing world trust is often seen as a purely technical issue related to computer security. This is undoubtedly important but it is not the most significant form of trust for humans. Trust as outlined in this essay is a very rich concept and much of its importance is lost in situations in which it is reduced or lost. Monitoring and surveillance can threaten it in the workplace, it has been argued here. The argument is not that those activities are never justified, they clearly are, but rather that they should be restricted as much as possible and that those technologies and methods least likely to damage trust should be the first choice. Trust, in the rich sense described in this essay, is worth generating and maintaining in the workplace. In fact, it is the morally right thing to do.

Various parts of this essay are based on Weckert 2011, 2005, and 2002.

References

AMA (2007) "Electronic monitoring & surveillance survey," American Management Association, retrieved February 25, 2013 from http://press.amanet.org/press-releases/177/2007-electronic-monitoring-surveillance-survey/

Baier, A.C. (1986) "Trust and antitrust," Ethics, 96: 231–260.

Baier, A.C. (1994) "Trust and its vulnerabilities." In A.C. Baier, Moral prejudices: Essays on ethics, Cambridge, MA: Harvard University Press; 130–151.

Bali, S. (2011) "Beware! Your boss may be spying on you at work," The Economic Times, retrieved February 25, 2013 from http://articles.economictimes.indiatimes.com/2011-05-01/news/29493330_1_plumbers-monitoring-phones

Barker, J. (2009) "Businesses use RFID to track workers, pay for fewer hours," MEDILL Reports (Jan. 14), retrieved February 25, 2013 from http://news.medill.northwestern.edu/chicago/news.aspx?id=111561

Bewayo, E. (1996) "Electronic management: Its downside especially in small business." In J. Kizza (ed.), Social and ethical effects of the computer revolution, Jefferson, NC: McFarland; 186–199.

Blaze, M., Kannan, S., Lee, I., Sokolsky, O., Smith, J.M., Keromytis, A.D., & Lee, W. (2009) "Dynamic trust management," IEEE Computer (Feb.): 44–52.

Botan, C., & Vorvoreanu, M. (2005) "What do employees think about electronic surveillance at work?" In J. Weckert (ed.), Electronic monitoring in the workplace: Controversies and solutions, Hershey, PA: Idea Group Publishing, 123–144.

Ciocchetti, C.A. (2011) "The eavesdropping employer: A twenty-first century framework for employee monitoring," American Business Law Journal, 48: 285–369.

Coleman, J.S. (1990) *Foundations of social theory*, Cambridge, MA: Harvard University Press.

Cutler, P.G. (1998) "E-mail: Employees and liability," *Chemistry in Australia* (Mar.): 30–31.

Descartes, René (1964) *Meditations*. In E. Anscombe & P.T. Geach (eds.), *Descartes: Philosophical Writings*, London: Nelson.

Dr. Seuss (1973) "The bee watcher." In *Did I ever tell you how lucky you are?* New York, Random House.

Fukuyama, F. (1995) *Trust: The social virtues and the creation of prosperity*, London, Penguin Books.

Garner, B.A. (ed.) (2004) *Black's law dictionary* (8th ed.), St. Paul, MI: Thomson / West.

Govier, T. (1997) *Social trust and human communities*, Montreal: McGill-Queen's University Press.

Hume, D. (1975) *A Treatise of Human Nature*, ed. L.A. Selby-Bigge, Oxford: Clarendon Press.

Kolb, K.J., & Aiello, J.R. (1996) "The effects of electronic performance monitoring on stress: Locus of control as a moderator variable," *Computers in Human Behavior*, 12: 407–423.

Kuhn, T.S. (1970) *The structure of scientific revolutions* (2nd ed.), Chicago: University of Chicago Press.

Lagerspertz, O. (1998) *The tacit demand*, Dordrecht: Kluwer Academic.

Lakatos, I. (1974) "Falsification and the methodology of scientific research programmes." In I. Lakatos & A. Musgrave (eds.), *Criticism and the Growth of Knowledge*, Cambridge: Cambridge University Press; 91–196.

Miller, S., Freeman, P., Melser, P., Roberts, P., & Weckert, J. (2001) *eCorruption vulnerabilities in the NSW public sector*. Report for the Independent Commission against Corruption, Centre for Applied Philosophy and Public Ethics, Canberra, Australia, retrieved March 15, 2013 from http://www.cappe.edu.au/docs/reports/consultancy/ICACeCorruption.pdf

Miller, S., & Weckert, J. (2000) "Privacy, the workplace and the Internet," *Journal of Business Ethics*, 28: 255–265.

Net Spy Pro (n.d.) *Home page*, retrieved March 15, 2013 from http://www.retinax.com/netspypro/

Polanyi, M. (1967) *The tacit dimension*, London: Routledge and Kegan Paul.

Popper, K. (1963) *Conjectures and refutations*, London: Routledge.

Putnam, R.D. (1994) *Making democracy work: Civic traditions in modern Italy*, Princeton, NJ: Princeton University Press.

Quine, W.V. (1970) *Philosophy of logic*, Englewood Cliffs, NJ: Prentice-Hall.

Raven, B.H. (1993) "The bases of power: Origins and recent developments," *Journal of Social Issues*, 49: 227–251.

Rempe, J.K., Ross, M., & Holmes, J.G. (2001) "Trust and communicated attributions in close relationships." *Journal of Personality and Social Psychology*, 81: 57–64.

Schneiderman, F.B. (ed.) (1999) *Trust in cyberspace*, Washington, DC: National Academic Press.

Skogsrud, H., Motahari-Nezhad, H.R. Benatallah, B., & Casati, F. (2009) "Modeling trust negotiation for web services," *IEEE Computer (Feb.)*: 54–61.

SmartTrack (n.d.) *Home page*, retrieved February 25, 2013 from http://smarttrack.com.au/

Softactivity (n.d.) *Home page*, retrieved February 25, 2013 from http://www.softactivity.com/

Sprenger, P. (1999) "Sun on privacy: 'Get over it'," *Wired* (Jan), retrieved February 25, 2013 from http://www.wired.com/politics/law/news/1999/01/17538

TCG (n.d.) *Home page*, retrieved February 25, 2013 from http://www.trustedcomputinggroup.org/

Uslander, E.M. (2002) *The moral foundations of trust*, Cambridge: Cambridge University Press.

Weckert, J. (2002) "Trust, corruption, and surveillance in the electronic workplace." In K. Brunnstein & J. Berleur (eds.), *Human choice and computers: Issues of choice and quality of life in the information society*, Boston: Kluwer; 109–120.

Weckert, J. (2005) "On-line trust." In R. Cavalier (ed.), *The impact of the Internet on our moral lives*, Albany: State University of New York Press; 95–117.

Weckert, J. (2011) "Trusting software agents." In C. Ess & M. Thorseth (eds.), *Trust and virtual worlds: Contemporary perspectives*, New York: Peter Lang; 89–102.

Wittgenstein, L. (1968) *Philosophical investigations*, trans. G.E.M. Anscombe, Oxford: Blackwell.

The goal in this series is for you to be able to write an essay that critically evaluates a business problem involving ethical issues. Your essay should include an examination of business practice as well as related ethical dimensions. In Chapter 3, we discussed how to bring the ethical dimensions to the fore through the use of detection questions. These were put side by side with the principles of professional practice.

In this chapter, we compare these two types of issues. This comparison can be accomplished in multiple ways; the one offered here invokes a technique that rates professional practice as having three levels of embeddedness: surface, medium, and deep. *Embeddedness* refers to how deeply ingrained a proposition is to the essential nature of the subject area being examined. The level of interaction allows you to see at a glance how professional practice issues, cost issues, and ethical issues conflict.

You need a model of some type to evaluate the professional practice issues, cost considerations, and ethical principles that may conflict. When ethical issues and professional practical issues conflict, you do not *automatically* choose either. Some ethical problems can be solved easily and do not require forgoing the dictates of professional practice. At other times, an ethical problem must be solved in such a way that professional practices must be overridden.

You need a methodology for comparison. The *embedded concept model* is one such methodology. I illustrate how this works with several examples that employ a chart to clarify the ways the concepts conflict. You may also want to use computer technology to chart your responses. A conventional approach is to present these differences through narrative description. The chart is no substitute for solid narrative description, but it simplifies and makes visual the model I propose.

Case 1

You are vice-president for sales of a life insurance company. You have noticed that many policyholders have been given information regarding future interest rates on universal life policies that have proven to have been too optimistic. As a result, seven to ten years after taking out a policy, policyholders must cut back on their death benefit or pay higher premiums (because the cash values that were projected to accrue and offset higher mortality rates in later years never materialized). Since the cash values were not sufficient to support the policies, a policyholder must pay more or cut back on the benefits of the policy. Both alternatives cause policyholders to feel that they have been cheated.

As a result of this situation, you propose that all of your company's agents project interest rates one-half point *below* what the policies are currently paying when the agents attempt to make a sale. The agents are very reluctant to do this because they believe that they will lose many potential customers to agents from other companies who project rates *even higher* than the policies currently pay. The current professional practice is to quote the current interest rate.

Let us examine this situation via professional practice issues, ethical issues, and cost issues. Each of these areas is important in forming a business decision.

Professional practice issues

1. A professional is required only to follow the law and the guidelines of the professional association. Nothing in the insurance industry's standards requires projecting universal life policies at one-half point below current values offered by the company.
2. Going beyond the law and the association's guidelines could be perceived as raising the standard that other insurance companies would be required to follow. Meeting this additional standard could require the use of funds that had not been budgeted.

Ethical issues

1. A person who buys an insurance policy expects the rates quoted to be accurate projections. Such a policy seems to be a simple example of telling the truth.
2. *Informed* consent is necessary for autonomous decision making.

Cast issues

1. Stating interest rates one-half point below what is current may result in some lost sales, the problem is not considered serious. In fact, there are sales opportunities for companies associated with honest policies.
2. Additional costs would be incurred in implementing a new system.

Analysis of the Illustration Practices at XYZ Insurance

	Surface	Medium	Deep
Professional Practice Issues			
A professional is required to follow only the law and the professional association's guidelines		x	
The insurance company may be accused of raising the standard	x		
Ethical Issues			
Personal integrity and truthfulness should be followed.			x
Only a truly *informed* consent satisfies the conditions of autonomy			x
Cost Issues			
New guidelines may affect future sales		x	
Additional costs may be incurred in implementing a new system	x		

In this simple case, the ethical issues override those of cost or professional practice. That means that ethical guidelines are "easier" to follow. When a great disparity exists between the embeddedness of one alternative as opposed to the other (meaning deep as opposed to surface), that direction should drive the decision. One should implement the other side as it is possible. For example, in this case, the insurance company should implement the program of projecting life insurance company should implement the program of projecting life insurance cash values one-half point below the current rate it offers. It should do this because the professional issues are not deeply embedded, the ethical issues are deeply embedded, and the cost issues are not deeply embedded (and the policy may actually become an advantage).

Case 2

In other cases, the choice is not so simple. You are a regional director of the World Health Organization. One of your duties is to supervise the distribution of birth control devices to women in less-developed countries. The product of choice has been the intrauterine device (IUD) that has proved to be effective and inexpensive. The problem is that in the United States, several hundred users of the IUD have contracted pelvic inflammatory infections that have been linked to use of the IUD. These infections can cause sterility and death.[1]

ABC Corporation, a large multinational company, has a considerable inventory of IUDs that it cannot sell in the United States. The company would rather not write off its entire inventory and has consequently made a very attractive offer to sell the World Health Organization all of its existing inventory and assist in distributing the product regionally. As regional director, you must decide whether to accept ABC's offer to supply IUDs for the World Health Organization's program for women in less-developed countries.

Professional practice issues

1. As a professional in the public health field, your responsibility is to choose the policy that maximizes health and minimizes the health risks in the general population.
2. Sexual activity without birth control in less-developed countries will lead to an increasing population that, in turn, will lead to severe poverty and mass starvation.
3. Mass starvation kills millions; pelvic inflammatory infections kill hundreds. Thus, it is better to save the many (in the spirit of the profession's mission).

Ethical issues

1. Each person's life is precious.
2. The end of saving more lives does not justify the means of sacrificing others.

Cost issues

1. ABC Corporation is willing to give the World Health Organization a substantial price break on its existing inventory of IUDs. This price break will allow the World Health Organization to serve more women of child-bearing age than its original

strategic plan had projected. ABC's offer to assist in regional distribution will save the World Health Organization additional money.

2. White knights are not lining up at your door to help you fulfill the mission of this program, and profit is also a part of the company's mission.

Analysis of Population Control in the Third World

	Surface	Medium	Deep
Professional Practice Issues			
Public health mission to preserve the health of as many as possible			x
Sexual activity without birth control leads to mass starvation			x
The end justifies the means			x
Ethical Issues			
Human life is precious			x
The end does not justify the means			x
Cost Issues			
ABC's inventory problem can be used to serve many women			x
ABC's offer can be your gain			x
The World Health Organization needs help from someone or it may be unable to continue this program			x

This case differs from Case 1 because the professional, ethical, and cost guidelines are equal. In this case, the dictates of the ethical imperative must be followed because it is more deeply embedded in a person's worldview than is the imperative of professional practice or cost issues. The components of ethics enter the worldview generally as a feature of a person's humanity.[2] The imperatives of professionalism enter the worldview as one of many modes of personal fulfillment; the imperatives of cost enter the worldview as modes of day-to-day practical consumption. Although many people may create pessimistic scenarios (such as state of nature) to the contrary, most daily practical business decisions will not cause your death or that of a family member. It may cause you to be discharged, drastically affecting your lifestyle. In the United States (at the writing of this book), making such a decision almost never causes an individual to face starvation.[3]

My experience has been that businesspeople are prone to hyperbole when they describe the consequences of an ethical decision that entails the loss of money and worldly goods. This overstatement culture has the effect of blocking businesspeople from taking the right action because they fear exaggerated consequences.[4]

As with scientific theories, the dictates of a universally binding imperative founded on generic structures trump those of a particular person's individual interests. More details on this appear in the "Evaluating a Case Study" section in Chapter 6.

In this essay, the main concern is the ability to assess the levels of embeddedness. Some common problems that my students have made in performing the assessment follow:

1. *Not giving the imperatives of professional practice or cost issue their due.* Remember that whether you assess embeddedness via a chart or through narrative paragraphs,

you are working from your original analysis of the problem. A failure to uncover all the important facets will be reflected in your depiction of embeddedness. You will notice gaps in the reasoning and will feel that something is missing. If this happens, go back over the issues lists. Rewrite the case in your own words; expand or recast the case in some way. By doing this, you become the author and are forced to recognize key elements in the case as presented.

2. *Seeing everything at the same level of embeddedness.* You need to view embeddedness as a way to describe the degree to which the professional practice or ethical issues or cost issues, is essential to the case. A less essential issue should be given less consideration. To better understand the essential structure of a professional practice, prepare short justifications of your choice of that element as an issue in the case. As you prepare justifications, think about each element in its relation to the whole. If that relation could not be different without seriously altering the whole, then it is essential. If you can find substitutes that would work just as well, then the relation is incidental.

3. *Listing too many professional, ethical, and cost issues.* This is the flip side to step 1. You have given too much detail that is not essential to the case at hand, or you are listing one issue in a number of different ways. In either event, preparing an essential description of your elements (as in step 2) can help you shorten your issue list to only those required for your evaluation.

Good solid work avoiding these mistakes will enable you to create a more satisfactory result in the argumentative stage, in which you may finally apply your ethical theory to your annotated embeddedness charts.

Macro and Micro Cases[5]

Macro Case 1. You are the US vice-president for sales at Korean Motors of North America. The home office in Seoul is trying to break into the luxury car market in the USA. The initial sales plan had focused upon subcompacts, compacts, and mid-sized cars. This has gone on for 10 years. The sales and advertising campaign was focused on point-by-point product comparisons with your competitors (including crash test data on print ads) and having double the warranty that the other companies offer. However, now the home office wants to go in a different direction: they want you to sell *success!* The point of the ad campaign and the sales talking points will be that buying the Korean Motors Olympus luxury car will make you successful and even godlike. The target market is the young nouveau riche. You have been told that it doesn't matter how bizarre and false these exaggerated claims might be, but you have to make the customer feel that when he buys this car, all aspects of his life will become successful. This new approach bothers you. The company has made great inroads into the low-cost marketplace by creating a well-priced quality product with a great warranty. This new approach will change the company's branding. You are very concerned that this is going to blow up. Your options are: (a) to take your concerns to the home office in Korea; (b) merely go along with the campaign (after all it wasn't your idea); or (c) brush up your resume and look for another job. What do you do? And why?

Macro Case 2. You are the director of human resource development of a Fortune 500 company. You have become aware that the composition of the company's management workforce is almost exclusively white and male. The company has a very high percentage of women and minorities in the lowest-paying jobs so that if the Equal Opportunity Commission reviewed the total numbers, they would look pretty good. However, you brought this issue to the attention of another director, who thought your concerns were crazy: "What does it matter who is running the company? As long as we're both employed and there's no hanky panky going on, what's there to worry about?"

You believe that this director's comments reflect the company's general sentiment. You wonder, however, if the limited managerial diversity may limit the corporate strategic vision. After all, the U.S. marketplace is diverse and having people from varied backgrounds, genders, and races might actually enhance business prospects.

If you put yourself out on the line for an unpopular program, you may be fired. Is this issue worth *that*? You have a comfortable life and a great 401 K plan that is filled with company stock, although you have two mortgages on your house. Your daughter is headed for college next year. Is discretion the better part of valor?

On the other hand, if you say nothing and a problem should arise, you might be in a difficult position. To clarify your thoughts, write a policy memo addressed to the CEO. In the memo, describe the problem and what you believe should be done to remedy it. After you finish that memo, write a private note that determines whether you should or should not send the memo to the CEO. In each case, be sure to survey professional, practice, ethical, and cost issues.

Macro Case 3. You are the copartner of a famous fashion house, Maria Haut-bas, whose sales figures in the last few years have been lagging. You are considering switching your advertising account from Sacher & Sacher to Mortimer Grunge, Ltd. Sacher & Sacher created an image of elegance that worked for the high end of your line but seemed old-fashioned to younger buyers. As a result, the young market has not had much interest in your line.

Grunge has developed a theme to position you on the "edge." This means that people will notice you, and the contrast from your previous image will draw customers. Grunge suggests doing this by employing anorexic models with a light pallor who appear to the heroin addicts. These women are often in a state of undress or a situation that suggests prostitution as well as drug addiction. However, other aspects of the scene (such as the automobile behind them or the apartment in which they are placed) connote great material wealth.

You understand the concept behind Grunge's campaign. You also believe that it will work. The problem is whether you are doing anything wrong in creating such a campaign. Anorexia is a serious problem among young women. Are you glorifying it? Drug addiction is a terrible situation. Are you promoting it? Prostitution in such a setting connotes an exploitation of women who give up their dignity for money. Is this what being hip really means?

These are serious issues. Consider that this campaign will succeed. Do these possible consequences matter? Perhaps your concerns are overblown. Perhaps viewers of the ads will see them as impossible escapism. What do you think? How conscious should people be about possible implications of their ads?

You must make a recommendation to your partner at Marie Haut-bas about the way to proceed in this ad campaign. Describe the professional practice, ethical, and cost issues involved. Be sure to conclude with a recommendation to proceed or not.

Macro Case 4. You own a small business that employs 65 workers. Your bottom line has been rather sluggish lately. One of the reasons, you believe, is that workers have been wasting time on the Internet and making personal phone calls. Although you believe that you are not an overly controlling person, you have to be sensitive about profits since your core business has been flat.

You have the opportunity to purchase a new product, Employee Scan. It allows you to preset the phone numbers of your clients and those of employees' homes, children's schools, and spouses' work places. The software will tell you how often and how long the employee spends on personal calls and lists unidentified numbers called so that they might be checked at your discretion. The software also lists the Internet sites that employees log onto and the time they spend at the site. A number of sex or entertainment sites will be listed in the report, and others can be identified at your discretion.

Even if you do no further checking, this software claims to give you a profile of how an employee uses work hours as far as phone calls and Internet visits are concerned. This sounds beneficial to you since you believe that many employees may be guilty of abusing these devices. However, privacy issues are involved. Even though use of this product breaks no laws, is it ethical to check your employees' behavior? Do they invite such a system if they are abusing your trust?

You want to discuss this situation with your daughter who is vice-president of the company. Write a report outlining a course of action, making sure that you represent professional practice, ethical, and cost considerations.

Macro Case 5. As the head of the Federal Trade Commission, you have been approached by several groups suggesting that your agency should institute certain controls over Internet commerce. You realize that the heart of the Internet has been its freedom to develop unhindered. You also realize that day trading stocks and Ponzi and other schemes have become prevalent on the Net. The great difficulty on the Net is that there seems to be no accountability. The groups have suggested that you regulate the Internet.

You are conflicted as to what to do, so you ask Ms. A to write a report supporting such regulations. In the persona of Ms. A, write this report following professional practice, ethical, and cost considerations.

You have also asked Mr. B to write a report against instituting any regulation of the Internet. In the persona of Mr. B, write this report following professional practice, ethical, and cost considerations.

Be prepared to present the report that you support.

Micro Case 1. You work in the IT department for Headbook, a giant social networking company. The company recently changed its privacy settings so that only someone with a masters degree in computer science could possibly understand them. The point involved is a way of getting information from people using the service in order to sell to third parties. This includes companies wishing to make a sale and resumé factcheckers who are hired by employers to vet potential employees. There is a lot of very personal information that is being gathered by users who before the change had very tight privacy controls. You believe that because the disclosure of the new policy was so complicated many people do not realize what they are divulging. You went to your boss, Sally Forth, to confront her with these facts. She said, "Look, you are way too sensitive about all this. The people all checked the box that said they had read the information and gave their consent. We can prove this in every instance. We are in the clear. Look, these cheapskates just want a great service like Headbook for free. Well, we have to make a dollar, too, and this is a way to do it—and how!"

You are not so sure. You are considering whether to "leak" this information to a prominent blog. It violates your confidentiality agreement, but you are concerned about what your company is doing to unknowing clients. What should you do?

Micro Case 2. You are an assistant at a retail clothing store and provide bookkeeping services as part of your duties. Your immediate supervisor, Mr. Inkster (who works for Mrs. Forest, the owner), has asked you to file certain expenses as marketing costs that really do not fit into that category. For example, he has been spending company money on his girlfriend, Sally Tuls. Mr. Inkster has bought her gifts, paid for hotel rooms, and paid for her expenses on numerous business trips—all out of company money.

This is not marketing money, and you know it. You also know that if it came to your word against his, you would never be believed, but you could make a copy of a selective set of records on disk (in case Mr. Inkster decides to alter the records) and use them to support any accusations you believe should be made. Or you could just look the other way, get the accounting degree you are working on, and hope that this situation will not occur with your next employer.

You are conflicted about what to do. Your mother, with whom you live, is a fair-minded and reasonable person (although a bit oriented toward the practical). Write a letter to her about this situation detailing the problems (professional practice, ethical, and cost) and then explain how you understand each (according to embeddedness). Finally, conclude with plan of action.

Micro Case 3. You are the business manager of an in vitro fertilization (IVF) clinic. Your supervisor, Dr. Mary Reed, has told you to take an ad on local radio stations that you know makes false claims about your agency's success rate with infertile couples. It also implies that insurance carriers may pick up this cost when in your state they do not. The purpose of the ad is to get couples through the door and into consultation. Once they reach this point, the couples will do almost anything to become pregnant (including taking another job just to pay the expenses).

You are conflicted about what to do. You could take a hard stance against Dr. Reed's demands and possibly lose your job. You could take the ad and then tip off a watchdog agency that might confront the clinic. You could do nothing; after all, most of the other agencies in this work exaggerate claims of success. Why should you be any different?

Describe a personal action plan detailing all the issues involved in the professional practice case, the ethical case, and the cost case. Recommend an action plan.

Micro Case 4. You are a regional sales manager of a toy company, Kalon Toys. The company has just come out with a line of toys that encourage building skills. There are concerns about the safety of the toys. Should asthmatic children eat the smallest pieces of the building set and then have several glasses of whole milk, they might experience severe digestive problems. The company has put a warning label on all sets. This problem is expected to affect only seventy-five children.

You realize, however, that claims involving children are always sensitive. A competitor recently was sued on a frivolous claim that cost it millions of dollars. Thousands of people on the Net "chatted" about the claim and spread rumor and innuendo about the product. You want to protect yourself from falling prey to the same situation. Write a report on the actions you might proactively take to protect yourself and the company.

Micro Case 5. You are a software stringer at a major software company. You recently created a modification to the very popular, I Will Take Over the World game. In its 3.0 version, this game sold thousands of copies, but your modifications will triple its sales. However, the game was developed as a result of computer software piracy.

Express your thoughts in writing about why people pirate software, why they should not do so, and the extent of the problem. What ethical theories does piracy involve? What is the general categorization of what is going on? What should society do?

Notes

1 I have heard that many of the structural problems with the IUD that caused pelvic inflammatory infection have now been rectified. I am not competent to comment on this; nevertheless, for this case, let us assume that these problems still obtain.

2 For a further discussion of the mechanics, see Chapter 1 of *Basic Ethics*.

3 Of course, the dead hero problem applies here. Would one prefer to be a live coward (here understood to mean a moral coward) or a dead hero (here understood to mean someone who has suffered for his or her beliefs)? This is not an easy question and lies at the heart of all discussions of Business Ethics.

4 It is not the worst thing in the world to have to step back and live on less. It has been my personal experience that the essential elements of personal happiness have no price tag. Truly supported caring relationships cannot be taken away from a person no matter how hard times befall (except through some unrelated event—such as disease or accident).

5 For more on macro and micro cases, see the overview on p. 138.

Ethical Issues within the Corporation

General Overview: This chapter addresses four issues that have ethical implications for the corporation: working conditions, affirmative action, gender issues, and whistle-blowing. These issues pertain to the organizational culture that affects each worker's life. All workers have a right to be treated with respect and afforded dignity whenever possible based on any authentically created shared community worldview.

If it is true that work is a substantial part of a person's life and if it is reasonable to assume that everyone wants to create the most meaningful life possible, then these four topics have a vital (though often overlooked) significance for the workplace. No good corporation can ignore them.

A. Working Conditions

Overview: The conditions under which people perform their jobs are very important to them. One reason for this is that each person is an individual with his one worldview. This worldview is connected to that person's sense of individual dignity. It is ethically required that individual dignity be affirmed whenever possible. An employer can do this by making the workplace a safe and healthy environment for the employees. Safety is often an issue for manufacturing plants but can also be an issue in office work. Workers' physical and mental health must be addressed. Company cultures that cause undue stress or are hostile, sexist, or racist contribute to a community attitude that people are simply replaceable cogs—like machine parts. Kant phrased a general moral maxim that describes this dynamic: "Each rational being should treat himself and all others never merely as a means, but always at the same time as an end in himself."[1] This maxim forbids exploitation of another, which would be tantamount to treating another person as a means only and would not recognize the person's dignity (as being an end in himself). This Kantian understanding

Business Ethics, Second Edition. Edited by Michael Boylan.
© 2014 John Wiley & Sons, Inc. Published 2014 by John Wiley & Sons, Inc.

of an "end" is part of what I mean by worldview. Both are connected with recognizing the particularity of *individuals* and providing flexibility and accommodation for this whenever possible.

Employers can affirm a person as an end by paying a fair wage and meeting or exceeding the professional practices of an industry (see "The Principle of Fair Competition").

The essays in this section approach the issue of working conditions in different ways. In the first essay, William W. Lowrance questions how we evaluate risk, which he views as something that can be measured. He views safety as the logical complement of risk. In other words, if working in a cotton mill creates a 5% risk for lung disease, then our assessment of the risk indicates that a worker is 95% safe from lung disease. However, assessment based only on statistical risk has a flaw: we have not defined *acceptable* risk. The issue of acceptability introduces the moral dimension to the question. Lowrance raises several guides to acceptability, but each really begs the question of how much risk is acceptable. The reader is encouraged to look to one of the primary moral theories and the ought-implies-can principle as a guide to evaluate the proper level of risk in the workplace (and, by extension, of safety in the workplace).

In the second article Sheila M. Neysmith and Jane Aronson address some issues in home care (particularly for the aged). Although their study took place in Canada, the principles can be applied to the USA and elsewhere. (Recently, one workers' compensation study found that home care was in the riskiest category for back injuries—from lifting elderly patients.)

This essay raises many working condition issues. The reader might discern others. Highlighted especially are issues of gender and race and ethnic backgrounds. Caring for others has traditionally, in Occidental culture (and elsewhere), been assigned to women. The care has not been valued although those who need it certainly value the benefit they receive. When you add to this ingratitude the default bias against women and the factor of race or ethnic bias, a potentially hostile and demeaning work environment results.

The third essay, by David M. Schilling, deals with sweatshops. When an employer has the upper hand in a labor market, there is the potential for exploitation. (Note: that in "labor-short" environments, excesses can also result, although in our new global economy, companies with the resources will be able to tap the glut of poor people worldwide to their own company's advantage.) The reader must make several conclusions about justice to evaluate the sweatshop issue. If there is a willing employer and a willing employee, is there a valid working condition contract? If some fictitious sporting shoe company were to pay a star basketball player $40 million a year in promotional fees and then pay $7.5 million to its 10 000 workers in foreign countries (some of whom are children or prisoners), is something wrong? Or is this merely an instance of rewarding according to some system of desert?

The important issue, of course, is whether the average consumer is willing to spend $15 more for a pair of shoes that has been produced under proper working conditions? Is this merely a case of an individual, Mary, not wanting to work under bad conditions (herself) but willing to pay only the lowest price when it comes to personal shopping decisions?

B. Affirmative Action

Overview: Affirmative action is the policy adopted in the late 1960s and early 1970s. Affirmative action has many versions but in general it involves the assessment of equally qualified candidates for a job, school admission, or government contract that adds a positive selection criterion based on a candidate's membership in particular race or other identified group or (in some cases) gender.

Affirmative action does not mean automatically getting a job, admission to school, or contract merely by being a member of one of the identified groups. This would constitute selection based *solely* on membership in a particular group, which might result in unqualified candidates receiving preferences. Instead, affirmative action involves making a selection among a group of qualified candidates and using race, gender, or another characteristic as a positive selection criterion (such as being a veteran). In other words, all things being equal this one factor results in the selection of the targeted candidate.

The policy of affirmative action based upon race and gender is controversial and has been the subject of numerous court cases in the USA. However, affirmative action based upon prior military service has not been controversial. The reader must think about this and decide whether this constitutes an inconsistency in the shared community worldview.

In the first article Judith Jarvis Thomson narrows her purview to affirmative action in university hiring. She contends that a problem has existed and continues to exist concerning discrimination against African Americans and women, a problem she believes should be redressed. She argues that affirmative action is a plausible (albeit imprecise) tool to do so.

Robert Simon's response to Thomson asserts that affirmative action is not an appropriate remedy because it blurs the individual versus the group distinction (this is similar to the discussion about the nature of the corporation discussed in Chapter 3). Did the wrongs of discrimination affect the groups or individuals? If the former, then a group remedy is in order. If the latter, then an individual remedy should be made. Affirmative action blurs this distinction and thus, he argues, is an ineffective remedy.

I contend in the third essay that the governmental policy of affirmative action is grounded in a theory of distributive justice (based upon positive rights). Many writers on the topic have suggested that the most useful way to view this process is either from the perspective of the small picture (i.e., each individual's person's desert) or from the view of the large picture (i.e., each ethnic, racial, or gender group's share of the total goods and services within the economy). This essay begins with a review of some strengths and weaknesses of each position and then attempts to identify a solution using criteria from a theory of distributive justice and considerations of shared community worldview.

C. Gender Issues

Overview: A myriad of gender issues face the modern US corporation. Integrating women fairly into the corporate community is the ultimate goal. Standing in the way of that goal are latent attitudes, stereotypes, and communication issues. These issues must be addressed from both practical and ethical points of view.

In the first essay, Rekha Karambayya examines issues of race and gender discrimination and the way they affect the day-to-day practice of business. She asserts that these issues are very subtle and create a series of paradoxes for those involved. Overt discrimination (shouts) and subtle discrimination (whispers) are featured as a structural given. "Belonging" is an important element in this equation; we all desire to belong. But what happens when we belong to several groups that pull us in different directions? Do we attempt to break free of such paradoxes or use them to our advantage?

In the second essay Jane Uebelhoer takes up the issue of compensation inequality between men and women in the workplace. In the beginning of the essay Uebelhoer sets out a definition of job discrimination as a logical exclusive operator. Next, she documents that job discrimination exists against women in the US workplace. Women make $0.77 to every $1.00 that men make for comparable jobs. This is a 13% rate of discrimination. Next, Uebelhoer argues why compensation discrimination is morally wrong, and then pivots into the reason for the extent of this sort of job discrimination. Various ideas are brought forward that should lead classes into productive discussion. The bright light is that this sort of discrimination in the long run will hurt business! And if there is anything to energize corporations, it is increased profits.

There is a distinction between "disparate treatment" and "disparate impact." The former requires intent while the latter is a fact based upon current data. The latter is a more accurate assessment tool for wage discrimination. This real problem (like many intransient social problems) cannot depend upon the wisdom of far-sighted legislators. Political action in democratic countries requires a boots-on-the-ground response. Democracy, in principle, listens to public protests. Perhaps this is the only way to change employment discrimination against women.

D. Whistle-Blowing

Overview: Whistle-blowing occurs when an employee goes outside the normal chain of command within his company to bring attention to actions that are either against the company's stated mission, unethical, or illegal. Sometimes this means jumping to a higher authority within the company or a designated ombudsman. At other times this means going outside the company to the police, newspapers, or professional organizations.

The way that whistle-blowers are treated depends upon the venue. For example, if you are employed by the US Federal Government, then your job is protected if you are a whistle-blower. However, in many other industries this is not the case. It is often the case that whistle-blowers are fired (with no positive recommendations for future jobs). Sometimes a whistle-blower is blacklisted in that type of job so that they will never work in that sort of employment again. In extreme cases, say an accountant who finds illegal activity by a crime-front business, the whistle-blower's life is at risk. With all these downside potentials, why would anyone want to be a whistle-blower? Simply because it is the right thing to do: ethical behavior does not guarantee positive rewards.

To counteract some of these downsides there are two mitigating factors. Some instances of whistle-blowing (such as turning in a tax cheating scheme) is rewarded by the IRS (Internal Revenue Service). The FBI also has a witness protection program which tries to protect the lives of whistle-blowers and their immediate families.

In the first essay Terrance McConnell sets out some paradigmatic cases of whistle-blowing. McConnell sees whistle-blowing as an instance of organizational ethics. This is because when one makes an accusation against an organization these claims call attention to alleged instances of negligence, abuse, or practices that damage the public interest or harm others. Whistle-blowers make public their charges of wrongdoing. The effect of the accusation is likely to affect adversely the interests of multiple parties: the organization itself, employees of the organization allegedly responsible for wrongdoing, clients of the organization, and the whistle-blower herself. Because of the possible personal harm the whistle-blower faces conflicting obligations (to ethics and the truth versus personal, prudential interest).

Organizations can be backward or forward looking regarding whistle-blowing. A backward approach would be to hush everything up and punish the squealer. A forward-looking approach would be to rectify the problem. McConnell sees that there is an inclination toward the backward approach—though there is more to the forward approach than is often recognized. This is the position that McConnell supports both for the individual perspective and for the organizational perspective (that overlaps with the societal perspective). A shared community worldview that is open to explore claims of wrongdoing with the forward perspective will be rewarded with an increased ethical presence and a more efficient business environment.

In the second essay, Erika Henik introduces the presence of emotions into the whistle-blowing model. In contrast to "cold" economic calculations and cost–benefit analyses to explain the judgments and actions of potential whistle-blowers, Henik argues that "hot" cognitions—value conflict and emotions—should be added to these models. Henik proposes a model of the whistle-blowing decision process that highlights the reciprocal influence of "hot" and "cold" cognitions and advocates research that explores how value conflict and emotions inform reporting decisions. Henik draws on the cognitive appraisal approach to emotions and on the social-functional value pluralism model to generate an account of just how these two sorts of cognitions might work and the structure of future empirical studies that might validate her conjectures.

Note

1 Immanuel Kant, *Groundwork of the Metaphysics of Morals*, trans. H.J. Paton (London: Hutchinson, 1948); 64/428.

A. Working Conditions
Of Acceptable Risk

WILLIAM W. LOWRANCE

Few headlines are so alarming, perplexing, and personal in their implications as those concerning safety. Frightening stories jolt our early morning complacency so frequently that we wonder whether things can really be *that* bad. We are disturbed by what sometimes appear to be haphazard and irresponsible regulatory actions, and we can't help being suspicious of all the assaults on our freedoms and our pocketbooks made in the name of safety. We hardly know which cries of "Wolf!" to respond to; but we dare not forget that even in the fairy tale, the wolf really did come.

The issues: X-rays, cosmetics, DDT, lead, pharmaceuticals, toys, saccharin, intrauterine contraceptive devices, power lawn mowers, air pollutants, noise....

The questions: How do we determine how hazardous these things are? Why is it that cyclamates one day dominate the market as the principal calorie-cutting sweetener in millions of cans of diet drinks, only to be banned the next day because there is a "very slight chance" they may cause cancer? Why is it that one group of eminent experts says that medical X-rays (or food preservatives, or contraceptive pills) are safe and ought to be used more widely, while another group of authorities, equally reputable, urges that exposure to the same things should be restricted because they are unsafe? At what point do debates such as that over DDT stop being scientific and objective and start being political and subjective? How can anyone gauge the public's willingness to accept risks?...

Judging Safety

...Safety is not measured. *Risks* are measured. Only when those risks are weighed on the balance of social values can safety be judged: *a thing is safe if its attendant risks are judged to be acceptable*.

Determining safety, then, involves two extremely different kinds of activities....

Measuring risks—measuring the probability and severity of harm—is an empirical, scientific activity;

Judging safety—judging the acceptability of risks—is a normative, political activity.

William W. Lowrance, "Of Acceptable Risk." From *Of Acceptable Risk* (Los Altos, CA: William Kauffmann, 1976).

Although the difference between the two would seem obvious, it is all too often forgotten, ignored, or obscured. This failing is often the cause of the disputes that hit the front pages.

We advocate use of this particular definition for many reasons. It encompasses the other, more specialized, definitions. By employing the word "acceptable," it emphasizes that safety decisions are relativistic and judgmental. It immediately elicits the crucial questions, "Acceptable in whose view?" and "Acceptable in what terms?" and "Acceptable for whom?" Further, it avoids all implication that safety is an intrinsic, absolute, measurable property of things.

In the following two examples, risk-measuring activity is described in Roman type, and safety-judging in italics....

A scientific advisory committee is charged by the government with recommending radiation exposure standards. The committee reviews all the animal experiments, the occupational medical record, the epidemiological surveys of physicians and patients exposed to X-rays, and the studies of the survivors of the Nagasaki and Hiroshima explosions. It inventories the modes of exposure; it reviews present radiation standards, including those of other nations and international organizations; and it examines the practical possibility of reducing exposures. *It weighs all the risks, costs, and benefits, and then decides that the allowed exposure has been unacceptably high; it recommends that because the intensity of some major sources, such as medical X-rays, can be reduced at reasonable cost and with little loss of effectiveness, the standards should be made more restrictive.*

Over a three-year period, William Ruckelshaus, administrator of the Environmental Protection Agency, considered many different petitions from the various interested parties before acting on his agency's inquiry into the use of DDT. Finally, in 1972, he ruled that the scientific evidence led him to conclude that DDT is "an uncontrollable, durable chemical that persists in the aquatic and terrestrial environments" and "collects in the food chain," and that although the evidence regarding human tumorogenicity and other long-term effects was inconclusive, there was little doubt that DDT has serious ecological effects. Ruckelshaus reviewed the benefits of DDT in the protection of cotton and other crops and affirmed that other equally effective pesticides were available. *Summing the arguments, then, he ruled that "the long-range risks of continued use of DDT for use on cotton and most other crops is unacceptable and outweighs any benefits...."*[1]

... In heading down the slopes a skier attests that he accepts the risks; at a later stage of his life he may reject those very same risks because of changes in his awareness, his physical fragility, or his responsibilities to family or firm. While one woman may accept the side effects of oral contraceptives because she doesn't want to risk pregnancy, another woman may so fear the pill that she judges a diaphragm to be a more acceptable compromise among the several risks. Even though he is fully aware of the mangled fingers, chronic coughs, or damaged eyes or ears of those around him, a worker may accept those risks rather than endure the daily nuisance and tedium of blade guards, respirators, goggles, or ear protectors; but his employer, for reasons of cost, paternalism, or government requirement, may find this risky behavior unacceptable....

Acceptance may be just a passive, or even stoical, continuance of historical momentum, as when people accept their lot at a dangerous traditional trade or continue to live near a volcano. Acceptance may persist because no alternatives are seen, as in the case of automobiles and many other technological hazards. Acceptance may result from ignorance or misperception of risk: variations on "I didn't know the gun was loaded" and "It won't happen to me" show up in every area. Acceptance may be simply acquiescence in a majority decision, such as a referendum-based decision on fluoridation, or in a decision by some governing elite, as with the average person's tacit approval of most public standards. Acceptance may even be an expression of preference for modern but known risks over perhaps smaller but less well understood risks, as with preference for coal- and oil-fired power plants over nuclear plants. ... It is important to appreciate that such decisions may or may not be—and are certainly not necessarily—fair, just, consistent, efficient, or rational.

There is a great deal of overlap between the two decisionmaking domains implied by our definition of safety. Scientists, engineers, and medical people are called upon by political officials to judge the desirability of certain courses for society. Panels of scientists recommend exposure limits. Physicians prescribe medicines and diets. Engineers design dams, television sets, toasters, and airplanes. All of these decisions are heavily, even if only implicitly, value-laden.

On the other hand, by adopting particular risk data in their deliberations, political and judiciary agents at least implicitly rule on the correctness of measurements. The business of determining risk must often be settled operationally in hearings or other political deliberations, because the day-to-day management of society can't always wait for scientists to complete their cautious, precise determinations, which may take years. Congressional committees and regulatory agencies conduct hearings and issue rulings on the risks of food additives and air pollutants. Courts rule on the dangers of DDT. Risk and its acceptability are weighed by both manufacturers and consumers in the push-and-pull of the marketplace.

Between the two activities—measuring risk and judging safety—lies a discomforting no-man's-land ... or every-man's-land. Scientists on the fringe of the political arena, attempting to avoid charges of elitism, are looking for more objective ways to appraise society's willingness to accept various risks. At the same time, political officials confronted by scientifically controversial "facts" that never seem to gain the clarity promised by textbooks are exploring the possibilities of advisory assistance, fact-finding hearings, and formal technology assessments.

Guides to Acceptability

"Reasonableness." This is by far the most commonly cited and most unimpeachable principle in safety judgments. For instance, the legislative charter of the Consumer Product Safety Commission directs it to "reduce unreasonable risk of injury" associated with consumer goods.[2] Panels of experts frequently invoke a "rule of reason" in rendering advice. The concept of reasonableness pervades economic analyses of hazard reduction and the structures of legal liability.

Unfortunately, reference to reasonableness is in a sense a phantom citation. It provides little specific guidance for public decisionmakers, for whom reasonableness is presumably a requirement for staying in office. Not surprisingly, the Consumer Product Safety Act does not venture to define reasonableness. As guidance, the Safety

Commission quotes the description given by the final report of its progenitor, the National Commission on Product Safety:

> Risks of bodily harm to users are not unreasonable when consumers understand that risks exist, can appraise their probability and severity, know how to cope with them, and voluntarily accept them to get benefits that could not be obtained in less risky ways. When there is a risk of this character, consumers have reasonable opportunity to protect themselves; and public authorities should hesitate to substitute their value judgments about the desirability of the risk for those of the consumers who choose to incur it.
>
> But preventable risk is not reasonable
>
> (a) when consumers do not know that it exists; or
> (b) when, though aware of it, consumers are unable to estimate its frequency and severity; or
> (c) when consumers do not know how to cope with it, and hence are likely to incur harm unnecessarily; or
> (d) when risk is unnecessary in … that it could be reduced or eliminated at a cost in money or in the performance of the product that consumers would willingly incur if they knew the facts and were given the choice.[3]

The point of safety judgments is indeed to decide what is reasonable; it's just that any rational decision will have to be made on more substantive bases, such as the following, which are in a sense criteria for reasonableness.

Custom of Usage. The Food and Drug Administration has designated hundreds of food additives as "generally recognized as safe" (GRAS). The GRAS list, established in 1958, includes such substances as table salt, vitamin A, glycerin, and baking powder, whose long use has earned them wide and generally unquestioned acceptance.[4] Being classified as GRAS exempts those substances from having to pass certain premarket clearances. From time to time this sanction is challenged, but most critics of the GRAS list have argued not so much that it should be abandoned as that individual items should be subjected to periodic review. In 1969, following its decision to ban the popular artificial sweetener cyclamate (until then GRAS), the Food and Drug Administration initiated a full review of the GRAS list. That review is still in progress, and "so far nothing has been found to lead to any further bans similar to the one on cyclamate."[5]

Prevailing Professional Practice. Long established as the criterion for physicians' clinical practice, this principle is increasingly being invoked in evaluating the protection that engineers, designers, and manufacturers provide their clients. Buildings are said to conform to the "prevailing local standards." Toys are "of a common design." X-ray machines are operated "at normal intensities." In many instances the wisdom of such deference to convention can be questioned. The underlying assumption is that if a thing has been in common use it must be okay, since any adverse effects would have become evident, and that a thing sanctioned by custom is safer than one not tested at all.

Best Available Practice, Highest Practicable Protection, and Lowest Practicable Exposure. Air and water quality regulations have stipulated that polluters control their emissions by the "best available means." So have noise abatement laws. Obviously, although such a requirement does provide the public regulator with a vague rationale, he must still exercise judgment over what constitutes "best" practice for every individual case and what economic factors should be considered in defining "practicable." Hardware for pollution control or noise abatement may exist, but only at a cost that many allege to be prohibitive; is it to be considered "available"?…

"No Detectable Adverse Effect." Although such a principle is applied frequently in our everyday lives, and although it has a certain operational value, it is a weak criterion which may amount to little more than an admission of uncertainty or ignorance. Many hazards now recognized, such as moderate levels of X-rays or asbestos or vinyl chloride, could at an earlier time have been said to have "no detectable adverse effect." …

The Threshold Principle. If it can be proven that there is indeed a level of exposure below which no adverse effect occurs, subthreshold exposures might be considered safe. But determining whether there really is a threshold, for the especially vulnerable as well as for the average populace, is usually a nearly impossible task. As we mentioned earlier, for loud noises there are clearly thresholds of annoyance, pain, and ear damage. But whether there are thresh-olds for effects of radiation, chemical carcinogens, and mutagens has never been firmly established.…

On Being, and Being Held, Responsible

In essence the issue is posed by the following questions: Should technically trained people be expected to bear any social responsibilities different from those borne by others? Why? What are the unique obligations? And further, can all the obligations be met simply by individuals working alone, or are there in addition some responsibilities requiring technical people to act collectively?.…

Scientists, engineers, designers, architects, physicians, public health experts, and other technically trained people *do* have special responsibilities to the rest of society with respect to personal safety. Some principal kinds of risks which ought to be taken upon the conscience of the technical community are:

1. Technically complex risks whose intricacies are comprehensible only to highly trained people;
2. Risks that can be significantly reduced by applying new technology or by improving the application of existing technology;
3. Risks constituting public problems whose technical components need to be distinguished explicitly from their social and political components so that responsibilities are assigned properly;
4. Technological intrusions on personal freedom made in the pursuit of safety; and
5. Risks whose possible consequences appear so grave or irreversible that prudence dictates the urging of extreme caution, even before the risks are known precisely.

Notice that we have said that these problems *should be taken as matters of conscience* by the technical community. Whether the verb describing the action should be *protecting*, or *watching over*, or *looking out for*, or *issuing a warning*, depends on the situation. The specific response might be doing an experiment, raising an issue before a professional society, blowing the whistle on an employer, exerting political leverage, or aiding a legislator or administrator in untangling the parts of a public issue.

…These responsibilities have several deep origins. Basically they arise, in congruence with all major moral philosophies, from the conviction that every person has a general responsibility for the well-being of his fellow men. Reflecting this, the common law has held through the centuries that anyone who becomes aware of the possibility of danger has a responsibility to warn those at risk. But we are obliged to push further and ask whether, in this age of cultural specialization, there isn't more to the issue—for if we don't press, we may be left simply making vague exhortations to virtue.

When we examine what society expects, we find that it does look to the technical community for warning, guidance, and protection, in the kinds of situations we have described and in others as well. Highly trained people are definitely seen as having special status. Given this, a key to developing a compelling ethical argument, and to understanding why the lay public feels as it does, seems to reside in the notion of professionalism.

Over the years a tacit but nonetheless real compact has developed. Society *invests in* training and professional development of scientists and other technical people. It invests heavily; substantial public subsidy of one form or another goes to virtually every college, university, medical school, field station, and research facility in the United States. By and large the professions are left free to govern themselves, control admission to membership, choose their direction of research, enforce the quality of work, and direct the allocation of public funds within their subject area.

Concomitantly, society *invests with* the professions and their institutions certain trusts, among them a trust the professions will watch over the well-being of society, including its safety. As Berkeley sociologist William Kornhauser has expressed it, "Professional responsibility is based on the belief that the power conferred by expertise entails a fiduciary relationship to society."[6] This "fiduciary relationship," or what we have called a tacit compact, is what gives rise to the ethical "oughts."

… As this century has careened along it has brought an increasing need for a collective shouldering of responsibility. The one-to-one personal relationships that once governed ethical conduct have been supplanted by more diffuse ones involving many intermediaries. Industrial scientists plan their research by committee. Engineers who design tunnels and dams interact with their ultimate public clients only indirectly, through managers, attorneys, and the officials who supervise public contracts. Physicians may still carry the wand of Aesculapius, but they do so in the context of one of the nation's largest businesses. Two sorts of diffuseness enlarge the collective dimension. First, the cliency is expanding, often in the interest of social justice: a national health care system that intends to reach every citizen has quite different ethical dimensions from a free-market private physician system. And second, as we confront hazards that are more diffuse, we often realize that *nobody* has considered that the problem was specifically his concern: there is no International Agency for the Supervision of the Ozone Layer.

We try to manage these problems by government action, building in mechanisms of accountability where possible; and we test the justice of specific actions in the courts, as when people feel that they are being unfairly denied medical care. Beyond that, and usually leading it, we have to depend on action by communities of scholars and coteries of professionals—hence the obligations we listed earlier.

Two current cases exemplify some of the difficulties. Three engineers in California, backed to a limited extent by several engineering societies, have pressed suit against the Bay Area Rapid Transit (BART) system for firing them after they publicly protested that the automatic train control systems their companies were developing for BART were inadequate and not up to the best professional standards with regards to passenger safety. The dispute raises complex questions about how great the risks really were, whether they should have been considered acceptable, how engineers should play their roles, how corporations should handle dissension, and what the professional societies should do.[7] In another case, an international group of biologists has voluntarily convened itself to discuss whether and how to control certain genetics experiments that would have bizarre, disastrous consequences if they ran amok.[8]

There is little precedent for either case, so it is not surprising that neither has been handled with assurance. In the BART case, the engineering societies were not well prepared to act and could muster only limited support. Perhaps for lack of experience and guidance, the three engineers party to the suit were not able to pursue the case through the courts to completion; the case has reportedly had to be settled out of court, thus setting only weak legal precedent. In the genetic experiments case, the scientists involved continue to suffer the anguish of not even being able to reach a firm consensus on the issue, and they are hard pressed to take any action other than to issue stern pronouncements, plead for prudence, and cross their collective fingers that researchers will be careful.

We have developed the above arguments because we believe they are important. They are by no means the sole guide to action. There can be no substitute for honesty, courage, sacrifice, and the other manifestations of high morality. Nor should legal and other sanctions fail to be applied: enforceable building codes can be adopted to supplement voluntary action; duties can be made a matter of contractual responsibility; and falsification of records is cause for lawsuit. There are many obligations in addition to ethical ones. The ethical ones are of a special sort, though, and urgently deserve to be developed.

The great questions of responsibility will remain with us. Is simply providing information or issuing warnings a sufficient response, or ought those with the knowledge do more? How is responsibility passed up through administrative and managerial hierarchies? In what sense is tacit acquiescence in a misleading scheme irresponsible (as when corporate scientists who know better say nothing when their company makes false claims for its products or evades pollution control laws)? To what extent should those who generate scientific and technological innovations be responsible for their subsequent application?

Notes

1   U.S. Environmental Protection Agency, "Consolidated DDT hearings," 37 *Federal Register*, 13369–13376 (July 7, 1972).

2   Consumer Product Safety Act, *Public Law* 82–573 (1972).

3   National Commission on Product Safety, *Final Report*, 11 (1970).

4   21 *U.S. Code of Federal Regulations*, 121.101 (subpart B).

5   Alan T. Spiner, Jr., "Food ingredient review: Where it stands now," *FDA Consumer*, 23–26 (June 1974).

6   William Kornhauser, *Scientists in Industry*, 1 (University of California Press, Berkeley, 1962).

7   Gordon D. Friedlander, *IEEE Spectrum*, 11: 69–76 (October 1974); Gordon D. Friedlander, "Fixing BART," *IEEE Spectrum*, 12, 43–45 (February 1975).

8   Nicholas Wade, "Genetics: Conference sets strict controls to replace moratorium," *Science* 187, 931–935 (1975); Stuart Auerbach, "And man created risks," *Washington Post* (March 9, 1975.)

Working Conditions in Home Care
Negotiating Race and Class Boundaries in Gendered Work

SHEILA M. NEYSMITH AND JANE ARONSON

Since the early eighties, industrialized countries have been developing long-term care policies in efforts to respond to the joint realities of population aging, the rising costs of institutionally based care, and the desire expressed by groups of seniors to remain in their communities. Home-based services are seen as basic ingredients in programs designed to meet these three concerns. However, the understanding of care that underlies these models seems to be rooted in familial images where the carer is a spouse or daughter, it is as if formal home care services were simply a paid version of informal care. Such assumptions are at odds with a reality in which service is provided by strangers, usually employed by an agency in which organizational priorities take precedence over those of individual care recipients or their families. Not only are home care workers not family, in Canada they are drawn from low-paid labor pools increasingly made up of immigrant women. Thus, immigration policy determines some of the behavioral and attitudinal distances that have to be traversed when a home care worker and a frail elderly person meet to negotiate the terms and conditions under which care is to be provided and received.

This article focuses on a group of workers who are immigrants from the Caribbean and from the Philippines. The usual ambiguities and conflicts that are part of doing home care work are compounded when the worker is visible as both an immigrant and a woman of color in a racialized society.[1] The experiences of these service workers are important because they provide us with a way of understanding how policy decisions on immigration, health care funding priorities, organizational structures, and community care cumulatively shape the labor processes and conditions of home care workers and, thus, the care received by elderly clients....

This work was supported by the Social Sciences and Humanities Research Council of Canada—Women and Change through a research grant (822-92-0015) and a network grant (816-94-0003).

Sheila M. Neysmith and Jane Aronson, "Working Conditions in Home Care: Negotiating Race and Class Boundaries in Gendered Work." Reprinted by permission of the publisher from *International Journal of Health Services* 27, 3 (1997): 479–499. Copyright © 1997 Baywood Publishers.

Home Care Workers: A Changing Labor Force

Long-term care policy discourse continues as if home care workers were middle-aged, working-class, white women who fitted in home care work around their own family obligations and shared many cultural similarities with their elderly clients. Maintaining such a stereotype in the face of a rapidly changing home care labor force means that policies and practices will reinforce rather than challenge existent gender, race, and class inequities. Conflicting interests are at work amongst the various players in the home care arena. For instance, minimalist service models mean that community care is limited to services provided in the isolation of people's homes by individual home care workers. The availability of a pool of immigrant women makes it possible for higher income families to hire such persons to do this home-based work. Feminist policy analysts have called for expanding services to care for children and elderly persons. The questions not raised are: who is going to do the work, under what conditions, and who will benefit from increased services? The employment patterns of recent immigrants, combined with the demographic characteristics of Canada's aging population, suggest that it will be low-waged women of color who will do the work. Who will receive the service will vary depending on how the current struggle over the mix of market, voluntary, and public services in the economy of care is resolved.

Examination of the employment patterns of immigrant women shows that services rather than manufacturing is now a major source of jobs [27]. Immigration patterns also indicate that service sector employees such as home care workers will increasingly be women of color. This pattern is already quite evident in Canadian as well as in U.S. urban centers (28, p. 17). Immigrants, however, come into a society where established structures determine how newcomers experience class, race, and gender disparities [29–31]. Home care policy exists within the broader political economy of a nation and thus reflects the assumptions and institutional practices of that society. The fact that home care workers are women, low-paid, and drawn from an immigrant labor force is not a given but, rather, a social phenomenon that needs to be examined. Home care workers who are women of color move into a type of work that is closely related to traditional domestic service work. Research on domestic workers has documented the oppressive conditions that frequently characterize this work [32–36]. This research also shows that women who have worked as domestics are convinced that factory or service jobs in organizations are preferable to domestic service work. They appreciate not being personally subordinate to an individual in that person's household and not having to do that household's dirty work on their property. In long-term care facilities and service agencies, relations with supervisors and clients may be hierarchical but at least they are embedded in impersonal structures governed by more explicit contractual obligations and limits. Also important is the presence of a work group for sociability and support (37, p. 23).

Examining the experiences of home care workers against a backdrop of domestic service research was helpful to us in understanding some of the issues emerging in our study. Furthermore, it provided a useful framework for assessing agency and policy responses to concerns raised by home care workers. Specifically, the parallels between home care work and domestic service reveal how racism unfolds in home-based care work in ways that it does not in institutionally based care work. The parallels are not exact; for example, home care workers are seldom live-ins and they are not hired primarily as domestic servants. However, home care workers' experiences of their work and its location suggest that when home care tasks are done by women of color in private homes, elderly clients and their families may respond as if to domestic servants. Elderly clients' and families' inevitable frustrations at having to rely on home care services were often directed at their individual workers—the only or closest target. All workers in our study, white women and women of color, regularly experienced the diminishment of being referred to as a "cleaning lady." This class-based diminishment certainly affected white workers and was something they strove to resist and, sometimes, reframe with their clients. However, for nonwhite home care workers, clients' frustrations could also be articulated in terms of their ethnoracial characteristics. In other words, an additional discourse, concerned not with class but with race, was available as a medium of expression for clients and families who, variously, sought targets for their complaints about meager home care services or who were, in a more diffuse fashion, struggling with their own diminishment as people deemed dependent and needy....

Methodological Considerations

Racism as ideology exists at the level of daily actions and their interpretations and, at another level, in the refusal by those in the dominant group to recognize and take responsibility for their race privilege. For instance, it is said that to be white in North America means not to have to think about race. This study uses the concept of "everyday racism" developed by Essed [39] to explore how differences between worker and client were structured and experienced at the micro level of providing and receiving help with household and personal needs (see also 40 and 41 for a discussion of race and class bias in research on women). The term "everyday racism" refers to a process in which (*a*) socialized racist notions are integrated into meanings that make these practices immediately definable and manageable by those who encounter them; (*b*) practices with racist implications become in themselves familiar and repetitive and thus rendered invisible; and (*c*) underlying racial and ethnic relations are actualized and reinforced through these routine or familiar practices in everyday situations (39, p. 52). Thus, we would expect home care workers of different ethnoracial groups to experience and talk about their work differently. DeVault's [42] report on interviews with African American nutritionists cautions researchers that adhering to the methodological rule to let findings emerge from the data can result in the researcher failing to hear race-ethnicity in the accounts of informants because it is implicit rather than explicit. Thus, workers' accounts may include personal experiences or knowledge of others' experiences, but in either case women of color place these within a general knowledge of racism to determine whether a specific event is defined as a racist incident. In other words, race, class, and gender disparities are socially constructed systems, but their effect must arise at specific moments, in particular circumstances, and will change as these circumstances change. ...

The focus groups were held several months after the interviews had been completed and analyzed. Their purpose was to explore more systematically the tensions and conflicts that emerged in the interviews around clients referring to the home care worker as a "cleaning lady." We wanted to get a better understanding of how the domestic service component of home care work was interpreted by women of color, how workers handled the routine racist attitudes and behaviors encountered in carrying out their work assignments, and how this affected the dynamic of relationship maintenance that undergirds home care work. The process for recruiting focus group members was very similar to that used when seeking participants for the interviews. The purpose of the focus groups was announced and volunteers were requested. Participants were remunerated at the rate of $11.25 per hour, the average wage at that time. On the advice of experienced agency workers one group consisted entirely of women from the Caribbean countries, the other group of women from the Philippines. Some focus group participants had taken part in the earlier interviews, others had not. Each focus group had seven members. A group for supervisors was also held. Supervisors represent the bridge between individual workers and the management of home care services, and, ultimately, the link between the daily structuring of home care workers' labor and the overarching policy discourse on meeting the needs of old people. A part of this focus group explored how encounters with racism were dealt with when they were brought to the attention of supervisors. With participants' signed consent, all interviews and focus groups were taped and transcribed. A computer software program [45] allowed us to do word/phrase searches and to code emerging conceptual categories, thus facilitating the practical management of the data.

Everyday Racism in Home Care Workers' Work

Home care work, like other caring labor, is underspecified and undervalued. Descriptions focus on practical tasks such as cleaning, meal preparation, laundry, bathing, and other aspects of personal care. This emphasis on concrete measurable units of work allows home care work to be classified as semi-skilled labor, basically able to be done by most women with minimal training. Pay scales reflect this. The following excerpts from transcripts of the interviews and focus groups reveal how home care work—carried out in the setting of an old person's home, usually combined with at least a minimum fee for service, but disconnected from the relational assumptions that frame familial care— easily gets categorized as domestic labor. If the home care worker is also an immigrant and a woman of color (the two are often not differentiated) the classification is reinforced. Home care work becomes the site for these women to experience the racism that permeates the larger society. As will become evident, home care workers were regularly called upon to interpret, explain, and respond to the spectrum of racial issues that routinely surface in large multicultural cities.

Dealing with the "Cleaning Lady" image

Being seen as a cleaning lady emerged as an issue in virtually every interview. Part of the problem seems to be the ambiguous definition of what a home care worker does. She performs some tasks that look like cleaning, are in fact cleaning, but she is there not for the purpose of cleaning but because of the health and social situation of the elderly person. Although home care workers were clear on the purpose and function of their role, they doubted that many elderly clients and their families were (see 46 for a parallel discussion of nanny ambiguity). The trigger for this definitional assignment seems to be the setting—that is, the work is done in an individual's home.

> This is a new kind of job. A lot of ladies and men we visit, they say we're the cleaning lady. They don't know that we have responsibility for everything about them, not just the house. We have to care about them; observe how they are doing; how they are eating; if something is happening.

> In general we are treated as a cleaning lady. You try. You tell them. You talk to them about food, but if the nurse doesn't say it, they don't listen to it.

> She [client] asked him [client's son] who I was. He said "That's the cleaning lady." I said "No, I am not. I'm the homemaker." "That's the same thing," he said. I said, "No, it is not," and I kind of felt upset.

Health and social service professionals were seen as contributing to the confusion by giving mixed messages: "I think it comes about because the information wasn't given out proper to them by the case worker. Or whoever was interviewing them didn't tell them what it was all about." Home care workers stated quite clearly that case coordinators and other health personnel were as much in need of education as clients and their families.

Home care workers are aware that they go along with the cleaning lady designation rather than continuously battle it. On other occasions they avoid the issue if they think to do so helps a client.

> I had one lady. She was very depressed. I tried every which way to cheer her up. She also thought I was only in there do to the cleaning. I didn't want to be offensive and make her feel that she couldn't cope. I want to make them feel that they are still able to take care of themselves and they just need a little help with the cleaning part. Yes, I let them think that way.

Clients are old, and home care workers use this knowledge to explain, but also excuse, behaviors:

> But I don't blame the people we care for because they are sick, they are in trouble. Sometimes we explain our work to them; that we are not just cleaning ladies and they understand. But some are very confused and we don't have the time. So we just forget about it.

The increasingly widespread practice of two rather than three or four hour work assignments aggravated the situation. The restriction on hours heightened the emphasis on cleaning—a clear client, if not worker, priority. This was confirmed in discussions with supervisors:

> Some clients don't like you to call their homes because they think you are holding up the homemaker from doing her work [group agrees]. When you phone some clients will actually say "She is doing work now, you cannot talk to her."

In the focus group discussions, participants connected being seen as a cleaning woman to several factors. Most clients had never encountered a home care worker; while they knew from past experience what physicians, nurses, and even physiotherapists do, a home care worker is an unfamiliar designation. Furthermore, clients are told by case coordinators that the home care worker is coming in to help them around the house with such things as meal preparation and cleaning—a translation into lay language of the professional category of providing assistance with the activities of daily living. Much more difficult to convey is the notion of social support that undergirds these surface activities. Whatever the original intent of the description, it seems that the elderly person interprets it in terms that are meaningful to her or his lived experience and current needs. Thus, depending upon class background, the client can draw on knowledge that someone who helps around the house is a servant, domestic, or cleaning lady. In addition, the limited physical capacity of most home care users means that getting cleaning done is a major concern. An elderly person can turn to a nurse or family member to give her a bath, take her for walks, or to do some shopping. Getting someone to do the kind of work that is required to keep even a small apartment clean is more difficult to negotiate. Walker and Warren's (47, p. 156) review of the Neighborhood Support Innovations in the United Kingdom found that the greatest cause of dissatisfaction amongst elderly users was that they gave help with cleaning a high priority whereas the designers of community support services neglected it.

The meaning of "Immigrant" for women of color

If the social support aspect of home care work remains invisible, if cleaning is a priority for elderly service users, and if the home care worker is a woman of color, elderly clients and their families assume she is an immigrant—clearly a negative label for our respondents:

> I'm here 22 years but I'm still an immigrant!

> I have been here since 1981. I did a lot to become an immigrant. I didn't just take it away from anybody. I became a landed immigrant in 1989 and last year I became a citizen.

> I'm here for 5 years. As far as I see, this is the only job you can get.

> Oh yeah, there are a lot of Filipinos in this country, but we're paying taxes, you know, we're working hard.

> There was one lady who said "Well then you should go back to where you come from." You know, immigrants should go where they belong. So I said, "Where did your mother come from?" And she said that she came from such and such. So I said "What does that make you? An immigrant just like me." You do hear it, you know.

We asked homemakers if and how language, culture, and race became issues in their daily routines. Language and cultural differences were fairly easy to negotiate, often recalled with a sense of humor. For instance, a home care worker recalled with a smile her education while cleaning up a kosher kitchen for one elderly couple. Around issues of race, responses were more equivocal:

> They know most Filipinas take jobs in the house. If you are not a nanny, you are a cleaning lady.

> Some people think our jobs are very demeaning. [example] There was a little girl, not a little girl, but she was young looking and she was white—and very pretty. And this lady had a black homemaker going there all the time—and it was ok. But when she saw this white girl she said "What you doing this kind of work for?" It comes back to us. How do you think we feel? We are good enough but as soon as they see somebody that they feel [pause] then you realize how much they think of you and your job. You know?

> Sometimes you can't even describe it but you know it's there. I'm trying to think. "All you people"; a lot say, meaning black people. Not "you people, YOUR people," that's the word—"YOUR PEOPLE." If you say you need a mop to wash the floor, you need modern things, well, "Why should I have to buy a mop when you are not used to a mop in your country?" That kind of thing, little things, you know.

It seems that clients', and their families', reactions to home care workers who are immigrant women of color range from genuine misunderstandings of what home care workers do to racist attitudes toward particular groups.

Negotiating ethnoracial tensions

These statements from individual interviews describe and offer some interpretations of the situations encountered by home care workers. In the focus groups, we asked home care workers how they responded to such incidents. Participants observed, with sighs, that they frequently handle them poorly—that is to say, they avoid, ignore, or are angry inside but remain silent. As one participant put it: "You cannot be educating all the time." The examples cited are everyday incidents that are familiar and repetitive:

> This lady, she had some candies, and I said "Can I have a candy?" She said "Eenie, meenie, minie, moe, catch a ..." and she stopped. I guess she was gonna use the nigger word. And she stop and look at me and I just took the candy and walked away. I didn't say anything. She just stopped on "catch a." I didn't make a fuss, no hard feelings. Like I don't hear, I just blank it out. And I'm still going there.

> They [the family] were wondering why when they come to visit their sister, I am wearing new clothes. They are wondering where I am getting the money to buy the clothes. I almost said, "I'm receiving $800 every two weeks." But I wanted to finish my job because I had the meeting tonight so I didn't want to have a discussion about it.

On occasion home care workers do respond and counter the interpretations dealt out to them:

> She said "Well a white person wouldn't do that [referring to cleaning]." So then I said, "Well, that is why the white person has to go on welfare because they don't wanna do the job. Most of us, I said to her, are employed because we will do the job." That kind of made her think a little bit.

I said [to a client] not all the provinces in the Philippines are poor. All the people who come here are not uneducated because I don't come like that. I answered that there are lots of Philippine people in Canada, but we come here as educated people. We're not all the poorest in the Philippines. It's not like that in our country. [The client] said, "Oh yeah? Are you [educated]?" I said, "Yes, do you want to see my certificate?"

Many Filipino health care professionals emigrate to Canada but their training is not recognized unless they acquire Canadian experience or recertification. Such persons possess skills that are attractive to employers in the home care market. Employees, however, see these jobs as temporary, second-choice options imposed by professional and other dominant interest groups.

In both the interviews and focus groups home care workers attributed much of the negative attitudes and behaviors they encountered to the powerful influence of the media. It was noted that elderly clients watch a lot of television:

They are older and they don't get out much and they look at that [points to TV]. That's where they get the negative thing about Black people.... As soon as you open the door, they say "Did you hear the news?" You can hardly have a conversation without the issue being talked about. We don't bring it up.

Sometimes they [elderly clients] watch those talk shows, like Oprah, where they are talking about race and stuff. If I feel it's getting too hot I'll just kinda go and find something else to do. I don't really discuss things about that 'cause then I get too touchy and then I'm gonna feel offended or something, or they're gonna feel [voice trails off].

Home care workers from the Caribbean saw as problematic stories on television about black crime. When clients attempted to engage the home care worker in such discussions, a variety of response strategies were used—including some courageous attempts at consciousness raising: "I said 'Well, in all races there are good and bad people. When one person does something you do not have to condemn us all. When a white person does something, we do not condemn all whites.'" Another home care worker pointed out to a client belonging to the same ethnic group as a man who was currently making the headlines for embezzling large sums that his crime and his cultural community were not associated. However, when a crime is committed by a person of color you read about black crime for days. In another case the home care worker explained to an elderly client her reluctance to discuss an incident by saying these things hurt her as a member of that community and thus it was difficult to talk about....

In sum, in everyday home care work and its management, the class, race, and gender disparities existing in the broader society are understood as individual cases of prejudice to be handled on an ad hoc basis. This understanding and the institutional practices that result reinforce the very patterns that perpetuate the problem. This is not intended as a critical comment on the way the cases were handled. Elderly clients, home care workers, and supervisors have no other options when conflicts arising from decreases in service hours, labor market inequities, and prevailing definitions of socially created dependencies must be treated as personal problems rather than public issues. As the above discussion highlights, each incident extracts time, emotional, and mental costs from these three sets of players who, in order to make home care happen, must daily negotiate tensions arising from structural inequities of race, class, and gender. The compromises they negotiate are never satisfactory but represent their best efforts in the face of, seemingly, a complete lack of resources to support alternative resolutions. There are, for example, no policies in place to support or broaden their efforts and no language to politicize or contextualize their individually borne discomforts and struggles. This dearth of institutional and discursive resources raises important questions about the purpose and structure of community-based care. We consider some of these in the following section.

Transforming Community Care

Revisiting assumptions in home care models

When policy makers talk about community-based care, they tend to assume that a consensus exists as to its ingredients. The familial model of care that permeates most discussions is justified by appealing to preference statements made by old people that they would like to have their care provided by family members. Limited attention is paid to the fact that elderly respondents, like their younger counterparts, hold idealized images of family. In such images, not only do family members have knowledge of the particular needs and preferences of the elderly person, but they also have the capacity, time, and commitment to provide the desired level of care. An extensive body of research suggests that this is seldom the case. Likewise, taking preference statements at face value fails to recognize that, when trying to respond to questions about how their needs might be met, research participants, like all of us, are limited to concepts and knowledge that are part of their experiences. In the North American context, there is little guarantee of care by sources other than a family member. This situation can be contrasted to that of old people in Norway [48] where home care has been available for over 25 years. There, surveys show, old people prefer not to have family members provide personal care....

Obviously missing from the data presented here are the voices of service users. Bringing their voices in is essential to developing the type of remodeling that we are suggesting. However, if including elderly service users and their families in decision-making is restricted to consumer surveys, we will only get more of what we already know—a list of preferences that reflect an idealized female family carer. If these narrowed preferences become the basis for developing long-term care policy, community-based care in the future will be limited to bolstering the lone carer and promoting opportunities for development of a personal care market for those with the resources to purchase such services. Under such conditions, old people, the family members who care for them (if available), and immigrant women of color who take up such jobs will all be losers. Old people will not have any guarantee of services should they need them. Family carers, primarily women, will bear increasing responsibility with only the hope of some occasional help or relief under a minimalist social policy that shrouds the lack of services to the elderly under the deceptive guise of "helping carers to care." Home care workers will be hired in a low-wage market where training, quality control, and working conditions are of little public concern.

The challenge today is to raise questions about what is required to enable elderly persons to remain a part of their community, however defined. What kinds of supports and guarantees are needed to promote this possibility? Projecting images of youthful active seniors or of severely debilitated elderly persons serenely accepting continuous care by a loving spouse or daughter as the norm is misleading because they are so at odds with the reality facing aging persons. The shape of community care programs is open to debate but can only be meaningful if service users are central to policy decision-making, as distinct from being occasionally consulted [51], and if home care workers can negotiate the content and organization of their work. One writer has phrased it this way: a vision is needed for community care which is both user-centered and worker friendly [52].

Conclusion

Redirecting the community care project will take considerable effort because the debates within it are frequently isolated. Feminist literature on caring has concentrated primarily on its effects for unpaid female kin. When formal caring is examined, the focus has been on the specification of tasks, their associated skills or professional expertise, and the organization and funding of services. An understanding of nonfamilial care would transform current models of community care. Recently the caring professions, nursing and social work, have begun to document the skill component of care work and separate it out from an amorphous idea of caring—perhaps most graphically conflated in the idea of caring communities. Caring work is attending physically, mentally, and emotionally to the needs of another and giving a commitment to the nurturing, growth, and healing of that other (53, pp. 18–19). Such a definition allows us to begin to specify what is competence in caring. It indicates that the adequate performance of tasks, such as meal preparation, is not the subject matter of caring; to define it as such misses the relationship-based components of the work. Caring is unpredictable, emotional work which, while not the equivalent of love, does involve commitment to developing and sustaining a relationship [54–57]. Such work can occur in a variety of interpersonal relationships and in different institutional contexts. Admittedly, this is difficult to accomplish in bureaucratic work settings or in those that rely on a transient labor force. The recognition of these difficulties highlights just how profoundly care work is affected by the restructuring of health and social services. The long-term care agenda is, currently, the product of a host of economically driven policy directions. At the time of writing, these directions are encouraging new providers in the form of voluntary and paid-for neighborhood service schemes; the development of a mixed economy of care where profit-making agencies compete with public sector and non-profits for service contracts; and the casualization of the labor force. Until there is a fundamental reexamination of the effects of these policy directions on the three most vulnerable players in home care—old people, their informal carers, and women of color who make up the home care workers labor market—gendered and racist policies will support practices that impede care. We hope that by documenting these effects, this study has taken a step toward this transformative task.

Note

1   Adjectives such as "racialized" and "gendered" are used as descriptors of social institutions, such as labor markets, where practices reinforce race and gender divisions within a society. In this article the term "women

of color" is used because the term includes Caribbean black, East Indian, and Asian women. These groups are frequently referred to by policy makers in Canada as "visible minorities," although group members describe themselves as "women of color."

References

1 Benjamin, A. E. An historical perspective on home care policy. *Milbank Q.* 71(1): 129–166, 1993.

2 Szasz, A. The labor impacts of policy changes in home care; how federal policy transformed home health organizations and their labor practices. *J. Health Polit. Policy Law* 15: 191–210, 1990.

3 Burbridge, L. The labor market for home care workers: Demand, supply and institutional barriers. *Gerontologist* 33(1): 41–46, 1993.

4 Estes, C., et al. *The Long Term Care Crisis: Elders Trapped in the No-Care Zone.* Sage, Newbury Park, Calif., 1993.

5 Kenney, G. How access to long-term care affects home health transfers. *J. Health Polit. Policy Law* 18(4): 937–965, 1993.

6 MacAdam, M. Home care reimbursement and effects on personnel. *Gerontologist* 33(1): 55–63, 1993.

7 Daatland, S. Recent trends and future prospects for the elderly in Scandinavia. *J. Aging Soc. Policy* 6(1/2): 181–197, 1994.

8 Special issue on policy issues in care for the elderly in Canada. *Rev. Can. Vieillement/Can. J. Aging* 14(2): 153–446, 1995.

9 Evers, A., and van der Zanden, G. (eds.). *Better Care for Dependent People Living at Home: Meeting the New Agenda in Services for the Elderly.* Netherlands Institute of Gerontology, Bunnick, The Netherlands, 1993.

10 Kraan, R., and Evers, A. (eds.). *Care for the Elderly: Significant Innovations in Three European Countries.* Westview Press, Boulder, Colo., 1991.

11 Lesemann, F., and Martin, C. *Home-Based Care, the Elderly, the Family and the Welfare State: An International Comparison.* University of Ottawa Press, Ottawa, 1993.

12 Wistow, G., and Henwood, M. Caring for people: Elegant model or flawed design. In *Social Policy Review 1990–91*, edited by N. Manning, pp. 78–100. The Longman Group, Harlow, Essex, 1991.

13 Applebaum, R., and McGinnis, R. What price quality? Assuring the quality of case managed in-home care. *J. Case Manage.* 1(1): 9–13, 1992.

14 Eustis, N., Kane, R., and Fischer, L. Home care quality and the home care worker: Beyond quality assurance as usual. *Gerontologist* 33(1): 64–73, 1993.

15 Feldman, P. Work improvements for home care workers: Impact and feasibility. *Gerontologist* 33(1): 47–54, 1993.

16 Kane, R., and Caplan, A. (eds.). *Ethical Conflicts in the Management of Home Care: The Case Manager's Dilemma.* Springer Publishing, New York, 1993.

17 Kramer, A., et al. Assessing and assuring the quality of home health care: A conceptual framework. *Milbank Q.* 68(3): 413–443, 1990.

18 Schmid, H., and Hasenfield, Y. Organizational dilemmas in the provision of homecare services. *Soc. Serv. Rev.* 67: 40–54, 1993.

19 Bartoldus, E., Illery, B., and Sturges, P. J. Job-related stress and coping among home care workers with elderly people. *Health Soc. Work*, August 1989, pp. 204–210.

20 Eustis, N. N., and Fischer, L. R. Relationship between home care clients and their workers: Implications for quality of care. *Gerontologist* 31(4): 447–456, 1991.

21 Kaye, L. W. Worker views of the intensity of affective expression during the delivery of home care services for the elderly. *Home Care Serv. Q.* 7: 41–54, 1986.

22 Mercer, S., Heacock, P., and Beck, C. Nurses aides in nursing homes: A study of caregivers. *J. Women Aging* 6(1/2): 107–121, 1994.

23 Warren, L. We're home helps because we care: The experience of home helps caring for elderly people. In *New Directions in the Sociology of Health*, edited by P. Abbott and G. Payne, pp. 70–86. Falmer Press, London, 1990.

24 Abel, E. Family care of the frail elderly. In *Circles of Care: Work and Identity in Women's Lives*, edited by E. Abel and M. Nelson, pp. 65–91. The State University of New York, Albany, 1990.

25 Dwyer, J., and Coward, R. *Gender, Families and Elder Care.* Sage, Newbury Park, Calif., 1992.

26 Lewis, J., and Meredith, B. *Daughters Who Care.* Routledge, London and New York, 1988.

27 Boyd, M. Gender, visible minority and immigrant earnings inequality: Reassessing an employment equity premise. In *Deconstructing a Nation: Immigration, Multiculturalism and Racism in '90s Canada*, edited by V. Satzewich, pp. 279–321. Fernwood Publishing, Halifax, Nova Scotia, 1992.

28 Foner, N. *The Caregiving Dilemma: Work in An American Nursing Home.* University of California Press, Berkeley, 1994.

29 Anthias, F., and Yuval-Davis, N. (with Cain, H.). *Racialized Boundaries: Race, Nation, Gender, Colour and Class and the Anti-Racist Struggle*, Routledge, London and New York, 1992.

30 Boris, E. The racialized gendered state: The construction of citizenship in the United States. *Social Politics: International Studies in Gender, State and Society* 2(2): 160–180, 1995.

31 Stafford, J. The impact of the new immigration policy on racism in Canada. In *Deconstructing a Nation: Immigration, Multiculturalism and Racism in '90s Canada*, edited by V. Satzewich, pp. 69–92. Fernwood Publishing, Halifax, Nova Scotia, 1992.

32 Arat-Koc, S. In the privacy of their own home: Foreign domestic workers as solution to the crisis of the domestic sphere in Canada. In *Feminism in Action: Studies in Political Economy* edited by M. P. Connelly and P. Armstrong, pp. 149–174. Canadian Scholars Press, Toronto, 1992.

33 Calliste, A. Canada's immigration policy and domestics from the Caribbean: The second domestic scheme. In *Race, Class, Gender, Bonds and Barriers*, Ed. 2, edited by J. Vorst et al., pp. 136–168. Garamond Press, Toronto, 1991.

34 Colen, S. "With respect to feeling": Voices of West Indian child care and domestic workers in New York City. In *All American Women: Lines that Divide, Ties that Bind* edited by J. B. Cole, pp. 3–70. Free Press, New York, 1986.

35 Dill, B. T. "Making your job good yourself": Domestic service and the construction of personal dignity. In *Women and the Politics of Empowerment*, edited by A. Bookman and S. Morgen, pp. 33–52. Temple University Press, Philadelphia, 1988.

36 Donovan, R. Work stress and job satisfaction: A study of home care workers in New York City. *Home Health Serv. Q.* 10: 97–114, 1989.

37 Glenn, E. N. From servitude to service work: Historical continuities in the racial division of paid reproductive labor. *Signs* 18(1): 1–43, 1992.

38 Tellis-Nayek, V., and Tellis-Nayek, M. Quality of care and the burden of two cultures: When the world of the nurse's aide enters the world of the nursing home. *Gerontologist* 29(3):307–313, 1989.

39 Essed, P. *Understanding Everyday Racism: An Interdisciplinary Theory.* Sage, Newbury Park, Calif., 1991.

40 Andersen, M. Studying across difference: Race, class and gender in qualitative research. In *Race and Ethnicity in Research Models*, edited by J. Stanfield II and R. Dennis, pp. 39–52. Sage, Newbury Park, Calif., 1993.

41 Cannon, L., Higginbotham, E., and Leung, M. Race and class bias in qualitative research on women. *Gender and Society* 2(4): 449–462, 1988.

42 De Vault, M. Ethnicity and expertise: Racial-ethnic knowledge in sociological research. *Gender and Society* 9(5): 612–631, 1995.

43 Aronson, J., and Neysmith, S. "You're not just in there to do the work": Depersonalizing policies and the exploitation of home care workers' labour. *Gender and Society* 10(1): 59–77, 1996.

44 Neysmith, S., and Aronson, J. Home care workers discuss their work: The skills required to "use our common sense." *J. Aging Stud.* 10(1): 1–14, 1996.

45 Folio Corporation. Folio VIEWS *2.1.* Provo, Ohio, 1992.

46 Gregson, N., and Lowe, M. *Servicing the Middle Classes: Class, Gender and Waged Domestic Labour in Contemporary Britain.* Routledge, New York and London, 1994.

47 Walker, A., and Warren, L. *Changing Services for Older People*, Open University Press, Buckingham and Philadelphia, 1996.

48 Daatland, S. What are families for? On family solidarity and preference for help. *Ageing and Society* 10: 1–15, 1990.

49 Bakan, A., and Stasiulis, D. Making the match: Agencies and the racialization of women's household work. *Signs* 20(2): 303–335, 1995.

50 Razack, S. What is to be gained by looking white people in the eye? Culture, race, and gender in cases of sexual violence. *Signs* 19(4): 894–923, 1994.

51 Aronson, J. Giving consumers a say in policy development: Influencing policy or just being heard? *Can. Public Policy* 19(4): 367–378, 1993.

52 Carpenter, M. *Normality Is Hard Work: Trade Unions and the Politics of Community Care*, Lawrence and Wishart, London, 1994.

53 Davies, C. Competence versus care? Gender and caring work revisited. *Acta Sociol.* 38: 17–31, 1995.

54 Fisher, B., and Tronto, J. Toward a feminist theory of caring. In *Circles of Care: Work and Identity in Women's Lives*, edited by E. Abel and M. Nelson, pp. 35–62. The State University of New York, Albany, 1990.

55 Graham, H. Social divisions of caring. *Women's Studies International Forum* 16: 461–470, 1993.

56 James, N. Care = organization + physical labour + emotional labour. *Sociol. Health Illness* 14: 488–509, 1992.

57 Thomas, C. De-constructing concepts of care. *Sociology* 27(4): 649–669, 1993.

Sneakers and Sweatshops
Holding Corporations Accountable

DAVID M. SCHILLING

A 12-year-old worker in Pakistan earns 60 cents per day stitching soccer balls that are sold for more than $10 in the United States; an Indonesian worker needs over a month's pay to purchase a pair of shoes she makes for Nike; Mexicans employed by Alcoa must choose between buying food and paying rent.

Although sweatshop conditions in factories throughout the world are not new, they became headline news when the public learned that clothes made under Kathie Lee Gifford's label were sewn by children at Global Fashions, a maquiladora factory (where products are made for export) in Honduras. Gifford, a television talk-show celebrity and children's advocate, was appalled when the National Labour Committee announced that clothes bearing her name were made by girls ages 12 to 14 who were forced to work 13-hour shifts under armed guard for 31 cents an hour. When she found that the charges were true, she convinced Wal-Mart to withdraw its contract from Global Fashions.

It would have been easy for Kathie Lee Gifford to end her involvement there. But she met with Secretary of Labor Robert Reich, who urged her to join the Department of Labor in its effort to end sweatshop conditions in the U.S. and abroad. Since that meeting, Gifford has recruited other celebrities in that effort.

On July 16 the Department of Labor sponsored the Fashion Industry Forum at Marymount University in Virginia. Retailers, buyers, designers, manufacturers, endorsers, contractors, consumers, unions and social responsibility groups gathered to discuss strategies for eradicating sweatshops in the garment industry. As Gifford observed, "The problems are not simple, but insidious and pervasive."

Nancy Penaloza, a sewing machine operator in New York City, described the sweatshop conditions under which she has worked for nine years: "I sew high-quality women's suits priced at $120 or more. I get paid $6 per suit. I work at least 56 hours a week, Monday through Saturday, and get paid $207 a week ($3.75 an hour), off the books. If there are deadlines, we work till the job is done. My boss screams at me all the time to work faster. There is only one bathroom for 100 people. We do not have a union. If you complain, you get fired and someone else takes your job." When Reich asked her, "What if you want to work 40 hours a week, can you?" Penaloza answered, "I have to work the number of hours my boss tells me."

David M. Schilling, "Sneakers and Sweatshops: Holding Corporations Accountable." Reprinted by permission from *The Christian Century*, October 9, 1996: 240–244. Copyright © 1996 Christian Century Foundation.

Who is responsible for these substandard labor conditions? Corporate giants in the U.S. apparel industry rarely own the factories that produce their goods. As part of a globalized economy, companies like Levi Strauss, Nike and Reebok contract with suppliers who produce their goods. The working conditions of many suppliers fall far below the most basic standards of fair and humane treatment. Companies typically distance themselves from responsibility for workplace conditions and low wages by contending they do not own or operate these facilities. Yet their orders enable these facilities to operate.

In an interconnected world, both consumers and investors are hearing about child and exploited labor conditions via the evening news or the Internet. Most Americans do not want to purchase a soccer ball made by a Pakistani child who is paid six cents an hour. As both consumers and investors, Americans are pressing U.S. companies and their suppliers to address exploitative work conditions. According to a survey released by Marymount University, more than three-fourths of Americans would avoid shopping at stores if they were aware that the stores sold goods made in sweatshops. The challenge is to make companies enforce their codes of conduct and use their economic power to see that their suppliers observe basic standards of human and labor rights.

The Interfaith Center on Corporate Responsibility (ICCR) has been working with labor groups, companies in the apparel industry, the Department of Labor and the newly formed presidential advisory committee to explore strategies to eradicate sweatshops. ICCR is not new to this work. For 25 years it has been challenging corporations to pay a living wage, provide safe working conditions, and contribute to the communities where they operate. ICCR members have raised their voices in corporate boardrooms and shareholder annual meetings since 1971, when the Episcopal Church filed the first religious shareholder resolution calling on General Motors to divest of its operations in apartheid South Africa. Currently, ICCR has 275 Catholic, Protestant and Jewish institutional investors, including denominations, religious communities, pension funds, dioceses and health-care corporations with combined portfolios worth over $50 billion.

ICCR members combine a principled and pragmatic approach. As religious shareholders, they are "in" but not "of" the corporation—insiders because they are part owners of the company, outsiders because they believe the exclusive focus on bottom-line profits is idolatry. As board member Sister Barbara Aires, S.C., explains, "Economic decisions have profound human and moral consequences. Faith communities measure corporate performance not only by what a corporation produces and its profitability, but also by how it impacts the environment, touches human life and wheather it protects or undermines the dignity of the human person. Protection of human rights—civil, political, social and economic—is a minimum standard for corporations seeking to act responsibly."

ICCR, along with two religious counterparts in Great Britain and Canada, has released a draft document titled "Principles for Global Corporate Responsibility: Benchmarks for Measuring Business Performance." This is the first time that religious groups have developed comprehensive global standards for responsible corporate citizenship. The Principles urge companies to envision themselves as one of many stakeholders in the global community and to set high standards for how they treat their employees, the environment and the communities where they operate.

ICCR's approach to corporations involves talking with company officials, filing shareholder resolutions that address changes in policies and practices, running public campaigns focusing on media and public education, and screening out investments in companies whose actions violate members' principles.

In many instances, ICCR uses all these tools at once. Sometimes it takes a public campaign for a company to agree to dialogue. In other cases the filing of a shareholder resolution gets a company's attention and leads to constructive dialogue and change. (In 1996 ICCR members filed 172 shareholder resolutions with 118 companies.)

Like many U.S. corporations, Alcoa operates manufacturing plants in Mexico's maquiladora sector, where goods are assembled for export. In 1965 the Mexican government set up the Border Industrialization Program, creating low-tariff, low-wage export platforms for U.S. companies on favorable terms—long before NAFTA was instituted and made all of Mexico an export platform. U.S. companies shift work to Mexico to cut labor costs. The rapid expansion of this sector has created jobs, but jobs at poverty-wage levels.

ICCR members, along with the Coalition for Justice in the Maquiladoras (CJM)—a broad-based coalition of labor, environmental and religious groups from Mexico, U.S. and Canada—were concerned about Alcoa. Among the concerns were low wages and poor health and safety conditions, including the gas poisonings of Alcoa workers in 1994. In 1995 the Benedictine Sisters of Boerne, Texas, filed a shareholder resolution calling on Alcoa to initiate a review of its maquiladora operations and to recommend changes. Alcoa was urged to participate in a survey to determine the purchasing power of the wages of its Mexican workers. A similar resolution was filed with ten other U.S. companies, including General Electric, Johnson & Johnson and Zenith.

Alcoa and other U.S. companies rationalize paying poverty-level wages in two ways. They point out that wages paid to workers are competitive with what other companies are paying in a specific area and that the wages paid to workers are above the minimum wage set by governments. But workers in Mexico and elsewhere can be paid a competitive wage well above the minimum required by law and still not be able to feed themselves and their families.

Before the 1994 Mexican economic crisis, the average pay of a maquiladora worker was $30 to $50 for a 48-hour week, or barely a subsistence wage. As a result of the peso devaluation and the inflation of over 50 percent that accompanied it, the purchasing power of maquiladora wages plunged below subsistence level.

In January 1996 a group of Alcoa workers in Ciudad Acuña did an informal market study which revealed that basic food items (not including meat, milk, vegetables or cereal) cost $26.87 a week, while wages averaged between $21.44 and $24.60 a week.

How can companies like Alcoa determine what a sustainable wage is, particularly in countries where standardized wage data are difficult to obtain and legal minimum wage levels are so low as to be meaningless? Sister Ruth Rosenbaum, T.C., co-chair of ICCR's Global Corporate Accountability Issue Group and director of the Center for Reflection, Education and Action, has devised an innovative method to determine wage levels. Rosenbaum has developed the Purchasing Power Index Study (PPI), which is based on the standard "market basket" survey similar to the Consumer Price Index done by the U.S. Department of Labor.

The PPI takes the market basket survey an important further step by calculating the intersection of wages and prices documented in the survey. Rosenbaum writes: "Based on wages paid, calculations are performed to determine the number of work minutes required in order to purchase any given item. Since each week contains a limited number of minutes, the calculations reveal how many items the worker can possibly purchase. The purchasing power of the wages is made evident, and the effect of the wage scale upon the life of the worker and the community is clarified in an objective way." (See Rosenbaum, *In Whose Interest?*, January 1996.) A sustainable wage is defined by religious shareholders as one that allows a worker to meet basic needs, set aside money for future purchases, and earn enough discretionary income to support the development of small business in the community.

How has Alcoa responded to religious shareholders? In January the company agreed to come to the U.S.-Mexico border for a meeting with maquiladora workers. But at the same time the Securities and Exchange Commission ruled in the company's favor that the Benedictine Sisters' resolution would be kept off the proxy statement and would not be brought up for a vote at Alcoa's shareholder meeting. Susan Mika, primary filer of the resolution; CJM Executive Director Martha Ojeda; and two Alcoa workers from Mexican plants traveled to Alcoa's annual shareholders' meeting. Workers Juan Tovar and Irma Valadez described the starvation wages, the lack of protective equipment and sanitary conditions and the lack of toilet paper in the workers' bathrooms. The Pittsburgh Labor Action Network on the Americas and the United Steelworkers of America helped draw press attention to the workers' concerns by distributing leaflets outside the meeting.

Mika called on Alcoa CEO Paul O'Neill to meet with the delegation after the annual meeting. O'Neill agreed and promised to review the wages and working conditions in Alcoa's Mexican plants. The combined pressure of religious shareholders, key labor groups, religious investors and maquiladora workers had an impact. In July Alcoa announced that its workers in Ciudad Acuña would receive a 40-pesos-per-week (about $5.25) raise. Said Mika: "This small wage increase, as applied to the reported 5,600 workers in Acuña, would nonetheless represent an additional investment of $30,000 per week in salaries received by workers."

O'Neill visited the plants, checked out workers' allegations, fired a human resources person for not reporting health and safety violations, put soap and toilet paper in plant bathrooms and raised wages.

The next step is to secure Alcoa's participation in a Purchasing Power Index study that could lead to a systematic wage increase for all of Alcoa's Mexican workers. Two U.S. companies that operate maquiladora plants in Mexico—Baxter International and W. R. Grace—have already agreed to participate. If ICCR can persuade a few key companies to raise wages, they can put pressure on all companies to pay a sustainable wage, whether the workers are in Michigan or Mexico, Indiana or Indonesia.

Sometimes work with a corporation produces results in one area but not in another. For example, two years ago General Motors endorsed the CERES Principles on the environment, a major mutual victory for environmental responsibility. In regard to its maquiladora operations in Mexico, however, GM has demonstrated little interest in participating in a study or in raising the wages of its 62,000 workers.

GM executives from Detroit and local GM managers did agree to visit GM workers at their homes in Reynosa, Mexico, which are made from corrugated metal and have no running water or electricity. At the time these workers were making 180 pesos (less than $26) a week in take-home pay. As a result of this trip, GM pledged to raise its workers' standard of living. CEO John Smith announced a housing initiative that "would make affordable housing a reality for thousands of its workers." ICCR supported the initiative but argued for more. "The housing program is a generous and compassionate response to the deplorable living conditions of some of GM's Mexican workers," said Barbara Glendon, O.S.U., of Mercy Consolidated Asset Management Program, for years a key sponsor of GM resolutions. "But compassion without justice is not enough to fulfill the obligations of our company to its employees. We are morally and ethically responsible to provide a sustainable wage to the people whose daily labor benefits us who are GM shareholders." A shift in wage policy from a competitive to a sustainable wage would improve the lives of over 700,000 GM workers worldwide and set a standard for other corporations to meet.

A public campaign over working conditions at a supplier in El Salvador turned into a collaborative relationship between ICCR and The Gap, a San Francisco-based clothing chain. The National Labor Committee Education Fund in Support of Worker and Human Rights in Central America (NLC) had found violations of The Gap's "Sourcing Principles and Guidelines" at Mandarin International, a shop in San Salvador owned by a Taiwanese firm. Workers had complained to the NLC about the use of child labor, forced overtime, unsafe working conditions, threats to prevent workers from organizing and firing of union leaders. After six months of leafleting at stores, letter writing by religious and community groups and face-to-face discussions, The Gap agreed to explore independent monitoring at Mandarin International and to urge Mandarin to rehire union leaders who had been fired.

Four widely respected Salvadoran institutions agreed to form the Independent Monitoring Group: the secretariat of the Archdiocese of San Salvador, Tutela Legal (the human rights office of the archdiocese), the Human Rights Institute of University of Central America, and CENTRA (a labor research organization). These institutions now monitor Mandarin on a regular basis for worker abuses. In addition, when Mandarin receives enough work orders to restore the workforce to former levels, union leaders will be rehired.

This development is historic. The Gap is the first company to agree to develop an independent monitoring mechanism for its contract suppliers. Other companies have hired third-party consultants (like Emst and Young, the accounting firm hired by Nike to do social audits of their contractors), but their reports are not independently generated or publicly disclosed. There are signs that independent monitors, made up of respected local institutions committed to human rights, will play a crucial role in ensuring that worker rights are respected, company codes of conduct upheld and sweatshop conditions eliminated.

Individuals and congregations can make a difference by refusing to purchase products made under sweatshop conditions, by writing to companies to inquire about their code of conduct and how it is enforced, by getting the directors of denominational pension funds involved in sweatshop issues and by voting for socially responsible resolutions.

There are companies that are willing to look for ways of doing business responsibly in the global economy; others are reluctant to enter the unknown territory where business operations and human rights intersect. But the consumers' growing concern about conditions under which products are made will not go away. As corporations struggle to do the right thing, we must hold them accountable and support those organizations that are helping to find principled and practical solutions to the challenges posed by the new global economy.

B. Affirmative Action

Preferential Hiring

JUDITH JARVIS THOMSON

Many people are inclined to think preferential hiring an obvious injustice.[1] I should have said "feel" rather than "think": it seems to me the matter has not been carefully thought out, and that what is in question, really, is a gut reaction.

I am going to deal with only a very limited range of preferential hirings: that is, I am concerned with cases in which several candidates present themselves for a job, in which the hiring officer finds, on examination, that all are equally qualified to hold that job, and he then straightway declares for the black, or for the woman, because he or she *is* a black or a woman. And I shall talk only of hiring decisions in the universities, partly because I am most familiar with them, partly because it is in the universities that the most vocal and articulate opposition to preferential hiring is now heard—not surprisingly, perhaps, since no one is more vocal and articulate than a university professor who feels deprived of his rights.

I suspect that some people may say, Oh well, in *that* kind of case it's all right, what we object to is preferring the less qualified to the better qualified. Or again, What we object to is refusing even to consider the qualifications of white males. I shall say nothing at all about these things. I think that the argument I shall give for saying that preferential hiring is not unjust in the cases I do concentrate on can also be appealed to justify it outside that range of cases. But I won't draw any conclusions about cases outside it. Many people do have that gut reaction I mentioned against preferential hiring in *any* degree or form; and it seems to me worthwhile bringing out that there is good reason to think they are wrong to have it. Nothing I say will be in the slightest degree novel or original. It will, I hope, be enough to set the relevant issues out clearly.

I

But first, something should be said about qualifications.

I said I would consider only cases in which the several candidates who present themselves for the job are equally qualified to hold it; and there plainly are difficulties in the way of saying precisely how this is to be established, and even what is to be established. Strictly academic qualifications seem at a first glance to be relatively straightforward: the hiring officer must see if the candidates have done equally well in

Judith Jarvis Thomson, "Preferential Hiring." Reprinted with permission of Princeton University Press from *Philosophy and Public Affairs* 2.4 (1973): 364–384. Copyright © 1973 by Princeton University Press.

courses (both courses they took, and any they taught), and if they are recommended equally strongly by their teachers, and if the work they submit for consideration is equally good. There is no denying that even these things are less easy to establish than first appears: for example, you may have a suspicion that Professor Smith is given to exaggeration, and that this "great student" is in fact less strong than Professor Jones's "good student"—but do you *know* that this is so? But there is a more serious difficulty still: as blacks and women have been saying, strictly academic indicators may themselves be skewed by prejudice. My impression is that women, white and black, may possibly suffer more from this than black males. A black male who is discouraged or down-graded for being black is discouraged or down-graded out of dislike, repulsion, a desire to avoid contact; and I suspect that there are very few teachers nowadays who allow themselves to feel such things, or, if they do feel them, to act on them. A woman who is discouraged or down-graded for being a woman is not discouraged or down-graded out of dislike, but out of a conviction she is not serious....

II

... Suppose two candidates for a civil service job have equally good test scores, but that there is only one job available. We could decide between them by coin-tossing. But in fact we do allow for declaring for A straightway, where A is a veteran, and B is not.[2] It may be that B is a nonveteran through no fault of his own: perhaps he was refused induction for flat feet, or a heart murmur. That is, those things in virtue of which B is a nonveteran may be things which it was no more in his power to control or change than it is in anyone's power to control or change the color of his skin. Yet the fact is that B is not a veteran and A is. On the assumption that the veteran has served his country, the country owes him something. And it seems plain that giving him preference is a not unjust way in which part of that debt of gratitude can be paid.

And now,... we should turn to those debts which are incurred by one who wrongs another. It is here we find what seems to me the most powerful argument for the conclusion that the preferential hiring of blacks and women is not unjust.

I obviously cannot claim any novelty for this argument: it's a very familiar one. Indeed, not merely is it familiar, but so are a battery of objections to it. It may be granted that if we have wronged A, we owe him something: we should make amends, we should compensate him for the wrong done him. It may even be granted that if we have wronged A, we must make amends, that justice requires it, and that a failure to make amends is not merely callousness, but injustice. But (a) are the young blacks and women who are amongst the current applicants for university jobs amongst the blacks and women who were wronged? To turn to particular cases, it might happen that the black applicant is middle class, the son of professionals, and has had the very best in private schooling; or that the woman applicant is plainly the product of feminist upbringing and encouragement. Is it proper, much less required, that the black or woman be given preference over a white male who grew up in poverty, and has to make his own way and earn his encouragements? Again, (b), did we, the current members of the community, wrong any blacks or women? Lots of people once did; but then isn't it for them to do the compensating? That is, if they're still alive. For presumably nobody now alive owned any slaves, and perhaps nobody now alive voted against women's suffrage. And (c) what if the white male applicant for the job has never in any degree wronged any blacks or women? If so, *he* doesn't owe any debts to them, so why should *he* make amends to them?

These objections seem to me quite wrong-headed.

Obviously the situation for blacks and women is better than it was a hundred and fifty, fifty, twenty-five years ago. But it is absurd to suppose that the young blacks and women now of an age to apply for jobs have not been wronged. Large-scale, blatant, overt wrongs have presumably disappeared; but it is only within the last twenty-five years (perhaps the last ten years in the case of women) that it has become at all widely agreed in this country that blacks and women must be recognized as having, not merely this or that particular right normally recognized as belonging to white males, but all of the rights and respect which go with full membership in the community. Even young blacks and women have lived through down-grading for being black or female: they have not merely not been given that very equal chance at the benefits generated by what the community owns which is so firmly insisted on for white males, they have not until lately even been felt to have a right to it.

And even those who were not themselves down-graded for being black or female have suffered the consequences of the down-grading of other blacks and women: lack of self-confidence, and lack of self-respect. For where a community accepts that a person's being black, or being a woman, are right and proper grounds for denying that person full membership in the community, it can hardly be supposed that any but the most extraordinarily independent black or woman will escape self-doubt. All but the most extraordinarily independent of them have had to work harder—if only against self-doubt—then all but the most deprived white males, in the competition for a place amongst the best qualified.

If any black or woman has been unjustly deprived of what he or she has a right to, then of course justice does call for making amends. But what of the blacks and women who haven't actually been deprived of what they have a right to, but only made to suffer the consequences of injustice to other blacks and women? *Perhaps* justice doesn't require making amends to them as well; but common decency certainly does. To fail, at the very least, to make what counts as public apology to all, and to take positive steps to show that it is sincerely meant, is, if not injustice, then anyway a fault at least as serious as ingratitude.

Opting for a policy of preferential hiring may of course mean that some black or woman is preferred to some white male who as a matter of fact has had a harder life than the black or woman. But so may opting for a policy of veterans' preference mean that a healthy, unscarred, middle class veteran is preferred to a poor, struggling, scarred, nonveteran. Indeed, opting for a policy of settling who gets the job by having all equally qualified candidates draw straws may also mean that in a given case the candidate with the hardest life loses out. Opting for any policy other than hard-life preference may have this result.

I have no objection to anyone's arguing that it is precisely hard-life preference that we ought to opt for. If all, or anyway all of the equally qualified, have a right to an equal chance, then the argument would have to draw attention to something sufficiently powerful to override that right. But perhaps this could be done along the lines

I followed in the case of blacks and women: perhaps it could be successfully argued that we have wronged those who have had hard lives, and therefore owe it to them to make amends. And then we should have in more extreme form a difficulty already present: how are these preferences to be ranked? shall we place the hard-lifers ahead of blacks? both ahead of women? and what about veterans? I leave these questions aside. My concern has been only to show that the white male applicant's right to an equal chance does not make it unjust to opt for a policy under which blacks and women are given preference. That a white male with a specially hard history may lose out under this policy cannot possibly be any objection to it, in the absence of a showing that hard-life preference is not unjust, and, more important, takes priority over preference for blacks and women.

Lastly, it should be stressed that to opt for such a policy is not to make the young white male applicants themselves make amends for any wrongs done to blacks and women. Under such a policy, no one is asked to give up a job which is already his; the job for which the white male competes isn't his, but is the community's, and it is the hiring officer who gives it to the black or woman in the community's name. Of course the white male is asked to give up his equal chance at the job. But that is not something he pays to the black or woman by way of making amends; it is something the community takes away from him in order that *it* may make amends.

Still, the community does impose a burden on him: it is able to make amends for its wrongs only by taking something away from him, something which, after all, we are supposing he has a right to. And why should *he* pay the cost of the community's amends-making?

If there were some appropriate way in which the community could make amends to its blacks and women, some way which did not require depriving anyone of anything he has a right to, then that would be the best course of action for it to take. Or if there were anyway some way in which the costs could be shared by everyone, and not imposed entirely on the young white male job applicants, then that would be, if not best, then anyway better than opting for a policy of preferential hiring. But in fact the nature of the wrongs done is such as to make jobs the best and most suitable form of compensation. What blacks and women were denied was full membership in the community; and nothing can more appropriately make amends for that wrong than precisely what will make them feel they now finally have it. And that means jobs. Financial compensation (the cost of which could be shared equally) slips through the fingers; having a job, and discovering you do it well, yield—perhaps better than anything else—that very self-respect which blacks and women have had to do without.

But of course choosing this way of making amends means that the costs are imposed on the young white male applicants who are turned away. And so it should be noticed that it is not entirely inappropriate that those applicants should pay the costs. No doubt few, if any, have themselves, individually, done any wrongs to blacks and women. But they have profited from the wrongs the community did. Many may actually have been direct beneficiaries of policies which excluded or down-graded blacks and women— perhaps in school admissions, perhaps in access to financial aid, perhaps elsewhere; and even those who did not directly benefit in this way had, at any rate, the advantage in the competition which comes of confidence in one's full membership, and of one's rights being recognized as a matter of course.

Of course it isn't only the young white male applicant for a university job who has benefited from the exclusion of blacks and women: the older white male, now comfortably tenured, also benefited, and many defenders of preferential hiring feel that he should be asked to share the costs. Well, presumably we can't demand that he give up his job, or share it. But it seems to me in place to expect the occupants of comfortable professorial chairs to contribute in some way, to make some form of return to the young white male who bears the cost, and is turned away. It will have been plain that I find the outcry now heard against preferential hiring in the universities objectionable; it would also be objectionable that those of us who are now securely situated should placidly defend it, with no more than a sigh of regret for the young white male who pays for it.

III

One final word: "discrimination." I am inclined to think we so use it that if anyone is convicted of discriminating against blacks, women, white males, or what have you, then he is thereby convicted of acting unjustly. If so, and if I am right in thinking that preferential hiring in the restricted range of cases we have been looking at is *not* unjust, then we have two options: (a) we can simply reply that to opt for a policy of preferential hiring in those cases is not to opt for a policy of discriminating against white males, or (b) we can hope to get usage changed—e.g., by trying to get people to allow that there is discriminating against and discriminating against, and that some is unjust, but some is not.

Best of all, however, would be for that phrase to be avoided altogether. It's at best a blunt tool: there are all sorts of nice moral discriminations [*sic*] which one is unable to make while occupied with it. And that bluntness itself fits it to do harm: blacks and women are hardly likely to see through to what precisely is owed them while they are being accused of welcoming what is unjust.

Notes

1 This essay is an expanded version of a talk given at the Conference on the Liberation of Female Persons, held at North Carolina State University at Raleigh, on March 26–28, 1973, under a grant from the S & H Foundation. I am indebted to James Thomson and the members of the Society for Ethical and Legal Philosophy for criticism of an earlier draft.

2 To the best of my knowledge, the analogy between veterans' preference and the preferential hiring of blacks has been mentioned in print only by Edward T. Chase, in a Letter to the Editor, *Commentary*, February 1973.

Preferential Hiring
A Reply to Judith Jarvis Thomson

Robert Simon

Judith Jarvis Thomson has recently defended preferential hiring of women and black persons in universities.[1] She restricts her defense of the assignment of preference to only those cases where candidates from preferred groups and their white male competitors are equally qualified, although she suggests that her argument can be extended to cover cases where the qualifications are unequal as well. The argument in question is compensatory; it is because of pervasive patterns of unjust discrimination against black persons and women that justice, or at least common decency, requires that amends be made.

While Thomson's analysis surely clarifies many of the issues at stake, I find it seriously incomplete. I will argue that even if her claim that compensation is due victims of social injustice is correct (as I think it is), it is questionable nevertheless whether preferential hiring is an acceptable method of distributing such compensation. This is so, even if, as Thomson argues, compensatory claims override the right of the white male applicant to equal consideration from the appointing officer. For implementation of preferential hiring policies may involve claims, perhaps even claims of right, other than the above right of the white male applicant. In the case of the claims I have in mind, the best that can be said is that where preferential hiring is concerned, they are arbitrarily ignored. If so, and if such claims are themselves warranted, then preferential hiring, while *perhaps* not unjust, is open to far more serious question than Thomson acknowledges.

A familiar objection to special treatment for blacks and women is that, if such a practice is justified, other victims of injustice or misfortune ought to receive special treatment too. While arguing that virtually all women and black persons have been harmed, either directly or indirectly, by discrimination, Thomson acknowledges that in any particular case, a white male may have been victimized to a greater extent than have the blacks or women with which he is competing. However, she denies that other victims of injustice or misfortune ought automatically to have priority over blacks and women where distribution of compensation is concerned. Just as veterans receive preference with respect to employment in the civil service, as payment for the service they have performed for society, so can blacks and women legitimately be given preference in university hiring, in payment of the debt owed them. And just as the former policy can justify hiring a veteran who in fact had an easy time of it over a nonveteran who made great sacrifices for the public good, so too can the latter policy justify hiring a relatively undeprived member of a preferred group over a more disadvantaged member of a non-preferred group.

But surely if the reason for giving a particular veteran preference is that he performed a service for his country, that same preference must be given to anyone who performed a similar service. Likewise, if the reason for giving preference to a black person or to a woman is that the recipient has been injured due to an unjust practice, then preference must be given to anyone who has been similarly injured. So, it appears, there can be no relevant *group* to which compensation ought to be made, other than that made up of and only of those who have been injured or victimized.[2] Although, as Thomson claims, all blacks and women may be members of that latter group, they deserve compensation *qua* victim and not *qua* black person or woman.

There are at least two possible replies that can be made to this sort of objection. First, it might be agreed that anyone injured in the same way as blacks or women ought to receive compensation. But then, "same way" is characterized so narrowly that it applies to no one except blacks and women. While there is nothing logically objectionable about such a reply, it may nevertheless be morally objectionable. For it implies that a nonblack male who has been terribly injured by a social injustice has less of a claim to compensation than a black or woman who has only been minimally injured. And this implication may be morally unacceptable.

A more plausible line of response may involve shifting our attention from compensation of individuals to collective compensation of groups.[3] Once this shift is made, it can be acknowledged that as individuals, some white males may have stronger compensatory claims than blacks or women. But as compensation is owed the group, it is group claims that must be weighed, not individual ones. And surely, at the group level, the claims of black persons and women to compensation are among the strongest there are.

Suppose we grant that certain groups, including those specified by Thomson, are owed collective compensation. What should be noted is that the conclusion of concern here—that preferential hiring policies are acceptable instruments for compensating groups—does not directly follow. To derive such a conclusion validly, one would have to provide additional premises specifying the relation between collective compensation to groups and distribution of that compensation to individual members. For it does not follow from the fact that some group members are compensated that the group is compensated. Thus, if through a computer error, every member of the American Philosophical Association was asked to pay additional taxes, then if the government provided compensation for this error, it would not follow that it had compensated the Association. Rather it would have compensated each member *qua* individual. So what is required, where preferential hiring is concerned, are plausible premises showing how the preferential award of jobs to group members counts as collective compensation for the group.

Thomson provides no such additional premises. Moreover, there is good reason to think that if any such premises were provided, they would count against preferential hiring as an instrument of collective compensation. This is because although compensation is owed to the group, preferential hiring policies award compensation to an arbitrarily selected segment of the group; namely, those who have the ability and qualifications to be seriously considered for the jobs available. Surely, it is far more plausible to think that collective compensation ought to be equally available to all group members, or at least to all kinds of group members.[4] The claim that although compensation is owed collectively to a group, only a special sort of group member is eligible to receive it, while perhaps not incoherent, certainly ought to be rejected as arbitrary, at least in the absence of an argument to the contrary.

Accordingly, the proponent of preferential hiring faces the following dilemma. Either compensation is to be made on an individual basis, in which case the fact that one is black or a woman is irrelevant to whether one ought to receive special treatment, or it is made on a group basis, in which case it is far from clear that preferential hiring policies are acceptable compensatory instruments. Until this dilemma is resolved, assuming it can be resolved at all, the compensatory argument for preferential hiring is seriously incomplete at a crucial point.

Notes

1   Judith Jarvis Thomson, "Preferential Hiring," *Philosophy & Public Affairs*, 2, no. 4 (Summer 1973): 364–384.

2   This point also has been argued for recently by J. L. Cowen, "Inverse Discrimination," *Analysis*, 33, no. 1 (1972): 10–12.

3   Such a position has been defended by Paul Taylor, in his "Reverse Discrimination and Compensatory Justice," *Analysis*, 33, no. 4 (1973): 177–182.

4   Taylor would apparently agree, *ibid*, 180.

The Future of Affirmative Action

Michael Boylan

For approximately thirty years, the United States has been struggling with a public policy known as *affirmative action*. Since controversial public policies often have a short life, it is remarkable that affirmative action has lasted as long as it has. In its inception, it was a strategy to reverse the clear and pervasive underrepresentation of African Americans (first) and women (second) in medicine, law, academia, government, and business. Over time, the policy has been expanded to include any clearly defined group that is underrepresented in the most desirable occupational classes, school admission, and government contracts.

Michael Boylan "Affirmative Action: Strategies for the Future." Reprinted with permission from *Journal of Social Philosophy* 33.1 (2002): 117–130.

Recently, some retrenchment toward affirmative action has occurred. The State of California passed Proposition 209 banning affirmative action in admissions in state colleges and universities. A 1996 court decision, *Hogwood v. Texas*, prohibited the use of racial preferences in determining admissions to state higher education facilities. Thus, two major states have recently discarded affirmative action in their university and college admissions policies. Municipalities are discarding minority set-asides for public contracts. Fewer companies are employing affirmative action criteria in hiring.

Clearly, we are at the crossroads regarding this policy. Either affirmative action will redefine itself and continue into the future, or it will gradually fade away. This essay examines the policy from the point of view of both distributive justice and worldview to suggest which direction the United States should take.

Defining Affirmative Action

For the purposes of this essay, *affirmative action* refers to a policy that gives a preference to individuals based on their membership in designated groups that are underrepresented in the most desirable occupational classes, school admissions, and/or government contracts. This preference can take many forms, including extra point(s) added to some rubric for evaluating candidates, recruiting funds allocated for the expressed purpose of obtaining representation from individuals from a disadvantaged group (even when no rubric credits are given), and special training, education, and/or counseling given to individuals from a disadvantaged group to enable them to compete equally with individuals from advantaged groups.

Individuals from an advantaged group refers here to individuals from some clearly defined socioeconomic, racial, or gender group that is statistically well represented (or overrepresented) in the most desirable occupational classes, school admissions, and government contracts.

Individuals from a disadvantaged group describes individuals from some clearly defined socioeconomic, racial, or gender group that is statistically underrepresented in the most desirable occupational classes, school admissions, and government contracts.

Advantaged describes individuals or groups possessing (or seeming to possess) properties, work habits, general demeanor, and/or work production that are/is valued in the general society by those empowered to make the decisions ("the establishment"). The assumption is that individuals from families that are advantaged will also tend to be advantaged.[1]

Disadvantaged describes individuals or groups not possessing (or seeming not to possess) properties, work habits, general demeanor, and/or work production that are/is valued in the general society by the establishment. The assumption is that individuals from families that are disadvantaged will also tend to be disadvantaged.

Deserving refers to anyone who through *his or her own effort* fulfills some functional requirement of action and as a result achieves a functionally specific result. As an overlay to this basic definition, however, additions and subtractions can be made on the basis of what constitutes "his or her own effort." For example, if A has a 100-piece puzzle that is 80 percent complete and B has the same 100-piece puzzle that is only 10 percent complete, and after some time, A completes the puzzle while B achieves the level of only 80 percent, some adjustment in our calculations is in order.[2] It is true that only A completed the puzzle, but it is also true that B did more of the puzzle than A (and at a stage of it being rather amorphous—which is harder, as any puzzle maker knows).

Thus, A may deserve the title of puzzle finisher, but B deserves of the title of person who completed more of the puzzle and *a fortiori* is more deserving of the title better puzzle maker.[3]

This is a tortured issue, but I believe that A is often given full credit for desert while B is said to be a loser. This is not fair because A and B have been given puzzles at different stages of completion. The work necessary to fulfill the functional requirements for A is markedly less than for B. In this way, "deserts" become skewed.[4]

I suggest a qualitative subtraction of "credit" from A so that we might see his achievement as less than or equal to that of B.

The context of these preferences supposes the following:

1. We are considering only applicants capable of performing the job (i.e., performing work in a profession, doing the academic work at a comparable level, and executing the contract according to the request for proposal.

2. Identically qualified candidates do not exist (so that all such models that refer to them must be fictions). The impact of this requirement is that when we are assessing what it means to fulfill the functional requirements listed in 1, we must have broad enough vision of *how* a candidate might fulfill these requirements. A colleague mentioned to me recently that a position in her department that had been advertised had not been filled because no one had the qualifications of the person who was leaving. This is a common situation. People imagine only one type of person as capable of filling a particular position. What is needed is a broader, more flexible vision.

3. Aptitude tests and other models of prognostication are most effective when applied to individuals from the advantaged rather than the disadvantaged groups (i.e., they may work for those already in the mainstream but are not necessarily good predictors for those out of the mainstream).[5] Thus, to suppose that A (from an advantaged group) is more qualified for some situation because he scored N on some test than B (from a disadvantaged group) because she scored $N-X$ (where $X > 0$) is perhaps to engage in a faulty comparison. The fault occurs because no present testing mechanism exists to measure both A and B on the same methodology.[6]

The Problem

What problem does the policy of affirmative action seek to redress? There are many candidates.[7] The most persuasive of these refers to past discriminatory actions. Under this view of the problem, a group that has been discriminated against in the past is entitled to reparations of some sort. Thus, if a case could be made that African Americans had been discriminated against in the past, then they are entitled to redress.

However, detractors will contend the following:

1. People who were guilty of causing the most viscous discrimination are not in positions of power today. The people most disadvantaged in the past are not those seeking assistance from affirmative action. Under this scenario, affirmative action may have been an effective strategy in the past but is no longer justified because things are now okay.
2. Wrongs committed against a group cannot be rectified by individual solutions. This is so because any sampling of individuals from the underrepresented group includes individuals who are not at a disadvantage from being a member of the affected group. In fact, many individuals from this group may be more advantaged than many individuals from the so-called advantaged group.
3. Affirmative action only prolongs the stereotypes of inferiority that have plagued disadvantaged groups from the beginning. To be a "token" hire, student, or contractor does nothing to address the ultimate problem of racism. Therefore, only when all people can be judged by the content of their character rather than by the color of their skin (or other characteristic) can we assert that we are beyond discrimination.

No matter what position a person takes on this issue, most would agree that certain clearly defined socioeconomic, racial, and gender groups are markedly underrepresented in the most desirable occupational classes, school admissions, and government contracts.

What is one to make of these facts? Three common responses follow.

1. Certain groups are just inferior per se.
2. The underrepresentation is a blip in the present statistical environment and will work out differently in the future by some invisible hand.
3. Sociological dynamics distort reality; in fact, everyone at present competes rather well under fair rules. Those who do not succeed do not succeed. They have no one to blame but themselves.

All of these (and other) responses admit to a problem. Response 1 admits to some purported theme of racial, ethnic, or gender superiority, a very difficult claim to assess. The most obvious version of the argument is patently absurd. It smacks of bad science and eugenics. Some modern versions of this argument exist, but I do not believe that they fare better than their ancestors.

Another position seeks to describe different behavioral traits on the model of evolutionary biology. The strongest version of this argument is suggested by the sociobiologists. According to one version, *behaviors* are subject to the same sort of evolutionary pressures as any ordinary phenotypical (physical) trait. This is to say that there is no such thing as a good or a bad trait but only a trait that is adaptive in some environment.

For example, if one were to summarize Kettlewell's classic experiment with moth wing color, the results would be as follows: subspecies (a) has variegated wing color, and subspecies (b) has black wing color. In Environment-1, the trees that constitute the habitat of the moths are variegated in color. In Environment-2, pollution has made the trees black with soot. Kettlewell noticed that the normally populous subspecies (a) [in Enviroment-1] were giving way to subspecies (b) as a result of industrial pollution [creating Environment-2]. By cleaning the trees, Kettlewell was able to reverse the trend, making subspecies (a) again more populous by re-creating Environment-1.

Does this mean that subspecies (a) is *better* than subspecies (b)? Certainly not, for in Environment-2, subspecies (b) flourished and dominated subspecies (a). All that the experiment shows is that no traits are good or bad per se but are so only within certain environments.

Another example of this can be found in the human realm. Today, young male children are five times more likely than young female children to be diagnosed as being hyperactive, meaning (among other things) that they are easily distracted and will readily move from one task that they are working on to another and another. This often leads to trouble in the first grade (Environment-1). As a result, the teacher may report that these children need to be put on medication right away if they are to be able to make it in the challenging world of the second grade.

However, when a person with this same trait works in a stockbroker's office (Environment-2), things are rather different. The individual who can move on seven planes at once and interrupt himself without a problem to make a trade or to react to fast-breaking market events is a prized commodity. This trait that was deleterious in Environment-1 is highly sought in Environment-2.

In evolutionary biology, phenotypical traits are not good or bad; they simply are. Variation in any species is a dogmatic given. This is what allows the species to survive in changing environments.

If behavioral traits also operate according to the rules of environmental evolutionary biology, then it could be possible that different groups within the human family might be different. To be different does not mean to be *absolutely better* or *absolutely worse*. It refers only to the functional expression of that trait in a given social environment. If Asians outperform Native Americans in competition for the prizes within twenty-first century America, this describes a fact about only certain behavioral traits within this environment but says nothing about how these two groups might fare within a *different* environment.

The crux of this analysis (if correct) is that various groups (as groups, not as individuals) are predisposed (by nature or ethnic nuture) to be more or less successful in different environments. As a result, one must conclude that there may be structural issues of justice and fairness at stake. (These will be addressed in the next section of the essay.)

The second response suggests that the invisible hand of the *market* will solve the problems of job discrimination. I have no doubt that this is true. The question is, however, *how* the problem will be solved. Simply to solve a problem is not enough. Hitler aspired to solve the "problem of the Jews" by killing all of them, which is unacceptable. What is needed is a theory of justice that advocates a solution and a theory (and its application) that are submitted to rational scrutiny.

The third reply is quite common these days. Many claim that problems with discrimination among selected groups in the American experience no facts about reality necessary to make possible a dialogue between individuals of disparate worldviews to forge mutually acceptable principles on which social and/or political institutions might be created. An example of this might be the Constitutional Convention that created the document that governs the United States of America. The members of the Constitutional Convention had various visions of what the newly formed country would be like that often conflicted with each other.

The best way to avoid such deadlocks is to establish a great conversation among the people involved. Sometimes such impasses are "solved" merely by someone gaining a power position over his opposition ("might makes right," a form of *kraterism*).

The best solution for creating a common body of knowledge is to agree to a procedure by which individual issues might be resolved. It is often easier to agree to such a procedure (because it is grounded in an abstract, rational procedure that strips individual interests from its decision-making process) than it is to agree on other points that are more empirical.

However, consensus is not always possible. For example, if Group A had as a part of its worldview that all people of type-x were totally worthless and if Group B had as a part of its worldview that all people of type-x were the most worthy of choice, then, the two could not form a common body of knowledge on that particular issue (unless there were radical compromise or fundamental change by Group A or B or both). The result would probably be that Group A and Group B could not form a shared community worldview. In this case, the only way that social and/or political institutions could be formed would be by the *krateristic* means cited earlier.

The second point is that the institutions and policies that result from those institutions must flourish. This means that impractical proposals are not acceptable. A proposal is impractical if the shared community worldview is so dissonant from the personal worldview of the individual that that individual will not accept ownership of the directives that flow from the shared community worldview. In this case, the individual reacts either in apathy or in defiance (depending on how much force has been used to subvert the oppressed group to the will of those in power).

Thus, to flourish, a significant number of people from all diverse groups within the society must continually strive to renew and to invigorate the great conversation on the fundamental principles that underlie our social and/or political institutions. One way to measure the health of a society is to observe whether the great conversation is ongoing and freely inclusive of all members (the principle of diversity).

The third point to notice about the shared community worldview is that the conversation must take place within the constraints of ethics, aesthetics, and truth (including religion). These are the highest principles by which we live, which are necessary to ensure that the conclusions of the great conversation are good principles. Without this constraint, despotic and repressive regimes could emerge.

Given these principles of personal and shared community worldview, how do they bear on the question of affirmative action? Certainly, one can identify the underlying problem as being one that the great conversation is meant to address (there are clearly identifiable groups based on social, ethnic, racial, and or gender factors that are not participating in the most desirable occupations, educational opportunities, or government contracts).

Diversity and the common body of knowledge are critical here. To engage authentically in the great conversation, we must include all groups. Everyone must be brought into process so that each might make her contribution. This aim at consensus is crucial if all parties are to agree with the result.

Within this context, affirmative action is simply one policy to solve a problem. Other policies may be more or less effective than affirmative action. If people are upset with affirmative action (as presently implemented)—and many are—then they must either revise affirmative action or replace it with something better. Merely to pass a law (such as California's Proposition 209) or take legal action (as in *Hogwood v. Texas*) is not sufficient to solve the problem; it exists and demands a solution.

The worldview perspective offers a foundation to support continued dialogue on problems such as affirmative action within certain constraints that ensure diversity in the process. This dialogue promotes fairness and the practical flourishing called for by shared community worldview.

Perhaps a new policy will emerge from the current debate on affirmative action. If it provides a more effective strategy that is accepted in the fashion described, then so be it. But until a better policy is in effect, I suggest modifying affirmative action at the income extremes as described as the best remedy for this important societal problem.

Since the great conversation is ongoing, we may find ourselves tinkering with this and other public policies in the future. In time, affirmative action may not be needed because the United States will have no severely disadvantaged groups. We are not there yet.

Notes

1   There are certainly many exceptions to this, the most obvious being someone who comes from advantage parents but has various disabilities that render him disadvantaged or a person from a family that is advantaged but who is given insufficient nurturing measured by that person's needs. In the first case, we have a genetic cause, in the second, we have an environmental cause. In both cases, the paradigm I describe is excepted.

2   The point of this example is not that B *could not* have finished the puzzle since the last portion is the easiest and if she had been able to complete earlier portions, then she could have completed later portions as well. But there might have been other factors that stopped B from the completion of the task. Let's assume that these factors are beyond her control. Then if we ask who is the better puzzle maker, the issue becomes more difficult. Do we honor results only or process? The former supports A while the latter supports B. My vote is with B because she has exhibited more effort and thus fulfills my definition of deserts.

3   One of the many difficulties with this type of analysis is that one is never sure whether A *could* have done the same job if he were presented the same puzzle as B. In some ways, this analysis can disadvantage the one who has been given the advantaged position.

4   For a fine discussion of different senses of "desert," see, Louis P. Pojman and Owen McLeod (eds.), *What Do We Deserve? A Reader on Justice and Desert* (New York: Oxford University Press, 1999).

5   The ability of aptitude tests to predict how intelligent people are (i.e., to predict success in school or employment) is a very controversial issue. One fundamental underlying issue is whether intelligence tests measure something that is, in fact, invariant. If it does not, it is not an aptitude test. (Achievement tests are rather different and are not at issue here.) The primary candidate for such an invariant factor is some sort of innate intelligence or heritability. It is here that the discussion usually has been engaged. Traditional advocates of the accuracy of such tests include R. M. Yerkes, "Testing the Human Mind," *The Atlantic Monthly* 131 (1923): 358–370; C.C. Bringham, *A Study of American Intelligence* (Princeton, NJ: Princeton University Press, 1923); and L. M. Terman, *The Measurement of Intelligence* (Boston: Houghton Mifflin, 1916). One of the most prominent detractors of the accuracy of such tests during this time period is Horace Mann Bond. For a discussion of his work, see Micheal Fultz, "A Quintessential American: Horace Mann Bond, 1924–1929," *Harvard Educational Review* 55 (November 1985): 416–442; and Wayne J. Urban, "The Black Scholar and Intelligence Testing: The Case of Horace Mann Bond," *Journal of the History of the Behavioral Sciences* 21 (October 1989): 323–333.

Contemporary opinion leans in the opposite direction. The following writers support the link between heritability and intelligence: C. Burt, "The Inheritance of Mental Ability" in *The Discovery of Talent*, ed. D. Wolfe (Cambridge, MA: Harvard University Press, 1969); A.R. Jensen, "How Much Can We Boost IQ and Scholastic Achievement," *Harvard Educational Review* 39 (1969): 1–123; and Richard J. Hernstein, who most recently with Charles Murray, wrote, *The Bell Curve: Intelligence and Class Structure in American Life* (New York: Free Press, 1994). On the other side are N.J. Block and G. Dworkin, "IQ, Heritability, and Inequality" in Block and Dworkin (eds.), *The IQ Controversy* (New York: Pantheon, 1976); S.J. Gould, *The Mismeasure of Man* (New York: Norton, 1981); M.W. Feldman, James Crouse, et al., *The Case Against the SAT* (Berkeley, CA: University of California Press, 1988); and R.C. Lewontin, "The Heritability Hang-up," *Science* 190 (1975): 1163–68. Various environmental variables that might skew results are documented by T.B. Brazelton et al., "The Behavior of Nutritionally Deprived Guatemalan Infants," *Development Medicine and Child Neurology* 19 (1977):

364–72; and J. Brozek (ed.), *Behavioral Effects of Energy and Protein Deficits*, NIH publication No. 79–1906 (Washington, DC: National Institutes of Health, 1979). For some evidence of the most recent scholarship, see Daniel Seligman, *A Question of Intelligence: The IQ Debate in America* (New York: Carol Publishing Group, 1992), and especially Audrey Shuey, *The Testing of Negro Intelligence*, 2d ed. (New York: Social Science Press, 1996).

6   It is instructive to consider whether this is a practical problem or an "in-principle" problem. I believe that clearly it is, at least, the former (see footnote 5), but it may be the latter as well. This is so because the number of variables that must be considered to generate a definitive response is impossibly high. It is analogous to the "three-ball problem" in Newtonian mechanics being transformed into the "three hundred-ball problem." There is a point where impracticability may become impossibility.

7   For an excellent summary of most of the arguments in favor of affirmative action, see Louis P. Pojman, "The Moral Status of Affirmative Action" *Public Affairs Quarterly* 6.2 (April 1992): 181–206.

C. Gender Issues

In Shouts and Whispers
Paradoxes Facing Women of Colour in Organizations

REKHA KARAMBAYYA

Racial discussions tend to be conducted at one of two levels—either in shouts or in whispers. The shouters are generally so twisted by pain or ignorance that spectators tune them out. The whisperers are so afraid of the sting of truth that they avoid saying much of anything at all.

Ellis Cose (1993, p. 9)

Rekha Karambayya, "In Shouts and Whispers: Paradoxes Facing Women of Colour in Organizations." Reprinted with kind permission of Springer from *Journal of Business Ethics* 16 (1997): 891–897. Copyright © 1997.

While there has been a recent proliferation of research on issues of gender in organizations, there has been relatively little work on issues of race, and even less on the intersections of race and gender (see Bell, Denton and Nkomo, 1993; Bell and Nkomo, 1992; Calas, 1992; for notable exceptions). For the most part, research on women in organizations is based on the implicit assumption that concerns raised are those of all women, and that results generalize to all women. This paper frames the experience of women of colour in organizations as a series of paradoxes, outlining the consequences for individuals and for organizations, and attempts to chart a research agenda for the future.

Bell et al. (1993) point out that research on women in organizations was initiated by the need to correct biases in organizational research. Much of organizational research implicitly excludes or ignores women, yet research on women that was directed at correcting that imbalance is itself guilty of making an "exclusivity error" with respect to women of colour. In framing this paper as dealing with the experience of women of colour I may be accused of making similar oversimplifying assumptions that all women of colour face the same issues and have the same experience. In the interest of simplicity, I refer throughout this paper to women of colour as a group. The issues here are likely to be part of their work lives, to a greater or a lesser degree depending on their unique situations, cultural heritage and identity. However, this discussion of the intersections of race and gender is only the beginning. The concerns raised here may be either magnified or subordinated to others, when factors such as age, class, physical ability and sexual orientation are considered.

For purposes of discussion I have chosen to use the term 'women of colour' rather than 'visible minority'. The latter term has often been perceived as negative (Mukherjee, 1993), at least in part because the term describes how people of colour appear to others, and because it defines them in relation to the majority, thereby reinforcing existing patterns of discrimination and exclusion (Mighty, 1991). The focus of interest here is the organizational experience of women who belong to racial minorities. However, it is important to acknowledge that women of colour are not a homogeneous group, and that this discussion cannot do justice to the diversity of their personal and professional experience. Also important is recognition that for women of colour their gender and racial identity are immediately obvious to those they come in contact with, requiring neither personal disclosure of gender and racial identity, nor significant ethnic influence in their lives. Their interaction with others is inevitably shaped by their gender and race in subtle and pervasive ways.

Bell and Nkomo (1992) point out that much of the research on women in organizations relies on one of two theoretical perspectives. The first of these is the gender-centred perspective in which women are compared to men along various criteria, and usually implicitly or explicitly accorded inferior status. The second is the organization-structure perspective which investigates the ways in which the structural characteristics of organizations restrict and impede women's progress in the workplace. They accuse both perspectives of oversimplifying the issues, the first by creating binary systems of thinking about sex role characteristics, and the second by treating individuals and organizations as separate, rather than interactive, systems.

Bell and Nkomo (1992) suggest using a conceptual framework in which an individual is represented in terms of four core identity elements: gender, race, ethnicity and class.

They propose that research be developed based on identity theory by exploring the unique effects that each of these core elements have had on a woman's life. One way that such an approach could evolve is based on the use of individual biographies. This, in their view, would correct some of the limitations of studying the work life of women as if it were divorced from the rest of their life experience. Biographies would provide a way of capturing the interplay among dimensions of a person's identity by offering a "holistic portrayal" of women's lives.

This paper recognizes the importance of such a holistic portrayal, and the critical need to centre research in the individual, unique experiences of women. First, the experiences of women of colour in organizations are portrayed as a series of paradoxes, based on the work of Smith and Berg (1987) on group processes. The organizational experience of women of colour is framed in terms of paradoxes, some occurring at the intrapersonal level, and others at the interpersonal level. With an emphasis on gender and race, this paper points out that organizations and their members socially construct a work environment that poses several double bind situations for women of colour. These paradoxes of organizational membership are raised with a view to drawing attention to their complex nature and the choices they entail. The use of paradox as a conceptual framework reveals the conflicts among dimensions of a person's core identity, and the implications of those conflicts for organizations and their members. Finally, the paper moves on to speculate on how we may begin to pay more explicit attention to the complexity of race and gender issues in organizational research.

The main purpose of this paper is to focus attention on the subtle and unacknowledged ways in which race and gender are woven into the fabric of organizational life. It is also my contention, in line with those of others such as Bell et al. (1993), that organizational research has, for the most part ignored the importance of race, particularly as it shapes the professional lives of women of colour. This paper is an attempt to begin to correct that deficit, and to offer one approach to conceptualizing race and gender in organizations.

On Paradox

A paradox is one or more statements that are self-referential and contradictory, and that taken together trigger a vicious circle. The typical response to a conflict of this nature is to attempt to resolve it by disentangling the contradictions. Paradoxes, however, are beyond most traditional forms of resolution. Accepting one element of the paradox brings one up against the other which is both contradictory in content, and rooted contextually in the first.

Smith and Berg (1987) used paradox as a conceptual tool to explore the conflicts and tensions inherent in group membership and process. This paper is based on their conceptual framework and its implications for individuals and organizations. Race and gender issues in organizations may be seen as membership in multiple groups whose interests are not entirely compatible. A woman of colour then may belong to groups reflected in her core identity: racial, gender, class, and ethnic. She may concurrently associate herself with professional groups, such as an organizational work unit, a professional association, etc. In that sense, much of what Smith and Berg (1987) describe as tensions between individuals and the groups they belong to may apply to the condition of women of colour in organizations.

In order to set the stage for the discussion that follows, it is necessary to restate some of the underlying assumptions in Smith and Berg's (1987) work on groups. They point out that their use of paradox is not meant to invalidate other concepts and theories of groups. It is instead an attempt to add another perspective for viewing groups and the experience of group life. While paradox may appear to enslave members of groups, and the groups themselves, recognition of their existence may be a necessary step in liberation from vicious circles. Smith and Berg (1987) introduce the possibility that paradox may arise at least partially out of interpretive framing processes, and that the processes of reality creation are central to understanding the behaviour of groups and their members.

This paper makes very similar assumptions about human interaction. First, it assumes that the processes of organizational interaction are influenced by individual and collective psychological processes, some conscious and others unconscious. Second, it acknowledges that this interaction is embedded in a social context that shapes and defines it. Recognition of that social context is critical to any discussion of race and gender in organizations. Finally, the paradoxical perspective applied to the intersections of race and gender is used as a conceptual tool to offer new perspectives on research in this area.

There is no test here of the empirical validity of this framework, and no attempt to develop prescriptions, either for organizations or for individuals. Instead the hope is that we may gain new insight from the use of paradox, and develop alternative research strategies that acknowledge and capture the ways in which race and gender influence organizational experience.

Paradoxes Facing Women of Colour

The nature of the specific paradoxes discussed here do not mirror those of Smith and Berg (1987). While some are similar, others are unique to the ways that issues of race and gender are played out in organizations. No attempt has been made to exhaustively list a series of paradoxes facing women of colour. Instead a few are used for purposes of illustrating how use of paradox may be informative and useful.

Issues of identity

Smith and Berg (1987) begin their discussion of the paradoxes of group life with what they refer to as the paradoxes of belonging. These paradoxes involve trade-offs around membership in a group. One of these paradoxes is about the tension between individuality and group membership. In order to become a member of a group an individual must experience some degree of similarity with other members, and yet remain separate, unique and maintain some individuality.

Women of colour face a number of circumstances in which the core elements that form their identity are in conflict with each other. They are often faced with explicit or implicit choices between expressing their interests in terms of their gender or in terms of their race, knowing that there are conflicts between the two sets of interests. It has been widely recognized that, for the most part, women's issues in organizations are those of white, middle-class women. Women of colour who draw attention to that fact are often accused of "diluting" the issues (Bell et al., 1993).

Women of colour can then either align themselves with women in organizations, knowing that such association is unlikely to fully address their concerns, or risk alienating white women, who are usually the majority, by creating an alternative forum that more accurately reflects their interests at the intersections of race and gender. Yet they may not have either the strength in numbers or the organizational power to address issues unique to women of colour. So they are faced with a double bind in which each of the available options requires a costly compromise.

The conflicts among core dimensions of one's identity present themselves in other ways as well. Women of colour must decide, either consciously or unconsciously, how they will attempt to "fit in". In order to be recognized as legitimate professionals they may adopt some of the norms of the dominant culture. This may sometimes result in what Bell (1990) calls a bicultural lifestyle, in which women of colour experience the stress of living in a professional world in which they adopt the white male cultural patterns in their work and professional lives, while their private lives remain embedded in their racial/ethnic roots. Aside from the very real problems of managing this participation in two very different cultural worlds, this kind of pattern may be dysfunctional for these women because it involves a suppression or denial of a core part of her identity in each sphere of her life. Cox (1994, p. 58) refers to this as "the cost of acting unnaturally." Not only must these women keep their professional and private lives separate, they are often denied opportunities for expressing themselves fully in each.

The paradox of identity is captured in the experience of a professional black woman interviewed by Cose (1993, p. 64):

> ...Eventually she realized that "I was never going to be vice president for public affairs at Dow Chemical." She believed that her colour, her gender and her lack of a technical degree were all working against her. Moreover, "even if they gave it to me, I didn't want it. The price was too high." Part of that price would have been accepting the fact that her race was not seen as an asset but as something she had to overcome.

Cose reports that this woman drew favourable attention from colleagues because she did not fit racial stereotypes, but in her view she did not achieve her potential. She felt that her colleagues were telling her "You're almost like us, but not enough like us to be acceptable" (Cose, 1993, p. 64).

Attributions of success, price of failure

Associated with issues of identity are patterns of attributions used by women of colour and their organizational colleagues to make sense of success or failure. These attributions and the decisions that arise out of them pose another set of paradoxes.

As proposed in the previous section on identity, women of colour often have to overcome negative stereotypes of their race as well as their gender. They are most often fully aware that their race and gender will inevitably influence organizational decisions. Even when they do achieve success against considerable odds, that success is attributed to their having overcome the limitations of their race and gender, rather than credited to it. Worse, their success may be used by the organization as proof that discrimination does not exist, and that organizational processes are gender and race neutral (Caplan, 1993).

Having achieved success, these women are not always credible role models for other women of colour because they have acquired success through assimilation into the dominant, usually white male, culture. In addition, their behaviour may be interpreted as a denial of one's racial or gender identity by other women of colour. One black lawyer interviewed by Cose (1993, p. 61) said of her success, which was often held up as an exception to the norm, "I don't like what it does to my relationships with other blacks."

If and when attributions involve career failures, characteristics associated with race and gender may play a significant role in explanations. Taken together these patterns suggest that individuals and organizations are socialized into seeing race and gender in a negative light; always associated with failures, never with successes. This set of paradoxes is eloquently summed up by Caplan (1993, p. 71) in her work on women in academia:

> Women—especially those who are targets of multiple forms of discrimination—are less likely than others to be hired; but when they **are** hired, they are assumed to be **less** competent than others and pressured to perform in **supercompetent** ways. (emphasis in original)

Some of the characteristics of managerial jobs may compound this set of paradoxes. In most managerial jobs success and failure involve some interpretation of outcomes, and at least a degree of subjectivity. This subjectivity and uncertainty in performance evaluations may mask gender and race bias, and has been referred to as "static" (Ella Bell as quoted in Cose, 1993) or "yes, but" feedback (Jones, 1973). Previous experience with prejudice or discrimination poses what Cox (1994) calls "attribution uncertainty" for members of minority groups. There is always the problem of trying to untangle discrimination from other factors that might influence performance evaluations. While receiving and responding to performance feedback is necessary for organizational success, women of colour may have to work exceptionally hard to separate legitimate performance feedback from bias. Whether or not bias exists, perceptions that it plays a role may have an effect on responses to it. Joe Boyce, who was interviewed by Cose (1993), speaking about the effects of race said:

> Your achievement is defined by your colour and its limitation. And even if in reality you've met your fullest potential, there's an aggravating, lingering doubt ... because you're never sure. (p. 59)

This uncertainty is compounded by issues of gender for women of colour. Recent research on appraisal processes in a Fortune 500 company showed that women rated the process lower on fairness despite that fact that on average women in this firm achieved higher appraisal ratings than men during that performance period (Cox, 1994).

There is also the possibility that a self-fulfilling prophesy may be at play in organizational situations (Merton, 1948). The terms refers to an effect whereby expectations of an outcome actually induce the outcome. For instance, with respect to women of colour it is likely that low expectations of performance are communicated by the climate set in the organization, the work assigned to an individual or the nature of feedback offered. If in fact some forms of racial and gender prejudice exist in organizations, the processes by which women of colour are evaluated and selected may predispose them to failure, and reinforce that prejudice.

Faced with attribution uncertainty and the possibility that discrimination and bias still exist in their organizations women of colour must face the difficult dilemma of setting their own expectations for career success. If they allow themselves to be overwhelmed by anger and bitterness they are likely to fail, whatever the circumstances, because they expect nothing else. Yet if they expect race and gender to be inconsequential, and do all the "right things" they are liable to be disillusioned when they find that success is still beyond reach. For many the middle ground has been to measure success relative to the set of options available to them, rather than by comparing themselves to their colleagues who do not face similar biases (Cose, 1993).

Speaking Out and Being Heard

It has been widely acknowledged that there is a curious reluctance to address issues of race in organizations (Bell et al., 1993; Cose, 1993; Nkomo, 1992), even as issues of gender are being raised. From the perspective of the individual woman of colour this may arise out of a hope that despite inequities in the outside world, they will receive fair treatment in the workplace. This need for fairness may be particularly enduring because of the importance of work, and its central role in their personal identity. Eventually, many are forced to realize that "the racial demons that have plagued them all their lives do not recognize business hours" (Cose, 1993, p. 55). Even so there is a pervasive silence about discrimination based on race and gender. Perhaps this reluctance to speak above a whisper stems from a fear that to give expression to the dissatisfaction arising out of unfair treatment would alienate and anger those members of majority groups in whose hands the power lies (Cose, 1993). Women of colour who speak of gender and racial bias would likely face the additional jeopardy of being labelled "shouters" (Cose, 1993) and seen as "troublemakers" (Caplan, 1993).

From the perspective of the organization, it is possible that inequities exist in part because organizations are unaware of them and members of majority groups are blind to their own privilege. These conditions create a paradox in which the organization cannot address issues of race and gender unless they are voiced as concerns by some of their members. Unfortunately, those organizations that are most discriminatory are also those in which such concerns are least likely to be expressed for fear of reprisal (Kabanoff, 1991; Smith and Berg, 1987).

These examples of the paradoxes involved in any consideration of race and gender issues, and their intersections, are merely illustrations of the pervasive and subtle ways in which these factors influence the organizational experience of women of colour. They demonstrate that although race and gender are embedded in organizational life, they are for the most part ignored by those who benefit from their gender and racial identity, and avoided by others who pay a price for theirs. Conceptualizing organizational experience in terms of paradox offers new perspectives on how research may approach race and gender in organizations.

Using Paradox

The use of paradox as a conceptual framework makes several contributions to research on gender and race in organizations. First, articulating the forms that these paradoxes may take draws attention to the multi-level nature of the phenomena at work. Race and gender issues manifest themselves at the intrapersonal level, at the interpersonal level and at the organization-person interface. At the intra-personal level they may take the form of conflicting dimensions of an individual's identity, and incompatible demands made by various identity groups. At the interpersonal level they may be reflected in ambiguous or different attributions of success and failure, and in racial and gender stereotypes. Other issues may create paradoxes at the organization-individual interface as in the case of the relationship between speaking out and the organizational distribution of power. These paradoxes may arise either concurrently or sequentially depending on the organization, its membership and context. Any attempt to create egalitarian workplaces will have to recognize the relationships and tensions among these levels of analysis.

Secondly, the use of paradox suggests how and why individuals and organizations may find themselves caught in vicious circles, making compromises that alternatively paralyse them and avoid the real concerns. Any attempts to deal with each horn of a dilemma without awareness of the other is likely to lead to "stuckness" (Smith and Berg, 1987), a phenomenon in which one is endlessly circling the issue without really addressing it.

Smith and Berg (1987) suggest that in order to break out of such a vicious circle, one has to confront the paradox. This response to dealing with contradictions is itself paradoxical. It proposes that the first step in dealing with a significant conflict, usually one that elicits negative emotions, is to move toward rather away from it.

In order to fully engage the paradox, each level at which the paradox exists must explore its own role in it. Individual and groups must attempt to acknowledge their own ambivalence and contribution to the paradox. In the context of this paper that may imply that women of colour, and the organizations that they participate in, must engage in self-reflection and examine how they define themselves and others around them. This approach requires all parties to the paradox to undertake some responsibility for its existence and resolution. The resolution may take on a cyclical nature, moving from one horn of the dilemma to the other. This conceptualization leads us to thinking about race and gender in dynamic, non-linear ways. It also suggests that the issues may be evolving and interactive, never quite reaching a resolution, but moving progressively closer to it.

Viewing the social construction of race and gender in the workplace in terms of paradox also forces us to contend with the processes by which these factors influence organizational life. Research on women of colour has been accused of being concerned with outcomes rather than process (Bell et al., 1993). Using the paradoxical framework highlights the importance of the processes by which these outcomes emerge, and suggests that each woman may have a unique experience of the workplace based on her personal identity and the characteristics of her workplace. It also recognizes how her experience is shaped by the interactive perceptual and interpretive processes that link her to her environment.

It is important to recognize here that at least part of our inability to adequately address race and gender issues, and particularly their intersection, stems from our flaming of organizations and organizational life. We frame organizations as stable, and unchanging, and assume that individuals that participate in them must be willing and able to assimilate into the organizational culture. While the value placed on assimilation suggests that diversity may be dysfunctional for the organization, it also implicitly assumes that organizations are gender and race neutral. Both of those assumptions are highly debatable (Cox, 1994; Nkomo, 1992). At the level of the individual organizational member, such an approach presupposes that gender and race identity may be (or even should be) suppressed, or at least contained, in the interests of organizational success.

One way to address these paradoxes is to reframe them so that the nature of the relationship between women of colour and their employers is reconceptualized as dynamic and interactive (Smith and Berg, 1987). This view recognizes that organizations are both the product of and a significant influence on their members. It also acknowledges the uniqueness of each woman's experience, given her unique situation and identity. At the very least this would suggest that the race and gender issues exist at both the organizational and the individual level, and that each partner in that relationship needs to assume some responsibility for recognizing and responding to them.

References

Bell, E.L.: 1990, 'The Bicultural Life Experience of Career-oriented Black Women', *Journal of Organizational Behavior* 11: 459–477.

Bell, E.L. and S.M. Nkomo: 1992, 'Re-visioning Women Manager's Lives', in A.J. Mills and P. Tancred (eds.), *Gendering Organizational Analysis* (Sage Publications, Newbury Park, CA); pp. 235–247.

Bell, E.L., T.C. Denton and S. Nkomo: 1993, 'Women of Colour in Management: Toward an Inclusive Analysis', in E. Fagenson (ed.), *Women in Management: Trends, Issues, and Challenges* in *Managerial Diversity*, Vol. 4: 105–130. Women and Work: A Research and Policy Series. Series Editors: L. Larwood, B.A. Gutek and A. Stromberg (Sage Publications, Newbury Park, CA).

Calas, M.B.: 1992, 'An/Other Silent Voice? Representing "Hispanic Woman" in Organizational Texts', in A.J. Mills and P. Tancred (eds.), *Gendering Organizational Analysis* (Sage Publications, Newbury Park, CA); pp. 201–221.

Caplan, P.J.: 1993, *Lifting a Ton of Feathers: A Woman's Guide to Surviving in the Academic World* (University of Toronto Press, Toronto).

Cose, E.: 1993, *The Rage of a Privileged Class* (HarperCollins, New York).

Cox, T.: 1994, *Cultural Diversity in Organizations: Theory, Research and Practice* (Berrett-Kohler, San Francisco).

Jones, E.W.: 1973, 'What It's Like To Be a Black Manager', *Harvard Business Review*. July–August 1973.

Kabanoff, B.: 1991, 'Equity, Equality, Power, and Conflict', *Academy of Management Review* 16(2): 416–441.

Merton, R.K.: 1948, 'The Self-fulfilling Prophesy', *The Antioch Review* 8, 193–210.

Mighty, J.: 1991, 'Triple Jeopardy: Employment Equity and Immigrant, Visible Minority Women', *Proceedings of the Administrative Sciences Association of Canada* (Niagara Falls, Ontario).

Mukherjee, A.: 1993, *Sharing our Experience* (Canadian Advisory Council on the Status of Women, Ottawa, Ontario).

Nkomo, S.M.: 1992, 'The Emperor Has No Clothes: Rewriting "Race in Organizations"', *Academy of Management Review* 17(3): 487–513.

Smith, K.K. and D.N. Berg: 1987, *Paradoxes of Group Life* (Jossey-Bass, San Francisco).

Compensation Inequality

Jane Uebelhoer

Bread and Roses

By James Oppenheim, Dec. 1911
On the occasion of the historic strike of textile workers in Lawrence, Massachusetts

As we go marching, marching, in the beauty of the day,
A million darkened kitchens, a thousand mill lofts gray,
Are touched with all the radiance that a sudden sun discloses,
For the people hear us singing: Bread and Roses! Bread and Roses!

As we go marching, marching, we battle too for men,
For they are women's children, and we mother them again.
Our lives shall not be sweated from birth until life closes;
Hearts starve as well as bodies; give us bread, but give us roses.

As we go marching, marching, unnumbered women dead
Go crying through our singing their ancient call for bread.
Small art and love and beauty their drudging spirits knew.
Yes, it is bread we fight for, but we fight for roses too.

As we go marching, marching, we bring the greater days,
The rising of the women means the rising of the race.
No more the drudge and idler, ten that toil where one reposes,
But a sharing of life's glories: Bread and roses, bread and roses.

Our lives shall not be sweated from birth until life closes;
Hearts starve as well as bodies; bread and roses, bread and roses.

First the bad news: job discrimination against women in the USA remains extremely common. Now the worse news: almost nobody believes this. How is the community going to fight discrimination if people don't believe it exists? What gives?

In what follows we will define job discrimination, describe its most common types, and cite evidence of the extent of job discrimination against women. We will then summarize the arguments that such discrimination is morally wrong, and attempt to explain the puzzling reluctance of Americans to believe that women are still victims of widespread discrimination. Finally, we will look to some social, economic, and legal factors related to reducing the incidence of job discrimination against women.

Job Discrimination Defined

Job discrimination is a decision against an employee which is not based on merit, is rooted in stereotypes about a group or groups to which the person belongs, and which harms the person (Velasquez, 2010, p. 351). To refuse to hire a person to drive a truck because that person does not have a current driver's license is *not* discrimination, but to refuse to hire a person to drive a truck because she was born in South Dakota *is* job discrimination. The first decision is not immoral or illegal; it is based on merit—it is the right thing to do. The second decision, while not illegal (more on this later), is immoral because it is grounded in a negative stereotype about people from South Dakota and so has nothing to do with merit. If I hire a person solely because he attended Duke University, my decision is not job discrimination with regard to the Duke graduate, because the decision does not harm that person. If I refuse to consider anyone but a Duke grad for a job at my large trucking company, it may constitute job discrimination—immoral but not illegal—against other applicants.

Hiring is not the only point at which discrimination can take place. Discrimination is common in decisions about who to promote, and about who to dismiss. Discrimination can also take place with regard to conditions of employment, such as whether to hire someone as a contractor—a temporary employee who receives no job benefits—or as a regular, permanent employee. An employer can discriminate with regard to wages, work assignments, or training. An employer can discriminate by requiring some people to travel, or to move cross country. Discrimination, as defined above, can take place in assigning work hours or shifts, in allocating office space, support staff, vacation time, or equipment. Any decision that is not based on merit, that is based on a stereotype, and that harms a person can be discrimination.

Some types of discrimination injure only or predominantly women. Discrimination against a woman because she is pregnant, or might become pregnant, is the major example. Job discrimination against women because they were married, especially in two careers most open to women—nursing and teaching—was near universal until the USA entered World War II, and in some places well beyond. As we will see below, employers discriminate against pregnant women due to the false assumption that pregnant women are incapable of working.

Now, especially as women have begun to move into formerly all-male occupations, employers often discriminate by failing to make accommodation for the physical changes women undergo during pregnancy (Grossman 2010). Examples of such failures include requirements for running, climbing, lifting—whether cases of canned goods or patients in a nursing home—standing or sitting for long periods, stretching, reaching, and balancing. Pregnant women must urinate frequently, ought to visit medical professionals for frequent prenatal exams, and are heat intolerant.

While pregnant women find some activities more difficult, in other ways the pregnant body performs too well.

> Many maternal physiologic functions operate at peak efficiency during pregnancy. It is a time of maximal production, storage and turnover of maternal body constituents. It is a time when the woman's body insures that it gets full access to oxygen and nutrients. Ironically, in an environment full of toxins, this physiologic efficiency probably magnifies a woman's exposure . . . (Chavkin 1984)

The right to be accommodated at work during pregnancy creates not only a duty of employers to pregnant women, but also an obligation to promote the health of developing children (Calloway 1995).

Employers also sometimes discriminate against women who are breastfeeding, and who must pump and then freeze their breast milk during break times. Parents of young children are sometimes unavoidably absent from work—when all child care resources fall through, when school is closed due to a weather emergency, or when a child is ill and cannot be taken to a sitter who also cares for other children. The same problems face people who must care for elderly or disabled relatives. Although these burdens might be split between two working spouses or partners, traditionally women do this work. In fact, employers help keep the tradition of "women's work" alive when they penalize fathers who cannot work nights and weekends because they must care for their children. This injustice is so common that it has its own widely used acronym, FRD—family responsibility discrimination (Williams & Tait 2011).

Evidence of Job Discrimination against Women

Several branches of the US government, as well as every state government, collect statistics which show ongoing discrimination. The 2010 census is continuing to do comparative analyses, but most are broken out by state. The Department of Labor's Bureau of Labor Statistics is a rich and useful source. The most often quoted statistic regards the ratio of women's and men's median annual earnings for full-time year-round workers. This ratio was 77.0 in 2009; in other words, women earned $0.77 for each dollar men made—that's $11,027 less a year.

Other statistics regard the wages earned in occupations almost exclusive to men—termed the most desirable occupations, as compared to the least desirable occupations, those occupied by very high concentrations of women. Women comprise 95% of child care workers whereas 95% of airplane pilots are men. Controlling for education, men far out-earn women. Men with PhDs earn $44,500 more than women with PhDs. Men with professional degrees earn $64,200 more than women with professional degrees. Men who graduate from high school earn $7,500 more than female high school graduates.

How do these statistics prove discrimination? The answer to this question is fairly simple, although the explanation is a bit involved. The inside of an organization should look like the outside of the organization. Corporate boundaries should be permeable, with employees moving in and out and up with no stickiness caused by membership in one or more protected groups. Consider any employer looking for an employee to hire. Some jobs are very desirable, for example, jobs with high salaries and attractive working conditions, or both, like executive at a large corporation, orthodontist, or petroleum engineer. People are willing to relocate their families across the country or around the globe to get such jobs. Jobs at the other extreme, like entry level employees at fast food restaurants or aides in nursing homes, will normally not prompt people to relocate—although undocumented workers are an exception.

There are many sources of information about how many people are qualified for a given job, or who could be easily trained to do a job, and where those people live. The Census Bureau and the Department of Labor are major sources. In addition, taking one of the examples of very desirable jobs used above, to work as a petroleum engineer a person is generally required to have a degree in petroleum engineering. Universities know the race, gender, ethnicity, veteran status, etc. of their graduates. Most of those graduates will become members of one or more professional organization—another source of data.

Low desirability jobs often require little education and training. McDonalds, for example, requires no more than proof of legal residency in the USA, has no educational requirement for entry level jobs, and conforms to child labor laws as to minimum age—these differ by state. So, to find out how many members of protected classes are qualified for a given low-desirability job, one doesn't need to know much more than the number of members of protected groups, between certain ages, who live within commuting distance. That employee will be recruited from a specific geographic distance if the job is not attractive enough to prompt people to move to relocate (e.g., McDonald's *n.d.*).

These inequities would concern us, but not *too* much, if everyone earned heaps of money. The 2010–11 gender gap in Hollywood is illustrated by the fact that top male earners Leonardo DiCaprio ($77 million) and Johnny Depp ($50 million), trounced top female earners Angelina Jolie and Sarah Jessica Parker, tied at $30 million (Derschowitz 2011). If you prefer musicians: U2 earned $311 million in gross box office receipts, AC/DC grossed $226 million on a worldwide tour, whereas #3 earner Beyonce grossed *only* $86 million from her tour.

But multimillion-dollar jobs are thin on the ground. Job discrimination is a leading cause of poverty among women, and among female-headed households. Poverty among women climbed to 13.9%, or 16.4 million women, in 2009, the highest rate in 15 years and the largest single-year increase since 1980. More than 40% of poor women lived in extreme poverty, with incomes *less than half* of the federal poverty level. The federal poverty level in 2011 is $10,890 for a family of one (Sebelius 2011). The poverty rate for single mothers rose to 38.5% and the child poverty rate jumped to 20.7%. This means more than one in five US children live in poverty. More than half of poor children lived in female-headed families in 2009 (Vogtman 2010).

> [O]nce women become mothers, many encounter workplace penalties no matter how they behave. This point was proved when a leading 2007 study gave subjects resumes that were identical except in one respect--one resume, but not the other, mentioned member-ship in the PTA. The mothers were seventy-nine percent less likely to be hired, one hundred 5percent less likely to be promoted, offered $11,000 less in salary, and held to higher performance and punctuality standards. (Correll, Benard, & Paik, 2007)

And no one is "just" a woman. Every person has a race, economic class, age, marital status, caregiver status, level of educational attainment, and more.

It is important to note that many men suffer from job discrimination too—because they are members of racial, ethnic, or religious minorities, or are relatively old, or have a disability, or because they have been out of the workforce serving in the military—or because they have been convicted of a crime. One in four African American men are pulled into the criminal justice system as teens and many of those never get completely free. The per capita incarceration rate among blacks is seven times that among whites. African Americans make up about 12% of the general population, but more than half of the prison population. They serve longer sentences, have higher arrest and conviction rates, face higher bail amounts, and are more often the victims of police use of deadly force than white citizens. The problem has its own acronym—DMC, disproportionate minority contact (Cole 1999). Some scholars are calling attention to the fact that a group of men are the objects of job discrimination *because they are men*. (This is not "reverse discrimination," a term used to criticize a poorly designed affirmative action program.) Consider maquiladora in Mexico and Central America. These are factories which import materials for assembly and export the finished goods, mostly to the USA. Their numbers have multiplied since the North American Fair Trade Agreement (NAFTA) went into effect in 1994 (Kamel & Hoffman 1999). Women are generally more tractable, more easily controlled, than men. Teenaged women are more nimble than any other group, and tend to be healthier, and have more patience and stamina than most other groups. This accounts for the strong preference for young women in garment factories, many of which are sweatshops. But the situation is not simple.

When men are employed in the maquiladoras, and they increasingly are, they are often involved in more active, thoughtful jobs and earn higher salaries, consistent with the norms of a patriarchal order. However, the preferred laborers in many of the industries are women; thus, men often are unemployed, marginalized, and left with the options of returning to their villages or crossing an increasingly militarized border. (Mutua 2001, p. 1197; cf. Arriola 2000)

Job Discrimination Is Morally Wrong

Is employment discrimination immoral? Generally, yes. Why this weak response? The moral life is seldom tidy. People are sometimes ignorant about the nature of their actions, and are always ignorant of at least some of the consequences of their actions. People often encounter situations in which they are unable to fulfill all of their moral obligations, when to fulfill one obligation is to violate another. To cut our way through this tangle, it is useful to distinguish intentional from unintentional discrimination (Velasquez 2010, p. 2).

Philosophical ethics points out that "ought implies can." To say that I ought to do something, that I have a moral obligation to act in a certain way, entails that I have a choice in the matter. It makes no sense to say that a person has a moral duty to breathe because people cannot prevent themselves from breathing. Further, a person must know what he or she is doing in order to morally responsible for the act. A favorite device in both comedy and tragedy is to set the protagonist up—a character innocently starts her car not knowing that turning the key triggers a bomb. Or a student pushes opens the door to his dorm room and a bucket of soapy water dumps on his head. Moral responsibility requires both that we know what we are doing and that we are free to do otherwise.

The first type of discrimination—intentional discrimination—meets these requirements. Intentional institutional job discrimination is committed when an individual within an organization knowing and freely performs a discriminatory act in line with the organization's policies. A clear example of intentional institutional discrimination against relatively short people occurred in December 2001 when Jiang Tao, a 5ft 5in law student at Sichuan University was refused a job at the Chengdu Branch of People's Bank of China (PBOC). The bank enforced a minimum height rule: male candidates were required to be at least 168cm (5ft 6in) tall and females 155cm (5ft 3in) (Zeng 2007).

Other instances of job discrimination can be classified as unintentional. Consider a certain manager of a retail store who did not know, and could not have been expected to know, that observant Jews are restricted by religious law from working on Shabbat, the weekly day of rest lasting from shortly before sundown on Friday to nightfall Saturday. When this manager makes and enforces a rule that all employees must work on Saturday, the rule and hence her rule making, discriminates against observant Jews, but, in the situation as described, the manager did not knowingly bring about this harm, and so is not morally responsible for it. As in other cases in which we unintentionally injure people because of ignorance, we have an obligation to work toward ever-increasing awareness of the consequences of our actions. The more resources we have, the greater this obligation.

At times our duties not to discriminate are in direct conflict with other obligations. In the case of the Chinese bank, many (or perhaps all) people at the bank share responsibility for the bank's discriminatory practices, but not everyone at PBOC is equally responsible. The most junior members of the firm's human resources department will have little opportunity to influence policy, and, if they press their case for change too forcefully, they risk being dismissed. Jobs at banks in China are desirable and relatively well paying. Assume that a junior PBOC employee is supporting a spouse, children, aged parents, and perhaps sending money to relatives in the country. The obligation not to risk the livelihood of all of these people is at odds with the obligation to refuse to participate in discrimination.

But step back and assume that every employer in Sichuan province enforces a policy not to hire men under 5ft 6in and women under 5ft 3in, resulting in a situation not unlike that suffered by African Americans in the southern USA for many generations. This universal discrimination would represent such a massive injury, such an injustice, that the obligation to act to change the policy would be strong and broadly shared.

How can we justify the claim that intentional job discrimination is immoral? We can do so by appealing to general ethical standards. First, job discrimination is immoral because it violates fundamental moral rights. It is wrong to treat others in ways we would not be willing to be treated, and—everything else being equal—no one would be willing to be live in a world in which, due to discrimination, they could not get and keep a decent job (Boylan 2004, p. 53).[1]

Why? Without access to a decent job a person, generally, cannot have a good life. Without a decent job a person cannot comfortably support himself and his family. A person cannot enjoy a range of choice and life opportunities, cannot save for retirement or own a home. Without a decent job it is very difficult to maintain self-respect, to stand with pride before one's family, or to command the esteem of the broader community. No rational person would be willingly subjected to widespread job discrimination. Job discrimination violates moral rights.

A business which is known to discriminate risks moral censure and legal sanctions (more later!). Such a business will lose potential clients and customers, and not just those from the groups against which the firm is discriminating. People in general will view the firm as morally suspect and out of step with social trends. The most talented and productive people will choose not to work for businesses known to discriminate. (The strength of this effect is what keeps the system of academic tenure in place at colleges and universities.) If large groups of people are not represented among a business's employees, that business is unlikely to reach the best decisions—the absence of women, or young people, or people with disabilities, etc., at the conference table is a hole in the firm's understanding which will manifest in business failures. So, businesses which discriminate are unlikely to flourish. Hence, since managers have a moral obligation to do their jobs well, it is in this way also that it is immoral to discriminate.

Groups against which businesses discriminate in employment are unable to build economic and political power, and move into the social mainstream. Such groups are less able to provide models to shape their young people's aspirations. These groups remain "foreign" to others in society and so continue to be easily stereotyped and excluded.

Societies which condone discrimination harbor a lie at their hearts—the lie that some people are fundamentally less worthy of respect and dignity than others, that some people are less morally entitled to job opportunity than others. Societies which condone intolerance and promote intergroup conflict are unstable, and diminish the wellbeing of all of their members.

Why Do People Underestimate the Extent of Job Discrimination against Women?

People believe that they are not biased. To what extent is this true by definition? Bias is the tendency to systematically make errors in some circumstances, but does it make sense to say that I am erring intentionally? If I knowingly write "6" when I am aware that the answer to an arithmetic problem is "4," am I erring? Am I biased in favor of "6"? I may say, "I have a bias in favor of my own children." If this is true, and I know it to be true, am I in error when I choose my children over your children? Does saying that people believe they are not biased mean nothing more than saying that people believe that they are not in error?

The history of modern psychology is heavy with theories holding that people always, sometimes, or never know their own minds. Sigmund Freud famously held that dark, libidinous urges resulted in neuroses. Little boys want to kill their fathers and gain sexual control over their mothers. Little girls despise their own genitalia and envy those with penises, believing that the penis is the source of power.

Much from the Victorian age has been swept away, but psychologists still posit an unconscious mind with influence that runs the gamut from slightly affecting our conscious lives to completely ruining them. Anthony Greenwald began in the 1990s to talk about "implicit cognition," using implicit/explicit as roughly synonymous with the older conscious/unconscious. "The signature of implicit cognition is that traces of past experience affect some performance even though the influential earlier experience is not remembered in the usual sense—that is, it is unavailable to self-report or introspection" (Greenwald & Banaji 1995).

In 1995 Greenwald invented the Implicit Association Test (IAT; Greenwald, McGhee, & Schwartz 1998), which was launched on a "demo" website at Yale and University of Washington in 1998. An Oracle database was added to collect trial-by-trial data, along with a study design framework, before the server was relocated to Harvard in 2002 (Project Implicit *n.d.*). The 11 millionth study session was completed in 2011, at which time the "demo" site was available in 22 languages, and hundreds of publications have been based on IAT data.

The IAT reveals that most people harbor unconscious stereotypes that support the status quo. Participants are often surprised by their IAT scores (Lane, Banaji, Nosek, & Greenwald 2007). Is this just another way of saying that people do not make mistakes on purpose? Not exactly. Before taking an IAT, the subject answers a few questions about their beliefs. The test itself measures the time it takes a subject to associate terms with groups of people. Eleven million iterations later, the keepers of the IAT can report with confidence that what we think we believe differs dramatically from what we actually believe. People overwhelmingly are much quicker to associate positive terms with young people than with old people. People self-report as either overweight or normal weight; both groups are much quicker to associate positive terms with people of normal weight. Both Blacks and Whites are quicker to associate positive terms with Whites than with Blacks. Both males and females are much faster to sort males with science and females with liberal arts.

Might our unconscious attitudes be more defensible than those we openly avow? Do people get what they deserve? White males *are* better than other people and so their privilege is earned? All is right with the world. People are loathe to say "I am a racist," or "I am a sexist." But people are inclined to believe others get what they deserve and deserve what they get. To believe that the world is fundamentally just in this way apparently reduces our anxiety, even though it leads us to blame many victims for misfortunes not within their control. The world favors youngish white men of normal weight—just as it should.

Discussion of cognitive bias brings up the term 'heuristics'—a term loosely synony- mous with rule of thumb, or educated guess. Before we pick up a screwdriver or wrench, we do well to remind ourselves "righty-tighty/lefty-loosey." If in an emergency we must ask a stranger for a ride, we will probably be safer selecting an old woman in a well-maintained car, than seeking a ride from several young men riding in a "beater." Many cognitive shortcuts have proven reliable and hence have come to be used habit- ually. Some of these are thought to be hardwired by evolution, and others have been arrived at by the individual's trial-and-error efforts to solve complex problems. These rules of thumb are derived from inductive inferences, rather than deduction; hence heuristics can lead us astray. Cognitive bias can lead to discrimination.

How does this relate to the problem of job discrimination against women? After a subject takes an IAT she or he is immediately informed about the correlation between her conscious/explicit and unconscious/implicit attitudes, and then about the statistical performance of all test takers. Typically we are told that we, like almost everyone else, are not who we think we are.

Writing about a US Supreme Court case, *St. Mary's Honor Center v. Hicks*, Deborah Calloway states that the

> Court joined academics, judges, and a growing segment of the American population that has come to believe that discrimination no longer exists. Under this view, the failure of African Americans, women, and other groups protected by Title VII to achieve equal employment opportunities results not from discrimination, but rather from inadequate motivation or deficient personal and work skills. (Calloway 1994)

Charles Sullivan expands this point while discussing *Desert Palace, Inc. v. Costa*:

> the core problem . . . which is the rejection by both the public and the courts of the prop-
> osition that employers frequently discriminate against blacks (or other minorities) and
> women . . . a plaintiff will rarely prevail because judges and juries believe discrimination
> is a thing of the past. They believe, for example, that decisions disadvantaging a minority
> result from a differing but legitimate judgments about merit. They believe, for example,
> that decisions are a result of . . . "cronyism." They believe, for example, that decisions are
> the result of personal animosity. They think it's the fickle finger of fate, random unfair-
> ness. But what they don't think is that the decision is a result of racism or the other kinds
> of isms our society has tried to address with the antidiscrimination laws. (Slater, Zimmer,
> Sullivan, & Blumrosen 2005)

Is there any way out of a tangle of unsupportable generalizations? Stepping
cautiously we can find at least some firm ground. There *is* much less job discrimination
against women in the USA than there used to be. Indisputably, the participation of
women in the labor force has grown steadily. In 1999 77% of women between the ages
of 25 and 54 were labor force participants. From 1940 to 1999 women workers
increased from 25 to 47% of the labor force (Blau, Ferber, & Winkler 2002, p.84). This
does not mean that women get the jobs they want, or jobs for which they are qualified, or jobs for which they could easily become qualified. But progress has been made
in the last 70 years. There are fewer cases in which women are paid less than men for
performing the same job. And there is less job segregation. Some women do jobs that
were formerly performed exclusively by men, such as driving trucks, and serving
as soldiers in combat zones, and holding senior executive positions in corporations.
Job discrimination against women in the USA has decreased to the point, as noted
above, that many or perhaps most people now deny that it exists or that it is a serious
problem!

An "all or nothing" approach ignores both the massive improvement in opportunity
and the current dismal condition of many minorities and women. Neither vision is
valid. We are less racist and sexist, and therefore the assumption of discrimination
whenever any harm befalls a minority or women is not valid. Statistics of improved
employment opportunities conceal continued subordination, and the overall condition
of minorities in relation to whites has not improved. Improvement in proportions of
jobs held by women is almost entirely in the higher level jobs of officials and managers, professional, technical, and sales workers. But the difficulties of minorities and
women are not as attributable to employment discrimination as was the case in the
1960s (Blumrosen 1990; cf. Blumrosen & Blumrosen 2003).

Robert M. Jackson argues that these improvements were caused by two forces. First,
individual women, and groups of women, challenged and rebelled against their
inferior status.

> [A]t the very least a feminist is someone who holds that women suffer discrimination
> because of their sex, that they have specific needs which remain negated and unsatisfied,
> and that the satisfaction of these needs would require a radical change . . . in the social,
> economic, and political order. (Jackson 1998, p. 190)

Feminism is therefore a tool that can be used to fight against sex-based discrimination and ultimately remedy the inequality between men and women in all areas of law and society (Jackson 1998, p. 191; cf. Blackman 2011, p. 104).

Second, the transition to modern institutions began to pull the props out from under of gender inequality: "as organizations accumulated ever more social power, their interests and actions became increasingly indifferent to people's gender" (Jackson 1998, p. 249). As production moved out of households, social power moved from families to firms. Male economic advantages could not be permanently reconciled with the economic interests of firms. Jackson compares and contrasts inequality of status with inequality of position. A high or low status is produced by a person's position. Women were of low status because they were in a subordinate position in the family. As firms took over, men initially gained control over all the new economic and political positions, but this monopoly couldn't last.

> *To be effective, all systems of status inequality, including gender inequality, must be embedded in positional inequality.* For one status group such as men to retain superior social standing over another status group such as women the higher status group must sustain preferential access to high-ranking economic and political positions. (Jackson 1998, pp. 246–251)

A similar point is made by neoclassical economists who hold that markets are hard on discrimination. An employer who refuses to hire qualified blacks and women will lose out to those who are willing to draw from a broader labor pool. Employer discrimination amounts to a self-destructive "taste"—self-destructive because it adds to the costs of doing business. Added costs can only hurt. To put it simply, bigots are weak competitors. The market will drive them out (Sunstein 1991).

It is now a fringe position that unregulated markets can solve social problems on their own. Instead, large-scale shifts are both facilitated by changes in law and likewise produce changes in law. In 1963, President Kennedy signed The Equal Pay Act as an amendment to the Fair Labor Standards Act, to prohibit discrimination on account of sex in the payment of wages by employers. The Equal Pay Act protects both men and women, and includes coverage for administrative, executive, and professional employees who were excluded from protection under the original Fair Labor Standards Act. After Kennedy was assassinated in November 1963, President Johnson called for passage of Kennedy's civil rights legislation. After a jaw-dropping 534 hours of debate in the Senate, Congress passed and Johnson signed the Civil Rights Act of 1964.

> SEC. 2000e-2. *[Section 703] of Title VII of the Civil Rights Act of 1964*
> (a) Employer practices
> It shall be an unlawful employment practice for an employer—
>> (1) to fail or refuse to hire or to discharge any individual, or otherwise to discriminate against any individual with respect to his compensation, terms, conditions, or privileges of employment, because of such individual's race, color, religion, sex, or national origin; or
>> (2) to limit, segregate, or classify his employees or applicants for employment in any way which would deprive or tend to deprive any individual of employment opportunities or otherwise adversely affect his status as an employee, because of such individual's race, color, religion, sex, or national origin. (US Equal Employment Opportunity Commission *n.d.*)

This passage, known in short as Title VII, remains central to civil rights and fair employment law. In 1978 Title VII was amended to make it illegal to discriminate on the basis of pregnancy. In 1967, a separate law, the Age Discrimination in Employment Act, made it illegal to discriminate against people over 40.

Less Disparate Treatment but Disparate Impact Still Runs Riot

A key distinction with regard to Title VII is that between "disparate treatment" and "disparate impact." Disparate treatment takes place when an employer treats one employee less favorably than another employee, based on a direct comparison of at least two identified employees (Maikovich & Brown 1989, p. 33). For an action or policy to be judged disparate treatment, the employer must intend to discriminate—have a discriminatory motive. In contrast, "Disparate impact cases involve employment practices that appear neutral on their face, but result in different employment outcomes for different groups. Proof of discriminatory intent is not required" (Nelson & Bridges 1999, p. 30).

Intentional job discrimination is not nearly as common as it was in the 1960s, but it remains a serious problem. A press release issued by the US Equal Employment Opportunity Commission (EEOC) in June 2011, titled "Employers Still Barring Large Groups of People from Jobs Based on Race, Sex, Age, Other Prohibited Bases," opened with "Deliberate discrimination against job seekers based on their race, sex, age, national origin or other prohibited basis remains a major national problem, a battery of experts told the U.S. Equal Employment Opportunity Commission (EEOC) . . .".

Title VII forbids discrimination not just against women because they are women, but also against men because they are men, and against Caucasians because they are Caucasians. In a highly publicized recent case *Ricci v. Steffano*, which dominated the confirmation hearings of Sonia Sotomayor to the Supreme Court, disparate treatment squared off against disparate impact. In 2003 the fire department of New Haven, Connecticut administered exams for promotion to lieutenant and captain. Of the 118 firefighters who took the exams, no Blacks and at most two Hispanics became eligible for promotion to captain, and no Blacks or Hispanics became eligible for promotion to lieutenant.

> Confronted with arguments both for and against certifying the test results—and threats of a lawsuit either way—the City threw out the results based on the statistical racial disparity. Petitioners, white and Hispanic firefighters who passed the exams but were denied a chance at promotions by the City's refusal to certify the test results, sued the City and respondent officials, alleging that discarding the test results discriminated against them based on their race in violation of, *inter alia*, Title VII of the Civil Rights Act of 1964.

The Supreme Court issued its decision on June 29, 2009, holding 5–4 that New Haven's decision to ignore the test results violated Title VII of the Civil Rights Act of 1964 (FindLaw 2009).

Another antidiscrimination case—a case involving many superlatives—is *Dukes v. Wal-Mart*, and, in turn, *Wal-Mart v. Dukes*. What began as a suit filed in 2000 by Wal-Mart employee Betty Dukes was certified in 2004 as a class action representing 1.6 million women. Wal-Mart appealed the class certification and for the next seven years the matter worked its way through courts. On June 20, 2011 the US Supreme Court ruled in Wal-Mart's favor, saying that the plaintiffs did not have enough in common to constitute a class (Supreme Court 2010).

We can conclude, at minimum, that in the USA we cannot rely upon legislators and the courts to eliminate discrimination against women. Italian scholar Ruth Rubio-Marin cites many examples to the effect that in Europe "instruments and policies dealing with gender equality both at the national and supra-national level reflect a move from a narrow antidiscrimination frame to a broader model that tackles the under-participation and disempowerment of women in public and private life as a deficiency of democracy and a problem of citizenship" (Rubio-Marin 2012). Rubio-Marin discusses specific "parity measures," such as gender quotas for the boards of publicly held companies, and for election to public office in the European Union (EU) and in EU member states. She further holds that "a combination of legal, historical, cultural, ideological and political factors make it unlikely that a similar development will take place in the United States" (Rubio-Marin 2012).

One need go no further than the term "quota" to hear alarm bells go off in the USA. Since at least 1978, when the Supreme Court ruled in *Regents of the University of California v. Baake* that setting aside seats in a medical school class for minority students was unconstitutional, quotas have been loudly condemned as reverse discrimination. But differences between the EU and the USA go much deeper, according to Rubio-Marin. Europeans have begun to understand "manifestations of citizenship" to include not just politics and the market—as has been the case for at least a century—but also to include care and social reproduction. It has never been the case that men are independent and women dependent; the appearance of independence has been made possible for men because they rely on women for uncompensated labor.

Presumably Rubio-Marin's important article went to press before the recent full emergence of the Occupy Movement, so perhaps we can be a bit more optimistic about the future position of women in the USA. Some hope and some fear that the Occupy Movement portends social changes on a par with those brought about by the French Revolution. But at least, as in the words of "Bread and Roses," quoted above, the Occupy Movement, by pointing out the 1–99% dichotomy, allows the ideological fog to clear enough so that we can see that "ten toil where one reposes," and that this is deeply immoral. Uncompensated and undercompensated labor create working conditions that are ethically wrong. It's time to make a commitment to equal pay for equal work that applies to everyone.

Note

1 For a thorough, cogently argued treatment of goods
  necessary for human action, see Boylan (2004).

References

Arriola, E.R. (2000). Voices from the barbed wires of despair: Women in the maquiladoras, Latina critical legal theory and gender at the US–Mexico border. *DePaul Law Review*, 50(2): 731–752.

Blackman, A.M. (2011). Manufactured home displacement and its disparate impact on low-income females: A violation of the fair housing act in Boise Idaho. *The Crit: A Critical Studies Journal*, 4(1): 67–111.

Blau, F.D., Ferber, M.A., & Winkler, A.E. (2002). *The economics of women, men and work*, 4th edn. Upper Saddle River, NJ: Prentice Hall.

Blumrosen, A.W. (1990). Society in transition II: Price Waterhouse and the individual employment discrimination case. *Rutgers Law Review*, 4: 1023–1066.

Blumrosen, A.W., & Blumrosen, R.G. (2003). First statistical report on international job discrimination against women. *Women's Rights Law Reporter*, 25(1): 63–65.

Boylan, M. (2004). *A just society*. Lanham, MD: Rowman & Littlefield.

Calloway, D.A. (1994). St. Mary's Honor Center v. Hicks: Questioning the basic assumption. *Connecticut Law Review*, 26(3): 997–1010.

Calloway, D.A. (1995). Accomodating pregnancy in the workplace. *Stetson Law Review*, 25(1): 1–53.

Chavkin, W. (1984). Walking a tightrope: Pregnancy, parenting and work. In W. Chavkin (Ed.), *Double exposure: Women's health hazards on the job and at home* (pp. 196–202). New York: Monthly Review Press.

Cole, D. (1999). No equal justice: How the criminal justice system uses inequality. *The Champion: National Association of Criminal Defense Lawyers* (Sept./Oct.): 20–25.

Correll, S.J., Benard, S., & Paik, I. (2007). Getting a job: Is there a motherhood penalty? *American Journal of Sociology*, 112(5): 1297–1339.

Derschowitz, J. (2011) *Leonardo di Caprio is Hollywood's highest paid actor*. CBS News, August 3. Retrieved March 15, 2013 from http://www.cbsnews.com/8301-31749_162-20087389-10391698.html

FindLaw. (2009). *Ricci et al. v. DeStefano et al.* Retrieved March 1, 2013 from http://caselaw.lp.findlaw.com/scripts/getcase.pl?court=US&vol=000&invol=07-1428

Greenwald, A.G., & Banaji, M.R. (1995). Implicit social cognition: Attitudes, self-esteem and stereotypes. *Psychological Review*, 102(1): 4–27.

Greenwald, A.G., McGhee, D.E., & Schwartz, J.L.K. (1998). Measuring individual differences in implicit cognition: The implicit association test. *Journal of Personality and Social Psychology*, 74(6): 1464–1480.

Grossman, J.L. (2010). Pregnancy, work and the promise of equal citizenship. *Georgetown Law Journal*, 98(3): 567–628.

Jackson, R.M. (1998). *Destined for equality*. Cambridge, MA: Harvard University Press.

Kamel, R., & Hoffman, A. (Eds.). (1999). *The maquiladora reader: Cross border organizing since NAFTA*. Washington, DC: American Friends Service Committee.

Lane, K., Banaji, M.R., Nosek, B.A., & Greenwald, A.G. (2007). Understanding and using the implicit association test: IV: What we know (so far) about the method. In B. Wittenbrink & N. Schwarz (Eds.), *Implicit measures of attitude* (pp. 59–102). New York: Guilford Press.

Maikovich, A.J., & Brown, M.D. (1989). *Employment discrimination: A claims manual for employees and managers*. Jefferson, NC: McFarland.

McDonald's (*n.d.*). *Best job descriptions*. Retrieved March 15, 2013 from http://www.bestjobdescriptions.com/customer-service/mcdonalds-crew-job-description

Mutua, A. (2001). Why retire the feminization of poverty construct? *Denver University Law Review*, 78: 1179.

Nelson, R.L., & Bridges, W.P. (1999). In M. Granovetter (Ed.), *Legalizing gender inequality: Courts, markets and unequal pay for women in America*. Cambridge: Cambridge University Press.

Project Implicit (*n.d.*). *Home page*. Retrieved March 1, 2013 from https://implicit.harvard.edu/

Rubio-Marin, R. (2012). Evolutions in antidiscrimination law in Europe and North America: A new European parity-democracy model and why it won't fly in the United States. *The American Journal of Comparative Law*, 60(Winter): 99–126.

Sebelius, K. (2011). Annual update of the HSS poverty guidelines; Office of the Secretary: Department of Health and Human Services. *Federal Register*, 76(13): 3637–3638.

Slater, J.E., Zimmer, M.J., Sullivan, C.A., & Blumrosen, A.A. (2005). Proof and pervasiveness: Employment discrimination in law and reality after Desert Palace, Inc. v. Costa: Proceedings of the 2005 annual meeting, Association of American Law Schools, sections on employment discrimination, civil rights, labor relations and employment law, and minority groups. *Employee Rights and Employment Policy Journal*, 9: 427–457.

Sunstein, C.R. (1991). Why markets don't stop discrimination. *Social Philosophy and Policy*, 8(2): 22–37.

Supreme Court. (2010). *Wal-Mart Stores, Inc. v. Dukes et al.* Retrieved March 1, 2013 from http://www.supreme-court.gov/opinions/10pdf/10-277.pdf

US Equal Employment Opportunity Commission. (n.d.). Title VII of the Civil Rights Act of 1964. Retrieved March 1, 2013 from http://www.eeoc.gov/laws/statutes/titlevii.cfm

US Equal Employment Opportunity Commission. (2011). *Employers still barring large groups of people from jobs based on race, sex, age, other prohibited bases*. Press release,

June. Retrieved March 15, 2013 from http://www.eeoc.gov/eeoc/meetings/6-8-11/index.cfm

Velasquez, M.G. (2010). *Business ethics: Concepts and cases*, 7th edn. Upper Saddle River, NJ: Pearson.

Vogtman, J. (2010). *Women's poverty soared in 2009*. National Women's Law Center. Retrieved March 1, 2013 from http://www.nwlc.org/our-blog/womens-poverty-soared-2009

Williams, J.C., & Tait, A. (2011). Mancession or momcession: Good providers, a bad economy and gender discrimination. *Chicago-Kent Law Review*, 86(2): 857.

Zeng, X. (2007). Enforcing equal employment opportunities in China. *University of Pennsylvania Journal of Labor and Employment Law*, 9(4): 991–1024.

D. Whistle-Blowing

Whistle-Blowing

TERRANCE McCONNELL

When a referee in a game blows the whistle, this is typically to indicate that a fou or a violation of the rules has occurred. Now when a person alerts the public to some misdeed perpetrated by an organization of which he or she is a member, we say that this person has blown the whistle. Thus was born a now popular metaphor in the English language. This chapter will discuss several examples of whistle-blowing, will outline some of the main elements of whistle-blowing, and will address some of the (sometimes neglected) ethical issues raised by this phenomenon for individuals, for organizations, and for society at large.

Some Examples

The phrase "whistle-blowing" is most commonly used in the context of business ethics. But it is more properly situated in the larger arena of organizational ethics.

Terrance McConnell, "Whistle-Blowing." Reprinted with permission of John Wiley & Sons Ltd from R.G. Frey ed., *A Companion to Applied Ethics: Blackwell Companions to Philosophy* (2003); 570–582.

Example 1

Jeffrey Wigand held a PhD in chemistry and worked in research and development for the Brown and Williamson Tobacco Company. He was making a handsome salary and doing quite well until he voiced objections to a plan implemented by Brown and Williamson. The company wanted to enhance the potency of nicotine in their cigarettes. By a process called impact boosting. Brown and Williamson developed a cigarette that allowed nicotine to be absorbed more rapidly by the body. Such cigarettes were apparently more addictive and more dangerous to smokers. Because of this, Wigand took exception to marketing them. As a result, he was fired by Brown and Williamson. He subsequently revealed some of the information to a reporter for the television show, *60 Minutes*, and his interview was eventually aired. Among other things, Wigand exposed as perjurious testimony by tobacco executives that they had no reason to believe that nicotine is addictive. During this time, Wigand was followed, harassed, and even received death threats. He ended up teaching chemistry in high school.

Example 2

In 1966, the physician, Henry Beecher, published an article in *The New England Journal of Medicine* (Beecher 1966). After examining published studies, Beecher identified fifty experiments involving human subjects that he said were unethical or ethically questionable. For reasons of space, the published article discussed only twenty-two of these studies. In a recent book, Jonathan Moreno referred to the publication of this article as an unprecedented act of whistle-blowing and said that it was "greeted as scurrilous by many of his [Beecher's] colleagues" (Moreno 2000: 242). While it is difficult to assign causal efficacy in such a complex array of human activities, it is nevertheless plausible to hold that the impact of Beecher's article was enormous; for it was in the early 1970s that the popular press began exposing ethically questionable scientific research, including the Tuskegee syphilis experiment and the research on hepatitis at the Willowbrook State Hospital (McConnell 1997: ch. 6). The most important result of Beecher's article was not to expose any particular study, but to turn the ethical spotlight on academicians and physicians, individuals whose work until then was merely assumed to be morally acceptable. Today, the extant ethics literature on the use of human subjects in experiments is vast, and most revelations have been after 1970.

Example 3

On July 13, 2000, the newspaper *USA Today* published an article about Cherylynn Mathias, a registered nurse from Tulsa, Oklahoma (Pound 2000). In the spring of 1999, Mathias responded to a job ad for a research nurse at the University of Oklahoma's College of Medicine in Tulsa. Though Mathias had limited experience in clinical research, she was hired. But, in the year that followed, Mathias became a thorn in the side of her supervisors and, ultimately, a whistle-blower.

On June 1, 1999, Mathias went to work as a coordinator on a clinical trial studying a cancer vaccine. The principal investigator of this study was Michael McGee. In the months that followed, Mathias became alarmed about numerous irregularities and violations of federal rules. These included injecting subjects with a potentially dangerous vaccine before it was tested on animals, overstating the likely benefits for the subjects, and subsequently trying to cover up these violations. During the fall of 1999, Mathias repeatedly raised these concerns with McGee, but she was ignored. In October she notified officials of the College's Institutional Review Board, and in December these officials met with McGee and Mathias. The meeting resulted in an agreement to bring in an outside company to evaluate the study. In March 2000, that firm issued two reports that were critical of the study and recommended that it be suspended because it was endangering the welfare of subjects. In April, Dr McGee did suspend the study, but he told subjects that the reason he was doing so was that he had run out of vaccine. Mathias pressed the college's top officials to report the consultants' findings, but they failed to do so. Because of this refusal, Mathias wrote to federal regulators about the improprieties, the outside report, and the failure to alert federal officials. Thus the scandal became public. The College of Medicine publicly acknowledged that twenty-six of the ninety-eight subjects who had participated in the melanoma trial had died, but they insisted that there was no evidence that these deaths were caused by the vaccine. Mathias still has her job, but fears that she will be ostracized for not being a good team player. She did report that one of the subjects in the trial had called her and thanked her for standing up for them.

Principal Features of Whistle-Blowing

Because of the complexity of the phenomenon and the variety of contexts in which it can occur, it is difficult to state the necessary and sufficient conditions for an action's counting as an apt instance of whistle-blowing. We can, nevertheless, highlight some of the prominent features associated with this practice.

A whistle-blower makes *accusations* against an organization. The accusations call attention to alleged instances of negligence, abuse, or practices that *damage the public interest or harm others*. The accusations typically single out individuals or groups within the organization as *responsible for* the harm being perpetrated. I say "organization" rather than "business" deliberately. For though famous early instances of whistle-blowing occurred within for-profit businesses, it can also occur within charities, universities, and other not-for-profit organizations (as some of the examples above show).

Whistle-blowers *make public* their charges of wrongdoing. If one were merely to tell a spouse or a friend about the questionable practices, this would not count as whistle-blowing. There are many different ways in which one might go public with the information, including telling one's story to a reporter for a newspaper, television station, or magazine. One might also alert an outside agency that has the authority to take action; this is what Cherylynn Mathias did. Henry Beecher's whistle-blowing went public in a more complicated way; he published an article in a prestigious medical journal. But, one might ask, since many of the studies to which Beecher called attention were themselves already published in journals, was the information not already public? In one sense, the answer here is "yes." These studies, however, were scattered in many places and the ethically problematic aspects of them—that subjects were put at risk and that informed consent was often absent—were but one part of a bigger and more complicated picture, and not something that the authors themselves emphasized. It took someone with Beecher's training and expertise to bring these details together and to show how widespread within the scientific community certain behavior was. Publishing this information in *The New England Journal of Medicine*, Beecher no doubt knew, magnified the attention that these morally troubling practices would receive.

Taking responsibility by *identifying oneself* as the source of the allegations is central to typical instances of whistle-blowing. Whether this is a necessary condition is arguable, and certainly difficult to prove. But it is questionable whether an act is an instance of whistle-blowing when the person who makes the allegations insists that his or her identity should not be revealed. In this regard, think of "Deep Throat." the pseudonym that Carl Bernstein and Bob Woodward assigned to the person leaking information to them about activities in the Nixon White House (Bernstein and Woodward 1974). "Leaking" of this sort fails to be a case of whistle-blowing for a second reason, I think (Bok 1983: 216–17). "Deep Throat" gave Bernstein and Woodward only bits of information at a time. Whistle-blowers, intent on putting an end to the injustice they are revealing, give all of the information they have at the time they make their revelations.

Whistle-blowers have *expertise* or *inside knowledge* on which their charges are based. Again, whether this is a necessary condition is not obvious. But, typically, the whistle-blower is uniquely positioned to be cognizant of the allegedly wrong behavior, and this positioning is usually due to a combination of the person's place in the organization and his or her ability to understand what is going on. This is clearly the case with Jeffrey Wigand. And think again about Cherylynn Mathias. Her training in a medical field and her knowledge (though limited) of what is expected in medical research were crucial to her being able to see the problems and as a credible source when the charges were made. Somebody with no training in medicine and no knowledge of the hazards that subjects sometimes encounter in experiments probably would not have recognized the irregularities spotted by Mathias.

Whistle-blowers, though possessing knowledge and having position within the organization, typically have *no means of ending the harmful practices* within the organization's structure. Blowing the whistle is usually the last resort, an act engaged in only because working within the organization's structure has proved to be fruitless. In most cases, anyway, if the morally dubious acts or practices could be stopped without making public revelations, the would-be whistle-blower would choose that course of action.

The act of whistle-blowing is likely to *affect adversely the interests* of multiple parties: the organization itself; employees of the organization allegedly responsible for wrongdoing; clients of the organization; and the whistle-blower himself or herself. Since the whistle-blower's charges are no doubt serious, the organization will have its good name and reputation tarnished. If the organization is for-profit, its bottom line may be adversely affected too. If the charges prove to be true, at least some of the organization's employees are likely to be penalized, possibly even fired. If the organization is circumventing norms in order to supply clients with a product, then calling this to the public's attention will have negative consequences for the clients as well. And, of course, retaliation against whistle-blowers themselves is common.

Finally, would-be whistle-blowers are apt to see their situation as one of conflicting obligations. To even arrive at the point of considering the act of whistle-blowing, the agent must believe that the organization is engaged in serious wrongdoing and that it is his or her obligation to take steps to stop such conduct. At the same time, the would-be whistle-blower is probably under obligations to the organization, including an obligation of confidentiality. The case of Beecher, described above, may seem to be an exception to this; for it was not an organization, let alone one that employed him, against which he blew the whistle. Even here, however, the point holds. Beecher blew the whistle against medical researchers. And not only did Beecher himself engage in medical research, but he was no doubt committed to the claim that such research does enormous good for many people. Beecher's act of exposing ethically suspect conduct among medical researchers had the obvious potential of setting back the entire enterprise. So, even here, Beecher no doubt felt the pull of conflicting obligations.

Ethical Context

Before discussing some of the issues raised for individuals and for institutions by whistle-blowing, let us look at the broader context in which these questions arise. When the possibility of blowing the whistle on one's own organization present itself as a plausible option, the would-be whistle-blower is likely to experience conflict. Here I shall explain one way of understanding why there is such a moral conflict, and then I shall explain two broad ethical perspectives for thinking about how to resolve the conflict.

The possibility of blowing the whistle presents an agent with a moral conflict. A would-be whistle-blower is a member of the organization which he or she believes is doing wrong. Membership typically carries with it obligations. These are *role-related obligations*, moral requirements that a person has in virtue of his or her position, job, or role. A physician's obligation of confidentiality to her patients is an instance of a role-related obligation. A lifeguard's requirement to assist struggling swimmers is another example. Loyalty to the organization and keeping secret company information are important role-related obligations that create conflict for would-be whistle-blowers. By contrast, *general obligations* are requirements that one has simply because one is a moral agent. Examples include obligations not to kill not to steal, and not to assault others. If one can easily prevent significant harm to others, most will concede that there is a general obligation to do so; in most cases, this is the general obligation that conflicts with the whistler-blower's role-related obligations owed to his or her organization.

If role-related obligations always prevailed over general obligations in cases of conflict, or if general obligations always took precedence over role-related obligations, then any would-be whistler-blower would have a structural answer to his or her conflict. Neither of these generalizations seems plausible, however. One suspects that it would be easy to produce examples where intuitively role-related obligations should take precedence, and other examples where general obligations should prevail. And, in any case, such a structural solution would not assist all whistle-blowers; for in some cases the conflict is between two role-related obligations. Consider again the situation of Cherylynn Mathias. As an employee of the College of Medicine, Mathias has obligations to the institution and to her research colleagues. But, as a nurse, she has obligations to the patient/subjects. Thus, she is faced with a conflict between two role-related obligations. Instead of looking for simplistic structural solutions to such conflicts, we need a more general ethical perspective.

Such a perspective is available. The dominant account seems to be what one might call the *future-oriented view* of rightness. According to this view, it is morally right to blow the whistle and thus publicly affix responsibility to one's own organization only if doing so will put an end to a current wrong. The idea is that blowing the whistle, and thus breaching loyalty, is right only if doing so prevents harm now or in the near future. Sissela Bok seems to endorse such a view when she suggests that a whistle-blower's accusations should concern "a present or an imminent threat." She goes on, "Past errors or misdeeds occasion such an alarm only if they still affect current practices" (Bok 1983: 215). Such a view need not be purely consequentialist; it need not imply, for example, that it is permissible to blow the whistle only if the harm prevented to others is greater than the harm that will occur to the organization because of the agent's revelations. But it does imply that merely exposing past wrongdoing is not a sufficient reason to blow the whistle; instead, doing so must prevent present or near future harm to others.

The future-oriented view contrasts with a position that is analogous to the retributivist theory of punishment: an agent should blow the whistle just in case the organization did in fact commit the wrong in question. The point is to call attention to wrongdoing, even if doing so will not prevent additional harm. While here I shall not try to resolve the dispute between the future-oriented view and the retributivist account, I do want to suggest that, with slight alterations, the future-oriented view has far more resources than it appears at first glance to have.

The suggested alteration is minor. Bok states the view in terms of affecting current practices. She seems to have in mind the practices of the *organization* on whom the whistle is to be blown. If we expand this to include not just the practices of the organization in question but also the practices of similar organizations, and if we also count as a relevant factor making reparations to living victims or heirs of the deceased (even if the unjust practice has ceased), then the future-oriented view has considerable resources.

Consider first the idea of making reparations. Suppose that an organization did engage in practices that harmed others, but has since abandoned those practices. You are a member of this organization and you discover documents which demonstrate that your organization behaved in a manner that harmed others, was aware of this, hid this information from the public, but did cease the harmful behavior. If we focus only on the organization's current practices, blowing the whistle will not prevent harm to others. But it remains a fact that the organization's past activities did cause harm and that those victims (or their heirs) have not been compensated. When there are victims, surely it is not enough for an organization merely to stop perpetrating injustices; it must also make amends to those whom it has wronged. If you are not able to convince your organization to do this, then blowing the whistle is warranted even though the organization does not currently engage in practices that cause harm. The altered version of the future-oriented view accommodates this intuition by counting as a relevant good the fact that it is made more likely that victims will be compensated.

Sometimes exposing a past injustice can open people's eyes to similar injustices. This is a second factor that the altered version of the future-oriented view can take into account. Consider again Beecher's (1966) article on unethical medical research. Because Beecher was an "insider" of sorts—one who himself engaged in medical research—one might say that he blew the whistle on colleagues. And, though assigning causal consequences to human actions embedded in complex social practices is difficult, one suspects that the spate of articles and books published in the 1970s and 1980s exposing ethically questionable medical research owes its origin to Beecher's seminal piece (for examples, see McConnell 1997: 192–9). Note too that most of these critical studies were done by "outsiders." Thus one act of blowing the whistle prompted many outside the relevant professions to examine questionable practices and to expose serious injustices. And it is at least possible that all of this could occur even if the original practice singled out by the whistle-blower had long since ceased.

A third factor that the altered version of the future-oriented view can take into account is the educational value of exposing corruption. When an organization has been shown to have wronged its clients or customers, we can expect people to be more alert to this possibility with similar organizations. And if customers and clients are more alert, this should result in fewer wrongs being perpetrated. Thus, when companies in the cigarette industry are shown to have systematically deceived customers about the dangers of their product, this should create a more informed and suspicious clientele. When a tire manufacturer is shown to have knowingly marketed a defective product, the public is rendered more alert. And when it is shown that the government of the United States sponsored numerous research projects that exposed unwitting subjects to serious dangers—as was done with the revelations about the human radiation experiments of the 1940s and 1950s (Faden 1996; Welsome 1999; Moreno 2000)—this should make citizens question both the medical establishment and projects initiated by the government. This can of course, have a serious down side: citizens may become paranoid and trust no one. But to the extent that suspicions are kept in perspective and channeled properly, they should serve both individuals and our society well.

Issues for Individuals

If (for the sake of simplicity) we focus on the modified version of the future-oriented view, then an individual contemplating an act of whistle-blowing should ask him or herself what good will result and what bad will result if he or she carries out the act. And while we need not say with utilitarians that whistle-blowing is justified only if the balance of good over evil is better for all affected parties than if the whistle were not blown, we surely do want to say that the good done (or harm prevented) by blowing the whistle must be significant if it is to be justified.

The most basic questions that would-be whistle-blowers must ask themselves are these: Is blowing the whistle in this situation *permissible*? Is it *obligatory*? Here it would be too ambitious to attempt to state the necessary and sufficient conditions for the permissibility and obligatoriness of whistle-blowing. Instead, I shall more modestly deal with *some* of the pertinent factors.

First, let us consider the *permissibility* of whistle-blowing. As noted earlier, acts of whistle-blowing will affect one's organization and some of its members adversely. It is a breach of loyalty, it ascribes wrongdoing to the organization and some members, it creates mistrust, and it may sever important relationships permanently. If such an act is nevertheless permissible, it will have to produce significant good (or prevent significant harm) to offset these bad effects. If an organization is doing something ethically questionable but the harm done is minor, it seems unlikely that an act as drastic as blowing the whistle will be permissible. One hopes that this can be handled behind the scenes, but if it cannot blowing the whistle may not be the best option.

If a would-be whistle-blower has decided that the harm being done by her organization is significant enough to warrant going public, then she should ask herself certain questions. Given the complexity of the normative judgment involved, she should ask herself how confident she is in her assessment. Is she sure about the facts? Is she sure that others are being harmed or unwittingly put at risk? Is all of this just a major misunderstanding? These questions are especially important if the would-be whistle-blower believes that her organization and the people who work for it are by and large good. People and organizations do not change their character over night. If something appears to be morally askew, make sure that it is. Because of the complexity involved, nothing can eradicate doubt completely, but seeking the advice of a trusted colleague may help.

Before blowing the whistle, our agent should also make sure that she has accurately estimated the damage that her act will do to the organization. Accusations of wrongdoing do harm to organizations, even if they prove to be false; and this harm reverberates to the employees and/or clients. A business against whom a false charge is made may suffer enough that it is forced to layoff employees. And a not-for-profit organization may find its funding cut back severely because of an accusation.

One other point is worth noting here. It is commonly said that before blowing the whistle, a person has an obligation to see that all existing avenues for change within the organization have been explored (Bok 1983: 221; Dougherty 1995: 2552). This seems plausible, of course, because many bad consequences can be avoided if the whistle is not blown. The agent will be forced neither to breach confidentiality nor to be disloyal. And the organization will not suffer embarrassment or more tangible harm. There is a reason for questioning this widely accepted claim, however. Within the context of the future-oriented view, more may be at stake ethically than simply stopping the organization's currently wrong behavior. At least two possibilities come to mind. First, if some have already been victimized by the organization's behavior, they should be compensated in some way. But it is hard to compensate victims without acknowledging in a quasi-public way that one has done wrong. Second, if one chooses not to blow the whistle because the organization has made appropriate changes, an indirect good may be lost, namely, prompting the examination of comparable organizations for similar practices. In some contexts, this latter point may be unimportant. Enough scandalous behavior by cigarette companies, automobile makers, supermarket chains, and medical research protocols have been exposed that it is unlikely that many remain naive about these organizations. The overall point is this: the mere fact that an organization is willing to alter the practices identified by the would-be whistle-blower is not alone sufficient to entail that people outside the organization should not be informed about these practices. The final judgment is complex, and other relevant factors should not be overlooked.

Now let us consider the other question that individuals must face, namely, whether blowing the whistle on one's organization is *obligatory*. Assuming that the agent has assessed the situation correctly, he will be revealing the existence of a serious moral wrong and rendering more likely that the wrong will cease and that the victims will be compensated. Why would anyone deny that such an action is required? Here we shall consider but one reason for such a denial.

As is well known, whistle-blowers often do not fare well. Some have been fired and others have been demoted or reassigned to far less desirable positions (see Shuchman 2000: 1013–15). Some have even been required to undergo psychiatric examinations, thus enabling the accused company unfairly to diminish the credibility of the whistle-blower. Often whistle-blowers are portrayed by employers as disgruntled and insubordinate. Jeffery Wigand was portrayed as psychologically unstable, and many apparently irrelevant incidents from his past were leaked to the press. In short, whistle-blowers and their families are apt to suffer as a result of their revelations. Given the size of these sacrifices, some will argue that the actions are beyond the call of duty.

Ethicists not only categorize actions as morally required, morally forbidden, and neutral, but also reserve for some acts the label "supererogatory." These are act that are above and beyond the call of duty. They are morally good but not required: their agents typically deserve praise, but would not be worthy of blame if they omitted the act (for an account, see Heyd, 1982, and Mellema, 1991). Acts involving great sacrifice are often thought to be supererogatory, such as a soldier covering an exploding grenade to protect his comrades. But it is doubtful that sacrifice is either necessary or sufficient for making an act beyond the call of duty. It is not necessary because a small favor done for a stranger is sometimes supererogatory. It is not sufficient because sometimes sacrifice is required, such as when a parent sacrifices for a child or a lifeguard risks his life to save a swimmer. Nevertheless because sacrifice is often supererogatory and because whistle-blowers put themselves at risk, some may hold that blowing the whistle is never obligatory. I shall without argument, reject this view. A plausible position, I think, is that the moral status of whistle-blowing is context-dependent. In some cases it may be wrong especially if the harm being done is minimal and will be stopped (and victims compensated) immediately. In other cases it may be justifiable—sometimes required, sometimes supererogatory.

I doubt that any formula can be devised for distinguishing when whistle-blowing is required and when it is supererogatory. I suggest, again without argument, that three factors are critical in determining whether blowing the whistle is obligatory or beyond the call of duty. The first factor is the degree of harm being perpetrated by the organization. The more serious the harm, the more likely it is that the agent is required to go public with her charges. The second factor is the degree of sacrifice that the whistle-blower must make. The greater the sacrifice, the more likely it is that blowing the whistle is supererogatory. The third factor is the whistle-blower's profession and/or his relationship with the victims. As the example of the lifeguard above suggests, in some roles sacrifices are justifiably expected. During times of plague, physicians take it to be their duty to treat quarantined patients even though they are put at risk. Imagine now our would-be whistle-blower wearing two hats—she is a physician and a researcher. If she finds out that the experimental drug being given to her patient/subjects is harmful but her employer orders her to continue and remain silent, both her profession and her relationship with the victims suggest that she is required to violate these orders, even at great cost to herself. None of this tells us how to distinguish precisely whether blowing the whistle is obligatory or optional, but such precision is difficult to attain.

Issues for Organizations

Officials acting on behalf of organizations must ask themselves how to respond to each case of whistle-blowing. More important, though, organizations must have within their structure ways of dealing with such cases. Assuming that organizations want to be ethical, what should their approach be?

Organizations must make their commitment to ethics known to employees through widely promulgated policies. At least three things are needed to succeed. First, there should be an internal mechanism for handling employees' complaints, such as an internal review board. In order to be more than mere window-dressing, such a board must listen seriously to complaints and be willing to act if necessary. And such a board must have support from the organization's top. Second, employees who use this mechanism must be protected from retaliation. The whole point is to resolve the problem internally, and so employees must know that they will be protected if they do not go public. Recall that Jeffrey Wigand raised his objection within the company structure, but was nevertheless fired. Because of cases like this, some have suggested that companies adopt a bill of rights for employees. Third, organizations should engage in self-assessment regularly and give due weight to employees' concerns raised in this context. (On these points, see Bok 1983: 225–6 and Dougherty 1995: 2552.) These are preventive measures, designed to make whistle-blowing unnecessary. But if for some reason they fail and a member does go public with a charge, then the case must be dealt with on its own merits. The public's perception, I suspect, is that organizations typically deny charges and attempt to cover up wrongdoing and hide their dirty laundry. And, in many cases, this may be true. Independent of the accuracy of the charges, however, it is a natural human response for organizational officials to feel betrayed, especially if they themselves are hearing the charges for the first time. At this point in the dispute, one can only hope that each side will be honest and seek a just solution. Beyond that, it is hard to say anything useful.

There is, however, one point that often comes up during such a public dispute that deserves special comment. In many of these cases, the employee in question has signed a contract that includes a confidentiality clause. And the organization often cites this clause as its moral (and legal) trump card, showing that the disgruntled member has acted unethically. As an ethical solution to the dispute, this strategy should be rejected. There are, of course, good reasons for confidentiality clauses. Businesses need to protect information vital to their workings; it is obviously legitimate to try to stay ahead of the competition and employees who give away trade secrets should be penalized. But these contracts do not show that *morally* employees should never blow the whistle. There is a major difference between an employee selling a trade secret to the competition for personal profit and blowing the whistle because of company improprieties that the employee proved powerless to stop. Moreover, such a contract can never entail that it is *always* wrong to blow the whistle. To hold otherwise commits one to an implausible absolutism. For the wrongdoing that the agent proposes to expose could be of any magnitude at all, including the most horrendous evil. To argue that a contractual obligation ethically prevents one from revealing this evil entails that such a contractual obligation overrides *any* other requirement with which it conflicts. But this lacks credibility no promise has such moral efficacy. A promise never to do something, even if one believes that doing so is morally required, can never be valid (for the full argument see, McConnell, 2000: ch. 3).

Issues for Society

Not all organizations will conduct themselves ethically, and, even if they did, not all of their members would so assess them. As a result, there will be cases of whistle-blowing, and they will likely trigger disputes. How should society deal with these?

One's first instinct, I think, is to protect the whistle-blower. The big organization against a single member is a classic mismatch, and the underdog needs assistance. Some states have in fact passed legislation designed to protect employees against various types of reprisals. Such laws are well intended, but there are two serious difficulties with them. First, some charges against organizations are false, sometimes maliciously motivated, sometimes brought to cover the employee's own incompetence. Second, organizations have many ways of making life difficult for members, so many ways that effective legislation is difficult to craft. Because of these complexities, in particular cases tough judgments of fact and culpability will have to be made no matter what statutes society has. Of course, individuals and organizations may also avail themselves of the civil law when they believe that their rights have been violated; with just verdicts, false charges from individuals and organizational retaliation should be discouraged.

In the end, however, the best that we can reasonably hope for is good-faith efforts by all parties: caution and deliberation before acting by would-be whistle-blowers: a repudiation of acts of revenge by organizations; and a search for the truth by the courts. These are clichés, but a neater structural solution appears elusive.

I close with another case. Barry Adams was a nurse at Youville Health Care Center, an extended-care facility in Cambridge, Massachusetts. Adams was fired in 1996 by his supervisor, Ann Poster. He says that he was fired for speaking out about working conditions (in part, serious downsizing) that created safety hazards for patients; she says it was because of insubordination. This case drew a lot of attention, in part because it raises questions about the accountability of nurse-managers who implement cost-cutting measures imposed by their organization. Adams charged Poster with unprofessional conduct and patient neglect. Officials of the Board of Registration in Nursing (for Massachusetts) ruled that Adams failed to prove that Poster fired him because of his complaints rather than insubordination, and therefore dismissed his charges. David Schildmeier, a spokesman for the Massachusetts Nurses Association, professed to be outraged by the decision.

From afar, most of us have no idea who was right in this situation. But independent of this, the case raises broader questions. In the United States, some professionals, including physicians, nurses, dentists, pharmacists, and attorneys, are given considerable latitude by society to police themselves. How diligently these professions do this job is open to debate. Many suspect, however, that peer-review committees are reluctant to make rulings against one of their own. If this is true, it puts members of any of these professions who blow the whistle on colleagues—as Barry Adams did—in a difficult position. If these peer-review committees indeed are seldom willing to sanction colleagues, members of these professions will understandably be hesitant to blow the whistle, even if the wrongs being done are great. Even if blowing the whistle in these cases is obligatory—not supererogatory in spite of the sacrifices the agent will undergo— it is both prudent and right for society to protect those who come forward. Perhaps a detailed study of professions given the privilege of policing themselves is in order; and if the results bear disappointing news, perhaps society should revoke the privilege.

Conclusion

Whistle-blowing occurs when a member of an organization openly accuses colleagues of professional wrongdoing through a public medium. Because such an action is likely to affect the organization adversely and be contrary to role-related obligations, it requires ethical justification. Such justification is most readily found in stopping harm to the public, effecting compensation for victims, and opening people's eyes to similar wrongdoing. When such good effects clearly outweigh the bad, whistle-blowing is permissible; whether it is obligatory depends, in part, on the degree of sacrifice the would-be whistle-blower is apt to undergo. Organizations committed to being ethical must provide internal mechanisms for listening to employees' concerns seriously and evaluating them fairly. Just societies must protect, to the degree feasible, individuals who blow the whistle in good faith.

References

Beecher, Henry K. (1966) Ethics and clinical research. *The New England Journal of Medicine*, 274: 1354–60.

Bernstein, Carl and Woodward, Bob (1974) *All the President's Men*. New York: Warner Communications.

Bok, Sissela (1983) *Secrets: On the Ethics of Concealment and Revelation*. New York: Vintage Books.

Dougherty, Charles J. (1995) Whistle blowing in health care. In Warren T. Reich (ed.), *Encyclopedia of Bioethics*; pp. 2552–3, New York: Simon and Schuster.

Faden, Ruth (ed.) (1996) *The Human Radiation Experiments: Final Report of the Advisory Committee on Human Radiation Experiments*. New York: Oxford University Press.

Heyd, David (1982) *Supererogation*. New York: Cambridge University Press.

McConnell, Terrance (1997) *Moral Issues in Health Care*, 2nd edn. Belmont, CA: Wadsworth.

McConnell, Terrance (2000) *Inalienable Rights: The Limits of Consent in Medicine and the Law*. New York: Oxford University Press.

Mellema, Gregory (1991) *Supererogation, Obligation, and Offence*. Albany, NY: State University Press of New York.

Moreno, Jonathan D. (2000) *Undue Risk: Secret State Experiments on Humans*. New York W. H. Freeman.

Pound, Edward T. (2000) Nurse's clues shut down research. *USA Today*, July 13.

Shuchman, Miriam (2000) Consequences of blowing the whistle in medical research. *Annals of Internal Medicine*, 131: 1013–15.

Welsome, Eileen (1999) *The Plutonium Files: America's Secret Medical Experimentation in the Cold War*. New York: The Dial Press.

Mad as Hell or Scared Stiff?
The Effects of Value Conflict and Emotions on Potential Whistle-Blowers

Erika Henik

The decision to speak out against perceived wrongdoing can be value-laden and emotionally charged. As A. Dale Console said when reflecting on his reasons for blowing the whistle on his employer, pharmaceutical maker E.R. Squibb, "While I am convinced that I am motivated by a deep sense of moral indignation, I am equally motivated by a deep personal feeling of resentment" (Nader et al., 1972: 122). Nevertheless, scholars have largely ignored the important role of values and emotions in shaping the whistle-blowing decision process, favoring instead demographic, individual difference and situational predictors and subjectively rational (or, "cold") decision-making processes (March and Simon, 1958; Miceli and Near, 1984, 1988; Miceli et al., 1991; Near and Miceli, 1996).

This oversight is important because values and emotions have been shown to influence cognition, judgments, and behaviors in response to wrongdoing in non-whistle-blowing contexts (e.g., Fiske and Tetlock, 1997; Goldberg et al., 1999; Tetlock et al., 2000; Weiner, 1985, 1986; Weiner et al., 1982, 1987). Perhaps it is no surprise, then, that the traditional models of whistle-blowing have had a hard time identifying consistently strong predictors of this type of reporting (Miceli and Near, 1992).

The present article addresses this gap in the literature by interweaving the traditional literature on whistle-blowing with the cognitive appraisal approach to emotions and the social-functional value pluralism model (Smith and Ellsworth, 1985; Tetlock, 1986). I propose a new model of whistle-blowing that incorporates emotions and value conflict—i.e., "hot" cognitions – and recognizes the reciprocal influence of "hot" and "cold" cognitions on behavior. Thus, the model complements Gundlach et al.'s (2003) social information processing model of whistle-blowing, with its focus on emotions and attributions, and extends it by incorporating the value conflict and emotions that observers experience after they make attributions of responsibility for wrongdoing.

This new model should help account for what currently seem to be irrational, impulsive or self-defeating decisions and behaviors by potential whistle-blowers

Erika Henik, "Mad as Hell or Scared Stiff? The Effects of Value Conflict and Emotions on Potential Whistle-Blowers." Reprinted with permission of Springer from *Journal of Business Ethics* 80.1 (June 2008): 111–119.

(Gundlach et al., 2003). Risky decisions, like the decision to blow the whistle, feature ambiguity and emotion, which "can lead to behavior which *appears* irrational, foolish, or unintelligent to others" (McLain and Keenan, 1999: 258; emphasis added). This model should also help scholars identify several patterns of whistle-blowing activity, as research on emotions suggests that each distinct emotion or combination of emotions is likely to have a distinct impact on the unfolding of the whistle-blowing process (Ellsworth and Smith, 1988). Thus, identifying the different emotions that are active among potential whistle-blowers as they move through their decision processes should allow us to identify multiple whistle-blowing paths and junctures of path divergence.

Literature Review

The traditional model of whistle-blowing

Whistle-blowing represents "the disclosure by an organization's member [or former member] of illegal, immoral, or illegitimate practices under the control of their employers to persons or organizations that might be able to effect action" (Miceli and Near, 1992: 15). As such, it is a form of voice, an attempt to change organizational practices, policies, and outputs by appealing to a higher authority, and a form of principled organizational dissent, an attempt to change the status quo because of one's conscientious objection to current policy or practice (Graham, 1986; Hirschman, 1970; Rusbult, et al., 1988).

The traditional model of whistle-blowing contains five stages, summarized as follows: A trigger event occurs in Stage 1. An observer recognizes the event as problematic and decides what action to take in Stage 2, and then acts in Stage 3. The process shifts to the organization in Stage 4, as it reacts to the report. Stage 5 returns the process to the observer (now the whistle-blower) and involves his/her assessment of the organization's response and a decision regarding future activities (e.g., further escalation, silence). The model draws on theories of moral judgment, bystander intervention, power/dependence, and expectancy for its predictions (Dozier and Miceli, 1985; Graham, 1986; Green-berger et al., 1987; Kohlberg, 1969; Lataéne and Darley, 1970; McLain and Keenan, 1999; Miceli and Near, 1985, 1991, 1992; Near and Miceli, 1985, 1987; Parmerlee et al., 1982; Pfeffer and Salancik, 1978; Vroom, 1964).

The present article focuses on Stage 2, decision-making. In the traditional whistle-blowing model, this stage comprises four distinct, though not necessarily sequential, judgments. First is the judgment that the observed activities are problematic. Second is an assessment about whether the activities are deserving of action, including an assessment of the seriousness of the consequences. Third is the determination that one is personally responsible to act. And fourth is the judgment of what action is possible and appropriate, including an assessment of opportunity costs and benefits and of the risk of retaliation.

Each of these judgments is said to be informed by different factors. Problem recognition, for example, can be colored by group norms regarding right and wrong, access to information and moral development (Greenberger et al., 1987; McLain and Keenan, 1999; Kohlberg, 1969). Assessment may be shaped by characteristics of the activity itself (e.g., its frequency) or by others' reactions to the activity; for example, the perceived apathy of others may inhibit one's own response (Jones, 1991; Latané and Darley, 1970). The assumption of personal responsibility to respond can be enhanced by high moral reasoning or mitigated by a "diffusion of responsibility" if there are many other observers (Kohlberg, 1969; Latané and Darley, 1970). Action choice is said to be based on a cost-benefit analysis involving perceived self-efficacy and perceived risk of retaliation (Pfeffer and Salancik, 1978).

Model and Propositions

The proposed model of the whistle-blowing decision process extends the traditional model and the social information processing model by adding emotion and value conflict as both outcomes of subjectively rational assessments and predictors of whistle-blowing behaviors (Miceli and Near, 1992; Gundlach, et al., 2003) (see Figure 5.1). Specifically, the model integrates the cognitive appraisal approach to emotions and the social-functional value pluralism model into these previous models (Smith and Ellsworth, 1985; Tetlock, 1986). The cognitive appraisal approach facilitates predictions about which whistle-blowing behaviors will result from different emotional responses to observed wrongdoing. The social-functional value pluralism model facilitates predictions about how integrative complexity, a cognitive style that can result from value conflict, moderates the effect of emotions on whistle-blowing behaviors.

The presentation of the model begins with a discussion of emotions. I provide evidence that emotions have a place in whistle-blowing (and dissent) models and review the cognitive appraisal approach to emotions. I then introduce propositions about the effects of emotions on whistle-blowing behaviors. Next, I review the value pluralism model and its effect on integrative complexity, and offer propositions about the moderating relationship of integrative complexity and emotions on whistle-blowing behaviors.

Emotions

Emotions may play a role at various stages in the whistle-blowing decision process. Emotions have been found to help direct attention toward problems and to initiate attribution processes (Goldberg et al., 1999; Weiner, 1985, 1986). Thus, observed activities that violate one's expectations about what should be occurring at an organization may trigger surprise, which can lead an individual to recognize the activity as wrongful and set off a search for the causes of the wrongdoing. Emotions may also inform cost-benefit calculations and risk assessments regarding action choices. For example, anger has been found to lead to more optimistic risk assessments, while fear leads to more pessimistic expectations (Lerner and Keltner, 2000, 2001).

The above examples treat emotions as predictors of the subjectively rational assessments posited by the traditional model's Stage 2. However, emotions may also result from those assessments, and these resulting emotions are the focus of the present paper. Due to space constraints, the present discussion is restricted to the emotions of anger and fear, both of which are active in whistle-blowing episodes. Potential whistle-blowers often express outrage at the violations they have uncovered (Westin,

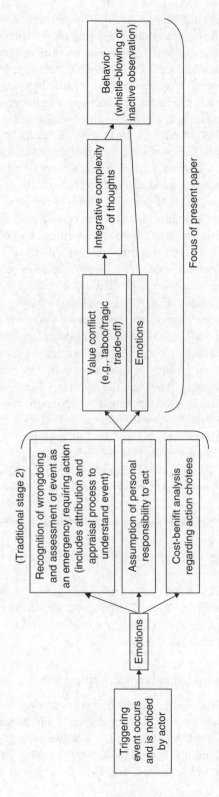

Figure 5.1 Proposed model of the whistle-blowing decision process

The boxes and labels in the figure read:

Triggering event occurs and is noticed by actor

Emotions

(Traditional stage 2)

Recognition of wrongdoing and assessment of event as an emergency requiring action (includes attribution and appraisal process to understand event)

Assumption of personal responsibility to act

Cost-benifit analysis regarding action chotees

Value conflict (e.g., taboo/tragic trade-off)

Emotions

Integrative complexity of thoughts

Behavior (whistle-blowing or inactive observation)

Focus of present paper

1981; Rothschild and Miethe, 1994). This outrage may be directed at the perpetrator, at peers or at the organization, depending on the circumstances. Gundlach et al. (2003) proposed that anger and resentment toward perpetrators would predict whistle-blowing among observers of wrongdoing, but anger toward peers or the organization (e.g., management) may also predict whistle-blowing. Anger has displayed a role in determining both pro-social and anti-social behaviors, and scholars have considered whistle-blowing as both a pro- and anti-social act (Betancourt and Blair, 1992; Dozier and Miceli, 1985; Miceli and Near, 1997; Schmidt and Weiner, 1988; Weiner et al., 1987). As for fear, fear of retaliation emerges as a concern of potential whistle-blowers in many case studies and surveys, and avoidance of retaliation is a prominent theme on whistle-blowing advice and advocacy websites (Glazer and Glazer, 1989; Keenan, 1995; Miceli and Near, 1984; Miceli et al., 1988; Government Accountability Project, 2006; Kohn, Kohn & Colapinto, 2006; Project on Government Oversight, 2006).

The cognitive appraisal approach to emotions holds that different emotions are associated with differences in the way an individual appraises his/her circumstances (Smith and Ellsworth, 1985). The theory identifies six appraisal dimensions: pleasantness, self/other responsibility, attentional activity, anticipated effort, certainty and human/situational control. Anger is associated with certainty regarding outcomes and the belief that one can take control of events, while fear is associated with uncertainty regarding outcomes and the belief that events are beyond one's control. As for the effects of emotions on future judgments and behaviors, Lerner and Keltner (2000, 2001) posited that each emotion has its own "appraisal tendency," or propensity to judge future events in line with the appraisal dimensions of that particular emotion. Lazarus (1991) assigned action tendencies to each emotion, including approach/attack for anger, avoidance/escape for fear.

Thus, the assessments posited by the traditional whistle-blowing model and the resulting attributions posited by the social information processing model can give rise to a variety of emotions, including anger and fear. We can infer the following relationships between anger and fear on one hand and whistle-blowing behaviors on the other:

Proposition 1:   *Anger predicts whistle-blowing over inactive observation.*

Proposition 2:   *Fear of retaliation predicts inactive observation over whistle-blowing.*

Gundlach et al. (2003) also expect anger to predict whistle-blowing and fear to predict inactive observation. The contribution of the present model is the integration of the cognitive appraisal perspective, while Gundlach et al. (2003) derive their propositions from attribution theory.

Value conflict and integrative complexity

Potential whistle-blowers who observe activities that they consider wrongful may experience a value conflict as they decide if and how to respond. For example, if the conclusion of their "recognition and assessment" judgments is that a wrongdoing is due to controllable and intentional acts by company officials, they may have conflicting loyalties to the public welfare and their employer (Graham, 1986). They may try to balance perceived moral/ethical obligations with their commitment to support their families (Jensen, 1987). They may hold strong allegiances to extra-organizational principles, like the right to free speech or a professional code of ethics (Graham, 1986; Rothschild and Miethe, 1994; Van Dyne et al., 1995). Whistle-blowers in Brewer and Selden (1998) reported feeling an "extended sense of responsibility" when confronted with a moral or ethical dilemma.

Tetlock's (1986) value pluralism model proposes that a person will think about an issue in integratively complex ways to the degree that the issue activates a conflict among values that the person holds as both (a) important and (b) approximately equally important. Weak value conflict, which occurs when conflicting values are of unequal strength, can be resolved by denying the less important value and bolstering the more important one (Abelson, 1959; cf. Festinger, 1964). Moderate value conflict can be resolved by screening options based on the most important value, then the next-most-important value, etc. (a.k.a. elimination by aspects; Tversky, 1972). The most intense levels of value conflict engender integrated strategies that specify the conditions under which one or another value should prevail, consider when reasonable individuals would assign different weights to the same values, and place the conflict in a broader, systemic context (Abelson, 1959; Tetlock et al., 1996).

Integrative complexity is a cognitive style that refers to the structure of thought – specifically, to the dimensionality of thought – rather than to the content (Harvey et al., 1961; Schroder et al., 1967; Streufert, 1978; Streufert and Streufert, 1978). Integrative complexity consists of two components. The first, differentiation, refers to the number of bipolar (thesis-antithesis) dimensions or categories that a person uses to conceptualize, organize and understand a phenomenon (Streufert and Nogami, 1989; Tetlock and Tyler, 1996). The more dimensions a person uses, the more his/her thinking and judgments are based on non-evaluative information (Schroder, 1971). The second component, integration, refers to the interrelations a person makes between differentiated dimensions. These interrelations are ways of or rules for resolving dialectical contradictions, such as explaining how reasonable people can view the same events differently or specifying the forms that trade-offs between conflicting values should take under various circumstances. Integration is impossible without prior differentiation (Streufert and Nogami, 1989; Tetlock and Tyler, 1996). Because it is systematic and effortful, integratively complex thinking is believed to occur only under conditions of high motivational involvement to solve a problem, such as strong value conflict (Kruglanski, 1996).

We can expect the value pluralism model to operate as follows in the whistle-blowing context, consistent with existing theory:

Proposition 3: *Stronger value conflict predicts more integratively complex thoughts among potential whistle-blowers.*

Interactions between emotions and value conflict/integrative complexity

Value conflicts may trigger emotions as well as cognitions. Taboo trade-offs, for example, are decisions that pit a sacred value, like life or liberty, against a secular value, like profit or efficiency (Fiske and Tetlock, 1997). Taboo trade-offs represent weak-value-conflict dilemmas because of how socially unacceptable it is to even consider choosing the secular value. Thus, they are boundary conditions for complex trade-off reasoning (Tetlock et al., 1996; Tetlock, 2000).

Tetlock et al. (2000) found that people who engage in taboo trade-offs provoke moral outrage among observers. This anger yields a particularly harsh mindset, dubbed the "intuitive prosecutor," that features simpler, more punitive attribution heuristics for inferring responsibility and assumptions of responsibility to defend the social or moral order (Goldberg et al., 1999). Scholars of emotion have found that strong emotional states like outrage can inhibit complex information processing and enhance the need for cognitive closure in other contexts, as well (Isen and Patrick, 1983; Isen and Geva, 1987; Suedfeld, 1992).

In the whistle-blowing context, observers of a wrongdoing that represents a taboo trade-off (e.g., toxic dumping to cut waste disposal costs) may express anger at the perpetrators or the organization and adopt a prosecutorial mindset as they seek to restore the moral order.

Proposition 4:   *Taboo trade-offs will provoke more expressions of anger, weaker value conflict, and lower integrative complexity than will non-taboo-trade-offs.*

The low integrative complexity that results from a weak-value-conflict situation like a taboo trade-off should moderate the main effect of anger on whistle-blowing decisions, as follows:

Proposition 5:   *The likelihood that anger will result in whistle-blowing will be stronger to the extent that value conflict is weak and integrative complexity is low.*

Thus,

Proposition 6:   *Taboo trade-offs predict whistle-blowing more than do non-taboo trade-offs.*

As noted above, individuals facing a whistle-blowing decision may experience their own value conflict as they choose between protecting the community (by blowing the whistle) and being a loyal employee (by remaining inactive observers). These types of conflicts are known as tragic trade-offs because they pit two sacred values against one another (Tetlock et al., 2000).

Because they entail strong value conflict, tragic trade-offs promote integratively complex thinking. Luckily, observers do not penalize actors for weighing tragic trade-offs. In fact, the longer individuals deliberate over a tragic trade-off, the wiser and more judicious observers deem them to be, regardless of the decision ultimately made (Tetlock et al., 2000).

The traditional and social information processing models of the whistle-blowing decision process include potential whistle-blowers' cost-benefit analyses of the risk of retaliation. While evidence of these assessments is strong – potential whistle-blowers often cite retaliation by management as a major risk factor in their decision processes – the outcome of these assessments is likely not simply a numerical estimate, but also an emotion or combination of emotions (Glazer and Glazer, 1989; Rothschild and Miethe, 1994). Further, the fear of retaliation may be an expression of the sacred value of protecting one's family, as retaliation may take the form of termination and loss of livelihood.

Proposition 7: *Tragic trade-offs will provoke more expressions of fear, stronger value conflict and higher integrative complexity than will non-tragic-trade-offs.*

The high integrative complexity that results from a strong-value-conflict situation like a tragic trade-off should moderate the main effect of fear on whistle-blowing decisions. Specifically, complex trade-off thinking that legitimizes both sides of a value conflict may facilitate an observer's choice of the less-risky course of action.

Proposition 8: *The likelihood that fear will result in inactive observation will be stronger to the extent that value conflict is strong and, therefore, that integrative complexity is high.*

Thus,

Proposition 9: *Tragic trade-offs predict inactive observation more than do non-tragic trade-offs.*

The prediction that fear of retaliation will be associated with integratively complex thinking would seem to contradict the threat-rigidity thesis, which holds that severe environmental threats lead to restricted information processing (Staw et al., 1981). However, the threat-rigidity thesis concerns an existing or imminent danger, while potential whistle-blowers are considering inviting a possible danger. The dimensions of certainty and time may allow potential whistle-blowers to engage in proactive integratively complex thinking rather than reactive integratively simple thinking.

Conclusion and Future Directions

Gundlach et al. (2003: 116) argued that "the most fruitful area of research [within whistle-blowing] is the investigation of how…emotions shape whistle-blowing decisions." This paper extends whistle-blowing scholarship by adding emotions and values – i.e., "hot" cognitions – to the traditional whistle-blowing model, which relies on "cold" economic calculations and cost-benefit analyses to explain the judgments and actions of potential whistle-blowers.

The model proposed here highlights the reciprocal influence of "hot" and "cold" cognitions, and the propositions identify the main effect of emotions on reporting decisions and the moderating effect of integrative complexity (which emerges from value conflict) on emotions. This model goes beyond the social information processing model of whistle-blowing (Gundlach et al., 2003) by demonstrating the potential effects of observers' attributions for perceived wrongdoing through the cognitive appraisal approach to emotions and the social-functional value pluralism model.

Because cognitive appraisal theory posits a unique appraisal tendency for each emotion, the proposed model can be used to predict distinct types of reporting behaviors, rather than just simple report/ no report decisions. For example, future work will explore the effect of hope on whistle-blowing decisions. The core relational theme of hope is fear of the worst but yearning for better, and its action tendency is vigilance/ commitment (Lazarus, 1991). Thus, hope may predict whistle-blowing to authorities within an organization (i.e., circumventions of the internal chain of command), while anger may predict whistle-blowing to external authorities (e.g., government or law-enforcement agencies).

In addition, both cognitive appraisal theory and the value pluralism model recognize the multiplicity of emotions and value conflicts that may be active simultaneously in a given situation. The proposed model facilitates explorations of the effects of combinations of emotions and varieties of value conflict on whistle-blowing judgments and decisions, and future work will pursue this question, as well.

References

Abelson, R. P.: 1959, 'Modes of Resolution of Belief Dilemmas', *Journal of Conflict Resolution* 3: 343–352.

Betancourt, H. and I. Blair: 1992, 'A Cognition (Attribution)-Emotion Model of Violence in Conflict Situations', *Personality and Social Psychology Bulletin* 18: 343–350.

Brewer, G. A. and S. C. Selden: 1998, 'Whistle Blowers in the Federal Civil Service: New Evidence of the Public Service Ethic', *Journal of Public Administration Research and Theory* 3: 413–439.

Dozier, J. B. and M. P. Miceli: 1985, 'Potential Predictors of Whistle-Blowing: A Prosocial Behavior Perspective', *Academy of Management Review* 10: 823–836.

Ellsworth, P. C. and C. A. Smith: 1988, 'From Appraisal to Emotion: Differences Among Unpleasant Feelings', *Motivation and Emotion* 12: 271–302.

Festinger, L.: 1964, *Conflict, Decision, and Dissonance* (Stanford University Press, Stanford, CA).

Fiske, A. P. and P. E. Tetlock: 1997, 'Taboo Trade-Offs: Reactions to Transactions That Transgress the Spheres of Justice', *Political Psychology* 18: 255–297.

Glazer, M. P. and P. M. Glazer: 1989, *The Whistleblowers: Exposing Corruption in Government and Industry* (Basic Books, Inc, New York).

Goldberg, J. H., J. S. Lerner and P. E. Tetlock: 1999, 'Rage and Reason: The Psychology of the Intuitive Prosecutor', *European Journal of Social Psychology* 29: 781–795.

Government Accountability Project: 2006, http://www.whistleblower.org/template/index.cfm.

Graham, J. W.: 1986, 'Principled Organizational Dissent: A Theoretical Essay', in B. M. Staw and L. L. Cummings (eds.), *Research in Organizational Behavior*, Volume 8 (JAI Press, Greenwich, CT); pp. 1–52.

Greenberger, D. B., M. P. Miceli and D. J. Cohen: 1987, 'Oppositionists and Group Norms: The Reciprocal Influence of Whistle-Blowers and Co-Workers', *Journal of Business Ethics* 6: 527–542.

Gundlach, M. J., S. C. Douglas and M. J. Martinko: 2003, 'The Decision to Blow the Whistle: A Social Information Processing Framework', *Academy of Management Review* 28: 107–123.

Harvey, O. J., D. Hunt and H. M. Schroder: 1961, *Conceptual Systems and Personality Organization* (Wiley, New York).

Hirschman, A. O.: 1970, *Exit, Voice, and Loyalty: Responses to Decline in Firms, Organizations, and States* (Harvard University Press, Cambridge, MA).

Isen, A. M. and N. Geva: 1987, 'The Influence of Positive Affect on Acceptable Level of Risk: The Person With a Large Canoe Has a Large Worry', *Organizational Behavior and Human Decision Processes* 39: 145–154.

Isen, A. M. and R. Patrick: 1983, 'The Effect of Positive Feelings on Risk Taking: When the Chips Are Down', *Organizational Behavior and Human Performance* 31: 194–202.

Jensen, J. V.: 1987, 'Ethical Tension Points in Whistle-Blowing', *Journal of Business Ethics* 6: 321–328.

Jones, T. M.: 1991, 'Ethical Decision Making by Individuals in Organizations: An Issue-Contingent Model', *Academy of Management Review* 16: 366–395.

Keenan, J. P.: 1995, 'Whistle-Blowing and the First-Level Manager: Determinants of Feeling Obliged to Blow the Whistle', *Journal of Social Behavior and Personality* 10: 571–584.

Kohlberg, L.: 1969, 'Stage and Sequence: The Cognitive-Developmental Approach to Socialization', in D. A. Goslin (ed.), *Handbook of Socialization Theory and Research* (Rand-McNally, Chicago); pp. 347–480.

Kohn, Kohn & Colapinto: 2006, http://www.kkc.com/index.jsp.

Kruglanski, A. W.: 1996, 'Motivated Social Cognition: Principles of the Interface', in E. T. Higgins and A. W. Kruglanski (eds.), *Social Psychology: A Handbook of Basic Principles* (Guilford, New York); pp. 493–522.

Latané, B. and J. M. Darley: 1970, *The Unresponsive Bystander: Why Doesn't He Help?* (Appleton-Century Crofts, New York).

Lazarus, R. S.: 1991, *Emotion and Adaptation* (Oxford University Press, New York).

Lerner, J. S. and D. Keltner: 2000, 'Beyond Valence: Toward a Model of Emotion-Specific Influences on Judgment and Choice', *Cognition and Emotion* 14: 473–493.

Lerner, J. S. and D. Keltner: 2001, 'Fear, Anger, and Risk', *Journal of Personality and Social Psychology* 81: 146–159.

March, J. G. and H. A. Simon: 1958, *Organizations* (Wiley, New York).

McLain, D. L. and J. P. Keenan: 1999, 'Risk, Information, and the Decision About Response to Wrongdoing in an Organization', *Journal of Business Ethics* 19: 255–271.

Miceli, M. P. and J. P. Near: 1984, 'The Relationships Among Beliefs, Organizational Position, and Whistle-Blowing Status: A Discriminant Analysis', *Academy of Management Journal* 27: 687–705.

Miceli, M. P. and J. P. Near: 1985, 'Characteristics of Organizational Climate and Perceived Wrongdoing Associated With Whistle-Blowing Decisions', *Personnel Psychology* 38: 525–544.

Miceli, M. P. and J. P. Near: 1988, 'Individual and Situational Correlates of Whistle-Blowing', *Personnel Psychology* 41: 267–281.

Miceli, M. P. and J. P. Near: 1991, 'Whistle-Blowing as an Organizational Process', in A. Bacharach, E. J. Lawler, S. B. Bacharach and D. Torres (eds.), *Research in the Sociology of Organizations* (JAI Press, Greenwich, CT); pp. 139–200.

Miceli, M. P. and J. P. Near: 1992, *Blowing the Whistle: The Organizational and Legal Implications for Companies and Employees* (Lexington Books, Lexington, MA).

Miceli, M. P. and J. P. Near: 1997, 'Whistle-Blowing as Antisocial Behavior', in R. Giacalone and J. Greenberg (eds.), *Antisocial Behavior in Organizations* (Sage Publications, Inc, Thousand Oaks, CA); pp. 130–149.

Miceli, M. P., J. B. Dozier and J. P. Near: 1991, 'Blowing the Whistle on Data Fudging: A Controlled Field Experiment', *Journal of Applied Psychology* 21: 271–295.

Miceli, M. P., B. L. Roach and J. P. Near: 1988, 'The Motivations of Anonymous Whistle-Blowers: The Case of Federal Employees', *Public Personnel Management* 17: 281–296.

Nader, R., P. J. Petkas and K. Blackwell (eds.): 1972, *Whistle Blowing: The Report of the Conference on Professional Responsibility* (Grossman Publishers, New York).

Near, J. P. and M. P. Miceli: 1985, 'Organizational Dissidence: The Case of Whistle-Blowing', *Journal of Business Ethics* 4: 1–16.

Near, J. P. and M. P. Miceli: 1987, 'Whistle-Blowers in Organizations: Dissidents or Reformers?', in B. M. Staw and L. L. Cummings (eds.), *Research in Organizational Behavior, Volume 9* (JAI Press, Greenwich, CT); pp. 321–368.

Near, J. P. and M. P. Miceli: 1996, 'Whistle-Blowing: Myth and Reality', *Journal of Management* 22: 507–526.

Parmerlee, M. A., J. P. Near and T. C. Jensen: 1982, 'Correlates of Whistle-Blowers' Perceptions of Organizational Retaliation', *Administrative Science Quarterly* 27: 17–34.

Pfeffer, J. and G. R. Salancik: 1978, *The External Control of Organizations: A Resource Dependence Perspective* (Harper and Row, New York).

Project on Government Oversight: 2006, http://www.pogo.org/p/x/expose corruption.html.

Rothschild, J. and T. D. Miethe: 1994, 'Whistleblowing as Resistance in Modern Work Organizations', in J. M.

Jermier, D. Knights and W. R. Nord (eds.), *Resistance and Power in Organizations* (Routledge, London); pp. 252–273.

Rusbult, C. E., D. Farrell, G. Rogers and A. G. Mainous III: 1988, 'Impact of Exchange Variables on Exit, Voice, Loyalty, and Neglect: An Integrative Model of Responses to Declining Job Satisfaction', *Academy of Management Journal* 31: 599–627.

Schmidt, G. and B. Weiner: 1988, 'An Attribution-Affect-Action Theory of Behavior: Replications of Judgements of Help-Giving', *Personality and Social Psychology Bulletin* 14: 610–621.

Schroder, H. M.: 1971, 'Conceptual Complexity and Personality Organization', in H. M. Schroder and P. Suedfeld (eds.), *Personality Theory and Information Processing* (Ronald, New York); pp. 240–273.

Schroder, H. M., M. J. Driver and S. Streufert: 1967, *Human Information Processing* (Holt, Rinehart and Winston, New York).

Smith, C. A. and P. C. Ellsworth: 1985, 'Patterns of Cognitive Appraisal in Emotion', *Journal of Personality and Social Psychology* 48: 813–838.

Staw, B. M., L. E. Sandelands and J. E. Dutton: 1981, 'Threat Rigidity Effects in Organizational Behavior: A Multilevel Analysis', *Administrative Science Quarterly* 26: 501–524.

Streufert, S.: 1978, 'The Human Component in the Decision Making Situation', in B. King, S. Streufert and F. Fiedler (eds.), *Managerial Control and Organizational Democracy* (V.H. Winston and Sons and Halstead Division, John Wiley and Sons, Washington, D. C. and New York, NY).

Streufert, S. and G. Y. Nogami: 1989, 'Cognitive Style and Complexity: Implications for I/O Psychology', in C. L. Cooper and I. Robertson (eds.), *International Review of Industrial and Organizational Psychology* (John Wiley and Sons, Inc, New York); pp. 93–143.

Streufert, S. and S. C. Streufert: 1978, *Behavior in the Complex Environment* (V. H. Winston and Sons and Halstead Division, John Wiley and Sons, Washington, D. C. and New York, NY).

Suedfeld, P.: 1992, 'Cognitive Managers and Their Critics', *Political Psychology* 13: 435–453.

Tetlock, P. E.: 1986, 'A Value Pluralism Model of Ideological Reasoning', *Journal of Personality and Social Psychology* 50: 819–827.

Tetlock, P. E.: 2000, 'Coping With Trade-Offs: Psychological Constraints and Political Implications', in A. Lupia, M. D. McCubbins and S. L. Popkin (eds.), *Elements of Reason: Cognition, Choice, and the Bounds of Rationality* (Cambridge University Press, New York).

Tetlock, P. E. and A. Tyler: 1996, 'Churchill's Cognitive and Rhetorical Style: The Debates Over Nazi Intentions and Self-Government for India', *Political Psychology* 17: 149–170.

Tetlock, P., O. Kristel, S. Elson, M. Green and J. Lerner: 2000, 'The Psychology of the Unthinkable: Taboo Trade-Offs, Forbidden Base Rates, and Heretical Counterfactuals', *Journal of Personality and Social Psychology* 78: 853–870.

Tetlock, P. E., R. S. Peterson and J. S. Lerner: 1996, 'Revising the Value Pluralism Model: Incorporating Social Content and Context Postulates', in C. Seligman, J. M. Olson and M. P. Zanna (eds.), *The Psychology of Values: The Ontario Symposium, Volume 8* (Lawrence Erlbaum Associates, Mahwah, NJ); pp. 25–51.

Tversky, A.: 1972, 'Elimination by Aspects: A Theory of Choice', *Psychological Review* 79: 281–299.

Van Dyne, L., L. L. Cummings and J. McLean Parks: 1995, 'Extra-Role Behaviors: In Pursuit of Construct, Definitional Clarity (A Bridge Over Muddied Waters)', in L. L. Cummings and B. M. Staw (eds.), *Research in Organizational Behavior, Volume 17* (JAI Press, Greenwich, CT); pp. 215–285.

Vroom, V. H.: 1964, *Work and Motivation* (John Wiley and Sons, Inc, New York).

Weiner, B.: 1985, 'An Attributional Theory of Achievement Motivation and Emotion', *Psychological Review* 92: 548–573.

Weiner, B.: 1986, 'Attribution, Emotion, and Action', in R. M. Sorrentino and E. T. Higgins (eds.), *Handbook of Motivation and Cognition: Foundations of Social Behavior* (Guilford Press, New York, NY); pp. 281–312.

Weiner, B., J. Amirkhan, V. S. Folkes and J. A. Verette: 1987, 'An Attributional Analysis of Excuse Giving: Studies of a Naïve Theory of Emotion', *Journal of Personality and Social Psychology* 52: 316–324.

Weiner, B., S. Graham and C. Chandler: 1982, 'Pity, Anger, and Guilt: An Attributional Analysis', *Personality and Social Psychology Bulletin* 8: 226–232.

Westin, A. F. (ed.): 1981, *Whistle-Blowing! Loyalty and Dissent in the Corporation* (McGraw-Hill Book Company, New York).

Evaluating a Case Study
Applying Ethical Issues

You are finally at the last stage of the process of evaluating ethical cases. By this point, you have (a) chosen a practical ethical viewpoint (including the choice of an ethical theory and practical linking principles, whose point of view you will adopt), (b) listed professional, ethical, and cost issues, and (c) annotated the issues lists by examining how embedded each issue is to the essential nature of the case at hand. What remains is to come to an action decision once these three steps have been completed. The final step is to discuss your conclusions. To do this, you must enter an argumentative phase. In this phase, I suggest that you create brainstorming sheets headed by the possible courses of action open to you. Prepare an argument on each sheet to support that particular course of action utilizing the annotated charts you have already prepared. Then compare what you believe to be the pivotal issues that drive each argument. Use your chosen ethical theory to decide which issue is most compelling. Be prepared to defend your action recommendation.

Let us return to the case of contraception in the less-developed countries. As you may recall, the case discussed in Chapter 4 was as follows.[1] You are a regional director at the World Health Organization. One of your duties is to supervise the distribution of birth control devices to women in less-developed countries. The product of choice has been the intrauterine device (IUD), which has proved to be effective and inexpensive.

The problem is that in the United States, several hundred users of the IUD have contracted pelvic inflammatory infections that have been linked to use of the IUD. Pelvic inflammatory infection can cause sterility and death. As a result, you have seriously considered removing IUDs from the list of approved birth control devices for the population control program.

As discussed in Chapter 4, ABC Corporation, a large multinational company, has a considerable inventory of IUDs that it cannot sell in the United States. The company would rather not write off its entire inventory and has consequently made a very attractive offer to sell the World Health Organization all of its existing inventory and to assist in distributing the product regionally.

As regional director, you must decide whether to accept ABC's offer to supply IUDs to women in less-developed countries.

Remember that in this case, the professional practice, ethical issues and cost considerations were deeply embedded, which creates an intractable conflict; there is no simple way to justify one instead of the other.

What you must do is (a) consult your worldview and see what it dictates that you do and (b) consult the ethical theory of your deepest convictions and see what it dictates that you do. Is there a synonymy between these? If not, then engage in a conversation between your worldview and the professional practice. Let each inform on the other. In the end, you should be able to come to some resolution.[2]

One step in this direction is to examine the arguments that support each position. What are the critical premises in these arguments?[3] In any argument, there is a conclusion. If you want to contrast two arguments, you must begin by contrasting two conclusions. Conclusions are supported by premises that (logically) cause the acceptance of the conclusion. Therefore, what you must do is to create at least two arguments that logically entail different conclusions. To do this, create brainstorming lists on the *key issue(s)* involved in the argument. The key issue of the disputation is that concept that makes all the difference. This case has a number of key issues. Let us try to construct arguments that are both for and against the position.

sample "Pro" Brainstorming Sheet for the Position

Position to be supported: Accept ABC Corporation's offer and continue to provide IUDs to women in less-developed countries.

Key Thoughts on the Subject

1. As a public health professional, you are enjoined to benefit the greatest number of people possible in your health policy.
2. It is a fact that in less-developed countries, millions die of starvation each year. The simple cause of starvation is too many people for the available food. When you decrease the number of people (given a level food source), more people can eat.
3. There are "blips" on any project. In this case, it is a few hundred or so cases of pelvic inflammatory disease. These casualties pale when compared to the number who will benefit from continuing to provide IUDs.
4. Utilitarian ethical theory dictates that the general good supersedes any individual's good.
5. In less-developed countries, the general good is advanced by continuing to distribute IUDs since more people (by far) benefit than are hurt.
6. ABC Corporation is willing to give a large discount on its present inventory and to provide some assistance in distributing the product regionally This will allow the organization to reach more people than ever before and thus fulfill the agency's mission.

Argument

1. In countries that have a limited amount of food that would feed only a certain population (n), increases in the population ($n + x$) will result in x not having enough food to live—fact.

2. Many less-developed countries experience the conditions mentioned in premise 1—assertion.
3. In many less-developed countries, x increase in population will result in y number of people starving to death—1, 2.
4. Many children who are born are not planned—assertion.
5. If you subtract the number of unplanned births from the total birth rate, the number of births would decrease significantly—assertion.
6. If all children were planned, the number (more than x) of births would decrease significantly—assertion.
7. If all children were planned, less-developed countries would not experience starvation (given constant crop production)—3–6.
8. The IUD is the most effective birth control device in less-developed countries—assertion.
9. The imperative of professional conduct in public health is to help as many people as possible—fact.
10. Public health professional standards dictate that the IUD be provided to women in less-developed countries—7, 8.
11. ABC Corporation is making an offer to provide the World Health Organization with substantial savings on the purchase of its IUD inventory and to assist in distribution—fact.
12. ABC Corporation's offer will allow the World Health Organization to reach more women than previously planned—fact.
13. Cost considerations bolster the professional practice—9–12.
14. The IUD poses potential health risks to some (less than 5 percent)—fact.
15. The ethical imperative of Utilitarianism dictates that the right ethical decision is to advance the cause of the common good—fact.
16. More people in less-developed countries are helped by distributing IUDs than are hurt by doing so—fact.
17. Utilitarianism dictates that IUDs should be provided to women in less-developed countries—14–17.
18. The regional director should accept ABC Corporation's offer and continue to distribute IUDs to women in less-developed countries—10, 13, 17.

Sample Brainstorming Sheet Against the Position

Position to be supported: Reject ABC Corporation's offer and stop selling IUDs in less-developed countries.

Key Thoughts on the Subject

1. As a public health professional, you are enjoined to benefit the greatest number of people possible through your health policy.
2. It is a fact that in less-developed countries, millions die of starvation each year. The simple cause of starvation is too many people for the available food. When

you decrease the number of people (given a level food source), more people can eat.

3. There are "blips" on any project. In this case, it is a few hundred or so cases of pelvic inflammatory disease. These casualties pale when compared to the number who will benefit from continuing to provide IUDs.

4. Human life is precious. No amount of practical gain can weigh against one human life.

5. Ends do not justify the means. One may have a very good end in mind, but unless the means to that end are just, the end cannot be willed.

Argument

1. In countries that have a limited amount of food that would feed only a certain population, (n), increases in the population $(n + x)$ will result in x not having enough food to live—fact.

2. Many less-developed countries experience the conditions mentioned in premise 1—assertion.

3. In many less-developed countries, x increase in population will result in y number of people starving to death—1, 2.

4. Many children who are born are not planned—assertion.

5. If you subtract the number of unplanned births from the total birth rate, the number of births would decrease significantly—assertion.

6. If all children were planned, the number (more than x) of births would decrease significantly—assertion.

7. If all children were planned, less-developed countries would not experience starvation (given constant crop production)—3–6.

8. The IUD is the most effective birth control device in less-developed countries—assertion.

9. The imperative of professional conduct in public health is to help as many people as possible—fact.

10. Public health professional standards dictate that the IUD be provided to women in less-developed countries—7, 8, 9.

11. The IUD poses potential health risks (less than 5 percent)—fact.

12. It is absolutely ethically impermissible (under Deontology)—no matter what the practical advantage—to knowingly jeopardize the essential health of any person—assertion.

13. ABC Corporation's offer is attractive from a mere cost perspective—fact.

14. It is absolutely ethically impermissible to provide IUDs to women in less-developed countries when they have been shown to be deleterious to the health of Americans—11, 12, 13.

15. In cases of conflict, an absolute ethical imperative trumps an absolute professional standards imperative—assertion.

16. The director must reject ABC Corporation's offer and halt the distribution of IUDs to women in less-developed countries—10, 14, 15.

Obviously, the crucial difference in these two arguments is the choice of an ethical theory and the way it is interpreted. Thus, whether a person takes a pro or con position is a function of the underlying value system that person holds. The way a person chooses a value system and the broader practical viewpoint is through the person's worldview and its accompanying baggage.

You must determine how to apply your practical ethical viewpoint. This requires careful attention to the theory and the linking principles you have chosen and the way they affect your evaluation of actual cases. To be an authentic seeker of truth, you must engage in this dialectical process. To do less is to diminish yourself as a person.

You are now ready to evaluate a case study.

Macro and Micro Cases[4]

Macro Case 1. You are the accounting liaison at the European Central Bank. You've just received a report from Betty Agathos, an accountant at Platinum-Women Investment Bank that had vouched for Greece's compliance with the EU's monitory over four years. Ms. Agathos has come out as a whistle-blower against Platinum-Women's previous glowing reports certifying Greece's compliance. Ms. Agathos maintains several very *troubling* red flags, but no *smoking gun*. Your job is to make sure everything runs smoothly. Should you follow-up on a report written by someone who has already lost her job for writing this? Set out what you recommend as a response to the Director of the European Central Bank—be sure to give both practical and ethical reasons.

Macro Case 2. You are the vice-president of student affairs (dean of students) at a private university. A student group that claims that the company that manufacturers the university's licensed or logo clothing employs sweatshops has protested this practice. You took the group's demands under advisement and decided to research its claims. Your research through two different sources indicates, to your amazement, that the claims are correct. The apparel is manufactured in the United States by illegal workers who are paid less than half the minimum wage for working a 60-hour week in non–OSHA conditions. Your information is from sources that could be used as evidence in court.

Therefore, you decide to contact the owner of the company, Mr. Big:

"I have heard from sources that the apparel that you are manufacturing for our university is produced in sweatshops."

"Where'd you hear that from, eh? We don't do none of that here. We run a clean business. Made in the U.S.A. What could be better than that?" said Mr. Big.

"Well, would you mind if we had the plant investigated officially so that we might be sure of your compliance?"

"Inspections ain't in our contract. What are you thinking about? You know when you allow inspections, it becomes public record and then your competition comes in and takes advantage of it. I don't think that we're in the mood for that. No, sir. We have a contract with you, and we expect to fulfill it. If you renege on us, we have a battery of lawyers on retainer. They'd love to take you to court and earn an end-of-the-year bonus."

You find that the university has a contract with the company to provide the specified apparel. This contract runs for one more year. If your supplier is in violation of the law, then the contract is broken, but the burden of proof is on the university to prove it. To prove malfeasance, you must conduct an investigation yourself (which is costly) or you must go to the authorities (which might result in a civil suit). Personally, you do not wish to encourage the sweatshops. The board of trustees of the university has shown little interest in this issue. Its concern is the bottom line.

What do you do? How do you justify your decision?

Macro Case 3. You are director of Human Resources Development at a major U.S. auto corporation. Following a recent settlement with a major Japanese auto maker over sexual harassment, the interest in the practices of employees and supervisors at auto manufacturing plant has increased. The problem is that most of the personnel attracted to assembly line jobs have a certain free-wheeling spirit that is often expressed in jokes, discussion, and behavior that many might consider offensive. However, it is impossible to prohibit all off-color jokes, sexist statements, and political and/or social opinions because they are ingrained in the behavior of many employees. They laugh at sensitivity training.

In a recent directors' meeting, someone suggested that the only way to completely "purify" the workplace is to set up a system of secret police who would create a network of informers to identify miscreants. By making an example of key offenders, the company might be able to avoid a potential lawsuit.

You want to create a work environment that is free from harassment, yet you are not sure that the cure is better than the illness. Write a memo to the directors outlining the course of action you believe should be taken and your reasons.

Macro Case 4. You are the city manager of Belleview, North Carolina, population approximately 200,000, located near the Research Triangle. Recently you issued a request for proposals for a new road to be constructed that will link two north-south roads. The cost of the project is $185 million. You had planned to have three companies work on the project. Belleview's municipal guidelines require minority contractors to be a part of the team. You have bids from seven teams, and the top four are from white-owned construction firms. Numbers five and seven are from minority-owned firms. Your feasibility study concluded that three was the best number of firms to work on the job, but a fourth could be added, although it would be inefficient. A fifth is out of the question.

You know that if race were not an issue, the process would be simple. You also know that affirmative action has received strong opposition lately. Federal courts recently released similar communities in a neighboring state from affirmative action requirements.

You are conflicted. You believe in a diverse America that serves and nurtures the needs of all peoples, yet you are a servant of the people of North Carolina and of Belleview. Write a report describing your position using issues of practicality and ethics to draw your final conclusion as to which firms to hire.

Macro Case 5. You are on the board of directors of a small to mid-size company that engineers software designed to solve crucial problems encountered in e-commerce. Since its inception ten years ago, employees of the company have worked extremely long hours and have received very low pay (but generous stock options). The board of directors is about to evaluate a gender bias complaint. It has been suggested that the long hours and hectic schedules discriminate against women since they bear most of the child care responsibilities. Child care is not available for all hours the company is open, nor does it provide for children who are ill or need special attention.

The frenetic pace of this company is not unusual for firms in the industry. If the company responds positively to this complaint, it might open itself to policies contrary to those that have resulted in much of its success. You muse that perhaps some work isn't appropriate for women with families. The men with families at the company are doing well. Is it your company's responsibility to be at the vanguard of some sort of social policy? If the women who made the complaint do not like the working conditions, then they can find work elsewhere; no one is forcing them to stay. However, outsiders might consider this to be gender discrimination. You have to bring up this issue to the board. Write a report highlighting the professional practice, ethical, and cost considerations and use them to support an action plan.

Micro Case 1. It's 2008 and you are an accountant at Platinum-Women Investment Bank. Your boss, Mike Wright, has asked you to review and approve your assessment of the sovereign country, Greece, concerning their compliance to macroeconomic policy as they promised to do as a condition to joining the eurozone. The report will be sent to the European Central Bank. You detect several serious red flags: contradictions from the data given and specifics mentioned in the notes on income and tax revenues. You bring these serious red flags to the attention of your boss. He says that he will look into it. But you follow up later on your own and discover that Mike Wright has sent your report forward without any of your reservations. It is as if you have given your professional *stamp of approval*. This bothers you so you confront Mike Wright on this. He prevaricates as he replies in logical gibberish. He pats you on the head for you to go on your way. But this doesn't sit right for you. If Greece has been submitting false reports, then the whole eurozone is at stake. You have a liaison at the European Central Bank. If you disclose to him your fears, then it might cost you your job. If you remain silent, it may cost the euro its very existence. What do you do and *why*?

Micro Case 2. You are a store manager at the Zap (a low-priced clothing store that markets to teens and those in their early twenties). You do the ordering for the store. On a buying trip, your visit to a major supplier, X-Z Liners, disturbs you. After you return home, you contact the garment workers union and discover that your fears were well founded—X-Z Liners is running a sweatshop.

At present, 15 percent of your merchandise is from X-Z Liners. You have strong personal and ethical beliefs about sweatshops. However, you realize that if you drop X-Z Liners as a supplier, your average costs will rise. When average costs rise, you risk losing your customers to other stores such as Bald Eagle Outfitters. Your spouse and family depend on your salary to pay the bills. What should you do? Do you bring in another line and risk losing business and your job? Do you forget your values and ignore the situation (after all, other stores buy from X-Z)? You are going to have to discuss this with your spouse. Write a defense of the position you plan to take.

Micro Case 3. You are an African-American male who works in a financial services company as a broker. You have just been informed that a sexual harassment complaint has been filed against you by a female co-worker. This has struck you like a lightning bolt; you cannot imagine what caused this complaint. You immediately think of your uncle who was fired from his position at Eastern-Western State College after forty years of service for supposedly referring to one of his twenty-year-old students as a "girl" (he was sixty-seven at the time).

You are not a ladies' man. You have had sexual relations with only one woman not your wife, and that was before you met your wife. You do not make lewd remarks. You do have fundamentalist Christian values and believe the passages in the Bible about a woman being subservient to her husband. You believe that this is a position dictated by God. Plenty of passages in the Bible support your beliefs.

The complaint states that your attitudes about women (albeit religiously motivated, although the complainant is an atheist) create a hostile work environment.

Write your response to this charge or write the charges that the woman making the complaint might bring.[5]

Micro Case 4. You are a woman attorney working in a prestigious law firm in a large city. You desire to become a partner, but you have noticed that the firm's partners (and from what you can tell, those at comparable firms) seem to (a) be very aggressive, (b) be highly competitive, (c) be convinced that every dispute must be resolved to the firm's considerable advantage (i.e., equitable resolutions that do not financially benefit the firm are considered to be failures), and (d) work long billable hours no matter what the personal cost. This combination does not agree with your personal worldview; you believe in being accommodating (when possible), but you do not believe in structuring deals that benefit one side at the expense of another. You value consensus is based on fairness and working hard, but your job is not your life. There is more to you than being an attorney.

Your problem is that you are in a profession in that seems to demand changing your values to meet the expectations of the norm. What do you do? You love the law and believe that it can work to promote your worldview. However, it appears that if you maintain your values, you will be unsuccessful in your profession (since the other top firms operate in the same fashion). If you change, you will feel that you have sold your soul.

Clarify your thoughts on this issue, and then write a report that examines your options. Then describe a particular action plan.

Micro Case 5. You are a twenty-eight-year-old first-generation Mexican American and are a registered nurse with a master's certification in geriatric care from the top school in your area. You and your husband make about the same salary and are somewhat financially leveraged with respect to your first home mortgage. You and your husband have two children and balance child care responsibilities with some help from your mother-in-law.

You are employed by A-B-C Health Care Corp., one of the nation's largest health insurance companies. A-B-C assigns you to four geriatric cases a day, which is a reasonable number. You go to the insured's home to perform the tasks that fall under your job description. However, there are problems. Your clients are generally economically upper middle class, but few of them have the education you have. Despite this fact, they frequently ask if you understand them, because you speak with a Spanish accent, they assume that you barely speak English, and they talk condescendingly to you. Because of their concept of you, they often ask you to perform tasks that are not in your job description, such as lifting heavy objects and doing housework. You feel sorry for these people, and you have a great affinity for the elderly. But you believe that you should be afforded some respect for who you are and what you do. Sometimes you became so angry that you want to quit. You can talk to your clients, of course, but they respond only to edicts from the company, which they trust because it is 100 percent American. You took this job knowing it would be tough, but sometimes it seems that it is more than you can bear. Jobs are difficult to find. If you go too far, you might lose your job and your salary, which is necessary to meet your mortgage payment.

Before you discuss the situation with your husband, who is very supportive, list the problems and what you plan to do about them.

Notes

1   I have heard that many of the structural problems with the IUD that caused pelvic inflammatory infection have now been rectified. I am not competent to comment on this; nevertheless, for this case, let us assume that these problems still obtain.

2   This dialectical interaction is described in Chapter 8 of *Basic Ethics*.

3   See my book, *Critical Inquiry* (Boulder, CO: Westview, 2010) on the details of this process.

4   For more on macro and micro cases, see the overview on p. 138.

5   This case is based on the actual experience of a former student.

The Context of Business
Nationally and Internationally

General Overview: So far in this book we have examined corporations via their definition, practices, and ethical issues within. This final chapter connects with the second in that it is about the context of business. Chapter 2 set this context as abstract theories of economic justice. In this final chapter the context is rather more concrete: the national and international environment that reciprocally interacts with corporations and how they can sustain profits.

Since the line between national and international has long since disappeared for large corporations, they are combined here. One crucial instance of this was in the financial crisis that was evidenced in 2008 (though some say June, 2007 is more accurate). There were two driving forces to this recession: the financial services industry and the housing bubble (in the US and elsewhere). New exotic financial services products, such as the credit default swaps that parsed a typical mortage many times more that was traditionally the case, and insurance on these products (that was not properly underwritten) created a context of overly speculative behavior that was not tagged as such. Some also say that the interaction between retail banking and investment banking that had become easier in the 1990s exacerbated this lack of information on the products that were being bought in many large investment portfolios.

A second perennial issue in international business practices is bribing. This practice brings to the fore the difference between the realist and anti-realist ethical positions described in Chapter 1. If there is a realist standard that bribery is wrong, then corporations should be punished for this practice. If antirealist standards hold true, then laws against bribery amount to cultural imperialism.

Finally, there is the issue of just what economic globalization is all about? How is it good, and how is it bad? What can we do to limit the excesses so that we get more good than bad?

A. The Financial Services Industry

Overview: This section begins with an essay by Ronald Duska. Duska begins by setting out the facts that the winners in the financial services industry are very well compensated. But being "very well compensated" does not constitute a crime in a modified capitalistic system. What we need to do as we explore "corruption" in the financial services industry is to look first to the purpose of markets. The ultimate purpose of markets is the production and exchange of goods and services.

This mission is not carried out when the purpose of financial markets is distorted because of greed and proper roles are abandoned because of the desire for profit. In these instances the entire system is corrupted.

The essay then turns to the individual perspective: financial services professionals. Society determines the rules for selling and trading. The ethical rules are very straightforward. However, people are fallible. In these cases, individual misdeeds occur. This is due to a lack of integrity on the part on the individual. Financial planners, for example, can run into conflicts of interest in the advice they give and the products that they represent (and are compensated for). Duska then lists a series of other potential misdeeds by individual professionals.

In the end, an Aristotelian call to examine functional purpose and staying on track with it is the best remedy for both individual and institutional corruption.

David E. McClean is both a university professor and a financial services professional. He has a rare oversight from both the theoretical perspective and the practical perspective. McClean begins with situating his article in the environment of cultural politics that examines broadly questions having to do with the organization of society and its social institutions. This is a communitarian perspective. From this vantage point, McClean begins his examination with the financial product called a "derivative." This product was often examined in the news media during the 2008–2009 financial crisis. McClean shows how derivatives are legitimate financial products. He then situates how derivatives and collateralized debt obligations fit into the financial crisis. It is McClean's contention that it is not the products themselves, but the lack of stewardship, that is to be faulted for the resultant debacle.

In the end, McClean believes that the best way to understand what happened in the financial crisis is to return to the broad shared community worldview of cultural politics that situates the purpose of financial institutions within the macro goals of the US (or any other national economy). Without some synergy between mission and in-the-trenches activity, there will always be crises as vague understandings are undercut by particularized strategies about how to work in the system. The broad vision must get into contact with boots on the ground.

The last essay in this section comes from Behnaz Z. Quigley and Mary Jane Eichorn. The authors are accountants and are interested in how to spot red flags on flagrant financial fraud—using examples of the most horrific thieves: Bernie Madoff and Ivar Kreuger. Laws and regulations alone are not the answer in preventing fraud, argue the authors. In the area of fraud, history continues to repeat itself. In 2008 Bernard L. Madoff was arrested for major investment fraudulent activities. In the 1920s Ivar Kreuger was known as the Match King and had international government match monopolies. Their stories are similar. It appears that Madoff used Kreuger's scheme as his template. Criminologists have borrowed from the fields of economics, sociology, and psychology to predict white collar criminal behavior. In this paper the authors focus on the supporting theories which underlie the fraud triangle / diamond: rationalization, incentive (pressure / motivation), opportunity, and capability are discussed in detecting fraudulent activities. From the authors comparison of Madoff and Kreuger, they contend that people who commit fraud appear to have the capability to control and manipulate others. In addition, red flags are often present when fraud is committed. However, it is the lack of due diligence by the auditors and principal investors that allows the fraud to continue. Therefore, due diligence is a requirement for investment activities and in the auditing process—including proactive assessments.

B. Global Business: Bribing

Overview: One of the most persistent problems in the international marketplace is that of bribery. This is a nagging problem because making "payments" to various officials to obtain contracts is ingrained in the way business is conducted in much of the world. It is a part of the shared community worldview in these countries. The issue is how US businesses should deal with officials in countries that follow a business standard that differs from US practice and is illegal in the USA.

Issues related to bribery are developed in Michael Philips's article. He argues that, in some contexts, accepting a bribe violates no promises or agreements and that in some cases there is no prima facie duty to refrain from offering a bribe.

The force of Philips's argument is to define what constitutes a bribe. His original definitions revolve around the taking of money to disobey the shared community worldview. But what if the shared community worldview were corrupt? This is to suggest that taking and accepting the bribe *simpliciter* are not sufficient for moral condemnation. The only time that this *is not* the case is when the bribe is offered in an environment that is free from taint of prior wrongdoing. Finally, unless there is a clear quid pro quo relationship, the bribe may merely be part of a cultural institution of gift exchange.

Thomas L. Carson replies to Philips by asserting that bribery is essentially wrong because it violates an implicit or explicit promise made to social and political institutions to act in accordance with the rules of that institution. For example, in athletics, the implicit agreement is that the athlete will perform to the best of his or her ability in the pursuit of victory. To do less (for example, when one is paid money to subvert that compact) is to act immorally. Since the duties involved are prima facie, they may be overridden by more primary moral duties.

An article by Scott Turow ends this section with a legal perspective on this issue. In the article he offers the following definition: "Bribery occurs when property or personal advantage is offered, without the authority of law, to a public official with the intent that the public official act favorably to the offeror at any time or fashion in the execution of the public official's duties." This is a narrower definition than used in the previous essays. In this case, the offer (to a public official) is itself sufficient to make the act immoral because all public officials have a duty to treat similar cases the same.

Giving a bribe materially changes things. The public official has a new and conflicting interest that is intended to make that public official abrogate her duty to the public at large. Thus, according to Turow, bribery of public officials undermines moral public institutions and threatens any society that claims to be based on ethical principles.

C. Globalization

Overview: 'Globalization' has a very wide set of meanings. In economics it refers to free trade without tariffs. In the grand vision, this extends further to the creation of a global marketplace in which all the processes involved with production are centered in the country best suited for it. So for example, if you are manufacturing high-end men's suits, you would seek quality tailors who will work for the lowest wages—anywhere in the world. Also, you would seek sources of cotton and silk from the cheapest suppliers. You would also seek the fewest number of governmental regulations and a stable society (relatively free from violence and discord) to locate your manufacturing center. The point is to maximize efficiencies over the globe to produce the best product at the lowest price.

The net effect of globalization is to promote interdependence between sovereign nations. Advocates say that this new world order with its overlapping of interests (caused by the process of production being split up among countries) will begin a process of global development. Much as the Zeroth Law of Thermodynamics dictates that equilibrium will be achieved by an outlier to a thermal system that has contact, so also does economic globalization suggest that the interdependence of countries in the world market will promote wider development throughout. This wider development model aspires to raise people from poverty and to promote democracy and world cooperation.

Critics of economic globalization as it is presently being carried out cite that the big losers are often manufacturing workers in developed nations (such as the G-8) who have benefits, safe working conditions, and union protection. These critics say that they will only get on board the globalization train if minimum working condition standards are set throughout the world. Otherwise, these critics say, the story changes from one in which international development is enhanced to one in which workers are kept at low wages and exploited by multinational corporations who want to make their extra profits on the backs of the poor of the world, who have few options.

Into this fray steps Farhad Rassekh with a generally positive appraisal of the promise of globalization based on what has already come to be. Rassekh begins by quoting Jeffrey Sachs, "Globalization, more than anything else, has reduced the number of extreme poor in India by two hundred million and in China by three hundred million since 1990." These are impressive numbers.

Rassekh then proceeds to give a history of globalization in the context of world poverty. He presents his case in detail with statistical foundation. He then extends from poverty, as such, to wellbeing (much as Amyarta Sen also does). If he is right, then economic globalization is a policy that cosmopolitans will all endorse.

But what of the detractors? Rassekh discusses these, too. He sets out their various arguments and offers considered refutation. Because economic globalization has been an orthodox part of mainstream economic theory for over 50 years, there is a good deal of weight behind Rassekh's arguments.

In the second essay, Nien-hê Hsieh harkens back to the opening of this book: Jeffrey Reiman's essay on negative rights in an expanded liberal context. The players in Hsieh's universe are the activities of multinational enterprises (MNEs). Many who write in the liberal context do not set out many instances of *harm*. (Remember, that advocates of the negative duty approach, believe that duties are only engaged when one actively engages in harming someone.) Hsieh begins his analysis with duties of forbearance. When seen in the context of the United Nations Declaration of Human Rights, there is some ambiguity about what it means to forebear from doing harm. What sort of side-constraints would be necessary to meet this requirement? Hsieh then examines possibilities for positive duty obligations. The complication in how one understands contexts for goods produced in a variety of venues makes such judgments more difficult.

If one seeks a different *piecemeal* approach some of these complications are more manageable. Since we are not committed to complete comprehensive change, we can more readily focus on specific negative duties—such as noninterference. These are important consideration as we consider the realm of liberty and security rights.

Next Hsieh considers an objection to his approach from the writings of Henry Shue (an advocate of positive rights). What follows is an interesting argument in which Hsieh contends that his model based upon duties of forbearance is the best approach to guide the behavior of MNEs and make a real (though minimalist) difference in the way global business goes forward. Readers of Chapter 3 of the book will also appreciate Hsieh's description of the agency status of corporations as he formulates his argument. This is, indeed, an essay that connects various parts of this book.

A. The Financial Services Industry

Ethics in Financial Services
Systems and Individuals

Ronald Duska

"Some turn every quality or art into a means of getting wealth; this they conceive to be the end, and to the promotion of the end they think all things must contribute."
Aristotle, *Politics*, Bk. 1, Ch. 9., 1258a, 13–14

Introduction

It is not uncommon for those looking to apportion blame for our current financial predicament to point to "greedy CEOs and corporate fatcats" as the culprits who place our nation in the bind that it currently finds itself. It is interesting to note who the top income earners were before the collapse of the financial markets in 2008. According to *The New York Times*, reporting on an *Alpha Magazine* study of hedge fund managers, that distinction would go to John Paulson, who earned an estimated $3.7 billion in 2007 and $2 billion in 2008. The second highest earner was James Simons of Renaissance Technologies with estimated 2008 earnings of $2.5 billion and estimated 2007 earnings of $2.8 billion. George Soros of Soros Fund Management had estimated 2008 earnings of $1.1 billion and estimated 2007 earnings of $2.9 billion. John D. Arnold of Centarus Energy made an estimated $1.98 billion in 2007 and 2008, while Ray Dalio of Bridgewater Associates made a mere $1 billion in those two years.[1]

What's more, the *Financial Times* pointed out that the 10 best-paid hedge fund managers in 2007 earned more than the combined GDP of Afghanistan and Mongolia. "John Paulson, who topped the list with $3Bn, who could have purchased Bear Stearns almost three-times over out of his gross earnings that year! Forget that $100 m or so Goldman CEO Lloyd Blankfein is said to have earned in 2006—these guys wouldn't get out of bed for that."[2]

At the time of the financial collapse many were complaining about the unfairness of CEOs' salaries. It was thought they were being overcompensated. Yet, if we compare Paulson's $3 billion income to the income of Goldman Sach's CEO, Lloyd Blankenfein, we see that Paulson made 30 times more money in 2007 than Blankenfein's comparatively measly $100 million. Clearly, if there is something inordinate about CEOs' salaries, there is certainly something inordinate about the earnings of some hedge fund managers. A large portion of the earnings of hedge fund managers was made from dealing with credit default swaps, collateralized debt obligations (CDOs), and other exotic financial instruments, in the subprime mortgage market, and in some cases from shorting the very financial packages they assembled for others.

It is an interesting and related fact that, in December 2007, the Bank for International Settlements reported derivative trades tallying in at $681 trillion—10 times the gross domestic product of all the countries in the world combined. As the author of the bank's report said, "Somebody is obviously bluffing about the money being brought to the game, and that realization has made for some very jittery markets."[3]

Jaime Jaramillo, was prescient, when he observed in 1994, long before the financial market meltdown, that:

> Today's financial economy is nothing more than a "great big fantasy," where promises made by people, firms, or even computers are taken so seriously that they are regarded as wealth. This fantasy eases economic transactions and enhances efficiency only to the extent that the instruments used in it are trusted by economic agents, and the entire system ceases to function when faith in these instruments collapses. The state's role in financial markets is necessary because of the "fiat" nature of monetary and financial instruments.[4]

Thus, we have either outrageous gambling or, worse, rigged games. Consider that, in the midst of the financial turmoil, Goldman Sachs and Company sold a mortgage CDO to customers, the development of which was heavily influenced by John Paulson. However, in the marketing materials used to promote the transaction to investors, Goldman Sachs failed to disclose that Paulson had played a role in the portfolio selection process and also failed to disclose that Paulson had adverse economic interests. As a matter of fact, knowing it was largely "junk," Paulson shorted the CDO he helped put together.[5]

The Securities and Exchange Commission (SEC) charged Goldman Sachs with misconduct and Goldman paid a record $550 million to settle the charges. In paying the fine Goldman made the following statement:

> Goldman acknowledges that the marketing materials for the ABACUS 2007-AC1 transaction contained incomplete information. In particular, it was a mistake for the Goldman marketing materials to state that the reference portfolio was "selected by" ACA Management LLC without disclosing the role of Paulson & Co. Inc. in the portfolio selection process and that Paulson's economic interests were adverse to CDO investors. Goldman regrets that the marketing materials did not contain that disclosure.[6]

Larry Kudlow of Cable National Broadcasting Company (CNBC) in musing about the case said the following:

> All this . . . raises the key question of whether Goldman Sachs' decision not to disclose Paulson's involvement was a correct judgment, or whether it was a material omission. It just seems to me that Goldman Sachs should have named Paulson in the offering circular for the CDO. They didn't. Is it because they didn't want investors to understand that this was a bear-market, short-the-bond CDO?
>
> Second point: Some highly placed, senior Wall Street sources who have been deeply engaged in structured mortgage-based CDOs tell me that this CDO in question was weak and appeared designed to unravel quickly. They go on to say, in general terms, that this CDO constructed by Goldman Sachs lacked sufficient cash; its covenants were weak; and it afforded less investor protection than usual in order to provide higher yields. This troubles me enormously.
>
> Creating something that's designed to fail? Well, you know what? If it's not illegal, it certainly appears unethical. So I must blame Goldman for this. Why sell it to customers if it's going to fail? Why go there in the first place? What kind of brokerage service is this?[7]

All these facts lead me to two ethical claims about the financial system. First: if the amount of money earned by CEOs is too much, the amount of money earned by hedge fund managers is obscene. Second: to the extent that such behavior is usual, the financial market system is corrupt, by which I mean many of the actors in it have failed to fulfill its legitimate purpose. I have in the past described this loss of purpose as losing one's soul.[8] I will return to that issue later.

I take it as a fundamental ethical principle that any social system is legitimated only if it serves the common good. I would argue that from society's point of view the fundamental purpose of business is not to maximize profit, but to create goods and services, that is, value.[9] Since financial services and financial markets are a subset of business activity, they must serve business's ultimate purpose, or else the tail will wag the dog. But, recently, financial markets have had a tendency to become independent entities of their own and subvert the common good. Hence the corruption.

In the light of the above, this paper will do five things:

1. Spell out more extensively the meaning of corruption.
2. Investigate what the legitimate purpose of financial markets is.
3. Inquire to what extent greed played a role in the corruption.
4. Show how financial markets lost sight of their purpose.
5. Consider the ethical role that individual financial services professionals play in the markets and their consequent role responsibility.

What Is Corruption?

As we indicated above, corruption can be viewed as a state of affairs which occurs when an individual, entity, or system does not perform as it was intended to perform, that is, it does not fulfill its purpose. According to Aristotle, all things aim at some good. Entities and activities come into existence for a reason. They have some purpose or use. Since goals energize and keep entities and activities alive and animated, not fulfilling that original purpose leads to a loss of vitality or the animating principle (which derives from the Latin word *animus*, which means "soul"). Now, any living entity (be it a system, institution, or individual) which fails to fulfill its purpose or function becomes corrupt and eventually dies away. That's why we associate the word "corruption" with rot and putrefaction. The recent market crisis shows the corruption in both government and financial markets.[10]

This corruption of markets, though, is not easy to recognize because it is abetted by a misconception of the true purpose of markets. Too often people think that the purpose of markets is to make profits for individuals. That view is not new. Markets do help people gain wealth, but that is not their societal purpose. While it is clearly the case that gaining wealth is an incentive to produce and exchange, incentives are not the same as purposes. The father of capitalism, Adam Smith, rightly noted that we would not get much market activity if there were no appeal to self-interest. He writes, "It is not from the benevolence of the butcher, the brewer or the baker, that we expect our dinner, but from their regard to their own interest."[11]

While Smith points out the obvious fact that self-interest is a great motivating factor and shows that self-interest is a great incentive to get people engaged in market activity, we should not confuse that incentive with the real purpose of the market. To confuse incentives with purposes is similar to confusing the engine of a plane with the destination of a plane. The engine is what drives you to your goal. It is not the goal. Accumulating wealth is what drives the market, but it is not the ultimate goal of markets. It is only a means to other more essential goals.

The ultimate purpose of markets is the production and exchange of goods and services. For any market to succeed, there need to be sectors which provide services necessary for the effective functioning of the market. There must be producers, consumers, traders, and any number of other actors fulfilling the roles necessary to have a vibrant and healthy market. Corporations or sectors of the economy can only survive in the long run if they provide a good or service that is needed. For example, we no longer need firemen on diesel train engines. Not everything needs to be sustained. Things that fulfill no purpose should die out.

The needs of society determine the purposes of financial markets. People need capital, loans, and money with which to purchase necessary items. To fulfill these purposes society has invented banks, insurance companies, and stock markets, along with any number of other agents, as well as financial instruments that are developed and sold by various actors in the financial markets. When the various sectors of the financial markets forget they are in business to provide those goods and services for clients, and concentrate solely on income generation, they fail to live up to their responsibility and become corrupted.

It is important to note that different sectors of the financial markets fulfill different needs. The responsibility of those in these sectors is to perform their role in such a way that it fulfills the specific needs of the clients. Let's examine a few.

One of the purposes of banks is to loan money. Banks make money doing that, but making money is not their purpose. Making money is the incentive to perform the business of servicing clients and customers well. For banks to persist they need to evaluate risk. It is unfair to their depositors to lend (depositors') money to those who are not creditworthy. Accountants exist to help give accurate and useful pictures of the financial holdings of companies. Rating agencies exist to give evaluations of the soundness of companies. The purpose of the hedge fund is to "hedge" or balance the risk of an investment when one's investments seem to be too extended. Becoming overleveraged, through buying short and long, is not prudent hedging—it is out and out gambling. If the solitary quest for profit in any of these sectors deflects them from fulfilling those functions, they are corrupted.

The fundamental goods in the financial services market are financial instruments. But instruments are things that are useful for other purposes. What is their basic purpose? What are they used for? Life insurance policies, annuities, securities, mutual funds, certificates of deposits (CDs), and other instruments are used to manage risk and provide financial security. They do not exist to be manipulated and arbitraged for the simple purpose of making more money for advisers or companies.

Given the above, it should be clear that there was rampant corruption leading to the economic crisis of 2008. Rating agencies failed in performing their tasks. Lending institutions failed by giving out loans to noncreditworthy individuals, thereby jeopardizing other clients. Accounting and auditing failed in their duty to make sure financial statements reflected the worth of the companies they were reporting on or auditing. Investment advisers like Madoff failed to fulfill their fiduciary duty. One's duty is not simply to be clever in doing something. One's duty is to fulfill one's role, which means fulfilling the purposes of that role. A clever financier can game the market and use his clients. An ethical financier will perform his or her function for the sake of the clients and public he or she serves.

That basic responsibility to serve the ends and purposes of the good of society was undermined by pursuing self-interest without constraint or regard for fulfilling their professional purpose. Ultimately, there seemed to be little concern for the good of the whole. In short, the pursuit of self-interest turned into selfishness, which is the unconstrained pursuit of self-interest at the expense of and without concern for others. That is the underlying corruption. Let's now turn to a consideration of the fundamental task and purpose of the financial markets.

The Purpose of Financial Markets

According to Robert Schenk,

> the primary purpose of financial markets is to allocate available savings to the most productive use. A well-functioning financial sector increases economic growth. If an economy does not allocate savings to the most productive uses, it will grow more slowly than it can grow.[12]

Joseph Stiglitz maintains that there are three important functions the financial markets serve: to allocate scarce capital more efficiently to benefit the rest of the economy; to manage risk; and to direct resources to the activities with the highest returns (i.e., to run the payment mechanism at low transaction costs). For Stiglitz, the stock market as one area of the financial market place is "first and foremost, a forum in which individuals can exchange risks. It affects the ability to raise capital (although it may also contribute to management's shortsightedness)." However, Stiglitz laments what it has become for "in the end, it is perhaps more a gambling casino than a venue in which funds are being raised to finance new ventures and expand existing activities ... new ventures typically must look elsewhere."[13]

One might then propose the thesis that the problem with financial markets is that they have turned into gambling casinos where wealth accumulation is the be all and end all of their activity, and hence they are not fulfilling their purpose. This is detrimental to the economies of the world, because, while financial markets create no goods, 40% of all profits are made in the financial sector. This straying from the basic purpose creates an opportunity for simply creating the fantasy world of financial instruments that Jaramillo warned about; where there is no "there" there.

> The ... free market would supposedly regulate itself. The problem with that approach is that regulations are just rules. If there are no rules, the players can cheat; and cheat they have, with a gambler's addiction. In December 2007, the Bank for International Settlements reported derivative trades tallying in at $681 trillion—ten times the gross domestic product of all the countries in the world combined.
>
> "Derivatives" are complex bank creations that are very hard to understand, but the basic idea is that you can insure an investment you want to go up by betting it will go down. The simplest form of derivative is a short sale: you can place a bet that some asset you own will go down, so that you are covered whichever way the asset moves.[14]

Financial systems mirror the complexities of a nation's economic system and its level of economic development, development being a normative term that implies a desirable end point. Financial markets are the bedrock of the financial system. As we saw, their purpose is to allocate savings efficiently to parties who use funds for investment in real assets or financial assets. An optimal allocation function will channel savings to the most productive use of those savings. In the US system the mediator in the allocation process is price, and price in a financial system is usually described in terms of an interest rate. Efficiency of allocation is critical to assure adequate capital formation and economic growth in a modern economy. System efficiency is achieved when the price reflected in the market is an equilibrium price; that is, a market clearing price. If disequilibrium exists, rapid adjustment to a new equilibrium is guaranteed. Efficiency will occur more readily if the number of buyers and sellers is large, both parties to a transaction easily obtain information, and transaction costs are kept to a minimum.

Is Greed a Factor in the Corruption?

There is a great deal of writing on the present fiscal crisis that claims the chief cause of the financial meltdown is greed on Wall Street. It is beyond an ethicist's expertise to comment on all the various economic factors, such as the use of credit default swaps as a form of reinsurance, or the causes of the failure of the rating agencies, or the leveraging of mortgage debt that led to the market freeze and collapse. But perhaps we can investigate the ethical claim that greed was the cause. Greed may have been one of the causes, but I think that is too simple. It leaves greed undefined. In a way, the present crisis has been aptly described as the perfect storm: too easy credit, too much leveraging, not enough information, overoptimistic ratings, easy money, and the desire of the public to acquire without the requisite thrift. Is that simply greed, avariciousness, or is it more subtle? I think a more complete answer is that the meltdown was the consequence of the promotion and adoption of an acquisitive form of life across all sectors of the economy. Human nature is what it is. Human beings look out for their own advantage. But the ethic that constrained that pursuit of self-interest was moribund.

We have already seen how Adam Smith recognized the power of self-interest. His famous quote about butchers and bakers continues: "We address ourselves not to their humanity but to their self-love, and never talk to them of our own necessities but of their advantages."[15] It is this addressing of people's advantages that makes capitalism so successful. But, by addressing people's self-love, are we promoting greed? If one looks at Max Weber, we can see that in many ways the recent collapse of the markets can be attributed to what he, in his classic work *The Protestant Ethic and the Spirit of Capitalism*, identified as the spirit of capitalism, a spirit that looks awfully like greed. For Weber, capitalism is involved in "the single minded pursuit of profit and forever renewed profit."[16] According to Weber, such a pursuit is what gives the capitalist society its shape or form of life. For him any business operating in a wholly capitalistic society, which does not always take advantage of opportunities for profit making, is doomed to extinction. But I would argue that single-mindedness is monomaniacal and such an unchecked pursuit of profit as a goal is an extreme, leading one to corruption.

Aristotle, the always temperate philosopher, would assert that virtue is always a golden mean and a vice is always an extreme. Oftentimes, in financial market transactions the unfettered pursuit of wealth for its own sake is paramount. How else can one explain, not the millions, but the billions of dollars of profit? As we saw, Aristotle describes the practice of accumulating wealth for the sake of accumulating wealth as greed. He deems greed unnatural and inordinate (out of order) in the sense that it is against the purpose of human beings, because the purpose of human beings is to live well, and the single-minded quest for wealth cannot be sufficient for living well. Rather, it corrupts the human being. Aristotle took note of those who "turn every quality or art into a means of getting wealth; this they conceive to be the end, and to the promotion of that end they think all things must contribute." Clearly for Aristotle, this is a picture of someone corrupt. Like Midas, those who accumulate wealth for its own sake are, "intent upon living only, and not upon living well."[17]

This would be analogous to the for-profit corporations if the sole purpose of existence of a corporation was the ever-increasing reach for more and more profit. In that case, the corporation loses its main purpose—the reason society allows it to flourish and exist—which is to produce goods or services. The pursuit of profit overrides concerns for those for whom the good or service is provided. This explains clearly what happened at places like Enron, and perhaps at some of the large commercial banks.

An examination of the recent cases of ethical lapses (in the sense of no one fulfilling their ethical responsibilities) in financial markets shows that the refocusing from the goals of production (What is a bank for? Who is it to serve? For what societal ends?) to the goal of financial growth has been an overriding cause of the collapse of the market.

The action of the traders does not seem to be rooted in some deep-seated evil cause. Rather it seems they were motivated by old-fashioned greed. Forgetting their major purpose, it appears they took on projects simply to accumulate wealth—for the company and the executives. This inordinate greed led to the corruption of the company. As we saw, where greed rules, there are no limits. What begins as a necessary service in a financial world became corrupted by forgetting what it was about . . . what it was for. If the only goal is to maximize wealth or profit, by definition there is no end—no place to stop. To maximize means there is never enough.

But Adam Smith never thought that way. He asserted that the pursuit of self-advantage is indeed a good thing, so that "Every man . . . is left perfectly free to pursue his own interest his own way, and to bring both his industry and capital into competition with those of any other man, or order of men."[18] But he puts a limit on that: "as long as he does not violate the laws of justice."

If we take justice to mean everyone gets his or her due, or if justice is balance, then one achieves the balance by doing what is to one's advantage, but always keeping in mind the purpose of one's pursuit. Commercial pursuits are necessarily societal. They involve others and the purpose of working for others. What does a lender owe the borrower? What is a mortgage company for? Is giving someone a mortgage they cannot afford, giving them their due? Is providing someone noncreditworthy with credit, giving them or the other stakeholders their due? Is failing to appraise securities properly giving those who trust the ratings their due? What is a bank for? What is a rating agency for? What are financial markets for? Is helping to destroy trust by failing to disclose giving society its due?

Losing Sight of the Purpose of Financial Markets

In an important book, *Infectious Greed*, Frank Partnoy gives a host of stunning examples, which eerily remind us of the situation today, where fundamental purposes were forgotten, and hence the balance required by justice was lost.[19] As far back as 1987, at Banker's Trust, Andy Krieger was successful in using currency options to manipulate unregulated currency markets with over the counter transactions. Krieger's success at Banker's Trust led Charles Sanford, the CEO, to encourage traders to speculate with bank's capital. Why? For the sake of ever-increasing profits. What began as investment that exploited inefficiencies in the market led to speculation when the inefficiencies were discovered and fully dried up. Speculation is never the primary business of a bank and engagement in it can lead to the downfall of a bank, as it did in the case of Banker's Trust. In that case, as Partnoy points out, "Investment positions [were] even hidden from investors at Banker's Trust . . . [but] there was nothing illegal about it."[20]

Another example is Gibson's Greetings, Inc., a company that produced and sold greeting cards. Gibson's Greetings got involved in interest-rate swaps on their loans, which at the time, in early 1992, yielded a profit of $260,000. The swaps were used to hedge debt and became, for a short time, profit generators. That is until interest rates went up. In 1993 Gibson got involved in $96 million worth of swaps. According to Partnoy, Banker's Trust, which took no risk, "made about $13 million from the swaps with Gibson, all of which supposedly began as an effort to find a low-cost hedge for a simple fixed-rate debt."[21] Gibson, instead of concentrating on the production of greeting cards, the purpose of its company, became an outright gambler for the sake of easy profits. Banker's Trust, instead of looking out for the interest of its client, Gibson, looked to its own bottom line.

Is Weber right? Is the collapse into greed a necessary aspect of the free market system? One would hope not, and the constant notion that certain behavior is scandalous underlies the fact that there is still an ethos that seeks human fulfillment, and recognizes that it won't be achieved by the pursuit of wealth for its own sake. Just as Midas awoke to the fact that his lust for gold kept him from achieving other more important goals, an enlightened society sees that profit maximization is not enough, because there is never enough. However, given the propensity of human beings to look out for their own advantage, we need to set up incentives that reward responsible behavior with worthwhile goals.

Aristotle pointed out that there are more things necessary to living well than the solitary pursuit of wealth. Businesses which discover the importance of serving their stakeholders will not only flourish as outstanding corporate citizens, they will provide a model of integrity for all to follow and be the foundation of trust that is necessary for markets to operate efficiently for the benefit of society.

In summary, the financial system is the complex array of financial markets, securities, and institutions that interact in facilitating the movement of capital among savers and borrowers. That financial system is also used for mediation of risk among parties. In the best possible model, this is all accomplished in a very efficient and hopefully ethical manner. But underlying all this is the belief that the other party can be trusted in the exchange. Once trust is gone, the market will not operate. If however, the system is gamed for the sake of ever-increasing profits, greed has taken over, the gatekeepers become the predators, and the foxes guard the chickens.

Financial markets have a role and purpose in society, but when that purpose is distorted because of greed and the proper role is abandoned for the sake of profit, the entire system gets corrupted. What has happened over and over again is that the markets have been manipulated and financial instruments misused. There are legitimate uses and purposes for hedges, special purpose entities (SPEs), derivatives, and swaps, such as to handle risk management. But, when accumulation is pursued and rewarded for its own sake, those purposes are forgotten.

Financial Services Professionals

Up to this point we have looked at the corruption of the system of financial markets. In spite of the systemic risks and corrupt practices, there are groups of financial services professionals who sell the various financial instruments and products. We will complete this article by looking briefly at their ethical responsibilities. Clearly, if Goldman's mortgage CDO was defective, and a broker knew that, he should not sell it.

There are various types of microbehavior within the market system that need to be examined. Generally there is agreement that a number of practices such as fraud, stock manipulation, and churning are unethical. However, there are also practices in financial dealings where it is unclear whether and how those practices are unethical. Questions can be raised about the following sorts of issues, such as insider trading, tax shelters, income smoothing, conflicts of interest, independence, demutualization, confidentiality and privacy, conflicting loyalties between clients and companies, and the responsibilities of professionalism among others.

Is insider trading really wrong? If so, what exactly is wrong with it? How much disclosure is necessary in sales of financial instruments? How much disclosure is necessary in financial statements that show the financial strengths and weaknesses of a company? Should mutual fund managers put themselves in unwarranted conflict of interest situations by engaging in private purchases of stocks that their company trades in? Should banks be able to sell insurance and investment products, and does such a capability create unnecessary conflicts of interest for them? Should one demutualize? What should the limits of privacy be in the credit industry? What climate should be created so that the interests of the broker do not conflict with those of his client? Do we need fee-based advising only, or is commission-based selling compatible with an agent's responsibility to give a client the best possible advice? Are financial service personnel professionals or simply salespeople, and what are their responsibilities as such?

Once again, the needs of society determine the purposes of the financial markets. Not everything needs to be sustained. Things that fulfill no purpose should die out. The ethical rules in the marketplace, even the marketplace of money, that individuals should follow, are fairly straightforward. Market transactions between individuals ought to be carried on without using others and without engaging in deception or fraud in accordance with one's role. However, human beings, being what they are, will for a variety of reasons fall short of fulfilling their responsibilities (and, in the worst cases, greedily and selfishly use others for their own gain). What follows is a list of ethically problematic ways of behaving in the financial services industry.

Perhaps the easiest form of being unethical is by lacking integrity. Ways of being deceitful or dishonest in the financial services industry include misrepresenting the financial product, including deceptive illustrations of possible returns, concealing risk factors, withholding full disclosure, misrepresenting one's ability, and other activities. Fraud is a legal concept and has specific meanings in specific instances, but generally involves "intentional misrepresentation, concealment, or omission of the truth for the purpose of deception or manipulation to the detriment of a person or organization."[22] Beyond deception and fraud, there are other ways of using a client, particularly in exchange situations, but possibly elsewhere, which involve coercing or manipulating the client, by fearmongering or other means.

A central concern in financial services arises from conflicts of interest. There is conflicting interest when either the broker or agent's interest is served by selling a product the client does not need or that is inferior to another product, typically a product that provides less remuneration to the salesperson. There is also conflict when an agent has two clients, and service to one will be detrimental to the other. If the interests in conflict are the interests of the agent against those of the client, professionalism demands that the agent subordinate his or her interests to those of the client. When the interests in conflict are those of two parties, both of whom the agent serves, solutions are more complex.

There are particularly difficult conflict of interest situations for accounting firms arising from providing external audit function for a publicly held firm while simultaneously selling consulting services to the same firm. Also, the audit function has inherent conflicts in balancing confidentiality to the client and duty to inform the public of possible illegal practices. The SEC has historically been concerned about the latter problem, but it is the mixing of auditing and consulting that concerns the SEC even more.

Financial planners routinely run into conflicts between the interests of their clients and the structure of fees for their services. There is an interesting juxtaposition in the field between fee-only planners and planners that sell product. A fee-only planner charges for their advice, but receives no commission from the client's implementation of that advice. Most planners are not fee only, rather do not overtly charge for their advice, but are remunerated through a commission on the implementation of that advice. This creates an interesting dilemma—does my advice purely service the needs of the client or do I shade my advice depending on the structure of a commission schedule?

In money management and investment banking, there are numerous examples of potential unethical practices, for example, money managers who trade personally in the securities their firms hold in portfolio. A manager with large holdings in a security can easily influence the price of that security as they buy and sell; therefore why not enter the market for a personal transaction before placing the firm's transaction. Investment bankers have ample opportunities to engage in practices that are either clearly a conflict of interest and often illegal, or border on a conflict of interest. Free riding and withholding securities from the public in an initial public offering (IPO) is illegal, but the temptation to compromise this rule is powerful when the issue is "hot"; that is, everyone knows the price will increase once the security begins to trade in the secondary market. In December 2000 the SEC commenced an investigation against three prominent investment banking firms for selectively providing shares of "hot" IPOs to certain clients. The investigation centered on a "quid pro quo" arrangement where the client is charged higher fees for other services in exchange for IPO shares that will surely rise in value.

Another unethical practice which occurs in the financial services industry is the scalping of securities: for example, an investment adviser who buys a security before recommending it, then selling out after the price has risen based on the recommendation. The most prominent case occurred in the 1980s, involving the *Wall Street Journal's* "Heard on the Street" column. This column was widely read and carefully followed by investors. The articles were very specific and often listed companies and recommendations, resulting in many readers buying upon the written recommendations. The author was accused of tipping off certain individuals about the contents of articles before they were published.

Cornering the market is obviously unethical and often illegal, especially when it is in direct violation of government regulations, as was the well-publicized case against Salomon Brothers in 1991. Salomon was one of the major primary dealers in US government securities. These dealers bid in the auctions for Treasury bills, notes, and bonds. The government has regulations concerning the percentage of successful bids that may go to individual firms, but firms may also bid for their customers. In one auction in early 1991 Salomon received over 80% of the offering under the pretense that a sizeable amount of the bids were for customers. In the subsequent investigation they were charged with illegal activity, but there was also evidence to suggest that Salomon had used agreements with customers that technically may not have been illegal, but surely bordered on the unethical given the intent of the government rules.

Companies can get involved in activities such as illegal dividend payments, where "dividend payments come out of capital surplus or that make the company insolvent,"[23] incestuous share dealing—buying and selling of shares in each other's companies to create a tax or other financial advantage,[24] compensation design, where they set up alternative forms of payment to allow agents to avoid rebating violations; discrimination in hiring and promoting; misrepresentation to new hires; invasion of privacy; and dubious claim settlement policies.

In insurance sales, there is needless replacement, and defective illustrations, which have been the basis of billion-dollar lawsuits against Prudential, New York Life, and Metropolitan Life among others. Brokers and agents get involved in churning accounts that benefit the agents at the expense of the clients. For brokers and dealers there is insistence on suitability rules, which demands you know and act in the best interests of the client you are selling to. There is a prohibition for financial planners and for those with control over clients' monies, as trustees or brokers or advisers, against commingling those funds with the financial service agent's.

For those on the exchanges, there is insider trading, which is, as the name implies, engaging in trading on the basis of inside information. This practice is viewed as unfair to other traders who do not have the information as it makes for an unequal playing field. There is free riding, in the form of withholding a new securities issue to resell later at a higher price, or in the form of buying and selling in rapid order without putting up money for the sale.

Finally, there are prohibitions against schemes such as pyramiding that build on nonexisting values, such as Ponzi schemes, rigging the market, manipulation, or running ahead (an analyst buying a stock before making the recommendation to buy to his or her client).[25]

Most of these unethical practices have in common, if not downright deception, the use of one's customers or clients for the benefit of the firm, the officers of the firm, or the financial services professional. This litany should help us begin to understand the tremendous range of possible conflicts of interest and outright possibilities of fraud in financial interaction. What can be done to avoid such problems?

Basic Ethical Principles: A Call to Reexamine Purpose

We have just provided a list of only some of the types of ethical misbehavior to occur in the financial services industry. Given the huge diversity of issues, what is the practical way to approach them? First, it would seem useful to come up with some general principles to follow. Second, it would be helpful to examine the various kinds of regulation governing financial services. Finally, it would seem helpful to examine how to make the environment more susceptible to ethical behavior. There is not time to deal adequately with these last issues, but we will briefly lay out some general principles.

Our experience show there are three valuable and overarching ethical principles that can be applied to the majority of issues in financial services: (1) avoid deception and fraud, (2) honor your commitments, (3) fulfill the true purpose of your professional role. Note that the different sectors of the financial markets fulfill different needs. The responsibility of those in these sectors is to perform the role in such a way that it fulfills those needs.

One can use the knowledge of financial markets to make predictions about what instruments will do, and that knowledge is important for the financial adviser. However, that knowledge can be used for good or ill. Integrity demands that one fulfill one's purpose. It demands aligning cleverness or skill with ends that serve those whom the professional is committed to serve. In the case of financial services professionals, that is the client. The primary purpose of the financial adviser is to give advice. That means determining and serving the needs of the advisee not the adviser. The adviser has a fiduciary responsibility to put the interests of the advisee first. Giving advice that is geared to enrich the adviser more than the advisee is not advice. It is corrupt behavior. It is the manipulation, by deceptive words, of the person for whose interests the adviser is supposed to look out.

It should be clear that there was rampant corruption leading to the economic crisis of 2008. Rating agencies failed in performing their tasks. Lending institutions failed by giving out loans to noncreditworthy individuals, thereby jeopardizing other clients. Accounting and auditing failed in their duty to make sure financial statements reflected the worth of the companies they were reporting on or auditing. Investment advisers like Madoff failed to fulfill their fiduciary duty. One's duty is not simply to be clever in doing something. One's duty is to fulfill one's role, which means fulfilling the purposes of that role. A clever financier can game the market and use his clients. An ethical financier will perform his or her function for the sake of the clients and public he or she serves.

As we said above, that basic responsibility to serve the ends and purposes of the good of society was undermined by pursuing self-interest without constraints and without a concern for the good of the whole. In short, the pursuit of self-interest turned into self-ishness, which is the unconstrained pursuit of self-interest at the expense of and without concern for others. That is the underlying corruption of financial markets.

Notes

1 Louise Story, "Top Hedge Fund Managers Do Well in a Down Year," *The New York Times*, March 24, 2009. Retrieved March 5, 2013 from http://www.nytimes.com/2009/03/25/business/25hedge.html

2 Vic Daniels, "And the Billy Big Bonus of 2007 Was . . . ," *HITC Business*, April 8, 2008. Retrieved March 5, 2013 from http://hereisthecity.com/2008/04/08/and_the_billy_big_bonus_of_200/

3 Bank for International Settlements, "BIS 77th Annual Report," June 24, 2007. Retrieved March 5, 2013 from http://www.bis.org/publ/arpdf/ar2007e.htm

4 Joseph E. Stiglitz, Jaime Jaramillo-Vallejo, and Yung Chal Park. 1994. "The Role of the State in Financial Markets." *Proceedings of the World Bank Annual Conference on Development: Economics Supplement*. Washington, DC: World Bank.

5 US Securities and Exchange Commission v. Goldman Sachs & Co. and Fabrice Tourre. Retrieved March 5, 2013 from http://www.scribd.com/doc/30032645/Goldman-Sachs-complaint Apr 16, 2010 11:22 EDT. For more on this we recommend three books: Michael Lewis, *The Big Short*, New York: Norton, 2010; Gretchen Morgenstern and Joshua Rosner, *Reckless Endangerment*, New York: Henry Holt, 2011; and William D. Cohan, *Money and Power*, New York: Anchor Books, 2011, among others.

6 US Securities and Exchange Commission, "Goldman Sachs to Pay Record $550 Million to Settle SEC Charges Related to Subprime Mortgage CDO," July 15, 2010. Retrieved March 5, 2013 from http://www.sec.gov/news/press/2010/2010-123.htm

7 Lawrence Kudlow, "The Case Against Goldman Sachs," *Kudlow's Money Politic$*, April 21, 2010. Retrieved March 5, 2013 from http://kudlowsmoney-politics.blogspot.com/2010/04/case-against-goldman-sachs.html

8 Ronald Duska and Julie Anne Ragatz. 2008. "How Losing Soul Leads to Corruption in Business." In Gabriel Flynn (ed.), *Leadership and Business Ethics*. Dordrecht: Springer.

9 Ronald Duska. 2007. "The Why's of Business Revisited." In *Contemporary Reflections on Business Ethics*. Dordrecht: Springer.

10 We would suggest that in this matter we can see similarities between the 20th-century philosopher Ludwig Wittgenstein and Aristotle. Two central claims for which Wittgenstein is famous are the claim that "The meaning is the use" and the claim that there are "forms of life" which constitute socio-logical relationships. According to Wittgenstein, we know what something is by knowing its use, what it is for, and that use constitutes a "form of life." Max Weber, in *The Protestant Ethic and the Spirit of Capitalism*, talks about the spirit of capitalism as being an ever-renewed search for profit. To tie these notions of Weber and Wittgenstein together, let me suggest that such a spirit (Geist) as Weber refers to constitutes for Wittgenstein a "form of life." The identification of form (formal cause) and purpose (final cause) is not only manifested in amorphous social organizations, it is also manifested in individual human beings. A person's purpose or ends is, in a sense, his or her soul, since those ends define what the person is. A person's mission (a collection of his or her ends) is the result of the person's commit-ments to particular projects and ideas. The mission one chooses defines their identity in a more mean-ingful manner than a description of their aggregate physical characteristics.

11 Adam Smith, *An Enquiry into the Nature and Causes of the Wealth of Nations*, I, ii, 2. Hereinafter referred to as WN.

12 Robert Schenk. n.d. "Overview: Financial Markets." Retrieved March 5, 2013 from http://ingrimayne.com/econ/Financial/Overview8ma.html

13 Stiglitz et al. 1994.

14 Dr. Ellen Brown, "Credit Default Swaps: Evolving Financial Meltdown and Derivative Disaster Du Jour," Global Research, April 11, 2008.

15 WN, I, ii, 2.

16   Max Weber. 1958. *The Protestant Ethic and the Spirit of Capitalism*. New York: Scribners; p. 17.

17   Aristotle, *Politics*, Book I, Ch. 9, 1258a.

18   WN, IV, ix, 51.

19   Frank Partnoy. 2003. *Infectious Greed*. New York: Henry Holt; p. 184.

20   Partnoy, *Infectious Greed*, p. 19, n. 24.

21   Partnoy, *Infectious Greed*, p. 53.

22   John Downes and Jordan Elliot Goodman. 2010. *Dictionary of Finance and Investment Terms*, 8th edition. Hauppage, NY: Barron's Educational Series, p. 148.

23   Downes and Goodman, *Dictionary of Finance and Investment Terms*, p. 174.

24   Downes and Goodman, *Dictionary of Finance and Investment Terms*, p. 175.

25   Downes and Goodman, *Dictionary of Finance and Investment Terms*, p. 352.

Derivatives and the Financial Crisis
Ethics, Stewardship, and Cultural Politics

David E. McClean

"Those of us who have looked to the self-interest of lending institutions to protect shareholders' equity, myself included, are in a state of shocked disbelief," [former Federal Reserve Chairman Alan Greenspan] told the House Committee on Oversight and Government Reform . . . "You had the authority to prevent irresponsible lending practices that led to the subprime mortgage crisis. You were advised to do so by many others," said Representative Henry A. Waxman of California, chairman of the committee. "Do you feel that your ideology pushed you to make decisions that you wish you had not made?" Mr. Greenspan conceded: "Yes, I've found a flaw. I don't know how significant or permanent it is. But I've been very distressed by that fact."

The New York Times, October 23, 2008

In what follows we will explore ethical issues concerning the creation and use of over the counter (OTC) financial derivatives. This is an exploration that is, arguably, worthy in its own right, but we will also consider larger questions and issues that have to do with how we draw ethical conclusions and engage in ethical deliberation in the face of complex and exigent commercial (and social) variables. There are a number of different ways to consider, critique, or reflect upon the power and role of derivatives subsequent to the financial crisis that took place (roughly) from 2007 through 2010. We will (a) consider where the singular ethical lapses were, if any, regarding the uses of derivatives, a market of more than $600 trillion (notional value, hereinafter, NV)—a gargantuan figure that, supposedly, posed and yet poses a huge threat to the stability of entire nations, and not just to the financial system comprised of commercial and investment banks and those firms that comprise the "buy side" of the markets—that is, investors such as mutual funds, hedge funds, pension funds, and the like. We will also (b) consider the realm of policy formation, that is, we will explore the role of regulators and lawmakers who, in their stewardship roles, allowed or paved the way for the use of certain derivative instruments, especially since 2000 when the Commodity Futures Modernization Act was passed by Congress—legislation that had very little to say about certain of what some have taken to be some of the most pernicious financial instruments ever devised (especially credit default swaps, or CDSs, which investment guru Warren Buffet dubbed "financial weapons of mass destruction"). Beyond this, we will, in closing (c), consider the debate about derivatives within the context of *cultural politics*, and the difficulties inherent in making ethical judgments about very complex practices and institutions, considering matters of risk management and corporate governance.

Before we proceed, a few words on cultural politics may be in order. Cultural politics has been aptly construed "not as something added to other more substantive domains but as an arena where social, economic, and political values and meanings are created and contested."[1] The frame of cultural politics permits us to ask more sweeping (and often more interesting) questions, questions that have to do with the organization of society and its social institutions—of civilization itself. This necessarily concerns values, and values are not always formed by the best uses of human intelligence but, often, by our animal spirits and prejudices, and by our scripted ways of seeing and organizing the world. What are the cultural politics of the derivatives debate, the debate about the need for and the extent to which there should be certain sorts of instrument called derivatives? Embedded within this question are other questions: What does the existence of more than $600 trillion (NV) say about the kinds of civilizations that have been constructed in (primarily) what is still called the West? What does the need for such instruments say about the hidden complexity that operates beneath the ordinary financial exchanges that are most ready to hand? Have we constructed civilizations that float upon seas of hubris, that is, assumptions that we can properly manage mind-numbing levels of complexity without the expectation of a series of "black swan" events? This may not sound like the normal fare for a business ethics text, but these are the sorts of questions that business managers and political leaders (and philosophers) should be asking themselves if they wish to help avert painful and world-disruptive crises in the future. It is by considering such questions that better policies may be constructed. On the other hand (and here is the twist), the cultural politics that has come to drive much of the hue and cry concerning derivatives may be misplaced, and may be part of a larger *anti*-finance, *anti*-business, *anti*-capitalist sentiment that itself may serve to undermine the construction of useful policy solutions concerning the creation, employment, and regulation of financial instruments and markets.

Derivatives, the Credit Crisis, and the Right to Contract

A "derivative" is generally defined as a financial contract, the value of which is "derived from" some other instrument(s), such as equities, bonds, or commodities. Given this rather broad definition, it becomes obvious that there are many plain

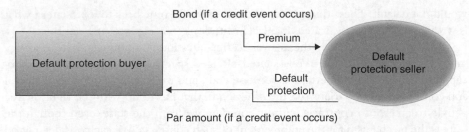

Figure 6.1 A basic credit default swap

vanilla investments that are "derivatives" but that do not spring to mind readily, along with the sorts of more sexy instruments that we have come to associate with the word. Mutual funds (i.e., mutual fund shares), for example, are "derivatives," since they fall under the definition just provided. A mutual fund share is itself a security, which invests in (usually) other securities, or other types of financial instrument. Clearly, a mutual fund share derives its value from the portfolio of other securities or financial instruments of which it represents a fractional ownership interest. The securities in the mutual fund portfolio derive their value from the success, or lack of success, of the businesses of which they represent a fractional interest of some kind, and so on.

But the sorts of derivatives that we will focus on here are those investment contracts that have been, somewhat arbitrarily, corralled to be the "proper" referent for the word "derivative." These include CDSs, total return swaps, and futures. In particular, we will be most concerned here with bilateral contracts such as CDSs. This is because, as of the printing of this book, CDSs are the type of derivative that has given rise to the most concern in recent years. Part of what we will explore here is why they have caused such alarm, whether there is something about the nature of these instruments that is morally problematic, and whether or not their existence represents something about the nature of finance, risk, and the public culture writ large.

Let us begin with the fact that, as defined, derivatives of the type we are considering are *contracts*. A CDS, for example, is a contract between two persons, usually non-natural persons (institutions), such as banks, hedge funds, and insurance companies, for the exchange of money or financial instruments under certain circumstances, that is, when there is a "credit event" or default on one or more credit instruments (bonds, for example), which are the referent instruments of the contract (see Figure 6.1). This type of derivative has all of the indicia of an insurance contract. The party seeking "protection" (or the "buyer of protection") is seeking to mitigate the risk that one or more credit instrument(s) in its portfolio will default. The "seller of protection" receives what have the indicia and function of insurance premiums for insuring the buyer of protection against loss.

For the moment, let us set aside the facts that CDSs were, prior to the credit crisis and subsequent economic downturn, regulated neither by state insurance commissions, nor by any federal agency. In the case of naked swaps (naked CDSs), that is, swaps where the buyer of protection has no actual exposure to loss, there was no regulation by state gaming (i.e., gambling) commissions either, even though these swaps were no more than bets (a gamble) that a referent credit or several referent credits would or would not default. These things aside for now (we will come back to them later), what is wrong with two sophisticated financial institutions entering into such contracts?

There are many who say the answer to this question is: nothing. There is a very sacrosanct freedom in the West, shared along a spectrum that contains anarcho-capitalists and extreme libertarians (on one end), and more nuanced forms of liberal and conservative libertarians (on the other end), that has to do with the right of free people to enter into contracts without interference from the state, even though the state is the mechanism for the enforcement of such contracts. We can consider a good many legal arguments and analyses, as well as a good many historical documents, to explore this fierce commitment to the right to freely contract, but the oft-cited Supreme Court case, *Lochner v. New York* (1905) (*Lochner*), is as good an exemplar as any. Joseph Lochner, the owner of a bakery, was convicted under a New York law that, for reasons of safety and the public interest, limited the number of hours bakery employees could work (no more than 10 hours per day and no more than 60 hours per week). Joseph Lochner argued that the law was "not a constitutional regulation of health and safety of a workplace under state police power." His argument was tested against New York's assumption that "The state has an interest in the health and safety of both the bakery workers as well as the quality of the bread that they make. Thus, these laws were passed under a valid exercise of the state's police power." Lochner is, among other things, a showdown between the camp that valorizes rights-based approaches to public policy and the camp that valorizes social utility-based approaches. In this case, the camp that valorized rights-based approaches, that is, the right of Joseph Lochner to enter into employment agreements with other freely consenting adults (and vice versa), won the day. The majority of the justices, in a narrow 5–4 decision, concluded as follows:

> [T]he power of the state to police the "liberty" of the individual to contract, which is protected by the 14th amendment, must be balanced against the state's interest. There is a limit on the police power of the states . . . The state's justification for this law under health and safety is a pretext because the public interest is not sufficiently affected by this act. There is no demonstrable causal link between labor hours of a baker and the quality of his product or his own health.

Justice John Marshall Harlan wrote a dissenting opinion in *Lochner*, arguing that:

> [T]he people of New York had decided that the health of an average man is endangered if he works more than 60 hours per week. Whether or not this is wise is not a question for the court to inquire. The only question for the court is whether the means devised by the state are germane to an end which may be lawfully accomplished and have a real or substantial relation to the protection of health of bakers. Common experience tells us that there is a logical relationship. There is abundant evidence that the workplace of a baker is hazardous to his health. Clearly, this is not a plain invasion of rights secured by "fundamental law."

Lochner was decided during a time in which the industrial tide, with all its promises for greater prosperity, was rising. That is, the social moment both favored and, perhaps, emboldened the Supreme Court to lay aside the generally hallowed notion of judicial restraint and play a more robust part in setting public policy that, in this case, favored business interests, establishing a robust right to contract that could ward off the states' attempts to create what they considered to be needed commercial reform.

In 1937 the court reconsidered its earlier position, in *West Coast Hotel Co. v. Parrish* (*Parrish*). In *Parrish*, the court let stand a Washington state law that required that women receive a minimum wage. The court indicated, quite clearly, that the right to contract was only relative to other exigent concerns. What we see in *Parrish* is another tradition in law, one that considers contracts from other than a rights-based point of view, that is, other than from the point of view of the inalienable rights or the "liberty" of the individual persons contracting. This tradition considers contracts from a more or less utilitarian perspective, one that undertook policy and judicial deliberation while leaning in the direction of social welfare considerations. Legal theorists of this persuasion, versed in economic thought, consider the real-world social advantages and disadvantages of contracts, among other things, arguing that the right to enter into certain contracts must be constrained even if the parties that would enter into them do so without coercion and in the absence of factors that would otherwise operate to undermine the contract, such as fraudulent inducement (although *Parrish* emphasized the imbalance in the bargaining position between employers and employees). For example, these theorists argue that efficiency and negative externalities matter as much as, if not more than, the rights of the parties seeking to contract. Thus, on this view, a policy maker would take into consideration the general social welfare and employ tools of economic analysis such as the Kaldor-Hicks criterion of efficiency/compensation principle, which holds that an outcome is more optimal from the perspective of utility if, at least in theory, those who gain from some change in policy (for example) would be in a position to compensate those who are made worse off by the policy. (This is a variant of the more well-known Pareto optimization. A Pareto optimal outcome is an outcome in which no person would be made better off without making someone else worse off.) This, along with much that applies a utility calculus of some kind, pulls into play all sorts of competing *values*. What does it mean, after all, to be made "better off" or "worse off" outside of the consultation of values, some of which can be wildly subjective and even idiosyncratic? Still, it is widely accepted that to be in poverty means to be "worse off" than someone who has adequate amounts of food, medical care, worker safety, housing, and the like, since in a condition of poverty these goods are missing or insufficient. It is as we approach the margins that the fuzziness concerning the meaning of "better off" and "worse off" becomes increasingly problematic.

What do *Lochner* and *Parrish* have to do with CDSs? These cases explicate the tensions, the competing goods, with which society must constantly contend, and concerning which easy answers are sometimes hard to come by. Most people wish to preserve the right to enter into commercial agreements as they see fit, without state interference. But this is a general preference. The same people, employing no more than normal, intelligent deliberation, would likely concede that laws that regulate the cleanliness of restaurants *they* patronize, or that address the general safety of the steelworker (such that the latter cannot contract away his or her right to safety in the workplace) are not extreme violations of the restaurateur's or the steel mill owner's right of free contract. A form of contract that can render society decidedly "worse off" by the less marginal standards would seem to be problematic indeed. A form of contract, say CDSs, that made the parties, in general, "better off" but that caused large numbers of persons to be made "worse off" is just the sort of thing utility-minded policy makers consider to be in need of constraints. The idea that CDSs meet the criteria for greater constraint because they were a major cause of the financial crisis, leading many to lose homes, jobs, and financial security, would seem to be a clear case for policy intervention. Of course, an important question regarding derivatives such as CDSs is—who is made worse off or better off by their use and proliferation?

This rights versus utility duality supervenes a long tradition in the philosophical literature in which some, on the one hand, hold (for good reasons) that rights remain inviolable, are trumps in the face of other moral exigencies, even if the utility of those affected by their exercise is severely diminished and, on the other hand, others who hold that the consideration of rights—especially natural rights—at the expense of considerations of utility is nonsensical at best.[2] It is no accident, then, that the arguments concerning the employment of derivatives such as CDSs have tracked these two traditional pathways of moral, legal, and economic thought, and in law more or less track the thinking explicated in the majority opinions in *Lochner* and *Parrish* (and, for that, matter in the dissenting opinions). Businesses need the ability to freely contract, especially with other businesses, and the last thing they want is to have worries about whether shifting sands of policy will undermine the validity of contracts. But experience changes thinking and priorities, both in legal analysis and in policy making. In the case of CDSs, because of new suspicions (and newly and widely disseminated data) surrounding them, the focus shifted away from the assumption that large financial institutions had the right to enter into contracts with one another, and in the direction of the social impact of these contracts. Concerns with *systemic risk* and social harm took center stage. Suspicions regarding them were made worse by the opacity of the world in which they were constructed, as well as the problematic moral reputation of that world, loosely known as "Wall Street." Of course, Wall Street's reputation is more than well deserved.

Still, can the financial crisis be laid at the doorstep of OTC derivatives such as CDSs? As one scholar, René M. Stulz, has put it:

> Credit default swaps are a subject of considerable ambivalence. On one side, they seem like straightforward financial derivatives that serve standard useful functions: making it easier for credit risks to be borne by those who are in the best position to bear them, enabling financial institutions to make loans they would not otherwise be able to make, and revealing useful information about risk in their prices. On the other side, in trying to understand the credit crisis, many observers have identified credit default swaps to be a prominent villain.

Stulz goes on to conclude:

> But it would be premature and quite misguided to turn 180 degrees from the presumption of innocence to a presumption of guilt. There is a dearth of serious empirical studies on the social benefits and costs of credit default swaps and other derivatives—not just in the last two years, but in the last several decades.

My own sense is that the deep dramatic problems of the financial credit crisis were not caused by credit default swaps, nor by other financial derivatives.[3]

Stulz wrote this for publication in late 2010. His observations jibe with the conclusions reached in the Financial Crisis Inquiry Report (the "Report"), published in January 2011, both in certain of the dissents written by Commissioners, as well as in the consensus conclusions of the report. For example, Commissioner Peter Wallison wrote, as part of his dissent:

> Despite a diligent search, the FCIC [Financial Crisis Inquiry Commission] never uncovered evidence that unregulated derivatives, and particularly credit default swaps (CDS), was a significant contributor to the financial crisis through "interconnections" [the notion that the connections between CDSs among financial institutions led to a domino effect of sorts]. The only company known to have failed because of its CDS obligations was AIG, and that firm appears to have been an outlier.[4]

In another dissenting essay, Commissioners Keith Hennessey, Douglas Holtz-Eakin, and Bill Thomas wrote:

> Rather than "derivatives and CDOs [Collateralized Debt Obligations] *caused* the financial crisis," it is more accurate to say:
>
> - Securitizers lowered credit quality standards;
> - Mortgage originators took advantage of this to create junk mortgages;
> - Credit rating agencies assigned overly optimistic ratings;
> - Securities investors and others failed to perform sufficient due diligence;
> - International and domestic regulators encouraged arbitrage toward lower capital standards;
> - Some investors used these securities to concentrate rather than diversity risk; and
> - Others used synthetic CDOs to amplify their housing bets.[5]

Derivatives and the Financial Crisis

I tend to agree with Hennessey, Holtz-Eakin, and Thomas (but would also emphasize that there was a good deal of outright *fraud* in the system, which originated with largely unregulated mortgage brokers and the complicit bankers with whom they had cozy relationships). Even though I believe, and believe firmly, that many of the practices in the financial services industry need reform, and even that much of the culture of Wall Street needs to be turned on its head, when one is serious about public policy one has an obligation to do justice to the facts and contexts, to not operate from prejudice or ideological blindness. The fact seems to be that there is nothing wrong with either CDSs per se, or with other derivatives per se. There is nothing unethical about seeking to insure oneself, legally, against loss by means of a sophisticated and fully informed party willing to provide that insurance, whether that other party is called "insurance company" or, simply, "swap counterparty." It is not even unethical, all else being equal, to lobby to create as many potential insurers as one can, or to lobby to be able to provide as much insurance as one can where the result will be increased revenue. As I discuss below, it is not the role of businesses to explore *all* of the possible public policy details of every product or service they wish to provide. Most of that responsibility lies elsewhere.

Much has been made, for shock value purposes, of the $600 trillion (NV) derivatives market, of which CDSs are but a part—albeit a large part. But once one considers that the notional default risk—the risk that a chunk of that notional value of referent securities in CDS contracts will default—the real risk that this gargantuan number might imply begins to attenuate, absent a "black swan event" of the type we recently lived through. Throwing astronomically large numbers at the public, which may not be in the best position to place those large numbers into context, can serve to obfuscate and lead to bad public policy, as is often the case with policy based upon populist consultation. By some estimates there is some $25 trillion to $30 trillion worth of real estate (commercial and residential) in the USA. But so what? By themselves the numbers mean little, other than as a general gauge or indicator of aggregate wealth. But the large numbers concerning the size of the derivatives market are, somehow, supposed to indicate the peril the world is in. There is a good counterargument that holds that it is because of the peril the world is in that we need robust derivatives markets—instruments (contracts) that permit the diffusion of risk, the transfer of risk from parties that are less able to absorb it to parties that are better able to do so. OTC derivatives, such as CDSs, may have exacerbated the financial crisis of recent years—in certain cases—but it seems hard to argue that these instruments *caused* it. This distinction is a critical one. Had there never been a burst housing bubble it is unlikely that OTC derivatives would be receiving the level of scrutiny they are now receiving. This is not to say that both the opacity and proliferation of these instruments were not, or would not one day become, problematic. Ironically, the housing market collapse shed light on these financial instruments, as it did on so many other areas of weakness or possible weakness in the financial system. It is arguable that, without such light, the unchecked proliferation of OTC derivatives might have set the stage for a far worse financial catastrophe down the road. Be that as it may, the *causes* of the most recent crisis lie elsewhere. One major factor, if not cause, among others, is that there was simply too much debt in the financial system, and too little savings to absorb the impact of the economic downturn that took place.

It is the job of regulators and legislators, drawing on the resources of informed experts (including those in the private sector) to consider and address systemic public policy issues. Businesses should not proceed as though public policy is completely irrelevant, but public policy and *systemic* risk are not the proper responsibilities of individual firms. Businesses seeking to build better mouse traps, even mousetraps of a kind that none had ever seen before, should not be required to study how the new mousetrap will impact, say, the butterfly population in another country, or whether the better mousetrap will impact populations of insects for which the mouse is a natural predator. They may, however, have some obligation to study how the better mousetrap will likely be used under strict liability considerations, how it will be discarded after use in view of environment impact considerations, and how the safety of the workers who manufacture it will be impacted in view of occupational health and safety concerns. Arguably, the same is true of the creation of better financial "mousetraps." For the most part, CDSs and other OTC derivatives work as intended, for parties who understand the nature of the bargain into which they are entering. Absent contractual fraud and internal risk considerations, a firm's analysis ends, so to speak, at the lobby door—at least for the most part. Most ethical and public policy issues that relate to or concern CDSs should be located at the level of policy makers on the outside of business organizations, beyond the lobby door.

There are certain internal actors, however, who do have special obligations to protect the firm from undue risk exposures, and when these actors are doing their part in this regard *systemic* risk is, we might say, naturally mitigated. These actors include boards of directors and risk officers (especially chief risk officers). It is here that we find that there were indeed failures in judgment, oversight, corporate culture, and responsibility, all of which led to the financial crisis in general—and all of which are salient from the point of view of business ethics. *For stewardship is squarely within the realm of ethics, and concerns the discharge of significant ethical duties to a firm's stakeholders, if not to society in general.* Let us turn our attention to the failures of policy makers, and then take up the failures of boards of directors and risk officers.

Failures of Stewardship

We return now to the Commodity Futures Modernization Act of 2000 (hereinafter the "2000 Act"), mentioned earlier. The 2000 Act exempted OTC derivatives, such as CDSs, from regulation by the Commodity Futures Trading Commission (CFTC), even though these derivatives had many of the characteristics of the financial futures contracts that were already regulated by the CFTC. CDSs would not be regulated by the CFTC *as a matter of law*. What is noteworthy, as well, is the implication that some OTC derivatives maintained the indicia of gambling (bets) of the sort referred to by the US Supreme Court in *Gatewood v. North Carolina*.[6] In *Gatewood*, the court defined a "bucket shop" as "[a]n establishment, nominally for the transaction of a stock exchange business, or business of similar character, but really for the registration of bets, or wagers ... on the rise or fall of the prices of stocks, grain, oil, etc., there being no transfer or delivery of the stock or commodities nominally dealt in." While many OTC derivatives have useful purposes, others, such as naked CDSs, where the buyer of protection is doing no more than placing a bet with no risk exposure to the referent security, are nothing more than gambling. The wording of the 2000 Act suggests knowledge of this fact, and thus the provisions to protect OTC derivatives, including naked CDS contracts, from regulation. But why? How did this happen?

It happened because, *at best*, ideology trumped stewardship, as government insiders, including such powerful figures as Lawrence Summers, Robert Rubin, Alan Greenspan, Senator Phil Gramm, and Arthur Levitt (then Chairman of the Securities and Exchange Commission, engaged in a turf war with the CFTC) joined hands with powerful interests within the financial services industry to beat back any suggestion that OTC derivatives, as just described, should be regulated—by any agency, including the CFTC. The then head of the CFTC, Brooksley Born, attempted to draft regulations that would have captured CDSs and other OTC derivatives in the same regulatory net as other financial derivatives that were regulated by the CFTC, largely because of the systemic risks they might pose. She was concerned that the hidden size and pervasiveness of these instruments could possibly lead to financial disaster down the road. I have already stated my agreement with some who wrote a dissenting opinion in the FCIC Report: derivatives exacerbated but did not cause the recent financial crisis. But that is now a side issue in the face of whether policy makers, as high as the White House and Treasury Department, turned a blind eye to bad public policy decisions under the ideological cloak of a commitment to "free markets." The answer seems clear—they almost certainly did. The lobbying pressure from banks and the large broker-dealers was enormous and effectively beat back Born's attempts to place some constraints on CDSs and other OTC derivative instruments, constraints similar to those found in the 2010 Dodd-Frank Wall Street Consumer Protection Act (typically referred to as "Dodd-Frank," named for Senator Christopher Dodd and Representative Barney Frank, co-sponsors of the legislation), now the law of the land. The law firm Skadden, Arps, Slate, Meagher, & Flom, in its analysis of Dodd-Frank, pointed out the impact of the legislation on OTC derivatives:

> Title VII of . . . Dodd-Frank . . . imposes a regulatory regime on over-the-counter ("OTC") derivatives and the market for such derivatives. The primary goals of the legislation and related rulemaking are to increase the transparency and efficiency of the OTC derivatives market and reduce the potential for counterparty and systemic risk. The main mechanisms for achieving this are: to require that as many product types as possible be centrally cleared and traded on exchanges or comparable trading facilities; to subject swap dealers and major market participants to capital and margin requirements; and to require the public reporting of transaction and pricing data on both cleared and uncleared swaps.[7]

This sounds sane indeed, and the reasons for such things as clearing houses—which lend transparency to the size and frequency of trades in OTC derivatives contracts—is precisely what Brooksley Born sought to accomplish years earlier. In 2009, before the enactment of Dodd-Frank, Born received the Profiles in Courage Award from the John F. Kennedy Presidential Library Foundation. In her acceptance speech she said "No federal or state regulator has market oversight responsibilities or regulatory powers governing the over-the-counter derivatives market or indeed has even sufficient information to understand the market's operations. The market is totally opaque and is now popularly referred to as 'the dark market.' . . . We now have a unique opportunity—a narrow window of time—to fashion and implement a comprehensive regulatory scheme for these instruments."[8]

The story of the ethics of derivatives is not merely a story about these instruments themselves, but rather it is a story about the swirl of the questionable decisions that surround them, a story about how policy makers breached a trust of stewardship to the country, a trust that required that they protect it from the rapacity of certain business interests, from the pitfalls of ideological blindness, and from certain types of "establishment," such as bucket shops, that spur rampant speculation rather than economic growth. It is noteworthy that under Dodd-Frank CDSs are still with us, and in a very big way, notwithstanding the hyperbole of some of the stellar critics of these instruments (such as Warren Buffet and George Soros). This speaks to the inherent utility of these contracts in mitigating risk, and even in generating revenue for firms. But we will now have, because of Dodd-Frank, much greater transparency in the contracts themselves as well as in those institutions that use them. Hedge funds and similar fund vehicles now have to report their exposures to CDSs and other derivatives, in some cases quarterly. It becomes clear in hindsight why the attempts by Born to institute similar sound regulation was so fiercely beaten back. It was Senator Phil Gramm, then head of the Senate Banking Committee, who made sure that the CFTC was blocked by force of law from actually *doing its job*—from regulating instruments that it made all the sense in the world for it, or some other government agency, to regulate. (Phil Gramm's spouse, Wendy Gramm, was once head of the CFTC herself, it might be of some interest to note.)

Was it all so that Wall Street could have a money party? Was it really all about greed? There are many who think so, and there is no doubt that many firms made lots of money in the OTC derivatives markets, and still do. But greed is the easy target in an ethical and public policy analysis of what happened, and to conclude that one has a full understanding of what happened by saying it was "all just greed" is to fail to do justice to the topic. People who peer into the ethics of business from the outside often do so with collections of prejudices about the nature of commerce in general. Commerce, for these persons, is nothing more than the haunt of greedy souls, of people who deliberately "turn away from the light" on their way to their hoped for fortunes. But the concerns that precluded the regulation of OTC derivatives, though attended by a desire for profit, also emanated from very serious *ideological views* about the nature of markets, contractual freedom (as previously discussed), and the role of capital. This takes us into a more interesting and useful analysis of what happened, of why OTC derivatives were not regulated before Dodd-Frank. Let us recall Alan Greenspan's exchange with Henry Waxman, from the epigraph:

> "Do you feel that your *ideology* pushed you to make decisions that you wish you had not made?" Mr. Greenspan conceded: "Yes, I've found a flaw. I don't know how significant or permanent it is. But I've been very distressed by that fact."

Suppose we take Mr. Greenspan at his word, and note that there was a "flaw" in his view of things—not merely complicity in a rapacious system, but "merely" an error in judgment—an error in judgment every bit as damaging as stark rapacity? This is the error in judgment that always attends tethering oneself to a model of reality, an ideology, a dogmatic conceptual scheme, from which you cannot extricate yourself and which blinds you to the facts at hand. To quote the great writer and literary critic, John Erskine, there is, among policymakers as among ethicists, a "moral obligation to be intelligent." Ideological commitments, such as Alan Greenspan's libertarian objectivism (Ayn Rand), or Phil Gramm's conservative libertarianism, can block the use of intelligence in sounding out issues and in attempting to derive the best answer to the question "What is to be done?" Philosophers such as William James and John Dewey often warned of commitments to dogmas and stifling, untested prejudices of the sort that led Mr. Greenspan to the discovery of a "flaw" in his way of looking at the economy and at markets. The flaw was Mr. Greenspan's assumption that executives would steer their firms away from untenable risk. He focused on data, on statistics, and did not notice other nonquantitative factors and trends taking place that threatened to undermine good corporate governance, such as the shorter tenures of CEOs and other executives, who came to see short stints at large banks and broker-dealers as ways to get rich quick and get out, often at the expense of the organizations they would leave behind.

One must be a little Aristotelian when considering matters as complex and sweeping as financial markets. One must be, to various degrees, philosopher, psychologist, sociologist, and culture critic. That is, one must use one's intelligence. Ideological commitments, whether they are of the left or the right, whether libertarian or statist, will only hamper the formation of good public policy. This does not mean theory is to be completely set aside, or can be. It only means that theories (whether capitalist or Marxist) tend to be riddled with questionable and untested assumptions, tend to impose an order on the world without sufficient empirical consideration and, often, need to be revised in the face of new evidence. Over the past 60 years or so, both capitalists and Marxists have learned that lesson the hard way.

Stewardship, Complexity, and the Interdependence of the Financial System

There is also the matter of the complexity and interdependence of today's financial system, which the recent financial crisis bears out as never before, and OTC derivatives are at the center of that complexity and interdependence. This complexity and interdependence makes it difficult for ethicists and other analysts to draw pat or easy conclusions about what went wrong and who is blameworthy. Yet stewardship requires accountability. The trading of financial instruments ripples or reverberates well beyond local markets, with consequences in the ordinary lives of ordinary people. Extreme market libertarians worry about the unintended consequences of government regulation and so-called "interference" in the free market. Ironically, a much dearer cost has been paid in recent years due to the unfettered use of a variety of products and services that originated in the laboratories of Wall Street, away from the eyes of regulators and beyond the effective reach of internal governance. The libertarian hue and cry regarding unintended consequences should by now be seen to have lost some of its tenability, though it would be naive to think it will ebb significantly since ideologues rarely admit the flaws in their conceptual schemes, the facts notwithstanding. In any event, since blameworthiness is increasingly difficult to determine in the midst of such complexity (which is why the search for actual criminality and criminals in the subprime meltdown has gone almost nowhere), policy makers have an obligation to make sure that the activities of market participants are regulated at each phase of product roll-out and at each level of a bank's or dealer's operation. As has been proposed by the SEC recently, more thought must be given to the nature, use, proliferation, and even the non-indicated uses of OTC derivatives, just as the issue of the suitability of such instruments for even institutional market participants must be an ongoing concern for banks and dealers who market these instruments or serve as counterparties (e.g., as sellers of protection in the case of CDSs).[9] It is difficult for policy makers and regulators to be proleptic without stifling innovation, but that, alas, is the balance that must be struck.

It would be imprudent to conclude that positive law or static regulation will provide the final checks on excessive risk and speculation in financial markets. It is, in part, the complexity and interdependence of those markets that led the Obama administration to propose a dynamic approach, which came into being under Dodd-Frank in the form of the Financial Stability Oversight Council (the "Council"). The Council "will provide . . . comprehensive monitoring to ensure the stability of our nation's financial system. The Council is charged with identifying threats to the financial stability of the United States; promoting market discipline; and responding to emerging risks to the stability of the United States financial system." The establishment of the Council extends the reach of Dodd-Frank beyond itself, so to speak, and provides a *dynamic* monitor that will think what others are not thinking, consider what others have failed to consider, and range over the financial system—internationally—asking the sorts of questions that did not get asked prior to the credit crisis because of self-serving concerns, ideological commitments, ignorance, or all of the preceding. Of all the things that arose from the recent crisis in the form of regulation, the establishment of a dynamic risk monitor with no water to carry for any particular constituency is one of the best, and should improve stewardship dramatically. The Council will be able to bring intelligence rather than ideology and politics to considerations of market risk in a way that has never been done before.

But this helps at the macro level. What about stewardship inside of banks, brokerages, hedge funds, and other financial institutions? For many years, boards of directors have been coming up short when it comes to understanding both the operations and risks associated with the organizations over which they serve as stewards. As was reported in *The New York Times* recently, "Many directors clearly lacked the educational or work backgrounds needed to understand the derivatives and other complex products whose risks eventually overtook their institutions. Worse, they forgot or never learned the many lessons of past bubbles and manias. And industry knowledge on bank boards is no more extensive today than it was four years ago."[10] Dodd-Frank does require the boards of certain large financial services firms to establish risk committees, which committees must "include at least 1 risk management expert having experience in identifying, assessing, and managing risk exposures of large, complex firms."

The problem of effective stewardship by boards of directors goes beyond the problem of insufficient expertise, however, and has to do, as well, with problems of corporate board culture generally. Robert A.G. Monks and Nell Minnow, experts in corporate governance, explain the problem this way:

Senator Carl Levin . . . provided perhaps the most authentic view into the nature of US boards at a hearing with the five most senior directors of recently bankrupt [December, 2001] Enron. These individuals are the ultimate example of America's director culture: they each had served for 17 years; they chaired the most important committees (executive, finance, compensation, and audit); three had earned doctorates; all were paid a minimum of $350,000 a year. They appeared voluntarily and at substantial personal inconvenience and legal hazard in order to articulate plainly and repeatedly that . . . they were not responsible *in any way* for the collapse of Enron or for the loss of investments, pensions, and jobs.[11]

Directors of public companies take great pains to insulate themselves from legal liability. They tend to be "lawyered up," so to speak (directors often have their own legal counsel, paid for by the corporation). They are able to invoke "the business judgment rule" and the protections afforded them by state law. They insist upon a proper understanding of their role— that they have a right to rely upon the expertise of the corporation's executive managers on all operational matters. Few people who are informed about governance blame corporate directors for wanting protection from the acts or failures to act of the executives, managers, and employees who, whether directly or indirectly, report to them. Yet, recent corporate and financial crises and scandals have turned up the heat on directors who think they can avert blameworthiness and liability completely. The Dodd-Frank requirement that risk experts be integrated into overall governance will undoubtedly lead boards to consider factors and issues that were once only considered at the executive and managerial levels. They will no longer be able to claim that they did not know the risks associated with certain activities or products—especially activities or products that have a significant impact on financial statements. At the same time, they will no longer be able to claim ignorance concerning risks, as they will have ample opportunities to pose questions directly to the risk committee or to the risk expert that is central to that committee.

Finally, senior risk and compliance officers should be given more autonomy and authority within banks and brokerages—autonomy and authority that will permit them to report their concerns directly to the board of directors (if there is one, but, if there is not, to firm owners or senior executives), without interference from business units. Risk officers, in many cases, have a kind of presumed authority in firms, and can be paid handsomely, but they often get outmaneuvered by production personnel (traders, bankers, etc.) who live and die by short-term results. Chief risk officers should have the authority to shut down or wind down trading strategies or market exposures that they believe place the firm at risk in the long term. This means that these professionals should be "off the desk"—not unduly influenced by the demands (and sometimes ravings) of traders and other producers in the firm. Also, there should be a rebalancing, a shift of emphasis from quantitative risk measures toward qualitative ones (such as conflicts of interest, dubious reporting lines, poorly established authority among business unit personnel, and subjective, professional assessments of conditions, such as corporate culture, that are not captured by quantitative risk models). This means moving toward an enterprise risk approach and away from a mere portfolio risk approach.

Derivatives and the Financial Crisis: Cultural Politics and Pedagogy

Some time ago, I was privy to a fellow academic's confession that she could not teach business ethics because of her antipathy toward the business world. I believe that her antipathy is shared by not a few philosophers who teach business ethics. That is, of course, her (and their) right and, for my part, I am glad that she would not expose students to such an attitude. I have heard fellow philosophers make reference to the financial system, "with all of these fancy instruments and crazy and useless activities that add nothing to society" (to paraphrase), with great revulsion. This reflects, at least often, a more general feeling of revulsion for capitalism and "neoliberal" economics.

There is certainly a good deal wrong with capitalism and neoliberal economic thought. But nothing, so far, has any credible chance to replace capitalism, while there are efforts within the profession of economics to challenge certain basic assumptions that drive neoliberal economic analysis. Amartya Sen, Joseph Stiglitz, and Jeffrey Sachs, to name a few thinkers, are on the frontlines of these challenges. Capitalism, while tending to lead to wild and unsustainable disparities between the rich and the poor, remains, at least arguably, the best engine for the creation of wealth—*generally*.

Philosopher Slavo Žižek, not usually known for measured analysis of capitalism or for melioristic approaches, had some interesting things to say about the recent financial crisis, demonstrating an insight into the complexity of the problems that led to it. In a radio interview with journalist Juan Gonzalez he warned against simplistic moral analyses, especially on the part of the left, of which he himself is a proud member:

> Juan Gonzalez: Well, I'd like to ask you, you say you are also critical of the progressive or the left response here. You say in your article in *Harper's*, "There is a real possibility that the primary victim of the ongoing crisis will not be capitalism but the left itself, insofar as its inability to offer a viable global alternative was again made visible to everyone." Could you elaborate?
>
> Slavo Žižek: I see—what worries me [are] two things about the left. First, it's more and more legalistic moralization. You know, it's kind of a pure form of protest against injustice. Then the only thing you can do is legal forums and so on. In this sense, many of the ex-leftists are getting depoliticized. They no longer ask the truly basic questions. Like even now, all the outcry was, "Oh, those bank profiteers," and so on. I totally agree with what we just heard. But don't you think that the truth is a little bit more complex . . . [12]

Rather than stand aside and cast stones, there are many philosophers and other intellectuals who might do better to admit defeat as to tenable challenges to, at least, the more basic tenets of capitalism: private ownership of the means of production, more or less unfettered markets, a well ordered system of regulation, market-based price discovery, and so on. This does not suggest—except in the minds of the most rabid market libertarians—that governments should have no control over important social institutions and processes. But absent a tenable replacement for capitalism, it would appear to be a more useful employment of one's critical skills to join the search for meaningful solutions to real problems that affect real people and real institutions. The working assumption must be that wholesale systemic change is a far-off goal and would require a tremendous moral shift, a sweeping change in sensibilities. There is little evidence that any such moral shift or change in sensibilities is on the horizon. Perhaps the time will come when the very idea of ownership will become a relic of the past. For the moment, however, I must join those who label such thinking "pie in the sky." The cultural politics that seems to suffuse philosophy departments, which departments tend to be the seat of the teaching of business ethics, is, for the most part, unhelpful when it comes to challenging problematic business practices, and so a pedagogy that clings to theories that exclaim that "the system is rotten to the core" is one that does not prepare the student to engage with that system.

The American philosopher Richard Rorty once wrote,

> When one of today's academic leftists says that some topic has been "inadequately theorized," you can be pretty certain that he or she is going to drag in either philosophy of language, or Lacanian psychoanalysis, or some neo-Marxist version of economic determinism . . . These futile attempts to philosophize one's way into political relevance [or commercial relevance?] are a symptom of what happens when a Left . . . adopts a spectatorial approach to the problems of its country. Disengagement from practice produces theoretical hallucinations.[13]

Philosophers and others who teach business ethics do a disservice when they teach the subject as though they, and the students they teach, should take the roles of spectator and critic concerning what amounts to no more than a sea of rapacity and corruption. They do well to get a deeper understanding of the important role of such areas of culture as the financial system and commerce in general, and do their parts to both explain the logics of the markets and to help shape, through pedagogy, the people who will one day lead commercial enterprises, whether banks, hedge funds, or tool-and-die factories—that those institutions will serve society as they should. The display of ignorance of many academics who have chimed in on the recent financial and credit crises has been, generally, disappointing, notwithstanding the insightful comments of Žižek and a few others. Some have mimicked the univocal populist commentators who have proffered that "Wall Street is completely unregulated" and that "what has happened is criminal." Both proffers are wrong, of course. Wall Street swims in a sea of regulation, and what is or is not criminal turns on facts that suggest the violation of certain criminal laws, not merely ethical lapses, blameworthiness, or failures of stewardship.

Cultural politics concerns the contestation of social, economic, and political values and meanings. Philosophers have a responsibility to enter this arena of contestation by restraining their biases and ideological commitments, as well as their assumption that abstract philosophizing is enough to affect behavior or policy. To the extent philosophy is still relevant in the public square (which is something that is itself contested) we philosophers might do better if we make sure that we have a firm grasp of all of the issues and facts before wading into public debates about policy. In an October 2010 *New York Times* article, philosopher Jay Bernstein wrote:

> In pondering [Wall Street and the idea of free markets] I want to, again, draw on the resources of . . . Hegel . . . Near the middle of the *Phenomenology of Spirit* (1807), he presents an argument that says, in effect: if Wall Street brokers and bankers understood themselves and their institutional world aright, they would not only accede to firm regulatory controls to govern their actions, but would enthusiastically welcome regulation.

He went on:

> We know that nearly all the financial conditions that led to the economic crisis were the same in Canada as they were in the United States with a single, glaring exception: Canada

did not deregulate its banks and financial sector, and, as a consequence, Canada avoided the worst of the economic crisis that continues to warp the infrastructure of American life. Nothing but fierce and smart government regulation can head off another American economic crisis in the future. This is not a matter of "balancing" the interests of free-market inventiveness against the need for stability; nor is it a matter of a clash between the ideology of the free-market versus the ideology of government control. Nor is it, even, a matter of a choice between neo-liberal economic theory and neo-Keynesian theory. Rather, as Hegel would have insisted, regulation is the force of reason needed to undo the concoctions of fantasy.[14]

I applaud Bernstein for his willingness to engage in such an important public debate, and to do so as a philosopher. But the upshot of his article represents the sort of aerial view philosophers too often have when addressing issues of commerce. Aerial views have their place, but public policy analysis requires more granularity—a better acquaintance with the nature of the subject under review. The relevance of Hegel to the financial crisis is, at best, curious, if not eccentric. Bernstein's invocation of *The Phenomenology of Spirit* (of all texts) as medicine for the financial crisis is probably unique. As to the allegations, the assertion that Wall Street is not already highly regulated is false, as I have already stated, and the deregulation of banks in the form of the repeal of Glass-Steagall had, in fact, little to do with the mess that the banks brought upon themselves (the exposures of the banks to bad loans and the securities backed by those loans is the principal cause of the crisis, and this had nothing at all to do with the separation of commercial and investment banking that Glass-Steagall instituted in 1933). Canadian banks were simply much less exposed to the subprime crisis than American banks were. Professor Bernstein had some interesting things to say about Wall Street, but none were of much use for the formulation of new policy. This does not mean that philosophers have no role to play, only that they must learn to take as much time to understand the commercial matters at hand as they do Wittgenstein's *Tractatus* or Dewey's *Experience and Nature*.

The cultural politics of academic departments of philosophy may often be in the way of sound policy advice, yet it is in these places that the more fundamental questions (what Žižek referred to as "the truly basic questions") about our kind of civilization get asked and debated. That is why it is important for philosophers to continue to enter the fray, armed with the proper understanding of the issues they seek to address. Analyzing naive or populist assumptions about basic and pervasive ideas concerning the nature and role of the state, the nature of freedom (and so of free markets), the nature of taxation, the idea of a political community, well, this is the bailiwick of the philosopher. The trick is to link her or his experience with respect to these sorts of questions to a solid grasp of the way the world actually works, and why it works that way. What is the nature of risk? Is it really contained by transferring it to other parties who, in turn, transfer it again? Are there really such things as "public" and "private" institutions? What is the purpose of compensation? What is an incentive? Should acute blameworthiness be criminalized? Good questions. How shall we go about answering them in a way that allows us to avoid real social pain in the future?

Notes

1 Cultural Politics (*n.d.*) *Home page*. Retrieved March 5, 2013 from www.culturalpolitics.net

2 Jeremy Bentham argued vigorously against the notion of rights unmoored from considerations of social utility: "Natural rights is simple nonsense: natural and imprescriptible rights, rhetorical nonsense—nonsense upon stilts."

3 R.M. Stulz (2010) Credit Default Swaps and the Credit Crisis. *Journal of Economic Perspectives*, 24(1): 73–92.

4 *Financial Crisis Inquiry Report*, January 2011. Washington, DC: US Government Printing Office; pp. 447–448.

5 *Financial Crisis Inquiry Report*, pp. 424–425.

6 Gatewood v. North Carolina, 27 S.Ct 167, 168 (1906).

7 *Skadden Insights* (legal practice newsletter of the law firm of Skadden, Arps, Slate, Meagher & Flom) (July 12, 2010). Retrieved March 5, 2013, from http://www.skadden.com/newsletters/FSR_Test_3_alt.html

8 Retrieved from the John F. Kennedy Presidential Library website, March 5, 2013, http://www.jfklibrary.org/Events-and-Awards/Profile-in-Courage-Award/Award-Recipients/Brooksley-Born-2009.aspx?t=3

9 Securities and Exchange Commission, Release No. 34-64766; File No. S7-25-11, RIN 3235-AL10: "Business Conduct Standards for Security-Based Swap Dealers and Major Security-Based Swap Participants."

10 Jeffrey Goldfarb and Antony Currie, "Usual Directors in Boardrooms," *The New York Times*, April 8, 2011.

11 Robert A.G. Monks and Nell Minnow (2008) *Corporate Governance* (4th edition). Chichester: John Wiley & Sons; p. 257.

12 Radio program, *Democracy Now!*, with hosts Amy Goodman and Juan Gonzalez, October 15, 2009.

13 Richard Rorty (1998) *Achieving Our Country—Leftist Thought in Twentieth Century America*. Cambridge, MA: Harvard University Press; pp. 93, 94.

14 J.M. Bernstein, "Hegel on Wall Street," *The New York Times*, October 3, 2010.

Madoff and Kreuger
Fraud Theories, Red Flags, and Due Diligence in the Auditing Process

BEHNAZ Z. QUIGLEY AND MARY JANE EICHORN

Introduction

The US Securities and Exchange Commission (SEC) is responsible for protecting investors and capital markets, and enforcing laws and regulations that apply to the US securities industry. Their main function is to detect white-collar crimes; this includes pyramid and Ponzi schemes. The Sarbanes Oxley Act (SOX) of 2002 was enacted in direct response to the Enron and other scandals of 2001. A portion of the law requires the SEC to implement rulings regarding auditing the financial statements of companies listed on the New York Stock Exchange (NYSE) (Sarbanes Oxley Act, executed in 2004). In direct response to the new auditing requirements, the Auditing Standards Board of the American Institute of Certified Public Accountants (AICPA) issued Statement of

Auditing Standards (SAS) No. 99, which replaced SAS No. 82. One of the components of this regulation refers to the "fraud triangle," which consists of rationalization, incentive, and opportunity, as a means to detect securities and commodities fraud.

Based on a KPMG 2003 fraud survey, Wolfe and Hermanson (2004) suggest adding 'capability' as an additional element to detect fraud. Therefore, the fraud triangle is converted to the "fraud diamond" (rationalization, incentive, opportunity, and capability). In 2008, Robert Mueller, Director of the Federal Bureau of Investigation (FBI), stated that due to the recent subprime crisis corporate fraud may increase (Ryan 2008). The most recent (2009) KPMG survey on fraud also suggests that corporate fraud will increase and that it will present significant challenges and management for their control systems. Before the 2009 study was published, Goldmann wrote an article for the Association of Certified Fraud Examiners (ACFE) stating that 'capability' should be added to the fraud triangle to strengthen an organization's internal controls systems (Goldmann 2008).

The FBI lists securities and commodities fraud cases (one of which is corporate fraud) as a separate category of white-collar crime. Their investigations include "cases that involve accounting schemes, self-dealing by corporate executives, and obstruction of justice" (Federal Bureau of Investigation 2007). These corporate fraud cases include Ponzi and pyramid schemes. According to the 2007 FBI statistics (see Figure 6.2), corporate fraud cases have been rising steadily.

Although the official term of "white-collar crimes" was not introduced until 1939 by Edwin Sutherland (Price and Norris 2009), we may include Charles Ponzi as a "white-collar criminal." During the early 1920s, Ponzi sold Americans the idea that their investment could be increased by using foreign (Spanish) market coupons. Ivar Kreuger seized on this "American belief" and in the early 1920s became known as "The Match King" (Partnoy 2009). To make his scheme work, Kreuger invented and used such financial instruments as convertible gold debentures and nonvoting B common shares. A recent article suggested that Bernard L. Madoff, CEO of Bernard L Madoff

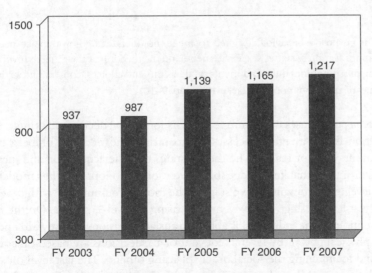

Figure 6.2 FBI pending cases of securities and commodities fraud
Source: Financial Crimes Report to the Public Fiscal Year 2007, Federal Bureau of Investigation.

Investment Securities, LLC (BMIS), former NASDAQ chairman, used Kreuger's model for his scheme (Masters and Chung 2009).

This essay will address three research questions. What are some of the theories that support the fraud triangle/diamond assumptions? Is the fraud diamond a better framework than the fraud triangle in detecting white-collar crime? Did Bernard Madoff use Ivar Kreuger's scheme and behavior as a model for his fraud scheme? We will then explore the Madoff Ponzi case in relation to the red flags that were present and the new SEC laws which have been implemented as a result of the forensic accounting investigation. Considering the continuous rise in white-collar crime and the recent Madoff conviction, this essay is a timely discussion on fraud and its detection.

Theoretical Framework

In this section we apply economic, psychological, and sociological theories to connect the fraudulent behavior of an individual to the framework of the fraud triangle/diamond. In doing so, we can explore some of the possible reasons why Kreuger and Madoff committed white-collar crimes—Ponzi schemes.

Criminologists borrow from the fields of psychology and the social sciences to explain the reasons why a person would make the decision to commit a white-collar crime. The rational choice theory of Clarke and Cornish, from economics; Kohlberg's cognitive moral reasoning and the theory of cognitive dissonance, from psychology; and the social structure learning model (Akers), from sociology are all attempts to explain the rationalization of unethical behavior, such as fraud.

The rational choice perspective of Clarke and Cornish derives its roots from G.S. Becker's economic theory. It revolves around certain assumptions, such as, the person is rational, cost–benefit analysis is considered, and the resulting behavior disregards the moral norms of the society. According to the definition of Cornish and Clarke,

> crime is purposive behavior designed to meet the offender's commonplace needs for such things as money, status, sex, excitement, and the meeting of these needs involves the making of (sometimes quite rudimentary) decisions and choices, constrained as they are by limits of time and money. (Clarke 1997, pp. 9–10)

Therefore, a person uses decision tree analysis for ethical decision-making.

Cognition is the mental processes of acquiring knowledge. Kohlberg based his theory on the work of Piaget. The theory states that the acquisition and incremental increases of intellectual knowledge influence moral development. His model consists of three levels each containing two stages. The model is cumulative, with development beginning at level 1; stage 1 and eventually rising to level 3, stage 2. On the first level (preconventional), the individual is able to translate decisions into reward and punishment or physical power. By level 2 (conventional), decisions are based on conformity, loyalty, and maintaining the social order (pleasing others). The last level (postconventional) decisions are based upon the individual's rights and values and individual conscience. In the last stage, unethical behavior can still appear because the individual's values can transgress society's ethical norms. Kohlberg acknowledges that moral decision-making is complex and having moral knowledge does not necessarily translate into moral action (Kohlberg and Hersh 1977).

The cognitive dissonance theory by Festinger assists in addressing ethical conflicts. These conflicts can be caused by attitudes, behaviors, and emotions and may result in additional psychological, social, or emotional tension. An individual resolves this conflict by according a hierarchy to moral and cultural decisions or changing behaviors to make them more consistent and aligned (Cano and Sams 2010). When confronted with the ethical decision to commit a crime, a conflict or dissonance occurs; therefore, the individual makes the decision concerning the risk. Then the individual becomes more apt to repeat the crime because dissonance has been alleviated. If new and different moral opinions are presented, the individual may choose to ignore them.

Akers applies Bandura's social learning theory to his social structure social learning model (SSSL) for explaining ethical behavior. While Kohlberg was developing his theory on moral development, Bandura was working on his social learning theory. The theory states that people can learn by watching others; the observer and the observee can learn concurrently. In addition, learning does not necessarily result in an immediate behavioral change, but a previously observed behavior may be exhibited at a later date. In this theory, cognition is recognized as a major part of the learning process, therefore, it can be said to be a bridge between the theories of behavior and cognition (Ormrod 1999).

In his application of Bandura's theory, Akers shapes his model into four different areas. The first area is differential association, that is, the expansion of an individual's social group to include others, such as business networks. The second area is differential reinforcement, that is, the power that an individual can derive from social status. The third area is favorable (peer approval) and unfavorable definitions (escape from negative social relationships). The last area is imitation or modeling. It is here that an avenue is initially provided for behavior such as crime. As in the rational choice model, positive and negative rewards are weighted against potential risks (Akers 2007).

The Fraud Triangle

Considering the above mentioned theoretical framework, we will explore the fraud triangle. In 1950 Donald Cressey developed what is known today as the "fraud triangle." He stated:

> Trusted persons become trust violators when they conceive of themselves as having a financial problem which is non-shareable, are aware this problem can be secretly resolved by violation of the position of financial trust, and are able to apply to their own conduct in that situation verbalizations which enable them to adjust their conceptions of themselves as trusted persons with their conceptions of themselves as users of the entrusted funds or property. (Cressey 1950; see Figure 6.3)

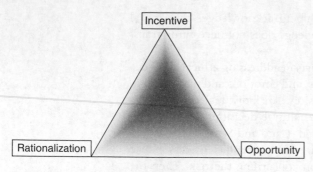

Figure 6.3 Cressey's fraud triangle (1950)
Source: *American Sociological Review.*

Rationalization, opportunity, and incentive (pressure or motivation) are the three legs of the triangle and all three must be present for fraud to be committed. (In addition, Cressey divided the "trust violators" into three different types. The first type he called independent business persons—those who borrow the money and will return it shortly; long-term violators were the second type—money was taken over long periods of time; and third were those that embezzled the money and left (Lynch 2007).) Of the three legs of the triangle, Cressey believed that incentive was the most important. At this point we will examine these three with reference to Madoff and Kreuger. It is important to consider that these three parts may not be clearly delineated.

Rationalization

According to Cressey (1950), a person must rationalize his or her decision before the fraud act can be committed. Rationalization implies a behavioral decision, where a person psychologically justifies his or her reasons to commit a fraudulent act. One of these reasons may be: "I really deserve to be paid more." Bernard L. Madoff used the idea "I am special and deserve to have power" as a psychological reason to justify his Ponzi scheme. We should note that some think that Madoff may have psychopathic tendencies (Creswell and Thomas 2009). These tendencies may assist in the rationalization of criminal behavior (Price and Norris 2009). Madoff's attitude can be seen as a manifestation of Kohlberg's moral development theory. Kreuger's mother suffered from mental anxiety (Partnoy 2009) and this may have some relevance for his business behavior.

To achieve a goal, a person needs to assess uncertainty (also known as randomness). No decision is 100% certain or uncertain but is rather on a continuum. Along this continuum, decisions are based on past events using probabilities (such as Bayesian probabilities) as a measurement. The more certain an event the higher the probability becomes and as a result the more credible the outcome is for future events (Tversky and Kahneman 1992). This concept explains why investors justify choosing an investment broker that has a "higher rate of return." Kreuger and Madoff used higher rates of return to lure investors, who believed that their returns were "legitimate." When the stock market crashed in 1928, Kreuger was concerned about disappointing his investors. Therefore, he became engaged in fraudulent activities, such as using his legitimate match business to fund his Ponzi scheme, showing false large profits, and forging Italian bonds (Partnoy 2009). Madoff did the same, using his broker-dealer business BMIS to cover his long-term Ponzi scheme. This concept is connected to the economic theory of the rational choice perspective of Clarke and Cornish.

Incentive

According to Cressey, this leg of the triangle (referred to by some as motivation or pressure) represents a perceived non shareable secret about financial affairs. When incentive is integrated with rationalization, this may cause a person to react and commit a fraudulent act (Cressey 1950). The two major sources of incentive are from society and industry. When we speak of society, we mean society in general and family in particular. Current US society emphasizes money and material goods as an indication of success. If an individual who has material wealth fears losing his or her wealth, high status, or economic security, then he or she may have a perceived non-shareable secret about financial affairs. Or the individual may have unrealistic expectations concerning material success (Price and Norris 2009). Those who commit fraud may measure wealth gains as a percentage increase (KPMG 2009). The percentage increases may appear less than the actual money earned, so that they may have added incentive to obtain more.

Madoff felt society's pressure, for he was very aware of his status in society and he feared both the loss of power and social status (Masters 2009). Like other addictions, the more money Madoff accumulated the more he wanted, therefore increasing the incentive to make more money. This was exacerbated because high society (high income) people begged him to take their money. In his trial he said: "I knew that I was doing wrong and believed it would end shortly and would be able to extricate myself and my clients. However, finding an exit strategy proved difficult and ultimately impossible" (Henriques and Healy 2009).

Because Madoff was cut off from his family (according to reports his sons did not know about the scheme, Margolick 2009), he may have felt isolated and unable to share his "financial problem" with anyone. Kreuger exhibited the same isolation from his nuclear family and the same need for power in high society, as exhibited by his Match Palace and international travel.

Besides society, incentive may come from within an organization or from an industry. In the financial industry, competition is intense for investor dollars. Bonuses, fees, and analyst's forecasts add to this intensity. In addition, the highest salaried people retain a high profile and status. Since this industry depends upon factors such as laws and regulations and political and economic climates, adverse economic conditions can strike suddenly. Kreuger's chief competitor was J.P. Morgan, and he would do anything to win a contract from him. When the French needed a loan and J.P. Morgan refused, Kreuger stepped in immediately. At that point, he did not have the funds but knew that America was experiencing an expansion so he planned to obtain the funds from Americans (Partnoy 2009).

Since the "incentive leg" of the triangle involves outside influences from both society and industry, it can be connected to Akers' social structure social learning model (SSSL).

Opportunity

In general, this leg of the triangle concerns the exploitation of the weaknesses in the internal control of a firm's accounting systems. Lack of approvals (different signatures) or having full access to accounting and information technology may contribute to this weakness (Murdock 2008). When presented with the opportunity, a person who has incentive, and has rationalized the act, now decides that the consequences are worth the risk. Since both Madoff (Bernard L Madoff Securities) and Kreuger (Kreuger and Toll Inc., International Match) were CEOs of their respective firms, they were able to create opportunities to exploit their own systems.

For example, Kreuger gave limited general record access to the young auditing firm of Ernst and Ernst and, when they requested data, he gave them falsified financial statements. Falsified records contained market value, not historical cost, for his assets, incorrect exchange rates, and incorrect incorporation dates. When the Wisconsin securities regulators questioned Kreuger's records, A.D. Berning, a junior accountant at Ernst and Ernst, accommodated Kreuger's mistakes with a letter of explanation. Berning's reward was international travel (Partnoy 2009). To foster his scheme, Kreuger created many of the financial products that are in use today, convertible gold debentures, convertible preferred shares, hedge funds with options, and class B common shares.

Like Kreuger, Madoff manipulated the auditing process by relying on small firms, such as Friehling & Horowitz (Gandel 2008). To further his ability to deceive the SEC, Madoff changed the programming of his financial records to produce falsified documents. He was able to accomplish this through the knowledge he gleaned from his brother, Peter, who ran the legitimate side of the business, as the chief compliance officer (Bandler and Varchaver 2009).

The Fraud Diamond

Capability

According to Wolfe and Hermanson (2004), a white-collar criminal is an individual who has rationalized that his or her fraudulent activity is justified. This individual possesses and realizes the necessary personalities and qualifications to attain his or her needed goal (see Figure 6.4).

There have been several studies concerning the personality attributes of white-collar criminals. In the extensive Bucy study, greed was the major underlying reason for leaders in committing white-collar crimes. In addition, leaders exhibited such characteristics as being arrogant, feeling entitled, and engaging in rationalization (Bucy et al. 2008). Since both Madoff and Kreuger were initially legitimately successful CEOs, we would conclude that according to the Bucy study, Madoff and Kreuger would be considered leaders. Also, overall, white-collar personalities include a need to control others, fear of losing status, being charismatic, and having a tendency to bully subordinates (Price and Norris 2009).

Kreuger was one of the first to realize that the financial markets were partially psychological in operation and always had a long-term vision. His company was one of the first to instigate vertical integration and his European construction contracts had an early finish profit clause. His reputation preceded him, and before he made an appointment with his next client he knew who the client was and what he or she needed (Partnoy 2009). His knowledge of financial products and his ability to know people contributed to his reputation, which helped him to increase his manipulation over others. In A.D. Berning he saw a person who regarded Kreuger's account as an opportunity. He exploited Higginson and Company partners because he knew that their group wanted to gain a lead over J.P. Morgan. One of the reasons why Kreuger created B common stock (eliminating shareholders' voting rights) was his need to control all aspects of his firms. Since his company was comprised of many firms, Kreuger made sure that only a few people knew about some of the other firms. He used the Match Palace as a physical defense to ward off people and continued to become emotionally isolated (Partnoy 2009).

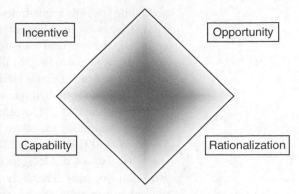

Figure 6.4 The fraud diamond
Source: Wolfe and Hermanson (2004).

Since both men were very intelligent, they elevated themselves legitimately to the highest socioeconomic level. This level contains very influential people with funds available to assist in keeping both Kreuger's and Madoff's schemes afloat. Each used his charisma and reputation as a catalyst to maintain access to these influential people.

Madoff used his Jewish background and his involvement in charities as a means of controlling whomever he allowed into his investment world. People invested with him because his investments were only open to certain people, and were perceived to be reliable, credible, and modest (Kaplan 2009). In an article by Mike Shedlock the suggestion is made that the smart money was invested with Madoff because investors believed the returns might be due to insider trading, not a Ponzi scheme (Shedlock 2008).

Like Kreuger, Madoff controlled all aspects of his firms through manipulation and secrecy. His sons ran the legitimate side of the business and did not know about the fraud (Bandler and Varchaver 2009; Margolick 2009). Brokers Bienes and Avellino were lured by Madoff to his company, made millions and were unable to alert the SEC when Madoff did not register them, for they were also benefiting from this scheme (Creswell and Thomas 2009). The SEC investigated Madoff's firm several times during his tenure. Unfortunately, the SEC did not do due diligence, and from 1999 did not acknowledge written warnings from the whistle-blower Markopolos concerning Madoff (Blodget 2008). Madoff was also very secretive about his dealings. For example, hedge fund investors could not report him as a manager (Arvedlund 2001).

The capability to make risk assessments would be a contributing factor in committing fraud. As stated in the rationalization section, certainty–uncertainty, which is based on prior experience or past events, contains elements of risk. Grable's study (2000), affirmed other studies that people who are Type A personalities, and have a higher level of both education and standard of living, are more prone to being risk seeking. It seems that both Kreuger and Madoff may fit into the risk-seeking category.

When Madoff and Kreuger decided to risk their ventures, they may have also accessed other factors, such as the current economic climate, political climate, and prevailing laws and regulations. When Kreuger decided on government match monopolies, they were not against the law, the Sherman Anti-Trust Act was not being enforced, the political climate was one of laissez faire towards business and the economy was expanding. In direct response to the Kreuger fraud, monopolies were outlawed and the SEC was established (Partnoy 2009). Madoff had to take greater risks than Kreuger, for he had started his scheme during the late 1990s, a time of contraction (Frontline 2009). However, government deregulation and the technology and housing expansions may have helped him to further his scheme for almost 20 years. Despite the SEC and the 2002 SOX, Madoff was able to avoid being caught because of the SEC's lack of due diligence, possible insider connections (Scannell 2009), and his fraudulent records. Therefore, it appears that laws and regulations alone are not the answer to preventing fraud, and adding "capability" to the fraud triangle may assist auditors in discovering new fraudulent acts. However, it must be reiterated that due diligence is a must requirement for an audit.

Since capability covers an individual's personality and social connections, all of the theories presented have application in this leg of the triangle. The need for control and secrecy relies heavily on resolving the conflict of an individual's attitudes, beliefs, and emotions; hence connection to the cognitive dissonance theory. Since an individual must work within economic and political environments, the social structure social learning theory is relevant. Kohlberg's moral development theory is present in the development of an individual's personality. Lastly, rational choice is present when an individual takes risks.

Due Diligence

As previously mentioned it was greed and the lack of due diligence on the part of the investors that allowed the Madoff and Kreuger Ponzi or pyramid schemes to continue. To be called a Ponzi scheme, the SEC states that certain elements must be present. Table 6.1 is a summary of those elements.

From Table 6.1 we can conclude that certain red flags would have been present while the scheme was in operation. Using information from Gregoriou and Lhabitant (2009) and Gandel (2008), we have created Table 6.2, which contains some of the characteristics of the Madoff securities investment firm, the red flags that were present, and the violation of the accounting or financial principles. Note that the SEC (which initially had authority to issue financial statement requirements) was not in existence at the time of Kreuger. However, the Madoff table can act as a template for Kreuger, postulating that the regulations or laws of US Generally Accepted Accounting Principles (GAAP) or the Financial Accounting Standards Board (FASB) did exist.

The Aftermath

Kreuger's business survived the beginning of the Great Depression; however, because he could not continue giving his constituents' promised funds, he decided to commit suicide. Because of the Kreuger scandal, the 1928 stock market crash, the

Table 6.1 Features of Ponzi and pyramid schemes

	Pyramid scheme	Ponzi scheme
Typical "hook"	Earn high profits by making one payment and finding a set number of others to become distributors of a product. The scheme typically does not involve a genuine product. The purported product may not exist or it may only be "sold" within the pyramid scheme.	Earn high investment returns with little or no risk by simply handing over your money; the investment typically does not exist.
Payments/profits	Must recruit new distributors to receive payments.	No recruiting necessary to receive payments.
Interaction with original promoter	Sometimes none. New participants may enter scheme at a different level.	Promoter generally acts directly with all participants.
Source of payments	From new participants—always disclosed.	From new participants—never disclosed.
Collapse	Fast. An exponential increase in the number of participants is required at each level.	May be relatively slow if existing participants reinvest money.

Source: Securities and Exchange Commission Frequently Asked Questions (FAQ) 2010.

Table 6.2 Red flags present in Madoff's pyramid/Ponzi scheme

Characteristics of Bernard Madoff Investment Securities (BMIS)	Red flags	Accounting/finance principle violated
Good (not great) consistent yearly returns	Wall Street knew Madoff's returns were obtained through fraudulent activity. Some banks refused to invest in Madoff	Efficient market portfolio theory
Cash given to investors	No electronic access to accounts. Lack of custodial accounts	Created deception transparency
Complicated investor financial statements	Required expert financial knowledge to decipher reports	Objectivity, reliability, and transparency
Family and close friends in key business roles	Weakness of internal controls and independent functions	Internal independent auditing and transparency. Business entity principal
Unknown and small independent auditing firm for BMIS	Inadequate auditing controls for the amount of business transactions. Lack of filing of company financial statement (2007)	No actual audit performed. Probable violation of all accounting principles including cost and revenue recognition
Audit of feeder funds by KPMG, PricewaterhouseCoopers, BDO Seidman, and McGladrey & Pullen	Underlying assets missing	Created deception. Unverified and incomplete audit
Client structure so that SEC registration is not required	Failure to register with SEC. Incomplete 13F form filing	Disclosure and SEC due diligence
Split/strike conversion strategy	Markopolos whistle-blower	Unsustainable results
Closed books to investors	Extreme secrecy	Deception and transparency

Great Depression, and public sentiment, the US Congress instituted the Securities Act of 1933 and the Securities and Exchange Act of 1934. These acts established the SEC and gave it the authority to require the submission of financial statements for publicly traded companies. Investors were also given the right to sue companies which committed fraud. The SEC later abdicated to US GAAP and the FASB (FASB 2011) to establish the rules and regulations for the financial statements of publicly traded companies.

Madoff decided to confess to his scheme in December 2008. He was convicted, and sentenced to 150 years in June 2009 (Frontline 2009). After he was sentenced, the SEC filed a lawsuit on behalf of Madoff's investors so that the investors have the opportunity to retrieve their funds from BMIS. Also, the auditors who reviewed Madoff's records are now being indicted for failing to discover that the underlying assets did not exist. The lawsuits pending include PriceWaterhouseCoopers (PWC) and KPMG (Farrell 2009). However, recently JP Morgan has been implicated in its choosing to ignore Madoff's red flags. The lawsuit states that JP Morgan knew of Madoff's Ponzi scheme and chose to be complicit (JP MorganChase was BMIS's principal banker) (Stempel 2011).

Similarities between Kreuger and Madoff continue. Because of the Madoff scandal, stock market crash of 2008, and public sentiment, the SEC as of December 2009 implemented enhancements to their auditing reviewing process, including revitalizing the enforcement division, changing how they assess whistle-blowers' information, and improving fraud detection methods with the addition of specialized staff (SEC 2010). Specialized staff now include forensic accountants. Although a detailed discussion of the qualifications and duties of forensic accountants is not within the scope of this essay, a broad overview of their functions will assist in understanding the duties and qualifications of these specialized auditors. Essentially, they are legal accounting experts who trace white-collar fraud through a cash flow investigative analysis of a company's books, looking for red flags. While investigating the possible fraud, they also focus on human behavior (Silverstone and Sheetz 2007). In addition, they will use their extensive knowledge of computers to prove their case in court. Since the Madoff case involves complicated broker/dealer relations, forensic accountants have been reconstructing Madoff's books to recover investor assets (WebCPA 2009).

To summarize the similarities and differences between Madoff and Kreuger, we have constructed Table 6.3 to compare the amount of investor fraud in 2009 US$ value and Table 6.4 as an overview of the Ponzi or pyramid schemes of Madoff and Kreuger.

Table 6.3 Correlating Ponzi scheme fraud to 2009 US $ (using calculations based on Officer and Williamson 2013)

	Year	Fraud amount	2009 $US
Kreuger	1932	$500,000,000	$7,850,000,000
Madoff	2008	$65,000,000,000	$64,800,000,000

Table 6.4 Overview of Madoff and Kreuger

	Madoff	Kreuger
Time frame	1980s–2008	1918–1932
Location	USA to Europe	Europe to USA
Business cycle	Several cycles, mainly expansion	Expansion then Depression
Company	Bernard L. Madoff Investment Securities	Kreuger and Toll Inc. International Match
Property and assets	$823M–$836M	More than 200 companies $100Billion (2000 USD)
Creativity	Electronic stock transfer "Pay as you go" Hedge funds with futures and options	Convertible gold debentures Preferred common stock Class B common stock Hedge funds
Scheme vehicle	Hedge funds to continue Ponzi/pyramid scheme	Government match monopolies to continue Ponzi/pyramid scheme
Best fraud asset	Jewish background Information technology	Markets are psychological Financial products
Demise	150 years in jail for massive fraud including perjury, money laundering, false statements to SEC	Committed suicide Actions were legal for the times
Regulations / Reform	SEC regulation reform Forensic accounting	SEC was established US GAAP and FASB accounting financial statements become the norm

Conclusion

There is a relationship between fraudulent behavior and economic rational choice theory, sociology's social structure social learning theory (SSSL), and psychology, cognitive moral development theory, and the theory of cognitive dissonance. Bernard Madoff's and Ivar Kreuger's unethical behavior were used as points of reference in this paper. According to Cressey's fraud triangle, rationalization, incentive (pressure/motivation), and opportunity must be present for a fraud to occur. The offender may justify his or her decision based on a psychological need and then determine a means–end goal to achieve that need, which can be based on the rational choice theory. When the incentive becomes too intense the goal must then be achieved when the opportunity is either presented or created.

By adding capability to the triangle, thereby making it a diamond, we can now incorporate personality traits, relationships between the offender(s) and the victim(s), socioeconomic factors, and the offender's ability to take risks. Victim(s) may be defined as employees, organizations, and investors. In the comparison between Madoff and Kreuger, it was the offender's capability which provided the necessary traits and qualifications, in using his expertise in the financial world and his knowledge of the people involved to exploit his relationships with his victim(s). Therefore, we believe that expanding the triangle to a diamond provides the extra facet needed to incorporate more factors when exploring financial fraud. Since the forensic accountant incorporates human behavior into his or her investigation, a practical application of the fraud diamond exists.

From our research, we also conclude that Madoff used Kreuger's Ponzi scheme and behaviors as his model. From a recent literature review, it seems that fraud increases when the economy contracts. However, further future research should include the possibility that fraud may increase during economic expansion as well, one arguable reason being that auditors are busier and due diligence is done less accurately.

References

Akers, R.L. (2007). *A Social Learning Explanation of White Collar Crime: Revisiting an Old Analysis*. Paper presented at the annual meeting of the American Society of Criminology, Atlanta, Georgia, November 13. Retrieved March 20, 2013 from http://citation.allacademic.com/meta/p_mla_apa_research_citation/2/0/0/0/7/p200078_index.html?phpsessid=4be67a9209d39b2ff2bdba6e1be74b5b

Arvedlund, E.E. (2001, May 7). Don't Ask, Don't Tell—Bernie Madoff Is So Secretive, He Even Asks Investors to Keep Mum. *Barron's*. Retrieved March 6, 2013 from http://www.sec.gov/news/studies/2009/oig-509/exhibit-0156.pdf

Bandler, J. and Varchaver, N. (2009, Apr. 30). How Bernie Did It. *CNNMoney.com*. Retrieved March 6, 2013 from http://money.cnn.com/2009/04/24/news/newsmakers/madoff.fortune/index.htm

Blodget, H. (2008, Dec. 17). Busting Bernie Madoff: One Man's 10 Year Crusade. *Business Insider*. Retrieved March 20, 2013 from http://www.businessinsider.com/2008/12/busting-bernie-madoff-one-mans-10-year-crusade

Bucy, P.H., Formby, E., Raspanti, M.S., et al. (2008). Why Do They Do It? The Motives, Mores, and Character of White Collar Criminals. *St. Johns Law Review*, 82: 401–571. Retrieved March 20, 2013 from http://www.stjohns.edu/media/3/bdca06c25e84422aa109aff032a289bb.pdf

Cano, C.R. and Sams, D. (2010). Advancing Cognitive Moral Development: A Field Observation of College Students. *Georgia College and State University: Journal of Academic and Business Ethics*. Retrieved March 20, 2013 from http://www.aabri.com/manuscripts/10556.pdf

Clarke, R.V. (1997). *Situational Crime Prevention, Successful Case Studies*, 2nd edition. Guilderland, NY: Harrow and Hester.

Clarke, R.V. and Felson, M. (1993). *R Routine Activity and Rational Choice. Vol. 5, Advances in Criminology Theory*. New Brunswick, NJ: Transaction.

Cressey, D.R. (1950). Criminal Violation of Financial Trust. *American Sociological Review*, 15(6): 738–743.

Creswell, J. and Thomas, L., Jr. (2009, Jan. 25). The Talented Mr. Madoff. *The New York Times*, Business section.

Farrell, S. (2009, Aug. 29). Billion-Dollar Lawsuit Could Destroy Top Accountancy Firms. *Telegraph*. Retrieved March 6, 2013 from http://www.telegraph.co.uk/finance/newsbysector/supportservices/6111149/Billion-dollar-lawsuit-could-destroy-top-accountancy-firms.html#

FASB (2011, Feb.) Financial Accounting Board Standards. *Reference for Business: Encyclopedia of Business*, 2nd edition. Retrieved March 6, 2013 from http://www.referenceforbusiness.com/encyclopedia/Fa-For/Financial-Accounting-Standards-Board-FASB.html

Federal Bureau of Investigation (2007). *Federal Bureau of Investigation: Financial Crimes Report to the Public Fiscal Year (2007)* (October 1, 2006 to September 30, 2007). Washington, DC: US Department of Justice.

Frontline. (2009, May 12). The Madoff Affair: Markers in His Four-Decade Career and Vast Deceptions. *PBS*. Retrieved March 6, 2013 from http://www.pbs.org/wgbh/pages/frontline/madoff/cron/

Gandel, S. (2008, Dec. 17). The Madoff Fraud: How Culpable Were the Auditors? *Times/Business&Money*. Retrieved March 6, 2013 from http://www.time.com/time/business/article/0,8599,1867092,00.html

Goldmann, P. (2008, July). The New Fraud Triangle: Another in Employee Fraud Motivation. *White-Collar Crime Fighter*. Retrieved March 13, 2013 from http://gatton.uky.edu/FACULTY/PAYNE/acc490/The%20New%20Fraud%20Triangle.pdf

Grable, J.E. (2000). Financial Risk Tolerance and Additional Factors that Affect Risk Taking in Everyday Matters. *Journal of Business and Psychology*, 14(4): 625–630.

Gregoriou, G.N. and Lhabitant, F.-S. (2009, Jan.). A Riot of Red Flags. Nice: EDHEC Risk and Asset Management Research Center. Retrieved March 20, 2013 from http://docs.edhec-risk.com/mrk/090210_Publication/EDHEC_PP_Madoff_Riot_of_Red_Flags.pdf

Henriques, D.B. and Healy, J. (2009, Mar. 13). Madoff Goes to Jail after Guilty Pleas. *The New York Times*, Business section.

Kaplan, M. (2009, Dec. 11). Trust Me: Why Ponzi Schemes Work. *Psychology Today*. Retrieved March 20, 2013 from http://www.psychologytoday.com/blog/bozo-sapiens/200912/trust-me-why-ponzi-schemes-work

Kohlberg, L. and Hersh, R.H. (1977). Moral Development: A Review of Theory. *Theory into Practice: Moral Development*, 16(4): 53–59. Retrieved March 13, 2013 from http://worldroom.tamu.edu/Workshops/CommOfRespect07/MoralDilemmas/Moral%20Development%20a%20Review%20of%20Theory.pdf

KPMG (2009). *Fraud Survey 2009*. KPMG Forensic. Retrieved March 13, 2013 from http://www.kpmginstitutes.com/aci/insights/2009/pdf/kpmg-fraud-survey-2009.pdf

Lynch, B. (2007, Feb.). Understanding Why People Commit Fraud Is the First Step In Preventing and Detecting Fraud in Your Company, Part 3. *Space Coast Business.Com*, 1(11): 72–73.

Margolick, D. (2009, July). The Madoff Chronicles: Did the Sons Know? *Vanity Fair*. Retrieved March 6, 2013 from http://www.vanityfair.com/politics/features/2009/07/madoff200907

Masters, B. (2009, Jan. 26). Madoff: Off the Fairway. *Financial Times*.

Masters, B. and Chung, J. (2009, June 24). Analysis: A Bitter Dividend. *Financial Times*: 11.

Murdock, H. (2008, Aug.). Risk Watch: The Three Dimensions of Fraud. *Internal Auditor*, 65(5): 81.

Officer, L.H. and Williamson, S.H. (2013). *Purchasing Power of Money in the United States from 1774 to Present*. MeasuringWorth. Retrieved March 20, 2013 from http://www.measuringworth.com/ppowerus/

Ormrod, J.E. (1999). *Human Learning*, 3rd edition. Upper Saddle River, NJ: Prentice-Hall.

Partnoy, F. (2009). *The Match King: Ivar Kreuger, the Financial Genius behind a Century of Wall Street Scandals*. New York: Public Affairs.

Price, M. and Norris, D.M. (2009). White-Collar Crime: Corporate and Securities Fraud. *Journal of American Psychiatry Law*, 37(4): 538–544.

Ryan, J. (2008, Apr. 18). Mueller Expects More Corporate Fraud Cases. *ABC News*. Retrieved March 6, 2013 from http://abcnews.go.com/TheLaw/FedCrimes/story?id=4677410

Scannell, K. (2009, Jan. 5). Madoff Chasers Dug for Years, to No Avail. *Wall Street Journal*. Retrieved March 6, 2013 from http://online.wsj.com/article/SB123111743915052731.html

SEC (2010, Oct 10). The Securities and Exchange Commission Post Madoff Reforms. Retrieved March 14, 2013 from http://www.sec.gov/spotlight/secpostmadoffreforms.htm

Sherlock, M. (2008, Dec. 13). Biggest Fraud in History $50 Billion in Madoff Ponzi Scheme. *Market Oracle*. Retrieved March 20, 2013 from http://www.marketoracle.co.uk/Article7769.html

Silverstone, H. and Sheetz, M. (2007). *Forensic Accounting and Fraud Investigation for Non-Experts*, 2nd edition. Chichester: John Wiley & Sons.

Statement on Auditing Standards No. 99 (2006). *Consideration of Fraud in a Financial Statement Summary*. Washington, DC: American Institute of Certified Public Accountants (AICPA).

Stempel, J. (2011, Feb. 3). JPMorgan Ignored Suspicions about Madoff: Lawsuit. *Reuters*. Retrieved March 20, 2013 from http://www.reuters.com/article/2011/02/03/us-madoff-jpmorgan-idUSTRE7127RW20110203

Tversky, A. and Kahneman, D. (1992). Advances in Prospect Theory: Cumulative Representation of Uncertainty. *Journal of Risk and Uncertainty*, 5(4), 297–323.

WEBCPA Staff (2009, May 15), Forensic Accountants Reconstruct Madoff Books. *AccountingToday.com*. Retrieved March 20, 2013 from http://www.accountingtoday.com/news/Forensic-Accountants-Reconstruct-Madoff-Books-50484-1.html

Wolfe, D.T. and Hermanson, D.R. (2004, Dec.). The Fraud Diamond: Considering the Four Elements of Fraud. *CPA Journal*, 74(12): 3842.

B. Global Business: Bribing

Bribery

MICHAEL PHILIPS

Although disclosures of bribery have elicited considerable public indignation over the last decade, popular discussions of the morality of bribery have tended largely to be unilluminating. One reason for this is that little care has been taken to distinguish bribes from an assortment of related practices with which they are easily confused. Before we can be in a position to determine what to do about the problem of bribery, we need to be clearer about what count and ought to count as bribes. Unfortunately, there is as yet very little philosophical literature on this topic.[1] In this essay I shall remedy this defect by presenting an account of the concept of bribery and by employing that account to clarify matters in three areas in which there is public controversy and confusion.

At least some confusion in discussions of bribery arises from a failure adequately to appreciate the distinction between bribery and extortion. This is true, for example, of accounts of the notorious case of Lockheed in Japan. I shall attempt to show that the morality of this and similar transactions is better assessed if we are clear on that distinction.

A second problem area arises out of the fact of cultural variability. As is generally recognized, the conduct of business, government, and the professions differs from culture to culture. In some places transactions that many Americans would consider bribes are not only expected behavior but accepted practice as well. That is, they are condoned by the system of rule governing the conduct of the relevant parties. Are they bribes? Are only some of them bribes? If so, which?

A third problem arises out of the general difficulty of distinguishing between bribes, on the one hand, and gifts and rewards, on the other. Suppose that a manufacturer of dresses keeps a buyer for a catalog company happy by supplying him with any tickets to expensive shows and athletic events that he requests. Are these bribes? Or suppose that a special interest group rewards public administrators who rule in its favor with vacations, automobiles, and jewelry. May we correctly speak of bribery here?

I

To answer such questions we need to say more precisely what bribes are. A bribe is a payment (or promise of payment) for a service. Typically, this payment is made to an

Michael Philips, "Bribery," *Ethics* 94 (July 1984): 621–636. © 1984 by The University of Chicago. All rights reserved.

official in exchange for her violating some official duty or responsibility. And typically she does this by failing deliberately to make a decision on its merits. This does not necessarily mean that a bribed official will make an improper decision; a judge who is paid to show favoritism may do so and yet, coincidentally, make the correct legal decision (i.e., the bribe offerer may in fact have the law on her side). The violation of duty consists in deciding a case for the wrong sorts of reasons.

Although the most typical and important cases of bribery concern political officials and civil servants, one need not be a political official or a civil servant to be bribed. Indeed, one need not be an official of any sort. Thus, a mortician may be bribed to bury a bodyless casket, and a baseball player may be bribed to strike out each time he bats. Still, baseball players and morticians are members of organizations and have duties and responsibilities by virtue of the positions they occupy in these organizations. It is tempting, then, to define a bribe as a payment made to a member of an organization in exchange for the violation of some positional duty or responsibility. This temptation is strengthened by our recognition that we cannot be bribed to violate a duty we have simply by virtue of being a moral agent. (Hired killers, e.g., are not bribed to violate their duty not to kill.) And it is further strengthened when we recognize that we may be paid to violate duties we have by virtue of a nonorganizationally based status without being bribed. (I am not bribed if—as a nonhandicapped person—I accept payment to park in a space reserved for the handicapped; nor am I bribed if—as a pet owner—I accept payment illegally to allow my dog to run free on the city streets.)

Still, it is too strong to say that occupying a position in an organization is a necessary condition of being bribed. We may also speak of bribing a boxer to throw a fight or of bribing a runner to lose a race. These cases, however, are importantly like the cases already described. Roughly, both the boxer and the runner are paid to do something they ought not to do given what they are. What they are, in these cases, are participants in certain practices. What they are paid to do is to act in a manner dictated by some person or organization rather than to act according to the understandings constitutive of their practices. Civil servants, business executives, morticians, and baseball players, of course, are also participants in practices. And their responsibilities, as such, are defined by the rules and understandings governing the organizations to which they belong. At this point, then, we are in a position to state a provisional definition of bribery. Thus, P accepts a bribe from R if and only if P agrees for payment to act in a manner dictated by R rather than doing what is required of him as a participant in his practice.[2]

One advantage of this account is that it enables us to deal with certain difficult cases. Suppose that a high-ranking officer at the Pentagon is paid by a Soviet agent to pass on defense secrets. The first few times he does this we would not hesitate to say that he is bribed. But suppose that he is paid a salary to do this and that the arrangement lasts for a number of years. At this point talk of bribery appears less appropriate. But why should something that has the character of a bribe if done once or twice (or, perhaps, on a piecework basis) cease to have that character if done more often (or, perhaps, on a piecework salaried basis)? In my account the explanation is that the frequency or basis of payment may incline us differently to identify the practice in question. Thus, if an American officer works for the Soviet Union long enough, we begin to think of him as a Soviet spy. In any case, to the extent to which we regard his practice as spying we are inclined to think of the payments in question as payments of a salary as opposed to so many bribes. A similar analysis holds in the case of industrial spies, undercover agents recruited from within organizations, and so forth.[3] We do not think of them as bribed because we do not think of them as full-fledged practitioners of the practices in which they appear to engage.

This practice conception is further supported by the fact that a person may satisfy my account of bribery on a long-term and regularized basis and still be said to be a recipient of bribes. This is so where his continued and regularized acceptance of payments does not warrant any change in our understanding of the practices in which he participates. Thus, we do not think of a judge who routinely accepts payments for favors from organized crime as participating in some practice other than judging, even if he sits almost exclusively on such cases. This may be arbitrary: perhaps we ought rather think of him as an agent of a criminal organization (a paid saboteur of the legal system) and treat him accordingly. My point, however, is that because we do not think of him in this way—because we continue to think of him as a judge—we regard each fresh occurrence as an instance of bribery.

The present account, however, is not entirely adequate as it stands. Consider the following counterexamples: (*a*) an artist is offered $5,000 by an eccentric to ruin a half-completed canvas by employing an unsuitable color and (*b*) a parent is paid $500 for the use of his eight-year-old son in a pornographic film.

It might be argued in relation to *a* that it is consistent with the practice of being an artist that one accept payment to produce whatever a client is willing to pay for. However, the conception of a practice that underlies this response seems to me questionable. What seems to me counterintuitive about speaking of bribery in *a* is that the act in question is private. By this I mean, roughly, that it affects no one who is not a party to the transaction. If I pay an artist to ruin a painting that has been commissioned by a museum, the oddity of speaking of bribery disappears. In general, where there is no violation of an organizational duty, we might say that a payment is a bribe only if it affects the interests of persons or organizations who are not parties to the transaction. To forestall counterexamples based on remote or indirect consequences, we must add that the parties affected must be parties whose interests are normally affected by the conduct of the practice in question and that they must be affected in the manner in which they are normally affected.

It is tempting to go further than this and claim that a bribe occurs only when the act agreed to by the bribed party violates the moral rights of some third party or organization. But this seems to me mistaken. We may speak of bribing officers of terribly corrupt institutions (e.g., concentration camps), but it is not at all clear that these officeholders necessarily violate the rights of any person or organization by violating their institutional duties (e.g., by allowing prisoners to escape). Or consider a society in which slaves are used as boxers and masters wager on the bouts. It seems clear that one can bribe a slave to lose a fight here, but it is not at all clear that a slave violates anyone's rights by accepting payment for so doing. (To say this would be to imply that a slave boxer has a prima facie duty to try to win his fight, and this seems to me untenable.)

What, then, of the second counterexample? Why are we reluctant to speak of bribery in the case of parents? One way to deal with this case is to attribute this reluctance to an anachronistic linguistic habit developed and sustained by centuries of thinking according to which children are the property of parents. According to this outmoded way of thinking, either there is no such thing as the practice of parenting or that practice far more resembles an account that Thrasymachus might offer of it than an account most of us would now accept. It sounds odd to speak of bribing parents, then, because our linguistic habits have not caught up with our new vision of parenting. But this is something we should change: we ought to allow that parents may be bribed.

But I am uncomfortable with this reply. Most of us now agree that children have rights which ought to be protected by law and/or community pressure and that parents have duties not to violate these rights. To this extent, we are coming to understand families as organizations. Thus, if we allow that parents are bribed, we will almost certainly hold that they are bribed in the way that members of organizations are typically bribed, namely, they are paid to violate their positional duties. But there is something disturbing about this. For despite our conviction that children have rights, many of us are uncomfortable thinking of the family as just another organization and thinking of a parent as just another functionary. Our reluctance to maintain that parents may be bribed, then, may express a healthy resistance to thinking of a parent on the model of an official. Just how we ought to think of the family, I cannot say; the challenge is to arrive at a conception that acknowledges that children have legally enforceable rights without reducing the family to just another institution.

If we exempt the family from consideration and we build in the condition required by the second counterexample, we are now in a position to present a tentative definition of bribery. Thus, P is bribed by R if and only if (1) P accepts payment from R to act on R's behalf,[4] (2) P's act on R's behalf consists in violating some rule or understanding constitutive of a practice in which P is engaged, and (3) either P's violation is a violation of some official duty P has by virtue of his participation in that practice or P's violation significantly affects the interests of persons or organizations whose interests are typically connected to that practice.

At least two additional important features of bribery deserve mention. The first is a consequence of the fact that bribes are payments. For, like other kinds of payments (e.g., rent), bribes presuppose agreements of a certain kind.[5] That is, it must be understood by both parties that the payment in question is exchanged, or is to be exchanged, for the relevant conduct. In the most typical and important cases, the bribed party is an official and the conduct in question is the violation of some official duty. In these cases we may say simply that an official P is bribed by R when she accepts payment or the promise of payment for agreeing to violate a positional duty to act on R's behalf. This agreement requirement is of great importance. As I shall argue in Section IV, without it we cannot properly distinguish between bribes and gifts or rewards.

Such agreements need not be explicit. If I am stopped by a policeman for speeding and hand him a fifty-dollar bill along with my driver's license, and he accepts the fifty-dollar bill, it is arguable that we have entered into such an agreement despite what we might say about contributions to the Police Benevolence Association. As I shall argue, some of the difficulties we have in determining what transactions to count as bribes may stem from unclarity concerning the conditions under which we are entitled to say an agreement has been made.

It is a consequence of this account that someone may be bribed despite the fact that she subsequently decides not to perform the service she has agreed to perform. Indeed, we must say this even if she has never been paid but has been only promised payment, or even if she has been paid but returns this payment after she decides not to abide by her part of the agreement. I see nothing strange about this. After all, if one accepts a bribe it seems natural to say that one has been bribed. Still, I have no strong objection to distinguishing between accepting a bribe and being bribed, where a necessary condition of the latter is that one carries out one's part of the bribery agreement. As far as I can see, no important moral question turns on this choice of language.

A final interesting feature of bribery emerges when we reflect on the claim that offering and accepting bribes is prima facie wrong. I will begin with the case of officials. The claim that it is prima facie wrong for someone in an official position to accept a bribe is plausible only if persons in official capacities have prima facie obligations to discharge their official duties. The most plausible argument for this claim is grounded in a social contract model of organizations. By accepting a position in an organization, it might be argued, one tacitly agrees to abide by the rules of that organization. To be bribed is to violate that agreement—it is to break a promise—and is, therefore, prima facie wrong.[6] While I concede that this argument has merit in a context of just and voluntary institutions, it seems questionable in a context of morally corrupt institutions (e.g., Nazi Germany or contemporary El Salvador). And even were it technically valid for those contexts, its conclusion would nonetheless be a misleading half-truth.

It is beyond the scope of this paper to discuss, in detail, the problems with the tacit consent argument in a context of corrupt institutions. In brief, my position is that actions which create prima facie moral obligations in just or ideal contexts do not necessarily create comparable obligations in unjust or corrupt contexts. Thus, for example, it does not seem to me that, if I join the Mafia with the intention of subverting its operations and bringing its members to justice, I have thereby undertaken a prima facie obligation to abide by the code of that organization. Of course, one could say this and add that the obligation in question is typically overridden by other moral considerations. But this seems to me an ad hoc move to defend a position. We use the expression "prima facie duty" to point to a moral presumption for or against a certain type of action. And surely it is strange to insist that there is a moral presumption, in the present case, in favor of carrying out the commands of one's Don.

But even if we grant that there is a prima facie duty here, we must be careful to qualify this assertion. For it is also clear that participants in unjust institutions have a prima facie right to interfere with the normal functioning of those institutions (at least where these functionings can be reasonably expected to produce unjust outcomes). Indeed, where the injustice is great enough they have a prima facie duty to interfere. And in some cases, the strength of this prima facie obligation will exceed the strength of any promise-keeping obligation generated by tacit consent. Thus we may say, other things equal, that the commandant of a concentration camp ought to act in a manner that frustrates the genocidal purpose of that institution. And, assuming that that institution is "rationally" designed to serve its purpose, there will be a strong moral presumption in favor of the violation of his positional duty.

What, then, of the morality of accepting bribes in such cases? If an official has no prima facie duty to satisfy her positional duties—or if the presumption in favor of satisfying them is outweighed by the presumption against so doing—then, other things being equal, it is difficult to see why it is prima facie wrong to accept payment for violating them. After all, there may be serious risks involved. This at least is so where the case against carrying out the purposes of one's organization is strong enough to permit one to violate one's positional duty but is not so strong that one has a prima facie obligation to do this. For it does seem prima facie wrong to make compliance with a prima facie duty contingent on payment (it ought rather to be contingent on an assessment of what one ought to do, all things considered). And it certainly seems wrong to demand payment for doing what is one's duty, all things considered.

Still, this may be too quick. Consider a concentration camp guard who lacks the courage to help inmates escape but who would be courageous enough to undertake the risks involved were he assured of sufficient funds to transport his family to another country and comfortably to begin a new life. If he is in fact reasonably certain that he would be brave enough to do what is required of him were he paid, it seems not improper of him to demand payment. In general, if the wrong of demanding payment for doing one's duty is outweighed by the importance of doing it and if demanding payment for doing it is causally necessary for doing it, then, all things considered, it is not wrong to demand payment.

If it is not wrong for an official to accept a bribe, one does not induce him to do something wrong by offering him one. Thus, we cannot say in all contexts that it is prima facie wrong to offer someone a bribe *because* this is an attempt to induce him to do something wrong or to corrupt him.[7] On the other hand, there may be cases in which it is prima facie wrong to offer a bribe despite the fact that it is perfectly acceptable for the bribed party to accept one. Recall the case of the boxer slave. Despite the fact that the slave has no obligation to try to win, a wagering master may have a prima facie obligation not to pay him to lose. For by so doing the master may gain an unfair advantage over his fellow wagerers. It might be objected that the master's obligation in this case is misleadingly described as an obligation not to bribe. He is obligated, rather, not to fix fights; or, more generally, not to take unfair advantage of his fellow wagerers. This objection raises issues we need not consider here. It is enough to point out that the purpose of offering a bribe is very often to seek some unfair or undeserved benefit or advantage and that this is one reason we are rightly suspicious of the morality of bribe offers.

We are now in a position to state a fifth interesting feature of bribery. Even if it is not prima facie wrong to offer and to accept bribes in all contexts, it is prima facie wrong to do so in morally uncorrupted contexts. Accordingly, a bribe offerer or a bribe taker must defend the morality of his act either by showing that there are countervailing moral considerations in its favor or alternatively by showing that the moral context is so corrupt that the factors that generate prima facie duties in uncorrupted contexts do not apply here. This strategy of moral justifications, of course, is not unique to bribery. It may hold in relation to a wide range of what are ordinarily taken to be prima facie duties. In the case of bribery, however, arguments to the effect that the moral context is corrupted will have a certain characteristic form. Thus, in the most important case—the case of officials—they will be arguments that challenge the legitimacy of an institution.

II

I now turn to the first of three problem areas I shall address in this paper, namely, the problem of distinguishing between bribery and extortion. Compare the following cases:

a) Executive P hopes to sell an airplane to the national airline of country C. The deal requires the approval of minister R. P knows that R can make a better deal elsewhere and that R knows this as well. P's researchers have discovered that R has a reputation for honesty but that R is in serious financial difficulties. Accordingly P offers R a large sum of money to buy from him. R accepts and abides by the agreement.

b) The same as *a* except that P knows that he is offering the best deal R can get, and R knows this too. Nonetheless, P is informed by reliable sources that R will not deal with P unless P offers to pay him a considerable sum of money. P complies, and R completes the deal.

According to my analysis *a* is bribery; *b* is not.

The difference between *a* and *b* is clear enough. In *a* P pays R to violate R's duty (in this case, to make the best deal that R can). In *b* P does no such thing. Instead, he pays R to do what is required of R by his institutional commitments in any case. Moreover, he does so in response to R's threat to violate those commitments in a manner that jeopardizes P's interests. Accordingly, *b* resembles extortion more than it does bribery. For, roughly speaking, R extorts P if R threatens P with a penalty in case P fails to give R something to which R has no rightful claim.

If this is true it may be that American corporate executives accused of bribing foreign officials are sometimes more like victims of extortion than offerers of bribes. For in at least some cases they are required to make payments to assure that an official does what he is supposed to do in any case. This is especially true in the case of inspectors of various kinds and in relation to government officials who must approve transactions between American and local companies. An inspector who refuses to approve a shipment that is up to standards unless he is paid off is like a bandit who demands tribute on all goods passing through his territory.

It does not follow that it is morally correct for American companies to pay off such corrupt officials. There are cases in which it is morally wrong to surrender to the demands of bandits and other extortionists. But it is clear that the moral questions that arise here are different sorts of questions than those that arise in relation to bribery. The moral relations between the relevant parties differ. The bribery agreement is not by its nature an agreement between victims and victimizers. The extortion agreement is. Moral justifications and excuses for complying with the demands of an extortionist are easier to come by than moral justifications and excuses for offering bribes.

Of course, the distinction in question is often easier to draw in theory than in practice. An inspector who demands a payoff to authorize a shipment is likely to fortify his demand by insisting that the product does not meet standards. In some cases it may be difficult to know whether or not he is lying (e.g., whether the shipment has been contaminated in transit). And given the high cost of delays, a company may decide that it is too expensive to take the time to find out. In this case, a company may decide to pay off without knowing whether it is agreeing to pay a bribe or surrendering to extortion. Since the morality of its decisions may well turn on what it is in fact doing in such cases, a company that does not take the time to find out acts in a morally irresponsible manner (unless, of course, it is in a position to defend both courses of action).

What sorts of justifications can a company present for offering bribes? It is beyond the scope of this paper to provide a detailed discussion of this question. However, I have already mentioned a number of considerations that count as moral reasons against bribery in a variety of contexts. To begin with, in reasonably just contexts, officials ordinarily are obligated to discharge the duties of their offices. In these cases bribe offers are normally attempts to induce officials to violate duties. Moreover, if accepted, a bribe offer may make it more likely that that official will violate future duties. Accordingly, it may contribute to the corruption of an official. In addition, the intent of a bribe offer is often to secure an unfair advantage or an undeserved privilege. Where this is the case, it too counts as a reason against bribery. To determine whether a bribe offer is wrong in any particular case, then, we must decide: (1) whether these reasons obtain in that case; (2) if they obtain, how much weight we ought to attach to them; and (3) how much weight we ought to attach to countervailing considerations. (Suppose, e.g., that it is necessary to bribe an official in order to meet an important contractual obligation.) It is worth remarking in this regard that, where officials routinely take bribes, the presumption against corrupting officials normally will not apply. Similarly, to the extent that bribery is an accepted weapon in the arsenal of all competitors, bribe offers cannot be construed as attempts to achieve an unfair advantage over one's competitors.

III

It is sometimes suggested that an environment may be so corrupt that no payments count as bribes. These are circumstances in which the level of official compliance to duty is very low, and payoffs are so widespread that they are virtually institutionalized. Suppose, for example, that the laws of country N impose very high duties on a variety of products but that it is common practice in N for importers and exporters to pay customs officials to overlook certain goods and/or to underestimate their number or value. Suppose, moreover, that the existence of this practice is common knowledge but that no effort is made to stop it by law enforcement officials at any level;[8] indeed, that any attempts to stop it would be met by widespread social disapproval. One might even imagine that customs officials receive no salary in N but earn their entire livelihood in this way. One might further imagine that customs officials are expected to return a certain amount of money to the government every month and are fired from their jobs for failure to do so. Finally, one might suppose that the cumulative advantages and disadvantages of this way of doing things is such that the economy of N is about as strong as it would be under a more rule-bound alternative. Are these officials bribed?

In my analysis, the answer to this question depends on how we understand the duties of the customs officer. If the official job description for the customs officer in N (and the written laws of N) is like those of most countries, the customs officer violates his official duties according to these codes by allowing goods to leave the country without collecting the full duty. The question, however, is how seriously we are to take these written codes. Where social and political practice routinely violates them, nothing is done about it, and few members of the legal and nonlegal community believe that anything ought to be done about it, it is arguable that these codes are dead letters. If we find this to be true of the codes governing the duties of the customs officials in country N, we have good reason for saying that the real obligations of these officials do not require that they impose the duties described in those written codes (but only that they return a certain sum of the money they collect to the central government each month). Anything collected in excess of that amount they are entitled to keep as salary (recall that they are officially unpaid). In reality we might say that duties on exports in country N are not fixed but negotiable.

Of course if we decide that the written law of N is the law of N, we must describe the situation otherwise. In that case, the official obligations of the customs officials are as they are described, and the system in N must be characterized as one of rampant bribery condoned both by government and by popular opinion. It seems to me that the philosophy of law on which this account rests is implausible. However, there is no need to argue this to defend my analysis of this case. My position is simply that whether or not we describe what goes on here as bribery depends on what we take the real legal responsibilities of the customs official to be. To the extent that we are inclined to identify his duties with the written law we will be inclined to speak of bribery here. To the extent that we are unwilling so to identify his duties we will not.[9]

IV

Let us now consider the problem of distinguishing bribes from rewards and gifts. The problem arises because gifts are often used in business and government to facilitate transactions. And to the degree to which a business person, professional person, or government official is influenced in her decision by gifts, it is tempting to conclude that she is violating her duties. In such cases we are tempted to speak of these gifts as bribes.

If I am correct, however, this temptation should be resisted. A bribe, after all, presupposes an agreement. A gift may be made with the intention of inducing an official to show favoritism to the giver, but unless acceptance of what is transferred can be construed as an agreement to show favoritism, what is transferred is not a bribe.

In some cases, of course, the acceptance of what is offered can be so construed. Again, if I offer fifty dollars to a policeman who has stopped me for speeding, he has a right to construe my act as one of offering a bribe, and I have a right to construe his acceptance in the corresponding manner. If I regularly treat the neighborhood policeman to a free lunch at my diner and he regularly neglects to ticket my illegally parked car, we have reason to say the same. Agreements need not be explicit. My point is just that to the degree that it is inappropriate to speak of agreements, it is also inappropriate to speak of bribes.

It follows from this that, if I present an official with an expensive item to induce him to show favoritism on my behalf, in violation of his duty, I have not necessarily bribed him. It does not follow from this, however, that I have done nothing wrong. So long as you are morally obligated to perform your official duty, normally it will be wrong of me to induce you to do otherwise by presenting you with some expensive item. Moreover, if you have any reason to believe that accepting what I offer will induce you not to do your duty, you have done something wrong by accepting my gift. To prevent such wrongs we have laws prohibiting persons whose interests are closely tied to the decisions of public officials from offering gifts to these officials. And we have laws forbidding officials to accept such gifts.

It might be objected that this account is too lenient. Specifically, it might be argued that wherever P presents Q with something of value to induce Q to violate Q's official duties P has offered a bribe.

But this is surely a mistake. It suggests, among other things, that an official is bribed so long as she accepts what is offered with this intent. Yet an official may accept such a gift innocently, believing that it is what it purports to be, namely, a token of friendship or goodwill. And she may do so with justifiable confidence that doing so will not in any way affect the discharge of her duty.

It may be replied that officials are bribed by such inducements only when they are in fact induced to do what is desired of them. But again, it may be the case that an official accepts what is offered innocently, believing it to be a gift, and that she believes falsely that it will not affect her conduct. In this case she has exercised bad judgment, but she has not been bribed. Indeed, it seems to me that it is improper to say that she accepts a bribe even when she recognizes the intent of the inducement and believes that accepting it is likely to influence her. There is a distinction between accepting a drink with the understanding that one is agreeing to be seduced and accepting a drink with the knowledge that so doing will make one's seduction more likely. To be bribed is to be bought, not merely to be influenced to do something.

From a moral point of view, whenever failure to perform one's official duties is wrong it may be as bad to accept a gift that one knows will influence one in the conduct of one's duty as it is to accept a bribe. And clearly we are entitled morally to criticize those who offer and accept such inducements. Moreover, we are right to attempt to prevent this sort of thing by legally restricting the conditions under which persons may offer gifts to officials and the conditions under which officials may accept such gifts. Nonetheless, such gifts ought not to be confused with bribes. If P accepts a gift from R and does not show the desired favoritism, R may complain of P's ingratitude but not of P's dishonesty (unless, of course, P led him on in some way). If P accepts a bribe from R and does not show the desired favoritism, P has been dishonest (perhaps twice).

This point is not without practical importance. People who work in the same organization or in the same profession often form friendships despite the fact that some of them are in a position to make decisions that affect the interests of others. Here, as everywhere, friendships are developed and maintained in part by exchanges of favors, gifts, meals, and so forth. Were we to take seriously the inducement theory of bribery, however, this dimension of collegial and organizational existence would be threatened. In that case, if P's position is such that he must make decisions affecting R, any gifts, favors, et cetera from R to P should be regarded with at least some suspicion. To guard against the accusation that he has been bribed by R, P must be in a position to offer reasons for believing that R's intent in inviting him to dinner was not to induce him to show favoritism. And for R to be certain that he is not offering P a bribe in this case, R must be certain that his intentions are pure. All of this would require such vigilance in relation to one's own motives and the motives of others that friendships in collegial and organizational settings would be more difficult to sustain than they are at present.

Since decision makers are required to show impartiality they must in any case be careful not to accept gifts and favors that will influence them to show favoritism. Moreover, if they are required by their position to assess the moral character of those affected by their decisions, they may be required to assess the intent with which such gifts or favors are offered. Most officials, however, are not required to assess character in this way. In order to avoid doing wrong by accepting gifts and favors they need only be justly confident of their own continued impartiality. Thus, they are ordinarily entitled to ignore questions of intent unless there is some special reason to do otherwise. If the intent to influence were sufficient for a bribe, however, they would not be at liberty to bestow the benefit of the doubt in this way.

Again, there are cases in which impartiality is so important that decision makers should be prohibited both from accepting gifts or favors from any persons likely to be directly affected by their decisions and from forming friendships with such persons. And they should disqualify themselves when they are asked to make a decision that affects either a friend or someone from whom they have accepted gifts or favors in the reasonably recent past. Judges are a case in point. In other cases, however, institutions and professions should be willing to risk some loss in impartiality in order to enjoy the benefits of friendship and mutual aid. For these are essential to the functioning of some organizations and to the well-being of the people within them. Consider, for example, universities. The practical disadvantage of the inducement account is that it may require us to be unnecessarily suspicious of certain exchanges constitutive of mutual aid and friendship (at least if we take it seriously).

V

An interesting related problem arises in cultures in which a more formal exchange of gifts may be partly constitutive of a special relationship between persons, namely, something like friendship. In such cultures, so long as certain other conditions are satisfied, to make such exchanges is to enter into a system of reciprocal rights and duties. Among these duties may be the duty to show favoritism toward "friends," even when one acts in an official capacity. Moreover, the giver may be expected to show gratitude for each occasion of favoritism by further gift giving. On the face of it, this certainly looks like bribery. Is that description warranted?

To begin with, we need to distinguish between cases in which the special relationships in question are genuine and cases in which they are not. In the latter case certain ritual or ceremonial forms may be used to dress up what each party regards as a business transaction of the standard Western variety in a manner that provides an excuse for bribery. I shall say more about this presently. But let me begin with the first case.

Where the relationships in question are genuine and the laws of the relevant society are such that the official duties of the relevant official do not prohibit favoritism, this practice of gift giving cannot be called bribery. For in this case there is no question of the violation of duty. All that can be said here is that such societies condone different ways of doing business than we do. Specifically, they do not mark off a sphere of business and/or bureaucratic activity in which persons are supposed to meet as "abstract individuals," that is, in which they are required to ignore their social and familial ties. Their obligations, rather, are importantly determined by such ties even in the conduct of business and governmental affairs. Favoritism is shown, then, not in order to carry out one's part of a bargain but, rather, to discharge an obligation of kinship or loyalty. Failure to show favoritism would entitle one's kinsman or friend to complain not that one reneged on an agreement but, rather, that one had wronged him as an ally or a kinsman.

This is not to say that one cannot bribe an official in such a society. One does this here, as elsewhere, by entering into an agreement with him such that he violates his official duties for payment. The point is just that favoritism shown to friends and kinsmen is not necessarily a violation of duty in such societies. Indeed, one might be bribed not to show favoritism.

The official duties of an official, of course, may not be clear. Thus, the written law may prohibit favoritism to kin and ally, though this is widely practiced and condoned and infrequently prosecuted. This may occur when a society is in a transitional state from feudalism or tribalism to a Western-style industrial society, but it may also occur in an industrial society with different traditions than our own. To the extent that it is unclear what the official duties of officials are in such cases it will also be difficult to say what count as bribes. Indeed, even if we decide that an official does violate his duty by showing favoritism to kin and allies who reciprocate with gifts, we may not be justified in speaking of bribery here. For the official may not be acting as he does in order to fulfill his part of an agreement. Rather, he may be acting to fulfill some obligation of kinship or loyalty. Again, his failure so to act may not entitle his kinsmen or allies to complain that he had welched on a deal; rather, it would entitle them to complain that he wronged them as kinsmen or allies.

Of course, all this is so only when the relationships in question are genuine. In some cases, however, the rhetoric and ceremonial forms of a traditional culture may be used to camouflage what are in fact business relations of the standard Western variety. To the extent that this is so, the favoritism in question may in fact be bribery in ethnic dress. The relationships in question are not genuine when they are not entered into in good faith. It is clear, moreover, that when American executives present expensive gifts to foreign businessmen or foreign government officials they do so for business reasons. That is, they have no intention of entering into a system of reciprocal rights and duties that may obligate them in the future to act contrary to their long-term interest. Rather, they perform the required ceremonies knowing that they will continue to base their decisions on business reasons. Their intention is to buy favoritism. And the foreign officials and companies with whom they do business are typically aware of this. This being the case, invitations of the form "First we become friends, then we do business" cannot plausibly be construed as invitations to participate in some traditional way of life. Typically, both parties recognize that what is requested here is a bribe made in an appropriate ceremonial way.

VI

On the basis of this analysis it seems clear that American officials are not always guilty of bribery when they pay off foreign officials. In some cases they are victims of extortion; in other cases, the context may be such that the action purchased from the relevant official does not count as a violation of his duty. The fact that American executives engaged in international commerce are innocent of some of the charges that have been made against them, however, does not imply that those who have made them are mistaken in their assessment of the character of these executives. One's character, after all, is a matter of what one is disposed to do. If these executives are willing to engage in bribery whenever this is necessary to promote their perceived long-term business interests, whatever the morality of the situation, it follows (at very least) that they are amoral.

Notes

1 At the time this paper was written there were no references to bribes or bribery in the *Philosopher's Index*. Since that time one paper has been indexed—Arnold Berleant's "Multinationals, Local Practice, and the Problems of Ethical Consistency" (*Journal of Business Ethics* 1 [August 1982]: 185–93)—but, as the title of this short paper suggests, Berleant is not primarily concerned with providing an analysis of the concept of bribery. However, three presentations on the topic of bribery were made at the 1983 "Conference for Business Ethics" (organized by the Society for Business Ethics at DePaul University, July 25–26) and have subsequently been accepted for publication. These are: Kendall D'Andrade's "Bribery" (forthcoming in a special issue of the *Journal of Business Ethics*, devoted to the DePaul conference, 1984); John Danley's "Toward a Theory of Bribery" (forthcoming in the *Journal of Business and Professional Ethics*, 1984); and Tom Carson's "Bribery, Extortion and the Foreign Corrupt Practices Act" (forthcoming in *Philosophy and Public Affairs*, Summer 1984). Where my position on substantive questions differs significantly from D'Andrade's, Carson's, or Danley's, I shall discuss this in the notes.

2 Danley defines "bribing" as "offering or giving something of value with a corrupt intent to induce or influence an action of someone in a public or official capacity." Carson defines a bribe as a payment to someone "in exchange for special consideration that is incompatible with the duties of his position." Both go on to discuss bribery as if it were restricted to officials of organizations. Since these are the most typical and important cases of bribery, their focus is understandable. But it does have at least one unfortunate consequence. For it leads both Danley and Carson to think that the question of whether it is prima facie wrong to offer or accept bribes reduces to the question of whether officials have obligations to satisfy their positional duties. Danley argues that they do not if the institutions they serve are illegitimate. Carson argues that they do on the ground that they have made a tacit agreement with their institution to discharge those duties (accepting a bribe, for Carson, is an instance of promise breaking). Whatever the merits of their arguments concerning the responsibilities of officials, both approach the question of the prima facie morality of bribery too narrowly. For different issues seem to arise when we consider bribery outside the realm of officialdom. Clearly it is more difficult for Carson to make his tacit consent argument in relation to the bribed athlete. For it is not clear that a runner who enters a race tacitly agrees to win it (if so, he would be breaking a promise by running to prepare for future races or by entering to set the pace for someone else). Nor is it clear that a boxer who accepts payment not to knock out his opponent in the early rounds violates a tacit agreement to attempt a knockout at his earliest convenience. Danley must expand his account to accommodate such cases as well. For it is not clear what it means to say that a practice such as running or boxing is legitimate.

3 Such cases present a problem for the accounts of both Danley and Carson. At the very least they must expand their accounts of positional duties such that we can distinguish between a bribe, on the one hand, and a salary paid to a spy recruited from within an organization, on the other.

4 Thus D' Andrade defines bribery as "alienation of agency." In his account bribery occurs when someone is seduced into abandoning his role as an agent of one person or organization and, for a price, becomes the agent of another. This highlights an important feature of bribery that is ignored by Carson and Danley and that was neglected in my own earlier thinkng on this subject, namely, that a brbe taker acts on behalf of someone. But D' Andrade's clam that agency is alienated when one accepts a bribe implies that the bribe taken necessarily is committed to act on behalf of some person or organization before he is in a position to accept a bribe. And it is difficult to see what helpful truth this might express in relation to the scientist, runner, or boxer of my examples. Surely it is not helpful to say that a bribe taker begins as his own agent in these cases and, for pay, alienates that agency to another. This applies to anyone who takes a job. Nor is it helpful to say—as D'Andrade did sat at one point—that he may begin as an agent of some abstraction (e.g.,truth). Surely the point behind ths obscure claim is better made by speaking of what is expected of someone as a participant in a practice. It is also worth noting that D' Andrade's alienation of agency account offers no basis for distinguishing between bribed officials, on the one hand, and undercover agents and spies, on the other. For these too alienate agency.

5 Carson fails to recognize the significance of this feature of bribery. This view of bribery, moreover, is inconsistent with Danley's account. Danley understands a bribe as an attempt to induce or influence someone. In this matter he appears to have most dictionaries on his side (including the OED). However, as I argue in more detail in Sec. IV he is mistaken.

6 This is Carson's argument.

7 Nor can we say that it is prima facie wrong because it is an attempt to get someone to do something that is prima facie wrong. This argument is flawed in two ways. To begin with, as we have seen, the premise expresses what is at best a dangerous half-truth. Were we to reason from the whole truth we must conclude that there are some contexts in which the presumption in favor of violating one's official duties is stronger than the presumption against it. In the second place, moreover, the inference is invalid: it is not necessarily prima facie wrong to induce someone to do something that is prima facie wrong. Rather, it is prima facie wrong to induce someone to do something that is wrong, all things considered. Thus, if it is prima facie wrong for P to do A, but P ought to do A, all things considered, there is no presumption against my inducing P to do A; I do not need to justify this by appealing to countervailing moral considerations. I require such justification only when it is wrong for P to do so. Cases of this sort are interesting but typically neglected by philosophers. (The following are examples: [a] P is a soldier in a war in which each side has equal claim to justice; R is a guard on the opposite side. Though it might be wrong for R to accept a bribe from P, it is not wrong for P to offer R a bribe. [b] P's father is certain to be convicted of a crime he did not commit because the evidence is overwhelmingly against him. It is permissible for P to offer a bribe to R, an assistant district attorney, to "lose" some evidence; but it is wrong for R to accept the bribe.) In any case, the upshot of this is that even if there were a general moral presumption against accepting bribes it would not follow that there is a comparable presumption against offering bribes.

8 In D'Andrade's account bribes are necessarily secret, so these could not count as bribes.

9 A corresponding point holds in relation to bribery outside the realm of officialdom. Consider the case of professional wrestling. Most of us believe that the outcome of professional wrestling matches is determined in advance. Are the losers bribed? (To simplify matters let us assume that they are paid a bit of extra money for losing.) The answer here depends on how we understand their practice. If we take them to be participating in a wrestling competition, we must say that they are bribed. In that case, by failing to compete they violate an understanding constitutive of their practice. It is reasonably clear, however, that professional wrestlers are not engaged in an athletic competition. Rather, they are engaged in a dramatic performance. This being the case the losers are not bribed. They are merely doing what professional wrestlers are ordinarily paid to do, namely, to play out their part in an informal script.

Bribery and Implicit Agreements
A Reply to Philips

THOMAS L. CARSON

In a paper that appeared recently in *Ethics*, Michael Philips defends at some length an analysis of the concept of bribery.[1] He also attempts to give an account of the moral status of bribery. Philips attacks several views defended in my paper, "Bribery, Extortion and the 'Foreign Corrupt Practices Act,'" *Philosophy and Public Affairs*, Winter 1985, pp. 66–90. In my paper, I argue that accepting a bribe involves the violation of an implicit or explicit promise or understanding associated with one's office or role and that, therefore, accepting a bribe is always *prima facie* wrong. Philips offers two separate criticisms of this position. (1) He argues that in at least some cases of bribery the person who accepts the bribe does not thereby violate any agreements or understandings associated with any offices or positions that he holds. (2) He argues that in "morally corrupt contexts" there may be no *prima facie* duty to adhere to the agreements or understandings implicit in one's role or position. I shall offer replies to both of these criticisms, although I make some concessions to the first.

(1) Standard cases of bribery involve paying an official of an organization to do things contrary to the obligations of his office or position. The following examples all fit this model of bribery: (1) paying a judge or juror to decide in one's favor, (2) paying a policeman not to give one a traffic ticket, and (3) paying a government official not to report violations of health and safety standards. Philips concedes that in cases in which a bribe is paid to an official it is plausible to suppose that the official's acceptance of the bribe constitutes the violation of a "tacit agreement."[2] However, he claims that there are cases of bribery in which the person being bribed is self-employed and in which his acceptance of the bribe cannot be said to constitute the violation of an agreement or understanding between himself and some other party. (Philips seems to imply that in such cases there is no identifiable party *with whom* one can be said to have made an agreement.) Philips gives the example of bribing a self-employed professional athlete. In such cases, he claims, the acceptance of the bribe cannot to said to constitute the violation of a tacit agreement.

> Clearly it is more difficult for Carson to make his tacit consent argument in relation to the bribed athlete. For it is not clear that a runner who enters a race tacitly agrees to win it (if so, he would be breaking a promise by running to prepare for future races or by entering to set the pace for someone else). Nor is it clear that a boxer who accepts payment not to knock out his opponent in the early rounds violates a tacit agreement to attempt a knockout at his earliest convenience.[3]

Thomas L. Carson, "Bribery and Implicit Agreements: A Reply to Philips." Reprinted with kind permission of Springer from *Journal of Business Ethics* 6 (1987): 123–125. Copyright © 1987.

But, Philips to the contrary, athletes, even self-employed athletes who are not members of teams or any other organizations, compete in *public competition* (as opposed to private matches or exhibition matches) on the understanding that they will do their best to win. This understanding constitutes an implicit promise or agreement between the athlete and (i) the sponsors or promoters of the competition, (ii) the spectators, fans, gamblers, and others who follow the competition (they take an interest in the competition only on the assumption that it is serious competition in which each athlete does his best to win), and (iii) his fellow competitors. The runner who enters a public competition tacitly agrees to do his best to win. To run the race with only the intention to 'warm up' for a future race is to violate an implicit agreement. Running so as to 'pace' a teammate violates no understanding, provided that one is competing as a member of a team. In such cases, we can say that one competes on the understanding that one will do the best one can to promote the victory of one's team. The boxer who accepts a bribe not to knock his opponent out in the early rounds violates a tacit agreement to try his best to win. For him to forego early opportunities to knock his opponent out is for him to fail to do his best to win. An athlete who participates in public competition tacitly agrees to do his best to win, short of injuring himself or others or breaking the rules of the sport. The promoters and/or sponsors of the competition, the spectators, and his fellow athletes all act on the assumption that the athletes will do their best to win. Of course, the fact that others *expect* one to do something does not suffice to show that one has consented or agreed to do it. However, there are other features in addition to the mere expectation that the athlete will do his best to win, which permit us to conclude that a tacit agreement exists in this case. The athlete knows that the others expect that he will do his best to win. Further, he knows that they play their roles in this competition only on the basis of this expectation. They would not do what they are doing (or even take an interest in the competition) if they came to believe that the athletes were not attempting to win.

Philips briefly mentions a somewhat different example that poses serious problems for my position. The case that he mentions is one in which a slave is bribed to lose a boxing match promoted by his master.[4] I find it a bit odd to refer to this as a bribe and am tempted to conclude that a necessary condition of bribery is that the person who receives the bribe accepts the payment in exchange for actions contrary to the duties associated with a position or role that he has accepted voluntarily. However, there are other cases of paying individuals to violate duties attached to positions or roles that they have not accepted voluntarily which we would not be hesitant to describe as bribes. Ordinary usage would allow that it makes sense to speak of bribing a conscripted soldier, even though he has not voluntarily accepted the duties attached to his position. Understandings or agreements entered into by slaves with their masters (or conscript soldiers with the armies of which they are a part) are not voluntary and thus do not create *prima facie* duties in virtue of implicit promises. (Perhaps some conscript soldiers do have a *prima facie* duty to fulfill the obligations of their positions, but these are not duties that they have in virtue of any promises or agreements.) I must, therefore, concede that in such cases the person accepting the bribe has not entered into any agreements or understandings of the sort that could generate a *prima facie* duty not to accept the bribe. However, it is well to note that my account still holds for the vast majority of cases of bribery. In almost all ordinary cases of bribery, the person who accepts the bribe violates duties associated with roles or positions that he has voluntarily assumed. The only exceptions are bribery of conscripted soldiers, some prostitutes, and others held as virtual slaves. The vast majority of us freely choose the roles and offices that we occupy.

(2) Philips argues that, even in those cases of bribery in which the recipient of the bribe is a member of an organization and can be plausibly said to be taking the bribe in violation of some implicit agreement or understanding, this understanding does not necessarily generate a *prima facie* duty not to accept the bribe.

> By accepting a position in an organization, it might be argued, one tacitly agrees to abide by the rules of that organization. To be bribed is to violate that agreement—it is to break a promise—and is, therefore, *prima facie* wrong. While I concede that this argument has merit in the context of just and voluntary institutions, it seems questionable in a context of morally corrupt institutions (e.g., Nazi Germany or contemporary El Salvador). And even were it technically valid for those contexts, its conclusion would nonetheless be a misleading half-truth. … Thus, for example, it does not seem to me that, if I join the Mafia with the intention of subverting its operations and bringing its members to justice, I have thereby undertaken a *prima facie* obligation to abide by the code of that organization. Of course, one could say this and add that the obligation in question is typically overridden by other moral considerations. But this seems to me an *ad hoc* move to defend a position. We use the expression *"prima facie duty"* to point to a moral presumption for or against a certain type of action. And surely it is strange to insist that there is a moral presumption, in the present case, in favor of carrying out the commands of one's Don.[5]

I fail to see the force of this argument. Philips thinks it 'dangerous' to suppose that we have a *prima facie* duty to keep all implicit agreements, lest we fail to see that it would be wrong to fulfill our institutional duties in many morally corrupt situations (see Philips' footnote 7). But surely this is not a convincing argument. In general, it is not a valid argument to claim that since it is very clear that *S* ought to do *x* (all things considered), it cannot, in any sense, be his *prima facie* duty not to do *x*. Conflicts of duties aren't necessarily cases in which it is difficult to determine what one ought to do, all things considered. Nor is it an *"ad hoc* move" to say that *prima facie* duties can be overridden by other more important duties. The concept of a *prima facie* duty is derived from Ross. Ross is perfectly prepared to allow that some *prima facie* duties create only a very *weak moral presumption* for certain kinds of acts. He would have no hesitancy to say that implicit promises in the context of morally corrupt institutions create *prima facie* duties—albeit duties that can sometimes be easily overridden by other considerations. If we accept Ross' view that breaking promises (or breaking voluntary promises) is *prima facie* wrong, then we should have no reluctance to say that it is always *prima facie* wrong to accept bribes to do things that are contrary to implicit agreements or understandings into which one has entered *voluntarily*.

Notes

1 Michael Philips, 'Bribery', *Ethics* 94 (July 1984): 621–636.
2 Philips, p. 623, n. 2.
3 Philips, p. 623, n. 2.
4 Philips, p. 625.
5 Philips, p. 627. Philips attributes this argument to me in his footnote 6.

What's Wrong with Bribery?

Scott Turow

The question on the floor is what is wrong with bribery? I am not a philosopher and thus my answer to that question may be less systematic than others, but it is certainly no less deeply felt. As a federal prosecutor I have worked for a number of years now in the area of public corruption. Over that course of time, perhaps out of instincts of self-justification, or, so it seems, sharpened moral insights, I have come to develop an abiding belief that bribery is deeply immoral.

We all know that bribery is unlawful and I believe that the legal concepts in this area are in fact grounded in widely accepted moral intuitions. Bribery as defined by the state of Illinois and construed by the United States Court of Appeals for the Seventh Circuit in the case of *United States* v. *Isaacs*, in which the former Governor of Illinois, Otto Kerner, was convicted for bribery, may be said to take place in these instances: Bribery occurs when property or personal advantage is offered, without the authority of law, to a public official with the intent that the public official act favorably to the offeror at any time or fashion in execution of the public official's duties.

Under this definition of bribery, the crime consists solely of an unlawful offer, made or accepted with a prohibited state of mind. No particular act need be specified; and the result is immaterial.

This is merely a matter of definition. Oddly the moral underpinnings of bribery are clearer in the context of another statute—the criminal law against mail fraud. Federal law has no bribery statute of general application; it is unlawful of course to bribe federal officials, to engage in a pattern of bribery, or to engage in bribery in certain other specified contexts, e.g., to influence the outcome of a sporting contest. But unlike the states, the Congress, for jurisdictional reasons, has never passed a general bribery statute, criminalizing *all* instances of bribery. Thus, over time the federal mail fraud statute has come to be utilized as the vehicle for some bribery prosecutions. The theory, adopted by the courts, goes to illustrate what lawyers have thought is wrong with bribery.

Mail fraud/bribery is predicated on the theory that someone—the bribee's governmental or private employer—is deprived, by a bribe, of the recipient's undivided loyalties. The bribee comes to serve two masters and as such is an 'unfaithful servant'. This breach of fiduciary duty, when combined with active efforts at concealment becomes actionable under the mail fraud law, assuming certain other jurisdictional requisites are met. Concealment, as noted, is another essential element of the crime. An employee who makes no secret of his dual service cannot be called to task;

presumably his employer is thought to have authorized and accepted the divided loyalties. For this reason, the examples of maitre d's accepting payments from customers cannot be regarded as fully analogous to instances of bribery which depend on persons operating under false pretenses, a claimed loyalty that has in truth been undermined.

Some of the stricter outlines of what constitutes bribery, in the legal view, can be demonstrated by example. Among the bribery prosecutions with which I have spent the most time is a series of mail fraud/bribery cases arising out of corruption at the Cook County Board of Appeals. The Board of Appeals is a local administrative agency, vested with the authority to review and revise local real estate property tax assessments. After a lengthy grand jury investigation, it became clear that the Board of Appeals was a virtual cesspool, where it was commonplace for lawyers practicing before the Board to make regular cash payments to some decisionmakers. The persons accused of bribery at the Board generally relied on two defenses. Lawyers and tax consultants who made the payments often contended that the payments were, in a fashion, a necessity; the Board was so busy, so overcome by paperwork, and so many other people were paying, that the only way to be sure cases would be examined was to have an 'in' with an official whom payments had made friendly. The first argument also suggests the second: that the payments, whatever their nature, had accomplished nothing untoward, and that any tax reduction petition granted by the bribed official actually deserved the reduction it received.

Neither contention is legally sufficient to remove the payments from the category of bribery. Under the definition above, any effort to cause favorable action constitutes bribery, regardless of the supposedly provocative circumstances. And in practice juries had great difficulty accepting the idea that the lawyers involved had been 'coerced' into making the boxcar incomes—sometimes $300 000 to $400 000 a year—that many of the bribers earned. Nor is the merits of the cases involved a defense, under the above definitions. Again, in practical terms, juries seemed reluctant to believe that lawyers would be passing the Board's deputy commissioners cash under the table if they were really convinced of their cases' merits. But whatever the accuracy of that observation, it is clear that the law prohibits a payment, even to achieve a deserved result.

The moral rationale for these rules of law seems clear to me. Fundamentally, I believe that any payment to a governmental official for corrupt purposes is immoral. The obligation of government to deal with like cases alike is a principle of procedural fairness which is well recognized. But this principle is more than a matter of procedure; it has a deep moral base. We recognize that the equality of humans, their fundamental dignity as beings, demands that each stand as an equal before the government they have joined to create, that each, as Ronald Dworkin has put, has a claim to government's equal concern and respect. Bribery asks that that principle be violated, that some persons be allowed to stand ahead of others, that like cases not be treated alike, and that some persons be preferred. This I find morally repugnant.

Moreover, for this reason, I cannot accept the idea that bribery, which is wrong here, is somehow more tolerable abroad. Asking foreign officials to act in violation of moral principles must, as an abstract matter, be no less improper than asking that of members of our own government; it even smacks of imperialist attitudes. Furthermore, even dealing with the question on this level assumes that there are societies which unequivocally declare that governmental officials may properly deal with the citizenry in a random and unequal fashion. I doubt, in fact, whether any such sophisticated society exists; more than likely, bribery offends the norms and mores of the foreign country as well.

Not only does bribery violate fundamental notions of equality, but it also endangers the vitality of the institution affected. Most bribery centers on persons in discretionary or decision-making positions. Much as we want to believe that bribery invites gross deviations in duty, a prosecutor's experience is that in many cases there are no objectively correct decisions for the bribed official to make. We discovered that this was the case in the Board of Appeals prosecutions where a variety of competing theories of real estate valuation guaranteed that there was almost always some justification, albeit often thin, for what had been done. But it misses the point to look solely at the ultimate actions of the bribed official. Once the promise of payment is accepted, the public official is no longer the impartial decision-maker he is supposed to be. Whatever claims he might make, it is difficult to conceive of a public official who could convince anyone that he entirely disregarded a secret 'gift' from a person affected by his judgments.

Indeed, part of the evil of bribery inheres in the often indetectable nature of some of its results. Once revealed, the presence of bribery thus robs persons affected of a belief in the integrity of *all* prior decisions. In the absolute case, bribery goes to dissolve the social dependencies that require discretionary decision-making at certain junctions in our social scheme. Bribery, then, is a crime against trust; and to the extent that trust, a belief in the good faith of discretionary decision-makers, is essential to certain bureaucratic and governmental structures, bribery is deeply corrosive.

Because of its costs, the law usually deems bribery to be without acceptable justification. Again, I think this is in line with moral intuitions. Interestingly, the law does not regard extortion and bribery as mutually exclusive; extortion requires an apprehension of harm, bribery as desire to influence. Often, in fact, the two are coincident. Morally—and legally, perhaps—it would seem that bribery can be justified only if the bribe-giver is truly without alternatives, including the alternative of refusing payment and going to the authorities. Moreover, the briber should be able to show not merely that it was convenient or profitable to pay the bribe, but that the situation presented a choice of evils in which the bribe somehow avoided a greater peril. The popular example in our discussions has been bribing a Nazi camp guard in order to spare concentration camp internees.

C. Globalization

Economic Globalization
An Empirical Presentation and a Moral Judgment

FARHAD RASSEKH

"globalization, more than anything else, has reduced the number of extreme poor in India by two hundred million and in China by three hundred million since 1990."

Jeffrey Sachs, 2005, p. 355

1. Introduction

The term globalization refers to the process of increasing interaction and integration of cultures, societies, and economies. The present essay focuses on the economic aspect of globalization and addresses the following question: has economic globalization improved the wellbeing of people in the low-income countries? If the answer to this question is in the affirmative, then further integration of economies is not only desirable but morally imperative. In a low-income country where a large number of people do not have access to adequate food, basic education, and primary healthcare—in such a country—reduction in hunger, illiteracy, and preventable diseases constitutes an improvement in wellbeing.[1]

Since, as we shall see, wellbeing is inversely correlated with poverty, this essay will analyze poverty in the light of globalization. More specifically, we will explore the relationship between globalization and poverty in the developing world. Additionally, we will address the issue of child labor and the environment in relation to globalization. We adopt an empirical approach and present the findings of many scholars who have analyzed and quantified the consequences of globalization. Although our analysis is entirely utilitarian, we will briefly analyze globalization from the perspective of the Rawlsian theory of justice.

A brief history of economic globalization

Adam Smith (1723–1790), the founder of modern economics, argued that "division of labor" results from "a certain propensity in human nature" which leads us to "truck, barter, and exchange one thing for another" (Smith 1981, p. 25). This propensity, which has existed in all societies at all times, gave rise to long-distance trade even in the early

Table 6.5 Growth in volume of world trade and output, 1500–2003
(annual average compound growth rates)

	World trade	World output	col. 1/2
1500–1820	0.96	0.32	3.0
1820–1870	4.18	2.94	4.4
1870–1913	3.40	2.12	1.6
1913–1950	0.90	1.82	0.5
1950–1973	7.88	4.90	1.6
1973–2003	5.38	3.17	1.7
1820–2003	3.97	2.25	1.8

Source: Maddison (2007, p. 81).

phase of civilization. Human beings quickly realized that voluntary exchanges are mutually beneficial regardless of with whom they conduct the exchanges. Throughout history, however, until the early decades of the 19th century, long-distance trade as a share of the economy was quite small and grew, if at all, at a very low pace.

Table 6.5 provides data on the growth rates of world trade and world output since the year 1500. Before the dawn of the Industrial Revolution in the early 19th century the world economy was almost stagnant, growing at an imperceptible rate of 0.32% per year. Although world trade during the years 1500–1820 grew faster (0.96% per year), this rate was also quite low. But international trade went under such a dramatic transformation in the early decades of the 19th century that the historians of globalization regard the year 1820 as the commencement of the modern era of globalization.[2] The unprecedented integration of the world economy between 1820 and 1913 was propelled by a number of factors, including the invention of steamship and trains that substantially reduced transportation costs, refrigeration that made the long-distance shipment of perishable foods possible, and the telegraph that made long-distance communication possible. Kevin O'Rourke and Jeffrey Williamson (1999, p. 36) estimate that these inventions from mid-19th century to 1913 reduced the transportation costs in real terms by 45% and led to an enormous increase in international trade and investment. Other factors include the repeal of the Corn Laws in 1846, which ushered in a period of free trade in England (the economic superpower of the time) and the conclusion of a number of trade treaties among the European countries.

The rapid economic globalization that had begun in 1820 came to a halt in 1914 with the onset of World War I, and was not resumed until after World War II. Since then, the world has experienced two phases of globalization. In the first one, roughly from 1950 to 1980, under the auspices of General Agreement on Tariffs and Trade (GATT), the developed countries went global by reducing their barriers to international trade, which resulted in the rapid growth of world trade, as we saw in Table 6.5.[3] During this period, however, most developing countries refused to globalize. Notable exceptions (in the developing world) that embraced globalization in the 1950s and 1960s include South Korea, Singapore, Taiwan, and Hong Kong, all of which now rank among the high-income countries.[4] The second phase of globalization started in the late 1970s and early 1980s when many countries in the developing world in the Americas, Africa, and Asia that had previously shunned globalization embarked on reforming their economic policies and included (in varying degrees) lowering barriers to international trade and investment.

2. Poverty and Globalization

Poverty has always and everywhere been a feature of human society. Consider that, as late as 1780, "four-fifths of French families devoted 90 percent of their incomes simply to buying bread—only bread—to stay alive" (Novak 1991, p. 16).[5] How has poverty evolved since then, especially in the developing world? To answer the question we adopt the global poverty line of one "international dollar" per day set by the World Bank, recently upgraded to $1.25 per day. In this analysis, the currency unit is based on purchasing power parity, which means it is adjusted for the cost of living differences between each country and the USA. Thus one international dollar anywhere in the world has the same purchasing power as one dollar in the USA. To make the analysis meaningful across years, the currency unit is corrected for price inflation over time.

Figure 6.5 presents the number of people living on less than one dollar per day since 1820. Here we see a steady rise in the number, reaching almost 1.4 billion in 1955, followed by a decline to nearly 1.3 billion in 1970 and then rising to 1.5 billion in 1980. Since 1980, however, this number has steadily fallen. World Bank economists and poverty experts Shaohua Chen and Martin Ravallion (2008, p. 41) estimate that the number fell from its peak (1.5 billion) in 1980 to 876 million in 2005.

Although the number of the very poor continued to rise throughout the 19th century and much of the 20th century, Figure 6.6 shows the world poverty *rate* has steadily decreased in the past two centuries—falling from 85% of the population in 1820 to under 20% in 2000. The rate further declined to 16.1% in 2005 (Chen and Ravallion 2008, p. 42). This dramatic and unprecedented *decrease* in the global poverty

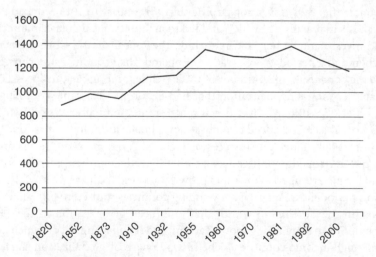

Figure 6.5 People living on less than $1 per day (millions)
Source: World Bank (2002, p. 8).

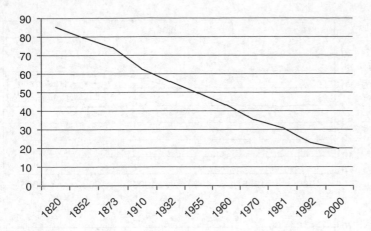

Figure 6.6 World poverty rate (%)
Source: Maddison (2003, pp. 232, 256).

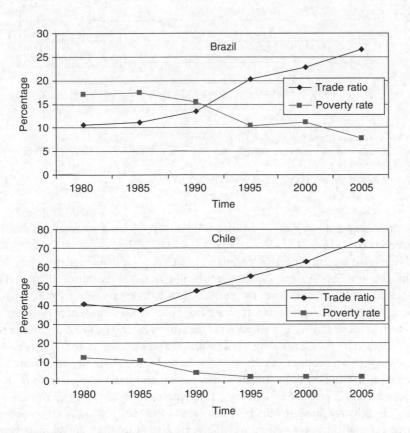

Figure 6.7 Trade share and poverty rate, Brazil and Chile
Source: Trade ratio data from Penn World Table, Version 6.3, http://pwt.econ.upenn.edu/php_site/
pwt63/pwt63_form.php.
Poverty rate data from Gwartney and Connors (2010, pp. 62–65).

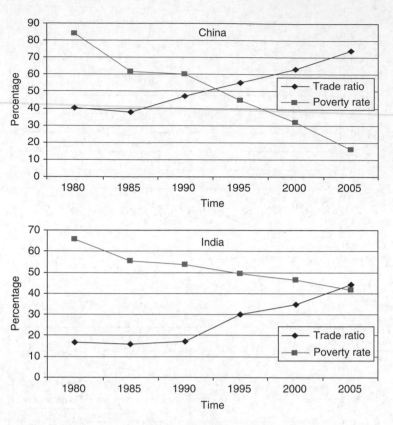

Figure 6.8 Trade share and poverty rate, China and India
Source: Trade ratio data from Penn World Table, Version 6.3, http://pwt.econ.upenn.edu/php_site/
pwt63/pwt63_form.php
Poverty rate data from Gwartney and Connors (2010, pp. 62–65).

rate is associated with an equally dramatic and unprecedented *increase* in globalization as documented in Table 6.5.

To demonstrate the negative correlation between globalization and poverty for individual countries, Figures 6.7, 6.8, and 6.9 illustrate the evolution of poverty rate and economic globalization over the period 1980–2005 for six countries: Brazil, Chile, China, India, Kenya, and Rwanda, representing three continents where poverty is concentrated. In these figures globalization is measured by the trade share (imports plus exports divided by the GDP), which is a common and standard criterion for evaluating the openness of an economy in the world. A bigger trade share means a more globalized economy. The figures for Brazil, Chile, China, and India show that they all experienced a decline in poverty as their trade share increased over the sample period. Most notably, the poverty rate in China fell from 84% in 1980 to 16% in 2005. For Kenya, the negative correlation is very clear over the period 1990 to 2005. In Rwanda between the years 1985 and 2000 the trade share fell from nearly 100% to about 25% while the poverty rate rose from about 60% to 80%. In the year 2000, both variables reversed their trends; that is, the trade share began to rise while the poverty rate began to fall.

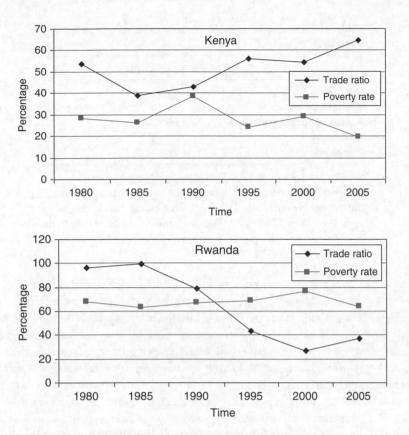

Figure 6.9 Trade share and poverty rate, Kenya and Rwanda
Source: Trade ratio data from Penn World Table, Version 6.3, http://pwt.econ.upenn.edu/php_site/pwt63/pwt63_form.php
Poverty rate data from Gwartney and Connors (2010, pp. 62–65).

Table 6.6 Dependent variable: Percentage change in poverty rate, 1980–2005

	Coefficient	t-stat
Constant	−34.17	−8.46
%Δ in trade share	−0.15	−2.93
R-squared	0.10	
Sample size	76	

Source: Author's estimation. The poverty rates ($1.25 per day) are from Gwartney and Connors (2010, Appendix C). The trade share data (based on purchasing power parity) are taken from Penn World Table, PWT 6.3 available from http://pwt.econ.upenn.edu/php_site/pwt63/pwt63_form.php.

Rwanda's experience, just like those of the other countries, confirms the inverse correlation between poverty and globalization.

The experience of this sample of six countries is quite common in the developing world. To demonstrate the point, Table 6.6 presents the regression results showing

Table 6.7 Dependent variable: Percentage in poverty rate, 1980–2005

	Coefficients	t-stat
Constant	−29.41	−7.28
%Δ in trade share	−0.12	−3.38
%Δ in economic growth	−0.12	−2.46
R-squared	**0.22**	
Sample size	**76**	

Source: Author's estimation. The economic growth rates are computed from the real GDP per capita data, which, along with the trade share data (based on purchasing power parity), are taken from Penn World Table, PWT 6.3 available from http://pwt.econ.upenn.edu/php_site/pwt63/pwt63_form.php.

the impact of globalization on poverty for 76 developing countries over the period 1980–2005. The dependent variable is the percentage change in the poverty rate and the independent variable is the percentage change in the trade share over the sample period. The coefficient of the trade share is negative and statistically significant, indicating that countries that have had a higher percentage increase in their trade share have experienced a larger reduction in their poverty rate. Table 6.7 shows the regression results with two independent variables: the percentage change in the trade share (as in Table 6.6) and the percentage change in economic growth over the sample period. The coefficients of both variables are negative and significant, which means that, even if we control for the impact of economic growth on poverty, a more heightened globalization continues to be correlated with a larger poverty reduction.

How does globalization reduce poverty? There are two channels through which globalization can reduce poverty. The first one involves investments by multinational enterprises (MNEs) along with their subsidiaries and franchisees that establish operations in the developing world. The MNEs' economic activities increase the demand for labor in the local area, causing employment or wages, or both, to rise, and thus poverty to fall. The MNEs also transfer relatively advanced technology and skilled labor to their host countries. The extension of economic activities by the MNEs to other countries is known as Foreign Direct Investment (FDI), which in 2007 stood at $2.5 trillion worldwide. Figure 6.10 shows FDI took off in the 1980s (when the developing countries went global), and soared in the 1990s and 2000s as globalization accelerated its expansion rate. The graph also shows that FDI is highly susceptible to economic booms and busts.

In 2008 the Organization for Economic Cooperation and Development (OECD) and the International Labor Organization (ILO) held a joint conference on the impact of the MNEs on the developing countries. In a report that the two agencies issued (OECD–ILO Conference 2008), they noted:

> An estimated 73 million workers, representing 3% of the global workforce, were employed in foreign affiliates of MNEs in 2006, almost three times more than in 1990. A disproportionate share of these workers is employed in the foreign affiliates of MNEs in developing and transition economies . . . (p. 11)

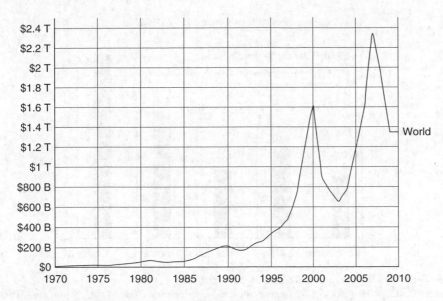

Figure 6.10 Foreign direct investment, net inflows
Source: World Bank (2011).

Moreover, "foreign-owned firms pay higher wages than their local competitors in developing countries . . . 12% higher for production workers and 20% for nonproduction workers" (p. 12). Quite clearly, globalization, channeled through the operation of the MNEs, has benefited the developing countries.[6]

The second (and a more sustained) channel through which globalization lowers poverty involves two stages. First, a higher level of economic integration increases economic growth; and second, a higher rate of economic growth, by increasing income per capita, reduces poverty. This leads to the question, how does globalization increase economic growth? Gene Grossman and Elhanan Helpman (1991) shed much light on this question:

> It is plausible to suppose that the foreign contribution to the local knowledge stock increases with the number of commercial transactions between domestic and foreign agents. That is, we may assume that international trade in tangible commodities facilitates the exchange of intangible ideas. This assumption can be justified in several ways. First, the larger the volume of international trade, the greater presumably will be the number of personal contacts between domestic and foreign individuals. These contacts may give rise to an exchange of information . . . Second, imports may embody differentiated intermediates that are not available in the local economy. The greater the quantity of such imports, the greater perhaps will be the number of insights that local researchers gain . . . Third when local goods are exported, the foreign purchasing agents may suggest ways to improve the manufacturing process . . . it seems reasonable to assume therefore that the extent of the spillovers between any two countries increases with the volume of their international trade. (pp. 166–167)

In an important study titled, "Does Trade Cause Growth?" Jeffrey Frankel and David Romer (1999) find, by employing sophisticated econometric techniques, that interna-

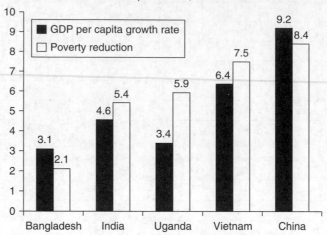

Percent per annum, 1992–1998

- GDP per capita growth rate
- Poverty reduction

Figure 6.11 Poverty reduction and economic growth rate in five countries
Source: David Dollar (2004), "Globalization, Poverty, and Inequality since 1980," World Bank Policy
Research Working Paper 3333.
© World Bank. With permission from World Bank.

tional trade increases income per capita in a sample of 150 countries. They use the
trade share, as defined above, in order to measure the degree of each economy's participation and integration in the world. They estimate that "a one-percentage point
increase in the trade share raises income per person by 2.0 percent" (p. 387). This has
been a highly important finding because of the very large sample, that encompasses
virtually the whole world, and also because of the estimation method that the authors
applied to the work.[7] But the "2.0 percent" estimate is an average over 150 countries
and does not show the distribution of economic growth caused by trade. Thus legitimate questions arise, such as: did the relatively poor economies benefit from trade at
all? If the answer is in the affirmative, did they gain as much as, more, or less than the
rich economies? To answer these questions, Farhad Rassekh (2007), using the Frankel-
Romer model and data, estimated the income growth caused by trade for the low-
income countries and the high income countries. He found that in the sample of 150
countries over the period 1960–1985 international trade actually boosted the income
of the relatively poor economies more than it increased that of the rich economies.
This finding implies that globalization tends to reduce global income inequality.[8]

To shed some light on the proposition that economic growth reduces poverty,
Figure 6.11 depicts the economic growth rates and the poverty reduction rates over the
period 1992–1998 for five countries: Bangladesh, India, Uganda, Vietnam, and China.

The data clearly show countries that have grown faster have been more successful
in reducing poverty. Uganda is an exception because, although it grew less rapidly than
India, it reduced its poverty more than India. Nevertheless, the correlation between
economic growth and poverty reduction is unmistakable. In fact, Ravallion (2001)
has found that a 1% increase in average income reduces the number of the very
poor (people living on less than one dollar per day) by 2.5%.[9] In a cross-section of 120

countries, World Bank economists David Dollar and Arat Kraay (2002) find that when an economy grows, all income groups, including the very poor in the lowest income bracket, experience an increase in their income equal to the average income growth. In a recent study, James Gwartney and Joseph Connors (2010) provide theoretical reasons as well as empirical evidence showing the effects of economic freedom, which includes liberalization of international trade, on economic growth and thereby on poverty reduction.[10] The authors identify four channels through which economic freedom enhances economic growth:

> First, countries with institutions and policies more consistent with economic freedom will attract more investment. Private investment will tend to flow toward countries with secure property rights and fewer trade barriers . . . Second, economic freedom encourages innovation and the discovery of valuable new products and lower cost production methods . . . Third, the market process encourages activities that are productive and discourages those that are unproductive . . . When property rights are protected and markets open, profits and losses perform this function . . . Fourth, a market economy is a network system and people integrated into the system will be able to achieve larger outputs and higher incomes than those outside of it . . . As the size of the market expands from the local town or village, to the region, nation and beyond, network participants derive larger and larger benefits from trade, specialization, and economies of scale. (pp. 48–49)

Gwartney and Connors (2010) conduct their statistical analysis for a sample of 63 countries over the period 1980–2005. They find that a one unit increase in economic freedom "at the beginning of the period reduced the extreme poverty rate by approximately 4 percentage points and the moderate poverty rate by more than 5 percentage points" (p. 54).[11] Dollar (2004) reports that over the decades of 1980s and 1990s "wages have generally been rising faster in globalizing developing countries than in rich ones, and in rich ones than in non-globalizing developing countries" (p. 24). To be more specific, during this period, wages in globalizing developing countries grew by 28%, twice as fast as the wage growth rate of 14% in nonglobalizing developing countries. The more rapid wage growth in globalizing countries provides them with an effective tool to reduce poverty.

In sum, the preponderance of evidence leads to the conclusion that globalization contributes to economic growth and reduces poverty.

3. Income and Selected Indicators of Wellbeing

The World Bank reports many indicators of wellbeing for all countries in an annual publication titled *The World Development Report* (available online as well as in print). A close examination of these indicators shows that they are correlated inversely with poverty and positively with per capita income across countries. Figure 6.12 plots on the horizontal axis the per capita incomes of 10 groups of countries from the lowest to the highest, and on the vertical axis five indicators of wellbeing; namely, literacy rate, life expectancy for female and male, infant mortality, and maternal mortality. Quite clearly, as income advances from the lowest income group ($2,000) to the middle income group ($6,500), the infant and maternal mortality

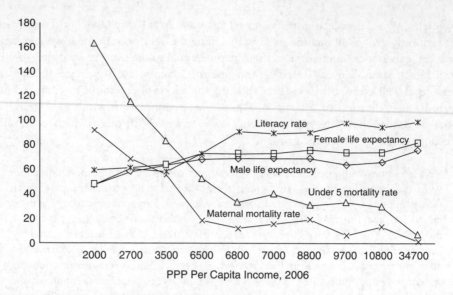

Figure 6.12 Income and selected indicators of wellbeing
Source: Rassekh and Speir (2010). "Can economic globalization lead to a more just society," from *Journal of Global Ethics*, 6, 1, pp. 27–43. With kind permission from Taylor and Francis www.tandfonline.com.

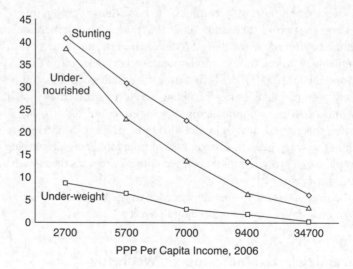

Figure 6.13 Income and the health of children
Source: Rassekh and Speir (2010). "Can economic globalization lead to a more just society," from *Journal of Global Ethics*, 6, 1, pp. 27–43. With kind permission from Taylor and Francis www.tandfonline.com.

rates fall sharply while literacy rate and life expectancy rise. The indicators of wellbeing continue to improve as income rises.

Figure 6.13 plots on the vertical axis the percentage of children suffering from stunting, undernourishment, and being underweight, all of which are manifestations of poverty. The horizontal axis of Figure 6.13 plots the per capita incomes of five groups of countries. Here we clearly see the remarkable difference that income levels make in the wellbeing of children. There are no surprises here. At higher levels of income a country is capable of acquiring the necessary resources to invest in education and in more effective healthcare that improve the wellbeing of its people. Since the preceding section documented that globalization has increased the per capita income, we should credit globalization with having contributed to the wellbeing of people in the developing world.

4. What about Child Labor and the Environment?

According to the International Labor Organization (ILO 2010) "The global number of child labourers stands at 215 million," of whom "a staggering 115 million at least, are subject to its worst forms."[12] Why do so many children (5–14-year-olds) work instead of going to school? The answer lies in the fact that hundreds of millions of parents are so poor that they depend upon their children's income. Schooling is a "luxury" they cannot afford. Since child labor is a symptom of poverty, wherever and whenever extreme poverty has existed, so has child labor. As Kaushik Basu, a leading scholar of child labor, points out, "This is not a new problem. In different parts of the world, at different stages of history, the laboring child has been a part of economic life" (1999, p. 1083).

To discern the impact of globalization on child labor, we examine its evolution in the postwar era during which globalization, as we saw above, continuously expanded its domain. In Table 6.8 the child labor participation rate is reported for the world as well as for three regions and four countries where child labor is heavily concentrated. The data, compiled and published by the International Labor Organization, strikingly show a downward trend over a period of 60 years from 1950 to 2010. Did globalization play a role in the downward trend? The answer is quite likely in the affirmative because over the period 1950–1980, when relatively few low-income countries embraced globalization, the child labor participation rate declined by 27%. But over the period 1980–2010, when many more low-income countries globalized, the rate fell by 78%, three times faster than in the previous 30 years. Note that such a substantial decrease in child labor occurred during the period when FDI soared, as documented in Figure 6.10.

Table 6.8 Child labor participation rates, 10–14 years, Source: Basu (1999, p. 1087). The figures for the years 2000 and 2010 are extrapolated and reported by the International Labor Organization

	1950	1960	1970	1980	1990	1995	2000	2010
World	27.57	24.81	22.30	19.91	14.65	13.02	11.32	8.44
Africa	38.42	35.88	33.05	30.97	27.87	26.23	24.92	22.52
Latin America & Caribbean	19.36	16.53	14.60	12.64	11.23	9.77	8.21	5.47
Asia	36.06	32.26	28.35	23.42	15.19	12.77	10.18	5.60
Ethiopia	52.95	50.75	48.51	46.32	43.47	42.30	41.10	38.79
Brazil	23.53	22.19	20.33	19.02	17.78	16.09	14.39	10.94
China	47.85	43.17	39.03	30.48	15.24	11.55	7.86	0.00
India	35.43	30.07	25.46	21.44	16.68	14.37	12.07	7.46

Cigno, Rosati, and Guarcello (2002), affiliated with the United Nations Children's Fund (UNICEF), have investigated the allegation that globalization increases child labor. For this purpose, they "assemble a set of relevant data on all developing countries for the relevant years available, namely 1980, 1990, 1995 and 1998" (p. 1579). Their careful statistical analysis leads them to note the following, "We could not find empirical evidence that exposure to international trade, and economic integration cross national borders, raise the incidence of child labor. If anything, the evidence points the other way" (p. 1587). This is an important finding on the impact of globalization on child labor. The authors, however, also note:

> We have addressed the concern that trade exposure *per se* could cause a rise in child labor, and found no empirical support for that proposition in crosscountry data. We do find support, on the other hand, for the proposition that countries with a largely uneducated workforce may be left out of the globalization process, and everyone in those countries, child or adult, will suffer as a result. There, however, the problem is not so much globalization, as the country's ability to take part in it. (p. 1588)

This conclusion stresses the crucial point that a nation may not be able to take advantage of the opportunities globalization provides if a substantial majority of people lack basic education. MNEs would not invest in a country where they face a largely uneducated workforce. In such a country, investment in education should rank highly on the list of appropriate policies. Once a basic level of education is attained, globalization can serve as a potent force in raising income, lowering poverty, and enhancing the wellbeing of people. The next part of this section focuses on the issue of the environment and globalization.

Does globalization contribute to environmental degradation? This question is motivated by an argument called "race-to-the-bottom," which maintains that polluting industries in rich economies move to countries that keep their environmental standards very low or do not enforce them in order to attract foreign investment. The race-to-the-bottom argument appears to be plausible: profit-seeking industries should be moving to countries where the cost of compliance with environmental standards are low and inspections by regulators less frequent. This seemingly sensible argument, however, as several scholars of globalization have pointed out, lacks empirical support.[13] Arik Levinson (1996), who has surveyed the literature, writes:

> The conclusions of both the international and domestic studies of industry location are that environmental regulations do not deter investment to any statistically or economically significant degree . . . the literature as a whole presents a fairly compelling evidence across a broad range of industries, time periods, and econometric specifications that regulations do not matter to site choice. (p. 450)

Moreover, Susmita Dasgupta and three coauthors (2002), all affiliated with the World Bank, write that if the race-to-the-bottom argument were valid, "pollution should be increasing everywhere" in the developing world (p. 160). The authors note that "China, Mexico and Brazil . . . received 60 percent of the total foreign direct investment for developing countries in 1998" (p. 160) and yet these countries "have all experienced significant improvements in air quality, as measured by concentrations of fine particulate

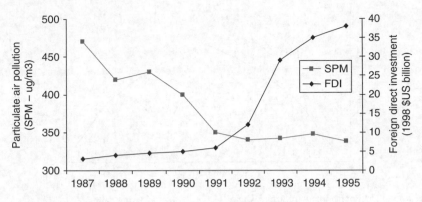

Figure 6.14 Foreign direct investment and air pollution in China
Source: Dasgupta et al. (2002, p. 161).

matter (PM-10) . . . or suspended particulate matter (SPM)" (p. 161). Figure 6.14 shows that the rising FDI in China is correlated with falling SPM. The illustrations for Mexico and Brazil (in Dasgupta et al. 2002) look almost identical to Figure 6.14.

Many researchers, who have studied the impact of globalization on the environment, argue that globalization is actually a potent force in *reducing* pollution. For example, Jeffrey Frankel and Andrew Rose (2005) note that exposure to international trade

> could have positive effect on environmental quality (even for a given level of GDP per capita) for a number of reasons. First, trade can spur managerial and technological innovation, which can have positive effects on both the economy and the environment. Second, multinational corporations tend to bring clean state-of-the-art production techniques from high-standard source countries of origins to host countries. Third is the international ratcheting up of environmental standards through heightened public awareness. (pp. 85–86)

Indeed, empirical studies have shown that economic growth, fueled by globalization, reduces pollution just as it reduces poverty. The relationship between income and pollution, however, is nonlinear. More specifically, Gene Grossman and Alan Krueger (1995) found that there is a bell-shaped relationship between many measures of pollution and per capita income across countries as depicted in Figure 6.15.[14]

This means income and pollution are positively correlated until income reaches a certain level, estimated to be in the range of $5,000–8,000 (in 1985 prices), beyond which the level of pollution diminishes as income continues to rise. The reason for the bell-shaped relationship is that low levels of income generally correlate with low levels of industrial activities and thus low levels of pollution. More industrial production increases the demand for labor, which in turn increases income per capita while also increasing pollution. However, beyond the per capita income threshold of $5,000–8,000, the economy begins to acquire the necessary resources to clean up the environment. Furthermore, people who are primarily concerned with wages and jobs at low levels of economic development demand a cleaner environment as their incomes rise.[15]

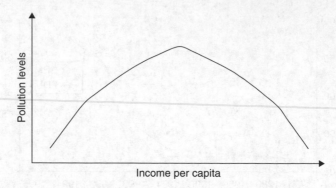

Figure 6.15   The Environmental Kuznetz Curve
Source: The curve is drawn based on the findings of Grossman and Kruger (1995).

In sum, globalization leads to cleaner environment because it increases economic growth and income and helps low-income economies pass beyond the threshold income sooner than otherwise.

5. Further Analysis of Globalization

The economist Bradford DeLong (2001) observes:

> The source of material prosperity seen today in leading-edge economies is no secret: it is the storehouse of technological capabilities . . . This storehouse is no one's private property . . . Governments, entrepreneurs, and individuals in poor economies should be straining every muscle . . . to do what Japan began to do in the mid-nineteenth century: acquire and apply everything in humanity's storehouse of technological capabilities.

In the mid-19th century Japan began to "acquire and apply everything in humanity's storehouse of technological capabilities" because it went global.[16] Peter Lindert and Jeffrey Williamson (2003, p. 7) refer to Japan's experience at that time as

> Probably the greatest nineteenth century "globalization shock." . . . Japan switched from virtual autarky to free trade in 1858. It is hard to imagine a more dramatic switch from closed to more open trade policy. In the 15 years following 1858, Japan's foreign trade rose 70 times, from virtually nil to 7% of national income.

To appreciate the impact of globalization on Japan's economy and the wellbeing of its citizens, consider the evolution of the Human Development Index (HDI) for Japan and a few other countries since 1870. HDI, constructed with three components (education, income, and life expectancy), measures the wellbeing of the residents of a country relative to others. In 1870 Japan's HDI equaled 0.160, which was well below Switzerland's index (0.457) and that of the USA (0.467). However, by 1995 Japan's HDI had reached those of the developed world; all of them around 0.94.[17]

A comparison between economic development of Japan and Brazil since 1870 sheds considerable light on the difference that globalization can make. In 1870 the incomes per capita in Japan and in Brazil were both $740 (in 1990 dollars). However, by 1996, Japan's per capita income stood at $19,582 and Brazil's at $5,346; in 2010, Japan's per capita income reached $34,692, while Brazil's was $10,607.[18] During much of the 20th century Japan embraced globalization while Brazil shunned globalization. But as we can see in Figure 6.7, Brazil changed course in the mid-1980s, which is precisely when its poverty rate began to fall. Japan eliminated its poverty decades ago.

What Japan did in the mid-19th century, South Korea, Hong Kong, Taiwan, and Singapore began to do in the mid-20th century, and China, India, as well as a number of other low-income countries began in 1980—go global. It is no surprise that these countries have succeeded in enhancing their economic growth and the wellbeing of their citizens. Without extensive and steady contact with other economies through open and relatively free international trade, it would be impossible to gain access to the storehouse of knowledge and technology a country needs to advance economically. MNEs invest in countries that adopt a global perspective and open their doors to international trade and investment. In addition to increasing the growth rate of an economy, globalization helps allocate resources efficiently. Through globalization a country exports goods and services in which it has a comparative advantage (that is, what it can produce at a lower cost than other countries) and imports goods and services in which it has a comparative disadvantage (that is, what it can produce at a higher cost than other countries). Such an exchange, based on comparative advantage, will benefit all trading countries.

Since the developing countries, for the most part, have a comparative advantage in agricultural goods as well as low-tech and labor intensive manufacturing, the developed countries have a moral obligation to eliminate their trade barriers that impede the exportation of such goods from the developing world. More specifically, the rich countries in the European Union and in North America ought to eliminate their agricultural subsidy (which puts farmers in the developing world at a disadvantage) as well as their quotas and tariffs on manufactured goods that reduce exports from low-income countries.

6. Does Globalization Have Any Downside?

When a country goes global, the export sector of the economy expands but the import-competing sector shrinks, and some workers in the shrinking sector will lose their jobs. In theory (and eventually) these workers should be able to find employment either in the expanding export sector or become creatively self-employed. But the process can be, and often is, lengthy and painful. To be more precise, according to the Stolper-Samuelson theorem, when an economy goes global, the real income of the abundant resource in the economy rises while that of the scarce factor falls. The abundant factor is the resource employed intensively in an economy's export sector. An example of the abundant factor in a developed economy such as Germany would be skilled labor. The scarce factor is the resource that is employed intensively in an economy's import-competing sector. Relatively low-skilled labor would be an example of the scarce factor in Germany.[19] Does this mean some people will necessarily suffer because of globalization? No, it does not. Here is why.

The Stolper-Samuelson theorem, which identifies the beneficiaries and losers of globalization, demonstrates that the gain to the abundant factor outweighs the loss to the scarce factor. As the economists Wolfang Stolper and Paul Samuelson (1994, p. 61) noted at the end of their paper:

> it has been shown that the harm which free trade inflicts upon one factor of production is necessarily less than the gain to the other. Hence, it is always possible to bribe the suffering factor by subsidy or other redistributive devices so as to leave all factors better off as a result of trade.

This conclusion can serve as an application to the influential theory of justice that John Rawls put forth in 1971. In an essay summarizing his theory, Rawls (1995), while speaking of "the whole social system," stated "The basic structure is just throughout when the advantages of the more fortunate promote the well-being of the least fortunate, that is, when a decrease in their advantages would make the least fortunate even worse off than they are" (p. 55). Let's label the beneficiaries of globalization "the more fortunate" and the losers "the least fortunate." Rawls would endorse globalization if the least fortunate could be compensated to the point that they would become actually better off with globalization than without. Since both theory (the Stolper-Samuelson theorem) and evidence (presented in this essay) inform us the gains of globalization outweigh the losses, an effective redistributive system can work out to everyone's advantage. Further, consider that the least fortunate in the developing countries are those whose wellbeing indicators are very low as depicted in Figure 6.12 and Figure 6.13. To the extent that globalization boosts their income and improves their wellbeing, globalization passes the Rawlsian test.[20]

7. A Final Note

Judged by the evidence presented in this essay, the case for globalization, especially for the developing world is quite strong. Since 1980, when a majority of low-income countries embraced globalization, for the first time in history the absolute number of the very poor has been declining. Concurrently, a number of indicators of wellbeing in poor countries have displayed much improvement, including a rapid decline in child labor. Nevertheless, it must be stressed, globalization is only a necessary (not a sufficient) condition for economic progress and the improvement of wellbeing. Sustained economic growth is a complex phenomenon, which no single policy can engender.[21]

Although globalization alone cannot guarantee higher income and wellbeing, the evidence clearly show that no country has ever achieved sustained economic growth without globalization. Lindert and Williamson (2003), who have surveyed the field, note that there is not even one country

> that chose to be less open to trade and factor flows in the 1990s than in the 1960s and rose in the global living-standard ranks at the same time. As far as we can tell, *there are no anti-global victories to report for the postwar Third World*. We infer that this is because freer trade stimulates growth in Third World economies . . . (emphasis added)

Indeed the preponderance of evidence in favor of globalization makes it a moral imperative for all developing countries to integrate into the world economy. But as noted above, the developed world also has a moral obligation to remove all obstacles the developing countries encounter in the integration process.[22]

The author gratefully acknowledges a Michael Pfaff research grant through the Barney School in support of this essay. The author thanks his graduate assistants Claudia Rohozneanu and Krishna Tayi for preparing most of the graphs and tables.

Notes

1   For a sophisticated and philosophical analysis of wellbeing, see the collection of articles in Martha Nussbaum and Amartya Sen (1993). In particular, see Sen's paper "Capability and Well-Being" in the collection.

2   See for example, Kevin O'Rourke and Jeffrey Williamson (2002) and Angus Maddison (1995).

3   GATT came into existence in 1947 and was transformed into the World Trade Organization in 1995.

4   The GDP per capita of these countries in 2008 based on purchasing power parity were: South Korea, $28,120; Singapore, $47,940; Taiwan, $35,800; and Hong Kong, $$43,960. In comparison, the GDP per capita of the USA in 2008 was $46,970. The data are from *World Development Report 2010* (World Bank 2010). Purchasing power parity is defined in the next section.

5   Although this statistic indicates the depth of poverty in France at the dawn of the French Revolution, most poor families grew their own food and made their own clothes at home, which did not require much income. Nevertheless, there is no denying that poverty was deep and pervasive in the late 18th century.

6   On the controversy over the manufacturing plants in low-income countries which are known as sweatshops, see Jeffery Sachs (2005). Sachs has been working with international agencies for more than two decades on poverty reduction, and has written extensively on global poverty. In his book, *The End of Poverty* (2005), Sachs recounts his close observation of how the sweatshops operate and how they benefit the local people.

7   In such studies, the trade share is an endogenous variable, which means if income and trade rise together, it may be that higher income is causing more trade and not the other way around. Frankel and Romer carefully take this potential problem into account and correct for it. Their estimated coefficient shows the effect of trade on income without the reverse causality from income to trade.

8   This essay does not address the impact of globalization on income inequality within and between countries. Readers interested in this subject may consult Francois Bourguignon and Christian Morrison (2002), Peter Lindert and Jeffrey Williamson (2003), and David Dollar (2004).

9   Since all statistical estimations are sensitive to the model specification, sample countries, and sample period, one may come across other studies whose estimated values are different from those presented here. Nevertheless, the proposition that economic growth reduces poverty enjoys immense empirical support.

10 Economic freedom is an "index that uses forty-two different components" (Gwartney and Connor 2010, p. 50). For more information, see Gwartney and Connor (2010).

11 Extreme poverty refers to the living conditions on less than $1.25 per day and moderate poverty refers to less than $2 per day, measured in 2005 international dollars (Gwartney and Connor 2010, p. 43).

12 See ILO (2010).

13 Prominent examples include Jagdish Bhagwati (2004) and Jeffrey Frankel (2005).

14 This is known as the Kuznets Environmental Curve.

15 Frankel and Rose (2005) validated this hypothesis by using regression analysis.

16 Japan did not go global voluntarily. In 1858 the US government forced Japan to switch from autarky to free trade (Williamson 2011, p. 13). We do not explore this issue here because we are concerned with the consequences of globalization for Japan, not with how or why it went global.

17 The HDI figures are from Nicholas Crafts (2000).

18 For the per capita income values in 1990, see Maddison (1995); for the values in 2010, see the Human Development Index in Human Development Reports of the United Nations (2011). The per capita income values are based on purchasing power parity.

19 For an analysis of the Stolper-Samuelson theorem, see any textbook on international economics.

20 For more detailed analysis of globalization form the Rawlsian perspectives, see Farhad Rassekh and John Speir (2010).

21 Economic growth has been a major research area in economics since Adam Smith. In the vast literature on economic growth, interested readers will do well reading David Landes (1998) and William Easterly (2001).

22 Readers who are interested in the broader impact of globalization than presented in this essay may consult two recent books on globalization (albeit with very different emphases and analyses) one by Jeffery Williamson (2011) and the other by Dani Rodrik (2011). Both authors are among the leading scholars of the field.

References

Basu, K. (1999) "Child Labor: Cause, Consequence, and Cure, with Remarks on International Labor Standards," *Journal of Economic Literature*, 37: 1083–1119.

Bhagwati, J. (2004) *In Defense of Globalization*, New York: Oxford University Press.

Bourguignon, F. and C. Morrison (2002) "Inequality among World Citizens: 1820–1992," *The American Economic Review*, 92: 727–744.

Chen, S. and M. Ravallion (2008) *The Developing World Is Poorer than We Thought, But No Less Successful in Fight against Poverty*, World Bank Policy Research Working Paper 4703. Washington, DC: World Bank.

Cigno, A., F.C. Rosati, and L. Guarcello (2002) "Does Globalization Increase Child Labor?" *World Development*, 9: 1579–1589.

Crafts, N. (2000) *Globalization and Growth in the Twentieth Century*, International Monetary Fund Working Paper WP/00/44. Washington, DC: International Monetary Fund.

Dasgupta, S., B. Laplante, H. Wang, and D. Wheeler (2002) "Confronting the Environmental Kuznetz Curve," *Journal of Economic Perspectives*, 16: 147–168.

DeLong, B. (2001) *"The Economic History of the Twentieth Century: Slouching towards Utopia?" Unpublished manuscript*, University of California at Berkeley.

Dollar, D. (2004) *Globalization, Poverty, and Inequality since 1980*, World Bank Policy Research Working Paper 3333. Washington, DC: World Bank.

Dollar, D. and A. Kraay (2002) "Growth Is Good for the Poor," *Journal of Economic Growth*, 7(3): 195–225.

Easterly, W. (2001) *The Elusive Quest for Growth*, Cambridge, MA: MIT Press.

Frankel, J.A. (2005) "The Environment and Globalization," in *Globalization: What's New*, ed. M. Weinstein, New York: Columbia University Press.

Frankel, J.A. and D. Romer (1999) "Does Trade Cause Growth," *American Economic Review*, 89: 379–399.

Frankel, J.A. and A.K. Rose (2005) "Is Trade Good or Bad for the Environment? Sorting Out the Causality," *The Review of Economics and Statistics*, 87: 85–91.

Grossman, G. and E. Helpman (1991) *Innovation and Growth in the Global Economy*, Cambridge, MA: MIT Press.

Grossman, G.M. and A.B. Krueger (1995) "Economic Growth and the Environment," *The Quarterly Journal of Economics*, 110(2): 353–377.

Gwartney, J.D. and J.S. Connors (2010) "Economic Freedom and Global Poverty," in *Accepting the Invisible Hand*, ed. M.D. White, New York: Palgrave Macmillan.

ILO (2010) *Facts on Child Labour 2010*, Geneva: International Labor Organization. Retrieved March 7, 2013 from http://www.ilo.org/wcmsp5/groups/public/@dgreports/@dcomm/documents/publication/wcms_126685.pdf

Landes, D. (1998) *The Wealth and Poverty of Nations*, New York: W.W. Norton.

Levinson, A. (1996) "Environmental Regulations and industry Location: International and Domestic Evidence," in *Fair Trade and Harmonization: Prerequisites for Free Trade?* ed. Jagdish Bhagwati and Robert Hudec, Cambridge, MA: MIT Press.

Lindert, P. and J. Williamson (2003) "Does Globalization Make the World More Unequal?," in *Globalization in Historical Perspective*, ed. M. Bordo, A.M. Taylor, and J.G. Williamson, Chicago: University of Chicago Press.

Maddison, A. (1995) *Monitoring the World Economy*, Paris: OECD Development Center.

Maddison, A. (2003) *The World Economy: Historical Statistics*, New York: Oxford University Press.

Maddison, A. (2007) *Contours of the World Economy, 1–2030 AD; Essays in Macro-Economic History*, New York: Oxford University Press.

Novak, M. (1991) *The Spirit of Democratic Capitalism*, New York: Madison Books.

Nussbaum, M. and A. Sen (1993) *The Quality of Life*, Oxford: Clarendon Press.

OECD–ILO Conference (2008) *The Impact of Foreign Direct Investment in Wages and Working Conditions*, Paris: OECD Conference Centre.

O'Rourke, K.H. and J.G. Williamson (1999) *Globalization and History*, Cambridge, MA: MIT Press.

O'Rourke, K.H. and J.G. Williamson (2002) "The Heckscher–Ohlin Model between 1400 and 2000: When It Explained Factor Price Convergence, and When It Did Not, and Why," in *Bertil Ohlin: A Centennial Celebration, 1899–1999*, ed. R. Findlay, L. Jonung, and M. Lundahl, Cambridge, MA: MIT Press.

Rassekh, F. (2007) "Is International Trade More Beneficial to Lower Income Countries?," *Review of Development Economics*, 11: 159–169.

Rassekh, F. and J. Speir (2010) "Can Economic Globalization Lead to a More Just Society?," *Journal of Global Ethics*, 6: 27–43.

Ravallion, M. (2001), "Growth, Inequality and Poverty: Looking Beyond Averages," *World Development*, 29(11): 1803–1815.

Rawls, J. (1995) "Distributive Justice," in *Perspective in Business Ethics*, 3rd edition, ed. L.P. Hartman, New York: McGraw-Hill.

Rodrik, D. (2011) *The Globalization Paradox*, New York: W. W. Norton.

Sachs, J.D. (2005) *The End of Poverty*, New York: Penguin Press.

Smith, A. (1981) *An Inquiry into the Nature and Causes of the Wealth of Nations*, Indianapolis: Liberty Fund. (Original pub. 1776).

Stolper, W.F. and P.A. Samuelson (2004) "Protection and Real Wages," in *The Stolper–Samuelson Theorem: A Golden Jubilee*, ed. A.V. Deardorff and R.M. Stern, Ann Arbor: University of Michigan Press. (Original pub. 1941 in *Review of Economic Studies*, 9, 58–73).

United Nations (2011) *International Human Development Indicators*, Human Development Reports. Retrieved March 7, 2013 from http://hdr.undp.org/en/statistics/

Williamson, J.G. (2011) "Trade and Poverty: When the Third World Fell Behind" Cambridge, MA: MIT Press.

World Bank (2002) *Globalization, Growth, and Poverty*, World Bank Policy Research Report, New York: Oxford University Press.

World Bank (2010) *World Development Report 2010, Development and Climate Change*. Washington, DC: World Bank.

World Bank (2011) *World Development Indicators*. Retrieved March 18, 2013 from http://www.google.com/public data/explore?ds=wb-wdi&met_y=bx_klt_dinv_cd_ wd&idim=count...

Multinational Enterprises and Incomplete Institutions
The Demandingness of Minimum Moral Standards

NIEN-HÊ HSIEH

In the business ethics literature, a long-standing subject of inquiry concerns the standards that ought to apply to the activities of multinational enterprises (MNEs).[1] MNEs operate across countries that vary widely in their legal, political, and regulatory institutions, and one question that arises is whether there are certain minimum standards that ought to guide managers in their decision-making independently of local institutional requirements. This essay puts forward one line of response to this question with an emphasis on the issue of the demandingness of minimum standards for MNEs.

One motivation for specifying minimum standards is as follows. From the perspective of many national governments, there are advantages to having MNEs locate operations in their countries. MNEs bring with them opportunities for economic growth through the infusion of capital, technology, and employment opportunities that in many cases are more favorable than local jobs (Navaretti and Venables, 2004, pp. 1–2). Given this, a concern raised by commentators is that, in order to compete for investment, national governments will lower standards in areas such as labor, consumer, and environmental protection (Cragg, 2000). This concern is compounded by the perception that many large MNEs possess bargaining power relative to the governments of the countries in which they operate (Navaretti and Venables, 2004, p. 1).[2] Identifying a set of minimum standards that ought to apply to the activities of MNEs independently of local institutional requirements is a way to begin addressing this concern.

The motivation to identify such standards can be framed more generally as a response to the fact that institutional arrangements structuring global economic activity may be incomplete. In this essay, these institutional arrangements are to be understood broadly, encompassing features that affect economic activity both directly (e.g., laws and regulation, and the officials and agencies that establish, adjudicate, and enforce them) and indirectly (e.g., the political and legislative processes and the social safety net). These institutional arrangements may be incomplete in a variety of ways. For example, they may be *weak* in the sense that what is formally required is unlikely to be enforced. They also may be *piecemeal*, by which is meant that requirements for important areas of economic activity are left unspecified. In some cases, institutional arrangements may be *contested*, meaning that the institutional requirements or the legitimacy of the institutions themselves are called into question. In situations such as these, it seems reasonable to ask if there are standards MNEs ought to respect at a minimum, independently of local institutional arrangements.[3]

Understood as moral duties, *duties of forbearance*—that is, duties to refrain from certain actions—promise one way to address this question. To say a duty is *moral* is to hold that it applies to agents independently of whether it is institutionally required, and, on most accounts, if there are duties that apply to all moral agents, they include at a minimum duties of forbearance. One reason for this is that duties of forbearance, such as duties not to harm or not to coerce, can be honored under most circumstances; the agent need only refrain from acting. This is in contrast to duties that require an agent to perform a specific action or to help bring about a certain state of affairs. Consider, for example, a duty to aid persons whose basic material needs are not met. For a moral agent to fulfill such a duty, she must actively contribute resources, either directly or indirectly, to those to whom she owes the duty. The assumption is that contributing these resources is costly to an agent; more is required of her than simply inaction as in the case of duties of forbearance. Duties of forbearance therefore provide a promising way to specify minimum standards for MNEs independently of institutional requirements.

At the same time, attributing duties of forbearance directly to MNEs poses something of a challenge. The challenge is that there is much debate as to whether MNEs, and business enterprises more generally, qualify as the kind of agents to which it is appropriate to attribute moral duties.[4] Accordingly, the approach taken in this essay is to focus on duties of forbearance as they apply to managers of MNEs in their capacity as moral agents. Because managers of MNEs are in a position to direct the activities attributed to MNEs, insofar as these duties place restrictions on what managers of MNEs are morally permitted to do, these duties specify moral standards that apply to the activities of MNEs. As part of this approach, this essay considers what must be the case about the moral responsibilities of individuals more generally for these duties not to place restrictions on the activities of MNEs. In the end, there is reason to hold that minimum moral standards for MNEs are more demanding than what the minimalist nature of duties of forbearance initially would suggest.

The essay is organized as follows. As a starting point, the essay summarizes the view that there are few, if any, standards that apply to MNEs apart from what is already required by the institutional contexts in which they operate. The essay then examines what follows for restrictions on the activities of MNEs by recognizing two kinds of duties of forbearance that are commonly held to be among the most basic moral duties. The first are duties not to harm. The second are duties not to interfere with the liberty and physical security of others. The essay closes by analyzing whether attributing duties of forbearance to MNEs entails acknowledging duties to aid persons whose basic needs are not met on the part of MNEs as well.

Not above the Law

According to what has been termed the "weak-side constraints" view (Arnold, 2003), there are few, if any, standards that apply to business corporations in addition to what is required by the institutional context in which they operate. This is a view most famously associated with Milton Friedman (1962, 1970). On Friedman's account, "there is one and only one social responsibility of business—to use its resources and engage in activities designed to increase its profits so long as it stays within the rules of the game, which is to say, engages in open and free competition without deception or fraud" (1962, p. 133).[5] For Friedman, it would be wrong for managers to adhere to standards that are more demanding than existing institutional requirements unless doing so could be justified in terms of increasing profits.

Part of Friedman's argument is that to do so would go against democratic principles, which is morally objectionable. According to Friedman, corporate managers who constrain profit-making activities when not institutionally required to so are engaged in "fundamentally subversive" behavior (1970). The thought seems to be that there are two basic mechanisms for allocating resources—the market system and the political system—and that in a democratic society, a nonmarket-based allocation of resources represents a form of political decision-making that requires the approval of a democratic majority. In constraining profit-making activities when not institutionally required to do so, managers expend resources that benefit parties through nonmarket-based allocations of resources, and, because managers are not democratically elected, they take upon themselves the decision to allocate resources in a manner that is contrary to democratic political principles. Call this the *political principle argument* for the weak-side constraints view.

Arnold (2003) argues against adopting the weak-side constraints view for MNEs operating in a global context. Rather than challenge the political principle argument directly, Arnold points out that many of the countries in which MNEs operate are not democracies (2003, p. 162).[6] In these countries, the weak-side constraints view does not apply and need not rule out adhering to standards that are more restrictive than local institutional requirements. For example, in a nondemocratic context, it would not be inappropriate, at least on grounds of the political principle argument, for managers to pay an above-market wage to workers or to have higher safety standards than required by law. Are there other arguments that give us reason to subscribe to the weak-side constraints view?

Another line of argument in Friedman's defense of the weak-side constraints view emphasizes the idea that managers are agents of shareholders because the shareholders own the corporation. According to this line of argument, the only common interest of shareholders that can be assumed is to make money. In turn, by adhering to standards not required by existing institutions, managers run the risk of forgoing profits, thereby failing in their obligation as agents of the shareholders. Call this argument for the weak-side constraints view, the *agency argument*.

To be certain, it is a matter of some debate whether corporate managers ought to be understood exclusively as agents of shareholders.[7] However, even if we were to grant that managers are agents of shareholders, there is reason to doubt that the agency argument provides an adequate defense of the weak-side constraints view. Recall that the question is whether there are standards other than local institutional requirements that apply to the actions of MNEs. The agency argument holds that a manager ought to pursue profit-making activity to the point of what is institutionally permissible because she is an agent. This assumes that the only standards the manager ought to observe as an agent are those specified by existing institutional requirements. The agency argument, it seems, is question begging. There must be some additional argument as to why it is morally permissible for her to adhere only to existing institutional requirements.[8]

To close this section, it will help to discuss an attempt to institutionalize universal standards for MNEs by way of the international human rights regime. The Universal Declaration of Human Rights (United Nations, 1948) specifies over two dozen rights that all states should respect. These include *security rights* (e.g., freedom from torture and a right to bodily integrity); *due process rights* (e.g., a right to a fair and public hearing); *liberty rights* (e.g., freedom of movement and freedom of thought, conscience, and religion); *political rights* (e.g., a right to vote); *equality rights* (e.g., protection against discrimination); and *welfare rights* (e.g., rights to education, to work, and to an adequate standard of living) (Nickel, 2010). Although the Universal Declaration of Human Rights is itself nonbinding, the rights it lays out have been given the form of law through subsequent covenants that aim to bind the states that ratify them (Campbell, 2006, p. 104). These rights then represent claims that ought to be protected by states for all persons, and the United Nations has sought to elaborate what follows for the activities of MNEs (Ruggie, 2008). One important requirement is that states help ensure that the activities of MNEs do not lead to violations of these rights (Ruggie, 2008).

If enacted and protected by states, human rights would provide a universal standard for the activities of MNEs across various local contexts under the weak-side constraints view. A difficulty arises, however, if local institutional arrangements do not provide adequate protection for these rights either because states lack the means or they have not formally recognized them. In such situations, the weak-side constraints approach is no better able to specify independent standards for MNEs. Human rights represent claims to be protected by states; they are not claims that ground duties on the part of all moral agents (Campbell, 2006).[9]

If there is a standard that has been elaborated for MNEs with respect to human rights, it is the principle to do no harm. In his report to United Nations Human Rights Council as the Special Representative of the Secretary-General, John Ruggie examines what responsibilities fall on MNEs with respect to enforcing human rights (Ruggie, 2008).[10] He concludes that the appropriate responsibility for MNEs is "put simply, to do no harm" (p. 9). This prompts consideration of an alternative to the weak-side constraints view, which is a view grounded in a duty not to harm.

Do No Harm

Call the argument that locates an independent standard for the activities of MNEs in a moral duty not to harm, the *no harm argument*. A number of features recommend this as an approach to ground minimum standards for MNEs. To begin, the moral duty not to harm others is widely thought to apply to all persons across varying institutional contexts. As Judith Lichtenberg writes, "no one disputes that people have duties not to harm others; these so-called negative duties are about as well established as any moral duties could be" (2010, p. 557).[11] In addition, the argument need not invoke any type of moral agency on the part of MNEs. Instead, the duty need only apply to managers who direct the activities of MNEs. Insofar as managers are under a duty not to harm to others, it would be wrong for them to enact policies or set into motion activities that cause harm (Lane, 2005, p. 238).[12]

In the first instance, the no harm argument may appear similar to the weak-side constraints view in what it requires of MNEs. Consider the question of whether there is a responsibility on the part of MNEs to provide assistance to parties beyond what they would receive from normal economic transactions. For example, it has been asked whether pharmaceutical companies have a responsibility to assist those suffering from diseases who cannot afford to pay for medication by donating the medication to governments and nongovernmental organizations, providing them at cost, or allowing the manufacture of generic versions (Griffin, 2004; Dunfee, 2006; Hsieh 2011). The no harm argument does not require the provision of such assistance. More generally, according to standard economic theory, voluntary transactions in normal economic activity are Pareto improving—that is, no one is made worse off and at least one party is made better off. So, the no harm argument may be thought to be similarly minimalist to the weak-side constraints view in what is required of MNEs.

There is reason to doubt this conclusion once we take into account the institutional context in which many MNEs operate. One precondition for the claim that normal economy activity is Pareto improving is that there is no harm to third parties. Many institutional arrangements, however, may be *piecemeal*. In such cases, existing institutional arrangements do not ensure that costs to third parties are internalized by those engaged in the activity or that those who are harmed by economic activity are fully compensated. A commonly cited example of this is the way in which current institutional arrangements do not ensure that social costs of greenhouse emissions are reflected in the market price of energy. Another assumption underlying the view that normal economic activity is Pareto improving is that institutional arrangements are not *weak*. As Leif Wenar (2008) argues, however, Western consumers may "buy stolen goods when they buy gasoline and magazines, clothing and cosmetics, cell phones and laptops, perfume and jewelry," because corrupt dictators in resource-rich countries do not fully compensate their citizens for the cost of producing those goods (p. 2). In other words, when institutional arrangements are incomplete, there is no guarantee that normal economic activity is free of harm to others. In situations such as these, there is reason to hold that the no harm argument requires MNEs to do more than simply comply with existing institutions.[13] Avoiding harm may require MNEs to curtail their activities, mitigate the harms that result, and, in some cases, strengthen existing institutional arrangements (Hsieh, 2009).[14]

Liberty and Security Rights

The duty not to harm focuses on the state of affairs that results from an agent's action—that is, it asks whether others are left worse off as a result of an agent's action. On many views of moral duties, however, states of affairs are not all that matter for evaluating an agent's actions. What also matters is whether an agent *wrongs* another person, where wronging consists in the violation or infringement of a person's moral rights. On most theories of rights, liberty rights (e.g., a right to freedom of movement) and security rights (e.g., a right to bodily integrity) are among the most fundamental rights that a person possesses in virtue of her humanity. In this section, I examine how recognition of liberty rights and security rights provides an additional approach to grounding standards that apply to the activities of MNEs. Call this the *noninterference argument*.

Liberty rights and security rights are generally said to ground duties of forbearance that are *perfect* and *general*. Perfect duties are "exceptionless duties that strictly bind agents' conduct at all times in their behavior towards every other person" (Ashford, 2009, p. 100). To be clear, although they are exceptionless, they do admit of qualifications that accommodate other moral considerations. For example, a duty not to violate the bodily integrity of another may allow for exceptions in cases of self-defense. Perfect duties also are "fully delineated." That is, they specify their content, by whom they are owed, and to whom they are owed. This is in contrast to *imperfect* duties, which grant discretion to a moral agent over when to fulfill the duty along with the content and recipient of the duty being met. Because a claim of noninterference can be honored in almost all circumstances (by noninterference), the duties to which liberty and security rights give rise are held to be perfect. In addition, because liberty and security rights are said to apply to all persons by virtue of their humanity, the nature of the duties to which liberty and security rights give rise are said to be *general*, as opposed to *special*, duties.[15] Special duties are owed to particular individuals "because of an act, event, or relationship of which a causal or historical account can be given" (Shue, 1988, p. 688). General duties are owed independently of such considerations.

As in the case of the no harm argument, the noninterference argument need not assume any degree of moral agency on the part of MNEs. Because the duties of noninterference to which liberty and security rights correspond are perfect and general, they apply to all moral agents in all circumstances, including managers of MNEs. Accordingly, these duties of forbearance place constraints on the sorts of activities that can be undertaken by MNEs independently of the local institutional contexts in which they operate. On the noninterference argument, activities that interfere with the liberty and security rights of persons are to be avoided.

In many ways, what is required by the noninterference argument tracks what is required by the no harm argument. Many forms of interference involve inflicting harm on another person. At the same time, the noninterference argument is potentially more restrictive in what it requires of MNEs in certain contexts. That is to say, it may rule out certain activities on the part of MNEs that are permitted by the no harm argument.

Consider a right not to be coerced, which is widely counted as a liberty right. On Onora O'Neill's (2000) account of coercion, it is possible for A to coerce B even if B is left no worse off than before and, hence, unharmed. Although the use of direct force is considered by many to be a paradigmatic case of coercion, for O'Neill what characterizes coercion is the making of an offer by A that B cannot refuse. In the case of a genuine offer, the "choice of one or another option can be seen as an expression of agency." A genuine offer can be refused—"no penalty, other than that of foregoing what is on offer, attaches to the refusal" (O'Neill, 2000, p. 90). In contrast, an "unrefusable" offer is one in which A seeks not only to make his preferred option (X) the preferred option for B, but also to make the other options "unsustainable" for B (O'Neill, 2000, p. 90). B cannot simply walk away from the offer, and as a result "the exercise of choice is corrupted by the structure of the offer" (O'Neill, 2000, p. 89). An offer in which A credibly threatens violence against B unless B chooses X is an instance of coercion. Although B may prefer X to suffering violence at the hands of A, B's choice of X is not a genuine expression of agency. On O'Neill's account, "take-it-or-leave-it" offers also can count as coercive if the alternative to not choosing X is a continued unsustainable situation, which includes continued deprivation or vulnerability. "If there is no other work and no welfare state," writes O'Neill, "those without other means must comply with the proffered wage bargain or face destitution" (2000, p. 95). In situations such as these, an offer of employment to B can count as coercive, even if B is left no worse off—and not harmed—by choosing the offer.

The preceding discussion provides one way to frame the debate about labor standards that have dominated much of the literature on the responsibilities of MNEs.[16] In debates about labor standards, questions about wages are frequently seen as distinct from those regarding working conditions. While it is not difficult to understand the concern with dangerous working conditions from the perspective of either the no harm argument or the noninterference argument, a responsibility to pay workers an above-market wage is often framed in terms of a duty to aid workers. The preceding discussion, however, provides one way to understand why a concern with paying an above-market wage need not invoke a duty to aid others, but simply a duty of forbearance—that is, a duty not to engage in coercion. If O'Neill's argument is correct, then, just as in the case of the no harm argument, the noninterference argument is more demanding with respect to what is minimally required of MNEs than might be initially thought.[17]

Duties of Assistance

On many views that acknowledge universal moral rights, liberty rights and security rights are not the only rights that persons are said to have in virtue of their humanity. Many of these other rights ground claims to assistance from others. That is, they ground *duties of assistance*, and not simply duties of forbearance on the part of others. In turn, the question arises whether acknowledging duties of forbearance entails acknowledging that duties of assistance also apply to MNEs. If the answer is in the affirmative, then the minimum standards for MNEs are even more demanding than the previous two sections would give us reason to believe.

This section takes up this issue by way of Henry Shue's influential argument that the *right to subsistence* is just as basic a right as a right to liberty or a right to security (1996).[18] By a right to subsistence, Shue has in mind a right to "basic economic security," which includes "unpolluted air, unpolluted water, adequate food, adequate clothing, adequate shelter, and minimal preventative public health care" (1996, p. 23). To say that a right is a *basic* is to hold that it is "the rational basis for justified demands the denial of which no self-respecting person can reasonably be expected to accept" (1996, p. 19). Basic rights, according to Shue, are "everyone's minimum reasonable demands upon the rest of humanity" (1996, p. 19). On Shue's account, the right to subsistence gives rise to the following duties in relation to a person's enjoyment of that right (1996, p. 60). They are duties:

I. To avoid depriving.
II. To protect from deprivation.
   1. By enforcing duty (I), and
   2. By designing institutions that avoid the creation of strong incentives to violate duty (I).
III. To aid the deprived.
   1. Who are one's special responsibility,
   2. Who are victims of social failures in the performance of duties (I), (II-1), (II-2), and
   3. Who are the victims of natural disasters.

In arguing that the right to subsistence is a basic right, Shue holds that the above duties—including duties of assistance of type (III)—apply to all persons.

In response, Thomas Donaldson (1989) argues that even if one recognizes a basic right to subsistence in the manner advocated by Shue, it does not follow that MNEs have a duty to assist those deprived in their exercise of the right to subsistence. Donaldson considers a range of rights—ranging from the right to freedom of physical movement to the right to subsistence—and concludes that whereas a duty of type (I) applies to MNEs with respect to all rights and a duty of type (II) applies to MNEs with respect to most rights, a duty of type (III-2) does not apply to MNEs (1989, p. 86). Donaldson puts forward two objections to attributing duties of assistance to MNEs. The first is that "it would be unfair, not to mention unreasonable, to hold corporations to the same standards of charity and love as human individuals" (1989, p. 84). In contrast to governments that have as their mission the advancement of their citizens' welfare, the "profit-making corporation is designed to achieve an economic mission and as a moral actor possesses an exceedingly narrow personality" (p. 84). Second, the business corporation is "an undemocratic institution" that is "ill-suited to the broader task of distributing society's goods in accordance with a conception of the general welfare" (p. 84). In certain aspects, these objections echo intuitions underlying previous arguments considered in this essay, such as the political principle argument, so it will be helpful to devote some time to examining them in more detail.

The first objection is that MNEs should not be held to the same standards as full moral agents, but Shue's account of basic rights points to a way to attribute duties of assistance to MNEs without attributing any degree of moral agency to them. Recall that in the case of duties of forbearance, liberty rights and security rights apply to the actions of MNEs by way of the people who manage and carry out the work of MNEs. No attribution of moral agency is required for duties of forbearance to apply to MNEs. On Shue's account, the right to subsistence is just as basic as a right to liberty or a right to security. This means that, in a manner similar to the noninterference argument, duties associated with the right to subsistence apply to managers of MNEs, who are in a position to direct the activities of MNEs to assist those deprived of economic security. Furthermore, the duties associated with the right to subsistence apply to other parties—such as shareholders, employees, and customers—who have claims over the way in which the resources of MNEs are used or claims to the benefits derived from their use. Unless their claims consistently override the claims grounded in a right to subsistence—which seems implausible if we accept that subsistence is a basic right—then it would be wrong for managers not to respect the right to subsistence, which includes providing assistance, when making decisions about the activities of MNEs.

To be certain, questions need to be addressed about the limits to what can be required of MNEs and the ability of MNEs to provide assistance, but there is reason to doubt that the answers to these questions count against this basic point. Consider first the limits to what can be required of MNEs. On the approach outlined above, the answer to this question depends on a more general discussion of the limits to what can be demanded of individuals more generally in the provision of assistance to persons who lack economic security. If the limits of what can be demanded of, say, shareholders are such that their requirements in fulfilling the duty of assistance are met even without MNEs having to take actions to help provide assistance, then MNEs are limited in what is required of them.

A similar point can be made about the ability of MNEs to provide assistance. In the institutional contexts under discussion, there is reason to hold that the activities of MNEs could be directed to help provide assistance to those deprived in exercising the right to subsistence. Consider, for example, the case of pharmaceutical, agricultural, and energy companies. These companies are involved in the production of goods that contribute directly to basic economic security. MNEs also can contribute to basic economic security by providing employment and related benefits, such as healthcare. Circumstances may be such that MNEs are limited in the ways they are able to help provide assistance. They may face, for example, financial constraints. None of these situations, however, presents a principled objection against including the provision of assistance among the minimal standards that apply to the activities of MNEs.

The second objection Donaldson raises is that the "undemocratic" nature of MNEs makes them "ill-suited to the broader task of distributing society's goods in accordance with a conception of the general welfare" (1989, p. 84). The objection echoes the political principle argument according to which the managers of MNEs lack the standing to direct the use of corporate resources for reasons other than normal business activity. Where the objection differs is that it does not presume the background institution of political democracy. The objection also differs in that it makes no claim about the violation of property rights on the part of shareholders or other stakeholders. Rather, the objection makes a more general claim about the inappropriateness of managers of MNEs making decisions that ought to be made politically. One way to interpret this claim without invoking property rights or assuming political democracy is with reference to the social or institutional role that MNEs are generally said to occupy. This role is commonly held to be distinct from a public one and, on this view, it would be inappropriate for MNEs to take up activities normally associated with public institutions, unless designated by them to do so. To help flesh out the second objection raised by Donaldson, what follows is one way in which to understand the way in which MNEs adopt a public role when helping to provide assistance.

Recall that duties of forbearance are said to be perfect. In contrast, duties of assistance are widely held to be imperfect. That is, there is a problem of allocation with regard to who it is that ought to fulfill the claims grounded in a right to subsistence. Public institutions serve to "perfect" these imperfect duties by playing a "mediating" role (Shue, 1988). To illustrate, following Beitz and Goodin (2009), suppose we grant that the rich have a duty to help the poor. This is an imperfect duty in the sense that no poor person has a specific claim against any given rich person. What a public institution—in this case, the state—does is to serve as a "consolidator" of these imperfect duties (p. 15). The rich have a perfect duty to pay taxes, and the state has a perfect duty to help the poor. In the account outlined above, the managers of MNEs play a mediating role for discharging the duties of assistance that are said to apply to the various parties associated with MNEs, such as shareholders and employees. That is, the managers of MNEs help to allocate resources in fulfilling the claims grounded in the right to subsistence. The problem, it may be said, is that they lack the status of public officials who have the authority to do so. Absent an account according to which they have such status, Donaldson's second objection stands.

None of this forecloses the possibility that MNEs have responsibilities to assist persons who lack economic security. First, other grounds have been advanced for a responsibility on the part of MNEs to provide assistance to those who lack economic security. One of these grounds, for example, is the principle of rescue (Hsieh, 2005, 2006; Dunfee, 2006).[19] Second, there may be situations in which it is appropriate for MNEs to take on responsibilities associated with states as a matter of justice. For example, O'Neill (2001) distinguishes between "primary agents of justice," which have "capacities to determine how principles of justice are to be institutionalised within a certain domain," and "secondary agents of justice," which contribute to justice by complying with these institutional requirements (p. 189). In line with the account in this essay, O'Neill classifies MNEs generally as secondary agents of justice. However, when states are weak and lack the means to bring about justice, O'Neill argues that "any simple division between primary and secondary agents of justice blurs" and that justice "has to be built by a diversity of agents and agencies" including MNEs (2001, p. 201). Third, more needs to be said about why MNEs and their managers do not have the sort of status that would make it legitimate for them to allocate resources to fulfill claims grounded in the right to subsistence. If this lack of status is largely a matter of societal norms and expectations and not a matter of moral principle, then it seems open for debate whether to assign MNEs a role in assisting persons who lack economic security.

Conclusion

When institutional arrangements structuring global economic activity are incomplete, it seems natural to ask whether there are minimum standards that ought to apply to the activities of MNEs independently of local institutional requirements. According to the weak-side constraints view, the answer is negative. On this view there are few, if any, standards that apply to MNEs apart from what is already required by the institutional contexts in which they operate. The discussion in this essay gave us reason to reject this view, prompting instead an approach to locating minimum standards for MNEs in duties of forbearance.

The approach taken was fairly minimalist. To begin, the approach focused on duties of forbearance widely held to be among the most basic: duties not to harm others and duties not to violate or infringe upon the liberty and security rights of others. These duties are held to apply to all moral agents in part because they can be honored in almost all circumstances; the agent need only refrain from acting. In addition, the approach did not presume any degree of moral agency on the part of MNEs. Rather, the approach focused on what follows for the activities of MNEs by acknowledging that these duties apply to managers and employees of MNEs as moral agents. In the end, despite this fairly minimalist approach, there is reason to hold that minimum moral standards for MNEs grounded in duties of forbearance are more demanding than what the nature of these duties of forbearance initially would suggest.

In closing, it should be noted that an approach based on duties of forbearance is not the only way in which to specific minimum standards for MNEs that are independent of local institutional requirements. It also should be noted that the approach in this essay takes for granted duties not to harm others and duties not to violate and infringe upon the liberty and security rights of others. In these respects, a complete account of minimum standards for MNEs along these lines will need to say more about the grounds for these duties as well as to defend this approach against competing approaches to specifying minimum standards for MNEs. What this essay has aimed to do is to show the promise of such an approach and to have laid out what more needs to be done to realize that promise.

I am grateful to Michael Boylan for his support and encouragement in writing this essay. I also thank the Zicklin Center for Business Ethics Research for funding part of this research and Harvard Business School for providing a hospitable environment in which to complete it.

Notes

1 An MNE is an enterprise chartered in one country (often referred to as the "parent enterprise") that controls the activities of one or more enterprises that operate in other countries (often referred as "affiliate enterprises" or "subsidiaries"). Control is usually exercised through the ownership of a significant share of equity in the affiliate enterprises. A key feature of MNEs is that they have a decision-making structure that allows for "coherent policies and a common strategy" across the parent and affiliate enterprises (United Nations Conference on Trade and Development, UNCTAD). For earlier treatments on the standards that ought to govern the activities of MNEs, see Donaldson (1989), De George (1993), and Donaldson and Dunfee (1999). For a recent survey of the literature on corporate responsibility, see Crane, McWilliams, Matten, Moon, and Siegel (2008).

2 Depending on the basis for comparison, for example, MNEs comprise anywhere from 29 to over 50 of the world's top 100 economic entities. In the case of countries, GDP is taken as the measure of their economic size. If the revenue of MNEs is used as a measure of their size, then MNEs comprise roughly half of the 100 largest economic entities in the world. However, as De Grauwe and Camerman (2003) point out, GDP is the sum of the value added by each producer, which is not the same as the sum of the revenue of these producers. Aggregating the revenue of producers is likely to involve counting more than once the value added by producers. Accordingly, the authors argue that counting the revenue of MNEs overstates their relative size. Following the authors' method of calculating the value added by MNEs, one estimate places 29 MNEs within the top 100 economic entities in the world (UNCTAD, 2002).

3 The criteria for completeness are minimal and intended to be fairly uncontroversial as evaluative criteria. A more comprehensive set of criteria for evaluating institutional arrangements might include, for example, criteria regarding the extent to which human rights are protected, the provision of public goods, the effective influence of citizens, and the ability of citizens to seek redress. As an illustration, see Rawls 1999, on the concept of a "well-ordered society."

4 For an insightful discussion of the literature and account of corporate moral responsibility that aims to avoid objections raised against previous accounts, see Dubbink and Smith, 2010.

5 In the frequently quoted *New York Times Magazine* article, Friedman provides a slightly different formulation of managerial responsibility. He writes (1970): "In a free enterprise, a private property system, a corporate executive is an employee of the owners of the business. He has a direct responsibility to his employers. That responsibility is to conduct the business in accordance with their desires, which generally will be to make as much money as possible while conforming to the basic rules of the society, both those embodied in law and those embodied in ethical custom." Strictly speaking, this formulation opens two avenues for managers to follow standards above and beyond what is required by the law: the desires of shareholders and ethical custom. However, most commentators interpret Friedman's view as consistent with the weak-sided constraints view.

6 In 2010, for example, according to the Economist Intelligence Unit (2010), 15.6% of all countries (26 countries) qualified as "full democracies," which included 12.3% of the world's population; 31.7% (53 countries) qualified as "flawed democracies," which included 37.2% of the world's population.

7 One question, for example, is whether shareholders can be said to own the corporation.

8 Elaine Sternberg (2000) claims to advance just such an argument for the weak-side constraints view. On her version of the weak-side constraints view, the constraints to be observed are "fairness and honesty" in relation to contracts and promises, and "refraining from coercion and physical violence, typically within the confines of the law." The difficulty with relying on her view as an alternative to Friedman's view, is that her view is based on Friedman's view (Arnold, 2003).

9 For an approach that aims to develop the moral dimensions of the international human rights regime with respect to business organizations, see Campbell and Miller (2004).

10 The United Nations Human Rights Commission's initiative is not the only United Nations attempt to institutionalize human rights requirements with regard to the activities of MNEs. The other prominent attempt to move beyond voluntary adherence on the part of MNEs is the *Norms on the Responsibilities of Transnational Corporations and Other Business Enterprises with Regard to Human Rights* (U.N. Doc. E/CN.4/Sub.2/2003/12/Rev.2 (2003)), which states that "within their respective spheres of

activity and influence, transnational corporations and other business enterprises have the obligation to promote, secure the fulfillment of, respect, ensure respect of and protect human rights recognized in international as well as national law, including the rights and interests of indigenous peoples and other vulnerable groups." Although the draft document was adopted by the United Nations Human Rights Commission's Sub-Commission on the Promotion and Protection of Human Rights in 2003, the Commission declared that the draft document had no legal standing. At that time, the Commission asked the Office of the High Commissioner for Human Rights to report on the relation of human rights to business conduct. This report forms the focus of the discussion in this essay. For discussion of the various attempts to relate human rights to business activity, see Voiculescu (2011).

11 De George (1993) for example, lists as the first ethical guideline for American multinational enterprises that they "should do no intentional direct harm" (p. 46).

12 For a nuanced treatment of the different kinds of harms that MNEs may cause and the varied responsibilities that MNEs have to avoid them, see De George (1993).

13 This is consistent with what Lichtenberg (2010) terms the "New Harms view." She writes, "over the past few decades, but especially in the past few years—with economic, environmental, and electronic globalization rapidly increasing; near consensus about the threat of severe climate change, whose effects will be felt most by the world's poorest people; knowledge that the provenance of products we use every day is compromised in a variety of ways; and finally, the growing impossibility of remaining ignorant of these phenomena—we have

learned how our ordinary habits and conduct contribute to harming other people near and far, now and in the future" (p. 558). All of this, according to Lichtenberg, makes it difficult to maintain the clean distinction between duties not to harm and duties to aid with respect to what they demand of citizens, especially those in developed economies.

14 For critical discussions, see Michaelson (2010) and Wettstein (2010).

15 Just what characteristics of human beings are said to justify attributing to them liberty rights is a matter of debate. For a helpful overview, see Wenar (2011). See also Campbell (2006) and Griffin (2008).

16 For some discussions of labor standards in the business ethics literature, see Hartman, Arnold, and Wokutch (2003), Snyder (2010), and Zwolinski and Powell (2011).

17 To be certain, O'Neill's account is not the only account of coercion, and some commentators may object that her account fails to locate the wrong in not paying an above-market wage in a violation of liberty. For another account of coercion see Wertheimer (1987). See also Hartman et al. (2003), Snyder (2010), and Zwolinski and Powell (2011).

18 For a wide-ranging discussion of Shue's approach, see Beitz and Goodin (2009). On the influence of Shue's account, see Pogge (2009, p. 125).

19 T.M. Scanlon (1998) provides one formulation of the principle: "(I)f you are presented with a situation in which you can prevent something very bad from happening, or alleviate someone's dire plight, by making only a slight (or even moderate) sacrifice, then it would be wrong not to do so" (p. 224). He notes that the "cases in which it would most clearly be wrong not to give aid . . . are cases in which those in need of aid are in dire straits: their lives are immediately threatened, for example" (p. 224).

References

Arnold, D. (2003) "Libertarian Theories of the Corporate and Global Capitalism." *Journal of Business Ethics* 48.2: 155–173.

Ashford, E. (2009) "The Alleged Dichotomy between Positive and Negative Rights and Duties," in *Global Basic Rights*, ed. C. Beitz and R. Goodin (Oxford: Oxford University Press): 92–112.

Beitz, C. and R. Goodin (Eds.) (2009) *Global Basic Rights* (Oxford: Oxford University Press).

Campbell, T. (2006) *Rights: A Critical Introduction* (New York: Routledge).

Campbell, T. and S. Miller (Eds.) (2004) *Human Rights and the Moral Responsibilities of Corporate and Public Sector Organizations* (Dordecht: Kluwer Academic).

Cragg, W. (2000) "Human Rights and Business Ethics: Fashioning a New Social Contract." *Journal of Business Ethics* 27: 205–214.

Crane, A., A. McWilliams, D. Matten, J. Moon, and D. Siegel (Eds.) (2008) *The Oxford Handbook of Corporate Social Responsibility* (Oxford: Oxford University Press).

De George, R. (1993) *Competing with Integrity in International Business* (New York: Oxford University Press).

De Grauwe, P. and F. Camerman (2003) "Are Multinationals Really Bigger than Nations?" *World Economics* 4.2: 23–37.

Donaldson, T. (1989) *The Ethics of International Business* (New York: Oxford University Press).

Donaldson, T. and T. Dunfee (1999) *Ties that Bind* (Boston, MA: Harvard Business School Press).

Dubbink, W. and J. Smith (2010) "A Political Account of the Corporation as a Morally Responsible Actor." *Ethical Theory and Moral Practice* 14.2: 223–246.

Dunfee, T. (2006) "Do Firms with Unique Competencies for Rescuing Victims of Human Catastrophes Have Special Obligations? Corporate Responsibility and the AIDS Catastrophe in Sub-Saharan Africa." *Business Ethics Quarterly* 16.2: 185–210.

Economist Intelligence Unit (2010) *Democracy Index 2010: Democracy in Retreat* (London: Economist Intelligence Unit).

Friedman, M. (1962) *Capitalism and Freedom* (Chicago, IL: University of Chicago Press).

Friedman, M. (1970) "The Social Responsibility of Business Is to Increase Its Profits." *New York Times Magazine* 13 September: 32.

Griffin, J. (2004) "Human Rights: Whose Duties?," in *Human Rights and the Moral Responsibilities of Corporate and Public Sector Organizations*, ed. T. Campbell and S. Miller (Dordecht: Kluwer Academic): 31–44.

Griffin, J. (2008) *On Human Rights* (Oxford: Oxford University Press).

Hartman, L., D. Arnold, and R. Wokutch (2003) *Rising above Sweatshops' Innovative Approaches to Global Labor Challenges* (Westport, CT: Praeger).

Hsieh, N. (2005) "Property Rights in Crisis: Managers and Rescue," in *Ethics and the Pharmaceutical Industry in the 21st Century*, ed. M. Santoro and T. Gorrie (New York: Cambridge University Press): 379–385.

Hsieh, N. (2006) "Voluntary Codes of Conduct for Multinational Corporations: Coordinating Duties of Rescue and Justice." *Business Ethics Quarterly* 16.2: 119–135.

Hsieh, N. (2009) "Does Global Business Have a Responsibility to Promote Just Institutions?" *Business Ethics Quarterly* 19.2: 251–273.

Hsieh, N. (2011) "Multinational Enterprises and Corporate Responsibility: A Matter of Justice?," in *Morality and Global Justice: The Reader*, ed. M. Boylan (Boulder, CO: Westview Press).

Lane, M. (2005) "The Moral Dimension of Corporate Responsibility," in *Global Responsibilities*, ed. Andrew Kuper (New York: Routledge).

Lichtenberg, J. (2010) "Negative Duties, Positive Duties, and the 'New Harms'." *Ethics* 120.3: 557–578.

Michaelson, C. (2010) "Revisiting the Global Business Ethics Question." *Business Ethics Quarterly* 20.2: 237–251.

Navaretti, G. and A. Venables (2004) *Multinational Firms in the World Economy* (Princeton, NJ: Princeton University Press).

Nickel, J. (2010) "Human Rights," in *The Stanford Encyclopedia of Philosophy* (Fall 2010 ed.), ed. E.N. Zalta. Retrieved March 7, 2013 from http://plato.stanford.edu/archives/fall2010/entries/rights-human/

OECD (2010) *OECD Benchmark Definition of Foreign Direct Investment*, 4th ed. (Paris: Organisation for Economic Co-operation and Development).

O'Neill, O. (2000) *Bounds of Justice* (Cambridge: Cambridge University Press, 2008).

O'Neill, O. (2001) "Agents of Justice," in *Global Justice*, ed. T. Pogge (Oxford: Blackwell): 188–203.

Pogge, T. (2009) "Shue on Rights and Duties," in *Global Basic Rights*, ed. C. Beitz and R. Goodin (Oxford: Oxford University Press): 113–130.

Rawls, J. (1999) *The Law of Peoples* (Cambridge, MA: Harvard University Press).

Ruggie, J. (2008) *Promotion and Protection of All Human Rights, Civil, Political, Economic, Social and Cultural Rights, Including the Right to Development*. Report to the United Nations Human Rights Council.

Scanlon, T.M. (1998) *What We Owe to Each Other* (Cambridge, MA: Belknap Press).

Shue, H. (1988) "Mediating Duties." *Ethics* 98: 687–704.

Shue, H. (1996) *Basic Rights: Subsistence, Affluence, and U.S. Foreign Policy*, 2nd ed. (Princeton, NJ: Princeton University Press).

Snyder, J. (2010) "Exploitation and Sweatshop Labor: Perspectives and Issues." *Business Ethics Quarterly* 20.2: 187–213.

Sternberg, E. (2000) *Just Business: Business Ethics in Action*, 2nd ed. (Oxford: Oxford University Press).

UNCTAD (2002) "Are Transnationals Bigger than Countries?" Press Release (Geneva: United Nations Conference on Trade and Development).

UNCTAD (2010) *Transnational Corporation Statistics*. Retrieved March 18, 2013 from http://unctad.org/en/Pages/DIAE/Transnational-Corporations-Statistics.aspx

United Nations (1948) *Universal Declaration of Human Rights*.

United Nations (2003) *Norms on the Responsibilities of Transnational Corporations and other Business Enterprises with Regard to Human Rights*.

Voiculescu, A. (2011) "Human Rights in Business Context: An Overview," in *The Business of Human Rights: An Evolving Agenda for Corporate Responsibility*, ed.

A. Voiculescu and H. Yanacopulos (London: Zed Books).

Wenar, L. (2008) "Property Rights and the Resource Curse." *Philosophy & Public Affairs* 36: 2–32.

Wenar, L. (2011) "Rights," in *The Stanford Encyclopedia of Philosophy* (Fall 2011 ed.), ed. E.N. Zalta. Retrieved March 7, 2013 from http://plato.stanford.edu/archives/fall2011/entries/rights/

Wertheimer, A. (1987) *Coercion* (Princeton, NJ: Princeton University Press).

Wettstein, F. (2010) "For Better or Worse: Corporate Social Responsibility beyond "Do No Harm." *Business Ethics Quarterly* 20.2: 275–283.

Zwolinski, M. and B. Powell (2011) "The Ethical and Economic Case against Sweatshop Labor: A Critical Assessment." *Journal of Business Ethics* 93: 449–472.

Evaluating a Case Study
Structuring the Essay

In previous sections, you have moved from adopting an ethical theory to weighing and assessing the merits of deeply embedded cost issues and ethical issues conflicts. The process involves (a) chosing an ethical theory (whose point of view you will adopt), (b) determining your professional practice issues and your issues lists, (c) annotating the issues lists by examining how embedded each issue is to the essential nature of the case at hand, (d) creating a brainstorming list that includes both key thoughts on the subject and arguments for and against the possible courses of action, (e) comparing pivotal premises in those arguments using ethical considerations as part of the decision-making matrix, (f) making a judgment on which course to take (given the conflicts expressed in d and e), and (g) presenting your ideas in an essay. The essay is your recommendation about what to do in a specific situation.

This section represents stage (g) in this process. If we continue with the IUD case, your essay might be something like the following.

Sample Essay

Executive Summary. Although my profession would advocate my continuing to distribute IUDs to women in less-developed countries and although cost issues also dictate continuing to distribute them through ABC Corporation's offer, it is my opinion that to do so would be immoral. Human life is too precious to put any one at risk for population control. If IUDs are too dangerous to be sold in the United States, then they are too dangerous to be given to women in poor countries as well. People do not give up their right to adequate health protection just because they are poor. For this reason, I am ordering a halt to the distribution of IUDs until such a time that they can be considered safe again. Furthermore, I will step up efforts to distribute alternate forms of birth control (such as the birth control pill) with better packaging that might encourage regular use.

The Introduction. In this case study, I have chosen the point of view of the regional director. This means that I must decide whether to continue distributing IUDs in less-developed countries despite a health hazard to 5 percent of the women who use this form of birth control. I will present my case against continuing the distribution based on an argument that examines: (a) the imperatives of my profession, public health; (b) cost implications; (c) the imperatives of ethics; and (d) the rights of the women involved. I will contend that after examining these issues, the conclusion must be that IUD distribution in the less-developed countries must cease until they no longer pose a significant problem to women's health.

The Body of the Essay. Develop paragraphs along the lines indicated in the introduction and executive summary.

The Conclusion. Although the dictates of the normal practice of public health and cost considerations seem to suggest that IUD distribution should continue, the ethical imperatives that human life is individually precious and that each woman has a right to safe medical attention overrule the normal practice of the profession. For these reasons, my office will suspend distribution of IUDs until they no longer pose a health risk to the general population.

Comments on the Sample. The sample provides an essay structure that contains a brief epitome and the essay itself. I often encourage my students to come in with their epitome, key issues, arguments for and against, and brainstorming sheets before writing the essay itself. This way I can get an "in-progress" view at the process of composition.

Obviously, the preceding sample represents the briefest skeleton of an essay proposing a recommendation. The length can vary as can any supporting data (charts, etc.) that will support your position. Your instructor may ask you to present your outcomes recommendation to the entire class. When this is the assignment, remember that the same principles of any group presentation also apply here including any visual aid that will engage your audience. It is essential to include your audience in your argument as it develops.

Whether it is a written report or a group presentation, the methodology presented here should give you a chance to logically assess and respond to business problems that contain moral dimensions.

The following are general questions that some of my students have raised about writing the essay, that is, the ethical outcomes recommendation.

What if I cannot see the other side? This is a common question from students. They see everything as black or white, true or false, but truth is never advanced by prejudice. It is important as rational humans to take every argument at its face value and to determine what it says, determine the objections to the key premises, determine the strongest form of the thesis, and assess the best arguments *for* and *against* the thesis.

What is the best way to reach my assessment of the best alternative? The basic strategy of the essay is to take the best two arguments that you have selected to support the conflicting alternatives and then to focus on that single premise that seems to be at odds with the other argument. At this point, you must ask yourself, Why would someone believe in either argument 1 or argument 2? If you do not know, you cannot offer an opinion—yet.

The rational person seeks to inform herself by getting into the skin of each party. You must understand why a thinking person might think in a particular way. If you deprecate either side, you lessen yourself because you decrease your chances to make your best judgment.

The rational individual seeks the truth. You have no need to burden your psyche with illogical beliefs. Therefore, you will go to great lengths to find the truth of the key premises that you wish to examine.

In your final essay, you will focus on one of the argument's premises and find the following:

A. The demonstrated truth of the conclusion depends on the premises that support it.
B. If those supporting premises are false, then the conclusion is not proven.
C. Since we have assumed that the premises are all necessary to get us to the conclusion, if we refute one premise, we have refuted the conclusion.

What if I place professional practice issues, or cost issues, or ethical issues too high in my assessment of the outcome? The purpose of presenting embedded issues analysis is to force you to see that not all ethical issues are central to the problem. Some issues can be solved rather easily. If this is the case, then you should do so. When it is possible to let professional practice issues determine the outcome without sacrificing ethical standards, then it is your responsibility to do so. Clearly, some ethical principles cannot be sacrificed no matter what the cost. It is *your* responsibility to determine just what these cases are and just which moral principles are "show stoppers."

Are ethical values the only values an individual should consider? Each person holds a number of personally important values that are a part of his or her world-view. These must be taken into account in real situations. Often they mean that although you cannot perform such and such an act, it is not requisite that the organization forgo doing whatever the professional practice issues dictate in that situation. For example, you may be asked to perform a task on an important religious holy day. Since your religion is important to you, you cannot work on that day, but that does not mean that you will recommend the company abandon the task that another person who does not share your values could perform.

What happens when you confuse professional practice issues and ethical issues? This often happens among managers at all levels. The problem is that one set of issues is neglected or is too quickly considered to be surface embeddedness. Stop. Go through the method again step-by-step. It may restore your perspective.

Macro and Micro Cases[1]

Macro Case 1. You are operations director in China for Victory Running Shoes (the world's largest athletic shoe company). Your largest factory near Shanghai recently has a one-day shut down as many of the women workers (85% of the company's employees) called in sick. You sent out a subordinate to get the facts. The women at the plant had been recruited from poverty farming lives. They were recruited and separated from their families. The women are provided room and board in company dormitories with other separated wives. These women say they feel like drones who work for long hours for wages that are then sent back to their husbands and children far away. This is a major cultural shift for these women (who also have an increasing suicide rate). They say that on the farm they had a respected social role. Here they have become machines.

They are nothing but machines. You are of two minds. Certainly, many of these women and their families would have starved to death had they stayed in rural agriculture. But you also understand that their present situation is not utopia, either. You must write a report to your corporation's vice president for operations about what you will do to address this situation. Remember to cite practical and ethical considerations.

Macro Case 2. You are the secretary of labor. You have become alarmed at the increased amount of apparel—economy brands as well as top-of-the-line labels—that recently has been documented to have been produced in sweatshops. It is obvious that regulations are in order, but you are baffled as to whether the regulations should come from and be enforced by the federal government or be initiated by the industry with internal sanctions and monitoring mechanisms as a positive incentive program with strong government encouragement.

You are conflicted by the arguments for each position. However, you believe that is necessary that your office take a stance, and you put the issue on the agenda for the next senior staff meeting. You must write a report justifying your position; make sure that your report represents both professional practice, ethical, and cost issues and highlights the advantages of the regulation you propose.

Macro Case 3. As the head of the Federal Trade Commission, you have been beset with requests from parents' groups throughout the country to do something about the violence in computer games. Because of numerous school shootings around the country recently, the issue has received increased support. You, however, are aware of no conclusive studies that link playing (violent) computer games to violent behavior.

You have decided to proactively address the problem at a meeting of the major software companies. At this meeting, you will present your proposal for regulation consisting of some monitoring or labeling system. There are two choices: creation and regulation of the system by the government or by an industry group.

Write two different proposals and show how each will work and then recommend one of them. State the reason you support this recommendation, be sure to include professional practice, ethical, and cost considerations.

Macro Case 4. You are an executive with a financial services company and are attempting to create a single e-network for all the major world markets. You have already gotten approval from a number of international firms, but you cannot receive it from one Japanese firm that is requiring a hefty bribe before it will enter into serious discussions.

An associate has suggested a way to get around U.S. sanctions on bribery. Although it is perhaps legal (meaning that you will not be jailed if you are discovered), it is certainly against the spirit of the law, but the bribery issue is contrary to your personal worldview. However, you recognize that you are an employee of a publicly owned company and owe the stockholders a fiduciary responsibility.

In your assessment, you have three options: not to offer a bribe and document why, take your associate's advice and do what is necessary to make the deal and cover yourself legally, or resign this position or ask for reassignment to a horizontal position in the company (although such a move is likely to freeze your career).

You are very conflicted about what to do. Part of this conflict concerns how to consider bribes in the ethical sense. Write a report clarifying your ideas on bribery and then on each of the three options. Conclude your report with a clear reason to adopt one of the three options (or another if you devise one) supported (by practical professional practice, ethical, and cost considerations).

Macro Case 5. You are the secretary of commerce. At a recent meeting of the G-8 nations, a proposal was made to establish some basic rules as to international business to be administered by the World Trade Organization (WTO). The WTO already monitors various multilateral trade agreements, but this plan would create new rules to ensure basic economic fairness. It would outlaw bribery and other uncompetitive practices and would include enforcement provisions that would not require an individual country to grant jurisdiction to the WTO.

This theory sounds promising, but one of the uncompetitive practices cited is monopolistic dominance. This means that any overly dominant market entity might be considered a monopoly and its business practices restricted (much as the U.S. Justice Department handles monopolies in the United States). Because the United States has most of these dominant companies, the regulations will benefit smaller countries at the expense of U.S. firms. Although this might fit perfectly in the model of capitalism (as modified in the twentieth century), it will hurt U.S. business, and possibly lower the standard of living (or at least slowing the growth of consumerism).

How should the control of uncompetitive practices such as bribery be balanced against policies that would restrict uncompetitive practices followed by U.S. businesses. Write a letter to the president of the United States describing your position. Be sure to cite professional practice, ethical, and cost issues in your recommendations.

Micro Case 1. You work for WOD Chemical, a multinational corporation. You were assigned to the Bombay, India office a year ago when your company sold its genetically modified wheat seed. The yields on this seed are 3x that of wild seed. The problem is this: farmers who did not buy your seed but are near to the farms that *did* benefited as natural cross-pollination brought them the benefits of the genetically altered seed in this year's crop. (You know this because you've sent around inspectors who were accompanied by the police.) Those who bought your seed are angry because their neighbors are "free riders" (getting something for no cost). But the local farmers are also mad because they said they preferred the wild seed and claim that WOD is polluting their crop and that not only do they refuse to pay WOD for the free enhanced seed, but they want cash for damages! Write a report to your home office suggesting a way to go forward citing practical and ethical issues.

Micro Case 2. You are a branch director of an automobile leasing company with two employees. Your firm does business east of the Mississippi River. A local municipality issued to several auto leasing companies in the region a proposal for a car-sharing program to be part of a welfare-to-work initiative. At a meeting of those intending to submit a bid, you find that most of your competitors plan to provide used cars with a new or remanufactured engine and a new chassis (so they can be registered as new), but these vehicles are *not* new. Although this practice satisfies the law, it seems wrong to you. You are also offended by several of your competitors who joked that these reconditioned vehicles are certainly better than the welfare-to-work persons deserve.

Various government regulations provide sanctions against failing to meet the specifications on a municipal bid. However, you prefer to create a consensus among bidders as to the criteria for making their bid. In other words, you seek regulation of the autos offered in the bid but from within the group.

You mention some of these concerns to your spouse, who asked you to refine your thoughts, which were disorganized. Therefore, your task is to write a report that you will first present to your spouse and then later to the other bidders about the autos that will be included in this bidding process. Do you threaten to go to the authorities? How much emphasis do you give to ethical arguments?

Micro Case 3. You are a telecommunications account executive (salesperson) who has been asked to handle the company's bid on the new telecommunications system for the country of X-Star (an oil-rich eastern European country). Your company is counting on this large contract for its strategic future. Your boss, Dick Sharpe, has given you a considerable wine and dine budget and told you not to skimp on anything you might need.

During the meeting with the U.S. branch procurement officer, Dewey Cheatum, he holds a manila folder in one hand and gestures with the other. Only the two of you are at the meeting:

"You know what I really live for is my boy, Alex" said Mr. Cheatum.

"Yes, sir," you responded.

"He's a talented boy, but you know he just doesn't fit in at the school he's going to. I don't think that he'll ever fit in at a public school. He needs a first-class private school like Excelsior to get that 'edge' in life—know what I mean?"

"Yes, sir," you replied.

"You know it's not how good you are in this world, but it's who you know and what they can do for you that brings success. Yep, that's what brings success. And Excelsior could give that to my Alex."

"So are you going to send Alex to Excelsior?" you naively asked.

"Ha! Fat chance on a civil servant's salary." Mr. Cheatum began hitting his free hand with the manila folder while he talked. "I'd need $45,000 to fall out of the sky to be able to afford four years at *that* tuition. Forty-five thousand. That's how much four years' tuition is at Excelsior."

You nodded as Mr. Cheatum excused himself to use the lavatory. He left the file folder that he had been playing with on the table. Naturally, you opened the folder that held all the specifications and preliminary bids of competitors—in duplicate. Naturally, you took the duplicates and put them in your briefcase. When Mr. Cheatum returned, you talked about several random topics and then you left.

When you got home, you suddenly felt panicked. What had you done? Had you entered into an agreement to pay the costs of Alex Cheatum's prep school education? The total cost was not out of line with your budget, but to put all your eggs in one basket that is the private property of the decision maker concerned you. The problem is that you *took* the information on the telecommunications contract. Suppose the room had a hidden camera.

You decided to take a long walk and think about it. When you got back you resolved to write a memo to yourself that would identify your thoughts on the practical and ethical considerations of the problem. You also need a plan of action. Therefore, after the preliminaries you plan to write out exactly how you should execute your eventual plan of action.

Micro Case 4. You are a newly stationed local official of SAVE THE WORLD, an international development organization. Your organization has convinced several world powers (including the United States) to participate with the World Bank in a key project for the construction of a dam in the western African country in which you are stationed. Your agency is overseeing the dispersal of moneys on the project. When you arrived, you decided to oversee the accounts and discovered that the local official employed a fraudulent accounting system to account for funds. With a little aggressive research, you discover that about half of the money has gone to private individuals and not to the project at hand.

This makes you furious. You do not know how this could have been allowed to transpire. The problem is this:

1. If you make a big deal about this (as fraud), the perpetrators may be caught and punished.
2. If you make a big deal about this (as fraud) and the perpetrators are punished, then your funding sources may pull out leaving a void where there is a legitimate need.
3. If you do not make a big deal of this (putting it all on different accounting methods), it allows the guilty to go free.
4. If you do not make a big deal of this, you (perhaps) become a part of the corruption.

You are conflicted about what to do. If you make the wrong choice it may mean not only your job, but your career in this line of work. Write out a plan of action using both practical issues and ethical issues to support your decision.

Micro Case 5. You are a bank auditor employed by a major U.S. bank doing business in a Russian republic. You are responsible for doing the taxes for your company. At present, however, the tax collection system in the republic is in its infancy. Large numbers of corporations and individuals simply do not pay. You could pay your fair share according to the regulations that presently exist in the Russian republic. No one else is really doing this, so you would put yourself at a competitive disadvantage with your competitors and perhaps are ignoring your fiduciary responsibility to your stockholders to make them money. You could pay what you think most comparable institutions are really paying on imaginative (a.k.a. fraudulent) accounting practices. In this case, you are doing what most other people in your situation are doing—even though it is contrary to the written law. Or you could take your chances and stiff the system. Worse case scenario on the last option is that you end up paying someone a big bribe (but it would still be less than the cost of option one).

You are not sure what to do. Should you follow one of these three alternatives or another one all together? Should you resign your post?

Write a report that will be directed to the branch manager stating what you plan to do and why. Be sure to cite both ethical and practical considerations.

Note

1 For more on macro and micro cases, see
  p. 138.

Further Reading

General Business Ethics

Bowie, Norman E. *Business Ethics: A Kantian Approach*. Oxford: Blackwell, 1999.

De George, Richard T. *Business Ethics*. 3rd Edition. New York: Macmillan, 1990.

Jones, Daniel. *A Bibliography of Business Ethics, 1971–1976; 1976–1980; 1981–1985*. 3 vols. Charlottesville: University Press of Virginia, 1977, 1982, 1986.

Soloman, Robert. *Above the Bottom Line: An Introduction to Business Ethics*. New York: Harcourt Brace, 1997.

Werhane, Patricia and R. Edward Freeman. *Dictionary of Business Ethics*. Oxford: Blackwell, 1998.

Westra, Laura, Patricia H. Werhane, George Brenkert, and Donald A. Brown. *The Business of Consumption: Environmental Ethics and the Global Economy*. Lanham, MD: Rowman and Littlefield, 1998.

Chapter 2 Theories of Economic Justice

Boulton, Jean. "Complexity Theory and Implications for Policy Development." *Emergence: Complexity & Organization* 12.2 (2010): 31–40.

Ege, Ragip and Herrade Igersheim. "Rawls's Justice Theory and Its Relations to the Concept of Merit Goods." *European Journal of the History of Economic Thought* 17.4 (2010): 1001–1030.

Mukesh, Sud and Craig V. VanSandt. "Of Fair Markets and Distributive Justice." *Journal of Business Ethics* 99 (2011): 131–142.

Rummens, Stefan. "No Justice without Democracy: A Deliberative Approach to the Global Distribution of Wealth." *International Journal of Philosophical Studies* 17.5 (2009): 657–680.

Schemmel, Christian. "Why Relational Egalitarians Should Care about Distributions." *Social Theory & Practice* 37.3 (2011): 365–390.

Chapter 3 What Is a Corporation?

A. The corporation as an individual

Donaldson, Thomas. *Corporations and Morality*. Englewood Cliffs, NJ: Prentice Hall, 1982.

Donaldson, Thomas. *The Ethics of International Business*. New York: Oxford, 1989.

Dubbink, Wim and Jeffery Smith. "A Political Account of Corporate Moral Responsibility." *Ethical Theory and Moral Practice* 14.2 (2011): 223–246.

French, Peter A. *Collective and Corporate Responsibility*. New York: Columbia University Press, 1984.

Garrett, J.E. "Redistributive Corporate Responsibility." *Journal of Business Ethics* 8 (1989): 535–545.

Gatewood, Elizabeth and Archie B. Carroll. "The Anatomy of Corporate Social Response: The Rely, Firestone 500, and Pinto Cases." *Business Horizons* 24 (1981): 9–16.

Gibson, Kevin. "Toward an Intermediate Position on Corporate Moral Personhood." *Journal of Business Ethics* 101 (2011): 71–81.

McMahon, Christopher. "Morality and the Invisible Hand." *Philosophy and Public Affairs* 10 (1981): 247–277.

Pfeiffer, R.S. "The Central Distinction in the Theory of Corporate Personhood." *Journal of Business Ethics* 9 (1990): 473–480.

Powell, John A. and Stephen Menendian. "Beyond Public/Private: Understanding Corporate Power." *Poverty and Race* 20.6 (2011): 5–8.

Ripken, Susanna K. "Corporations Are People Too: A Multi-Dimensional Approach to the Corporate Personhood Puzzle." *Fordham Journal of Corporate & Financial Law* 15.1 (2009): 97–177.

Strate, Lance. "The Supreme Identification of Corporations and Persons." *et Cetera* 67.3 (2010): 280–286.

Velasquez, M. "Why Corporations Are Not Morally Responsible for Anything." *Business and Professional Ethics Journal* 2 (1983): 1–18.

B. The corporation as a community: stakeholder theory

Bartkus, Barbara and Myron Glassman. "Do Firms Practice What They Preach? The Relationship between Mission Statements and Stakeholder Management." *Journal of Business Ethics* 83.2 (2008): 207–216.

Bowie, Norman and Ronald Duska. *Business Ethics*. 2nd Edition. Englewood Cliffs, NJ: Prentice Hall, 1991.

Dilling, Petra F.A. "Stakeholder Perception of Corporate Social Responsibility." *International Journal of Management & Marketing Research (IJMMR)* 4.2 (2011): 23–34.

Evan, William and R. Freeman. "A Stakeholder Theory of the Modern Corporation: Kantian Capitalism." In Tom L. Beauchamp and Norman E. Bowie (eds.), *Ethical Theory and Business*. 3rd Edition. Englewood Cliffs, NJ: Prentice Hall, 1988.

Frederick, William et al. *Business and Society: Corporate Strategy, Public Policy, Ethics*. 6th Edition. New York: McGraw Hill, 1988.

Freeman, R. Edward. *Strategic Management: A Stakeholder Approach*. Boston: Pitman, 1984.

Goodpaster, K. and Piper, T. *Managerial Decision Making and Ethical Values*. Cambridge, MA: 1989.

Marshall, John and Matthew Adamic. "The Story Is the Message: Shaping Corporate Culture." *The Journal of Business Strategy* 31.2 (2010): 18–23.

Mgbere, Osaro. "Exploring the Relationship between Organizational Culture, Leadership Styles and Corporate Performance: An Overview." *Journal of Strategic Management Education* 5.3/4 (2009): 187–201.

Posner, Barry and Warren Schmidt. "Values and the American Manager: An Update" *California Management Review* (Spring, 1984).

Wang, Heli and Cuili Qian. "Corporate Philanthropy and Corporate Financial Performance: The Roles of Stakeholder Response and Political Access." *Academy of Management Journal* 54.6 (2011): 1159–1181.

Werhane, Patricia. "Engineers and Management: The Challenge of the Challenger Incident." *Journal of Business Ethics* 10 (1991): 605–616.

Chapter 4 What Are Proper Business Practices?

A. Competition and the practice of business

Dean, P. "Making Codes of Ethics 'Real.'" *Journal of Business Ethics* 11 (1992): 285–290.

Delios, Andrew. "How Can Organizations Be Competitive but Dare to Care?" *Academy of Management Perspectives* 24.3 (2010): 25–36.

Dima, Alina Mihaela and Radu Musetescu. "Business Ethics and Anti-Competitive Behavior." *The Business Review, Cambridge* 15.2 (2010): 178–184.

Duro, R. and B. Sandstrom. *The Basic Principles of Marketing Warfare*. New York: John Wiley & Sons, 1987.

Gordon, I. *Beat the Competition*. Oxford: Blackwell, 1989.

Hamel, G., Y. Doz, and C. Prahalad. "Collaborate with Your Competitors and Win." *Harvard Business Review* 67.1 (1989): 133–139.

Leonardo, Becchetti, Giorgio Federico, and Solferino Nazaria. "What to Do in Globalised Economies if Global Governance Is Missing? The Vicarious Role of Competition in Social Responsibility." *International Review of Economics* 58.2 (2011): 185–211.

McManis, G. "Competition's Failure Means It's Time for Collaboration." *Modern Health Care* 20.3 (1990): 57.

Paine, Lynn. "Corporate Policy and the Ethics of Competitor Intelligence Gathering." *Journal of Business Ethics* 10 (1991): 423–436.

Quairel-Lanoizelée, Françoise. "Are Competition and Corporate Social Responsibility Compatible?" *Society and Business Review* 6.1 (2011): 77–98.

Ries, A. and J. Trout. *Marketing Warfare*. New York: McGraw-Hill, 1986.

B. Advertising

Bakir, Aysen and Scott Vitell. "The Ethics of Food Advertising Targeted Toward Children: Parental Viewpoint." *Journal of Business Ethics* 91.2 (2010): 299–311.

Beheish, M.D. and R. Chatov. "Corporate Codes of Conduct: Economic Determinants and Legal Implications for Independent Auditors." *Journal of Accounting and Public Policy* 12 (1993): 3–35.

Berman, R. *Advertising and Social Change*. Beverly Hills, CA: Sage Cushman, 1990.

Drumwright, Minette E. and Patrick E. Murphy. "The Current State of Advertising Ethics." *Journal of Advertising* 38.1 (2009): 83–107.

Dyer, G. *Advertising as Communication*. New York: Methuen, 1982.

Gold, P. *Advertising, Politics, and American Culture: From Salesmanship to Therapy*. New York: Paragon House, 1987.

Miller, Felicia M. and Gene R. Laczniak. "The Ethics of Celebrity-Athlete Endorsement." *Journal of Advertising Research* 51.3 (2011): 499–510.

Schlegelmilch, Bodo and Magdalena Öberseder. "Half a Century of Marketing Ethics: Shifting Perspectives and Emerging Trends." *Journal of Business Ethics* 93.1 (2010): 1–19.

Stankey, M.J. "Ethics, Professionalism, and Advertising." In R. Howland and G.B. Wilcox (eds.), *Advertising in Society*. Lincolnwood, IL: NTC Business Books, 1990.

Synder, Wally. "Making the Case for Enhanced Advertising Ethics." *Journal of Advertising Research* 51.3 (2011): 477–483.

Weis, E.B. "What's Ahead for Admen, Starting Third 100 Years." In *Advertising Age* (ed.), *How It Was in Advertising: 1776–1976*. Chicago: Crain Books, 1976; 298–319.

C. Information technology

Allen, Lori and Dan Voss. *Ethics in Technical Communication: Shades of Grey*. New York: John Wiley & Sons, 1997.

Crandall, Richard and Marvin Levich. *Logic and Responsibility in the Computer Age*. New York: Springer, 1998.

Floridi, Luciano. "Network Ethics: Information and Business Ethics in a Networked Society." *Journal of Business Ethics* 90 (2009): 649–659.

Gunkel, David J. "Thinking Otherwise: Ethics, Technology and Other Subjects." *Ethics and Information Technology* 9.3 (2007): 165–177.

Johnson, Deborah G. *Computer Ethics*. Upper Saddle River, NJ: Prentice Hall, 1993.

Migga, Joseph, D. Gries, and F.P. Schneider (eds.). *Ethical and Social Issues in the Information Age*. New York: Springer, 1997.

Mingers, John, and Geoff Walsham. "Toward Ethical Information Systems: The Contribution of Discourse Ethics." *MIS Quarterly* 34.4 (2010): 833–854.

Pourciau, Lester J. and G.T. Mendina (eds.). *Ethics and Electronic Information in the Twenty-First Century*. West Lafayette, IN: Purdue University Press, 1999.

Santana, Adele, Antonino Vaccaro, and Donna Wood. "Ethics and the Networked Business." *Journal of Business Ethics* 90 (2009): 661–681.

Stichler, Richard N. and Robert Hauptman (eds.). *Ethics, Information, and Technology: Readings*. Jefferson, NC: McFarland, 1997.

Vallor, Shannon. "Social Networking Technology and the Virtues." *Ethics and Information Technology* 12.2 (2010): 157–170.

Weckert, John and Douglas Adeney. *Computer and Information Ethics*. Westport, CT: Greenwood Publishing, 1997.

Chapter 5   Ethical Issues within the Corporation

A. Working conditions

Blades, Lawrence E. "Employment at Will vs. Individual Freedom: On Limiting the Abusive Exercise of Employer Power." *Columbia Law Review* 67 (1967): 1405–1435.

Carbo, Jerry and Amy Hughes. "Workplace Bullying: Developing a Human Rights Definition from the Perspective and Experiences of Targets." *WorkingUSA* 13.3 (2010): 387–403.

Dawkins, Cedric. "Beyond Wages and Working Conditions: A Conceptualization of Labor Union Social Responsibility." *Journal of Business Ethics* 95.1 (2010): 129–143.

Ewing, David W. *Freedom inside the Organization*. New York: McGraw-Hill, 1977.

Ezorsky, Gertrude (ed.). *Moral Rights in the Workplace*. Albany: State University of New York Press, 1987.

Gibson, Mary. *Workers' Rights*. Totowa, NJ: Rowman and Allanheld, 1983.

Jönsson, Berth. "The Quality of Work Life—The Volvo Experience." *Journal of Business Ethics* 1 (1982): 119–126.

Pfeffer, Richard M. *Working for Capitalism*. New York: Columbia University Press, 1979.

Snyder, Jeremy. "Exploitation and Sweatshop Labor: Perspectives and Issues." *Business Ethics Quarterly* 20.2 (2010): 187–213.

Sollars, Gordon G. and Fred Englander. "Sweatshops: Kant and Consequences." *Business Ethics Quarterly* 17.1 (2007): 115–133.

Stouten, Jeroen et al. "Discouraging Bullying: The Role of Ethical Leadership and its Effects on the Work Environment." *Journal of Business Ethics* 95 (2010): 17–27.

Werhane, Patricia H. *Persons, Rights, and Corporations*. Englewood Cliffs, NJ: Prentice-Hall, 1985.

Westin, Alan, F. and Stephan Salisbury (eds.). *Individual Rights in the Corporation*. New York: Pantheon Books, 1980.

B. Affirmative action

Blackstone, William T. and Robert Heslep. *Social Justice and Preferential Treatment*. Athens: University of Georgia Press, 1977.

Burns, Prue and Jan Schapper. "The Ethical Case for Affirmative Action." *Journal of Business Ethics* 83.3 (2008): 369–379.

Cohen, Marshall, Thomas Nagel, and Thomas Scanlon. *Equality and Preferential Treatment*. Princeton, NJ: Princeton University Press, 1976.

Demuijnck, Geert. "Non-Discrimination in Human Resources Management as a Moral Obligation." *Journal of Business Ethics* 88.1 (2009): 83–101.

Glazer, Nathan. *Affirmative Discriminination*. New York: Basic Books, 1975.

Greenawalt, Kent. *Discrimination and Reverse Discrimination*. New York: Alfred A. Knopf, 1983.

Lauring, Jakob and Christa Thomsen. "Ideals and Practices in CSR Identity Making: The Case of Equal Opportunities." *Employee Relations* 31.1 (2009): 25–38.

Petersen, Lars-Eric and Franciska Krings. "Are Ethical Codes of Conduct Toothless Tigers for Dealing with Employment Discrimination?" *Journal of Business Ethics* 85.4 (2009): 501–514.

Triana, María del Carmen and María Fernanda García. "Valuing Diversity: A Group-Value Approach to Understanding the Importance of Organizational Efforts to Support Diversity." *Journal of Organizational Behavior* 30.7 (2009): 941–962.

C. Gender issues

Baier, Annette C. *Postures of the Mind: Essays on Mind and Morals*. Minneapolis: University of Minnesota Press, 1985.

Card, Claudia. "Gender and Moral Luck." In Owen Flanagan and Amélie Rorty (eds.), *Identity, Character, and Morality: Essays in Moral Psychology*. Cambridge, MA: MIT Press, 1990.

Collins, Patricia Hill. *Black Feminist Thought: Knowledge, Consciousness, and the Politics of Empowerment*. New York: Routledge, Chapman and Hall, 1991.

Donoho, Casey, Timothy Heinze, and Christopher Kondo. "Gender Differences in Personal Selling Ethics Evaluations: Do They Exist and What Does Their Existence Mean for Teaching Sales Ethics?" *Journal of Marketing Education* 34.1 (2012): 55.

Friedman, Marilyn. "Beyond Caring: The De-Moralization of Gender." In Marsha Hanen and Kai Nielsen (eds.), *Science, Morality and Feminist Theory*. Calgary: University of Calgary Press, 1987.

Friedman, Marilyn. "The Social Self and the Partiality Debates." In Claudia Card (ed.), *Feminist Ethics*. Lawrence: University of Kansas Press, 1991.

Gilligan, Carol. *In A Different Voice: Psychological Theory and Women's Development*. Cambridge, MA: Harvard University Press, 1982.

Gilligan, Carol. "Moral Orientation and Moral Development." In Eva Feder Kittay and Diana T. Meyers (eds.), *Women and Moral Theory*. Totowa, NJ: Rowman and Littlefield, 1987.

Grosser, Kate. "Corporate Social Responsibility and Gender Equality: Women as Stakeholders and the European Union Sustainability Strategy." *Business Ethics: A European Review* 18.3 (2009): 290–307.

Grosser, Kate and Jeremy Moon. "Developments in Company Reporting on Workplace Gender Equality?: A Corporate Social Responsibility Perspective." *Accounting Forum* 32.3 (2008): 179–198.

Held, Virginia. *Feminist Morality: Transforming Culture, Society, and Politics*. Chicago: University of Chicago Press, 1993.

Held, Virginia (ed.). *Justice and Care: Essential Readings in Feminist Ethics*. Boulder, CO: Westview Press, 1995.

Jaggar, Alison. *Feminist Politics and Human Nature*. Totowa, NJ: Roman and Allanheld, 1983.

Morrell, Kevin and Chanaka Jayawardhena. "Fair Trade, Ethical Decision Making and the Narrative of Gender Difference." *Business Ethics* 19.4 (2010): 393–407.

Noddings, Nel. *Caring: A Feminine Approach to Ethics and Moral Education*. Berkeley: University of California Press, 1984.

O'Brien, Mary. *The Politics of Reproduction*. London: Routledge, 1983.

Rorty, Amélie (ed.). *Explaining Emotions*. Berkeley: University of California Press, 1980.

Ruddick, Sara. *Moral Thinking toward a Politics of Peace*. Boston: Beacon Press, 1989.

Tannen, Deborah. *You Just Don't Understand: Women and Men in Conversation*. New York: Ballantine Press, 1991.

Thomas, Lawrence. "Sexism and Racism: Some Conceptual Differences." *Ethics* 90 (1980): 239–250.

Thomas, Lawrence. *Living Morally: A Psychology of Moral Character*. Philadelphia: Temple University Press, 1989.

Tong, Rosemarie. *Feminist Thought: A More Comprehensive Introduction*. Boulder, CO: Westview, 2008.

Westbrook, Kevin W., C. Steven Arendall, and Walton M. Padelford. "Gender, Competitiveness, and Unethical Negotiation Strategies." *Gender in Management* 26.4 (2011): 289–310.

Williams, Patricia J. *The Alchemy of Race and Rights*. Cambridge, MA: Harvard University Press, 1991.

Wolf, Susan. *Feminism and Bioethics: Beyond Reproduction*. New York: Oxford University Press, 1996.

D. Whistle-blowing

Fredin, Amy. "The Unexpected Cost of Staying Silent." *Strategic Finance* 93.10 (2012): 53–59.

Kaptein, Muel. "From Inaction to External Whistleblowing: The Influence of the Ethical Culture of Organizations on Employee Responses to Observed Wrongdoing." *Journal of Business Ethics* 98.3 (2011): 513–530.

Lindblom, Lars. "Dissolving the Moral Dilemma of Whistleblowing." *Journal of Business Ethics* 76.4 (2007): 413–426.

Somers, Mark and Jose C. Casal. "Type of Wrongdoing and Whistle-Blowing: Further Evidence that Type of Wrongdoing Affects the Whistle-Blowing Process." *Public Personnel Management* 40.2 (2011): 151–163.

Teo, Hayden and Donella Caspersz. "Dissenting Discourse: Exploring Alternatives to the Whistleblowing/Silence Dichotomy." *Journal of Business Ethics* 104.2 (2011): 237–249.

Chapter 6 The Context of Business: Nationally and Internationally

General international issues

Barnet, Richard and Ronald Mueller. *Global Reach: The Power of Multinational Corporations.* New York: Simon and Schuster, 1974.

Beitz, Charles. *Political Theory and International Relations.* Princeton, NJ: Princeton University Press, 1979.

Brown, Peter G. and Henry Shue (eds.). *Boundaries: National Autonomy and Its Limits.* Totowa, NJ: Rowman and Littlefield, 1981.

Falk, Richard, Samuel S. Kim, and Saul H. Mendlovitz (eds.). *Toward a Just World Order*, vol. 1. Boulder, CO: Westview, 1982.

Meager, Robert F. *An International Redistribution of Wealth and Power.* New York: Pergamon Press, 1979.

Turner, Louis. *Multinational Companies and the Third World.* New York: Hill and Wang, 1973.

A. The financial services industry

Block, Walter, and Laura Davidson. "The Case Against Fiduciary Media: Ethics is the Key." *Journal of Business Ethics* 98.3 (2011): 505–511.

Martin, William. "Socially Responsible Investing: Is Your Fiduciary Duty at Risk?" *Journal of Business Ethics* 90.4 (2009): 549–560.

Palazzo, Guido, and Lena Rethel. "Conflicts of Interest in Financial Intermediation." *Journal of Business Ethics* 81.1 (2008): 193–207.

San-Jose, Leire, Jose Luis Retolaza, and Jorge Gutierrez-Goiria. "Are Ethical Banks Different? A Comparative Analysis Using the Radical Affinity Index." *Journal of Business Ethics* 100.1 (2011): 151–173.

Sifah, David. "Ethics: An Essential Prerequisite of the Financial System." *Finance & the Common Good/Bien Commun* 33 (2009): 46–57.

B. Global business: bribing

Baughn, Christopher et al. "Bribery in International Business Transactions." *Journal of Business Ethics* 92.1 (2010): 15–32.

Cleveland, Margot et al. "Trends in the International Fight against Bribery and Corruption." *Journal of Business Ethics* 90 (2009): 199–244.

McKinney, Joseph and Carlos Moore. "International Bribery: Does a Written Code of Ethics Make a Difference in Perceptions of Business Professionals." *Journal of Business Ethics* 79.1 (2008): 103–111.

Sanyal, Rajib and Turgut Guvenli. "The Propensity to Bribe in International Business: The Relevance of Cultural Variables." *Cross Cultural Management* 16.3 (2009): 287–300.

Tian, Qing. "Perception of Business Bribery in China: The Impact of Moral Philosophy." *Journal of Business Ethics* 80.3 (2008): 437–445.

C. Globalization

Eaton, Heather. "The Ethics of Gender and Globalization: Military Madness and Ecological Stress." *Political Theology* 10.4 (2009): 671–684.

Preble, John F. "Toward a Framework for Achieving a Sustainable Globalization." *Business and Society Review: Journal of the Center for Business Ethics at Bentley College* 115.3 (2010): 329–366.

Rassekh, Farhad and John Speir. "Can Economic Globalization Lead to a More Just Society?" *Journal of Global Ethics* 6.1 (2010): 27–43.

Sklair, Leslie. "The Globalization of Human Rights." *Journal of Global Ethics* 5.2 (2009): 81–96.

Strahovnik, Vojko. "Globalization, Globalized Ethics and Moral Theory." *Synthesis Philosophica* 24.48 (2009): 209–218.